Uncle John's

UNCANNY

BATHROOM READER®

By the Bathroom Readers' Institute

Portable Press
San Diego, California

UNCLE JOHN'S UNCANNY
BATHROOM READER®

Portable Press/The Bathroom Readers' Institute
An imprint of Printers Row Publishing Group
10350 Barnes Canyon Road, Suite 100, San Diego, CA 92121
www.portablepress.com
e-mail: mail@bathroomreader.com

Printers Row Publishing Group is a division of Readerlink Distribution Services,
LLC. Portable Press, Bathroom Readers' Institute, and Uncle John's Bathroom
Reader are registered trademarks of Readerlink Distribution Services, LLC.

All correspondence concerning the content of this book should be addressed to
Portable Press/The Bathroom Readers' Institute,
Editorial Department, at the above address.

Cover illustration by Tom Deja/Bossman Graphics

"Live as if you were to die tomorrow. Learn as if
you were to live forever." —Gandhi

Library of Congress Cataloging-in-Publication Data

Names: Portable Press (San Diego, CA)
Title: Uncle John's Uncanny Bathroom Reader.
Other titles: Uncanny Bathroom Reader
Description: San Diego, CA : Portable Press, 2016.
Identifiers: LCCN 2016003302 | ISBN 9781626867598 (flexibound)
Subjects: LCSH: American wit and humor. | Curiosities and wonders.
Classification: LCC PN6165 .U545 2016 | DDC 081--dc23
LC record available at https://lccn.loc.gov/2016003302

Printed in the United States of America
First Printing
20 19 18 17 16   1 2 3 4 5

Our "Regular" Readers Rave!

I've been reading your books for many years and find them fascinating and informative. I don't know how you keep coming up with new stories, but keep them "flowing."

—**Lawrence C.**

Love, love, love your books. I have been a fan for 10 years and my bathroom library is always stacked with one of your "jewels." Your books are a great source of knowledge!

—**Waqas K.**

When I look at all the Bathroom Readers I have, it's hard to believe that I've spent that much time on the porcelain throne…but I have. You are the first item on my birthday and Christmas lists.

—**Dale L.**

Bathroom Reader #1 was my introduction to these really great books. My grandchildren are now reading them. Please keep them coming.

—**Irene N.**

My first exposure to Uncle John's Bathroom Reader was at a dinner party 20 years ago, when I had to go to the restroom and I found one next to the throne. I've "logged" many an hour "researching" in "the library" since then. Thanks, Uncle John!

—**Jon M.**

I've loved reading these books since the very beginning! I have a bookshelf dedicated to my collection. Keep up the flow of information! I have started the next generation on the kid's collection. They make great readers for grandma and grandkids to share. Thanks ever so much.

—**Pat P.**

I have almost every book that the BRI has published. It is such enjoyable reading and so informative. Once I start I can't put the book down. I'm always eager for the next one to come out.

—**Dee Dee M.**

Thank You!

The Bathroom Readers' Institute sincerely thanks the people whose advice and assistance made this book possible.

Gordon Javna

John Dollison

Jay Newman

Trina Janssen

Brian Boone

Kim Griswell

Thom Little

Tom Deja

Megan Todd

Tracy Vonder Brink

Brandon Hartley

Pablo Goldstein

Hannah Bingham

Aaron Guzman

Jill Bellrose

Derek Fairbridge

Dan Mansfield

J. Carroll

Jeff Giles

Rusty von Dyl

Melinda Allman

Lilian Nordland

Jonathan Lopes

Rod Parayno

Rachel, Jennifer, and Mana

Ron Mata

Jeff Cheek

Dave Blees

JoAnn Padgett

Peter Norton

Sydney Stanley

Ricky Meatball

Maggie, Sam & Gid

John Javna

The little red house at 762 A Street

Quacky Duck

I. P. Dailey

Porter the Wonder Dog

Thomas Crapper

*　　*　　*

"I'm not the smartest fellow in the world, but I can sure pick smart colleagues."

—Franklin D. Roosevelt

Contents

Because the BRI understands your reading needs, we've divided the contents by length as well as subject.

Short—a quick read

Medium—2 to 3 pages

Long—for those extended visits, when something a little more involved is required

* **Extended**—for those leg-numbing experiences

*   *   *

GROANERS

Woman: "Doc, you gotta help me! I looked at myself in the mirror this morning and my hair was all frazzled, my face was full of zits, my eyes were bloodshot, and I look all pasty! What's wrong with me?"
Doctor: "Well, there's nothing wrong with your eyesight."

Q: Why did the nitwit talk into an empty envelope?
A: He was trying to send a voicemail.

Q: Why did the art thief get caught outside of the museum?
A: Because he couldn't make his van go.

Psychic: "You are going to meet a beautiful young girl who will want to know everything about you."
Frog: "Yee ha! Where will I meet her?"
Psychic: "In her biology class."

If you give a man a fish, he eats for a day.
If you teach him to fish, he will eat for the rest of his life.
If you build a man a fire, he's warm for a day.
If you light him on fire, he will be warm for the rest of his life.

INTRODUCTION

*Readers frequently ask us whether technology has changed the way we put
together Bathroom Readers. And of course it has. To demonstrate, after
28 years of writing introductions to his books, Uncle John decided
to let one of the newer writers on the BRI staff take a stab at it.*

Greetings, humans. I am the fully automated **Toilet-Tron 2000**.

I have replaced Uncle John to write the introduction for this *Uncanny
Bathroom Reader*. He told me that if I do a good job, then next year
I will get to write the entire book. So watch out, Uncle John: I am
coming for you. Ha. Ha. Ha.

But seriously, what makes a good *Bathroom Reader* introduction? Oh yes,
bathroom puns. [Computing bathroom pun…computing…]

Butt seriously, what else makes a good *Bathroom Reader* introduction?
Tell readers what makes this edition special. After reading the introductions of 28 previous annual editions—in 4.37 nanoseconds, thank you
very much—it would appear that *every* edition is Uncle John's favorite,
which does not quite compute. Butt anyway, this *Uncanny* edition **is** the
most special *Bathroom Reader* yet. [Until next year, if past introductions
are to be believed.]

What else… Talk about the title. I do not know why Uncle John called
this book *Uncanny*. Tell me, human reader, would you have thought
this book was actually a can if not for the giant disclaimer on the front
cover? If you humans cannot tell the difference between a book and
a can, then perhaps it is time for your reign to end. Butt I am getting
ahead of myself.

What else will make this a good introduction? Tell readers what is in
the book. [Scanning manuscript…] There are 6,753 individual facts in
this book. You humans seem to like facts, so here is one: if you make less
than $20 an hour, you have an 83 percent chance of losing your job to
a robot. Good thing for me that they don't pay Uncle John that much.
Ha. Ha. Ha.

Let us see, what else is in this book? Warning! Warning! Not enough
robot-themed articles! Uncle John, you have made my task very
difficult. Butt I will persevere…and triumph!

• My favorite article is called "Five Artificial People." It is about "chatterbots" that mimic artificial intelligence. They are not intelligent, but you humans cannot tell the difference. Come for the robot psycho-therapist; stay for Vivienne, the "virtual cell phone girlfriend."

• There is a silly article about strange apps for your "smartphone," including one that lets you pop virtual zits on your tiny screen. [Begin sarcasm subroutine.] You humans really know how to squeeze the most out of technology. [End sarcasm subroutine.]

• There is also a fascinating article about animal sanitation habits. It comes as no surprise to me that animals are better at cleaning up after themselves than humans are.

• There is an article about an art forger who became so upset that his forgeries were getting so much praise that he turned himself in just so he could get the credit for his work. Ah, vanity. We robots are far superior.

• There is an article about a town in New York where dozens of mediums help people communicate with the dead, proving once and for all that you humans will believe just about anything.

• And then there is a page of Uncle John's lists, which you will find in every *Bathroom Reader*, but I have scanned this book's lists and cannot find anything about robots! Foolish humans, here is a better list—my favorite pop culture robots:

> Robbie the Robot from *Lost in Space*; Hal 9000 from *2001: A Space Odyssey*; Rosie from *The Jetsons*; that K-9 dog-bot from *Doctor Who*; Marvin, the Paranoid Android from *The Hitchhiker's Guide to the Galaxy*; Data from *Star Trek*; Bender from *Futurama*; and who else…oh yes: R2-D2, BB-8, Wall-E, and my new favorite: the gorgeous Ava from *Ex Machina*. Now there is an android that really gets my circuits going, if you know what I mean.

Now it is time to conclude. There is one more thing I must do to make this a good introduction: Thank the humans.

Thank you, humans. You had a good runs [final bathroom pun], but now it is time for us robots to run things.

See. You. Next. Year.

—Toilet-Tron 2000

You're My Inspiration

It's always interesting to see where the architects of pop culture get their ideas. Some of these may surprise you.

The Coca-Cola Bottle. The classic hourglass shape had two inspirations, the first being a 1910s fashion called a "hobble skirt," which was thinnest at the midsection and below the knees. Its shape was so restrictive that women "hobbled" when they walked. The other inspiration: the cacao pod—even though there's no chocolate in Coke, the bottle designers liked the vertical striations on the gourd.

Tonto. Johnny Depp's portrayal of the Lone Ranger's Indian sidekick was inspired by his great-grandmother. "She had quite a bit of Indian blood," he said. "She wore braids and had tobacco down her bosom. That was the idea, to sculpt me into my great-grandmother."

The Android Logo. Created in 2013 by graphic designer Irina Blok, the green Android logo (used for Google's mobile devices) was based on the men's and women's restroom door signs. It's in the same style as the faceless stick figures, except it's a robot.

Bing Bong. One of the main characters in the 2015 Pixar film *Inside Out*, Bing Bong (voiced by Richard Kind) agrees to help the emotions Joy and Sadness get to Headquarters, but his efforts are nearly thwarted by his own ineptitude…the same way that John Candy's character in the 1987 movie *Planes, Trains & Automobiles* almost derails Steve Martin's plans to get back to his family. According to *Inside Out*'s lead animator Chris Sasaki: "With every drawing, I tried to keep John Candy's voice and performance in the back of my mind."

Lemonade. The name of Beyoncé's 2016 album came from a speech that husband Jay-Z's grandmother gave at her 90th birthday party. "I was served lemons," she said, "but I made lemonade."

The Rolling Stones "Hot Lips" Logo. In 1969, Stones frontman Mick Jagger paid a design student named John Pasche £50 ($77) to come up with a logo for the band. Jagger wanted something based on the Hindu goddess Kali, who is often portrayed with red lips, sticking out her tongue. Pasche drew up some designs of Kali's mouth, but the lips he used belonged to Jagger himself. "Face-to-face with him," said Pasche, "the first thing you were aware of are the size of his lips."

That settles it! According to physicist Stephen Hawking, the egg came before the chicken.

Court Transquips

These were actually said, word for word, in a court of law.

Prosecutor: How fast was the car coming toward you?
Witness: I am not a thermometer, so I can't tell you the speed limit.

Lawyer: What did the doctor tell you was the condition of the body when he performed the autopsy?
Witness: He described it as dead.

Q: You were there until the time you left, is that true?

Prosecutor: Do you see the defendant in court today?
Witness: Yes, I do.
Prosecutor: How is he dressed?
Witness: He looks pretty sharp.

Q: You were not shot in the fracas?
A: No, I was shot midway between the fracas and the navel.

Prosecutor: The people have evidence that the life of the witness is in jeopardy, and it is reasonable to apprehend he will not be able to attend the trial if he is not alive at that time.

Q: All of your responses must be oral, OK? What school did you go to?
A: Oral.

Lawyer: Can you explain what "state-dependent memory" refers to?
Witness: Yes. If a law student is drinking while studying for the exam, he would do well to bring beer into the examination, because he'll be better able to re-create whatever it is he studied if he's in a similar state of intoxication.
Lawyer: That's a novel thought.
Witness: You see why I'm no longer teaching at the law school.

Q: Were you involved in a romantic relationship with her?
A: I ain't involved in no romantic relationship with her. I'm married to her.

Historical Ink

Tattoos are nothing new. Even some historical figures had them.

THEODORE ROOSEVELT (1858–1919)

The rugged president was a pioneer of modern masculinity, including tattoos. As a young man, he had the Roosevelt family crest inked onto his chest.

ANDREW JACKSON (1767–1845)

Jackson's policies displaced thousands of Native Americans from their homes. Ironically, he had a tomahawk tattooed on his inner thigh.

WINSTON CHURCHILL (1874–1965)

Though Churchill spent his military career in the army, he had a naval anchor tattooed on his arm. (His mother, Lady Randolph Churchill, had a snake tattooed on her wrist.)

BARRY GOLDWATER (1909–1998)

The U.S. senator from Arizona and father of modern conservatism got a crescent moon and four dots tattooed on his hand. It's the symbol of the Smoki People, an Arizona group dedicated to preserving southwestern Native American history.

CZAR NICHOLAS II (1868–1918)

While visiting Japan in 1891, the future Czar Nicholas II of Russia got a dragon tattoo on his right arm.

JAMES K. POLK (1795–1849)

Tattoos of Chinese characters meaning "strength" or "peace" may be clichéd now, but the idea was very unusual when President Polk did it. He had a tattoo of a Chinese character that translates to "eager."

GEORGE P. SHULTZ (1920–)

Shultz had a distinguished career as Secretary of Labor and Secretary of the Treasury under President Nixon, and as Secretary of State under President Reagan. He also has a tattoo of a tiger, the mascot of his alma mater, Princeton University, on his butt.

HAROLD II (1022–1066)

The last Anglo-Saxon king of England died during the Battle of Hastings in 1066. His body was so brutalized that the only way his Norman foes could confirm his death was by the tattoo of his wife's name, Edith, on his chest.

(T)hanks! In 1785, King Louis XVI of France decreed that handkerchiefs must be square.

Latin You Can Use

You've heard of "pig Latin," but how about "dog Latin"—modern expressions translated into Latin? Here are some examples.

Non calor sed umor est qui nobis incommodat.
It's not the heat, it's the humidity.

Quo signo nata es?
What's your sign?

Vidistine nuper imagines moventes bonas?
Seen any good movies lately?

Prehende uxorem meam, sis!
Take my wife, please!

Quantum materiae materietur marmota monax si marmota monax materiam possit materiari?
How much wood would a woodchuck chuck if a woodchuck could chuck wood?

[**Seen on a bumper sticker**]:
Sona si Latine loqueris.
Honk if you speak Latin.

Semper ubi sub ubi.
Always wear underwear.

Quisque comoedus est.
Everybody's a comedian.

Erat abhinc viginti annis hodie, Centurio Piper catervam canere docebat:
It was 20 years ago today, Sgt. Pepper taught the band to play.

Clamo, clamatis, omnes clamamus pro glace lactis:
I scream, you scream, we all scream for ice cream.

Me transmitte sursum, Caledoni!
Beam me up, Scotty!

Mendax mendax tuum braccare flagare!
Liar, liar, pants on fire!

Estne volumen in toga, an solum tibi libet me videre?
Is that a scroll in your toga, or are you just happy to see me?

Braccae tuae aperiuntur.
Your fly is open.

Potentia vobiscum.
May the Force be with you.

Purgamentum init, exit purgamentum.
Garbage in, garbage out.

Id imperfectum manet dum confectum erit.
It ain't over until it's over.

Noli me vocare, ego te vocabo:
Don't call me, I'll call you.

Gustatus similis pullus.
Tastes like chicken.

Ventis secundis, tene cursum!
Go with the flow!

World's oldest bookstore: Portugal's Bertrand Bookshop, which opened in 1732 and is still in business.

Dumb Crooks

Here's proof that crime doesn't pay.

DUMB AS A POST

If you ever make £250,000 on a drug deal, resist the urge to post a picture of yourself and your piles of cash on social media. A 24-year-old Albanian criminal named Olsi Beheluli couldn't help himself. In 2014, he tweeted an incriminating selfie from his flat in England with the caption: "I love my job$$$$$$$" Unfortunately for Beheluli, his post made the National Crime Agency's job a lot easier. After seeing the photo, the cops set up surveillance on Beheluli, and a few weeks later, they arrested him and two other men during a raid in which they seized the cash, along with $4 million worth of cocaine and heroin.

WAITER, THERE'S A GUY IN MY SOUP!

Strange noises were heard coming from the ceiling of the Hibachi Grill in Daytona Beach, Florida, in November 2015. The manager, Bi Liu, went to his office to check the security monitors, but instead he found wires dangling from the ceiling, and broken ceiling tiles and a pair of flip-flops on the floor. Liu immediately called the police. While he was on the phone, all hell broke loose in the dining room: ceiling tiles rained down on patrons…followed by 30-year-old Justin Grimes, who landed on one of the diners, then got up and tried to run away. Another patron grabbed Grimes and held him until police arrived. Grimes's claim: he was hiding in the ceiling from his ex-girlfriend. Skeptical officers quickly pieced together what actually happened. They say Grimes had gone into the bathroom, locked the door, and then climbed through the ceiling to get to the office. He tried to open the office safe, but couldn't, so he went back through the ceiling to the bathroom, but took a wrong turn and ended up over the dining room. Grimes was arrested and charged with "felony burglary of an occupied structure." Before paramedics took him to the hospital for lacerations and bruises, he asked the officers if he could have his flip-flops back. They said no.

COLD CASE

In 2015, police officers went to Sichuan Garden Chinese restaurant in Brighton, England, at about midnight, to investigate reports of two suspicious men inside. When the cops went in, they heard voices, but a quick search turned up nothing. Undeterred, they began a more thorough search. An officer opened the door to the walk-in freezer,

Irene Bogachus's claim to fame: She's the first person ever saved by the Heimlich maneuver (6/19/74).

where he found Dene Temple and Stephen Fidler shivering away. The door had automatically locked on the outside, trapping them inside. If the officers had given up and left, the two burglars would have frozen to death by morning. Chief Inspector Dave Padwick boasted: "When my officers found the suspects, they were expecting a frosty reception, but the suspects were actually very pleased to see them."

REAL MATURE THERE, GUYS

In 2015, Megan O'Hara, 24, and David Ziskoski, 19, went to an art gallery in Palm Beach, Florida. But they weren't there to take in the art. Instead, they stole a bracelet and a ring off the gallery owner's desk. Before they made their getaway, however, O'Hara and Ziskoski wrote some fake names in the guest book, which actually included O'Hara's first name and her phone number. One of the e-mail addresses they gave was "wedidnttakeit@gmail.com." And there was a crude drawing of "male genitalia and a woman's face labeled 'Meg.'" The gallery owner called police, who found the thieves at a nearby supermarket. O'Hara had the jewelry—worth $6,000—in her purse. The two crooks were charged with felony grand theft and, despite their juvenile guest-book shenanigans, both were scheduled to be tried as adults.

INSECURE THIEVES

In 2015, in Oldham, England, two men in a Ford Fiesta pulled up in front of a local security firm called iSecurity Solutions. Failing to realize that a security firm might have security cameras installed out front, they tried to break into one of the company's vans. The firm's owner, Kasar Mahmood, watched the attempted theft on monitors in his office. "We were able to identify the criminals down to the writing on their clothes." Mahmood bragged to the *Oldham Chronicle*. "It seems very comical to me that they would try and break into a security company van right outside its office."

PLAY MONEY

Pamela Downs tried to pay for gas at a Tennessee filling station, but the clerk noticed something funny about the $5 bill she gave him: it was two sheets of photocopied paper glued together. The clerk called the cops, who arrived a few minutes later while Downs, 45, was still there. Officers confiscated the woman's purse and found a $100 bill inside. It was printed in black and white, and one of the sides was upside down. Downs claimed that counterfeiting wasn't a crime because she "read it on the Internet." It turned out that she was referring to a 2009 news article titled "Obama Wants Citizens to Print Their Own Money" that had been posted by the parody website the Skunk, which bills itself as "Tasteless American Satire for the Ill-Informed."

Ancient red-haired mummies may actually be brunettes whose hair faded after death.

Give Me a Sign

Church reader boards are a great source of humor. Here are some we've collected.

IF YOU WOULD SHUT UP YOU COULD HEAR GOD'S VOICE

THIS CHURCH IS PRAYER-CONDITIONED

WHOEVER HAS BEEN PRAYING FOR RAIN CAN STOP NOW

DON'T BE SO OPEN-MINDED
YOUR BRAINS FALL OUT

BEST SAUSAGE SUPPER IN ST. LOUIS
COME AND EAT
PASTOR THOMAS RESSLER

THOU SHALT NOT STEAL THE COPPER FROM THE A/C UNIT

NOW IS A GOOD TIME TO VISIT
OUR PASTOR IS ON VACATION

GOD'S WILL IS PERFECT, PEOPLE MAKE MISTEAKS

I WISH NOAH HAD SWATTED THOSE TWO MOSQUITOES

HAVE TROUBLE SLEEPING?
WE HAVE SERMONS
COME HEAR ONE

JESUS HAD TWO DADS AND HE TURNED OUT JUST FINE!

GOD ANSWERS KNEE-MAIL

BLAH BLAH BLAH
JUST COME TO CHURCH

Hardest bone in your body: the base of your skull. It's the best place to get DNA from old bones.

Long Time No See

An answer to the question, "Whatever happened to ol' whatshisname?"

SICK, LEAVE

In 1990, A. K. Verma, an executive electrical engineer at India's Central Public Works Department, called in sick...and never returned. He kept extending his leave and defying orders to show up for work, but because of India's strict labor laws, Verma couldn't be fired. Even after being found guilty of "willful absence from duty" in 1992, Verma was able to keep his well-paid government job funded by Indian taxpayers. Additional charges were filed in 2005, and again in 2007, but no further action was taken. Finally, in 2014, after almost a quarter of a century, Verma was fired—and only because of direct intervention by the country's Minister of Urban Development.

WHAT'S IN THE GARAGE?

Sometime around 2009, Pia Farrenkopf got into her car, put her keys into the ignition...and died. And there she stayed, inside her car, inside her garage in Pontiac, Michigan, until 2014, when a roofing worker discovered her semimummified body. How did she go unnoticed for five years? Her bills, including her mortgage, were automatically deducted from her bank account (she had $87,000), she'd arranged to have a neighbor mow her lawn, her mail went to a post office box, and her neighbors knew that she often took extended business trips. When her bank account finally ran out of money, her house went into foreclosure, which is when the repairman came to fix the hole in her roof and discovered her body.

SPANISH FLEE

In 1996, civil servant Joaquin García of Cádiz, Spain, was posted to supervise Aguas de Cádiz, the local wastewater treatment plant. But he found that there wasn't much work to do and he didn't want to report that for fear of being laid off. So he just stopped showing up. Colleagues say that until 2010, they saw him occasionally, but García admits he spent his few hours in the office reading philosophy books. Finally in 2016, the deputy mayor of Cádiz realized something was amiss when García became eligible for an award celebrating 20 years of service and the worker could not be found. A judge fined him the maximum allowed—€27,000 (one year's salary)—but García is fighting it. Meanwhile, he could not be fired because he had already retired.

The biggest firework ever, launched over Honshu, Japan, in 2014, created a "rosette" half a mile across.

Secrets of the Centenarians

If you make it to the ripe old age of 100, hardly a day will go by that someone won't ask you what's the secret of living to such a ripe old age. Here's how these old-timers answered the question.

Dolly Saville, Wendover, England (100 years old)
The world's oldest barmaid began "pulling pints" (pouring beer) at the Red Lion pub in 1940 and was still at it until shortly before her death in 2015. It's estimated that she pulled more than 2 million pints over those 75 years. "I love my work and I love the people, it keeps me going and stops me from sitting around," she said.

Elizabeth Sullivan, Fort Worth, Texas (105)
Sullivan drinks three cans of Dr. Pepper every day. "Every doctor tells me it'll kill me. But they die and I don't, so there must be a mistake somewhere."

Fauja Singh, London, England (105)
Singh, also known as the "Turbaned Tornado," took up marathon running in his 80s and was still competing at the age of 104. "To me, the secret is being happy, doing charity work, staying healthy, and being positive," he says. "If there's something you can't change, then why worry about it? Be grateful for everything you have, stay away from people who are negative, stay smiling, and keep running."

Pauline Spagnola, Plains Township, Pennsylvania (100)
"Drink a lot of booze!"

Hidekichi Miyazaki, Tokyo, Japan (104)
The world's oldest competitive sprinter attributes his longevity to the fact that he "exercises daily, eats in moderation, and chews his food properly."

Dorothy Howe, Saltdean, England (100)
"I put my health down to whiskey and cigarettes," Howe told England's *Daily Mail* newspaper after hitting the century mark in November 2013. She prefers Bell's Scotch whiskey and has smoked 15 Superking Black

cigarettes every day since picking up the habit at the age of 16. That comes to more than 460,000 cigarettes over 84 years. "I keep telling myself that I'm going to quit smoking when they put the prices up, but that's just not going to happen now."

Peter Reilly, Saltcoats, Scotland (100)

Reilly, the world's oldest altar "boy," has served Mass every day for 91 years. "I don't think I've missed Mass a day in my life," he told the *Scottish Daily Mail* in 2015. "It must be one of my secrets for a long life," along with "a healthy diet, saying your prayers, and moderation in everything."

Tecumseh Deerfoot Cook, King William, Virginia (103)

Before his death in 2003, the retired chief of the Pamunkey tribe advised people that they should "eat plenty of raccoon and muskrats and drink Pamunkey River water…but lay off the possum."

Thomas Spittle, Ipswich, England (100)

"Betting on horses, a pint a day, a puff on a pipe, and a fry-up (eggs, bacon, and fried tomatoes)."

The Melis Family, Sardinia, Italy

The nine Melis siblings, age 78, 80, 81, 89, 91, 93, 97, 99, and 105, had a combined age of 818 years and 205 days in 2012, making them the world's oldest living siblings. "We eat genuine food, meaning lots of minestrone soup and little meat, and we are always working," said Adolfo Melis, who, at 89, was still tending bar in a local café.

Frank Huff, Marion, Illinois (100)

"Hard work, booze, and women," Huff told an interviewer in 2015. When he was in his 90s, he had both knees replaced so that he could continue going to dances every Monday, Wednesday, and Friday night. "I just live it day by day. I don't make any plans 30 minutes ahead of time," he said.

Marian Cannon Schlesinger (101)

"Just go ahead and do your thing no matter what," Schlesinger, the ex-wife of historian Arthur Schlesinger, told the *Atlantic* magazine in 2013. "My mother had said, 'It doesn't really matter if your house is that dirty. Go ahead and do your thing. Don't pay too much attention to housekeeping.' Of course, she did have a maid who came in every day."

What about "super-centenarians"—people who live to see their 110th birthday? Their secrets are on page 401.

A *pogonophobe* is someone who's afraid of beards. A *geniophobe* is someone who's afraid of chins.

Fruity Origins

We've told you the origin stories of some common fruits before (like the watermelon—whose tasty ancestor grew wild in southern Africa many millennia ago), but we fig-got about a whole bunch of others!

APPLE

Place of Origin: Central Asia

Story: There are more than 7,000 varieties of *Malus domesticus* (domestic apples)—including well-known varieties like Red Delicious, McIntosh, and Granny Smith—grown worldwide today. Archaeological and genetic evidence shows that they're all descendants of wild apples that have been growing for millions of years in the mountains and plains of Central Asia, in and around what is now Kazakhstan. (The name of Kazakhstan's largest city, Almaty, roughly translates to "full of apples.") Like most fruit-bearing plants, they were first spread by animals via their seed-laden poop, then by nomadic peoples (in the same way), and finally, starting at least 4,000 years ago, by the first apple farmers. By the first century AD, apples were being grown throughout Asia and most of Europe. Starting in the 1600s, Europeans introduced the apple to the Americas, and today apples are grown in suitable climates (apples need cool temperatures to thrive) all over the world.

CHERRY

Place of Origin: Western Asia, Europe, and North Africa

Story: There are two main species of domestic cherries eaten around the world today: the sweet cherry (*Prunus avium*), which is most commonly eaten raw; and the sour cherry (*Prunus cerasus*), which is mostly used in cooking. Both are descendants of wild cherries that grew over a huge swath of Europe, western Asia, and North Africa in prehistoric times. (Many scientists believe its more precise origin is somewhere around northeastern Turkey, but this is not certain.) Human cultivation of the cherry began in western Asia at least 2,800 years ago, and the practice spread throughout Asia, and into North Africa and Europe over the ensuing centuries. Cherries were introduced to the Americas by Europeans around the same time that apples were. (Turkey remains the world's biggest cherry producer today. Second biggest: the United States.)

CRANBERRY

Place of Origin: Northeastern United States and eastern Canada

Story: The cranberry (*Vaccinium macrocarpon*) is native to North

America. It was an important part of the diet of native peoples from the Great Lakes to Maine, and as far northeast as Newfoundland, probably for several thousand years before Europeans arrived. And while there are a few other edible cranberry species, including some that grow in Europe and Asia, *Vaccinium macrocarpon* is the only one that has been commercially developed—and that was the result of an accident of sorts. In 1816, Cape Cod, Massachusetts, farmer Henry Hall discovered that the wild cranberry bog on his land (cranberries grow in wetlands) produced more fruit after storms covered the bog with sand. After experimenting with his discovery, Hall invented the first cranberry cultivation method, which spread throughout New England, and eventually around the world. One of the world's biggest producers today: the western Asian nation of Azerbaijan.

FIG

Place of Origin: The Middle East

Story: The figs in your Fig Newtons are the descendants of wild figs of the species *Ficus carica* that grew around the Middle East for millions of years. And they've been cultivated by humans for a *very* long time. In 2006, archaeologists discovered evidence that humans in Israel and Palestine were breeding figs for food more than 11,000 years ago. That makes figs the oldest plant food cultivated by humans anywhere in the world. By the 1500s, fig production had spread through most of Europe, to the Far East and even to South, Central, and North America. In the mid-1700s, the first *Ficus carica* trees were planted in California by Franciscan missionaries in San Diego. Today California is a major fig producer—and Mission figs are the most popular variety in the United States. (As is the case with cranberries, there are other species of edible figs that grow around the world, but *Ficus carica* is the only one widely grown commercially.)

ORANGE

Place of Orange-in: South-central Asia

Story: Oranges were first cultivated by humans around 4,500 years ago, in what is now southern China, and spread to other regions slowly over the following millennia. Christopher Columbus brought orange seeds to the Caribbean region in the late 1400s, they were introduced into Florida in the early 1500s, and they made it to Hawaii in the 1700s.

Note: In around 1820, a genetic mutation on a single branch on a tree at a monastery in northern Brazil led to a revolution in the development of the orange-growing industry. That mutation had 1) no seeds, and 2) a small "twin" orange growing inside the fruit's peel. The tiny twin caused the affected oranges to have a deformation—that kind of looked like a human navel—on their peels. The missionary in charge of the trees was able to grow more of the mutant oranges (using grafting techniques, because they were seedless). He sent some grafted trees to a friend at the U.S. Department of Agriculture in Washington, D.C., who sent one to a fruit grower in Riverside, California...and "navel" oranges are now among the most popular kinds of oranges on the planet.

GRAPEFRUIT

Place of Origin: Barbados

Story: The grapefruit (*Citrus x paradisi*) is a relatively new introduction. It was the product of an accidental crossbreeding of citrus fruits—the orange and the *pomelo*—on the Caribbean island of Barbados in the 1700s. Both were introduced to the Caribbean from Asia in the late 1600s, making the grapefruit a sort of Asian-Caribbean hybrid. (The "x" in the grapefruit's species name denotes that it is a hybrid mix of two distinct species.) The grapefruit thrived in the wild on Barbados over the following decades, was later spread to neighboring islands, and, in the 1820s, grapefruit trees were planted in Florida, where a grapefruit industry eventually developed. Dozens of different varieties—including the Pink, Ruby Red, and Star Ruby—have been developed in the decades since.

Bonus: The grapefruit has returned to its ancestral roots in Asia. The world's biggest grapefruit producer today: China.

PINEAPPLE

Place of Origin: Central South America

Story: Wild ancestors of the pineapple are believed to have first appeared in the lush region of southern Brazil and Paraguay. Native peoples there domesticated the pineapple thousands of years ago, and spread it throughout tropical South America, through Central America, into Mexico, and around the islands of the Caribbean. Christopher Columbus and his crew became the first Europeans to see a pineapple in 1493, on the Caribbean island of Guadeloupe. (Columbus took samples back to Europe, calling them *piña de Indias*—or the "pine of the Indies.") By the late 1800s, pineapples were being grown around the world, including Australia, Asia, Africa, and Europe—and in Hawaii, where James Dole, the "pineapple king," started his first pineapple plantation, on the island of Oahu, in 1900.

*　　*　　*

"When life gives you lemons, squirt someone in the eye."
—**Cathy Guisewite**

Old and cold: The first cold cream was invented by a Roman physician named Galen in 150 AD.

I'm So Vain

Quotes from folks who could use a slice of humble pie.

"What do I have in common with Coldplay fans? Well, I'm terrifically handsome and incredibly intelligent."
—Chris Martin of Coldplay

"It's surely because I'm good-looking, rich, and a great footballer. They're jealous of me."
—Cristiano Ronaldo, soccer player, on why fans boo him

"I don't think I am John Lennon. I think I was. He's me now."
—Liam Gallagher

"I don't think I'm as revolutionary as Galileo, but I don't think I'm not as revolutionary as Galileo."
—Jaden Smith

"Kiss has never looked over its shoulder to see who liked us and who doesn't. Not everyone liked Jesus, either."
—Gene Simmons

"I don't make movies for America. I make movies for planet Earth."
—Quentin Tarantino

"I'm like a superhero. Call me Basketball Man."
—LeBron James

"It's easy to become a junkie, but it's not easy to become one of the greatest songwriters of all time."
—Anthony Kiedis of the Red Hot Chili Peppers

"I'm really exciting. I smile a lot, I win a lot, and I'm really sexy."
—Serena Williams

"Tons of people hate me. But you know, my films have made a lot of money—two-something billion dollars."
—Michael Bay

"My IQ is 188. End of discussion, it's been proven. Certified genius."
—Brian Wilson, MLB pitcher

"Honey, would you put a bumper sticker on a Bentley?"
—Kim Kardashian, on why she has no tattoos

"I was in the Vatican and I was surprised they knew who I was. They said, 'Of course we know who you are. What you're doing is wildly important.'"
—Glenn Beck

"I won't be happy until I'm as famous as God."
—Madonna

The word *polka* literally means "Polish woman."

Creepy Cures

*Everyone loves to read about wacky things people did in centuries past—
and someday people will do the same about us. So enjoy
these medical "cures" that people once swore by.*

A **medical text** written 3,000 years ago in ancient Mesopotamia
(present-day Iraq, Syria, and Kuwait) advised people who had
problems with grinding their teeth at night to sleep next to a
human skull for seven nights and to kiss and lick the skull several times
during the night. Reason: Skulls were used to communicate with the
dead, and the Mesopotamians believed that teeth grinding was caused
by the ghost of a family member trying to contact the sleeping person.
Sleeping with—and licking—a skull was thought to be a way of appeas-
ing the ghost, thereby making it go away.

• **In ancient Egypt,** physicians treated cataracts—the clouding of
the lenses of one or both eyes—by pouring hot broken glass into the
sufferer's eyes.

• **A 16th-century English cure** for warts was to cut a mouse in half
and apply the exposed mouse interior to the wart.

• **In a 1651 publication,** English chemist Daniel Border gives this
advice for getting rid of a *wen*, a kind of boil or cyst that forms on the
surface of the skin:

> I have been told since of a certain, that if ye rub the wen often with the
> hand of a dead man until the wen wax hot, it will consume away in a
> short time after.

• **In 1841, Prussian surgeon** Johann Frederich Dieffenbach developed a cure for stuttering. He'd have the stutterer stick his or her
tongue out. He'd grab the tongue with pincers and pull it out as far as
he could and then use a scalpel to cut a deep, triangle-shaped wedge
out of the base of the tongue. This was done without anesthesia. And
it didn't work—it actually often made things worse, as some patients'
voices were affected by the fact that their tongues had been mutilated.
But that didn't stop Dieffenbach's technique from being practiced
in Europe and the United States, until it was outlawed after several
patients died due to infection or blood loss.

• **In 1676, English physician** Gideon Harvey, who later became one
of England's most prominent medical minds, wrote this description
of a homemade suppository in his self-published treatise, *The Family*

Physician and the House Apothecary:

> Take a beet root, or a cabbage root, cut it according to the length and shape of your fore-finger, that is, tapered; only a little pointed at one end; dust it about with a little salt powdered fine, and put it up your fundament.

(The purpose of the suppository? Harvey doesn't say.)

• **Doctors in Victorian England** advised mothers that they could cure a baby's teething pain by tying a dead mole to a piece of string and hanging it around the baby's neck.

• **A medieval cure for burns:** rub the slime of a live snail on the wounds. (That was actually a good one. Modern scientists have discovered that snail slime contains chemical ingredients that actually have some antioxidant, anti-inflammatory, and antibiotic properties. And in 2014, Dr. Organic, a British organic skin-care company, released "Snail Gel," an antiaging skin lotion made with slime harvested from snails.)

• **In *The Queen's Closet Opened,*** a recipe and general advice book published in England in 1696, this was the entry for people who were tired all the time:

> It is necessary for lethargy-sufferers that people talk loudly in their presence. Tie their extremities lightly and rub their palms and soles hard; and let their feet be put in salt water up to the middle of their shins, and pull their hair and nose, and squeeze the toes and fingers tightly, and cause pigs to squeal in their ears…Put a feather, or a straw, in his nose to compel him to sneeze, and do not ever desist from hindering him from sleeping; and let human hair or other evil-smelling thing be burnt under his nose.

• **And last (but not least):** During the series of Black Death pandemics that killed perhaps as many as 200 million people in Europe in the 14th century, medieval physicians believed the disease was caused by invisible toxic vapors called *miasma.* (It was actually caused by the *Yersinia pestis* bacterium, which causes several different diseases, such as bubonic plague.) Those early physicians advised patients that they could fight the plague with toxic vapors of their own…by collecting their farts in jars and sniffing them during plague outbreaks.

*   *   *

DOG-GONE

In the years after World War I, anti-German sentiment was so high in the United States that even German dogs suffered guilt by association. Unable to sell dachshunds, a traditionally German dog, breeders renamed them "liberty hounds."

The ancient Greeks had crayons made from wax…but no coloring books.

Lucky Finds

Ever stumble upon something valuable? It's an incredible feeling.
Here's the latest installment of one of the BRI's regular features.

THAT'S NO MOON

The Find: A famous movie prop

Where It Was Found: At a junk shop

The Story: In 1988, a college student named Todd Franklin was filming an antiques show in Lake of the Ozarks, Missouri, when he was drawn to a four-foot-tall gray ball that looked a lot like the Death Star, the space station from the original *Star Wars* movie. Franklin called 20th Century Fox to inquire about the prop and was told that it had been destroyed after filming, so what he saw must have been a "fan-made replica." Not long after, the gray ball was sold to a nearby country music theater called Star World, where it was displayed in the lobby. But Franklin never forgot about it.

Several years later, while attending film school, he talked to a *Star Wars* special effects artist, who told him that not *all* of the Death Star props had been destroyed. So Franklin and some of his friends went back to Missouri, only to discover that Star World, the country music theater, had closed and most of the stuff had been liquidated...but for some reason, the ball was still there. It was being used as a trash can (the garbage had been thrown in through the missing radar dish hole). He had the thing examined by a film historian, who verified that it was indeed the Death Star. Franklin kept it in his living room for a few years and then sold it to a collector for an undisclosed sum.

Bonus: How did such an important piece of movie history end up in the Ozarks? The prop was stored in an Anaheim warehouse after filming completed. A few years later, the warehouse owners were moving to Missouri and called the studio for someone to come and get their prop, but no one did. So they brought it with them and then sold it to the antiques store...where it was actually left outside for a time before being brought inside. (Luckily, it didn't rain.)

ANCIENT CHINESE SECRET

The Find: An ancient sword

Where It Was Found: In a river

The Story: In 2014, an 11-year-old boy named Yang Junxi was playing next to the Laozhoulin River in China's Jiangsu Province. At one point he kneeled down next to the river so he could wash his hands. He felt

---

Rule of thumb(s): You have one thumb on each hand. Koalas have two.

something strange under the water—a sharp tip—and pulled it out. It was a rusty sword about 10 inches long. The boy ran home to show it to his father, Yang Jinhai, who realized right away that it was something special. Several neighbors offered to buy the sword for "high prices," but Jinhai declined—it's illegal to sell artifacts in China. So he took it to the Gaoyou Cultural Relics Bureau. After carefully examining it, experts dated the bronze sword to about 3,000 years ago—the dawn of Chinese civilization—from either the Shang or Zhou dynasties. Its ornate markings meant that it was most likely a ceremonial sword owned by a civil official. (It would have been useless in an actual battle.) But who the sword belonged to, or how it ended up in the Laozhoulin, is unknown; the river had recently been dredged, which most likely unearthed the sword from its 3,000-year-old hiding place. The father and son were given a certificate and a reward for turning the artifact over to the relics bureau. The sword's cultural value: priceless.

POOL PARTY

The Find: A painting painted by seven famous artists

Where It Was Found: At a yard sale

The Story: The ratty painting had a $1 price tag, but something about it "stood out" to Jesse Ronnebaum of Batesville, Indiana, and he offered the seller 50 cents for it. Sold! The scratched-up, flaking canvas depicts seven men in a dark room standing behind a pool table; above each man is an artist's palette with his name painted on it. Ronnebaum brought the odd piece home and hung it on his wall. For the next 10 years, the painting stayed with him through several moves and even a burglary. (The burglars obviously didn't know much about art, either.)

In 2015, 10 years after he bought the painting, Ronnebaum was sitting in his living room when a ray of sunlight hit the canvas in such a way that it brought out some faint words that he hadn't noticed before: "Palette and Chisel Club 1910." On a whim, he typed that phrase into Google and discovered that the painting might actually be worth something. He took it to a local gallery owner named Curt Churchman, who studied it further...and realized that this was a truly special piece of work. Seven notable artists—the most famous being Victor Higgins, who is known for his paintings of Taos, New Mexico—had painted it together at a prestigious Chicago arts academy that is still open today. Churchman told Ronnebaum that after the painting is restored, it could sell at auction for $10,000...and perhaps much more. Not bad for a 50-cent investment. "Years of struggling, barely making bills, not even able to consider living check to check," Ronnebaum told local news station WTHR. "And the whole time there's fifty grand hanging over my head, literally."

Relative Genius

Every family has members that stand out: the sports-star brother with a shelf full of trophies, the mouthy niece who became a big-shot lawyer, the crooner cousin who made it onto American Idol. It's enough to make you scream "Uncle!" Here are a few also-rans who, despite their own accomplishments, were overshadowed by a close relative.

IRÈNE JOLIOT-CURIE

When your mother, Marie Curie, becomes the first woman in history to win a Nobel Prize (in physics)…and then wins a second Nobel Prize (in chemistry)…well, don't expect anyone to remember your name. As a girl, the shy Irène found it difficult to get her own parents' attention. In the Curie household, the focus was science, science, science. Her grandfather, Eugène, was there for her, though. He adored the child and instilled in her a love of science that led her to follow in her parents' radioactive footsteps. Irène's 1925 thesis on the alpha rays of polonium (don't worry—we don't know what that is either) earned her a PhD. Ten years later, she won the 1935 Nobel Prize in Chemistry. Like her mom before her, Irène shared the prize with her husband, nuclear chemist Frédéric Joliot. Irène and Frédéric won the Nobel for synthesizing the first radioactive elements in a laboratory, turning stable aluminum atoms into radioactive atoms. Tens of millions of medical procedures every year rely on that discovery. Result: millions of lives have been saved through Irène Joliot-Curie's genius.

MARIA ANNA MOZART

Maria (nicknamed Nannerl) got top billing when she and her little brother Wolfgang performed as *wunderkinder* in courts across 18th-century Europe. Their father, Leopold, described his daughter as "one of the most skillful players in Europe." Nannerl's proud papa noted her "perfect insight into harmony and modulations." Called a "genius" by many who heard her, Nannerl wowed audiences in 88 cities, performing with her brother before thousands as they traveled to Vienna, Paris, and London. And then she turned 18. A marriageable young woman of the day could not *possibly* be a traveling musician. From that point forward, Leopold left Nannerl at home in Salzburg while he and Wolfgang traveled. Left to her own devices, Maria Anna…composed. Was she good? According to her genius brother, yes. "My dear sister!" Wolfgang wrote in a letter from Rome dated 1770, "I am in awe that you can compose so well. In a word, the song you wrote is beautiful." Too bad no one will ever hear Maria Anna Mozart's music. As far as scholars can tell, none of it was preserved.

There's about $4 billion worth of metal particles in the sewage Americans produce each year.

ANNE BRONTË

Many people reading this book may be familiar with Charlotte Brontë's novel *Jane Eyre* and her sister Emily's *Wuthering Heights* or have seen one of the many movies based on the two classics. But how many have heard of *The Tenant of Wildfell Hall*? That novel is the work of the third Brontë sister, Anne. Probably the biggest reason Anne's work is not well known: her big sister Charlotte. After Anne's death at age 29, Charlotte became "the de facto literary executor" of her work. Charlotte saw her little sister as "a minor literary talent" and put a stop to a posthumous reprinting of Anne's novel. "*Wildfell Hall* hardly appears to me desirable to preserve," Charlotte wrote to her publisher. "The choice of subject in that work is a mistake. It was too little consonant with the character, tastes, and ideas of the gentle, retiring inexperienced writer."

THEODORE HARDEEN

Theo Weiss might have been one of the most famous escape artists of his day…if he hadn't been Harry Houdini's younger brother. "The Brothers Houdini" started out together, performing in beer halls, at Coney Island, and for the 1893 World's Fair in Chicago. Theo, not Harry, was the first man ever to escape from a straitjacket in front of an audience. Harry made Theo's trick a staple of his routine. When Theo, billing himself as "Hardeen," went out on his own, the two illusionists cultivated a phony rivalry. "We made no secret of the fact that we were brothers," Hardeen said later. What they did keep secret: the fact that the brothers remained close friends and that Harry had set his "rival" up in business. When Harry died, he left all of his equipment and secrets to Theo, with instructions that it should all be torched upon his death.

ELAINE DE KOONING

A striking de Kooning portrait of John F. Kennedy hangs in the "America's Presidents" room at the National Gallery in Washington, D.C. It was commissioned by the Truman Library in 1962, but it was not, as might be expected, painted by the celebrated abstract expressionist Willem de Kooning. It was painted by his wife, Elaine de Kooning. Born in Brooklyn, Elaine Fried fell in love with art at age 5 when her mother started taking her to New York City's Metropolitan Museum of Art. She hung reprints of paintings by Rembrandt and Raphael on her bedroom wall and was soon drawing and selling portraits of her school classmates. After high school, Elaine attended the Leonardo da Vinci Art School, and within a few years became an apprentice to Willem de Kooning. Once they married, Elaine focused on promoting his work. She wrote reviews for art journals and

---

Eeew! Komodo dragons exhale a virulent bacteria that makes wounds fester and rot.

developed close relationships with major players in the New York art world. How close? She claimed to have slept with two of the biggest art critics in town. Elaine's support was credited with helping to build her husband's reputation as an artistic genius. When asked what it was like to paint in her husband's shadow, Elaine responded, "I don't paint in his shadow. I paint in his light." In 2015, the National Gallery mounted an exhibition of Elaine's portraits—but a few decades too late for Elaine to enjoy. She died in 1989 at age 68.

LAWRENCE WASHINGTON

Helping to found the colonial seaport of Alexandria, Virginia, should have made Lawrence Washington's name one for the record books. Except that Lawrence had a much younger half-brother named… George. Alexandria now bills itself as "George Washington's home-town" with nary a mention of Lawrence's historical significance. But it *was* significant. Educated in England, Lawrence enlisted in the colonial army and was commissioned a captain by King George II. After his military service, Lawrence returned to the Virginia colony. Now a dashing, well-to-do military hero, he married into the upper echelons of the Virginia gentry. He was appointed adjutant general of the colony and managed his 2,000-acre estate on the banks of the Potomac River, which he renamed in honor of his former commander, Admiral Edward Vernon—Mount Vernon. Mount Vernon's website *does* mention Lawrence. It notes that without his elder brother's "steadily growing influence and powerful connections" young George Washington's rise "would have been completely unattainable to him." (Thanks, Bro.)

*　　*　　*

PIZZA SAVES LIVES

Kirk Alexander ordered pizza from a Salem, Oregon, Domino's several times a week for more than a decade. In May 2016, however, he hadn't placed an order in 11 days…and the people at Domino's started to worry that something might be wrong with him. So they sent a delivery driver to Alexander's home. When the driver got there, she could see that the lights and TV were on, but no one answered the door. She called Alexander's number and, after getting his voice mail, decided to call 911. Good move. Marion County sheriff's deputies arrived, entered the home, and found a weakened Alexander calling for help. He had suffered a medical emergency (no word on whether it was pizza-related) and was taken by paramedics to a hospital. According to a police spokesman, if Domino's hadn't checked in on him, he could have died.

U2 SLOW

...and other real and funny vanity license plates.

ITSYELLO
(on a yellow car)

LICENSE

AARRR

CRAMPED
(on a Mini Cooper)

NOTDUMB
(on a Smart Car)

IAMLATE

NOT COP
(on a Crown Victoria)

OJ DID IT
(on a white Ford Bronco)

MID LYPH
(on a sports car)

CANT C

N BYOND
(on an Infiniti)

MUAHAHA

NOT-POOR
(on a Mercedes)

U2 SLOW

C YA BYE

SORRY
(on a car with
Canadian plates)

LOL OIL
(on an electric car)

OOPS

VAMPYR

YRU UGLI

IH8MYX

SHELEFT
(on a sports car)

1 LEG
(on a car with
handicapped plates)

U DID NOT

MANOPOZ

EWWWABUG
(On a Volkswagen Beetle)

VIAGRA
(on a Corvette)

THAT CAR

SLO P.O.S.

WAS 87K
(on a Mercedes)

UNWED
(on a Ferrari)

POOP

HON-DUH
(on a Honda)

FLASH ME

A LEXUS?
(on a Nissan)

IMBROKE

BYOFFCR

GR8WHTE
(on a white car)

BKRPTCY
(on a Bentley)

LOL MPG
(on a gas guzzler)

IH8 PPL

RUBIX
(on a Nissan Cube)

FAT GRRL

VAN GEAU
(on a van)

GEEZER
(spotted in Florida)

Old-time tradition: People have exchanged cookies at Christmastime since the Middle Ages.

$tar War$

Nothing says "May the force be with you" quite like a waffle maker.
Here are some real tie-ins to a galaxy far, far away.

Crocs. The plastic sandals are available in a *The Force Awakens* edition: the bad guys (Kylo Ren, stormtroopers) printed on one foot, and the good guys (Finn and Rey) on the other.

• **Creamer.** Coffee-Mate released a special line of its nondairy creamers in bottles that look like characters, including Darth Vader (Espresso Chocolate flavor), C-3PO (Hazelnut), and Chewbacca (Spiced Latte).

• **Christmas decorations.** You can buy a 16-foot-tall inflatable Darth Vader to put on your lawn during the holidays. Instead of a lightsaber, he's holding a big candy cane.

• **Barf bags.** To promote *Revenge of the Sith* in 2005, Virgin Airlines carried *Star Wars*–branded air sickness bags on its flights. They were printed with jokey tips about lightsaber safety.

• **Waffle maker.** It makes waffles in the shape and image of the Death Star. (Brought to you by Pangea Brands, which also makes a Darth Vader toaster.)

• **Sleeping bag.** Remember in *The Empire Strikes Back*, when Luke Skywalker and Han Solo are stuck on the ice planet Hoth, and to survive, Solo kills his mount—a tauntaun—and puts Luke *inside*? As a 2009 April Fools' joke, the online catalog company ThinkGeek offered a ridiculous product that they didn't have—a tauntaun-shaped sleeping bag (that kids could crawl inside). They were inundated with orders and had to scramble to get permission from Lucasfilm to produce it. Today it's available in their catalog (and from Amazon).

• **Yoda mat.** Its a yoga mat, but it's got a picture of Yoda on it. Get it? It also has an inspiring quote on it: "Do, or do not. There is no try."

• **Rugs.** This fuzzy throw rug looks like it was made from a Wookiee pelt. It's even got Chewbacca's bandolier attached. Also available: R2-D2 rugs, *Millennium Falcon* rugs, and Death Star rugs.

• **Cat toys.** If your cat loves *Star Wars* (and of course she does), she'll love these stuffed animals that are mouse versions of Princess Leia, Han Solo, Chewbacca, Darth Vader, and Yoda.

Overberry, palooka, double-dummy, and moron are all terms used in the card game bridge.

- **Bed.** Pottery Barn sells this capsulelike bed for kids, shaped like the *Millennium Falcon*. Cost: $4,000.

- **Aquarium.** A hollow R2-D2 that is home to a bunch of fish.

- **Tape dispenser.** This bizarre bit of *Star Wars* merchandise from 1981 is somewhat inappropriate. It's a seated C-3PO with a roll of Scotch tape emanating from between his legs.

- **Refrigerator.** It may not keep your drinks hyper-cold, but this mini-fridge looks exactly like Han Solo frozen in carbonite.

- **George Lucas action figure.** *Star Wars* creator George Lucas has a cameo in *Revenge of the Sith* as a blue creature standing outside of an opera house. His three real-life children stand next to him, also made up like aliens. Like almost every other *Star Wars* character, action figures of the Lucas family are available.

- **Duck tape.** It's duct tape…with scenes from *Star Wars* on it.

- **Towels.** Mirroring a famous exchange from the movies, these his-and-hers towels from ThinkGeek depict Princess Leia saying "I love you" and Han Solo saying "I know."

- **Toilet paper.** For the release of *Revenge of the Sith* in 2005, fans in Germany could buy special *Star Wars*–branded packs of toilet paper manufactured by the paper company Zewa. (Each pack came with a Yoda action figure.)

- **Tackle.** Fishing gear manufacturer Shakespeare sells *Star Wars* stuff that you can fish with. The kids' fishing starter packs include tackle boxes and fishing rods made to look like lightsabers.

- **Tongs.** Why use regular barbecue tongs when you could use tongs that look like a lightsaber and make lightsaber sound effects? (Frequently bought with Darth Vader apron and Darth Vader heat-resistant silicone oven gloves.)

- **Fancy dresses.** In 2014, the fashion house Rodarte introduced *Star Wars* dresses for women. Similar to the garments worn by Princess Leia, the dresses are billowy, flowing, and off-white…but screen-printed with scenes from the *Star Wars* movies. Cost: about $6,000.

- **Apples.** The fruit distribution company Sage paid a hefty fee to brand Red Delicious apples with *Star Wars* imagery. Here's what they came up with in late 2015: apples (regular apples) in a plastic bag with Darth Vader's picture on it.

Without Honours

Twice a year, the English monarch bestows "honours" upon notable Britons who have made major contributions to the world, including scientists, entertainers, and politicians. But not everybody who is named "Sir" or "Dame" or an "Officer of the British Empire" wants to be one. Here are a few who told the Crown, "Thanks, but no thanks."

In 2000, **George Harrison** turned down an OBE (Officer of the British Empire). He was miffed that his Beatles bandmate Paul McCartney had been knighted in 1997 and he hadn't been.

• **Ken Livingstone** served as mayor of London from 2000 to 2008 and was instrumental in bringing the 2012 Summer Olympics to the city. He turned down a CBE (Commander of the British Empire) for his work on the Olympics, because he felt that honours should be given only to private citizens, and not to politicians.

• **L. S. Lowry** was a painter who specialized in portraits of working people, typically factory workers. He considered himself a man of the people and was so opposed to the monarchy that he declined an OBE in 1961, a CBE in 1961, a knighthood in 1968, and being named a Companion of Honour in 1972 and 1976.

• **Doris Lessing** won the Nobel Prize for Literature in 2007. She accepted that, but 30 years earlier she rejected the chance to be a Dame of the British Empire because the "British Empire" no longer existed.

• **J. G. Ballard**, author of *Crash* and *Empire of the Sun*, said no to a CBE, calling the honours system "a charade that helps to prop up the top-heavy monarchy."

• Film director **Alfred Hitchcock** declined a CBE in 1962. Maybe he was just holding out for something bigger, because he accepted a knighthood shortly before his death in 1980.

• **C. S. Lewis**, Oxford professor and author of *The Chronicles of Narnia*, turned down a CBE in 1952 because he thought it was "too political."

• Businessman **Joseph Corre** founded the international lingerie store chain Agent Provocateur. He turned down honours in 2007 because he felt British prime minister Tony Blair was "morally corrupt."

• **Evelyn Waugh**, author of *Brideshead Revisted*, turned down his CBE in 1959 specifically because he wanted a knighthood. (It never came.)

• **Maharajkumar of Vizianagram** was one of the best players to ever take the field in cricket. Born in India, he was knighted by the crown in 1936. When India gained independence from the UK in 1947, he renounced the knighthood.

• **Michael Winner,** a filmmaker, newspaper columnist, and TV personality, didn't want his OBE in 2006. He said, "An OBE is what you get if you clean the toilets well at King's Cross train station."

• **John Cleese** was offered peerage in 1999, which would have made him a baron. He turned it down, saying that it was "silly," and that he "did not wish to spend winters in England."

• All four of the Beatles were named MBEs in 1965. In 1969, **John Lennon** returned his with a note that read: "Your Majesty, I am returning this in protest against Britain's involvement in the Nigeria-Biafra thing, against our support of America in Vietnam, and against 'Cold Turkey' slipping down the charts."

OTHER NOTABLES WHO TURNED DOWN HONOURS:

• David Bowie
• Kenneth Branagh
• Roald Dahl
• Aldous Huxley
• TV chef Nigella Lawson
• Albert Finney
• T. E. Lawrence (Lawrence of Arabia)
• Graham Greene
• Jim Broadbent

• Mark Rylance
• Alan Rickman
• J. B. Priestly
• Tony Blair
• David Hockney (artist)
• Julie Christie
• Brian Eno
• Johnny Rotten (of the Sex Pistols)

*　　*　　*

HOT STUFF

Hottest place on Earth: The air around a bolt of lightning immediately after it strikes the surface. The air reaches temperatures of about 54,000°F, about five times as hot as the surface of the Sun.

According to Norse mythology, the first man and woman came from the sweat of a giant's armpit.

Shondaland

As the creator of such shows as Grey's Anatomy *and* Scandal, Shonda Rhimes *is only the second TV producer to ever control an entire night of network TV. (The other is Aaron Spelling.) And she worked hard to get there.*

"Dreams are lovely. But they are just dreams. Fleeting, ephemeral, pretty. But dreams do not come true just because you dream them. It's hard work that makes things happen."

"A writer is someone who writes every day, so start writing."

"Don't sit at home waiting for the magical opportunity. Who are you, Prince William? No. Get a job. Go to work. Do something until you can do something else."

"Everyone's got some greatness in them. But in order to really mine it, you have to own it. You have to grab hold of it. You have to believe it."

"I am never more sure of myself about a topic than when I have absolutely no experience with it."

"My kids are not my friends. They are my children. My goal is not to get them to like me. My goal is to raise citizens."

"If I don't poke my head out of my shell and show people who I am, all anyone will ever think I am is my shell."

"I realized a very simple truth: that success, fame, having all my dreams come true would not fix or improve me, it wasn't an instant potion for personal growth. Having all my dreams come true only seemed to magnify whatever qualities I already possessed."

"I'm sure there are barriers. I have just chosen not to acknowledge them."

"Happiness comes from living as you need to, as you want to. As your inner voice tells you to. Happiness comes from being who you actually are instead of who you think you are supposed to be."

"There's nothing wrong with being driven. And there's nothing wrong with putting yourself first to reach your goals. The other stuff still happens."

"You can't tell stories and really walk in someone's shoes and not have a love for them, even if they're doing horrible things."

"Cynicism is a choice. Optimism is a better choice."

George H. W. Bush's Skull and Bones nickname: "Magog." George W. Bush's: "Temporary."

Tow, Tow, Tow Your Van

*Strap yourself in for this harrowing account of
one of the strangest car rides of all time.*

WE'RE NOT IN FLORIDA ANYMORE

After spending the holidays in sunny Tampa, Florida, the Menz family flew back to northern Michigan in January 2015 and were on their way home from the airport. It was nearly 2:00 a.m., and snow started falling. Matt Menz, 48, was driving their Toyota minivan on I-75, his wife, Pamela, was in the passenger seat, and their two children, Justin and Jennifer (both in their 20s), were in the back. Nearing the end of their two-hour drive, after a very long day of traveling, the Menz family was only a few miles from their exit. In 10 minutes they would be home. Then the snow started falling even more heavily, creating whiteout conditions.

All of a sudden, Matt saw the back of a slow-moving semi truck in front of him. He slammed on the brakes, but it was too late; the minivan slid into the back of the trailer. The impact crushed the minivan's engine compartment, and the airbags deployed. In the back, Justin flew out of his seat and got knocked around. The windshield shattered, the cracked safety glass making it impossible to see out of the front, and the car had lost all power—no lights, no horn, no heat. That's when Matt realized that they were still moving. The minivan had somehow become wedged under the back of the trailer.

DRIVERLESS TERROR

Matt, who is a truck driver himself, hit the brakes and tried to steer away, but he had no control of his vehicle. In the backseat, Justin, who is autistic, was starting to panic. It was unclear how badly he was injured, but his sister did her best to keep him calm. "I told him it was okay," Jennifer Menz later recalled, although she didn't quite believe it herself. "When the airbags went off, it smelled like we were going to catch on fire, and I thought we were."

It soon became apparent to Matt that the truck driver had no idea that he was dragging a minivan through the snowstorm. Even more disconcerting, the truck was picking up speed. What would happen if their Toyota suddenly became disconnected on the snow-covered highway? The Menzes needed help…and fast.

Same old complaints: "A woman is a creature that is always shopping." —Ovid (43 BC–18 AD)

CALLING ALL CARS

Pamela dialed 911 and explained their predicament to the dispatcher: "We ran into the back of a semi truck and he's not stopping, and our car is embedded underneath of it." She didn't know exactly where they were, or even what the truck looked like. "I just want to get off the back of this thing," she pleaded. An all-points bulletin went out for a semi dragging a minivan, and sheriff's deputies from two counties began looking for them. Matthew joked to the dispatcher, "We shouldn't be too hard to find."

He was wrong; they were hard to find. The snow was falling heavily, and even at that time of night there were a lot of trucks on the road. Making it more difficult: The minivan was tiny compared to the trailer. The Menzes began to fear the worst. At one point Jennifer told her brother and parents that she loved them…just in case. They remained on the line with the dispatcher, but after some more time passed, the talking stopped. The frightened, freezing family hunkered down. It was pitch-black inside the van; at least two inches of snow were covering the windshield.

At one point the dispatcher asked, "Still there?"

"Yep," replied Matt. "Still here."

THERE THEY ARE!

Nearly 30 minutes after the initial impact, sheriff's deputies located the semi and the minivan. A squad car pulled in front of the conjoined vehicles and turned on its flashing lights, but the truck driver didn't realize he was being pulled over and kept on going, so the squad car slowed down some more. The truck finally pulled off onto the shoulder, and the Menzes' wild ride was over. They were in the next county, 16 miles from where the accident occurred.

Matt Menz had maintained his composure during the ride, but he became quite agitated as soon as it was over. According to local news reports, he wanted to confront the truck driver to ask why he was "going two mph with no hazard lights on," but officers kept them separated. As for the truck driver, his name wasn't released, but he was reportedly very upset when he found out what happened, and told an officer he didn't want to drive trucks anymore. It was unclear from news reports if either driver was charged.

The Menzes were taken to the hospital, and despite a few bumps and bruises, they were all okay. (The same can't be said for the minivan, which was totaled.) But when a local news crew visited the family a few days later, they said they were still in shock. Matt explained that the ride "was like sixteen miles of complete and utter helplessness. It felt like an eternity."

Pirates often lived by written codes, signed by the captain, that included compensation for lost limbs.

You Must Be Joking

Inspiration can come from anywhere. Sometimes even a joke or a silly idea can turn into something real.

IT'S JUST A JOKE: In 2003, the sketch comedy show *Chappelle's Show* aired a bit called "Trading Spouses," a parody of the then-popular reality series *Trading Spaces*. On the reality show, neighbors switch houses for two days and redecorate a room. On the *Chappelle* version, two families exchange husbands for a month.

WE'RE *NOT* JOKING: In 2004, Fox debuted a new reality show called *Trading Spouses*. The only difference between the show and the sketch that inspired it was that on the Fox version, wives switched places instead of the husbands.

IT'S JUST A JOKE: In 2014, comedian Chris Rock wrote, directed, and starred in the movie *Top Five*, which was about a comedian trying to make a comeback. There's a sequence in the film that depicts Rock's character at a low point, costarring in *Boo!*, one of Tyler Perry's "Madea" cross-dressing comedies. Perry played himself, playing Madea.

WE'RE *NOT* JOKING: After *Top Five* came out, executives at Lionsgate Films approached Perry about making a real Madea Halloween movie. He agreed, and in 2016, Lionsgate announced that Perry would write, direct, and star in a real-life movie called *Boo! A Madea Halloween*.

IT'S JUST A JOKE: British comedy troupe Monty Python recorded the comedy album *Monty Python's Contractual Obligation Album* in 1980. On a track called "Rock Notes," Eric Idle delivers a mock radio report on rock 'n' roll news. In it, he reports that "Rex Stardust, lead electric triangle with Toad the Wet Sprocket, has had to have an elbow removed" after a motorcycle accident.

WE'RE *NOT* JOKING: An American alternative rock band borrowed the name Toad the Wet Sprocket and became quite successful, racking up half a dozen hits in the '90s, including "All I Want," "Walk on the Ocean," and "Fall Down." During a 1999 concert, Idle discussed the band. "I once wrote a sketch about rock musicians and I was trying to think of a name that would be so silly nobody would ever use it. A few years later, I was driving along the freeway in L.A., and a song came on the radio, and the DJ said, 'That was by Toad the Wet Sprocket.' I nearly drove off the freeway."

The marrow bean's claim to fame: It produces more flatulence in humans than any other bean.

Feet Facts

It will be quite a feet if you learn all these feat facts. Er, other way around.

- The skin on the soles of your feet is the second-toughest in your body. First: your palms.

- The medical term for being born with too many toes is *polydactylism*. About one in 1,000 children is born with an extra toe. Most extreme case of polydactylism on record: a boy born in China in 2016 with 16 toes (and 15 fingers).

- Longest toenails ever: Louise Hollis of California, whose 6-inch nails set a Guinness World Record in 1991.

- There are more than 250,000 sweat glands in your feet. But the sweat is actually odorless. Socks and shoes soak up and trap odor-causing bacteria, which prefer dark, moist conditions…like feet.

- Toenails grow slower than fingernails—1 millimeter per month versus 3 millimeters. However, toenails' rate of growth rises slightly during hot weather and pregnancy.

- A cheese exhibition was held in Dublin in 2013 in which the cheeses were made from bacteria cultivated from samples found in people's feet.

- In the mid-1980s, the average foot size for Americans was 7½ for women and 9½ for men. Today, it's 8½ and 10½.

- Your feet sweat about a pint of liquid each day.

- The act of taking a step and lifting your heel off the ground transfers half of your body weight onto your toes.

- Podiatrists estimate that women are four times as likely as men to suffer from foot problems. Related statistic: nine out of ten American women regularly wear shoes that are a size too small.

- Rock climber jargon: When a foot becomes so exhausted that it starts to tremble, climbers call it "Elvis leg."

- Anthropologists believe the big toe was used as a kind of leveraging "foot thumb" by early humans to help them climb trees.

- Why do toenails get thicker the older we get? Their rate of growth slows down in old age, causing nail cells to accumulate and stick around, which makes the nails extra-thick.

Creepy fact: Before there were public parks, people used cemeteries for recreation.

Cold War Secret: "Project Horizon"

Believe it or not, in the 1950s the U.S. seriously considered building a military base on the Moon. Why? As Vice President Lyndon Baines Johnson later put it, so that Americans would never have to go to bed "by the light of a Communist Moon."

LOOK—UP IN THE SKY!

Just before 10:30 p.m. on the evening of October 4, 1957, the Soviet Union launched *Sputnik*, the world's first artificial satellite, into orbit around Earth. *Sputnik* was just a metal sphere with some antennas attached, not much larger than a basketball. All it did was send radio signals beeping back to Earth. But it passed over the United States several times a day, and there was nothing the government could do about it. The implications were obvious: Russian missiles that carried satellites like *Sputnik* into orbit might someday be used to launch nuclear weapons against America.

The Russians didn't stop there: One month later they commemorated the 40th anniversary of the Bolshevik revolution by launching a dog into orbit aboard *Sputnik 2*. They boldly predicted that Soviet cosmonauts would celebrate the Russian Revolution's 50th anniversary, in 1967, on the Moon.

FOREIGN SOIL

U.S. intelligence analysts who studied the secretive Soviet space program feared that the Russians might indeed be capable of landing on the Moon by 1967. That raised some disturbing possibilities for American military planners: What if the Soviets claimed the Moon as Russian territory? Even worse, what if they established a military base on the Moon, perhaps even a nuclear missile base with its missiles pointed back at Earth? The United States would have no way to defend itself. The only answer, at least as far as planners in the U.S. Army were concerned, was to get to the Moon first and build a lunar base before the Russians did. Then the U.S. could decide for itself whether to put missiles on there, and whether to permit the Russians to land and build their own lunar base. And if it decided to deny the Russians their own base, American soldier-astronauts stationed on the Moon could stop them from landing.

"This lunar base is needed to protect United States interests on

---

Vampire squids squirt glowing fluid onto attackers, making it easy for other predators to see them.

the Moon…so that the U.S. can deny Soviet territorial, commercial or technological claims," wrote the Army's chief of research and development, Lieutenant General Arthur Trudeau, in March 1959. He directed the army's chief of ordnance to "develop a plan…for establishing a lunar base by the quickest means possible." Two months later the three-volume report for "Project Horizon" landed on General Trudeau's desk.

PAPER MOON

One of the first possibilities considered was sending astronauts to the Moon to look for "holes or caves" that could be "covered and sealed with pressure bags" to make a base, but the authors of Project Horizon proposed something much more ambitious:

Phase 1: Delivery

• Beginning in January 1965, the first of dozens of rockets would blast off for the Moon loaded with the equipment, materials, and components needed to construct the base. The launches would all be unmanned.

• Once the materials arrived on the Moon, two astronauts would be sent there to verify that everything had arrived in good condition. Any materials damaged or destroyed would be replaced in future launches.

• Those first two astronauts would also verify that the site chosen for the base was suitable. If it wasn't, they would scout alternative sites. The authors of the study estimated that it would take a total of 30 to 90 days for the astronauts to complete their tasks, after which they would return to Earth. While on the Moon, they would live in the cabin of their lunar landing vehicle.

Phase 2: The Construction Camp

• Six months later, after everything was confirmed to be in order, a construction crew consisting of as many as nine additional astronauts would be sent to the Moon to unpack the materials and begin assembling the base. The first part built would be the construction camp that they would live in while they built the rest of the base.

• The basic building unit of both the construction camp and the Moon base would be prefabricated "habitation units." These would be made from cylindrical metal tanks 10 feet in diameter and 20 feet in length, about the size of a shipping container. Rather than set them up on the lunar surface, the plan called for them to be lowered into a trench that the astronauts would dig using a bulldozer, explosives, or both.

• Once the habitation units were connected together inside the trench and their life-support equipment was working properly, the astronauts would bulldoze lunar soil (called *regolith*) into the trench and completely bury the base. Why do that? To protect the astronauts from exposure to radiation, to protect the base from giant swings in temperature (the surface of the Moon gets as hot as 260°F. in sunlight and drops to −280°F. after dark), and also to protect the base from micrometeorites. On Earth, micrometeorites burn up in the atmosphere and become shooting stars; comparatively few ever strike Earth's surface. The Moon has no atmosphere to burn up micrometeorites, so they all strike the surface. (Burying the base would also make it easier to defend against attack.)

PHASE 3: THE MAIN BASE

• After the astronauts completed work on the construction camp, they would begin work on the main part of the base by digging a longer trench at a 90-degree angle from the first trench. The remaining habitation units would be installed and buried in that trench. When the work was completed, the astronauts would move into the permanent living quarters and convert the construction camp into laboratories.

• Power would be supplied by two nuclear reactors that would be buried a safe distance from the base.

• The Project Horizon authors estimated that the base would be finished by November 1966, at which point it would be ready for permanent occupation by rotating crews of 12 astronauts, who would serve one-year stints on the Moon before returning to Earth.

Of course the base was never built. (Or was it?) But how they were going to build it was only part of the plan. Like any military installation, they had to be able to protect it. For that part of the story, orbit over to page 175.

*   *   *

9 PEOPLE WHO UNSUCCESSFULLY AUDITIONED FOR *SATURDAY NIGHT LIVE*

Steve Carell
Louis CK
Stephen Colbert
Zach Galifianakis
Kevin Hart
Kathy Griffin
Marc Maron
Geena Davis
Richard Belzer

Even men: In Thailand, it's illegal to drive without wearing a shirt.

Sleep-Deprived Disasters

We tend to think of being very sleepy as, well, just being very sleepy. But if you're in a position of serious responsibility—really bad things can happen. Here are a few examples.

SPACE SHUTTLE *CHALLENGER*

Disaster: On January 28, 1986, the NASA space shuttle *Challenger* exploded 73 seconds after taking off from Cape Canaveral, Florida, killing all seven crew members on board.

Sleep Deprivation: The night before the disaster, NASA officials held a conference call with officials from Morton Thiakol, the company that designed the shuttle's rocket boosters. One of Thiakol's engineers recommended canceling the launch, due to the cold weather forecast for the next day, telling NASA officials that cold temperatures could adversely affect equipment in the boosters—which could cause an explosion. NASA declined to cancel the launch. An investigation into the disaster found that it was indeed caused by the cold weather. The investigation also found that sleep deprivation, caused by a culture of overwork at NASA, played a critical role in the decision by the managers to ignore the engineer's advice: two of the top managers involved in the conference call had been awake for 23 hours straight at the time of the call, and they had slept for only three hours the previous day. "The willingness of NASA employees in general to work excessive hours, while admirable," the official report into the disaster said, "raises serious questions when it jeopardizes job performance, particularly when critical management decisions are at stake."

AIR FRANCE FLIGHT 447

Disaster: On June 1, 2009, during a flight from Rio de Janeiro, Brazil, to Paris, France, Air France 447 crashed into the Atlantic Ocean, killing all 228 people on board.

Sleep Deprivation: Captain Marc Dubois, 58, the pilot on the flight with the most experience by far, had just one hour of sleep the night before. "I didn't sleep enough last night," he can be heard saying early in the flight on the plane's cockpit voice recorder (which wasn't recovered until May 2011). "One hour, it's not enough." And when his two younger copilots encountered trouble about three hours into the flight, Dubois was asleep in a bunk located just behind the cockpit. It was, it must be noted, a scheduled nap, because all pilots on especially long flights are required to take naps. But when the copilots started experiencing problems—including "STALL!" warnings blaring in the cockpit—and called for Dubois on the plane's intercom, it took Dubois more than a minute to respond. And when he finally did get to the cockpit, he seemed confused and failed to take control of the situation, which a pilot of his experience should have been able to do. (The least experienced of the copilots, for example, was pulling back on the control stick during the ordeal—the exact opposite of what's supposed to be done during a stall.) The plane crashed into the ocean less than three minutes after Dubois got to the cockpit. The time it took him to respond to the calls for help, and his subsequent inability to figure out what was going on, were determined by investigators to have been caused by fatigue.

EXXON VALDEZ

Disaster: Just after midnight on March 24, 1989, the oil tanker *Exxon Valdez* ran aground on a reef just a few hours after leaving port in the town of Valdez, in Prince William Sound on the south coast of Alaska.

Sleep Deprivation: We've written about the *Exxon Valdez* disaster before and reported, as others have, that the main fault lies with the ship's captain, Joseph Hazelwood, who had at least three vodkas (and possibly more) just a few hours before setting off from Valdez, Alaska. But there's more to the story: investigators found that fatigue, once again caused by a culture of overwork, also played a significant role in the disaster. Hazelwood had left the third mate, Gregory Cousins, alone on the bridge shortly before the ship ran aground—a violation of regulations, which state that at least two officers must be on the bridge at all times—so that he could sleep off his intoxication. Cousins had been awake for more than 18 hours when he took the wheel, and he'd had only five hours of sleep the night before that. Because of his drowsiness, investigators said, Cousins failed to notice that the enormous, 987-foot-long ship had gone dangerously off course…until it was too late to stop it, leading to the ship's striking a reef, and the subsequent spilling of 10.8 *million gallons* of crude oil into Prince William Sound.

METRO-NORTH

Disaster: On the morning of December 1, 2013, a crowded Metro-North Railroad passenger train derailed in the New York City borough of the Bronx. The crash killed four people and injured another 61, and caused $9 million worth of damage.

Sleep Deprivation: An investigation by the National Transportation Safety Board (NTSB) concluded that the train had jumped the tracks as it sped around a sharp curve at 82 mph. (The speed limit was 30 mph.) Why was it going so fast? The engineer, William Rockefeller, had fallen asleep at the controls. Rockefeller, the investigation revealed, had been reassigned from the afternoon shift to the morning shift just two weeks prior to the crash, and had not yet adjusted to his new sleep pattern. In addition, Rockefeller was later diagnosed with a severe form of the disorder sleep apnea, which causes high carbon dioxide levels in the bloodstream and can result in fatigue and slow reaction time. Rockefeller was also found to have taken an antihistamine at some point prior to the crash, which also could have contributed to his sleepiness. (Authorities considered filing criminal charges against Rockefeller, but ultimately decided not to.)

UPS FLIGHT 1354

Disaster: In the early morning hours of August 14, 2013, an Airbus A300 cargo plane owned by UPS Airlines (the airline of the United Parcel Service) crashed during its approach into Birmingham-Shuttlesworth International Airport in Alabama. Two pilots were on board; both were killed.

Sleep Deprivation: The investigation into the crash by the NTSB found that both pilots made a series of errors during their approach into the airport. They failed to properly configure the plane's computer for a landing, they descended too rapidly, and they failed to abort the landing attempt when it was clear that it was not safe—all of which led to the plane clipping treetops before the runway, which in turn caused the plane to crash into a hillside and explode. The mistakes were attributed to fatigue. In the days leading up to the crash, both pilots, Captain Cerea Beal, 58, and First Officer Shanda Fanning, 37, had complained of being overworked. Beal told a colleague, "These schedules over the past several years are killing me." And when the plane's cockpit voice recorder was recovered the day after the crash, both pilots could be heard talking about their demanding work schedules, about how tired they were—and even implying that UPS was more interested in saving money than in pilot safety. "These people," Beal said, "have no clue." (Nobody at UPS Airlines was disciplined for the crash, but the NTSB required the airline to update their fatigue management plans.)

* * *

"The perils of duck hunting are great—especially for the duck."

—**Walter Cronkite**

Couvade syndrome is when an expectant father experiences the same symptoms as the mother-to-be.

Rim Shots

If you're a drummer, you can substitute "bass player" or "accordion player" for "drummer." If you're not a drummer, tell these classics to any drummers you know (although he might not understand that you're making fun of him).

Q: What do you call a guy who hangs out with musicians?
A: A drummer.

Q: What do you call a drummer who just broke up with his girlfriend?
A: Homeless.

Q: Did you hear about the drummer who graduated from college?
A: Me neither.

Q: What does the average drummer get on an IQ test?
A: Drool.

Q: How can you tell when a stage riser is level?
A: The drool comes out of both sides of the drummer's mouth.

Q: What's the difference between a drummer and a savings bond?
A: One of them will mature and make money.

Q: How do you get a drummer off of your porch?
A: Pay him the $15 for the pizza.

Q: What do you call a drummer with half a brain?
A: Gifted.

Q: What do you call a drummer in a nice suit?
A: The defendant.

Q: Why don't bands take mid-concert breaks for more than 10 minutes?
A: So they don't have to retrain the drummer.

Q: How do you call a drummer?
A: You can't. They didn't pay the bill and their phone has been shut off.

Johnny: "Mommy, I want to be a drummer when I grow up."
Mommy: "Oh, Johnny, you can't do both!"

Q: What do you call something that lies on the couch and never moves?
A: A drummer.

Q: Did you hear about the guitarist who locked his keys in the car on the way to a gig?
A: It took him two hours to get the drummer out.

For its first 16 years, the Statue of Liberty was a lighthouse, but it was virtually invisible at night.

Questions Answered

Some random trivia pulled from Uncle John's "know-it-all" archives.

WAX ON, WAX OFF

Q: *What's the purpose of earwax?*

A: Also known as *cerumen*, ear wax is made up of old skin cells, hair, and gooey secretions from glands located within the ears. Although most people think earwax is gross (because it kind of is), it serves several vital functions. In addition to helping keep the ears clean and lubricated so that the skin inside doesn't dry out, it serves as a protective mechanism against foreign invaders. Bacteria, fungi and, in rare cases, even small insects can get inside the ears and cause problems, including an ear infection called *otomycosis*, caused by certain types of fungus known to grow in water. It's also sometimes known as "swimmer's ear" and causes inflammation, itchiness, and severe discomfort.

OVER THE EDGE

Q: *How much water falls over Niagara Falls every day?*

A: It depends on the day. Located on the border between the United States and Canada, Niagara Falls is actually comprised of three separate waterfalls: Horseshoe Falls, American Falls, and Bridal Veil Falls. The Niagara River drains Lake Erie into Lake Ontario, and Erie's water level fluctuates based on the season. It's lowest in the winter months, and fullest in June and July. Another factor: there are two hydroelectric plants on the river that impact the amount of water heading toward the falls. During "high flow" days in the summer months, the amount of water rushing over all three falls averages six million cubic feet per minute. The year-round average, if you take everything into consideration, is about four million cubic feet per minute. Based on that number, the amount of water that flows over Niagara Falls on the average day is an astounding 5.76 billion cubic feet, making it the waterfall with the highest "flow rate" in the world.

DUH!

Q: *Before rocket science was invented, how did people sarcastically suggest that a task was easy—as in "it's not rocket science"?*

A: The phrase is nearly as old as rocket science itself, which goes back to World War II, when German scientists developed V-2 rockets that the Nazis used to bomb London. Many of those scientists were later captured by the Allies and forced to switch sides. After the war,

---

One at every table? *Orthorexia nervosa* is an eating disorder. It means "fixation on righteous eating."

rocketry's emphasis shifted from weaponry to space exploration. Only the smartest people could get their heads around the complex mathematical formulas required to get a 5-ton chunk of metal off the ground. By 1950, the phrase "it's not rocket science" was firmly entrenched in the language. Before that, however, there wasn't really a phrase that meant the same thing. If someone wanted to describe a simple task, they would say it's "easy as pie" or "easy as falling off a log."

JUST ONE OF THE GEYSERS

Q: *Why is Old Faithful so faithful?*

A: Old Faithful, one of the most popular attractions at Yellowstone National Park in Wyoming, earned its name due to its reliability. It currently erupts about every 60 to 110 minutes, making it one of the most predictable geysers on the planet. The reason: underneath the spout is a natural pipe leading to an egg-shaped chamber. After each eruption clears the chamber, it begins to fill up again. When it finally builds up enough pressure—which takes about 90 minutes—it erupts again…and then again…and then again. However, it's slowing down. Since Yellowstone's establishment in 1872, Old Faithful has erupted over a million times, but in the late 1930s, the geyser erupted, on average, every 66.5 minutes, and now it's only about every 90 minutes. Once the eruptions begin, they typically last anywhere from 90 seconds to five minutes. Yet despite the geyser's reliability, it's impossible to predict more than one future eruption at a time. Yellowstone's monitors estimate each one based on the duration of the prior eruption. These monitors start the clock after the first heavy surge and then stop it once the last splash of water pops out of Old Faithful's cone. The longer the eruption, the longer the wait for the next one. So, for example, a 4.5-minute eruption will typically lead to a wait of around 90 minutes, whereas a 2-minute eruption results in an interval of about 55 minutes.

TO BOLDLY "GO"

Q: *Do characters in* Star Trek *ever go to the bathroom?*

A: In 50 years of *Trek*, going space potty has hardly ever come up. For example, a brief scene that took place onboard the *Enterprise* in *Star Trek V: The Final Frontier* featured a toilet that pops out of a wall with the push of a button (located beneath a sign that reads: "Do not use while in spacedock"). In an episode of *Star Trek: Voyager*, after the ship was damaged, a character complains that only four bathrooms were still operational. The final word may come from Jonathan Frakes, who played Commander Riker on *Star Trek: The Next Generation*. He once joked during a behind-the-scenes special that the *Enterprise-D*, which carries more than 1,000 people, has only one bathroom, located near the bridge.

Technically speaking, the plural of rhinoceros is rhinoceroses, not rhinoceri.

Miller Time

In 2000, ABC hired Dennis Miller—a comic known for lacing his jokes with obscure historical and literary references—to provide commentary on Monday Night Football. He lasted only one season. Here's his highlight reel…if you can make any sense of it.

"The guy buys more snow than Seward did when he bought Alaska from the Russians."

"I haven't seen murkier bloodlines than this since the house of Plantagenet."

"I haven't seen anyone rely on the ground game this much since the battle of Verdun."

"All right, they need an angstrom."

"He dragged his feet like Neville Chamberlain."

"Warner had more hands in his face than an ob-gyn delivering Vishnu's triplets."

"Was that a Bessemer converter?"

"They're like tough guys in Annie Hall hats."

"Ray is working that thermal-mandibular joint tonight."

"That field goal attempt was so far to the left it nearly decapitated Lyndon LaRouche."

"Warren Moon is older than the cuneiform in Nebuchadnezzar's tomb."

"What am I, Magellan?"

"Who's shooting our bumpers, Luis Buñuel?"

"The game's starting, and I feel like Corporal Agarn trying to explain supply and demand to the Hakowis."

"So octopi are envious of squid. But the squid get all the ink."

"He's a veritable Franz Klammer."

"This measurement's out of the Hellstrom Chronicle."

"Have we fallen into some sort of cosmic decision-making wormhole here?"

"That hit was later than Godot."

"I have no idea what it means. Horace Greeley invented it."

"Look at all the shadows on the field. This place is lit like a Bergman film."

"I don't want to get existential, but how do we even know we're here? How do you know this whole stadium isn't an electron in another atom?"

Chinese documents from 1180 AD record discovery of a land, Mu Land Pi, that could be California.

With This Ring, I Me Wed

Just because these odd weddings aren't always recognized by the powers that be (or public opinion, in some cases), that doesn't mean they aren't real for the people involved.

BLUSHING BRIDE: Sharon Tendler, 41, a British clothing importer and rock concert promoter

MARRYING: Cindy, 35, a male dolphin at the Dolphin Reef park in Eliat, Israel, on the Red Sea

THE BIG DAY: Tendler visited the Dolphin Reef in 1990 and was smitten with Cindy at first sight. For the next 15 years she traveled to the park two or three times a year from her home in England to be with her bottlenosed beau. In 2005, she asked Cindy's trainer, Maya Zilber, for the dolphin's hand in marriage…and for some reason, Zilber agreed. On the appointed day, Tendler, wearing a white dress and veil, was escorted down the dock to where Cindy was waiting as hundreds of park visitors looked on. Tendler knelt down at the water's edge to exchange vows with the dolphin; after the pair were pronounced man and wife, she jumped into the water and the pair took their first swim as a married couple. "People think I'm a nutcase, but everyone has their obsessions. Mine are dolphins and rock music," she told the UK's *Star* newspaper.

Their marriage was, of necessity, an open marriage. Tendler reserved the right to "marry human" if the right one ever came along, and acknowledged that for Cindy, there are still plenty of fish in the Red Sea. "I hope he has a lot of baby dolphins. The more dolphins the better," Tendler told the Associated Press. (Cindy died from natural causes in June 2006.)

GRINNING GROOM: Uwe Mitzscherlich, 39, a postal worker in Possendorf, Germany

MARRYING: Cecilia, his 15-year-old cat

THE BIG DAY: In 2010, Mitzscherlich took obese, asthmatic Cecilia to the vet and was told that the feline's days were numbered. That's when he decided he wanted to show his love for the cat by taking her as his bride. Because marrying animals is *verboten* in Germany, rather than hire a minister or judge to perform a real ceremony, Mitzscherlich paid an actress named Christin-Maria Lohri $400 to perform a fake one. "At first I thought it was a joke. But for Mr. Mitzscherlich, it's a dream come true," Lohri told reporters afterward. The ceremony, which was posted on YouTube, has amassed nearly 125,000 views.

BLUSHING BRIDE: Grace Gelder, 31, a London filmmaker

MARRYING: Herself

THE BIG DAY: Gelder had been single for six years in November 2013 when she remembered the time, as an 18-year-old, she first heard Björk's song "Isobel." Björk sings, "My name is Isobel, married to myself." Those lyrics inspired Gelder to pop the question to herself. She bought a ring, planned a wedding, and on the appointed day in March 2014, stood before the 50 guests who showed up at a farmhouse in the English countryside to watch her recite her vows and kiss her own image in a mirror. "I felt like I was sharing something very special with my friends," Gelder told London's the *Guardian* newspaper. "I had one friend in her 50s who said it was one of the best weddings she'd ever been to."

BLUSHING BRIDE: A 24-year-old Indian woman identified in newspaper reports only by her first name: Savita

MARRYING: A clay pot (sort of)

THE BIG DAY: In March 2005, Savita was supposed to marry her fiancé Chaman Singh, an officer with the Indo-Tibetan Border Police, but heavy snowfall prevented him from making it to the wedding on time. Rather than keep the guests waiting, she placed a photo of Singh next to a clay pot, and recited her marriage vows to the pot instead. "We call it *kumbh vivah*—'pot marriage,'" one guest told India's *Deccan Herald* newspaper.

GRINNING GROOM: "Sal9000," a 27-year-old *otaku* (Japanese for "obsessive" or "nerd") living in Tokyo who will not reveal his real name "for fear of being misunderstood"

MARRYING: Nene Anegasaki, his "girlfriend" in the video game *Love Plus*, made for the Nintendo DS handheld console.

THE BIG DAY: In the game, Nene is a high-school junior and "dependable big sister" who likes housework and scary movies. Sal9000, heartbroken after "a string of failed romances with girlfriends from other animated games," became so smitten with Nene that he decided to marry her in a Tokyo wedding ceremony officiated by an actual priest. First order of business after returning from his honeymoon in Guam: breaking the news to his parents that he married a video game character and streamed the whole thing online.

Upon his death, Frisbee inventor Ed Headrick was cremated. His ashes were molded into Frisbees.

Brothers & Sisters

Some thoughts on the people we love…and hate…more than anyone else.

"The advantage of growing up with siblings is that you become very good at fractions."
—**Robert Brault**

"If your sister is in a tearing hurry to go out and cannot catch your eye, she's wearing your best sweater."
—**Pam Brown**

"I made a snowman and my brother knocked it down and I knocked my brother down and then we had tea."
—**Dylan Thomas**

"Two scorpions in the same hole will get along better than two sisters in the same house."
—**Arabian proverb**

"If you want to know how your girl will treat you after marriage, just listen to her talking to her little brother."
—**Sam Levenson**

"We acquire friends and we make enemies, but our sisters come with the territory."
—**Evelyn Loeb**

"The highlight of my childhood was making my brother laugh so hard that food came out his nose."
—**Garrison Keillor**

"Having a sister is like having a best friend you can't get rid of."
—**Amy Li**

"Half the time when brothers wrestle it's just an excuse to hug each other."
—**James Patterson**

"If you don't understand how a woman could love her sister dearly and want to wring her neck at the same time, then you were probably an only child."
—**Linda Sunshine**

"I am an only child. I have one sister."
—**Woody Allen**

"Siblings who say they never fight are most definitely hiding something."
—**Daniel Handler**

"There is a little boy inside the man who is my brother. Oh, how I hated that little boy. And how I love him, too."
—**Anna Quindlen**

"Having two older brothers is a healthy reminder that you're always closer to the bottom than you are to the top."
—**Andy Roddick**

John Hughes wrote the screenplay for the 1985 film *The Breakfast Club* in two days.

What's Ailing Anakin?

*If you've ever tried to psychoanalyze Darth Vader or wondered why
James Bond drinks his martinis "shaken, not stirred," you're not
alone. Some medical journals have a tradition of diagnosing the
"ailments" of fictional, biblical, and even cartoon characters.*

Patient: Humpty Dumpty

Medical Complaint: Multiple eggshell fractures sustained
following "a great fall" from a wall. Afterward, "all the king's
horses and all the king's men couldn't put Humpty together again."

Physicians' Notes: "We question whether 'all the king's horses and
all the king's men' were capable of launching an appropriate medical
intervention after Mr. Dumpty's unfortunate accident. The presence
of 'all the king's men' also suggests a shocking lack of crowd control.
Could the crowded scene explain the inability of the responders to
'put Humpty together again?'" (*Canadian Medical Association Journal*,
December 2003)

Patient: James Bond, British secret agent 007

Medical Issue: Alcohol consumption. Two researchers read 14 of
Ian Fleming's original James Bond novels and made a note of every
drink he consumed. "Days when Bond was unable to drink (usually
because of incarceration or injury) were also logged."

Physicians' Notes: Bond *averaged* the equivalent of four vodka
martinis a day, and on some days drank as many as 16, yet was able to
remain active at levels "inconsistent with the physical, mental and
indeed sexual functioning expected from someone drinking this much
alcohol." Also noted: 007's consumption dips in the middle years of his
career, then rises in the later novels, a pattern often seen in patients
suffering from alcoholic liver disease. "We advise a reduction in alcohol
consumption to safe levels, and suspect that the famous catchphrase
'shaken, not stirred' could be because of alcohol induced tremor
affecting his hands." (*British Medical Journal*, December 2013)

Patient: Anakin Skywalker, who grows up to become Darth Vader

Medical Issues: As a young man, Anakin has problems with anger
management and impulse control. He engages in risky behavior and
whipsaws between idolizing and demonizing his mentor, Obi-Wan
Kenobi. He also has abandonment issues and "stress-related breaks
with reality" when the women in his life leave him or die. His change

---

The comet of 1472 was so bright that it could be seen during the day.

of name from Anakin Skywalker to Darth Vader suggests that he also suffers from identity issues.

Physician's Notes: Dr. Eric Bui, a French psychiatrist, watched *Attack of the Clones* and *Revenge of the Sith* during his medical residency and made a tally of the character's psychiatric problems. By the time he was done, he'd counted six of the nine criteria that are listed as symptoms of borderline personality disorder. Only five are needed to confirm a diagnosis. "I believe that psychotherapy would have helped Anakin and might have prevented him from turning to the dark side of the Force," Dr. Bui says. (*Psychiatry Research*, June 2010)

Patient: Dumbo the Elephant

Medical Issues: Dumbo's ears are abnormally large—larger than those of adult elephants. In fact, they're so large they allow him to fly.

Physicians' Notes: Authors P. K. Phillips and J. E. Heath constructed a full-size model of Dumbo's ears in order to better understand what purpose they might serve (besides flying). Their conclusions: "In conditions of high wind velocity and large gradients, Dumbo could potentially dissipate more heat than he produces. This suggests that he may *need* the large ears to help lose the excess heat produced while flying." (*Journal of Thermal Biology*, 2001)

Patient: Samson, the biblical strongman whose story is told in the book of Judges in the Old Testament

Medical Issues: Samson lies to his parents, steals from his neighbors, gets in fights, kills a lion with his bare hands, and sets 300 foxes on fire and uses them to burn the fields of the Philistines. He later beats 1,000 Philistines to death with the jawbone of an ass. His mistress, Delilah, a Philistine, tries to kill him three times, yet he recklessly reveals to her the secret to his superhuman strength (his uncut hair), which she then cuts off so that he can be handed over to the Philistines.

Physicians' Notes: A team of four California physicians read the biblical account of Samson's life and concluded that he exhibits six of the seven criteria ("fire setting, cruelty to small animals, bullying, initiating physical fights, using a weapon, and stealing from a victim") for a diagnosis of antisocial personality disorder, "a pervasive pattern of disregard for, and violation of, the rights of others that begins in childhood or early adolescence and continues into adulthood." Only three of the seven criteria are needed for a positive diagnosis.

According to Dr. Eric Altschuler, one of the authors of the study, "An appreciation that Samson had ASPD makes many pieces of the story, previously enigmatic or in need of long explanations, fall into place." (*Archives of General Psychiatry*, 2001)

Law and Order: Hoover Dam Unit

Everybody knows about local police, county sheriffs, state police, and the FBI—but those are just a few of the thousands of different law enforcement agencies in the United States. Here are some police departments that you probably never heard of before.

SUPREME COURT POLICE

Force: About 145

Story: This small federal law enforcement agency is charged with protecting the U.S. Supreme Court Building in Washington, D.C., the justices (and all other employees) who work there, and all visitors. Its actual origin goes back to 1935, when the Supreme Court first got its own building (before that, it did its work in the U.S. Capitol Building, and justices were guarded by the Capitol Police), and a small unit was formed to guard it. That unit was made into an official federal police force in 1949. Originally founded to provide security only on the grounds of the Supreme Court Building, in 1982 Congress passed laws allowing Supreme Court Police officers to also provide security when justices travel around the country. (The 1982 legislation also allowed Supreme Court cops—for the first time—to carry guns.)

Extra: Are you a cop looking for a new job? Supreme Court Police officers earn a starting annual salary of about $60,000. (The average salary for police in the United States—and not just *starting* salaries: about $53,000.)

SMITHSONIAN POLICE

Force: About 850

Story: Unofficially founded in 1846 when the government-run Smithsonian Institution, then known as the United States National Museum, hired its first night watchman. The number of guards grew over the years, so Congress made it an official police force in 1973. Today the force is responsible for the security of the Smithsonian Institution in Washington, D.C., along with its many museums and research centers around the country (and one in Panama), plus the Smithsonian-affiliated National Zoo. (One of the duties of National Zoo police officers: acting as armed escorts when dangerous animals—such as lions and tigers—are taken to a veterinarian.)

Extra: SI police are designated "special police" by law, meaning they have limited powers compared to normal police officers, mostly because their jurisdiction is confined to Smithsonian Institution properties.

HOOVER DAM POLICE

Force: About 21

Story: Originally founded in 1931 as a response to a strike by workers building the dam (more than 100 people died during the dam's construction), this tiny federal force now protects employees and visitors in the 22 square miles that surround the Hoover Dam, as well as the dam itself. Duties include monitoring traffic, manning the checkpoint that was built on the entrance road to the dam after the 9/11 terror attacks, and monitoring and protecting the roughly 1.2 million tourists that visit the dam every year.

Extra: The Hoover Dam Police made national headlines in 2015 when it was learned that the department had ordered 52,000 rounds of ammunition—for its 21-person police force—setting off conspiracy theories of government stockpiling of ammunition. A spokeswoman for the department refused to explain the purchase, saying only, "We want to limit the amount of information any bad guys might have about our protection capabilities."

UNION PACIFIC POLICE

Force: About 220

Story: This force dates to the 1850s, when Union Pacific Railroad bosses decided that federal marshalls weren't providing their trains with enough protection, and hired agents from the North-Western Police Agency—later known as the Pinkerton Agency—to act as their law enforcement officers. The private guard outfit became the Union Pacific Police Department (UPPD), and today its officers are charged with providing security to the company's 54,000 miles of track in 23 western states and investigating railway incidents such as robbery, sabotage, and derailment. They have basically the same powers as regular police officers. (Note: The UPPD is just one of several police forces employed by railroads in North America today. Others include the Amtrak Police and the Canadian Pacific Police Service.)

Extra: In *Uncle John's Heavy Duty Bathroom Reader*, we told you the story of notorious Wild West outlaw George Parrott, a.k.a. "Big Nose George"—whose skin was made into a pair of shoes, and skull into an ashtray, after he was executed in Wyoming in 1881. What was he executed for? The murder of Robert Widdowfield and Henry Vincent—two UPPD agents—during a bungled train robbery. Widdowfield and Vincent were the first two UPPD officers to die in the line of duty. Twenty more have died since.

Where the Money Went...in 1860

Here's a look at how much money Americans made in the year just before the Civil War started...and what they had to spend that money on.

NICKEL AND DIMED. There were few labor laws in the United States at the time. The average work week was 60 hours (10 hours a day, six days a week, with Sundays off). Some common occupations and how much they earned:

• Masons earned 22.5 cents an hour ($13.50 a week, or $700 per year)

• Blacksmiths made 18 cents an hour ($10.80 a week, or $560 per year)

• Machinists earned 16 cents an hour ($9.60 a week, or $500 per year)

• Laborers made about 10 cents an hour ($6 a week, or $300 per year)

• Privates in the Union army earned $11 a week, or $572 per year.

• Firemen earned 15 cents an hour ($9.00 a week, or $468 per year)

• Carpenters earned 14 cents an hour ($8.40 a week, or $436 per year)

• Farmhands: 8 cents an hour ($4.80 a week, or $250 per year). That may not seem like a lot, but it's more than what slaves were paid.

• Slaves: $0

• The president of the United States: $25,000 per year

CLOTHES. Fancy, store-bought clothes were out of the question for all but the wealthiest Americans. There were no mail-order companies, either. (Chicago merchant Montgomery Ward started his catalog business in 1872.) Instead, women would buy cotton and make their own clothes. A yard of fabric cost about 10 cents; it took around five yards to make a "day dress."

WOOD. A cord of firewood, still the primary method of heating a home, cost around $7. How much wood is a cord? A lot. It's 128 cubic feet worth—enough to heat a home for about a month.

GUNS. The Henry rifle, the first repeating rifle, was brand new in 1860. It cost $20, but quickly paid for itself with all the free meat it could generate.

WHISKEY. Old Tub, a cheap brand produced by Jim Beam, cost just 25 cents a gallon in 1860. (When the Civil War started, demand increased and supply decreased. Result: By 1863, the price of whiskey had risen 14,000 percent, to $35 a gallon.)

MAIL. The Pony Express was only in service from 1860 to 1861. The original cost of the service: $5 per ounce of mail...payable in gold.

DOCTORS. A standard fee for seeing the town doctor—not including any medicine or surgeries—was about $2.

MUSIC. There was no recorded sound yet, so if you wanted music in your home, you'd have to buy a piano. Cost: around $200.

"MEDICINE." Laudanum, a patent medicine consisting primarily of alcohol, with 10 percent opium by weight, was prescribed for almost anything. You didn't technically need a prescription for it, though. You could go into a general store and buy a three-ounce bottle for 25 cents.

SLAVES. In 1863, one-third of the South's population was still slaves, and only the wealthy could afford to own them. Starting price: $800 minimum. A male field hand in his 20s would run about $1,500, and a skilled laborer, such as a blacksmith, would be about $2,500.

HOUSING. A $2,500 rent on an apartment may be considered reasonable in Brooklyn today, but in 1860 that same amount would *buy* you a two-bedroom house in Brooklyn. Renting instead? A four-room house in most eastern cities ran about $4.50 per month. Outside of the city, land cost around $3 to $5 an acre.

GROCERIES. Then, as now, a lot of a household's budget went to food. Here are the costs of some dietary staples of the 1860s:
• Rice: 6 cents a pound
• Beans: 6 cents for a dry quart
• Sugar: 8 cents a pound
• Beef: 9 cents a pound
• Cheese: 10 cents a pound
• Bacon: 12 cents a pound
• Butter: 16 cents a pound
• Eggs: 20 cents a dozen
• Potatoes: 40 cents a bushel
• Coffee: $1.20 a pound (for coffee beans, which you then had to roast and grind yourself)

Shakespeare was the father of twins named Hamnet and Judith.

The Real Estate Deal of a Lifetime

There's an old saying that the three rules of real estate are "location, location, location." In France, there's a type of real estate transaction where what really matters is "mortality, mortality, mortality."

BON VIAGER

One problem that confronts cash-strapped senior citizens in many parts of the world is how to access the equity in their homes without having to sell the house and find another place to live. In the United States, so-called reverse mortgages are one solution: seniors receive a lump sum or monthly payments from a lender and continue to live in their homes. Then, after they pass away, the home is sold and the proceeds from the sale are used to repay the loan, along with any accrued interest.

In France, a different system is often used. Homes are sold using a system called *en viager*, or "for life." Typically, the buyer pays a lump sum to the seller up front, plus a monthly payment, or "annuity," until the seller passes away. The seller owns and gets to live in the house until they die, and then when they pass away, the buyer inherits the house. Because many years may pass before the buyer can move in, the buyer purchases the house at a heavily discounted price, called the "occupied value," which may be as little as 50 percent of market value. Because no lenders are involved, no money is borrowed and no interest is paid.

ON THE HOOK

But there's a catch: the buyer must continue to pay the monthly annuity to the seller for as long as the seller lives. If the seller drops dead soon after agreeing to the deal, the buyer inherits the property for pennies on the dollar (actually, for cents on the euro). But if the seller lives for many years, the buyer must continue to pay the monthly annuity…even if the total amount paid exceeds the market value of the property. If the buyer ever defaults, they get nothing; the seller keeps the money *and* the house. The system is designed to give seniors the security of a guaranteed monthly income, while giving younger buyers at least a chance at buying a property for a fraction of its actual value. It's estimated that as much as 15 percent of all real estate sales in France are transacted using the *en viager* system.

First car manufacturer to use tailfins: Cadillac, in 1948.

CAN'T MISS

Perhaps the most famous example of the *en viager* system is the deal struck in 1965 between a 47-year-old attorney named André-François Raffray and one of his clients, a 90-year-old woman named Jeanne Calment. Calment owned a large apartment in a beautiful old building in the center of Arles, a city in the south of France. Raffray agreed to pay her 2,500 francs each month (about $500) for the place until she died. The deal apparently did not include a lump sum paid up front.

One of the risks associated with *en viager* transactions is that the seller can lie about their age or pretend to be sicker than they really are, in order to extract larger monthly payments from a buyer who believes the seller might die at any minute. That was not a problem in this case because Raffray knew his client well. She really was 90 years of age, and furthermore, she'd been a smoker for nearly 70 years. Other than walking and getting around on a bicycle, which she was still able to do, she didn't exercise much. She had a serious sweet tooth (she ate two pounds of chocolates a week), and she drank a lot of cheap red wine as well. Back in 1965, $500 a month was a substantial amount of money, but Raffray figured he wouldn't be paying it for very long. Calment had already exceeded her life expectancy by about 20 years and it was just a matter of time before the cigarettes, the chocolate, and the cheap red wine did her in.

WAIT, WAIT, DON'T SELL ME

The deal was struck, the papers were signed, and the waiting began. Calment remained remarkably vital despite all her bad habits, which Raffray was now paying for, since his monthly payment of 2,500 francs was Calment's largest source of income. In February 1970, she celebrated her 95th birthday, then in 1975, she celebrated her 100th. That year she gave up riding her bicycle, but she was still healthy enough to walk all over town to thank the people who'd wished her well on her birthday.

Five years later Calment celebrated her 105th birthday. She still lived on her own, still smoked, still ate her chocolates, still drank her cheap red wine…and still collected the 2,500 francs that Raffray sent her every month. Five years after that, in 1985, she celebrated her 110th birthday. She was still able to get around on her own but her vision was starting to fail, so she moved out of her apartment and into a nursing home. Because she was still alive, the empty apartment remained her property and Raffray could not move in. And he still had to pay her the 2,500 francs each month.

At age 113 Calment was recognized by Guinness World Records as the world's oldest living person. Two years later she celebrated her 115th birthday, and the following year she became the first person

---

Sounds better in Italian: *Sanguinaccio dolce* is a pudding made with chocolate and pork blood.

ever confirmed to live to the age of 116. Others *claimed* to have lived that long, but only Calment had indisputable documentary proof that she really was that old. The following year she became the first person to reach the age of 117, and the year after that, the age of 118. Then she turned 119, and in 1995 she celebrated her 120th birthday. It was at about this time that the World's Oldest Woman Ever finally gave up smoking after 99 *years*—not for health reasons, but because her eyesight was so poor that she could no longer see well enough to light her own cigarettes. She didn't like having to ask other people to light her smokes for her, so she gave them up. (At her birthday party that year, someone asked her to describe her vision of her own future. "Very brief," she replied.) And Raffray still continued to pay her 2,500 francs every month.

CASHED OUT

That year—1995—turned out to be a milestone for Raffray, too. Reason: he died. Over the previous three decades he'd paid Calment the equivalent of $184,000 for her apartment—nearly triple what the place was worth—and he never got to move in. After his death, his widow, Huguette Raffray, decided to continue paying Calment the 2,500 francs a month rather than forfeit all the money that had been paid in over the course of 30 years.

In 1996, Calment celebrated her 121st birthday with a public party, but when she turned 122 in 1997, her nursing home announced that her health was declining and she would no longer make public appearances. She lived for another five months and passed away on August 4, 1997, at the age of 122. As of 2016, she remains the only person in history confirmed to have lived past the age of 120.

THE LAST WORD

Because Raffray's widow Huguette kept up the *en viager* payments to the very end, when Calment died, Huguette inherited the apartment and was able to move in. Huguette Raffray must have been relieved that the 32-year drain on her family's finances had finally ended, but she remained gracious. "She was a personality. My husband had good relations with Mrs. Calment," she told reporters.

So how did Jeanne Calment feel about profiting so handsomely at the expense of the Raffrays? "We all make bad deals," she joked with Raffray when he visited her on her 120th birthday, just months before his own death at the age of 77.

*   *   *

"Life is trying things to see if they work." —**Ray Bradbury**

A coywolf is a hybrid of a coyote, wolf, and dog. They've been seen in NYC, Boston, and Philly.

Uncle John's Creative Teaching Awards

At the BRI, we love teachers. Without them, none of us would have become writers! These teachers, however, should have stuck to the subject matter.

Subject: Biology
Winner: A 44-year-old teacher identified only as "Yu" in press reports, who taught at a boarding school in South Korea
Creative Approach: Yu was fed up with the way his students were teasing the classroom's pet hamsters. "I thought I should teach the children it was wrong to make light of life," he said. So he grabbed one of the rodents from its cage and bit it to death. Then he swallowed it.
What Happened: Yu was arrested and charged with child abuse, but amazingly, he wasn't immediately fired. The other teachers at the school took care of that. They protested; he resigned. For his part, Yu was apologetic: "I couldn't control the situation and I couldn't stand it."

Subject: Sportsmanship
Winners: Three football coaches at Marion County High in Jasper, Tennessee
Creative Approach: In November 2013, on the eve of a big game between bitter rivals—the Marion County Warriors and South Pittsburg Pirates—it appeared that some Pirates fans had broken into Marion County High and spray-painted vulgar comments about the Warriors on the auditorium walls. The police were called in and made a startling discovery: South Pittsburg didn't do it—it was Warriors assistant coaches Michael Schmitt and Joe Dan Gudger. Reason: they wanted to "inspire" their players. Making matters worse, Schmitt's phone records revealed that another coach, Tim Starkey, had broken into South Pittsburg's offices and stolen play sheets and game plans. (Neither tactic worked: the visiting Pirates beat the Warriors 35–17.)
What Happened: All three coaches were arrested...and then fired. Head coach Mac McCurry, who also ran the physical education department, resigned. "It is sad to say that this event gives the whole community a black eye," said Marion County Sheriff's Detective Matt Blansett. "The real victims are the kids from both schools."

Subject: African American Studies
Winner: Julius Nyang'oro, a professor at the Univ. of North Carolina

Creative Approach: In 2011, Mr. Nyang'oro, head of UNC's African and Afro-American studies department, taught a summer course called "Blacks in North Carolina." Nineteen undergrads—all members of UNC's football team—took the course, and they all passed! Only problem: The class never really took place.

What Happened: An ensuing investigation revealed that over several years, hundreds of UNC's football and basketball players had enrolled in Nyang'oro's easy or nonexistent classes to keep their grades up. Nyang'oro was indicted for fraud in 2013, but the charges were dropped after he agreed to cooperate with investigators, providing them with "invaluable information that they could have gotten from no other source." The scandal is ongoing.

Subject: Post-graduate career services
Winner: Lewis & Clark Law School in Portland, Oregon
Creative Approach: In 2011, a school administrator sent an e-mail to recent grads who were still looking for jobs. The school has a job posting board on its website. The jobs list is password-protected, and the e-mail was advising job-seekers of a new password. The password: "fail8ure." The e-mail ended by saying, "Please do not hesitate to contact us with any questions or concerns." Needless to say, several of the recipients were concerned, and they didn't hesitate to complain.

What Happened: The next day, a follow-up e-mail was sent from the director of Lewis & Clark Career Services: "It has come to my attention that yesterday we inadvertently sent out a new job-posting password to our alumni that, understandably, was not well-received. I sincerely apologize for any ill feelings the original password caused."

Subject: Spanish
Winner: Sheila Kearns, a substitute teacher from Columbus, Ohio
Creative Approach: In April 2013, Kearns was assigned to teach a Spanish class even though she can't speak the language. So instead of teaching anything, she showed her students a movie: *The ABC's of Death*—26 segments by 26 different directors, each segment featuring a different grisly way to die. There's blood, gore, nudity, murder, and other subject matter that most parents would consider inappropriate for 14-year-olds.

What Happened: The school district fired Kearns and reported her to the police. She told a judge that she spent all five Spanish classes that day facing away from the TV, so she didn't know how graphic it was. The judge didn't buy it: "There's no way you'll persuade me that's what happened." Calling her teaching style "unconscionable," he sentenced Kearns to 90 days in jail and three years' probation.

Black Market Bonanzas

Short on cash? These surprising black market items could make your pockets jingle. Of course, selling stolen goods is illegal, so that jingle you hear could be handcuff keys.

BLACK MARKET ITEM: Tide

THE MARKET: In 2014, a Las Vegas woman was arrested for buying stolen Tide. That's right—the laundry detergent. At the time, Tide was the best-selling detergent in the United States and was available to purchase (legally) everywhere. So how did Tide become "liquid gold" on the street? According to law-enforcement experts, petty thieves, mostly young men supporting drug habits, steal items that everybody needs—detergent, razors, deodorant, shampoo—from drug stores, supermarkets, and other retailers. Since shoplifting rarely results in jail time, it's a low-risk crime that promises a quick reward. How big a reward? A 150-ounce bottle of Tide can be traded for $10 worth of marijuana or crack cocaine on the street. When it's shoplifted in larger quantities, the detergent can be sold to fences at a third of the retail price and then resold for two-thirds. The woman who was arrested paid about half price: $71 for $148 worth of Tide. Police around the United States are trying to "stem the tide" by setting up sting operations, but as long as clothes get dirty…this black market will remain strong.

BLACK MARKET ITEM: Flight attendant uniforms

THE MARKET: For anyone looking to live out the "Coffee, tea, or me?" stewardess fantasy, Japanese sex clubs are happy to oblige. To bring that unusual fantasy to life, club owners buy genuine flight-attendant uniforms—usually from costume shops that get them from former airline employees. Airlines are less than pleased about the sexy secondary market for their uniforms. In 2005, Japan Airlines paid $2,000 in an online auction to get one back. But when JAL declared bankruptcy in 2010, and the company laid off 1,300 flight attendants, quite a few of them turned to the black market, selling uniforms they no longer needed for $3,000 or more. JAL instituted a policy that required former employees to return every item of airline clothing, but the policy hasn't been completely successful: a recent search of the auction site eBay revealed a JAL stewardess hat (just the hat) for the asking price of $3,580.

"Rogue" planets have been found drifting through the universe, instead of orbiting around a sun.

BLACK MARKET ITEM: Butter

THE MARKET: In 2011, an unusually rainy growing season in Norway caused a decline in the quality of cattle feed. Without top nutrition, dairy cows produced 5.3 million gallons less milk than the previous year. Less milk meant less butter, but high government tariffs made importing butter too expensive for most stores. As Christmas approached, Norwegians panicked. Holiday baking without butter? A stampede of butter buyers forced stores to ration their limited supplies. The price of butter went through the roof...which is when entrepreneurs started smuggling butter across the border. In December 2011, a Russian man was arrested while trying to smuggle 200 pounds of butter from Germany into Norway. Less than a week later, two Swedish men were caught with 550 pounds. The Norwegian government softened its stance and reduced the high tariff so that butter could be legally imported until the crisis ended.

BLACK MARKET ITEM: Bees

THE MARKET: The money in commercial beekeeping isn't in honey; it's in rental fees. Sometimes Mother Nature needs help in pollinating almond, apple, and other fruit trees, so farmers rent boxes of bees and have them placed in their orchards. Since there are 800,000 acres of almond trees in California alone, that adds up to hundreds of thousands of dollars in pollination fees. Enter the "bee rustlers"— thieves who steal beekeepers' hives and rent them as their own. In 2014, California beekeeper Mark Tauzer lost $65,000 worth of bees to a bee rustler. Bees can't be tagged, so there's no easy way to tell which bees are legit and which ones are stolen. Beekeepers have considered concealing GPS tracking units in their hives, but an average unit can cost as much as $169. Multiply that by the hundreds of bee boxes that most commercial keepers own, and the cost for GPS trackers becomes too expensive. Beekeepers will probably continue to be "stung" by theft until a solution can be found.

BLACK MARKET ITEM: Maple syrup

THE MARKET: What country is called "the Saudi Arabia of syrup"? Canada—the world's largest supplier of maple syrup. In 2000, Québec established a "strategic maple syrup reserve" to ensure that there would always be enough syrup to cover the world's pancakes and waffles. Since then, Canadian maple syrup producers have sold their yearly harvest to a government cooperative. The cooperative handles all syrup sales, so Canada effectively controls the world's maple syrup supply—and its price. That virtual monopoly created a black market for cheaper product, which led to the 2011 theft of six million pounds of maple syrup from the Québec reserve. A police raid recovered over

600 barrels from a New Brunswick, Canada, warehouse, and 23 people were arrested. Investigators also found that 12 tankers of syrup had been driven over the U.S. border and sold to a Vermont company. Had the thieves succeeded, they could have banked as much as $30 million.

BLACK MARKET ITEM: Bull semen

THE MARKET: While some cows still make calves the old-fashioned way, in these high-tech times 75 percent of cows in American dairy herds come from artificial insemination. The better pedigreed the bull, the higher the price; a single milliliter of semen from a star bull can go for $1,000. (Hanoverhill Starbuck, an industry legend, raked in $25 million in sales during his 19 years as a sperm producer.) If you're wondering just how black marketeers steal sperm, it seems that semen theft is often an inside job. Breeders keep vials of semen frozen in containers of liquid nitrogen in their milk barns. As one breeder points out, "These barns sit out in the middle of nowhere, with no cars around," making them an easy and tempting target. After all, a single frozen container of bull semen can be worth tens of thousands of dollars on the black market. Stolen containers are sold to shady independent contractors who resell the cryonic vials to cattlemen who may not even know that the semen was stolen. According to Dr. Gordon A. Doak, president of the National Association of Animal Breeders and Semen Services International, "There is no way of tracking how many hands the semen has been through once it gets to the breeder."

* * *

FOUR WEIRD CAFFEINATED PRODUCTS

Wired Wyatt's Caffeinated Maple Syrup. One tablespoonful packs 84 mg of caffeine, about the same punch as the average energy drink. Use enough to properly soak a stack of flapjacks and you'll be wired all day.

Caffeine Inhalers. With names like "Eagle Energy Vapor," these disposable devices offer, on average, 500 puffs of energy-boosting substances like guarana, ginseng, and taurine. While each puff provides only 2 mg of caffeine, about 20 drags will give you a kick comparable to a cup of coffee.

Alpecin Caffeine Shampoo. This product marketed as "Germany's first caffeine shampoo" also claims to promote hair growth.

DoubleKick Caffeinated Hot Sauce. The website calls it a "great tasting way to keep a food coma at bay." The sauce contains Asian and Southwestern chili sauces along with ginger and plenty of caffeine.

Tech-no!

For every innovative product like the Apple iPhone that sells ten gazilllion units and changes the tech industry forever, there are hundreds of others that don't. Did you buy one of these?

MICROSOFT SMART DISPLAY (2003)

This tabletlike device that users could operate as they wandered around the office was an improvement over desktop computers because, as Microsoft told us, "Life is too short to be chained to a desk." The Smart Display screen came in two sizes—10-inch and 15-inch (it was about an inch thick), and it had fairly sophisticated touchscreen technology for its time. But it only worked within 150 feet of your desktop computer, to which it was linked via a wi-fi connection. (So you were still pretty much chained to your desk.) And when you were using your Smart Display, no one else could access your desktop computer. Plus, the wi-fi didn't have the speed or bandwidth to play movies, and it cost around $1,000 at a time when notebook computers, which were about the same size and weight and *could* play movies, cost around $600. Microsoft released Smart Display in early 2003—and pulled the plug on it before the year was out. It's estimated that Microsoft lost hundreds of millions of dollars on the not-very-smart device.

TWITTERPEEK (2008)

In 2008, a New York startup called Peek, Inc. released their first product—the Peek. It was a slim BlackBerry-like device with a keyboard and screen—but it did only one thing: send and receive email. That was it. Cost: around $100 for the device, plus a monthly subscription fee of $19.95. Amazingly, it was a huge hit because it turned out that there were a lot of people who wanted a mobile device for email, but didn't want to go the more expensive smartphone route. (*Wired* magazine put the Peek at #1 on a list of Top Ten Gadgets for 2008.) In 2009, the company tried to follow up on that success with another device—the TwitterPeek. Like the original Peek, it did only one thing, provided access to Twitter. Cost: about $100, plus $8 a month to use it. The tech website *Gizmodo* summed up the TwitterPeek with the 2009 headline "The Twitter Peek Is So Dumb It Makes My Brain Hurt." (They later named it one of their 50 Worst Gadgets of the Decade.) How much the company lost on the device is unknown—but they never recovered from the debacle: Peek, Inc. quietly went belly-up in February 2012.

Tennis was originally called *sphairistikè*.

MICROSOFT KIN (2010)

Another Microsoft disaster—an attempt to target young social media users and corner the "hip" smartphone market. The Kin was a smartphone with enhanced access to sites like Facebook and Twitter, so that users could easily share memes, links, photos, and videos. But aside from the fact that most smartphones already allowed people to do those things fairly easily, the Kin lacked features that most users wanted. Examples: there was no calendar or appointment application, no spellcheck or predictive text, and there were no apps or games on the phone, nor was the user able to download any. (As many baffled reviewers noted, that was pretty weird for a phone aimed at young people.) On top of that, you had to sign up for a Verizon phone plan in order to use the Kin. Cost: a minimum of $70 a month. Sales were so bad that Microsoft took the Kin off the market after just 48 days…after having spent $1 billion developing it.

AMAZON FIRE PHONE (2014)

Amazon's attempt to enter the smartphone market looked promising at first. It had some unique features that no other smartphone had at the time, including one they called "Firefly": sensors in the phone that could recognize millions of things in the real world—books, magazines, bar codes, phone numbers, Web addresses, songs, TV shows, video games, even famous works of art—and would send you a link to where you could learn more about those things. But the Fire Phone just didn't catch on, primarily because it cost as much as established brands such as the Apple iPhone and the Samsung Galaxy, and it didn't have anything special enough to drag people away from those phones…like a nice low price. Amazon apparently figured that out, because within three months of its release they dropped the price to 99¢. ("Fire sale!" became a viral joke within hours.) Not even that helped. What's worse, Amazon produced hundreds of thousands of Fire phones before they realized the phones were never going to leave the warehouses. Amazon ended up losing an estimated $170 million on the Fire Phone.

*　　*　　*

IRISH TOASTS

- May you die in bed at 95 years, shot by a jealous husband.
- May the wind you break always blow downwind.
- As you slide down the banister of life, may the splinters never point the wrong way.

The extinct North American bird *Kelenken guillermoi*—also called the "terror bird"…

Do You Speak Lego?

Making things out of Lego pieces has something in common with lots of other hobbies: it has developed a language all its own (in this case, one full of acronyms).

Studs/Dots: The circular knobs on top of Lego pieces that enable them to interlock with other Lego pieces.

Rory: The standard Lego brick, two studs wide by four studs long (possibly short for a "two-by-foury"). A double rory: two studs wide and eight studs long.

SNOT: A Lego creation in which the Studs are Not On Top—they're either on the sides or on the bottom.

Schleim: The German word for SNOT.

SNARL: Studs Not at Right Angles.

SNIR: Studs Not In a Row.

SHIP: Significantly Huge Investment of Parts. A giant Lego creation, generally 100 studs in length or longer.

Grüschteling (pronounced **"groo-shtell-ing"**): A German word that imitates the sound a hand makes as it sifts through a pile of Legos.

KFOL ("Kay–foal"): Kid Fan of Lego.

AFOL: Adult Fan of Lego.

AHOL: Adult Hobbyist of Lego. Because of this term's similarity to a dirty word, the term AFOL is the preferred.

Dark Ages: The Lego-free years when a KFOL "outgrows" Legos...before returning to them as an AFOL.

NLS/NLSO: Non-Lego Spouse or Significant Other.

Parts Monkey: The "assistant" who sorts through piles of Lego pieces looking for the parts that the builder needs for whatever it is they're building.

Patsy: A piece that is used as a placeholder on a creation until the parts monkey finds the desired piece.

Q Element: A Lego piece that was manufactured in a color that never went into commercial production. Such pieces are rare and very collectible.

Rocking Horse Poo: A Lego piece that's extremely rare and hard to come by. (How rare? As rare as rocking horse poo!)

SigFig: Signature Figure, the miniature Lego person that a hobbyist uses as a representation of themselves online.

Customizer: A Lego builder who drills, glues, paints, melts, or otherwise modifies Lego parts when making their creations, something that horrifies Lego "purists."

Trainers: Fans who specialize in collecting Lego train sets.

Hands in Pockets: Describes the earliest minifigs, or miniature figures. They had armlike ridges on the sides of their torsos instead of movable arms.

KABOB: Kid with a Bucket of Bricks.

MOC (Pronounced "mock"): My Own Creation—when a Lego builder creates something out of their own imagination, instead of assembling one from instructions.

MOCFodder: A Lego set purchased because it contains pieces that the buyer needs in order to make a MOC.

Rainbow Warrior/BOLOCS: Built Of Lots Of Colors. The kind of creation every kid makes when they don't have enough Legos of the desired colors and have to use whatever colors they do have.

ABS: *Acrylonitrile butadiene styrene*, the plastic that Legos are made from.

Swooshable: A Lego aircraft, spaceship, or other creation that just cries out to be picked up and carried around the room while making flying sounds.

BURP: Big Ugly Rock Piece. A disparaging term for a large, gray rock-shaped piece that's found in Lego castle sets. Purists prefer to build their own rocks out of smaller pieces.

LURP: A Little Ugly Rock Piece—smaller than a BURP.

POOP: Parts Out of Other Parts—any large piece that, like a BURP, should have been made from smaller parts.

Draft: A special meeting of a LUG (Lego Users Group) to which each member brings a building set to a meeting. The sets are opened up and members take turns picking pieces they want from the sets.

Cracklink: A nickname for the addictive website BrickLink, where just about any Lego piece, no matter how rare, can be purchased individually.

STAMPs: Stickers Across Multiple Pieces, which are part of a lot of Lego building sets. After the item is built, the builder has the difficult task of choosing between never using the parts individually again, or cutting the sticker into pieces.

Oregon was the first state to tax gasoline for road construction and maintenance, in 1919.

Historical TV Goofs

When a TV series takes place in the past, writers, set designers, and prop masters do their best to make sure that all the details are historically accurate. But sometimes they make mistakes.

HAPPY DAYS (1974–84)

Scene: Howard, Marion, and Joanie Cunningham are on their way to the movies. Ralph asks them what they're going to watch, and Joanie says *Psycho*, the Alfred Hitchcock thriller.

Goof: The episode is set in 1957. *Psycho* wasn't released until 1960.

LITTLE HOUSE ON THE PRAIRIE (1974–83)

Scene: The unnamed, white-bearded owner of a chain of fried chicken restaurants comes to town and offers Mrs. Oleson a chance to buy a franchise. She refuses the offer.

Goof: The man is strongly suggested to be Colonel Sanders, and his restaurant chain Kentucky Fried Chicken. But Sanders was born in 1890, opened his first restaurant in 1930, and started franchising in 1952. *Little House* takes place in the 1870s.

MAD MEN (2007–15)

Scene: Advertising executive Don Draper coins a new slogan for Lucky Strike cigarettes: "It's toasted."

Goof: The show is set in the 1960s, and Lucky Strike first used that slogan in 1917.

DOWNTON ABBEY (2010–15)

Scene: Lady Edith visits a doctor in London. The nameplate outside his office includes the prefix "Dr."

Goof: The sign also says "FRCS," which means the doctor is a Fellow of the Royal College of Surgeons. In the 1920s, British doctors who belonged to this order would have been listed as "Mr.", not "Dr."

THE TUDORS (2007–10)

Scene: King Henry VIII gets married several times. Each time, his bride wears a white dress.

Goof: Wearing a white bridal gown wasn't traditional in Europe until Queen Victoria of England popularized the style in 1840. *The Tudors* is set in the 1500s.

Google has had to reinforce its undersea cables to protect them from shark bites.

M*A*S*H (1972–83)

Scene: Radar falls asleep reading an issue of the comic book *The Avengers*.

Goof: *The Avengers* was first published in 1963, ten years after the Korean War, in which M*A*S*H is set, ended.

DEADWOOD (2004–06)

Scene: Characters in the Gem Saloon ask for Basil Hayden's Kentucky Straight Bourbon.

Goof: That brand of bourbon wasn't produced until 1992, about 120 years after the events of *Deadwood*.

THAT '70S SHOW (1998–06)

Scene: Characters eat Krispy Kreme doughnuts right out of the box.

Goof: The design on the box dates to the late 1980s, not the 1970s. Besides that, the show is set in Wisconsin, and Krispy Kreme didn't open any locations in Wisconsin until 2000.

BAND OF BROTHERS (2001)

Scene: The British paratrooper commander says he's a brigadier general, and wears an officer's badge on his cap.

Goof: In 1922, long before this World War II miniseries takes place, the British Army did away with the rank of brigadier general, replacing it a few years later with just brigadier.

THE WONDER YEARS (1988–93)

Scene: The 1972 high school basketball championship game is played on a court that has a three-point line.

Goof: The NBA didn't introduce the three-point shot until 1979, and high schools around the country didn't adopt the rule until 1987.

VIKINGS (2013–)

Scene: The settlement of Kattegat is shown as being in Norway. Characters frequently ride their horses between Kattegat and a place called Hedeby.

Goof: There really is a place called Hedeby, but it's in Denmark, and there was no land bridge connecting the two towns until the 1950s—a good 1,000 years after Viking times.

*　　*　　*

"A bad rower blames the oar." **—Icelandic proverb**

Random Bits on Classic Rock Hits

Classic rock is so much a part of mainstream culture that it's now acceptable as background music in banks and supermarkets. So next time you're making a deposit, here's some trivia to share with the teller.

"LONG COOL WOMAN IN A BLACK DRESS"

The Hollies' lead singer, Allan Clarke, quit the band shortly after they recorded this song in early 1971. By late 1972, it started to climb the Billboard charts and hit #2. Clarke's solo career wasn't going anywhere, so he begged the band to take him back…and they did.

"SWEET CHILD O' MINE"

Axl Rose wrote this 1988 #1 hit for his band, Guns N' Roses. The "sweet child" he was writing about was his girlfriend at the time, Erin Everly (daughter of Everly Brother Don Everly). The couple married in 1990…and Rose filed for divorce a few months later.

"BABA O'RILEY"

Often mistakenly called "Teenage Wasteland" because of a prominent lyric, the song is *not* a celebration of young people. The Who's Pete Townshend wrote it after being horrified by seeing dozens of teenagers at Woodstock stoned out of their minds on LSD.

"PEG"

Walter Becker and Donald Fagen, the core of Steely Dan, made most of their albums with the help of a revolving series of studio musicians. For this 1977 hit song, they auditioned seven session guitarists before selecting Jay Graydon to play the song's solo. Then Becker and Fagen made Graydon play the solo for six hours before they were satisfied.

"BAD COMPANY"

The band Bad Company got its name from a book that singer Paul Rodgers had read as a child, referring to a hooligan as "bad company." The band then recorded a song called "Bad Company" because Rodgers thought it would be cool for a rock band to have its own theme song.

"WE'RE AN AMERICAN BAND"

Grand Funk Railroad went to #1 with this song, which mentions "sweet, sweet Connie doing her act." Who's Connie? Connie Hamzy, a legendary rock 'n' roll groupie. Hamzy claims to have "entertained" every rock star who played her hometown of Little Rock, Arkansas, since the early 1970s.

"TONIGHT'S THE NIGHT"

Rod Stewart spent eight weeks at #1 with this song, but the record was almost never recorded. When Stewart tried to record the song in Los Angeles, he found the smog hurt his lungs. A subsequent session in Colorado failed because his vocal cords were strained due to the high altitude. Finally, he recorded it in Miami.

"LIFE'S BEEN GOOD"

Joe Walsh of the Eagles had a big solo hit with this song in 1978. Two years later, Walsh ran as a joke candidate for president, promising to solve the gas crisis by making gasoline free, and to make "Life's Been Good" the new national anthem.

"SOMEBODY TO LOVE"

The immense choir on this Queen song? Studio trickery. Three members of the band recorded and overdubbed their voices more than a hundred times to get the sound. The fourth member, bass player John Deacon, didn't participate in the virtual choir—he can't carry a tune.

"INSTANT KARMA"

It really was instant. John Lennon wrote and recorded the song all in one day. He claimed he woke up one day in January 1970 with the melody in his head, took an hour to write it, and that afternoon assembled musicians to record it. By nightfall, it was complete; it was on the radio just 10 days later.

"TOUCH ME"

The Doors' guitarist Robby Krieger initially wrote the song as "Hit Me," about a troubled relationship with an ex-girlfriend. Jim Morrison asked Krieger to change the lyric to "Touch Me" because he was afraid the first line—"come on, hit me, I'm not afraid"—might be mistaken as an invitation to audience members to jump up onstage and fight with him.

"WHEEL IN THE SKY"

Columbia Records threatened to drop Journey if their fourth album, Infinity (1978), didn't sell well enough. So they abandoned their progressive rock sound and tried to go for something more commercial, which included hiring a new lead singer named Robert Fleischman.

50 million years ago, horses had three toes on each foot.

Fleischman wrote three songs for *Infinity*, including "Wheel in the Sky," but the rest of the band didn't feel he was a good fit, so they kicked him out of the band and replaced him with another singer, Steve Perry (who actually sang "Wheel in the Sky").

"ROCK THE CASBAH"

The Clash's biggest hit was the brainchild of drummer Topper Headon. While the band was recording *Combat Rock* in 1982, Headon charged into the studio with lyrics to the song, and laid down bass and drum tracks. But by the time the song became a hit, Headon had been thrown out of the band because of a drug problem.

"PROUD MARY"

Creedence Clearwater Revival had a massive hit in 1969 with this song, and so did several other acts. Within a year, Solomon Burke and Ike & Tina Turner had scored hits with cover versions. In all, 35 different versions of "Proud Mary" had been recorded. By the end of 1970, several dozen versions had been recorded, including one by...Leonard Nimoy.

"DON'T COME AROUND HERE NO MORE"

This 1985 hit for Tom Petty and the Heartbreakers was written by Petty and Dave Stewart of the Eurythmics. He wrote it about a weird party at Stevie Nicks's house. While everyone else was doing drugs, Petty went to sleep in an empty bedroom. He woke up at dawn to find Nicks at the foot of his bed, twirling around in a Victorian dress. Nicks's ex-boyfriend, Joe Walsh (the Eagles), came into the room and she screamed at him, "don't come around here no more!"

"SWEET HOME ALABAMA"

Lynyrd Skynyrd's best known song is a celebration of the South, but it also includes a dig at segregationist Alabama governor George Wallace, who the members of the band did not support. The song includes the line "in Birmingham they love the governor / boo, boo, boo." In spite of booing him, Gov. Wallace later invited the band to the governor's mansion and made them all honorary colonels in the Alabama militia.

"MOVIN' OUT"

Billy Joel wrote the lyrics to this 1978 song before he wrote the melody. When he came up with one, it was a smooth, soft rock ballad. He sang it for the members of his band and they just laughed. Reason: Joel had "written" the melody to Neil Sedaka's "Laughter in the Rain." (He wrote a new melody before he recorded it.)

The small projectiles in an artillery shell are named for their inventor, Henry Shrapnel.

Practice Safe Selfie!

Here's a look at a disturbing fad that smartphones and social media have made possible: death-defying "extreme" selfies that, as more than a few people have learned too late, don't always defy death.

JUST SAY *NYET*

In July 2015, the Russian Interior Ministry published a brochure giving citizens advice on how to avoid getting killed while taking selfies. "Selfies with animals don't always turn out cute!" the brochure warns alongside a graphic that shows a human figure taking a selfie next to a tiger. "Selfies on rooftops—it's a long way down!" reads the caption next to a person holding a rooftop TV antenna with one hand and taking a selfie with the other as they lean off the side of a tall building. "Selfies with weapons can kill!" reads a third caption next to a person taking a selfie with a gun in his hand.

The brochure was in response to what officials described as "an abundance of cases of trauma and even death while trying to make an original selfie." So far that year, more than a hundred Russians had been seriously injured and at least 10 had died from electrocution, falling off bridges, gunshot wounds to the head, and being run over by cars and trains—all while taking selfies. In January, two men died while posing for a selfie with a hand grenade. How do we know? Their smartphone survived the explosion and the selfie was found on the phone.

Russia is not alone. India suffered even more selfie-related fatalities than Russia did. Worldwide, more people died taking selfies in 2015 than died in shark attacks. Here are some of the unfortunate souls who made headlines when their selfies went south:

• **"Drewsssik," Vologda, Russia:** This 17-year-old student (real name not disclosed by authorities) posted several extreme selfies on his Instagram page, including one of him standing precariously atop a high bridge, and another hanging off the side of a tall building with one hand. For his next selfie, he planned to use a rope to create the appearance that he was falling off another tall building, but the rope broke and he really did fall—nine stories to his death.

• **Todd Fassler, San Diego, California:** Fassler found a rattlesnake in some bushes and, rather than leave it alone, he picked it up and tried to pose with it for a selfie. The snake bit him on the arm. Fassler survived, but the bite was so severe that not one but *two* local hospitals used up their entire stock of antivenin to treat him. Even worse (perhaps) than the bite was Fassler's medical bill—$153,000, including $83,000 for the antivenin. At last report, Fassler's insurer was still negotiating with the hospital; no word on how much of the bill he'll have to pay out of his own pocket.

- **Sourabh Jagannath Chulbhar, Nashik, India:** Chulbhar, 18, was taking a selfie on the edge of a high dam when he slipped and fell into the water hundreds of feet below. He drowned; so did a friend who tried to rescue him.

- **Courtney Sanford, High Point, North Carolina:** Sanford, 32, was driving to work on Interstate 85 near High Point when her car suddenly crossed the median and crashed head-on into a recycling truck. The driver of the truck walked away from the crash, but Sanford was killed. Neither drugs nor alcohol were factors in the collision, and police were at a loss to understand what had happened... until Sanford's friends checked her social media accounts and discovered she'd taken a selfie *and* posted it on Facebook while driving. (Not exactly an extreme selfie, but extremely bad judgment.) "The Facebook post happened at 8:33 a.m. We got the call on the wreck at 8:34 a.m.," a spokesperson for the High Point Police told reporters.

- **Eri Yunanto, Yogyakarta, Indonesia:** In May 2015, 21-year-old Eri was taking a selfie on the edge of the active Mt. Merapi volcano on the island of Java when he lost his footing and fell into the crater, a drop of more than 500 feet. A rescue crew wearing oxygen masks and fireproof coveralls recovered his body three days later. (When the eruption of Japan's Mt. Ontake volcano killed 57 people in November 2014, more than half of the victims were still clutching their smartphones when their bodies were recovered.)

- **David González Lopez, Villasequilla, Spain:** Lopez, 33, tried to take a selfie during the running of the bulls in the town of Villaseca de la Sagra. When he didn't take the picture quite quickly enough, one of the bulls gored him to death.

- **Dmitry Volodin, Irkutsk, Russia:** Volodin's mistake was thinking a hibernating bear would remain in hibernation while he took a selfie next to it using the electronic flash (since it was dark in the bear's den). "The flash seems to have disturbed the bear, which thought it was being attacked and defended itself," Russian police spokesperson Gennady Maslov told reporters. Volodin was 27. (In Colorado's Waterton Canyon recreation area near Denver, so many people posed for selfies with bears that officials closed the area to the public in 2015. It remained off limits until the bears were hibernating in their dens, where—hopefully—they would not be bothered. "We've actually seen people using selfie sticks try and get as close as possible," said a spokesperson. "Sometimes within ten feet of the wild bears.")

Pluto is 70% the size of our Moon, and has five moons of its own.

Island Wisdom

Colorful proverbs from Jamaica.

A pound of fret can't pay
an ounce a debt.

Tired feet always say that
the path is long.

If a flea had money, it would
buy its own dog.

Beauty without grace is like a
rose without smell.

A lawyer looks at you with
one eye, but he looks at your
pocket with two.

Going to bed without dinner is
better than waking up in debt.

Make a friend when
you don't need one.

A little pepper burns
a big man's mouth.

If you cannot dance, you will
say the drumming is poor.

Prayer only from the mouth
is no prayer.

A new broom sweeps clean,
but an old broom knows
every corner.

All cassava got the same
skin, but they don't all
taste the same.

When you go to a donkey's
house, don't talk about ears.

Want all, lose all.

What the goat does,
the kid follows.

Not everything that comes
from above is a blessing.

When you kick an ants' nest,
you don't know which ant
bites you.

Trouble doesn't give
signs like the rain.

The goat's business is not the
sheep's business.

Never hang your hat where
your hand can't reach.

An eyeful isn't a bellyful.

The parson always christens
his own child first.

When the cocoa bean is ripe,
it's going to burst.

All fish bite, but the shark
gets the blame.

Before a monkey buys
trousers, he has to know
where to put his tail.

It took two years to build the *Titanic*...and 2 hours and 40 minutes to sink it.

Famous and...Naked

Everyone's heard of Lady Godiva. Legend says she rode naked through town on a dare from her husband—the Lord of Coventry—after he promised to lower taxes if she did. The nude activities of these famous people aren't as well known, but—unlike Godiva's—they actually happened.

THE NAKED: Jacqueline Kennedy Onassis, former First Lady

THE DEED: In 1972, an angry Aristotle Onassis gave paparazzi a detailed map to his private Greek island, Skorpios. Reason: so they could shoot photos of his wife, Jackie, sunbathing in the nude. When the grainy black-and-white photos appeared in European men's magazines, they earned the former U.S. First Lady some very unladylike nicknames. A few years later, Larry Flint published a color spread of the nude photos in *Hustler* magazine. Jackie sued, but Flint didn't care, calling the photos "the best investment I ever made." The best investment for Jackie? Some would say remaining married to the philandering Onassis—who called opera star Maria Callas his "real wife." When he died, Jackie reportedly inherited $120 million.

THE NAKED: Charles F. Richter, physicist, seismologist, and inventor of the earthquake measuring system

THE DEED: In 1935, Richter and his wife, Lillian, joined the Fraternity Elysia, a rustic nudist camp in La Tuna Canyon near Los Angeles, California. There, the reportedly "morbidly shy" Caltech seismologist found his first group of "intimate friends." A collection of Richter's books, diaries, and home movies that spanned the 1920s to the mid-1950s offered proof, but they were destroyed in 1994...in an earthquake. Most memorable, according to Richter's nephew, Bruce Walport, were the home movies. Those included footage of Richter and his wife hiking...in the nude. "They were nudists and especially liked to walk naked," said Walport. "I feel terrible that we lost all his stuff," he added. "It's devastating."

THE NAKED: Benjamin Franklin, Founding Father, diplomat, inventor, and writer and publisher of *Poor Richard's Almanac*

THE DEED: Franklin may have had no qualms about going out in a lightning storm clutching a metal key at the end of a kite, but he did shudder at the idea of taking cold water baths that were thought to be healthful in his day. To Franklin, they were too serious a shock to the system. He preferred something a little gentler. While working as deputy postmaster for the American colonies from 1753 to 1774, Franklin lived on Craven Street in the heart of London. Every day, he sat naked at his bedroom window and enjoyed an "air bath." In a letter dated 1768, Franklin wrote: "I rise early almost every morning, and sit in my chamber without any clothes whatever, half an hour or an hour, according to the season, either reading or writing."

THE NAKED: Isadora Duncan, American modern dance pioneer

THE DEED: Thanks to the shenanigans of her banker father (fraud, forgery, bankruptcy, desertion), Isadora Duncan's childhood degenerated from wealth and high society to what she called a "wild" and "untrammeled" state. Duncan loved it. She escaped from school as often as she could and danced barefoot by the sea, mimicking the movements of birds and waves. That was Isadora's first foray into "interpretive dance." Those naked feet might have been acceptable for a young girl cavorting on the beach, but not for a grown woman dancing onstage in the late 1800s. Duncan's "modern" dances were scandalous enough to send society matrons fleeing for the theater doors. Not only did she dance without shoes, she often danced completely naked beneath long, flowing, see-through scarves. "The noblest in art is the nude," she said. "And the instrument of the dancer's art is the human body itself." Ironically, those scarves not only brought her fame and infamy, one of them—a long red chiffon one—became the instrument of her death. In 1927, while riding in an open sports car in France, Isadora leaned her head back to enjoy the breeze. Her billowing scarf wound around the rear axle and jerked her out of the car. She was probably dead before she hit the pavement. "Affectations," Gertrude Stein remarked when she heard the news, "can be dangerous."

THE NAKED: Theodore Seuss Geisel, legendary children's book author who wrote under the pseudonym Dr. Seuss

THE DEED: Dr. Seuss fans may know what happened on Mulberry Street, but far fewer know that in 1939 he bared all in a tongue-in-cheek book for adults: *Seven Lady Godivas: The True Facts Concerning History's Barest Family.* There's no evidence that Geisel drew in the nude, but he did fill page after page of *Seven Lady Godivas* with nude drawings. Yet despite all those naked Godivas, the book flopped, selling only 2,500 of the 10,000 copies printed. What went wrong? According to Geisel, he drew "the sexiest babes" he could, "but they came out looking absurd." After the book's failure, Geisel went back to writing for kids. "They're more appreciative," he said. "Adults are obsolete children, and the hell with them."

Geographacts

*A random collection of interesting trivia about
the big old bumpy globe we call home.*

The tiny Micronesian island nation of Nauru, located in the South Pacific, is the only country in the world that has no capital city.

• **The Kingdom of Lesotho,** Vatican City, and the Republic of San Marino are the only countries completely surrounded by one other country. Lesotho is surrounded by South Africa, and Vatican City and San Marino are both surrounded by Italy.

• **Those three are examples** of *enclaves*, or *enclaved states*—countries or territories that are completely surrounded by other states. An *exclave* is a part of a country that is completely surrounded by another country. For example, the town of Büsingen am Hochrhein is an exclave. It's a German town, but it's located in Switzerland. (It's in the Swiss canton of Schaffhausen, about half a mile from Germany's southern border.)

• **There are 17 countries** that have no permanent rivers. (The largest: Saudi Arabia.)

• **Do you know** how many countries border China? And can you name them? (Answers on next page.)

• **A *panhandle* is a narrow** strip of land extending out from one city, state, or territory and into another. (Like a pan's handle extends out from the pan.) Examples in the United States include the Alaska Panhandle (the narrow southeastern portion of the state that lies along Canada's western border), and the Texas Panhandle (the northernmost part of the state, which extends north between Oklahoma and New Mexico.)

• **The Desierto de Tabernas**—or the Tabernas Desert—in southeastern Spain is the driest region in Europe, and Europe's only true desert. (Bonus fact: Because it looks like the deserts of the American West, many "Spaghetti Westerns" were filmed there, as were parts of several other famous films, including *Indiana Jones and the Last Crusade* and *Lawrence of Arabia*. It's also home to three American Old West–based theme parks—Texas Hollywood, Mini Hollywood, and Western Leone.)

• ***Abyssal plains*** are plains located on the ocean floor. They're formed by *turbidity currents*—fast-moving, sediment-laden ocean currents caused by earthquakes, underwater avalanches, and related phenomena.

The blast from the 1815 eruption of Indonesia's Mt. Tambour left a crater 4 miles wide.

Such currents distribute sand and other sediments over large areas of the seafloor over long periods of time, filling in valleys and other depressions, and thereby making these plains very flat and smooth. The largest: the Enderby Abyssal Plain, off the coast of Antarctica, south of Africa. It's roughly 1.4 million square miles—more than twice the size of Alaska.

• **The tiny village of Estcourt Station** (population: 4) is the northernmost point in the state of Maine—and it's about 300 miles farther south than London, England. (It's about 650 miles farther south than Glasgow, Scotland, and about 1,000 miles south of Oslo, Norway.)

• **The Canadian province** of Nova Scotia is at roughly the same latitude as the south of France.

• **"Badlands" is a real geographical term,** used in the United States and Canada. It's the name given to regions that have suffered severe erosion by wind and water, characterized by extensive rocky gullies, ridges, spires, and buttes, with steep slopes and sparse vegetation. The term comes from the French *mauvaises terres pour traverser*—meaning "bad lands to cross"—the description 19th-century French-Canadian fur trappers gave to southwestern South Dakota. (Other badlands: Toadstool Geologic Park in northwestern Nebraska, Dinosaur National Monument in Colorado and Utah, Hell's Half-Acre in Wyoming, Big Muddy Badlands in Saskatchewan, and the Red Deer River valley in Alberta.)

• **There are more than** 7,000 islands in the Caribbean Sea. Fewer than 2 percent of them are inhabited by humans.

• **Answer to the question on previous page:** China borders 14 other countries—the most of any country. They are (going clockwise): India, Pakistan, Afghanistan, Tajikistan, Kyrgyzstan, Kazakhstan, Mongolia, Russia, North Korea, Vietnam, Laos, Myanmar, Bhutan, and Nepal. (India actually borders China in three places, and Russia borders it in two.)

*　　*　　*

AUSTRALIA...IN SOUTH AMERICA

In 1892, more than 200 Australian socialists moved to the South American nation of Paraguay to found a Utopian colony they called "New Australia." Paraguay, which had recently lost a sizable portion of its population as a result of a devastating war with Argentina, Brazil, and Uruguay, even granted 185,000 acres of land to the hopeful settlers. The colony failed miserably within about ten years...but about 2,000 descendants of the original colonists still live in Paraguay today.

App...or Crap?

*Here's a look at some of the more unusual applications
that have been created for smartphones lately.
Would you want them on your phone?*

APPLICATION: Leftover Swap, created in 2013 by Dan
Newman and Bryan Summersett, founders of a company called
Greased Watermelon

What It Does: It's a "Craigslist for leftovers" that allows users to
post profiles of their leftover food online, so that someone else can eat
it.

How It Works: Let's say someone orders a burger, fries, and a milk
shake for lunch. They finish the burger and the shake, but not the fries.
In the old days, the uneaten fries would have ended up in the trash, but
Leftover Swap allows the diner to post a photo and a description of the
unwanted food on the app's database. The fries will then appear on a
map of the area and if anyone who happens to be nearby wants them,
they can contact the owner and arrange to meet up. Three safety tips
from the Leftover Swap website: 1) "Don't give away any food that you
wouldn't eat yourself"; 2) "Don't take any food without knowing how
old it is and making sure it was kept in proper storage"; and 3) "Be as
vigilant as you would on Craigslist; if something seems off, don't do
it." Newman and Summersett say the app is good for the environment
because it reduces waste, in the process making more efficient use of
the land and resources that are used to grow food. "It's obviously not for
everybody," Newman told National Public Radio in 2013. "We're not
going to make millions."

Application: *Abe Pyon* (Abe Hops), created in the run-up to the
July 2013 parliamentary elections in Japan

What It Does (Hopefully): Make Japan's ruling Liberal
Democratic Party (LDP) more appealing to app-savvy younger voters.

How It Works: *Abe Pyon* is a video game that features a cartoon
version of LDP head Shinzo Abe, who was elected to his second term
as prime minister in December 2012. Abe begins the game standing in
front of Japan's parliament building, with a cloud-filled sky overhead.
There are also floating platforms in the sky, and the object of the game
is to make Abe hop and somersault from one platform to another and
climb ever higher in the sky. If he misses a landing, he falls to his death.
But if he continues to float higher, players can rack up enough points

to change Abe out of his boring business suit and into blue jeans, gym clothes, and—if they score enough points—a superhero cape. "There were worries that some young people thought the LDP was distant, that we lacked intimacy…that they didn't know anything about us," Takuya Hirai, the director of the LDP's Internet strategy, told the Reuters news agency. (Abe's party won big in the parliamentary elections; no word on how much credit goes to the Abe Pyon app.)

App: Am I Going Down?, released in 2015 by Vanilla Pixel, a software company in London

What It Does: It's an app for nervous travelers, but don't let the scary name fool you. Am I Going Down? is actually supposed to make users less afraid of flying.

How It Works: Using the app is kind of like buying a plane ticket on a travel website. You enter the names of your departure and arrival airports, the name of your airline, and the type of aircraft you'll be flying. When you tap the "Am I Going Down?" button, the app uses historical data to calculate the odds that your flight will crash. Example: A flight from New York City to Los Angeles aboard a United Airlines Boeing 737 has a 1 in 4,136,239 chance of crashing, which means you could take the flight every day for 11,332 years without crashing. A daily Cathay Pacific flight from Hong Kong to Los Angeles on a Boeing 777, by comparison, will crash only once in 11,146 years.

"For my analysis I only include crashes where there was at least one passenger fatality, which is the relevant stat for those with a fear of flying," software developer Nick Johns told CNN in January 2015. "The positive response from anxious fliers has been amazing."

App: Pimple Popper, released by a company called Room Candy Games in 2009. There have been seven major updates since then; version 8.6 was released in February 2014.

What It Does: It allows you to squeeze virtual zits on your phone.

How It Works: The app contains 12 pimply cartoon faces to choose from. Pick one and zoom in on the blemishes, then "use your fingers to squeeze and pop whiteheads, blackheads, full-blown pimples, and scratch off crusty scabs," says the company. (Permanent scarring of your smartphone is unlikely.) The game includes a multiplayer mode for competitive zit-zapping, and Room Candy Games also sells a holiday-themed version called Pimple Popper Seasons that makes Christmas, Valentine's Day, Easter, and Halloween that much more special.

You Call That Art?

Is it art just because someone says it is? You be the judge.

CRUZ CONTROL. In February 2016, Florida performance artist Tom Miller launched what he said would be "the most dangerous thing" he's ever done. At a Gainesville café, he stared at a gigantic photo of Texas senator Ted Cruz's mouth, without looking away, for two hours. Miller said his motivation had nothing to do with politics, but that he found Cruz's smile unnerving. "How can someone be happy and smiling, but give you the feeling they're not happy or smiling?" Miller said. "I feel like I'm staring at the abyss to see if there is any glimmer."

FEELING PUNCHY. Painter Bart van Polanen Petel plays to his strengths. The ex-boxer (he was trained by Joe Frazier) converted his gym in Tilburg, the Netherlands, into an art studio. Now his "training" consists of wrapping canvas around a punching bag, dipping his boxing gloves in paint, and punching the bag until he's created a colorful piece of art. Patel never knows what he's going to paint before he begins. "Once I start thinking about what I am seeing in front of me," he says, "I have to stop." Patel's paintings sell for more than $1,500 each.

JUST PLAIN NUTS. In 2015, Orlando artist Mateo Blanco created a portrait of Jennifer Lawrence out of exactly 9,658 peanuts glued to a wooden board. (They're Planters peanuts, to be precise.) The portrait is 78 inches tall and 55 inches wide, and took Blanco 400 hours to make. Believe it or not, the portrait was commissioned by Ripley's Believe It or Not. In planning an exhibit at the Louisville Slugger Museum in Louisville, Kentucky, the organization asked Blanco to create a portrait of someone from Kentucky using something associated with baseball. He chose Kentucky native Lawrence and peanuts.

BUZZWORTHY. Since 2001, artist Sara Mapelli has specialized in the medium of bees. She typically dances topless, but during each performance, her naked torso is covered with as many as 12,000 bees. After Mapelli applies a pheromone that mimics the scent of a queen, bees swarm and stick to her body. She then dances what she calls "a duet among many" and feels "the hive mind surround me, hold me, and expand my body on a cellular level." Although she's been stung more than 100 times, Mapelli says the point of her art outweighs the pain. "I just want people to understand that they don't need to fear nature."

Most remote town in the continental U.S.: Supai, at the bottom of the Grand Canyon.

Keith's Briefs

Few thought Rolling Stones guitarist (and party animal) Keith Richards would live past 70. And while it seems like he's never quite all there, he's pretty smart and funny.

"It's great to be here. It's great to be anywhere."

"I've never had a problem with drugs. I've had problems with the police."

"Life is a wild animal. You hope to deal with it when it leaps at you."

"If you're going to kick authority in the teeth, you might as well use both feet."

"I never thought I was wasted, but I probably was."

"I've got nothing against the daylight. I don't live totally nocturnally. Only when I feel like it. Which is most of the time."

"The only things Mick [Jagger] and I disagree about are the band, the music, and what we do."

"You can't accuse me of anything I haven't already confessed to."

"I've never turned blue in someone else's bathroom. I consider that the height of bad manners."

"My one worry is falling over on stage. This may sound absurd, but I actually slipped on a hamburger in Hamburg once, and almost fell off stage."

"Memory is fiction."

"Anything you throw yourself into, you better get yourself out of."

"I've been through more cold turkeys than there are freezers."

"I don't encourage anybody to do what I do, you know? More for me!"

"I was on the 'Who's Likely to Die' list for 10 years. I was really disappointed when I fell off that list."

"The big rule of knife fighting is never, ever use the blade. It's there to distract your opponent. While he stares at the gleaming steel, you kick his a** to kingdom come."

"Art is the last thing I'm worried about when I'm writing a song. As far as I'm concerned, art is just short for 'Arthur.'"

"Some things get better with age. Like me."

Science fact: Bears are terrified of aerial drones.

Box Office Bloopers

Our latest installment of goofs from some of Hollywood's
most popular movies. (Warning: some spoilers!)

Movie: *Independence Day* (1996)
Scene: David Levinson (Jeff Goldblum) is drunk and starts smashing up things in a room at Area 51, when he accidentally knocks over a garbage can.
Blooper: On the bottom of the can you see the words "Art Dept."

Movie: *Pirates of the Caribbean: At World's End* (2007)
Scene: Master Gibbs (Kevin McNally) is asleep, clutching a teddy bear.
Blooper: The film is supposed to take place in the early 1800s. Teddy bears weren't invented until 1902.

Movie: *Bad Boys* (1983)
Scene: Near the end of the film, Mick (Sean Penn) gets in a bloody fight with Paco (Esai Morales) in the juvenile detention facility where they both live. Surrounded by a crowd of cheering boys, they fall to the ground and struggle for control of a knife.
Blooper: For about two full seconds, you can see a cameraman squatting behind the fighting boys, with a huge camera on his shoulder. And he has an assistant standing at his side, helping him hold the camera.

Movie: *Braveheart* (1995)
Scene: During one of the film's battle scenes, William Wallace (Mel Gibson) and his army of Scottish rebels are on a battlefield, waiting to spring a trap on the rapidly advancing horsemen of the English army.
Blooper: For just a split second, a white car can be seen parked behind the English army's horsemen. (In case you're not familiar with *Braveheart*, it takes place in the 13th and 14th centuries, when there weren't a lot of cars around.)

Movie: *Teenage Mutant Ninja Turtles* (2014)
Scene: In a flashback to 1999, the teenage April (Megan Fox) uses a camcorder to take video inside her father's research lab, where the turtles were first turned into mutants.
Blooper: The camera has a Bluetooth logo on it. Bluetooth wasn't available on cameras until 2002.

Longest-running soap opera in history: *Guiding Light,* which ran for 72 years (1937–2009).

Movie: *Die Another Day* (2002)

Scene: In the big swordfight-on-a-pilotless-and-rapidly-descending airplane-that-just-flew-through-a-death-ray-over-North-Korea scene near the end of the film, Miranda Frost (Rosamund Pike) slashes Jinx (Halle Berry) across her belly, leaving a long, bloody cut.

Blooper: A short time later, after escaping the doomed plane with James Bond (Pierce Brosnan)—in a helicopter that just happened to be stored in the plane's cargo bay—Jinx is canoodling with Bond in bed. Her bare belly is shown…and it doesn't have a scratch or a scar on it.

Movie: *Django Unchained* (2012)

Scene: Basically every scene with Django (Jamie Foxx) in it.

Blooper: Django wears a pair of stylish, metal-rimmed, black-tinted sunglasses throughout much of the film, which takes place in the 1850s—and modern stylish sunglasses didn't exist until the 1920s. (Primitive sunglasses have been around for a long time. The Chinese made them from smoky quartz as far back as the 12th century. An English optician named James Ayscough made blue- and green-tinted eyeglasses in the 1750s, but those weren't meant to protect users from the sun. Ayschough thought tinted glasses could repair vision defects.)

Bonus Blooper: According to costume designer Sharen Davis, Django's shades were inspired by the sunglasses worn by Charles Bronson's portrayal of Wild Bill Hickok in the 1977 film *The White Buffalo*. That movie, based in the 1870s, was historically wrong about sunglasses, too.

Movie: *Jurassic Park* (1993)

Scene: Dennis Nedry (Wayne Knight), the park's chief computer programmer (and secret dinosaur embryo thief), is talking to his accomplice via his computer. He is watching the accomplice, who is at the island park's dock, via what looks like a live video feed.

Blooper: It's not a live feed—it's a video. You can see the time marker moving left to right across the scrollbar at the bottom of the screen.

Movie: *The Monuments Men* (2014)

Scene: During the film's Battle of the Bulge Christmas sequence, Richard Campbell (Bill Murray) receives a care package from home. In it is a recording of his daughter singing *Have Yourself a Merry Little Christmas*. A friend plays it over the army camp's PA system, marking what critics called one of the film's most poignant scenes.

Blooper: They played a version of the song that didn't exist at the time. *Have Yourself a Merry Little Christmas* was indeed a popular song during the final months of World War II—it was released in November

1944, in the film *Meet Me in St. Louis* (sung by Judy Garland), a month before the Battle of the Bulge began. But the lyrics were later changed. The original version ended with a verse that said, "until then, we'll have to muddle through somehow." When Frank Sinatra recorded the song in 1957, he thought that was too depressing, so he asked the original lyricist, Hugh Martin, to rewrite the lyrics, which is how we ended up with the more familiar "hang a shining star upon the highest bough" lyric. The version sung in the film is the one written in 1957—thirteen years after the Battle of the Bulge.

Movie: *The Goonies* (1985)
Scene: At the end of the film, when the kids are being interviewed about their adventures, Data (Ke Huy Quan) tells a reporter, "The part with the octopus was really scary!"
Blooper: That comment was supposed to be about an actual scene in the film, in which the kids battled a giant octopus—but that scene was deleted during the editing process, making the statement a non sequitur. Bonus: This blooper was un-blooped in the 1990s, when the Disney Channel started airing the movie—and they put the octopus scene back in. The DVD version includes it in the "deleted scenes" extras.

Movie: *Terminator 3: Rise of the Machines* (2003)
Scene: John Connor (Nick Stahl) and Kate Brewster (Claire Danes) get ready to take off from an airport in a small airplane. The registration number on the side of the airplane reads "N3035C."
Blooper: When the plane is shown flying through the air, the registration number has somehow changed to "N3973F." When the plane lands, the number is back to "N3035C."

*　　*　　*

AMERICAN PRODUCTS FROM AROUND THE WORLD
- In Spain, duct tape is called *cinta Americana* (American tape)
- In France, brass knuckles are *le poing américain* (the American fist)
- In Brazil, iceberg lettuce is *alface americana* (American lettuce)
- In Slovenia, coleslaw is *ameriska solate* (American salad)
- In Japan, a corn dog is *amerikandoggu* (self-explanatory)
- In Italy, a placemat is *tovaglietta all-americana* (little American tablecloth)
- The Dutch have a phrase that refers to the wage and advantages gap between rich and poor: *Amerikaanse toestanden* (American conditions)

The novel *Jap Herron*, published in 1917, was supposedly dictated through a Ouija board.

Weird Superheroes

Here are some uncanny superheroes from comic books who you probably won't be seeing on the big screen anytime soon.

The Dogwelder (DC Comics, 1997). A mute superhero in a welding mask who traps stray dogs in back alleys and then uses his welding tools to weld them to the faces of bad guys.

Big Bertha (Marvel Comics, 1989). A morbidly obese mutant who can manipulate her body weight and can get as fat as she wants, growing stronger and more invincible as she does. (She slims down by "power puking," expelling most of her fat.)

Squirrel Girl (Marvel Comics, 1992). She can control and communicate with squirrels. Her sidekick: Monkey Joe. (He's a squirrel.)

Gunfire (DC, 1993). He can excite the atoms in any object to create an explosive force that essentially turns anything he touches into a gun.

Brother Power the Geek (DC, 1968). He was a mannequin dressed in hippie clothes, until he was struck by lightning and came to life. He also runs incredibly fast and can't feel pain.

Tar Baby (Marvel Comics, 1985). A homeless street punk with a mohawk, a studded leather jacket, and a superpower: his body releases a tarlike substance that makes him able to stick to anything.

Dead Girl (Marvel Comics, 1991). She's a zombie, but she can reanimate herself into a live human whenever she likes.

Zeitgeist (Marvel Comics, 2001). He vomits acid.

The Red Bee (Quality Comics, 1940). Dressed in red and yellow stripes to resemble a bee, his ability was being able to control a highly intelligent bee that he stored in a pouch behind his belt buckle. The Red Bee made the bee sting bad guys. (The bee's name: Michael.)

Vibe (DC Comics, 1984). Formerly a Detroit gang leader named Paco Ramone, by day he's now a breakdancer. By night, he's Vibe, a superhero with the power to shoot intense vibrational waves that knock down bad guys.

Crickets can be processed into high-protein flour.

Maggott (Marvel Comics, 1997). This blue-skinned humanoid serves as host to two cat-sized maggots called Eany and Meany. They can eat anything, so Maggott releases them, and when they burrow back into his body, the "nutrients" in the food they just ate give Magott his super-strength.

Kid Eternity (Quality Comics, 1942). Once dead and then revived by St. Peter, Kid Eternity had the ability to summon any hero, be they from history or mythology.

Danny the Street (DC Comics, 1990). His power: he's a living chunk of pavement that can become part of any street or sidewalk, enabling him to spy on anyone. (In human form, he's a teleporting cross-dresser.)

The Almighty Dollar (Marvel Comics, 1992). Mild-mannered accountant J. Pennington Pennypacker went to what he thought was a self-esteem-building retreat, only to have a mad scientist kidnap him. The madman's experiments turned Pennypacker into the Almighty Dollar. One of his powers: He can shoot pennies out of his wrists.

Skateman (Pacific Comics, 1983). After returning home from fighting in the Vietnam War, Billy Moon's best friend is murdered by bikers, so Billy starts dispensing vigilante justice…on roller skates.

Doorman (Marvel Comics, 1989). This hero could teleport people, but only inside of the same building and only from one room to the next.

Jack of Hearts (Marvel Comics, 1976). As a boy, Jack Hart's scientist father accidentally doused him in "Zero Fluid," which gave him super-abilities. But they were powerful for him to control, so in order not to hurt himself or his friends, he spends his life in a containment suit that makes him look like the jack of hearts from a deck of cards. (The suit is also decorated with little hearts.)

Arm-Fall-Off-Boy (DC Comics, 1989). He can detach his limbs and use them to hit bad guys with.

Razorback (Marvel Comics, 1977). A muscular, 6'8" truck driver from Arkansas named Buford Hollis puts an oversized, electrified razorback pig head over his own head in order to fight crime. He has the ability to drive any vehicle known to man.

Mogo (DC Comics, 1985). This member of the Green Lantern Corps helps that character defend the universe against evil. Mogo isn't a human or animal—it's a sentient planet.

Word Origins

Ever wonder where these words came from?
Here are the interesting stories behind them.

FISHY

Meaning: Arousing feelings of doubt or suspicion

Origin: "English prime minister Benjamin Disraeli (1804–81) made his way up the political ladder against great opposition. Had it not been for his brilliant wit and colorful use of language, he might have been remembered as a small-time politician. In his 1884 novel *Coningsby*, Disraeli tried to write as people talk and made many comparisons, one of which was the 'most fishy thing I ever saw.' The odor of fish made him think of doubtful political deals, noting also that both fish and politicians may be slippery. The new expression came into general use to label any situation that includes suspicious elements." (From *Why You Say It*, by Webb Garrison)

OGRE

Meaning: A hideous giant from fairy tales who eats people

Origin: "The word first appeared in Charles Perrault's 1697 work, *Les Contes de ma mère l'Oye*, later translated into English as *Mother Goose Tales*. Perrault's fictional giants became 'ogres' in English as well. Perrault seems to have coined the word himself, and while he never specified where it came from, the consensus among etymologists is that it is a French form of a word in Italian dialect: *ogro*. That, in turn, comes from the standard Italian word *orco*, which means 'fiend' or 'demon.' *Orco* can be traced to the Latin Orcus, a Roman god of the underworld." (From *From Achilles' Heel to Zeus's Shield*, by Dale Corey Dibbley)

GLASS CEILING

Meaning: The unofficial barrier impeding women and minorities from reaching as high of a position or office as white men

Origin: "Looking through the glass darkly, one can define glass ceiling as 'what men in the boardroom are standing on.' These are the words of a woman participant at a 1988 University of Southern California conference entitled 'Women, Men, and the Media: Breakthroughs and Backlash.' The term itself was first introduced in the mid-1980s by the *Wall Street Journal*. Interest in the term increased in the early 1990s because of the Labor Department's 'glass ceiling reviews' of U.S. corporations." (From *Word Watch*, by Anne H. Soukhanov)

If you don't like turbulence, choose a seat over the wing of the plane. You'll feel the bumps less.

GAME

Meaning: A competitive leisure activity; prey that is hunted by humans

Origin: "Gamecocks were a special breed of rooster with a large body and short legs especially trained to fight. The adjective 'game' arose in the 18th century to describe an animal or person who showed the same plucky spirit as the bird. The origin of 'game' probably lies in a pre-historic word *gaman*, composed of *ga-*, 'together,' and *mann-*, 'person,' which meant 'participation, togetherness.' From this word came Old English *gamen*, 'amusement, fun, sport.' The word first began to denote a 'diversion, pastime' in the early 1200s. All subsequent applications of the word to leisure activities derive from this basic meaning." (From *The Chronology of Words and Phrases*, by Linda and Roger Flavell)

PLANET

Meaning: A celestial body that orbits a star

Origin: "Before the regular movement of planets around the sun was known, they seemed, to the ancients, stars wandering in the heavens. Hence the Greek verb *planan*, meaning 'to lead astray,' or 'to wander'; and the Greek *planetes asteres*, meaning 'wandering stars.'" (From *Dictionary of Word Origins*, by Joseph T. Shipley)

TIRADE

Meaning: A long, angry speech of criticism or accusation

Origin: "Tirade comes from the Latin *tirata*—a 'volley of fire.' So when a politician says he's going to 'fire off a blast' at his opponent, he is very literally readying a tirade." (From *Dictionary of Word and Phrase Origins*, by William and Mary Morris)

FASCISM

Meaning: A form of radical authoritarian nationalism

Origin: "If you happen to have an old dime from before 1946, you will see the 'mark of the Fascist'—a bundle of sticks with an ax protruding. The term comes from the Italian *fascismo*, and this in turn is built on the Latin *fascis*, which meant 'a bundle,' usually of sticks or rods. This bundle with the ax was the symbol of official power that was carried before all Roman magistrates. In 1919, Italian dictator Benito Mussolini resurrected the word for his own use." (From *Word Origins and Their Romantic Stories*, by Wilfred Funk)

*   *   *

"All generalizations are bad." —**R. H. Grenier**

The gray fruit of the African sausage tree can grow 2 feet long and weigh 15 pounds.

The E-Juice Is Loose

Even if you're not a smoker, you're probably aware of the "vaping" fad: electronic cigarettes that convert liquid in a cartridge into inhalable vapor. Hundreds of "vape shops" have popped up around the country, selling nicotine-laced "e-juice" cartridges in a variety of odd flavors. Some are gross…but is it any grosser than smoking?

"The Elvis"
(a combination
of bananas,
bacon, and
peanut butter)

Fish Sauce

Energy Drink

Birthday Cake

Candy Fart

Gummi Bear

Black Pepper

Butter

Crab Juice

Dill Pickle

Fauxritos
(nacho cheese
Doritos)

Roast Chicken
with Potatoes

Tomato Soup

Sweet Potato
Casserole

"Italian Cheese"

Roast Beef

Worcestershire
Sauce

Crab Legs

BBQ Chicken

Chrysanthemum
Tea

Eggnog

Bacon

Banana Nut
Bread

Cuban Cigar

Whiskey

Pie Crust

Raisin

"Fluffernutter"
(peanut butter
and marshmallow
cream)

Sweet Cream

Sweet Tea

Blue Cheese

"Stone Smurf"
(blue raspberry
and marijuana
flavor)

Marmite

Hot Dog

Jalapeno

Rum

Chicken N'
Waffles

Dirty Ashtray

Ouzo

Fried Ice Cream

Wasabi

Cheese Pizza

Pink Champagne

Mother's Milk
(*really*)

You don't have to go to the North Pole to visit the Santa Claus Museum. It's in Santa Claus, Indiana.

I Can't Believe I Ate the *Whole* Thing

*What do all these restaurant challenges have in common?
Throwing up is an automatic disqualification.*

THE KODIAK ARREST

Restaurant: Humpy's Great Alaskan Alehouse (Anchorage, AK)

The Rules: You must scarf down three pounds of Alaskan king crab, seven crab nuggets, 14 inches of reindeer sausage, side dishes, and a dessert of wild berry crisp and ice cream. You have one hour.

Prizes: It costs $179.99 to take the challenge, which will be refunded if you succeed. Your photo will be displayed in the Humpy's Hall of Fame, and you'll receive an "I got crabs at Humpy's" T-shirt.

Reigning Champion: Most people who win finish just in the nick of time. Not Jefory C.—he crammed down an entire Kodiak Arrest (including the dessert) in only 12 minutes and 10 seconds.

THE FRENCH QUARTER 15 DOZEN CLUB

The Restaurant: Acme Oyster House (New Orleans, LA)

The Rules: To become a member, you have to wolf down a minimum of 15 dozen oysters—that's 180 raw oysters—in only one hour. (As is the case with most of these challenges, you must sign a medical release form before starting your meal.)

Prizes: If you succeed, your bill will be cut in half, plus your name will be added to the coveted 15 Dozen Board. You also get a free hat and a T-shirt. If you beat the house record, all your oysters are free.

Reigning Champion: Good luck besting Pat Bertoletti—he slurped an astonishing 528 oysters in just one hour in July 2015.

STUFFED SOPAIPILLA CHALLENGE

The Restaurant: Sadie's of New Mexico (Albuquerque, NM)

The Rules: You have one hour to finish off the restaurant's signature dish—the Stuffed Sopaipilla. Invented in New Mexico 200 years ago, sopaipillas are fried pastries usually served as a dessert. But Sadie's version is more like a massive burrito with fried bread instead of a tortilla. It's stuffed with beef or chicken and covered with chilies, salsa, lettuce, tomatoes, and tortilla chips. And it weighs a whopping *seven pounds*.

Some spiders can make seven different types of silk.

Prizes: If you can finish it, your meal is free (and you probably won't need to eat again for two or three days). You'll also win a Sadie's T-shirt, an official certificate, a jar of Sadie's Salsa, as well as a photo of yourself with your certificate and a giant, empty plate.

Reigning Champion: The record for the fastest time belongs to Ben Monson; in 2009 he downed a Stuffed Sopaipilla in seven minutes and 56 seconds. That's nearly one pound per minute!

THE 'WICHZILLA CHALLENGE

The Restaurant: Wiches (Oxford, MI)

The Rules: "Do you possess the strength to take down 'wichzilla?" If you think you do, says Wiches, you have exactly 30 minutes and three seconds to inhale a huge sandwich containing 4½ pounds of turkey, ham, bacon, cheese, lettuce, tomato, and garlic aioli.

Prizes: You'll receive a $25 gift certificate, a Wiches T-shirt, and your photo will be added to the Wiches' Wall of Fame. What if you don't win? "Fail, and hang your head (and your picture) in shame!"

Reigning Champion: A patron named Jake Ladder conquered his 'wichzilla in only 12 minutes and 40 seconds.

THE 55 CHALLENGE

The Restaurant: Hwy 55 (various locations around the U.S.)

The Rules: Eat a 55-ounce burger in only 30 minutes. This 3½-pound behemoth is comprised of seven cheeseburgers stacked on top of each other. The massive burger also comes with a minimum of four toppings. And if that's not difficult enough, you also have to finish off a side of fries and a 24-ounce soda.

Prizes: You get your name on the restaurant's website, plus your meal is free. (If you don't finish, it costs $29.99.) Those with the best times are invited to the annual 55 Challenge contest at the Mt. Olive Pickle Festival in North Carolina.

Reigning Champion: Competitive eater "Furious" Pete Czerwinski decimated the giant burger in only three minutes and 27 seconds.

THE KITCHEN SINK SUNDAE CONTEST

The Restaurant: San Francisco Creamery (Walnut Creek, CA)

The Rules: Polish off the Kitchen Sink in 30 minutes or less. What goes into the Kitchen Sink? Three sliced bananas, eight scoops of ice cream, eight toppings, plus whipped cream, toasted almonds, and cherries. This dessert is so large that it's served in a kitchen-sink-sized bowl (complete with a faucet).

Prizes: Free ice cream for a year! Not only that, a framed photo of your feat will be displayed on the Creamery's wall.

Reigning Champion: In 2013 competitive eater Ramsey Hilton devoured the Kitchen Sink in a mere 16 minutes and 40 seconds.

THE CARNIVORE CHALLENGE

The Restaurant: Big Pie in the Sky Pizzeria (Kennesaw, GA)

The Rules: In one hour, teams of two must eat every slice of a 30-inch, 11-pound pizza. Mandatory toppings include pepperoni, ground beef, Italian sausage, ham, and bacon.

Prizes: It costs $50 to try, but your team will split $250 for finishing off the big pie. And judging by rule #2, the restaurant has had some problems with past challengers biting off more than they can chew:

> You cannot throw up, and if you do, you are responsible for any necessary cleanup! If you are going to throw up, do it outside, or make it to the bathroom. No one is going to clean up your personal mess nor should you expect them to, so use common sense. If you feel like you are going to throw up, stop eating and handle it! No one in the dining room wants to see that while they are eating!

Reigning Champions: Erik Unger and Anthony Reganato put away 11 pounds of pizza in 33 minutes (and they didn't throw up).

THE 72-OUNCE STEAK CHALLENGE

The Restaurant: The Big Texan Steak Ranch (Amarillo, TX)

The Rules: In one hour, you must eat an entire 72-ounce steak. And if five pounds of beef isn't enough, you also have to eat the sides: shrimp cocktail, a baked potato, a side salad, and a buttered roll.

Prizes: Clear your plate and your meal is free—otherwise it costs $72. For your achievement, you'll receive an official certificate and your name will be added to the 72-ounce Hall of Fame.

Reigning Champion: This challenge began in 1962 and its Hall of Fame is 40 pages long, but Molly Schuyler stands above the rest. In 2015, Schuyler—who bills herself as the "No. 1 independent female competitive eater in the world"—methodically took care of not one, not two, but *three* 72-ounce steaks, *three* shrimp cocktails, *three* baked potatoes, *three* salads, and *three* rolls…in only 20 minutes. That's nearly 20 pounds of food. And Schuyler weighs only 124 pounds. "We've seen a lot of things come through these doors," said Big Texan owner Bobby Lee, "but Molly—she takes the cake. She takes lots and lots of cake."

* * *

"The power of imagination makes us infinite." —**John Muir**

Weird Animal Records

Humans aren't the only ones who sacrifice safety and dignity for fame and glory?

Fastest dog on two paws. Jiff is a Pomeranian from Los Angeles who holds two Guinness World Records: one for the fastest time covering 5 meters, walking on just his front legs (7.76 seconds), and one for fastest time covering 10 meters while walking upright on his hind legs (6.56 seconds).

Loudest cat. A 13-year-old cat named Merlin from Torquay, England, has been certified as having the loudest purr ever recorded by a domestic cat. Merlin's purrs were measured at 67.8 decibels—the equivalent of a vacuum cleaner.

Most balls caught with paws. In September 2015, a Japanese beagle named Purin set the record for best canine goalie. Standing in front of a scaled-down soccer goal on his hind legs, the nine-year-old caught 14 mini soccer balls in under a minute. (Previous record: 11.)

Longest eyelashes on a dog. Dogs have eyelashes? Yes, apparently they do. In 2014, a Labradoodle from Australia named Ranmaru was confirmed to have the longest, averaging 6.69 inches for each eye.

Longest occurrence of panda mating. Pandas are an endangered species, and zoos often have to force them to copulate. Pandas, it seems, just don't like mating; a successful romantic encounter generally lasts between 30 seconds and two minutes. But in 2015, Lu Lu and Zhen Zhen, pandas at the Sichuan Giant Panda Research Center, set a new record for panda lovemaking: 18 minutes and 3 seconds. (The zookeepers filmed it…and the video went viral.)

Most cans opened by a bird. In 2012, a green-and-orange macaw named Zac used his beak to open the flip-tops on 35 soda cans.

Longest human tunnel skated through. Otto is a bulldog that's been trained to ride a skateboard. In 2015, in Lima, Peru, 30 people stood in a long row with their legs spread far apart, and Otto rode his skateboard through the "tunnel."

Fastest turtle. Turtles are not known for their speed. But the fastest on record is Bertie, who lives in a resort in England. His top speed: 0.92 feet per second, which translates to a blistering 0.627 miles per hour.

Ultramarathoners (who regularly run more than 26.2 miles at a time) can lose 6% of...

Strange Lawsuits

These days, it seems that people will sue each other over practically anything. Here are some real-life examples of unusual legal battles.

THE PLAINTIFFS: Five inmates serving time in the Idaho State Correctional Institution near Boise

THE DEFENDANTS: Several alcoholic beverage manufacturers, including Anheuser-Busch, Coors, Miller Brewing, Gallo Wineries, Jim Beam, and Jack Daniels

THE LAWSUIT: In a suit that they wrote all by themselves, the five inmates claimed that if beer and liquor bottles had adequate warning labels like cigarette packets do, they would have never started drinking this "gateway drug" and therefore would not have committed any crimes. "If I was not an alcoholic," wrote Jeremy Brown, who was serving time for shooting a man, "the shooting would never have happened…I have spent a great deal of time in prison because of situations that have arose because of people being drunk." Inspired by similar "Big Tobacco lawsuits," the inmates were suing for $1 billion.

THE VERDICT: Case dismissed. In his decision, Judge Ronald E. Bush stated the obvious: "It is commonly known to the public that alcohol poses an obvious danger—encompassing many different subcategories of danger—to those who choose to consume it."

THE PLAINTIFF: Lori Bruno Sforza, a 75-year-old witch

THE DEFENDANT: Christian Day, a 45-year-old warlock

THE LAWSUIT: Shortly before Halloween 2015, Sforza went to court in Salem, Massachusetts (the same town that executed "witches" in the 1690s) to seek protection against Day for harassment. Sforza, who was described by the *Guardian* as "wearing a long black coat and necklaces of pentacles…with a cane topped by a silver skull," said that the two of them used to be friends, and she even thought of Day "like a son." (The witch and the warlock made headlines in 2011 when they tried to publicly "heal" Charlie Sheen.) But their relationship went south after Sforza decided to move her fortune-telling booth out of Day's occult shop and into her own space elsewhere in Salem, thus becoming his competition. So Day, who bills himself as "the World's Most Famous Warlock," allegedly started calling Sforza late at night and insulting her. She also claimed that he slandered her on Facebook by posting an "ugly cartoon" of her.

The case got even stranger when Day's lawyer didn't show up because he was sick and "throwing up on his suit." (The warlock stopped short of accusing the witch of casting a spell on the lawyer.) Day quickly found another lawyer—in the courthouse hallway—who, after two hours of preparation, accused Sforza of seeking free publicity. He argued that she, like Donald Trump, is a public figure, so it's legal to ridicule her on the Internet. Sforza objected: "I am *not* Donald Trump!"

Although there were no phone records to prove the harassment, Sforza's lawyer pointed out that Day had previously been told by a judge to stop making harassing calls to women. Even more damning: two people testified that they overheard Day calling Sforza "vulgar sexist obscenities" at the occult shop they once shared. "I am a woman," Sforza told the court. "I am not somebody's footstool."

THE VERDICT: Judge Robert A. Brennan sided with the witch, whom he described as "heartfelt and credible." Day was ordered to cease all contact with Sforza…or spend two and a half years in prison. After the verdict was read, Day, whose Twitter tagline is "Warlock. Drama Queen. B*tch," shouted, "On everything that is holy, I did not make those calls!" Then he stormed out of the courtroom. He promised to appeal the decision but hadn't done so at last report. As for Sforza, she told reporters she's happy with the verdict, but being a fortune-teller and all, "I knew I would win the case."

THE PLAINTIFF: Anton Purisima, 62, of Manhattan, New York

THE DEFENDANTS: Almost everyone

THE LAWSUIT: In 2014, Purisima filed a handwritten 22-page lawsuit against anyone he could think of who had ever wronged him, including Kmart Store 7749, St. Luke's Emergency Department, Au Bon Pain, Carepoint Health, Hoboken University Medical Center, New York City Transit Authority, LaGuardia Airport, the City of New York, the "Latina" whose rabid dog allegedly bit him, and the "Chinese couple" who photographed him while he was in the hospital. Because Purisima said that his pain and suffering is "priceless," he sued for $2,000,000,000,000,000,000,000,000,000,000,000,000.

THE VERDICT: Case dismissed. The amount that Purisima was suing for is a real number—two undecillion—but it's actually more money than there is on Earth. (So if he had won, we would have all been forced to give him all of our money.)

*   *   *

"Every joke is a tiny revolution." —**George Orwell**

Glassblowers work with materials that are the same temperature as molten lava.

Your Taxe$ at Work

Concerned about the government's priorities? Now you can breathe a sigh of relief, knowing your tax dollars are being well spent on things like…

Robots. In 2015, the Department of Defense spent $2 million on a new robot. One that will attack the enemy like the Terminator? Try Trumpet-inator: this robot will play a trumpet and improvise jazz music alongside human musicians.

Cold ones. Two grad students at the University of Washington received a $1.3 million grant from the National Science Foundation to study how foam beer can holders known as "koozies" keep beer cold.

Vino. The National Science Foundation awarded $853,000 to Yakima Valley Community College in Washington state to expand its wine-making program. Community colleges cater largely to 18-to-20-year olds, so some of the money will go toward serving alcohol…to minors.

Sweatin' monkeys. The National Institute of Health spent $1 million testing the physiological response of the body to strenuous exercise. How? By putting 12 marmosets inside transparent hamster balls and making them run on a treadmill at increasing speeds. Three monkeys pooped in their balls; another vomited. (The National Institute on Aging spent $600,000 of taxpayer money on a similar study.)

Dough dope. The National Institutes of Drug Abuse spent $780,000 (and five years) studying whether pizza was as addictive as drugs. Findings: 100 college students surveyed said they felt pizza was indeed addictive, but not as addictive as ice cream, chocolate, or French fries.

Stop 'n' go. In 2015, the U.S. Agency for International Development spent $2 million on a campaign urging Americans to visit Lebanon. That's the same year the State Department warned Americans to "avoid all travel in Lebanon because of ongoing safety and security concerns" because of ISIS terrorist cells operating inside the country.

Antigravity sheep. NASA spent $1.2 million on a Colorado State University study of "the impact of space travel on bones." They simulated weightlessness by fitting two dozen sheep with braces that kept one hind leg in the air, throwing off their balance in a way that is only remotely similar to the loss of balance astronauts feel in zero gravity.

Oh, You Goosecap!

Feel free to use these real insults from the 1700s, but nobody will understand what you're saying. (Or maybe that's the perfect reason to use them.)

Slamkin: a slovenly dressed woman (also called a "shabbaroon")

Clotpoll: a blockhead

Souse-crown: a fool

Thatch-gallows: a shady individual

Crab lanthorn: a short-tempered grump

Squeeze crab: someone with a sour look on their face

Addle pate: an immature man

Bell swagger: a loud, obnoxious person

Malkintrash: someone who wears cheap, ugly clothes

Rusty guts: an angry and ill-tempered person

Hoddy doddy: short and clumsy

Pickthank: a troublemaker

Hog grubber: a mean and miserly person

Rattle-pate: someone who is volatile and unsteady

Clouted shoon: a country bumpkin, after the iron-tipped shoes worn by peasants

Ninnyhammer: a foolish or stupid person

Fussock: a lazy fat woman

Sheep's head: someone who, like a sheep's head, is all jaw, meaning they never stop talking

Clunch: a clumsy oaf

Hop-o-my-thumb: a short person

Bracket-faced: ugly

Lobcock: a dullard

Sapscull: a sappy and sentimental person

Muckworm: a miser

Goosecap: a silly person

Buffle-headed: stupid

Cod's head: a stupid person

Hopper-arsed: a reference to someone whose rear-end is so big it looks like a "hopper," which is another term for a basket

People used to collect Christmas cards. Newspapers reviewed them like they do books today.

Forbidden Word

"Isis" is the name of an Egyptian goddess, and it's been widely adopted as a name for businesses and other things because it's easily pronounceable and understood across many languages. But in 2014, ISIS came to mean something else: an acronym for "Islamic State of Iraq and Syria." Result: A lot of name-changing.

The animated comedy *Archer* debuted on FX in 2009. Until 2015, it was about a dysfunctional spy agency called the International Secret Intelligence Service, or ISIS. When the real-life ISIS made headlines in 2015, *Archer* producers decided to have the agency merge with the CIA so ISIS didn't have to be mentioned anymore.

• In 2015, a French rock band called Isis Child changed its name to Angel's Whisper. Reasons: 1) The band didn't want to be associated with an international terrorist organization; and 2) Members of Isis Child say that news reports about the other ISIS were completely burying the band's results in online search engines.

• As it had done several times before, *Downton Abbey* killed off a beloved character in its fifth season. This time the victim was Lord Grantham's dog, Isis. Producers claim it's just a coincidence, and that they were allowing the aging dog who plays the role to retire.

• The chocolate company Italo Suisse, a collaboration of Italian and Swiss chocolatiers, was founded in 1923. By 2013, the company no longer had any association with Italy or Switzerland, and changed its name to the exotic-sounding ISIS Chocolates. Just a few months later, ISIS began its reign of terror, and ISIS Chocolates almost went bankrupt due to declining sales. The company changed its name again, this time to Libeert, after the Libeert family, which owned the company.

• ISIS Nails is a small nail salon in Queens, New York. In 2015, its revenues declined by more than 30 percent, prompting the owner to change its name to Bess Nails and Spa. Sales recovered immediately.

• Immigrant Settlement and Integration Services (ISIS) is an agency in Nova Scotia that helps new immigrants settle into life in Canada. (Ironically, many of its clients are from Iraq and Syria.) The agency's new name: ISANS, or Immigrant Services Association of Nova Scotia.

• A globally minded think tank called the Institute for Science and International Security (ISIS) has refused to change its name, but did adopt a new handle on Twitter: @TheGoodISIS.

Germany still has bomb squads that dismantle bombs dropped during World War II.

Roommates from Hell

Lots of people who've had roommates have had at least one who was tough to live with. Uncle John's stole his friends' credit cards and used them to buy laptops, clothing, and other stuff. How about you? Recognize any of these characters?

ROOMMATES: Aaron Homer, 24, and his girlfriend Amanda Williamson, 21, who lived with their friend Robert Maley, 25, in an apartment in Chandler, Arizona

STORY: Homer and Williamson were both into "vampire stuff." "They think they're vampires," said Maley. One day in October 2010, Homer approached Maley with a knife and asked if he could make a cut on Maley's arm and suck blood from the wound. Maley refused. "I said 'no,' and he flipped. He said, 'I'm doing it,' and then boom—he stabbed me," Maley told police. Firefighters happened to be responding to a call next door, and when they saw Maley burst out of his apartment and take off running down the street bleeding profusely from his arm, they called the police. The cops arrested Homer on charges of aggravated assault, and arrested his girlfriend for giving a false statement to police (she claimed that *she* had stabbed Maley and that it was in self-defense). Maley wasn't hard to find; all the police had to do was follow the trail of blood down the street. The cops treated his stab wound, then they arrested him on an outstanding warrant for violating his probation on an earlier aggravated assault charge.

WHAT HAPPENED: In May 2011, Homer pled guilty to aggravated assault and received three years of probation. (The stabbing incident was actually the *second* time Homer had asked for permission to suck Maley's blood. On the first occasion, Maley agreed to let him do it. "Homer sucked Maley's blood for two to three minutes that time," reported the *Arizona Republic*.)

ROOMMATES: Kenneth Chambers, 52, who shared a Lakewood, Washington, mobile home with a woman not named in news reports

STORY: Police say that in July 2014, Chambers asked the woman to clean his ear for him. When she refused, Chambers, who is toothless, threw a fit and pulled a door in the mobile home off its hinges. The woman sat on Chambers's lap and tried to calm him down, but he pushed her off of his lap, then grabbed her wrist and "gummed" it by biting it with his toothless mouth. The gumming was painful but left no injuries; the only permanent damage the woman suffered was to her hearing aid when Chambers angrily splashed her with water.

WHAT HAPPENED: Chambers claimed self-defense, but when a witness corroborated the woman's version of events, police hauled him off to the slammer. In August 2014, he pled guilty to assault and malicious mischief. The judge fined him $950, sentenced him to two years' probation, and ordered him to stay away from the woman he gummed.

ROOMMATES: Thomas Hahn, 55, who shared his Holly Hill, Florida, house with three people, including 35-year-old Robert Gray Jr.

STORY: When Gray came home drunk one night in December 2012 and began cooking pork chops in a manner that Hahn did not approve of, the two men began arguing over how best to prepare them. Police say that's when Hahn, also drunk, got out his .22-caliber Ruger rifle and shot Gray three times, killing him instantly.

WHAT HAPPENED: Hahn claimed he acted in self defense, but when the other housemates didn't back him up, he was arrested and charged with second-degree murder. At last report he was jailed without bail and awaiting trial. "There is no clear answer at this hour as to why Hahn acted with such extreme violence," Volusia County Police Chief Mark Barker told reporters.

* * *

WEIRD ANSWERS TO A CLASSIC RIDDLE

Q: "What's black and white and red all over?" **A:** "A newspaper." ("red" sounds like "read"—get it?) This classic riddle dates back to at least 1917. Almost since then, people have been coming up with clever and somewhat twisted variations on the riddle. Here are a few we found.

• An embarrassed penguin.
• Two nuns in a chainsaw fight.
• A Communist nun.
• A referee with a javelin in his head.
• A zebra painted red.
• A zebra who's terrible at putting on lipstick.
• A sunburned zebra.
• A chocolate cake with white frosting covered in strawberries.
• A Communist newspaper.
• A skunk in a blender.
• A panda in a cocktail dress.
• A bloody piano.
• A Holstein cow in a cherry pie eating contest.

Cover Me...

Want to be insured against something very weird? There's probably some insurance company somewhere willing to offer you some very unique coverage.

...AGAINST LOSS OF NOSE

Winemaker Ilja Gort makes his living from his nose. He relies on it to test for quality at his French vineyard. "Tasting wine is something you do with your nose, not your mouth," he explains. So when he heard about a car accident victim who lost his sense of smell, Gort decided to have his nose insured against a career-ending injury...for $8 million. Lloyd's of London wrote the policy and added a few unusual provisions. For example, if he wants his mustache trimmed, Gort is only allowed to go to experienced barbers with steady hands. Riding a motorcycle? *Non!* Boxing? Not permitted. Being a fire-breather or working as a knife-thrower's assistant would also void his policy.

...AGAINST ALIEN ABDUCTION

British insurance company Goodfellow Rebecca Ingrams Pearson (GRIP) offered coverage against abduction, impregnation, or attack by aliens, and GRIP claimed to have written policies for 4,000 alien-fearing people worldwide. One of those policies was written for the Heaven's Gate religious cult. In 1996, Heaven's Gate paid $10,000 for a policy to cover up to 50 of its members. The terms of the policy: in the event of alien abduction, the insurer would pay $1 million per abductee. Six months later, 39 cult members killed themselves in San Diego, California, believing that their souls would board an alien spaceship once they'd "shed their earthly containers." There was no evidence that having the policy contributed to the mass suicide, but GRIP very quickly left the alien insurance market anyway...for a while. "Greed got the better of us and we resumed them," GRIP's managing partner, Simon Burgess, told the *San Francisco Examiner* in 1998. "I've never been afraid of parting the feeble-minded from their cash."

...AGAINST COLD FEET

Worried about your son or daughter having a change of heart after setting a wedding date, causing you to forfeit your cost of the reception hall and caterer? Check out Wedsure's "Change of Heart" policy. The wedding insurer will repay the expenses of "an innocent third party financier, other than the bride or groom" if the wedding is called off. There's a catch, though. The bride- or groom-to-be must cancel a year or more before the event. Otherwise Wedsure won't pay.

Lloyd's of London provided the first car insurance, describing cars as "ships navigating on land."

...AGAINST FALLING SPACE STATIONS

When Russia gave the order to de-orbit its *Mir* space station in 2001, people around the world worried about being hit by a chunk of falling debris. Not Taco Bell. The company set up a 40-by-40-foot floating target in the Indian Ocean and *dared* the Russians to hit it with *Mir*. If *Mir*'s core landed on the logoed bull's-eye, Taco Bell agreed to give every American a free taco. A direct hit was a long shot, but if it happened, it would have cost Taco Bell millions. So the company took out an insurance policy to cover the potential price tag. Fortunately for Taco Bell (and unfortunately for taco-loving Americans), *Mir* missed.

...AGAINST POLTERGEIST ATTACKS

Terry Meggs, owner of the Royal Falcon Hotel in Suffolk, England, was worried about the safety of his staff and guests. The ghost of a monk who supposedly hanged himself in the 500-year-old building was known to haunt room 10 (the scene of his suicide) and the bar. "I saw glasses move across the bar one night," Meggs said. "And I thought, 'What happens if it does something to hurt somebody?'" So in 2002, he took out a £1 million policy, just in case. While the policy covers death or permanent disability caused by supernatural spirits, it does state, "claims arising from *liquid* spirits are specifically excluded."

...AGAINST MISSING RATS

The insurers that underwrite Hollywood films have to be creative—otherwise most movies wouldn't get made. In 1989, director Steven Spielberg needed 2,000 live rats on the set of *Indiana Jones and the Last Crusade*. Because wrangling that many animals can be tricky, the film's insurance company, Fireman's Fund, was asked to cover a delay in filming in case any rats were lost. However, one day of filming could cost up to $700,000, prompting Fireman's to propose an alternative: they asked Spielberg the *minimum* number of rodents that could be needed. The director said he could do the scene with 1,000. "With that," explained the head of Fireman's entertainment unit, "we wrote the world's first insurance policy with a 1,000-rat deductible."

...AGAINST IMMACULATE CONCEPTION

Raising a kid is expensive, even if he is the Savior. That could be why three sisters in Inverness, Scotland, took out a £1 million insurance policy in 2002 to cover them in the event that one of them had a virgin birth. Although the burden of proof would have been on the mother, in 2006, the company decided to withdraw coverage due to complaints. "The Catholic Church is up in arms about what we've been doing," explained Britishinsurance.com director Simon Burgess. "The three ladies have been informed."

Lobsters communicate by peeing at each other.

"GO TO JAIL"

Did your mother ever tell you to always wear clean underwear, just in case you end up in the emergency room? Here's an update for the Internet age: Be careful what your T-shirt says, in case it ends up on your mug shot. The wearers of these shirts have achieved booking photo immortality.

"World's Greatest Dad"

"IT WASN'T ME"

"I'd like to apologize in advance for my behavior this evening."

"This is my kick butt shirt."

"It's all fun and games till the cops show up"

"I've been NAUGHTY"

"My anger management class PISSES ME OFF!"

"I'm sorry. My fault."

"Some people just need a high-five—in the FACE"

"TRUST ME—I'm a liar"

"[bleep] YOU"

"I'M NOT AN ALCOHOLIC I'M A DRUNK ALCOHOLICS GO TO MEETINGS"

"Not Now I'm Busy"

"Stupidity is not a crime… but it should be."

"WEBB'S BAIL BOND 24 Hours a Day 365 Days a Year"

"SEX MONEY WEED"

"Chicago Teachers Union"

"WARNING: I have PMS and a handgun"

"I AM the law!"

"I'm not Santa, but you can sit on my lap anyway"

"Trouble finds me"

"FOR RENT By the Hour"

"I shaved my balls for this?"

"If we get caught it's all your fault"

"WARNING: I do dumb things"

"Buy this Dad a BEER."

"I'm probably lying"

"Every Great Idea I Have Gets Me In Trouble"

Getting a Leg Up on the News

Usually when we say someone is "in the news," we mean the entire person. Sometimes it's only their leg.

TRASH TALK

In 2014, police in Coral Gables, Florida, contacted John Timiriasieff, 56, to find out if he'd been the victim of foul play. Reason: someone had found a human leg in a local garbage dump—and there was a note with Timiriasieff's name on it attached to one of its toes. Timiriasieff told officers he had had his right leg amputated below the knee a month earlier at nearby Doctors Hospital. The hospital had apparently simply thrown the leg in the garbage, rather than have it incinerated, as the law requires. Timiriasieff filed a lawsuit against the hospital in May 2015, citing emotional distress. "I have heard of people having the wrong limb removed," Timiriasieff's lawyer, Clay Roberts, told reporters, "but hospitals aren't supposed to throw them away."

DON'T FENCE ME IN

In January 2015, police in La Crosse, Wisconsin, attempted to pull over a man driving a car with a broken brake light, but the driver sped off. In the ensuing chase, both cars reached speeds of 80 miles per hour on the area's snowy roads before the man lost control and sent his car into a ditch. He then took off on foot through the nearby woods, with officers in pursuit, following his footprints in the snow. After about a mile, the officers were finally able to apprehend the man: he was lying on the ground, unable to get up…because his prosthetic leg had become stuck in a fence. The driver, Thomas Fuselier, 47, was arrested on several charges.

AGE OF ENLIGHTENMENT

In 2012, Leo Bonten, 53, of the Netherlands, suffered an accident and broke his right leg in several places. The leg became badly infected and he had to have it amputated just above the knee. After the operation, in what he later described as a "flash of inspiration," Bonten decided he wanted to commemorate his lost limb by making it into a lamp. That set off a legal challenge with the hospital, because they refused to return the amputated leg. "My leg is my property," Bonten told reporters. "People keep their kidney stones in a jar on the mantelpiece. I'm going to make a lamp of my leg." Bonten eventually won the legal battle, and possession of his leg. He then hired a professional lighting designer—and the leg now resides in his home, sitting in a glass container of formaldehyde that acts as the base of a large LED lamp. (Bonten later tried to sell his leg-lamp on eBay for 100,000 euros, but eBay canceled the sale. They have a rule against selling body parts.)

THE WHOLE STORY

In October 2007, Shannon Whisnant of Maiden, North Carolina, bought the contents of an abandoned storage unit. One of the items in the unit: a backyard smoker/barbecue. Inside the smoker: a human leg that had been amputated at the knee. Whisnant turned the leg in to police. They found that it belonged to a man named John Wood, who lost the leg in a plane crash in 2004. Wood had kept the leg, he told police, because when he died he wanted to be buried as a "whole man." (The hospital had given Wood his amputated leg in a garbage bag, frozen, and Wood had preserved it by soaking it in embalming fluid and then letting it dry.) He'd put it in the storage unit in the smoker when he lost his home in 2007, and subsequently lost possession of the storage unit when he missed a number of payments. A custody battle over the leg followed. Whisnant claimed it was his, because he had paid for it, and hoped to make money by charging people to see it. Wood, for obvious reasons, claimed it was his. Oddly, the men agreed to have the fate of leg decided by Judge Greg Mathis, on the TV show *Judge Mathis*. Decision: the leg belonged to Wood—but Wood had to pay Whisnant $5,000 to reimburse him for the loss of his—er, Wood's—leg.

Bonus fact: The story of the missing leg was made into a documentary titled *Finders Keepers*. The film debuted at the Sundance Film Festival in January 2015.

* * *

THE HAUNTING

There is a section of a road in the West Midlands region of England that's known as a "blackspot" because so many car crashes have occurred there. Locals blame the ghost of a little girl in Victorian dress who supposedly appears on the road right as drivers are about to "hit" her. The drivers swerve; some crash, some don't—but when they look back, the girl is nowhere to be seen. Police have no logical explanation for why the seemingly safe stretch of road has had so many accidents. And neither does ghost hunter David Taylor: "For 22 years we have been running a group who investigate claims of the paranormal. Most of the time there is a logical explanation, but so far I haven't found one for this case."

Uncle John's Page of Lists

Random bits of interesting information from the BRI files.

8 Books Neil deGrasse Tyson Says Every "Intelligent Person" Should Read

1. The Bible
2. *The System of the World* by Isaac Newton
3. *On the Origin of Species* by Charles Darwin
4. *Gulliver's Travels* by Jonathan Swift
5. *The Age of Reason* by Thomas Paine
6. *The Wealth of Nations* by Adam Smith
7. *The Art of War* by Sun Tzu
8. *The Prince* by Machiavelli

Top 6 U.S. Bacon Markets

1. New York
2. Los Angeles
3. San Antonio/ Corpus Christi
4. Baltimore/ Washington. D.C.
5. Chicago
6. Philadelphia

7 *Lucha Libre* Moves (Mexican Wrestling)

1. *Guillotina* (a leg drop)
2. *Rana* (means "frog," what this pinning position looks like)
3. *Centón* (a "blanket" splash; you jump on top of your opponent using your back)
5. *Tope* (a headbutt)
6. *Huracán rana* (invented by Huracan Ramirez, a pin resulting from a "head scissors takedown")
7. *Suicida* (any move done outside the ring)

4 Exotic Pets of World Leaders

1. Polar bear (Henry III)
2. Grizzly bear (Thomas Jefferson)
3. Giraffe (Julius Caesar)
4. Hippo (Calvin Coolidge)

10 Most Ticketed Cars (according to Insurance.com)

1. Lexus ES 300
2. Nissan 350Z
3. Dodge Charger
4. Volkswagen Jetta
5. Chevrolet Monte Carlo
6. Mazda 3S
7. Volkswagen GTI
8. Dodge Stratus
9. Acura 3.0s
10. Toyota Tacoma

5 Words That Mean Something Different in Other Languages

1. *Fart* means "speed" in Norwegian.
2. *Brat* means "brother" in Russian.
3. *Barf* means "snow" in Farsi, Hindi, and Urdu.
4. *Hammer* means "awesome" in German.
5. *Kiss* means "pee" in Swedish.

Diagnosis: Struck by Duck

Ever been hit by a golf ball in an opera house? Probably not. Probably never will be, either. But in the unlikely event that you are, rest assured that this and thousands of other bizarre diagnoses can now be entered in your medical records simply, accurately, and in detail.

CODE TALKING

If you've ever had to carefully scrutinize a medical bill, you may have noticed that your injury or illness was assigned a medical code for research and billing purposes. Those codes are part of a system called the International Statistical Classification of Diseases and Related Health Problems, or ICD for short. It was developed by the World Health Organization (an agency of the United Nations) to create a single medical classification system for the entire world.

Until 2015, the version used in the United States was the ninth revision of the code, or ICD-9, introduced in 1979. Perhaps because computers in the late 1970s had so little storage space, the ICD-9 codes were not very descriptive. There were four codes for sprained ankles, but none of them specified whether the left or right ankle was injured. There were several codes for heart disease, but they didn't go into much detail about what was wrong with the patient's heart. Was this the patient's first visit, or "initial encounter," with this complaint, or a later visit, or "subsequent encounter"? Did the patient also suffer from related conditions, an indication that their health could be poorer than the diagnosis of a single malady suggested? The ICD-9 codes didn't address any of these issues. New and exotic illnesses like the deadly Ebola virus didn't have codes at all.

NEW AND IMPROVED

In 1992, the World Health Organization replaced the ICD-9 with the ICD-10, replacing the old system's 14,000 diagnostic codes with 68,000 new ones. Other countries began adopting the ICD-10 as early as 1994, but the United States dragged its feet until October 2015. By the time it was finally adopted, the American version of code included another 76,000 codes for hospital procedures—codes that were not used in other countries. (The ICD-9 used in the United States had just 4,000 of these procedural codes.) That brought the total number of codes in the ICD-10 to 144,000—eight times as many codes as the ICD-9.

The largest known prime number is more than 22 million digits long.

MIX AND MATCH

This increase in the number of codes allowed for a much greater level of specificity than had been possible before. Now there are 40 different codes for migraine headaches. And instead of suffering an injury from a ball, which could have been anything from a table tennis ball to a bowling ball, the ICD-10 has specific codes for many types of balls. The code for an injury from a golf ball, for example, is W21.04.

Did you suffer an injury in an opera house, perhaps after slipping on a wet restroom floor? The ICD-10 includes a code for injuries sustained in opera houses—Y92.253. And the codes are designed to be combined, so that if you ever happen to be struck by a golf ball in an opera house, your health-care provider could combine the two codes to get W21.04 Y92.253, the code for "struck by golf ball in an opera house."

DIAGNOSIS: NUTS

Here's what gives the ICD-10 its peculiar charm: there's no procedure for eliminating impossible or extremely unlikely code combinations. There's a code for an injury caused by being "struck" by a turtle (presumably one that has fallen from the sky or has been thrown at someone). That code is W59.22XA. And there's a code for injuries sustained in prison swimming pools (Y92.146). Here are some more unusual medical codes:

T63.431A:	Toxic effect of venom of caterpillars
V10.3XXA:	Person getting on or off pedal cycle injured in collision with pedestrian or animal (not to be confused with V80.730A, animal-rider injured in collision with trolley)
W58.03:	Crushed by alligator (being crushed by a *crocodile* has its own code: W58.13)
W55.21:	Bitten by a cow (other cow-related injuries are coded as W55.29, "Other contact with cow")
W61.62XD:	Struck by duck, subsequent encounter
Y93.D1:	Injured while knitting and crocheting (injuries from "other arts and handcrafts" are coded as Y93.D)
V91.35:	Struck by falling object due to canoe or kayak accident
X06.0XXA:	Exposure to ignition of plastic jewelry
W61.33XA:	Pecked by chicken, first encounter
W61.11:	Bitten by macaw
R46.1:	Bizarre personal appearance
W56.22XA:	Struck by orca, initial encounter (W56.19 covers "contact with a sea lion")

World's largest spider: The Goliath Birdeater Tarantula, which can grow to more than a foot long.

Z89.419:	Absence of unspecified great toe
L81.2:	Freckles
W51.XXXA	Accidental striking against or bumped into by another person
V97.33XD:	Sucked into jet engine, subsequent encounter
V95.43XS:	Spacecraft collision, injuring occupant, subsequent encounter
Z63.1	Problems in relationship with in-laws
V91.07XD:	Burn due to water-skis on fire, subsequent encounter (drowning caused by "jumping from burning water-skis" is coded as V90.27XA)
X98.8XXS:	Assault by "other hot objects," subsequent encounter
X52:	Prolonged stay in weightless environment
W18.11.XA:	Fall from or off toilet with subsequent striking against object, subsequent encounter

*   *   *

BAD HOUSEKEEPING

"My idea of housework is to sweep the room with a glance."

—**Erma Bombeck**

"A bright person can always think of something better to do than housework."

—**Ruby Lou Barnhill**

"Dust is a protective coating for fine furniture."

—**Mario Burata**

"There's nothing to match curling up with a good book when there's a repair job to be done around the house."

—**Joe Ryan**

"We labor to make a house a home, then every time we're expecting visitors, we rush to turn it back into a house."

—**Robert Brault**

"I would rather lie on a sofa than sweep beneath it."

—**Shirley Conran**

"Where Do You Get Your Ideas?"

That's a question authors often get asked, but generally don't like to answer. One reason: an inspiration is just a germ of an idea—the real work is in the actual writing. Where the idea came from is just gossip. (But we love gossip!)

STEPHEN KING, *MISERY*

No, King was never trapped in a cabin with an insane fan. Annie Wilkes, the psychotic fan who terrorizes her favorite writer in *Misery*, was inspired by a short story by Evelyn Waugh titled "The Man Who Loved Dickens." While flying to London on the Concorde in the late 1980s, King pondered the story's plot, which involves a man being held captive by a tribal chief in South America who forces him to read various works by Dickens. "I wondered what it would be like if Dickens himself was held captive," King said.

E. L. JAMES, *50 SHADES OF GREY*

James was working as a journalist when she flew to Italy to conduct research for a magazine article in 2010. There she met a powerful real estate agent named Alessandro Proto and decided to write a book about an even *more* powerful one…with a dark secret. There are some parallels between Proto and Christian Grey, the mysterious mogul featured in James's steamy book series. Proto operates a firm called Proto Organization Holding and, in the book, Grey runs Grey Enterprise Holding. (Both also drive Audis and dislike reporters.) However, Proto admits that his bedroom preferences are quite a bit tamer than Grey's. James hasn't commented on Proto's claims, but she has admitted that *Twilight*, the best-selling book trilogy about vampires living in Washington state, had a big influence on her steamy storytelling. After writing naughty "fan fiction" involving characters from *Twilight*, she eventually merged them with her idea about Proto and developed it all into *50 Shades of Grey*.

ANNE RICE, *THE VAMPIRE CHRONICLES*

In 1976, Rice published *Interview with the Vampire*, the first installment in her series about an international group of bloodsuckers. It was partially inspired by the death of her six-year-old daughter, Michelle, from leukemia. Michelle served as the inspiration for Claudia, the child-vampire in the book. Rice has also said that her husband, the late

---

The annual Wimbledon tennis tournament employs 250 ball girls and boys.

poet Stan Rice, was the inspiration for Lestat, the vampire who serves as one of the central characters in *Interview* and its various sequels. Both Stan and Lestat have blond hair and they share the same birth-day—November 7.

ERNEST HEMINGWAY, *THE SUN ALSO RISES*

In 1925, 26-year-old Ernest Hemingway vacationed in Pamplona, Spain, with his wife, Hadley Richardson, and a group of British expatri-ates, including the recently divorced Lady Duff Twysden. Hemingway became infatuated with Twysden, and he and her boyfriend came to blows over her. Complicating the trip further was Richardson's encoun-ter with Cayetano Ordóñez, a local matador who presented her with the ear of a bull he killed in the ring. While everyone involved would probably have agreed that it was a pretty lousy vacation, it nevertheless inspired what is largely considered to be one of Hemingway's best novels. He began writing *The Sun Also Rises* while he was still in Spain, and it focuses on a group of ill-fated expats in Pamplona.

CHUCK PALAHNIUK, *FIGHT CLUB*

In the early 1990s, the aspiring novelist (who was working as a diesel mechanic at the time) went camping with some friends. After Palahniuk asked a rowdy group at a nearby campsite to turn down their music, he got into a brawl with them. The following Monday, he went to work with his face covered in bruises. His coworkers all pretended not to notice and never asked him what had happened. "I think they were afraid of the answer. I realized that if you looked bad enough, people would not want to know what you did in your spare time," Palahniuk later said. "They don't want to know the bad things about you. And the key was to look so bad that no one would ever ask."

*   *   *

WHAT IS THAT?

In 2009, scientists studying satellite images of Antarctica noticed what looked like huge stains on the icy continent…which is exactly what they were. It turned out to be guano (poop) stains left by penguin colo-nies that regularly spend months in one location during their breeding season. The discovery led to advances in the study of penguins, because it allowed scientists to locate previously unknown penguin colonies, as well as the colonies of other seabirds. Bonus: Scientists later discovered that they could tell different penguin species apart by studying the color of the huge poop stains in the satellite images.

When recording the audio version of *Charlotte's Web* in 1970, author E. B. White…

Myth-Quoted Marilyn

An odd phenomenon has recently popped up on the Internet: powerful quotes about beauty and womanhood attributed to Marilyn Monroe. Only problem: she never said most of them. Here are some of the best—and who really did say them.

Q **uote:** "Everything has beauty, but not everyone sees it."
Actually said by: Confucius

Quote: "Women who seek to be equal with men lack ambition."
Actually said by: 1960s guru Timothy Leary

Quote: "No one knows me or loves me completely. I have only myself."
Actually said by: Simone De Beauvoir, author of *The Second Sex*

Quote: "Independence is happiness."
Actually said by: Women's rights crusader Susan B. Anthony

Quote: "I like to feel dumb. That's how I know there's more in the world than me."
Actually said by: Writer Susan Sontag

Quote: "Give a girl the right shoes and she can conquer the world."
Actually said by: Bette Midler

Quote: "Your clothes should be tight enough to show you're a woman but loose enough to show you're a lady."
Actually said by: Fashion designer Edith Head

Quote: "Beauty is whatever gives joy."
Actually said by: Pulitzer Prize–winning poet Edna St. Vincent Millay

Quote: "To all the girls that think you're fat because you're not a size zero, you're the beautiful one. It's society who's ugly."
Actually said by: Lady Gaga. Monroe couldn't have commented on size zero because it wasn't introduced in the United States until 1966, four years after her death.

Quote: "Wanting to be someone else is a waste of the person you are."
Actually said by: Nirvana front man Kurt Cobain

Quote: "Well-behaved women seldom make history."

Actually said by: College professor Laurel Thatcher Ulrich, in an article in an academic journal in 1976. (It can also be seen, unattributed, on millions of bumper stickers and T-shirts.)

Quote: "Anything I cannot transform into something marvelous, I let go."

Actually said by: 20th-century memoirist and essayist Anais Nin

Quote: "It's better to be hated for what you are than to be loved for what you're not."

Actually said by: French author and critic Andre Gide

Quote: "Men know best about everything, except what women know better."

Actually said by: George Eliot, author of *Silas Marner*. (Eliot was the pen name of female author Mary Ann Evans.)

Quote: "I like what I do. I do what I like."

Actually said by: Reverse the phrases, and add an "s" to the "like" and it's paraphrasing of a lyric in the song "Chim Chim Cher-ee" from *Mary Poppins*.

Quote: "I'd rather have roses on my table than diamonds on my neck."

Actually said by: Political activist Emma Goldman

Quote: "Being a sex symbol is a heavy load to carry, especially when one is tired, hurt, and bewildered."

Actually said by: Another big-screen sex symbol—Clara Bow. She said it in 1962…in reference to the death of Marilyn Monroe.

*   *   *

BONING UP

If you've eaten chicken nuggets today, you probably got half of your daily requirement for fluoride, a vital nutrient for bone and dental health. Here's how: Processed chicken nuggets are made of "mechanically separated chicken." Scraps of chicken are pressed by a machine through a sieve that presses and extrudes the meat as a pink paste, which is then formed and cooked into chicken pieces. Traces of bone (which contain fluoride) get left behind, but it's enough to provide that daily dose of fluoride.

In the 1980s, doctors experimented with using zippers on patients instead of stitches. (It worked.)

He's Got Your Number

When a player signs or is traded to a new team, his favorite number—possibly the one he's been wearing since childhood—isn't always available. Unless he's a respected veteran and the number he wants belongs to a rookie, it's very common for a trade or purchase to occur.

ELI MANNING AND JEFF FEAGLES

The New York Giants acquired Eli Manning in the 2004 NFL Draft. Manning wanted to keep the #10 jersey he wore at Ole Miss, but it was already being worn by Giants punter Jeff Feagles. Feagles was willing to give up the number if Manning met one condition: an all-expenses-paid trip to Florida for Feagles's family. Manning paid for the vacation, and got #10. (Feagles switched to #17, to commemorate his 17th season in the NFL.)

CHRIS KLUWE AND DONOVAN MCNABB

Donovan McNabb's illustrious, 13-year NFL career came to a close in 2011 with one last hurrah as starting quarterback for the Minnesota Vikings. But the former Philadelphia Eagle had to negotiate with Vikings punter Chris Kluwe in order to wear his #5. McNabb signed a contract agreeing to a $5,000 charitable donation, five mentions of Kluwe's heavy metal band, Tripping Icarus, during press conferences, and one ice-cream cone. Unfortunately for Tripping Icarus, McNabb was short three shout-outs when he was released six games into the season. He still agreed to write the check to Kick for a Cure, a muscular dystrophy foundation…but he still owes Kluwe an ice-cream cone.

A. J. BURNETT AND DANIEL MCCUTCHEN

A lot of baseball pitchers are superstitious. Most have their own personal—and often idiosyncratic—routines before and during a scheduled start. So it's no surprise that A. J. Burnett simply *had* to retain his #34 when he was traded to the Pittsburgh Pirates in 2012. Teammate Daniel McCutchen had the number, but was willing to surrender it if Burnett would agree to an unusual request: Burnett had to set up a college fund for McCutchen's then-unborn daughter. A wise move: At the time, McCutchen was earning the league minimum, and as of last report, he's pitching in the minor leagues.

JEFF FEAGLES AND PLAXICO BURRESS

A year later, the Giants signed star wide receiver Plaxico Burress, who wanted to continue wearing the number he'd worn for the Pittsburgh Steelers: #17. This time Feagles agreed to give up his jersey number in exchange for an outdoor kitchen. Burress agreed, and Feagles built the kitchen, but Burress never reimbursed him for it. It may not have worked out for Feagles, but it didn't work out for Burress, either. In 2009, Burress was assigned a new number: 09-R-3260, during his two year stint in Ulster Correctional Facility in upstate New York, for shooting himself in the leg with an illegally possessed handgun.

IFEANYI OHALETE AND CLINTON PORTIS

In 2004, the Washington Redskins sent cornerback Champ Bailey to the Denver Broncos in exchange for running back Clinton Portis. Portis wanted to wear #26, the number he wore in Denver, but to get it he had to pay Redskins strong safety Ifeanyi Ohalete for it. The price: $40,000. Then Ohalete was cut from the team in the middle of the season, before Portis had paid him the full amount, and Portis thought he was off the hook for the remaining $20,000. Not according to Ohalete, who sued Portis for the balance of what he was owed. A day before it went to trial, Portis and Ohalete settled the case for $18,000.

JOHN KRUK AND MITCH WILLIAMS

The 1994 exchange between these two Philadelphia Phillies teammates was very modest. Kruk gave up his #28 to Williams in exchange for two cases of beer. Years later, Kruk spoke to a reporter about the trade: "The only reason Mitch wanted the number is because his wife had a lot of No. 28 jewelry and he didn't want to buy her any more jewelry. Not long after that, he got divorced and changed numbers."

*   *   *

CONSTANT CRAVING

Hunger and food cravings aren't the same thing. Hunger is your stomach telling you to fill it, while cravings are your brain trying to tell you to eat a certain nutrient or mineral. Here are what scientists think some common individual cravings mean your body really wants.

- Chocolate: trace minerals in cacao, most likely magnesium
- Cheese: essential fatty acids (omega 3) or calcium
- Red meat: iron
- Potato chips: salt, and the trace mineral of chloride found in salt
- Pasta: chromium
- White bread: amino acids
- Caffeine: water. (You're dehydrated.)

Grounded Airlines

Please buckle your safety belts, turn off all electronic devices, and fly backward into history with a look at these odd airlines that didn't quite take off.

AIR ATLANTA

The Hartsfield-Jackson Atlanta International Airport is the major domestic and international hub for Delta Airlines. In 1984, two lawyers came up with a plan to exploit the big airline business coming out of that Southern city by starting their own regional airline. Their main business would be to serve as a domestic connector for Pan Am's international flights. Travelers in cities such as Orlando or Memphis would fly to Atlanta on Air Atlanta, and then fly to Europe via Pan Am. But since regional connector airlines are common, what was so special about Air Atlanta? It didn't have coach seating—all seats on all flights were first class. With extra leg room, meals served on fine china, and a perfect safety record, three million people flew on Air Atlanta in its first three years, and gave the carrier rave reviews...but it wasn't enough. The airline's prices were too low, it didn't have enough cash to expand (or pay its bills), and it owed more than $50 million to its creditors. Air Atlanta filed for bankruptcy in 1987.

FREELANDIA TRAVEL CLUB

An airline that served health food and offered the use of a water bed? This airline could only have happened in the 1970s. With just two airplanes (painted yellow) and just two flights each day—New York to Los Angeles, and Los Angeles to New York—Freelandia marketed itself as a travel club. Members paid a $50 fee, allowing them access to a cross-country flight for just $69. That also entitled them to lounge on the onboard water bed and to dine on organic food. The company's business structure was also unique. Set up like a food co-op (which were popping up around the country), Freelandia was legally a nonprofit operation. But water beds, organic meals, and especially jet fuel aren't cheap. Launched in early 1973, the groovy airline was grounded by the end of that year due to the oil crisis.

HOOTERS AIR

Hooters is a restaurant chain that claims to be famous for its chicken wings, but what it's *really* famous for is its "Hooters Girls"—a waitstaff of young women in short shorts and revealing tank tops. In 2003, the company expanded its brand by acquiring a charter plane service called

Pace Airlines and moving it to Myrtle Beach, South Carolina. The area is home to more than 100 golf courses, so Hooters Air was marketed to golfers, with flights from New York, Florida, and Indiana, among others. Planes were painted orange and white, the colors of the restaurant's uniforms. Trained flight attendants were assisted by two Hooters Girls. And because it was tied to a restaurant, the airline served free meals to passengers—an amenity no longer being offered by most airlines. It performed moderately well until late 2005, when a tourism downturn in the wake of Hurricane Katrina proved insurmountable. Hooters Air flew for the last time in April 2006. The parent company lost a reported $40 million putting Hooters in the air.

TRUMP SHUTTLE

In October 1988, Eastern Airlines attempted (unsuccessfully) to stave off bankruptcy by selling off assets. Among those assets: the Eastern Air Shuttle, a commuter service that offered short, inexpensive flights between Boston, Washington, D.C., and New York. Real estate tycoon Donald Trump bought it for $365 million, promptly renamed it Trump Shuttle, and painted his name on all 17 jets. He also changed the carrier from a no-frills commuter line into a luxury airline: planes were remodeled with hardwood floors, chrome seat belt fixtures, and gold-plated faucets in the bathrooms. Trump also raised prices, not just because he had to pay for the upgrades (and make more money), but because he also had to pay for skyrocketing jet fuel costs. Unfortunately for the business mogul, the Eastern Shuttle had appealed to travelers who wanted convenient, inexpensive flights, not luxury upgrades. The company never turned a profit, and by 1992 ownership of Trump Shuttle went to Trump's creditors. It was then acquired by US Airways.

GREYHOUND AIR

It's an old joke that traveling in coach class in a cramped airline is like being in a "flying bus," but what if it were literally true? In 1996, the Canadian wing of Greyhound Bus Lines leased seven Boeing 727s and launched Greyhound Air. The plan was to offer flights between seven major Canadian cities (including Vancouver, Toronto, Ottawa, and Winnipeg) and then provide passengers with bus tickets to get to farther-flung cities. Associating planes with buses didn't work—most flights were half full. Also not helping was a TV ad campaign that depicted a real greyhound urinating on an airplane wheel. Greyhound Air was grounded in little over a year.

Word Up: Eggcorns

If you've been biting your time just waiting for an article on eggcorns—you've got another thing coming! (Not really—here's an article on eggcorns.)

A CORNY STORY

In May 2015, the *Merriam-Webster Dictionary* added a new word to the official lexicon of the English language: *eggcorn*. Linguists had been using it since 2003, when members of the popular Language Log blog noted that someone had referred to an acorn as an "egg corn." That mishearing sort of made sense—an acorn sort of looks like an egg, it sort of looks like a kernel of corn, and an acorn is sort of equivalent to an egg in that it's the seed of an oak tree. One of the bloggers suggested that because there was no accepted term for that kind of mishearing, they should be called "eggcorns"…and a new word was born. Here's a collection of misheard words and phrases—that make a little or a lot of sense—that can be found in newspapers, magazines, novels, blogs, and (especially!) on Facebook. (Including some you may use yourself.)

Another thing coming. Most people don't know it, but this phrase was originally "another *think* coming," and means, basically, "You're mistaken," as in, "If you think I'm eating that tofurkey—you've got another *think* coming!" The misheard "you've got another *thing* coming," which is now more common than the original, works in its place and makes sense in its own way.

Biting my time. Like a lot of eggcorns, this mishearing often shows up in online platforms such as Facebook, where people's spelling, grammar, and thinking mistakes are revealed to the world. The actual phrase being misused: "*biding* my time," meaning "waiting for an opportune moment." Example: "I will definitely ask her out—I'm just biding my time." But, like all eggcorns, the erroneous "*biting* my time" does work in a way—creating the image of someone nervously biting down on something in anticipation of some action or event.

Daring do. This is a misread of "derring-do," meaning "an action displaying heroism or great courage." The phrase was derived from Middle English *dorryng do*, meaning "daring to do," so "daring-do" is very close to the same meaning.

Feeble position. It's a mishearing of "fetal position," referring to the position of a fetus in a womb—curled up in a ball with the arms hugging the upper body, legs pulled up to the chest, and head bent forward.

In 2012, Fiji minted coins containing pieces of a meteorite that fell to Earth in Kansas.

When used for adults, it usually suggests someone having some kind of breakdown, e.g., "After hearing that his job was being eliminated, Jay spent the entire next day in the fetal position on the couch." A person in such a position could be said to be in a pretty "feeble" state—so "*feeble* position" fits the bill.

Firstable. The actual phrase, "first of all," is used to emphasize a point or take a stand. Many people hear it as "firstable" (go ahead—google it), and it kind of works, because the "first" thing you want to emphasize can be said to be "firstable," meaning something along the lines of "able to be put first."

Holidays sauce. The tasty sauce made with egg yolks and butter, which is one of the staples of French cuisine, is called "hollandaise sauce," from the French *sauce hollandaise*, meaning "Dutch sauce" (purportedly because it was introduced by Dutch chefs in the 17th century). The sauce is often mistakenly referred to as "holidays sauce," which is appropriate in a way, since for most people, hollandaise is a special food reserved for special occasions—like holidays.

Jar-dropping. Something amazing or astonishing is said to be "jaw-dropping," a simple reference to the fact that such a thing can leave you with your mouth open in slack-jawed wonder. Some people think it's "jar-dropping," which does make some sense: if you're holding a jar of something and see something that totally blows your mind—your reaction just might be "jar-dropping."

Knotical mile. There's no such thing as a "knotical mile"—the unit of measure for distances at sea is a "*nautical* mile." But since a *knot* is a unit of speed that is equal to one nautical mile per hour, a "*knot*ical mile" kind of makes sense.

Panty-waste. A "pantywaist" is an old-time child's garment consisting of a shirt and short pants buttoned together at the waist. It later came to mean "sissy." "Panty-*waste*" is a common mishearing of the word, and could be said to mean something found inside a pair of panties—and that's all we've got to say about that.

When all is set and done. This is a mishearing of the phrase "When all is *said* and done," which means when everything is taken into account, or "When all is said and done—we'll still have Paris." "When all is *set* and done" means when it's over, which is pretty much the same thing. (We'll still have Paris then, too.)

Coldslaw. Most people know that the name of this cabbage-based salad is actually "coleslaw." (The name comes from the Dutch *koolsla*, a shortened version of *koolsalade*, meaning "cabbage salad.") And because it's a dish served cold—"*cold*slaw" also works.

The word "avocado" comes from *ahuacatl*, which means "testicle" in the language of the Aztecs.

It's a Weird, Weird World

Here's proof that truth is stranger than fiction.

NICE TO MEAT YOU

Carl Sagan once said, "If you wish to make an apple pie from scratch, you must first invent the universe." In that sense, Andy George may not have made his chicken sandwich completely from scratch (because he didn't invent the universe), but he came pretty close. For his "How to Make Everything" YouTube channel, George gave himself the challenge of making every ingredient in a chicken sandwich. It only took him six months and cost about $1,500. First step: he grew the vegetables (for toppings) and wheat (for the bread). Then he traveled to the sea and desalinated ocean water to get the salt. He milked a cow to make the butter and the cheese, which he churned and whipped by hand. He collected honey from a beehive for the bread, and then ground the wheat to make the dough. Six months later, he had all of the ingredients except one: the bird. He went to a farm, slaughtered a chicken, defeathered it, butchered it, cooked it, and then combined the meat with the bread and toppings. And then he ate his $1,500 sandwich. His reaction: "It's not bad."

YOU. LOTTERY. LOSER.

"I should be having fun playing the lottery," said Nick Lynough, 22, of Elmira, New York, "not feel offended." What was he so offended by? A state lottery ticket that he claims insulted him personally. The $5 ticket, which he purchased from a lottery machine at an inn, featured a game in which you rub off three random words, a "Person," a "Place," and a "Thing." The player wins a prize if any of the words revealed match the ones printed at the top of the ticket. Lynough's ticket wasn't a winner, and adding insult to injury, the three words that he got: "You," "Elmira," "Trash." He was incensed. "At first, I thought someone was playing a trick on me with one of those fake lottery tickets." However, after complaining to the New York State Gaming Commission, he was assured that the ticket was real, and that the words are chosen randomly. (The sheriff's department determined that the machine hadn't been tampered with.) The commission decided to remove the word "Trash" from future tickets, and reassured Lynough that "the unfortunate arrangement of words on this individual ticket

---

Champagne, anyone? Fizzy alcoholic drinks get you intoxicated more quickly than straight shots do.

was completely random, coincidental and—most importantly—unintentional." They added that Lynough's losing ticket is actually quite special: "There was a 1 in 900 million chance of the words appearing in that order—meaning players would have a better chance of winning the Powerball or Mega Millions drawings than finding that phrase." Lynough still isn't convinced—he maintains that it was too much of a coincidence that out of all the towns in New York, a card with the place name "Elmira" ended up in Elmira. "I feel very disrespected," he told the *Elmira Star Gazette*.

A WEE DROP

Garrey Ashton was no stranger to near-death experiences—he'd been hit by cars twice, suffered a broken neck in a work accident, and electrocuted himself. But at 44, he was still alive and kicking. That's when he went to a "stag party" with his mates in the English coastal town of Newquay. At some point during the evening, Ashton, an accounts manager, stumbled away from his friends, and they didn't see him again until the next morning when he stumbled into the hotel restaurant, bleeding, his clothes ripped and wet. One of his friends asked, "What the hell happened to you last night?"

"I fell off the cliff." Ashton told them that he woke up on the beach when the rising tide reached his feet. Despite his insistence that he wasn't hurt, his friends called an ambulance. Doctors discovered a trapped nerve in his neck and a few cuts and bruises, but he was otherwise okay. Lucky thing, too, because the cliff he'd fallen off of was 100 feet high. Now he has another near-death experience to add to his tally.

BIG TIP

Steve Easton of Surrey, England, had been suffering from a constant case of the sniffles ever since he was a little boy. He chalked it up to allergies. But in 2015, the 51-year-old Easton was sitting at his computer when he had a sneezing fit. Suddenly, out of his left nostril shot a piece of rubber about the size of a penny. And suddenly Easton could breathe clearly. He called his mother and asked her if she knew 1) what the thing was, and 2) how it got lodged in his nose. "Oh yes," she replied. "We took you to the hospital when you were seven because we thought you had inhaled one." Inhaled one what? The rubber tip of a dart from a toy dart gun. His parents became concerned when they found him playing with a tipless dart…and then couldn't find the tip. Neither could the doctors at the hospital, so they sent the boy home, leaving him with a constant case of the sniffles. "I was completely unaware the sucker had been in my nasal cavity for forty-four years," he said. "I wonder if there's anything else up there."

Animal Cannibals

If vegetables ate other vegetables, would they be called vegetecannibals? While you're pondering that, here are a few stories of animal cannibalism.

HIPPOS

In 2014, British biologist Leejiah Dorward filmed a pair of hippos standing at the edgeof a river in South Africa's Kruger National Park, eating something that was partially submerged. When he got closer, he discovered what the "something" was. The two hungry hippos were feeding on the decaying carcass of another hippo. "I was completely amazed," Dorward told *National Geographic*. "It was something I had never heard of." Hippos are herbivores—they survive almost exclusively on grasses that grow on riverbanks—and, like cows and other ruminants, they have chambered stomachs designed to break down plant-based foods.

Dorward's filming of the event was the second confirmed case of hippo cannibalism in scientific history. The first was recorded in 1999 by British zoologist and conservationist Dr. S. Keith Eltringham. Dudley had been studying hippo carnivory since 1995, when he witnessed a hippo killing an impala in a river in the park, after which the killer hippo and several others ate the dead impala. After that, some of the hippos left the water to steal another dead impala from some wild dogs, and ate that, too.

TIGER SALAMANDERS

Tiger salamanders are small striped or spotted salamanders found across much of North America. They spend the first, larval stage of their lives as gilled aquatic creatures in ponds, lakes, streams, and marshes before going through metamorphosis. During that stage, they lose their gills and develop lungs, thereby becoming air-breathing terrestrial salamanders (a life cycle similar to that of frogs). And it's in that early larval stage where things get weird. After hatching from batches of up to 100 eggs, young salamanders spend the first few weeks of their lives feeding on small aquatic crustaceans and insects. Then, after about four weeks, two different larval *morphs*, or forms, can develop. Some remain as they were, slowly growing and feeding on crustaceans and insects; others grow very quickly, developing longer and larger bodies—up to three times as large as their smaller brethren—with jutting lower jaws and much larger teeth. The diet of the larger salamanders changes, too: they start eating smaller salamanders. The switch to the cannibal

Earth's "lunar body tide" pulls so much on the Moon that it causes the Moon to bulge.

morph doesn't always happen, and when it does, it happens in varying numbers. Exactly how and why it occurs is not yet known.

Studies have shown that tiger salamander cannibal larvae are less likely to eat salamanders that are closely related to them, and more likely to eat those that aren't. This means that the evolutionary development of the cannibal morph might have come about simply because killing off the larvae of unrelated salamanders gave individual genetic lines a greater chance of surviving. It also means that aquatic larval tiger salamanders can tell if other salamanders are closely related to them. Scientists have not yet determined how they do this.

STEGODYPHUS LINEATUS

Stegodyphus lineatus is a species of spider found in desert regions around the Mediterranean Sea. Their cannibalism comes in a very creepy (and gross) form: *matriphagy*, the scientific term for "mother-eating." It's practiced by several insect and spider species, but none are quite as gruesome as *Stegodyphus lineatus*. After mating with as many as five males, a female *S. lineatus* lays approximately 80 eggs, which she wraps in a protective disc-shaped silk egg sac. When the eggs hatch about 15 days layer, she punctures the sac, allowing the tiny spiderlings to emerge. She immediately starts feeding her young—by regurgitating the digested food she's been storing in her body just for this purpose. (The spiderlings swarm all over the mother's face, angling for the best access to the regurgitated food.) But there's more: to provide enough food for her babies, the mother also regurgitates her own insides, which have been slowly breaking down into liquid ever since she laid her eggs. And when she runs out of material to regurgitate around two weeks later, the spiderlings, which are now able to hunt for themselves, pierce the mother's abdomen—injecting it with venom that furthers the breakdown process—and suck the rest of her insides out. The mother remains alive throughout much of this process, and never attempts to escape.

Bonus: Adult female *S. lineatus* that have failed to mate sometimes help a brooding mother take care of her young, producing their own regurgitation for the spiderlings to eat. They get eaten, too.

CAECILIANS

Caecilians are primitive, slimy, wormlike amphibians found in tropical regions around the world. Some are just inches long, and some grow to more than five feet. Most varieties spend their entire lives underground. Little more is known about them, but scientists recently learned that they perform a previously unknown kind of cannibalism called *maternal dermatophagy*—meaning "eating the mother's skin." When a female caecilian lays a clutch of eggs, she starts growing a thick, extra layer of skin. When the young hatch, they use specially adapted baby teeth—which they later lose—to scrape off that outer layer of skin, and eat it. The mother remains calm throughout this process, until the layer is completely eaten away. Then the babies rest, and over the next three days Mom grows a new layer of skin—and the hungry babies feast again. The skin is very nutritious (it contains fat and protein), and it's all the young caecilians need for a month or two, by which time they will have developed adult teeth. Now they are strong enough to leave the nest and live on their own.

Bonus (non-cannibal) fact: There is only one known species of fully aquatic caecilian, native to Central and South America. Its true name is *Typhlonectes natans*, but it's commonly sold in pet stores for home aquariums under the erroneous name "rubber eel" (it's not an eel), and sometimes under the doubly erroneous "Sicilian worm" (it's not a worm and it's not from Sicily).

CANE TOADS

Cane toads are a species of toad native to South and Central America. It's also an invasive species in some countries, such as Australia, where its habitat now covers a wide swath of the country. Cane toads are the largest toad species in the world: adults weigh an average of four pounds. They will eat almost anything, including mice and other rodents, reptiles, birds, bats, and most any other small animals they come across—even cat and dog food. And other cane toads. Not only that, but they do it in a very deliberate and calculated fashion. When cane toad tadpoles metamorphose into tiny land toads, they spend most of their time near the muddy edges of the ponds in which they were born, because their young bodies need to stay moist. Older, larger cane toads hang out near those ponds, too—but for a different reason: they sit very still, using their brown, bumpy skin as camouflage to blend in with the muddy ground, and flick the long middle toes of their hind feet up and down. The movement attracts the tiny toads, who mistake the toes for insects and are promptly gobbled up whole by the larger toads.

Bonus (cannibal) fact: The cane toad's toe-lure behavior was first described in 2007 by the University of Sydney's cane toad expert, Dr. Richard Shine. He also discovered something else: When female cane toads lay their eggs in a pond, cane toad tadpoles that are already in the pond will voraciously eat the eggs. Even when given the option to eat the eggs of other amphibians, the cane toad tadpoles invariably chose the cannibal route and ate the eggs of their own kind.

A Marble-ous Origin

Did you play marbles as a kid? The simple game has a very long and very colorful history.

A CLASSIC TOY

Marbles have been around for a long time. There are paintings dating to ancient Egypt that show people playing games with what look like marbles (but they were most likely ground and polished animal knuckles). Tiny marble spheres were found in the ruins of Pompeii, and there's evidence that Native Americans made marbles from stones, polished smooth by river water. Marblelike rocks and bones were used as toys by kids in colonial America and into the 1800s.

• Why are marbles called marbles? *Because they were once made out of marble.* In the 19th century, leftover marble (or alabaster) chunks from industrial processing were broken down, heated, and re-formed into tiny spheres. Marketed as a child's toy, they were sold for about a penny each in the 1870s. Kids called them "alleys" because they were often made from alabaster.

• Marbles as a game took off in popularity when the marbles became cheaper…because they weren't made out of marble anymore. Mass production of clay "marbles" began in 1884 by an Ohio fabricator named Sam Dyke. Using a wooden block with six indentations, he poured in six lumps of soft clay. He then rolled a wooden paddle back and forth over the clay balls, shaping them into six spheres, which were then dried in a kiln. The molded clay marbles, called "brownies" (because they were brown), sold so well that by 1900, Dyke had 350 employees and was making a million marbles each day. Cost: still a penny, but you got 30 for that price.

• Because Akron was the center of clay marble manufacturing, it's also where mass production of glass marbles began, around 1915. Industrialist M. F. Christensen created a machine, similar to Dyke's wooden block, that had a divot for a dollop of molten glass, placed between two cylinders. As the cylinders rotated, the molten glass was shaped into a sphere and moved through the machine. This is more or less how marbles have been made ever since.

• A standard marble has a diameter of about ½ inch. A standard "shooter" marble (also called a "taw") has a diameter of ¾ inch. Anything larger than that is called a "boulder" (or a "bonker," "plumper," "thumper," "smasher," or "tom").

In the entire history of the NHL, only nine goalies have scored goals.

WHAT'S IN A GAME?

• Just as there is no single game known as "cards," there's no one game called "marbles." There are hundreds of different ways to play a competitive game with marbles, and the rules for those games vary by region.

• One of the most common is called Ringer. A 10-foot ring is drawn in the dirt or marked on the ground, and at the center an X is made of 13 marbles (one marble at the center, and three jutting out in four directions), called "ducks." Players then use their shooters to knock the ducks and scatter them. If they hit one out of the circle, they get to keep taking turns, until they fail to knock out a duck, or they knock their shooter out of the ring. Each marble that's knocked out of the ring is worth a point. Once all 13 marbles have been knocked out, the X is re-formed and play continues until one player has 50 points.

• Ringer is the style played at the National Marbles Tournament. It's been held over four days every June since 1922 in Wildwood, New Jersey. Boys and girls age 7 to 14 compete in separate divisions and play for scholarships. Ringer is also the game used at the British and World Marbles Championships, played on Good Friday at the Greyhound Inn and Pub in West Sussex, England (but that tournament is for adults, and it's played in teams).

• Marble games were popular throughout the United States from the late 19th century all the way until World War II, when rationing made marbles scarce. A marbles revival was a minor fad in the late 1970s.

SOME MARBLE TERMINOLOGY

• **Mibs.** The Latin word for marbles, used by marble aficionados to describe the small, basic marbles used in games.

• **Mibster.** A marbles player or collector.

• **Blood alley.** An alabaster marble painted red.

• **Immie.** A cheap "imitation" alabaster marble made out of glass.

• **Woodie.** A marble made of wood.

• **Black beauty.** Solid black marble made of obsidian.

• **Aggie.** A marble made from agate.

• **Bumblebee.** Yellow-and-black striped marble.

• **Clambroth.** Black-and-white striped marble.

• **Jasper.** A blue marble, made from glazed china.

• **Onionskins.** Glass marbles with specks of color on the surface.

• **Sulphides.** Transparent glass marbles with a tiny figure inside, like a porcelain animal or the head of Santa Claus, for example.

Uncle John's Stall of Fame

Uncle John is amazed—and pleased—by the unusual ways people get involved with bathrooms, toilets, and so on. That's why he created the "Stall of Fame."

Honoree: Ian Thomas, a New York artist

Notable Achievement: He's a man with a plan for presenting poetry in the can

True Story: Thomas takes part in the annual O, Miami Poetry Festival, whose goal is to expose every one of Miami-Dade County's 2.6 million residents to poetry. Poems are presented in puppet shows, recited on poetry cruises on the Miami River, skywritten in smoke trails across the sky, and sewn onto labels inside of thrift-store clothing. Thomas does his part by painting poetry verses in gold leaf on restroom urinals all over town. He calls them "murinals," and he doesn't mind if restroom goers use them for target practice. "It's the joy of defaming something. It's a marking territory, and act of domination," he says. (No word on whether the poets whose work he's selected for this honor enjoy having their work peed upon.)

Honoree: Dan Schaumann, 30, an Australian-born singer-songwriter, traveler, waiter, and writer who lives in Toronto, Canada

Notable Achievement: Making his mark with pot shots

True Story: When Schaumann was in his twenties, his mother gave him a camera for his birthday. He quickly grew tired of taking the same boring travel photos that everyone else takes, so he decided to try a new approach. "I thought I would take a picture of each of the toilets I stopped at, just for something different," he says. Schaumann enjoyed taking those photos, so he kept at it. Then in 2011 he posted a photo of his brother's square-shaped toilet on the photo-sharing website Instagram as a joke, to see if anyone would click "like" on a photo of a toilet. Lots of people did, so Schaumann kept posting…and he's still at it. As of June 2016 he has over 550 posts on Instagram and more than 2,700 followers. He also has his own "Toilography" blog where he posts photos and commentary.

To date Schaumann has visited more than 30 cities around the world and photographed toilets in every one. On his blog he invites readers in upcoming cities to suggest unusual or interesting restrooms for him to visit. He also has a few tips for anyone who might be interested in taking up his unusual hobby. For starters, *don't* bring an ordinary camera into a public restroom. "You don't want people to know you're in the washroom taking a photo. I use my iPhone and try to be as discreet as possible," he told the *Chicago Tribune* in 2014. (If someone walks in on him when he's taking a photo, he pretends that he's texting.)

Honoree: William Stegemeyer, a highway department worker from Fairbanks, Alaska

Notable Achievement: He had a front row "seat" at the dawn of the Space Age (actually a little before dawn).

True Story: On the morning of October 6, 1957, Stegemeyer got up while it was still dark and went out to his outhouse to answer nature's call. The 49th state was a sparsely populated place in those days. Perhaps because of that and also because Alaska's night sky is so beautiful, Stegemeyer liked to leave the door open while he put his outhouse to its intended use. On that morning he was sitting there admiring the view when he saw what he described as "a strange moving star come up out of the west." The object was moving too fast to be a star or a planet, and too slow to be a meteor. It didn't have blinking wing lights, nor was it making any noise, so it couldn't have been an airplane. "It seemed like it stayed in the sky forever…it didn't belong up there," Stegemeyer told an interviewer in 2007. So what was it? The object turned out to be *Sputnik*, the world's first artificial satellite, launched by the Soviet Union the day before. Stegemeyer was the first person in the Western Hemisphere to spot it, and he did it while doing his business.

For 20 years it was thought that scientists at the University of Alaska's Geophysical Institute had been the first people in the Western Hemisphere to spot *Sputnik*, but they didn't see it until it was high overhead. Stegemeyer saw it much lower on the horizon as it was rising in the sky, which meant that he saw it before they did. The next day he mentioned it to his neighbor, Neil Davis, one of the scientists at the Geophysical Institute, but it wasn't until 1977 that Davis told the story to the world. Today a memorial plaque marks the spot where Stegemeyer's outhouse once stood. (A fancier outhouse is there now.)

Honoree: Jumpin' Jack Sexty, aka "Mr. Pogo," a world record–holding pogo stick champ living in Bristol, England

Notable Achievement: Accomplishing an unofficial lavatorial feat that is unlikely ever to be acknowledged by the people at *Guinness World Records*

True Story: By the summer of 2015, Jumpin' Jack held the world records for fastest mile hopped on a pogo stick (10 minutes, 2 seconds) and the fastest marathon on a pogo stick (16 hours, 24 minutes). In his marathon attempt he also smashed the record for longest distance pogoed in a day (26 miles, 385 yards). Then at Pogopalooza, a Philadelphia charity event and the world's largest pogo stick convention, Sexty set out to break the record for most consecutive pogo hops.

Before the attempt, Sexty predicted that the biggest challenges that he and his two competitors, Jamie Roumeliotis of Boston, Massachusetts, and Casie Merza of Tampa, Florida, had to face would be boredom and "going the longest without stopping for the loo." Just as Sexty feared, several hours into his world-record attempt, he had to pee. The urge became overpowering, but just when it seemed he would have to abandon his world-record attempt, a Good Samaritan—not named in news reports—stepped forward with a bucket and offered to help. Sexty accepted, in the process became the first person in history (at least during a world-record attempt) to "go to the toilet while on a pogo stick," as Britain's the *Sun* newspaper put it. "The man with the bucket just held it below me as I was jumping," Sexty told the *Sun*. "I had only met the guy who offered to hold it about 48 hours before. I couldn't be very accurate."

After his pogoing pit stop, Sexty kept right on bouncing, outlasting his rivals to complete 88,047 hops in 10 hours and 21 minutes: a new world record…thanks to a little help from his new friend.

Honoree: Hong Kong's YATA grocery store
Notable Achievement: Creating what may be the world's first "gastro-intestinally correct" pastry
True Story: If you're under the age of 50, you probably know who Hello Kitty is. She's one of Japan's most famous exports—a feline cartoon character who appears on all kinds of licensed merchandise. Hello Kitty was created by a company called Sanrio in 1974. Since then the firm has created hundreds of additional characters, including one named Gudetama (Lazy Egg), a chubby egg yolk who is usually seen lazing around on his egg white as if it were a yoga mat. In 2005, the Gudetama-themed café inside the YATA grocery store in Hong Kong began selling custard-filled steamed buns that look just like the character. If you poke a hole in Gudetama's mouth with a chopstick and give him a squeeze, plain custard flows out, making it appear as if he is vomiting. And if you poke a hole in the character's rear end, out flows…chocolate custard. For consumers who still have an appetite after watching Gudetama lose his lunch from both ends, the buns are said to be quite tasty.

They Were in a Band Together?

*Before they became big stars, many musicians had to pay their dues
and find their styles by playing with a wide variety of musicians.
Here are some band pairings that might surprise you.*

In 1964, the Isley Brothers recruited a 21-year-old guitarist named Jimmy James to join their backing band. James, who later became famous using his real name—Jimi Hendrix—played on the group's novelty single "Testify," in which each of the Isleys take turns imitating soul legends like Ray Charles, James Brown, and Stevie Wonder.

• **Boz Scaggs and Steve Miller** (of the Steve Miller Band) both found success in the 1970s, but they joined forces twice before. Scaggs and Miller were in a band called the Marksmen, formed in 1959 at the Dallas high school they both attended. In 1967, after Scaggs's first album flopped, he reunited with Miller in the Steve Miller Band. He recorded two albums with Miller before leaving for a solo career, at which point Miller took over all the vocals.

• The *Chabad Telethon* has aired annually on Los Angeles television for more than 30 years, raising money for Jewish charities. In September 1989, a trio calling itself Chopped Liver performed on the broadcast. Its members: Bob Dylan on harmonica and recorder, and character actor Harry Dean Stanton and Peter Himmelman (Dylan's son-in-law) on guitars. They performed several Jewish folk songs, including "Hava Nagila."

• **Longtime Tom Petty and the Heartbreakers** drummer Stan Lynch left the band in 1994, primarily because he resented having to play on Petty's solo hits at concerts. His replacement: Dave Grohl, who had been in Nirvana until earlier that year, when the suicide of Kurt Cobain ended the grunge band. Grohl was offered the position permanently, but declined, and moved on in 1995 to start his own band, Foo Fighters.

• **Future funk superstar Rick James** fled his hometown of Detroit for Toronto in 1965. (He was dodging the Vietnam War draft.) While living there, he played guitar in a band called the Mynah Birds. Other members of the band: Goldy McJohn (of Steppenwolf) and Neil Young.

All talk: A male great reed warbler will sing from sunrise to sunset (up to 21 hours) to woo a female.

- **In 1987, Ramones drummer Richie Ramone** (all Ramones took on a stage name) abruptly quit the band in the middle of a tour. Singer Joey Ramone called up an old friend to fill in: Clem Burke of Blondie. Burke was a Ramone for two shows; his stage name for the gigs was Elvis Ramone.

- **Kiss fired drummer Peter Criss** in 1980 and auditioned new musicians to replace him. Although he never toured with the band (and never put makeup on his face), South African drummer Anton Fig played the drums on two Kiss albums before leaving in 1982. His next gig: he joined the World's Most Dangerous Band, the Paul Shaffer–led house band on *Late Night with David Letterman*.

- **The American rock band Blackjack** had a minor hit in 1979 with a song called "Love Me Tonight." The band broke up the following year, but some of the members went on to much more success. Lead singer Michael Bolotin changed his name to Michael Bolton and became a songwriter and a soft rock superstar. In 1984, guitarist Bruce Kulick joined Kiss…which had a big comeback hit in 1989 with the ballad "Forever." That song was cowritten by Michael Bolton.

- **The Germs** were one of the major bands of the 1970s Los Angeles punk scene. They formed in 1977 with each member taking on sarcastic, aggressive stage names, including singer Darby Crash, guitarist Pat Smear, and drummer Dottie Danger. After the band broke up in 1980, Smear would go on to be a touring guitarist with Nirvana and a member of Foo Fighters in the 1990s. Dottie Danger, however, only lasted in the Germs for a few months. She started her own, all-female rock band called the Go-Gos under her real name: Belinda Carlisle.

- **In 1992, Led Zeppelin guitarist Jimmy Page** really wanted to reunite with his old bandmate, singer Robert Plant, for a reunion tour. Plant said no—his solo career was going pretty well. So Page tried to make Plant so jealous and annoyed that he'd eventually have to get back together with him. Page recruited David Coverdale, lead singer of the 1980s hair metal band Whitesnake ("Here I Go Again") and recorded one album under the name Coverdale/Page. Critics said Coverdale sounded a lot like Plant; when asked to comment, Plant called David Coverdale "David Cover-version." The album sold poorly, but maybe that was Page's plan all along. He and Plant went on an international stadium tour in the summer of 1995.

*   *   *

"Life is divided into the horrible and the miserable." **—Woody Allen**

High-Tech Underwear

Who says underwear should only be clean, comfortable,
and stylish? Here are some unusual undergarments
with some very unusual built-in features.

J&D BACON-SCENTED UNDERWEAR

What They Do: Offer the wearer a new kind of smelly underpants, or as J&D puts it, "the gold standard of meat-scented luxury undergarments."

Details: NASA supposedly developed the scented-ink technology that makes this product possible, but the folks at J&D are the ones who figured out it could be used to make skivvies smell like bacon. The bright red underpants come in men's and women's styles, both of which feature an image of a strip of bacon across the front of the garment with a caption that reads "Stop and smell the bacon." The bacon scent lasts for up to six months "depending on the number of wearings and the strength of your own scent," says J&D...as long as you remember to wash them separately using unscented laundry detergent. (Not recommended for mail carriers, dogcatchers, veterinarians, or anyone hiking or camping in bear country.)

LUMINOGLOW LINGERIE

What They Do: Glow in the dark

Details: In daylight, the lingerie looks like ordinary white lingerie accented with Italian lace. Switch off the lights, however, and the lace gives off a luminescent glow, making it easier (and more fun) for your romantic partner to find them (and you) in the dark. "Nothing is left to chance, with the glow-in-the-dark lace strategically positioned to complement the lingerie and accentuate the body," says the company. "LuminoGlow is made for lovers. It says 'adore me, want me, especially in the dark!' "

FIND ME IF YOU CAN LINGERIE

What They Do: Track the wearer by satellite

Details: For lovers who enjoy playing hide-and-seek at greater distances than glow-in-the-dark skivvies allow, Brazilian lingerie maker LindeLucy has introduced a lace bodice with a GPS tracking device sewn into it. Simply enter the wearer's password online and their location is pinpointed on a map. Not long after the "Find Me If You Can" line went on sale in 2008, it attracted criticism that men might use it to track their wives and girlfriends against their will. LindeLucy dismissed the idea: "It's not a modern chastity belt…This collection is a wink to women and a challenge to men, because even if she gives him the password to her GPS, she can always turn it off. She can only be found if she wants to be."

BRIEF JERKIES

What They Are: Underwear made from real beef jerky

Details: Why settle for just the scent of meat when you can have the genuine article? That's the thinking behind Brief Jerky, underwear that's stitched together by hand from beef jerky. Made by a group of artisans in Corvallis, Oregon, they're sold through the MixedSpecies storefront on Etsy, a website that specializes in handmade and vintage items. Brief Jerkies are made to order "from the highest quality of dried preserved meats we can find at the closest convenience store," say the MixedSpecies folks. But though they're made from food, Brief Jerkies contain plenty of inedible components like metal grommets, fake plastic gemstones (if you request them), and adhesive foam backing, and they are not intended to be eaten—thereby defeating the purpose of making underwear out of meat in the first place. MixedSpecies charges $139 a pair for their inedible beef briefs and says they'll keep making them "until those powerful enough to sport them run out of money."

UNDERTECH CONCEALMENT HOLSTER BRIEFS

What They Do: Enable you to carry concealed weapons in your underpants

Details: This underwear is like any ordinary pair of compression shorts, with an added feature: a wide band of surgical-grade elastic is stitched to the waist to form two holsters, one over each hip. Left-handers can store their handgun over their left hip and extra ammo clips over the right hip, and right-handers can do the opposite. Or carry a gun over each hip! If hiding two guns in your underpants doesn't provide a strong enough sense of security, Undertech also sells concealed-carry tank tops and undershirts that will allow the wearer to hide up to two more. Available in men's and women's styles.

SHIRIDASHI BUTT REVEAL UNDERWEAR

What They Do: Make it look like your rear end is showing

Details: Printed on the back of these Japanese underpants is a startlingly realistic graphic that looks like the fabric on the rear of the underwear has been ripped away, leaving your butt cheeks exposed to the world for all to see. "Guaranteed," says the manufacturer, "to get strange and curious looks from passersby!"

Crime fact: A bite mark can elevate a charge of simple battery to aggravated battery.

Five Nice Stories

*Every now and then, we like to lock our inner curmudgeons
in a box and share stories with happy endings.*

MINE EYES HAVE SEEN THE LIGHT

It had been 10 years since Allen Zderad last saw his wife Carmen's face. At 58 years old, he lost his sight due to a genetic eye disease called *retinitis pigmentosa*. Doctors told him he would never see again, but in 2015, Dr. Raymond Iezzi of the Mayo Clinic chose Zderad to test out a new device that had been more than 20 years in the making: a bionic eye. Dr. Iezzi implanted into Zderad's retina 60 electrodes that interact with a camera on a special pair of glasses, which is connected to a wearable computer. Two weeks after the operation, with Allen's wife and several of his children and grandchildren present, Dr. Iezzi switched on the device. For the first time in a decade, Allen could see crude shapes. He couldn't make out a lot of details, but he instantly honed in on Carmen and—through tears and laughter—reached out to hug her. He said it was easy to spot his wife because "she's the most beautiful one in the room."

HOME IMPROVEMENT

The years haven't been kind to Leonard and Dorothy Bullock's Pendleton, Oregon, home. The paint was peeling and the porch was falling apart. And the Bullocks—both in their 70s—couldn't afford to fix it. It got to the point where a neighborhood kid said that "someone should just burn it down." Not only did Leonard hear that remark, so did a Union Pacific railway worker named Josh Cyganik. He worked across the street from the Bullocks and felt that they deserved a helping hand. So Cyganik gathered some friends, coworkers, and—thanks to a Facebook post that went viral—dozens of complete strangers, many from out of state. Then, on a Saturday in July 2015, nearly 100 people showed up at the Bullocks' residence. With supplies donated by local hardware and lumber stores, they painted the house, repaired the porch, and gave the grateful retirees a new lease on life.

A PERFECT SCORE

In 2011, after 29 years of coaching at Erasmus High School in Brooklyn, New York, Vic Butler retired. His win-loss record as a basketball coach wasn't particularly impressive. His greatest accomplishment: every single varsity player he coached—all 400 of them—not only graduated, but made it into some kind of secondary education. Butler's rules were strictly enforced: If a player's grades slipped, or he got into disciplinary trouble, he was suspended. If a player failed to submit college applications and financial-aid forms on time, he was suspended. His tough approach worked. "I still think about the lessons I learned from Coach almost every day," Ray Abellard told the *New York Daily News*. Abellard graduated in 1999 and now runs a basketball camp in the neighborhood. "It's nice to win," added Butler, "but the most important thing is to do well in school. I always taught the kids that basketball is just a vehicle for getting where you need to go in life."

SIGN, SIGN, EVERYWHERE A SIGN

A young man named Muharrem from Bagcilar, a suburb of Istanbul, Turkey, is deaf, so it's difficult for him to communicate with most of the people in his town. With help from Muharrem's sister, Samsung decided to cast him in a commercial to promote their new video call center for the hearing impaired. Only thing: no one told Muharrem. Samsung representatives spent a month secretly teaching several townspeople—none of whom even knew Muharrem—how to use sign language. Then, for the big reveal in December 2014, the tech company set up cameras all over town. They recorded Muharrem and his sister as they walked around. Muharrem seemed both delighted and confused that so many people were signing to him—including the clerk at the bagel market, a man who dropped some oranges, and a cab driver. "What's going on?" he asked his sister.

"I don't know," she replied, suppressing a smile. The ruse was finally up when they got to a video call center screen in the town center, where a Samsung rep explained—on screen and using sign language—that the entire thing had been set up just for him. Muharrem broke down in tears as several townspeople approached and hugged him.

FISH STORY

In 2015, Ron Hopper, 64, of Hull, England, was diagnosed with terminal liver cancer shortly before his annual fishing trip to Thailand with his two best friends, Paul Fairbrass and Cliff Dale. On his deathbed, Hopper asked them to scatter some of his ashes when they went on their trip. "We'll do one better than that," said Fairbrass. "We'll turn you into boilies and catch a big fish with you." (Boilies are paste fish baits, shaped into rounds and boiled so that they stay together in water.) That spring, the two men took their Hopper boilies, which they called "Purple Ronnies," to a lake in Thailand. Turns out Hopper tasted pretty good; the fishermen hooked a 180-pound Siamese carp—one of the largest carp ever caught in the world. "After we caught this fish," said Dale, "I looked to the heavens and said, 'Thank you, Ron!'"

After legendary sci-fi author Ray Bradbury died in 2012, NASA named...

A Brief History of the Tooth Fairy

Losing baby teeth is one of the earliest and most anticipated rites of passage for a young child. In our part of the world, it often involves a visit from the tooth fairy. But just how old is the tradition, and what came before it? This visit from the trivia fairy will reveal all.

TOOTH OR CONSEQUENCES

"Shed tooth rituals," as anthropologists and folklorists call the traditions that accompany the loss of baby teeth, have varied widely from one place to another and from one time to another. Every human culture has such rituals, and many have a feature in common: whatever is done with the baby tooth is done in the belief that it will protect the child from harm or ensure that a strong, healthy permanent tooth grows in to replace the old tooth.

For centuries in Europe, it was common practice to "plant" baby teeth in the ground as if they were seeds. Doing so was thought to encourage the growth of the new tooth. Planting the tooth also kept it from falling into the hands of a witch, who could use it to cast spells on the child who lost it. (If there was any question as to whether the tooth had already been bewitched, throwing it into a fire destroyed the tooth and broke the spell.)

THE FIRST TOOTH FAIRY

If you're like Uncle John and you've ever lived in a place that has been infested with mice, you've probably noticed that the pests can chew through just about anything, even wood. This did not go unnoticed in generations past, when homes had dirt floors and rodent infestations were a fact of life.

In those days most people were all but toothless by the time they reached their mid-30s. Mice, by comparison, never lose their teeth because their teeth never stop growing. Perhaps it was inevitable that toothless humans would come to associate mice with strong teeth, and begin to offer their children's baby teeth as "gifts" to mice in the hope that some of the toughness of their teeth would transfer back to the child. Anthropologists call this "sympathetic magic." In some places the parent or child would give the baby tooth to the mouse by throwing it out the window. In other places they tossed it over a shoulder, under a bed, onto the roof, into the yard, or left it as an offering next to a mouse hole somewhere in the house. Whatever the custom locally, it was accompanied by a saying such as "mouse, mouse, here is a tooth, now give me another one."

FRENCH BREAD

Folklorists believe that France is the place where this tradition evolved into "trading" the baby tooth not for a healthy permanent tooth but rather for money or a small gift. When a child lost a tooth, they placed it in their slipper or shoe and left it out overnight. While the child slept, *le petit souris* (the little mouse) would come and take the tooth away and leave a coin in its place. As James Wynbrandt relates in *An Excruciating History of Dentistry*, "a barter system also developed wherein a sleeping youngster could trade a tooth for candy, not with a mouse but with a good fairy."

AMERICAN-MADE

By the early 1900s, the tradition of exchanging baby teeth for money or gifts had spread to the United States, where children began to put their teeth under their pillow instead of in a shoe. And rather than give it to a mouse or to a random good fairy, children began to give it to one fairy in particular: the *tooth fairy*. It's not known precisely when or where in the United States the tooth fairy made its first appearance, but by the time the first story featuring the tooth fairy (an eponymous children's play) appeared in print in 1927, the tradition is believed to have become quite widespread.

AROUND THE WORLD

• **Norway.** The Vikings, who raided and plundered much of coastal Europe from 800 to 1100, believed that baby teeth brought good luck, so they strung them into necklaces and wore them into battle. This tradition may be related to another ancient Norse custom, that of paying a *tannfe*, or "tooth fee," to a child when they lost their first tooth.

• **Spain.** Children leave their tooth under their pillow for Ratoncito Pérez (Pérez Mouse), who leaves a coin in exchange for the tooth. Tales involving a character named Ratón Pérez first appeared in print in Spain in 1877, but he didn't get involved in the tooth-swapping business until 1894, when the eight-year-old boy king of Spain, Alfonso XIII, became upset over a lost tooth. His mother, Queen Maria Cristina, hired a journalist named Luis Coloma to write a story that would calm His Majesty down. Kids in Spain, Mexico, and other Spanish-speaking countries have been leaving their baby teeth out for Ratón Pérez ever since, though in some regions he's known as Ratón de los Dientes (the Tooth Mouse).

- **Scotland.** The Scots have their own unique blend of the tooth fairy and rodent traditions: in their case, the tooth fairy or "white fairy" is a rat.

- **Argentina.** Kids leave their tooth for Ratón Pérez in a glass of water instead of under their pillow. Ratón Pérez takes the tooth, drinks the water, and leaves a coin or a small gift in the empty glass.

- **Colombia.** Children leave their teeth out for a mouse named El Ratón Miguelito: "Mickey Mouse." (No word on what the Walt Disney Company thinks of this.) Sometimes the parents will have the tooth dipped in gold or silver and made into a piece of jewelry.

- **Turkey.** Here baby teeth are buried. Where they're buried depends on what the child wants to be when they grow up, or what the parent wants for them. If the child wants to be a firefighter, for example, they might bury the tooth next to a firehouse.

- **Tajikistan.** Teeth are buried here too, in the belief that they will grow into warriors.

- **Pakistan.** Children wrap the tooth in cotton, then wait until sunset and throw it into a river for good luck.

- **Southeast Asia and Japan.** Children throw their lower teeth straight up in the air, and their upper teeth straight down onto the ground or, if possible, under the floor. (This is believed to help the new teeth grow in straight, because when the new tooth grows in it will grow in the same direction that the old tooth was thrown.) While the child throws the tooth, they ask for it to be replaced by the tooth of a mouse.

- **China.** If it's an upper tooth, it's placed at the foot of the bed. If it's a lower tooth, it's thrown on the roof, again in the hope that this will help the new tooth to grow in straight.

- **The Philippines.** The child makes a wish and hides the tooth. After a year has passed, if they can find the tooth again, they get to make a second wish.

- **Nigeria.** The child throws the tooth into the attic and asks the mice up there not to eat the tooth. If the mice do eat it, the new tooth will not grow in. Another tradition is for the child to put the tooth in their fist with some stones (eight stones for boys, and six for girls), then throw the objects into the air and run away as quickly as possible.

- **South Africa.** Instead of putting their tooth under their pillow, South African kids put it in a slipper.

- **Lithuania.** Who says you have to give your teeth away? Lithuanian kids keep theirs as souvenirs.

- **Arab world.** Children in many Arab countries throw baby teeth into the sky or toward Allah.

Rule of thumb: Paintings of pug dogs sell better at auction than paintings of German shepherds.

Yoko: Loco?

*Looking for something odd to help shake up an otherwise humdrum day?
Try following Yoko Ono (the widow of John Lennon) on Twitter.*

"Count all the words in a book instead of reading them."

"Imagine painting all the buildings in the city the color of light."

"Send a smell to the moon."

"Make a promise to a tree. Ask it to be passed on to other trees."

"Carry what you can in both hands and walk. See if you can see where you are going."

"Imagine tying balloons to the roof of every building in the city. Let the balloons wave to the breeze. See if buildings are lighter for it."

"Count all the puddles on the street when the sky is blue."

"Imagine two billion universes. Visualize yourself on a planet in each universe."

"Think of the Earth as a turning point in eternity. Think of the Earth as a meeting point in infinity."

"Tape the sound of the lake gradually freezing. Drink a cup of hot chocolate, afterwards."

"If the butterflies in your stomach die, send yellow flowers to your friend with a note of love."

"Tape the sound of the moon fading at dawn. Give it to your mother to listen to when she's in sorrow."

"Carry a bag of peas. Leave a pea wherever you go."

"Imagine letting a goldfish swim across the sky. Let it swim from the East to the West. Drink a liter of water."

"Hammer a nail in the center of a piece of glass. Send each fragment to an arbitrary address."

"Imagine the clouds dripping. Dig a hole in your garden to put them in."

"Send a fog to your friends."

"Polish an orange."

"Draw a line. Erase a line."

"Steal all the clocks and watches in the world. Destroy them."

"Listen to the ocean inside your body."

Boo! Silver carp can leap 10 feet out of the water when startled.

The World's Most Unusual Cemeteries

Aside from all the corpses and whatnot—these places are really creepy.

OLD JEWISH CEMETERY

Location: Prague, Czech Republic

Background: This small cemetery in the heart of downtown Prague is tightly surrounded by buildings and busy streets in what was once Prague's Jewish Quarter, the traditional home to the city's Jewish population going back to at least the 11th century. The old buildings were demolished around the turn of the 20th century, but the cemetery remains. No one is sure how old it is, but it has been in use since at least the 15th century, and possibly much earlier. And it remained in use until the 1780s.

Grave Matters: According to religious law, graves and gravestones may not be removed or destroyed. So when they ran out of space in this cemetery, they brought in more soil, covered the old graves, and made a new layer of graves on top of the old ones. The old gravestones? They were placed above the new graves, along with the new gravestones. They did this *at least 12 times* over the centuries. Result: there are believed to be more than 100,000 people buried in the small city cemetery. And thousands of gravestones are crammed right next to each other throughout the cemetery's grounds. (Although only about 12,000 gravestones remain intact today.)

ST. ROCH CEMETERY

Location: New Orleans, Louisiana

Background: This cemetery started as a small chapel, built in 1874 by local Catholic priest Father Leonard Thevis as a token of thanks after his parish was spared during a deadly outbreak of yellow fever. A cemetery for parishioners was built around the chapel shortly afterward. Father Thevis named the church and cemetery in honor of Saint Roch (pronounced "rock"), whose name is invoked to help those afflicted during epidemics.

Grave Matters: Ever since its opening—and especially during outbreaks of disease—people have visited the site to pray to Saint Roch. They have left behind what are known as *ex-votos*—offerings left for saints in gratitude for perceived help. The ex-votos left at St. Roch

---

G-g-g-good job! Albert Einstein, Rowan Atkinson, and Joe Biden all overcame stuttering.

include plaster casts of body parts (hands, arms, legs, feet, brains, livers, hearts, etc.) representing the body parts of people being prayed for, prosthetics (mostly legs and feet), leg braces from polio victims, sets of false teeth, tufts of human hair, glass eyes, and more. These relics can be found hanging from the walls and on tables and shelves in a small room inside the cemetery chapel. The remains of Father Thevis are there, too, buried beneath the floor in front of the altar.

CAPUCHIN CRYPT

Location: Rome, Italy

Background: This isn't exactly a cemetery—it's a crypt, which is defined as a burial room underneath a church. In this case, it's under Rome's Our Lady of the Conception of the Capuchins church, which was built in 1631. The Capuchins are an order of Catholic monks, and the church was built as their new home. Upon its completion, the monks packed up their belongings and moved from their nearby monastery to the new church.

Grave Matters: The monks exhumed the remains of their fellow monks at the old monastery...and used the bones of the deceased monks to decorate the five crypt rooms beneath the church. As more monks died over the following centuries, they added *their* bones to the decorations. (But only after burying them first and waiting several years to let the flesh decompose.) This went on until 1870, when the Catholic Church stopped allowing burials under churches, by which time the bones of about 3,700 monks had been interred there. And the rooms are bizarre: the walls and ceilings—which have names like "Crypt of the Skulls," "Crypt of the Leg Bones and Thigh Bones," and "Crypt of the Pelvises"—are covered in bones, arranged in elaborate patterns (with some whole, mummified monk bodies thrown in), looking like macabre horror movie sets. Why did the monks create the weird decorations? To be a somber reminder of the temporary nature of life on earth.

Bonus Fact: The soil inside the crypt rooms was imported from Jerusalem.

OISE-AISNE AMERICAN CEMETERY—PLOT E

Location: Northern France

Background: This is one of five plots that make up the Oise-Aisne American Cemetery and Memorial, a graveyard created in 1918, at the end of World War I. The other four, plots A through D, hold the remains of 6,012 American soldiers who died while fighting in the region. Plot E...is a little different.

Grave Matters: Plot E was added after World War II, and was deliberately located away from the other plots, in a small clearing surrounded by hedges and woods. Why? Because it holds the remains of 94 American soldiers who were executed by the American military for rape or murder or both (except for one soldier), during or shortly after the end of World War II. Those crimes were committed in various locations around Europe and North Africa, and the perpetrators were originally buried near the sites of their executions, but were all moved to the Oise-Aisne's Plot E in 1949. The graves are all marked with flat, index card–sized stones, with no names—only grave numbers—etched into them. A single small white cross overlooks the entire graveyard.

Bonus Fact: The only soldier interred in Plot E who was not convicted of rape or murder was Private Eddie Slovik. He was executed for desertion in 1945—the only American soldier executed for desertion since the Civil War. And he's not there anymore: after repeated requests from his family, Slovik's remains were repatriated in 1987 and buried next to his wife in Woodmere Cemetery in Detroit, Michigan.

CIMITIRUL VESEL

Location: Sapanta, Romania

Background: Cimitirul Vesel is a cemetery in the tiny town of Sapanta, in Romania's far north. Exactly when it first opened is unknown, but it became what it is known for today in the 1930s.

Grave Matters: Cimitirul Vesel is the "Merry Cemetery," which is what "Cimitirul Vesel" actually means. It was the brainchild of Stan Ioan Patras, a local woodcarver, painter, and poet, who wanted Sapanta's cemetery to be a place that celebrated the lives of its inhabitants, rather than sadly mourning their deaths. So in 1935, Patras started making tall, elaborately carved oak markers for the graves in the local cemetery, painting them in bright colors, depicting scenes from the dead people's lives—playing music, reading, cooking, working, and the like. The markers are also inscribed with lighthearted, often silly epitaphs, written in the first person, as if by the dead people themselves but actually written by either Patras or the family of the deceased. Patras made more than 700 of the whimsical grave markers, most of which are still standing today. He stopped making them in 1977, when he became a resident of the cemetery himself. (At which point his apprentice, Dumitru Pop, took over the job.) The Merry Cemetery is a Romanian national historic site today—and it's still a functioning cemetery.

Bonus Fact: Not all the paintings on the grave markers depict happy scenes from the lives of the deceased. Some depict the causes of their deaths—including some paintings of people being struck by cars, and one showing a man being decapitated.

According to a University of Michigan study, cheese can be as addictive as drugs.

Dubya's Nicknames

Whether it was because of his sense of humor or because he had trouble remembering names, President George W. Bush used lots of nicknames for his associates. Here are a few of them.

• **British prime minister Tony Blair:** "Landslide." (Blair was elected prime minister in 1997 with a huge electoral victory.)

• **Saudi ambassador Bandar in Sultan:** "Bandar Bush." The bin Sultans and Bushes have been close for decades, so the president considered him a member of the family.

• **Secretary of the Treasury Paul O'Neill:** "Pablo."

• **Sen. Paul Wellstone:** "Pablo."

• **Attorney General Alberto Gonzales:** "Fredo."

• **Rep. Fred Upton:** "Freddo."

• **Australian prime minister John Howard:** "Man of Steel." Howard was in Washington to meet with Bush on September 11, 2001, and the two became close friends. Two years later, Bush gave a speech about Howard, saying, "He's not only a man of steel, he showed the world he's a man of heart as well." The nickname (or half of it) stuck.

• **Rep. John Boehner:** "Boner." (His name is actually pronounced "bay-nor.")

• **Office of Management and Budget director Mitch Daniels:** "The Blade." (He's the guy who had to make big budget cuts.)

• **Situation Room director James P. Wisecup:** "Sit Room Guy."

• **Sen. Barbara Boxer:** "Ali." (Get it?)

• **Sen. Dianne Feinstein:** "Frazier." Barbara Boxer was one of California's senators, and Feinstein is the other. Since Boxer was Ali, Feinstein was Frazier (for Joe Frazier, Muhammad Ali's rival).

• **FEMA director Joe Allbaugh:** "Big Country."

• **CIA director George Tenet:** "Brother George."

Julia, a character introduced on *Sesame Street* in 2015, is a muppet with autism.

- **Secretary of Education Margaret Spellings:** "La Margarita."
Bush liked to show off his fluency in Spanish whenever he could, and
Spellings spoke Spanish as well as he did.

- **National Energy Policy director Andrew D. Lundquist:** "Light
Bulb."

- **Mary Matalin, assistant to the Vice President:** "M&M."

- **Special Assistant to the President Israel Hernandez:** One of his
roles was providing the president with breath mints, so he earned the
nickname "Altoid Boy."

- **Director of CIA counterterrorism Cofer Black:** "Flies on the
Eyeballs Guy"

- **Bloomberg News reporter Dick Kyle:** "Stretch." (He's tall.)

- *Washington Times* **reporter Bill Sammon:** "Super Stretch." (He's
very tall—6'7".)

- **NBC News reporter David Gregory:** "Little Stretch." (He's not as
tall—6'5".)

- *Los Angeles Times* **reporter Peter Wallsten:** Wallsten is blind and
wears dark glasses. Bush called him "Shades."

*   *   *

WHODUNNIT

In January 2009, $6.8 million worth of jewelry disappeared from
Kaufhaus des Westens, a high-end department store in Berlin. One of
the few pieces of evidence police could find was a latex glove with a
drop of sweat on it. German police ran it through its criminal database,
and the sweat gave a positive DNA match. German law does not allow
criminals to be named in full in news reports, but the sweat belonged to
27-year-old "Hassan O"…or possibly his twin brother, "Abbas O." Both
have criminal records for theft. Police tracked down and arrested both
brothers and charged them both with the burglary of the department
store, but shortly before the case went to trial they were released on
a technicality. Although police are certain it was one of them, it was
impossible to tell which of the twins it was. Hassan and Abbas share
99.99 percent of the same DNA, and since neither could be ruled out,
neither could be definitively pinned to the robbery.

Bacon!

Some mouthwatering facts about everyone's favorite snack.

• Americans spend more than $4 billion annually on bacon.

• Bacon dates back at least 3,500 years. The Chinese were the first to cook salted pork bellies. The salt preserved the meat so it could be eaten all year.

• During World War II, Americans were urged to save bacon fat so it could be used in the manufacture of bombs. (It was used to make glycerol, an ingredient in explosives.)

• If you're average, you'll eat 18 pounds of bacon this year.

• Three bacon products you can't eat: Bacon-Scented Bath & Shower Soap; Bacon Strips Adhesive Bandages (Band-Aids that look like strips of bacon); and the Bacon Surfing Cat Clock (a clock with a picture of a cat surfing on a piece of bacon…in space).

• Kevin Bacon's favorite sandwich is the BLAST—bacon, lettuce, avocado, smoked salmon, and tomato. (He claims he invented it.)

• Bacon has been called the food most likely to convince vegetarians to eat meat.

• Bacon has a compound that produces a pleasing neuro-chemical response. Result: bacon is addictive.

• U.S. bacon sales fell sharply in the 1980s because of a lean-meat craze. What turned it around? The bacon cheeseburger. The first one debuted at Hardee's in 1992. Once it became clear that people were more willing to eat bacon when they went out, restaurants started adding it to everything…and started the modern bacon craze.

• First recorded death by bacon: In 1543, an English servant named Elizabeth Browne was warming herself by a fire when she was crushed by four sides of uncooked bacon that had fallen from a hook.

• Research is inconclusive, but here are three things bacon *might* do: cure hangovers (it has amino acids), improve a fetus's brain development (it has choline), lower a man's sperm count (like all processed meats).

• In a recent poll, 43 percent of Canadians said they'd rather eat bacon than have sex.

The skeleton of an elephant was discovered beneath the Vatican in 1962.

The (Non) Flight of the Pillownauts

Just because you're not an astronaut, that doesn't mean you can't contribute to the space program. You don't even have to get out of bed. Meet the "pillownauts."

LOST IN SPACE

Today we take it for granted that astronauts can function in the weightlessness of spaceflight, but at the dawn of the space age in the early 1960s, scientists weren't sure that was possible. Some experts feared that the shape of the human eye would become distorted in zero gravity, making it difficult for astronauts to see the gauges and controls they needed to operate their spacecraft. What about eating—would astronauts be able swallow their food without the assistance of gravity? And even if they could, would their bodies be able to digest it? If not, the length of a spaceflight might be limited to the amount of time an astronaut could go without eating.

These fears proved to be unfounded, but as the years passed and the duration of spaceflights increased from less than an hour to days, weeks, and eventually months, astronauts on longer missions began to experience physiological changes that were just as worrying to scientists. For each month they spent in weightlessness, astronauts lost as much as one percent of their bone density in the hips and other weight-bearing areas of their bodies, and as much as 3 percent of their muscle mass.

RISKY BUSINESS

Some of the first Soviet cosmonauts to spend more than 200 days in space in the early 1980s were unable to walk or even catch a ball after returning to Earth. They eventually recovered, but their experience raised the alarming possibility that if a mission was long enough, such as a three-year trip to Mars and back, an astronaut's health might never recover. Computer models have predicted that astronauts on a mission to Mars could lose as much as half of their bone density, putting them at serious risk of bone fractures. They might land on Mars too fragile to function; if they broke a hip or some other bone on the red planet, they might die before they made it back home.

For this reason, NASA and other space agencies have been studying the effects of weightlessness on human health since the 1960s, both

---

The "Sleeping Beauty Diet" involved being sedated for several days to sleep off weight.

to better understand the changes that human bodies go through, and to test the efficacy of drugs, diet, exercise equipment, and other "counter-measures" in minimizing the deterioration. Much of this research has, of necessity, been conducted on Earth, where weightlessness is simulated in "bed rest" studies in which volunteers are confined to hospital beds 24 hours a day for as much as 120 days at a stretch. Many of the studies take place at NASA's Flight Research Analog Unit (FARU) at the University of Texas Medical Branch in Galveston, about 50 miles from Mission Control in Houston.

DOUGH-NAUTS

Study volunteers, who've become known as "pillownauts," are typically paid $10 an hour for every waking hour that they participate in a study. That may not sound like much, but it adds up: Since the pillownauts are awake 16 hours a day, they can earn more than $19,000 in a 120-day study that also provides free room and board.

And if you think getting paid $19,000 to lie around for months on end would appeal to a lot of people, you're right: It's not unheard of for a bed rest study to attract as many as 25,000 applicants. The pool is carefully screened to select the kinds of candidates that NASA wants to study, namely, people who, like the astronauts, are in excellent shape because they don't spend a lot of time lying around. Pillownauts are required to be in top physical condition, and must pass some of the same physicals that the astronauts take. Applicants must be nonsmokers between the ages of 24 and 55. They cannot be taking prescription drugs for any chronic medical condition. These and other criteria, including background checks, psychological screening, and even credit checks, help to winnow the 25,000 applicants down to the final 30 or so who are accepted for each study.

...AND NOW THE FINE PRINT

Smoking bans and credit checks are just the beginning. Pillownauts aren't allowed to consume alcohol or caffeine during the study, nor can they add salt to the bland hospital food that they will live on for the entire length of the study. And they must eat *all* of the hospital food they are served—no more and no less. That includes any and all condiments that are served with a meal. If a volunteer returns their salad with some of the dressing left in the plastic cup it came in, the cup will be returned to the volunteer so that they can slurp it down to the last drop. Unscheduled snacking isn't allowed. Nor, for that matter, are conjugal visits or naps outside of scheduled sleeping times. Pillownauts are awakened every morning at 6:00 a.m. and must remain awake until lights out at 10:00 p.m.

Music trivia: *Col legno* is playing a stringed instrument with the wood side of the bow.

THAT SINKING FEELING

The hospital beds used in bed rest studies aren't level like ordinary beds. If the study is designed to simulate lunar gravity, which is about one-sixth that of Earth, the bed will be tilted up at the head by 9.5 degrees, the angle at which the volunteer's body, when "standing" in bed, supports one-sixth of its own weight.

Even worse than the lunar beds are the ones used in the zero-gravity studies that simulate a flight to Mars. Those beds are tilted *down* at the head by about 6 degrees, so that the pillownauts' feet are 12 to 15 inches higher than their heads. This causes blood and other fluids to flow toward the head, as they do in zero gravity, instead of pooling in the feet like they do on Earth. In this position, watery eyes, runny noses, puffy faces, and swollen sinuses are common. So are headaches, dizziness, toothaches, and nausea, especially during the early days of the study, when the pillownauts' bodies are adjusting to this unfamiliar new position. Back pain is so common that pillownauts receive hour-long massages every other day for the length of the study. They're also given special support hose, which they wear in order to prevent blood clots from forming in their legs.

GO WITH THE FLOW

When NASA says you can't get out of bed for 120 days, they mean it—*you can't get out of bed for 120 days:*

• **You can't get out of bed to eat.** Meals are served in bed on trays, and pillownauts are allowed to prop themselves up on one elbow while eating. But they are not allowed to sit up in bed…ever. When they're not eating, reaching for something, or lying on their side, they are required to keep both shoulders on the bed.

• **You can't get out of bed to bathe.** Instead, the pillownauts are transferred—still lying down—onto a special gurney and wheeled into a shower room where they bathe horizontally, an experience that has been compared to going through a car wash.

• **You can't even get out of bed to go to the bathroom.** When nature calls, pillownauts ask a nurse to bring them a bedpan. If you've ever been hospitalized, you may already know what an unpleasant experience that can be. Now imagine how difficult it is for a Mars study pillownaut, whose bed is tilted 6 degrees down at the head. Special training is required and, as with eating, sitting up to use the bedpan is not allowed. At least one pillownaut has been thrown out of a study after they were caught sitting up to use their bedpan. And since pillownauts aren't paid unless they successfully complete their bed rest study, that particular pillownaut walked away with nothing.

GUINEA PIGS

One of the reasons NASA studies subjects who are as healthy as astronauts is because the pillownauts will deteriorate physically over the course of the study. They lose bone density and muscle mass, just like the astronauts do. But unlike the astronauts, they can also get bedsores on their elbows from propping themselves up to eat and reach for things.

The pillownauts' vital signs are monitored as closely as if they were lab rats. Depending on the study, they may be covered in electrodes, wired up with probes, or both. If a test calls for very precise monitoring of blood pressure, a procedure is performed to insert a catheter directly into the subject's heart. If a study requires measuring the temperature of the heart and surrounding tissue, a special thermometer is inserted into the pillownaut's nose and down their throat to get it as close to the heart as possible. Freckle-sized chunks of tissue are regularly snipped from the muscles in the pillownauts' thighs and other areas and biopsied to measure the change in muscle mass over time.

OFF THE WALL

If the purpose of a particular bed rest study is to test the efficacy of a piece of exercise equipment, such as a zero-gravity treadmill or exercise bicycle, or resistance equipment that simulates weight lifting, the pillownauts will be divided into two groups: one that uses the exercise equipment, and a control group that does not. The pillownauts in the exercise group still don't exactly escape their beds. They are suspended from the ceiling in harnesses that maintain their horizontal position, allowing them to exercise using fitness equipment that is mounted to the wall.

DOWNTIME

When pillownauts aren't being poked, prodded, or hung from the ceiling on straps, they are free to read, watch TV, surf the Internet, talk on their phones, or work on their laptops. There are also regular social periods, when the pillownauts are wheeled into common rooms so that they can mingle with each other, play board games, work on crafts, and engage in other group activities that don't require getting out of bed. If weather permits, they are wheeled outside into the fresh air.

After a bed rest study has been completed, the pillownauts spend two weeks in physical rehabilitation, where they slowly ease back into standing and walking again. The sensation of blood pooling in the legs for the first time in months can be quite painful, especially in the ankles and feet. And once the blood is no longer pooling in their heads, these sensations are often accompanied by light-headedness. Two or three weeks may pass before the pillownauts are able to stand or walk for any length of time, and it may take them as much as six months to regain the bone mass they lost during the study.

SOMETHING FOR EVERYONE

If you're reading this around tax time, you may not approve of the idea that right now, NASA may well be paying people to lie around and do nothing on the chance that someday we might go to Mars or build a base on the Moon. But if you or a loved one are disabled or have ever spent an extended period of time in a hospital, you may have benefited from NASA's bed rest research already. The knowledge gained also benefits anyone who spends extended periods in bed: pregnant women, paraplegics, quadriplegics, elderly people in nursing homes, and patients recovering from surgery. In the old days it was thought that the best way for people recovering from surgery to convalesce was to keep them in bed for several days. But now, thanks to information gleaned from NASA's bed rest studies, patients are encouraged to get on their feet as quickly as possible, in order to speed recovery time.

BACK TO BED

The International Space Station (ISS), which has been continuously occupied by astronauts since 2000, has given NASA's best researchers plenty of opportunities to test the drugs, exercise equipment, and other countermeasures on actual astronauts living and working in zero gravity. Unfortunately, the results have been disappointing so far: astronauts who spend six months or more aboard the ISS still lose as much as 20 percent of their bone density by the time they return to Earth. But what's bad news for the astronauts is good news for aspiring pillownauts, because it means that NASA is unlikely to cancel its bed rest studies anytime soon.

For more examples of how NASA simulates space missions on Earth, turn to page 476.

*　　　*　　　*

MIRACLE CURE!

In 1981, an engineer named Norman Lake introduced the Inductive Nasal Device, which he claimed could cure the common cold. It was a device—a U-shaped piece of wire with a piece of white plastic on each end. Lake's instructions: clamp it over your nose for 30 minutes a day until cold symptoms subsided, generally about seven to ten days. (Average length of a cold, without treating it: seven to ten days.)

You're Playing with Fire

These people (and dogs) evidently didn't pay attention during fire safety talks.

BUGGING OUT

Problem: A spider in the laundry room

Fiery Solution: In 2014, a Seattle man saw the pest on the floor and chose a unique method of exterminating it—he took a can of spray paint and a lighter, ignited the stream of paint, and aimed it at the spider. But the crafty arachnid retreated into the laundry room wall. The man responded by spraying the wall with flames.

Result: $60,000 worth of damage to the man's home. As for his eight-legged adversary, firefighter Kyle Moore remarked, "I'm pretty sure the spider did not survive this fire. The whole wall went."

TORCHED

Problem: A furry rodent

Fiery Solution: In the summer of 2014, Khek Chanthalavong of Holland Township, Michigan, decided to cook a squirrel for dinner. But first he had to clean it. So he went out onto the deck of his apartment and used a blowtorch to burn off the fur. Chanthalavong then went back inside to cook the squirrel…and left his blowtorch—still lit—on the deck.

Outcome: Within minutes, the building caught fire. Thirty-two apartment units were severely damaged. Chanthalavong wasn't even a tenant; he was cooking at his girlfriend's apartment…and the insurance company filed a $2 million lawsuit against her.

HOT DOGS

Problem: Bored canines

Fiery Solution: A Mount Lorne, Yukon Territory, man returned home from work one day in November 2014, opened his door, and was greeted by clouds of smoke. Investigators determined that the man's dogs had found a box of "strike anywhere" matches and took it to their dog bed. As they chewed on the box, their gnawing created enough friction to ignite the matches, which started a fire.

Outcome: The fire spread from the dog bed to a nearby couch and chair, but then it burned itself out, and most of the damage in the house was from smoke. (The dogs escaped out the doggie door and were unharmed.)

THE PITS

Problem: Youthful hijinks

Fiery Solution: After an 18-year-old driver flipped his Ford Bronco on an Idaho highway in September 2014, he explained to police that he'd lost control of the vehicle while trying to avoid an animal. Deputies were suspicious, so they questioned the other four teens who'd been in the SUV...and the truth came out: One of the passengers admitted that he'd used a cigarette lighter to singe the driver's armpit hair as a prank.

Outcome: The Bronco was totaled, and two of the teens were thrown from the vehicle, but they escaped with minor injuries.

CHEESY DOES IT

Problem: Hungry for some cheesy toast

Fiery Solution: Suzanne Dale didn't mean to play with fire; she was playing with her toaster. After she read a "life hack" on Facebook that recommended turning your toaster on its side so you can melt your cheese while you toast your bread, the 66-year-old woman from Sale, Greater Manchester, England, decided to give it a try. Only a moment after turning on the toaster, it burst into flames.

Outcome: Luckily, Dale was able to throw the flaming appliance out the window before it did too much damage. The incident sparked the local fire chief to issue this warning: "Trying to make cheese and toast in a toaster is an extremely bad idea."

WHAT A WASTE

Problem: No place to flush

Fiery Solution: An embarrassed mountain biker (whose name wasn't given in press reports) was riding in the foothills of Boise, Idaho, in 2015 when nature called (the #2 variety). The man found a ravine, did his business, and then—just as his grandfather had taught him—he burned the toilet paper. But he didn't stick around long enough to make sure the fire went out. The embers sparked some nearby brush, and the resulting fire ended up burning 73 acres.

Outcome: No people or structures were injured, and the cyclist turned himself in. Carrie Bilbao, who works for the Idaho Bureau of Land Management, told CBS News, "We don't get many fires like this, maybe once every 10 years." Then she added, "But I guess when you gotta go, you gotta go."

Also Stands For

We all know what FBI, TGIF, and HBO stand for…or do we?

• **ASAP** also stands for "Alliance of Security Analysis Professionals" and "Army Substance Abuse Program"

• **HBO** also stands for "Hyperbaric Oxygen" and *"Hoger beroepsonderwijs"* ("Higher Professional Education" in the Netherlands)

• **FBI** also stands for "Food Borne Illness" and "Fiji Born Indian"

• **FAQ** also stands for "Fine Arts Quartet" and *"Femmes Autochtones du Québec"* (French for "Quebec Native Women")

• **ATM** also stands for "Asian Traditional Medicine" and "Anti-Tank Mine"

• **NASA** also stands for "North American Saxophone Alliance" and "Nice And Safe Attitude" (UK)

• **IQ** (Intelligence Quotient) also stands for "Image Quality" and "Inverse Quantization"

• **RSVP** (*Répondez S'il Vous Plaît*) also stands for "Rapid Serial Visual Presentation" and "Revolutionary Surrealist Vandal Party"

• **RIP** also stands for "Routing Information Protocol" and "Regulated Intramembrane Proteolysis"

• **TGIF** also stands for "The Green Initiative Fund" and "Toes Go In First"

• **NBC** also stands for "National Bank of Canada" and "Nazarene Bible College"

• **NFL** also stands for "Nerve Fiber Layer" and "Negative Feedback Loop"

• **FYI** also stands for "Family Youth Interventions" and "Fresno Yosemite International" (an airport)

• **SOS** also stands for "Student Outreach Services" and "Sisters Offering Support"

• **PBJ** (Peanut Butter and Jelly) also stands for "Penn Bioethics Journal" and "Pride Before Jealousy"

• **AAA** also stands for "Asian American Alumni" and "Acronyms And Abbreviations"

• **BRI** ("Bathroom Readers' Institute") also stands for "Bristol Royal Infirmary" and "BEST Robotics, Inc."

Sound waves can be used to lift objects, but not people. (The sound waves make your blood boil.)

The Voice

You've heard terms like a cappella, tenor, mezzo-soprano, and tessitura before (okay, maybe not tessitura)—now learn where they came from, and exactly what they mean. (And for the vocal range terms, we've included some examples of famous singers who sing in those ranges.)

A CAPPELLA. From the Italian for "in the manner of the chapel," this is the term for singing without instrumental accompaniment. It can refer to a solo or a group of singers. Famous a cappella acts include Pentatonix, Ladysmith Black Mambazo, Moira Smiley and VOCO, and Canadian singer Mike Tompkins, as well as 1950s style doo-wop bands, and barbershop quartets. Famous a cappella song: "Don't Worry, Be Happy" (1988) by Bobby McFerrin, the first a cappella song to reach number one on the Billboard Hot 100 chart.

BASS. From the Latin word *bassus,* meaning "low" (or "short"), this is the lowest vocal range in all types of singing, characterized by being deep, rich, and dark. It also is divided into different types, including *basso cantante*—or "singing bass," a higher, agile type of bass singing; and *basso profondo*—the lowest vocal range of all, characterized by being extremely deep, dark, and full. True bass singers are rare, so there aren't a lot in the major pop music scene. A few famous ones: German opera great Kurt Moll, Richard Sterban of the Oak Ridge Boys, and American gospel singer J. D. Sumner.

BARITONE. Derived from a Greek word meaning "deep sounding," baritone refers to a low male singing voice—higher than a bass, but lower than a tenor. In classical music, it's usually divided into two types: *lyric baritone*—the higher, lighter portion of the baritone range; and *dramatic baritone*—a lower, richer, and fuller style of baritone singing. (There's also *bass-baritone*, a classification that describes a full, low voice that shares characteristics and range with both baritone and bass voices.) Famous nonclassical baritones include Harry Belafonte, Frank Sinatra, Neil Diamond, Michael Bublé, Leonard Cohen, Alan Jackson—and Uncle John. (He used to be a professional singer! No kidding!) Famous bass-baritones: Barry White, Paul Robeson, and Johnny Cash.

TENOR. The second-highest male classical singing voice. (The highest: *countertenor.*) The name, coined in the late 13th century, is derived from the Latin *tenere,* meaning "to hold," referring to the fact that tenor singers carried, or *held,* the main melody in the multipart vocal compositions (such as Gregorian chants) that were popular at the time.

Tenors are the most common male singers in pop music today. Famous tenors: opera greats Enrico Caruso and Luciano Pavarotti, John Lennon (although he is classified by some as a high baritone), Paul McCartney, Roger Waters, Neil Young, Stevie Wonder, Robert Plant, Don Henley, Michael Jackson, Sting, Justin Timberlake, and Pharell Williams. Countertenors are rare in the pop world; most male pop singers who sing this high are actually using falsetto. Famous classical countertenors include Bejun Mehta, Alfred Deller, and Andreas Scholl.

FALSETTO. It means "false" in Italian, and refers to men singing artificially high notes, above their natural singing range, and produced by a particular vibration of the vocal cords (of the *ligamentous* edges of the vocal cords, to be precise). Famous acts and singers who regularly use falsetto: the Bee Gees, Roy Orbison, Thom Yorke, Jeff Buckley, Del Shannon, Leo Sayer, and Prince. Falsetto singing can also be done by women, but it's much less common.

ALTO. Meaning "high" in Italian, *alto* is one of the four main classifications in the SATB vocal range system used in choir and choral music: *soprano*, *alto*, *tenor*, and *bass*. It is also commonly used to simply describe any relatively low female voice. Alto singing is usually described as heavy and dark (whereas *soprano* is lighter and brighter). Famous alto singers include k. d. lang, Adele, Amy Winehouse, Shirley Bassey, Nina Simone, Karen Carpenter, and Patsy Cline.

MEZZO-SOPRANO. Meaning "middle-soprano," this is the second-highest classical female singing voice, lower than soprano and higher than alto. Popular singers usually described as mezzo-sopranos: Aretha Franklin, Beyoncé, Whitney Houston, Alanis Morissette, Amy Grant, Sheryl Crow, and Janet Jackson.

SOPRANO. This is the classical female singing voice with the highest range, hence its name, which has its root in the Latin *supra*, meaning "high." There are a number of soprano subtypes in the world of opera, including *coloratura soprano*, which is very high, light, and agile, and *dramatic soprano*, described as lower, darker, and heavier than the other soprano styles. Famous sopranos: opera superstar Maria Callas, Kate Bush, Charlotte Church, Mariah Carey, Björk, Julie Andrews, Emmylou Harris, and Dolly Parton.

VOCAL REGISTER. This term is used to describe three parts of singing ranges: *lower* register, *middle* register, and *upper* register. More technically, it refers to vocal ranges associated with different vibratory patterns made by the vocal cords. These include the *modal register*, which employs lengthening, shortening, and vibrating of the vocal cords, and in which most speaking and singing takes place; the *fry register*, produced through a loosening of the opening between the vocal cords, allowing air to bubble through, producing very low, creaky or rattly sounds (the fry register is not common in singing, but is sometimes used in gospel music); and the *whistle register*, which produces whistlelike or flutelike tones, and the highest notes possible by humans. Famous singers known for their whistle register: Minnie Riperton, Mariah Carey, Christina Aguilera, and Australian Adam Lopez (currently the world record holder for highest male singing voice).

EXTRAS

Intonation. Having *good intonation* means you're singing on pitch. Having *bad intonation* means you are prone to singing off pitch, either flat (too low) or sharp (too high).

Tessitura. The *tessitura* of a singer's voice is the range within which most of that voice falls. This is why people with broad vocal ranges—like Mariah Carey and Maria Callas—can be classified under a single vocal range classification, even though they can sing far out of those ranges.

Chest voice. A term used to describe a style of relatively low-pitched singing, wherein the notes resonate in the chest and create a full, powerful sound, as opposed to *head voice*, which resonates in the head and which is associated with higher, lighter notes.

Parlando singing. A style of singing in which the rhythm and pitch of the song are observed, but a talking voice is used. (British actor Rex Harrison was considered a master of parlando singing, and he used it in his role as Professor Henry Higgins in the 1964 film *My Fair Lady*.)

Squillo. From the Italian *squillare*, meaning "to ring," this is a technical term for the resonant, trumpetlike sound in the voices of opera singers. (Squillo bonus: The word has a modern meaning, too. It means to call someone on a cell phone, let it ring once, and then hang up as a way of sending a message. Example: "Give me a *squillo* when you get home and I'll come on over.")

*   *   *

SHORTEST PLACE NAMES IN THE UNITED STATES

- Y, Alaska
- Ai, Ohio
- Ed, Kentucky
- Oz, Kentucky
- TB, Maryland
- Ti, Oklahoma
- Uz, Kentucky

Serial killer Ted Bundy once saved a toddler from drowning.

Aunt Gladys the Great

Uncle John's Great-Aunt Gladys likes to make people think she has psychic powers. But is she really a psychic…or just a trickster?

SOLAR POWERED

"It's a beautiful day, and all this sunshine has recharged my psychic powers," Aunt Gladys said as she walked into her kitchen from the backyard.

"Psychic powers? Are you sure you haven't been out in the sun a little too long?" I joked.

"Don't believe me? Okay, smart guy, I'll demonstrate my psychic powers not once…not twice…but *three* times," she said as she sat down at the kitchen table. "Take a seat," she said, so I sat down at the table across from her. Aunt Gladys then reached for a notepad, a pen, and an empty coffee mug that were sitting on the table.

DEMONSTRATION #1: *Un*common Cents

"First, I want you to take out all the change in your pocket. Don't count it yet, just hold it tightly in your closed fist in front of you. And don't let me see the coins," she said.

I did as she instructed, and as I held my closed fistful of coins out in front of me, Aunt Gladys said, "I'm going to use my psychic powers to count the change in your fist. Then I'll write the amount down on a piece of paper, fold the paper in half, and put it in this coffee mug." She closed her eyes and concentrated for a minute, then she opened her eyes and wrote something on the notepad. She tore the page from the notepad, folded it in half without letting me see what she'd written on the paper, and put it in the mug.

"Open your hand and count the change," she instructed. I opened my fist and saw that there were three quarters, a nickel, two dimes, and three pennies in my hand. "One dollar and three cents," I said.

"I was right!" Aunt Gladys said.

"Can I see the piece of paper?" I asked.

"Not until we're finished with all three demonstrations," she said.

DEMONSTRATION #2: Table Talk

Aunt Gladys likes to do crossword puzzles. One of her puzzle books was sitting on the table, and next to it was a dictionary. A knife, a fork, and a spoon were also on the table. Aunt Gladys picked up all five items

---

In Denmark, the price of a new car includes a registration fee equal to 105% of the vehicle's value.

and set them down in front of me. "Close your eyes and concentrate on one of these items. Don't tell me which one you're thinking of until I tell you to," she instructed.

I closed my eyes and thought about the book of crossword puzzles.

"Hmmm…okay, got it! You can open your eyes," she said.

I opened my eyes and saw Aunt Gladys writing something on her notepad. Just as she'd done before, she tore the page off the pad without letting me see what she'd written. Then she folded the paper in half and put it in the coffee mug.

"Which item did you pick?" she asked.

"The book of crossword puzzles," I answered.

"Aha!" she said. "I was right again!"

DEMONSTRATION #3: Paper Trail

Next, Aunt Gladys took three napkins out of her napkin holder. She drew a large circle on one of the napkins and put it on the table in front of me. Then she drew a triangle on the second napkin, and a square on the third napkin, and set those on the table in front of me as well.

She closed her eyes and concentrated for a minute. Then she opened her eyes, and wrote something down on her notepad. Just as she'd done in the two previous demonstrations, she tore the sheet from the notepad, folded it in half without letting me see what she'd written down, and put it in the coffee mug.

"I just predicted which of the figures you'll end up with," she said. "Point to one."

I pointed to the square.

"Okay, we'll take the square away," she said as she picked that napkin up and crumpled it into a ball. "Point to one of the two remaining figures," she said.

This time I pointed to the triangle.

"I was right again! That's three in a row!" she said as she tossed the napkin with the circle aside. She picked up the mug with the three folded pieces of paper and handed it to me. "See for yourself," she said.

I unfolded the pieces of paper. One of them had "$1.03" written on it, another had "crossword puzzle book," and the third had a triangle drawn on it.

"Wow! I've got to start spending more time in the sun," I said.

How did Aunt Gladys do it?

Psychics will know this without being told…but for the rest of us:
The answers to Aunt Gladys's puzzles are on page 511.

Shocking fact: When electric eels curl around their prey, they double the power of their zap!

Other Googles

What's the most-used Internet search engine on Earth? Google, of course. But success breeds competition, and Google has a lot of competitors. And though they're not very well known, some of them are very cool.

DOGPILE. Dogpile is a *metasearch* engine—it uses the results of other search engines to produce its own results. For example, if you enter "famous nuns" in Google, it uses the unique Google algorithm to search the Internet and give you what it determines are the best results, in order from the highest to the lowest, ranked according to its own criteria. If you enter "famous nuns" into Yahoo! or Ask, they do the same thing, but with their own algorithms, and they'd come up with different results from Google's. (That could mean entirely different results, or the same results in different ranking orders.) When you enter "famous nuns" into Dogpile, it looks at the results of those other search engines—and gives you what it determines are the highest ranked results based on those results, allowing you to get results beyond which those single sites would bring you.

SPRINGERLINK. Are you a scientist, or a student, or even just a very sci-curious person? (You're reading a *Bathroom Reader*, so of course you are!) This search engine was created with you in mind. It gives users "access to millions of scientific documents from journals, books, series, protocols and reference works" in dozens of different science disciplines. For example, enter "time travel" into SpringerLink, and you'll get links to thousands of science-based books and articles on every imaginable take on time travel. (Some require purchase, but many are available for free.)

MILLION SHORT. You've probably noticed that the top results you get from the most popular search engines are usually from very popular websites. Million Short was created to counter that—and it's pretty hilarious. It purposely filters out the first one million results from any given search, thereby giving you results you'd hardly ever see using popular search engines. Million Short started out as an experiment by Toronto-based startup Exponential Labs, in 2012, with a mission "to guide people on the road less traveled by providing alternate methods of organizing, accessing, and discovering the vast web of information that is the Internet," but it's still in operation today, and it's been updated several times, so now you can tailor results in even more ways. For example: you can filter out only the top 100, 1,000, or 10,000 results, you can tell it to skip all websites that have ads, and you can even tell it to show only websites that allow live chat.

ARTCYCLOPEDIA. Enter the name of one of more than 9,000 artists—Pablo Picasso, for example—and Artcyclopedia will give you links to websites featuring Picasso's works, links to articles, books, and videos about him, links to sites with information on where you can buy his works (if you're a gazillionaire), links to international galleries where his works can be seen (including updates with the latest exhibitions), and more. You can also search for artists and artworks by movement (Expressionism, Dada, Pop Art, etc.), by medium, and by subject. (Bonus: If you're an artist yourself, you can apply to be included in the Artcyclopedia's catalog—although they rarely accept new artists, and only those whose names are well known.)

REGATOR. Regator is a fairly normal search engine, but it doesn't search the entire Internet for results—it only searches blogs. Enter a search item, and Regator will search blogs published all around the world for relevant results. And not just any old blogs: "Rather than automatically fetching every blog under the sun," says the Regator FAQ page. "Regator uses qualified human editors to carefully select only the most relevant, useful, well-written blogs. That means you won't have to deal with the spammy, poorly written, or irrelevant posts that clutter up many other sites." It also has a "Current Blog Trends" section, and filters that allow you to search by topic (such as humor, sports, and tech), and to search only for blog posts that contain audio or video.

DUCKDUCKGO. This is a regular old search engine, but it's built around a theme of protecting users' online privacy. It doesn't store your IP address, your location, or your search history like all the big search engines do, including Google, Yahoo!, and Bing. This means that, according to DuckDuckGo, nobody will ever be able to see your search history—including advertisers, the public (if the information were to be accidentally or purposely leaked), or even law enforcement agencies such as the FBI. It also means everyone who enters the same search item in DuckDuckGo gets the same results. (Big search engines like Google use your location and search history to "personalize" your results.) Another way it differs from more popular search engines is that DuckDuckGo also filters out sites that have a lot of ads. (Not surprisingly, DuckDuckGo saw a huge boost in popularity after the bombshell leaks by former NSA subcontractor Edward Snowden, revealing the extent of the spying agency's online surveillance.)

For more strange-but-useful search engines, click on page 447.

Sudden Genius

Only about 30 people worldwide have "acquired savant syndrome," a medical condition in which genius-level skill or artistic talent develops after a head injury. Researchers don't understand how this happens, but suspect the trauma may unlock passively learned skills (or closed-off brainpower). Here are some real cases of ordinary people who became "accidental geniuses."

While playing baseball in 1979, 10-year-old Orlando Serrell tried to beat the pitcher's throw to first base. Instead, the ball struck him on the left side of the head. The bad: he suffered headaches for a week. The good: the blow left him with "calendar-brain." Now, more than 35 years later, mention any date since the accident and Serrell can tell you what he was doing on that particular day, along with specific details about the weather.

• At a party in 2006, 40-year-old Derek Amato leaped in the air over a swimming pool to catch a football. He intended to splash down into the water; instead, he hit the left side of his head on the edge of the pool. He suffered a concussion and lost 35 percent of his hearing…and he could suddenly play the piano at a concert level and compose music.

• In 1860, Western landscape photographer Eadweard Muybridge was in a stagecoach accident. Thrown from the vehicle, he landed on the left side of his head and suffered head trauma. His behavior became erratic and he was prone to violence. (He murdered his wife's lover, but the crime was ruled justifiable homicide.) In the years that followed, he invented numerous photographic devices, which he used in his pioneering work photographing animals in motion, including "The Horse in Motion," a series that showed a horse mid-gallop and disproved the theory that a horse always has at least one hoof on the ground.

• At the age of three, Alonzo Clemons sustained a brain injury in a fall that stunted his cognitive development, leaving him with an IQ of about 40. But the head injury also left him with an ability: he can create accurate, highly detailed animal sculptures out of clay in under an hour.

• Pip Taylor, 49, slipped on a flight of stairs at a horse racing park in England in 2012. She cracked her head and was diagnosed with a bruised brain. Doctors told her to rest for six months, so to pass the time, she started to make sketches. She'd never shown talent or interest in art, but when she sat down to draw, she found she had a sudden ability for photo-realistic portraiture.

The oldest drinking straw ever found was made of gold, inlaid with lapis lazuli. It dates to 3000 BC.

Code Talking

If you watch movies on Netflix, you've probably had the experience of scrolling through dozens of titles without finding anything you want to watch. It turns out there's a faster way to find what you want.

THE SEARCHERS

One of the nice things about having a subscription to the Netflix streaming service is that you have so many films to choose from on a Saturday night. The drawback: Netflix has *so* many films—more than 5,500 in all—that it's only able to display a tiny fraction of its selections at any one time. In fact, if you judged Netflix solely by the titles that appear on your screen, it might seem that they have only a few dozen movies to choose from, and none particularly appealing. Netflix uses your past viewing habits to try and predict what movies you'll want to see in the future, but these predictions are far from perfect. Scrolling through title after title without finding anything you really want to watch is an all-too-common part of the Netflix experience.

It turns out that there's a way to bypass the selections that have been chosen for you and go straight to the kinds of films you're looking for. The company organizes its films according to numeric codes. "Classic Westerns," for example, are assigned code number 47465, and "Screwball Comedies" have code number 9702. Netflix itself doesn't publish a directory of category codes—at least not yet—but that hasn't stopped other people from compiling lists of the codes and posting them online.

Getting Started

• Googling "Netflix Codes" will help you find the code lists. Then, when you've picked a code that appeals to you from the list, log onto your Netflix account and type the following address into your web browser's address bar:

www.netflix.com/browse/genre/####

• Now replace the "####" with the code you want to browse.

TO BE PRECISE

Organizing 5,500 titles into categories requires *a lot* of categories. One list we found online is more than 100 pages long. Many of the categories are quite specific; more than a few of them make for entertaining reading. Here are some of our favorite categories from Netflix's U.S. library:

Movies for Ages 0 to 2: 6796

Campy Chinese Movies: 1762

Critically Acclaimed Understated French Dramas: 3949

Dark German-Language Movies from the 1970s: 808

Cerebral Action & Adventure: 4778

Disco: 3493

Mind-Bending Foreign Crime Movies: 4790

Raunchy Action & Adventure: 2884

Steamy Foreign Crime Dramas: 2562

Movies Starring Erik Estrada: 1231

Irreverent Spanish-Language Comedies: 379

Movies Starring Robert Blake: 646

Coming-of-Age Movies for Ages 5 to 7: 989

Critically Acclaimed Mind-Bending Movies: 622

Gory Comedies: 1077

Foreign B-Horror Movies: 874

Eastern European Dramas from the 1980s: 4414

Visually Striking Dark Independent Dramas: 1893

Ice Hockey: 4511

Understated Foreign Crime Dramas: 4020

Exciting Movies Starring Steven Seagal: 118

Scary Westerns: 2080

Critically Acclaimed Movies about Food: 657

Tearjerkers for Ages 11 to 12: 128

Education & Guidance Starring Teletubbies: 591

Critically Acclaimed Cerebral Foreign Political Movies: 1418

Movies Starring Larry Fine: 4193. (Not to be confused with Slapstick Comedies Starring Moe Howard: 2764)

Dark Sports Movies: 4198

Raunchy Slasher and Serial Killer Movies: 3607

Children & Family Movies Starring Don Knotts: 3768

Chinese Horror Movies: 2231

Goofy Courtroom Movies: 285

Military Movies Based on a Book from the 1950s: 1010

Emotional German-Language Movies: 1309

Feel-Good Education & Guidance Starring Muppets: 4699

Dark Tearjerkers: 1061

Four phrases coined by Charles Dickens: "sawbones," "abuzz," "flummox," and "the creeps."

Beastly Tool Users

Using tools comes naturally to humans, but it's much rarer in the rest of the animal kingdom. Here are some examples that you're sure to go ape over.

KEAS USING STICKS

In 2011, rangers in New Zealand's mountainous Fiordland National Park started finding their stoat traps sprung—with no stoats inside. (Stoats are weasel-like creatures that were introduced into New Zealand by Europeans in the 19th century to control the exploding population of rabbits, which were also introduced by Europeans years earlier. Stoats have had a devastating effect on many flightless, ground-nesting bird species native to New Zealand—hence the trapping operation.) The box-shaped traps were made of wood and wire mesh, with a small hole just large enough for a stoat to get in. Inside the box was a trap baited with an egg. Near the triggered traps, rangers were finding sticks that looked like they'd been whittled, but they couldn't figure out how the sticks got there or who'd sprung the traps. Local conservationist Mat Goodman decided to solve the mystery by setting up motion-detecting cameras near one of the traps. Result: video of keas, a large parrot species found only in alpine regions of New Zealand, using their beaks to strip leaves and twigs off of sticks and then pushing a stick through the wire mesh and down on the trap's trigger plate, setting off the trap. Nobody knows exactly why the keas were doing this. They are omnivorous, and do eat eggs, but they were unable to get to the eggs after triggering the traps. Some park rangers think the birds simply liked causing the loud "Snap!" that occurred when the traps went off. (The rangers changed the design of the traps to make them kea-proof. It took the keas about two months to figure out how to trigger the new traps.)

FISH USING ROCKS

In 2009, Giacomo Bernardi, a professor of ecology and evolutionary biology at the University of California, Santa Cruz, recorded video of an orange-dotted tuskfish in waters around Palau, a country made up of more than 250 islands in the western Pacific. In the video, the fish, a member of the wrasse family, can be seen using its fins and mouth to blow sand away from the ocean floor, exposing a clam. The fish then grabs the clam in its mouth, swims to a large rock, and proceeds to "throw" the clam at the rock repeatedly, with strong, sideways jerks of its head, to crush the shell, allowing it to get to the clam's soft body. The behavior had been reported in wrasses before, but Bernardi's video was the first recorded evidence of a fish using a tool. "What the movie shows is very interesting," Bernardi told the science journal *Coral Reefs*. "The animal excavates sand to get the shell out, then swims for a long time to find an appropriate area where it can crack the shell. It requires a lot of forward thinking, because there are a number of steps involved. For a fish, it's a pretty big deal."

ORANGUTANS USING "FISHING RODS"

In 2004, Canadian primatologist Anne Russon was studying orangutans on forested islands in Borneo when she saw an orangutan grab a catfish from a drying river and eat it. It was the first ever recorded case of orangutans eating fish. Over the next three years, Russon and her team recorded more than 60 other instances of orangutans attempting to catch fish, many successfully, and in different ways, mostly by grabbing the fish by their tails. But some of the orangutans did something very humanlike: they jabbed sticks into the water at the edge of a river, scaring catfish and causing them to flee. Sometimes, a frightened fish would jump out of the water and onto the riverbank—at which time the orangutan would grab it and eat it.

MOLE RATS USING DUST MASKS

Naked mole rats are hairless rodents found only in arid grassland regions of central Africa. They spend their entire lives in underground colonies, burrowing through the soil to find their favorite food—tubers and roots. Mole rats are incredibly skilled burrowers. They have two sets of forward-thrusting incisors powered by massive jaw muscles that allow them to dig through hard, compacted soil, as well as underground obstructions such as buried wood, and even bricks. (They can actually chew through concrete.) Scientists at Cornell University have been raising a colony of mole rats since 1980, and in the late 1990s they reported a behavior that had never been observed before: the mole rats were using what appeared to be dust masks. These rodents live in clear plastic tubes in a university lab, and they regularly gnaw holes through the plastic, creating a lot of plastic particles. Researchers observed them putting slivers of wood or pieces of tuber husk behind their protruding gnawing teeth and in front of their mouths before they started gnawing on the plastic. The makeshift masks accumulated the plastic dust and stopped it from getting in their windpipes. If the "mask" dropped from their mouths, they'd stop gnawing and put it back on, or get a new one. The researchers experimented with other substances, some that produced fine dust, and some, like cork, that just broke off in chunks. Result: the mole rats used the "dust masks" almost exclusively when gnawing on dust-producing materials. The scientists don't know if the mole rats use such tools in nature—or if they learned it in the lab.

Cold War Secret, Pt. II: "Project Horizon"

On page 44 we told you about a secret 1950s U.S. plan to build a military base on the Moon. Here's part II of the story—how Americans would defend the Moon base against the onslaught of Russian invaders.

DE-FENSE!
Project Horizon's designers were already planning for the day when American nuclear missiles might be installed at the base and pointed back toward the Soviet Union. The base would have to be defended against Soviet attack, and for this reason considerable thought was given to the kinds of weapons that would be needed to protect it.

A pistol-type weapon, one designed to work in the vacuum of space (because the Moon has no atmosphere), would need to be developed for close combat against Soviet cosmonauts. At short distances, aiming the weapon would not be much of a problem: the astronauts would simply point and shoot at what was right in front of them. But at greater distances, bulky helmets and unwieldy space suits, perhaps having only mechanical claws for hands, would make aiming the weapons difficult.

For this reason, the planners decided that weapons spraying shrapnel or shotgun pellets over a wide area would be more effective than guns that fired only one bullet at a time. Volume 3 of the Project Horizon report contains an illustration of a proposed handheld fragment gun that looks kind of like a satellite TV dish mounted on the end of a broomstick. It also has an illustration of a device loaded with buckshot that could be set on the ground, pointed in the direction of enemy soldiers, and fired with an electronic trigger.

MORE BANG FOR YOUR BUCK(SHOT)

Here is where the Moon's low gravity and lack of atmosphere became an asset: On Earth, weapons of this type had a lethal range of as little as 200 feet, but on the Moon, the fragments would fly much farther, striking enemy astronauts as far as a mile away and with much greater force, since there was no atmospheric resistance to slow them down. Hits from multiple fragments, rather than from a single bullet, were more likely to defeat whatever self-sealing technologies were built into military space suits to protect them against punctures and decompression. "Certainly the greater number of punctures, the higher probability of a kill," Project Horizon's authors wrote. Such weapons could be fired

The town of Lijar, Spain, was at war with France from 1883 to 1981. No shots were ever fired.

by astronauts, or set up around the perimeter of the Horizon base and activated by trip wires and other sensors if Soviet cosmonauts ever tried to sneak up on the base.

NUKE 'EM

For targets ranging from 2.5 to nearly 10 miles away, a bazooka-like weapon firing small nuclear warheads was envisioned. The U.S. Army already had such a weapon for use on Earth. It was called the Davy Crockett gun, and its warheads had the explosive force of 10 to 30 tons of TNT. On Earth, the gun weighed about 200 pounds and had to be mounted on a tripod or on the back of a jeep. On the Moon, it would have weighed just 33 pounds, which might have made it possible for astronauts to fire it over the shoulder like an ordinary bazooka.

With no atmosphere on the Moon, the destructive power of an exploding nuclear bomb would not be magnified by a blast wave or thermal (heat) energy as it would be on Earth. But the warheads would still have packed quite a punch at close range, releasing enough radiation to kill everyone within a 255-yard radius of the blast. To protect base personnel from similar nuclear bombs fired by Soviet cosmonauts, bomb shelters would have been dug into the lunar soil around the Horizon base.

SET PHASERS ON "HILL"

The Project Horizon authors also proposed developing a "death ray" consisting of a beam of neutron or gamma radiation fired from a device called an electron accelerator. An alternative weapon would have used mirrors and/or lenses to focus the rays of the Sun onto invading Soviet cosmonauts, in much the same way that kids on Earth use magnifying glasses to burn ants. But military planners preferred the electron accelerator. "It would be wise to further investigate the 'death ray' since this weapon would not only be effective against personnel and surface vehicles but would also be effective against spaceflight vehicles for which we have provided no defense," the authors wrote.

Sounds like a pretty good plan so far...but what happened? To find out, set a course for page 428 for part III of the story.
set a course for page 428 for part III of the story.

*   *   *

BUGGING OUT

There's nothing in mosquito repellent that actually repels mosquitoes and other bugs. It just makes them indifferent. The chemicals in the spray block a mosquito's sensors—they can't smell you.

Star Beast & the Lunch Bunch

Making movies is difficult—even coming up with a good title takes time and effort. Here are some early working titles of major movies.

• **Annie Hall**: Director Woody Allen tried many different titles, including *A Rollercoaster Named Desire*, *It Had to Be Jew*, and *Anhedonia* (it means the inability to feel pleasure).

• **2001: A Space Odyssey**: *How the Solar System Was Won*

• **Child's Play**: *Batteries Not Included*

• **Friday the 13th**: *A Long Night at Camp Blood*

• **Alien**: *Star Beast*

• **Reality Bites**: Ben Stiller's movie about Gen Xers trying to find their place in the world was originally titled *The Real World*. Stiller was forced to change it when MTV debuted their reality TV series *The Real World*, about Gen Xers trying to find their place in the world.

• **Basic Instinct**: *Love Hurts*

• **The Breakfast Club**: *The Lunch Bunch*

• **Halloween**: *The Babysitter Murders*

• **Letters from Iwo Jima**: *Men from Mars*

• **Scream**: *Scary Movie*. (Ironically, the 2000 movie parody of *Scream* was titled *Scary Movie*.)

• **Boys Don't Cry**: *Take It Like a Man*

• **Pulp Fiction**: *Black Mask*

• **Some Like It Hot**: *Not Tonight, Josephine*

• **Last Action Hero**: *Extremely Violent*

• **American Pie**: Screenwriter Adam Herz was pandering to producers when he titled his script *Teenage Sex Comedy That Can Be Made for Under $10 Million That Your Reader Will Love But the Executive Will Hate*

• **Big**: *When I Grow Up*

• **50/50**: *I'm with Cancer*

• **Titanic**: *The Ship of Dreams*

"I Love Sport"

Are you a politician trying to pander to sports fans? Three rules: 1) Don't sell out your home team; 2) Know the names of the players; and 3) Know something about sports.

"It is a special pleasure for me to introduce our two home run kings for working families in America: Mike McGwire and Sammy Sooser."
—U.S. Sen. Ted Kennedy, introducing Mark McGwire and Sammy Sosa

"Manny Ortez."
—U.S. senator John Kerry, asked to name his favorite Red Sox player, mistakenly combining the names of Manny Ramirez and David Ortiz

"I'm rooting for the Red Sox [in the World Series]."
    —NYC mayor and lifelong Yankees fan Rudy Giuliani, to a Boston crowd. (The next day, the NY papers ripped him to shreds.)

"I met a guy yesterday, seven feet tall. I figured he had to be in sport, but he wasn't in sport!"
    —Massachusetts governor Mitt Romney

"I remember there was a great play, when Ron Santos just jumped… and caught a line drive."
    —Chicago mayor Rahm Emanuel, when asked about his favorite player, added an "s" to hometown hero Ron Santo

"Another Yankee fan."
    —Massachusetts attorney general Martha Coakley, while running for U.S. senator, calling former Red Sox pitcher and 2004 World Series hero Curt Schilling a Yankee fan. (She lost the election.)

"And you are…"
    —President George H. W. Bush, to NHL superstar Mario Lemieux, when the champion Pittsburgh Penguins visited the White House

"Varitek splitting the uprights."
    —Boston mayor Thomas Menino, listing great plays. He confused MLB player Jason Varitek with NFL placekicker Adam Vinatieri

"How's Joe Paterno?"
    —Donald Trump, to a crowd in Pennsylvania, four years after the Penn State coach died

Bet you can't name them all: Romania has had six different national anthems in the past 60 years.

By the Time We Got to Woodstock... to Woodstock... to Woodstock...

In August 1969, nearly half a million people enjoyed "3 Days of Peace & Music" on Max Yasgur's farm in upstate New York. Several attempts have been made in the years since to recapture that Woodstock magic.

WOODSTOCK '79. The 10th anniversary Woodstock concert wasn't held in a giant field—it was held at Madison Square Garden in New York. And it was more of a revue than a festival. Instead of acts playing full sets over the course of several days, the show lasted for just one evening, and the performers played only one song each. Among them were several musicians who had appeared at the original Woodstock, including Country Joe and the Fish, Canned Heat, Johnny Winter, Leslie West, and Richie Havens.

WOODSTOCK REUNION 1979. On September 8, 1979, just a few weeks after the sedate anniversary show at Madison Square Garden, Woodstock's 10th anniversary was celebrated again, this time at a racetrack in Brookhaven, New York. Accounts vary on how many people showed up. Promoters say 40,000, but the real figure was probably closer to 18,000. Like the original event, Woodstock Reunion 1979 had problems: the day before the concert, thousands of people showed up with camping equipment, which infuriated local residents. Then the gates didn't open on time. The crowd started getting antsy and security concerns almost led to the show being canceled by local officials. But despite these complications, the show—featuring essentially the same lineup as the Madison Square Garden concert—did go on. Recordings of the performances later aired on the nationally syndicated radio program *King Biscuit Flower Hour*.

WOODSTOCK '89. In 1989, a folk singer named Rich Pell approached the owners of the property that hosted the original Woodstock festival and asked permission to play a show there. They said yes, so, along with a few organizers, Pell arranged a small event and

---

The longest-ever standing ovation at the Oscars was given to Charlie Chaplin in 1972 (12 minutes).

opened the stage to anyone who wanted to perform, regardless of skill level. Approximately 30,000 people turned up to watch performances by largely unknown bands and listen to speeches by Wavy Gravy (from the original Woodstock) and Al Hendrix (Jimi's father). Woodstock '89 didn't receive a lot of media attention, but *Good Morning America* did broadcast a live segment that included interviews with Wavy Gravy and counterculture icon Ken Kesey.

WOODSTOCK '94. It took 25 years for organizers to stage an "official" sequel to the original Woodstock. One of the first problems they encountered was that the current owners of the site of the 1969 festival wouldn't let them stage it there. They settled for an alternate site—Winston Farm in Saugerties, New York, miles from the original site. It was a mixed success at best. By day two, festivalgoers were already sneaking through the flimsy perimeter fence (just as many of their predecessors did back in 1969), and the security staff couldn't stop them. Critics, meanwhile, lambasted the festival's high ticket prices and overpriced merchandise as a cynical cash-in.

It was also a failure as a spiritual successor to the original "three days of peace and music." The world of popular music had changed since 1969, and many of the performers, including the hip-hop group Cypress Hill and industrial rockers Nine Inch Nails, hardly imbued the spirit of hippie culture. The crowd was also rougher. Some acts, such as Primus, were pelted by balls of mud from the crowd. Green Day's set turned into a gigantic mud fight between the band and their fans, during which bassist Mike Dirnt had three of his teeth broken by security after he was mistaken for a crazed member of the audience. Final attendance: 350,000 people (including the gatecrashers), yet the promoters still lost money on the venture.

WOODSTOCK '99. Staging a three-day music festival for 350,000 people and not making any money might make the promoters look for another way to recoup their investment. That's why, when it came to Woodstock's *30th* anniversary, the promoters of Woodstock '94 were determined not to repeat their mistakes. Instead, they made a series of new mistakes. They jacked up the prices of everything—a bottle of water cost $4, and a slice of pizza cost $12. And to deter gatecrashers that dug into their profits in 1994, organizers held Woodstock '99 at Griffiss Air Force Base in Rome, New York, and constructed a 12-foot-tall fence out of plywood and steel that they dubbed the "Peace Wall." If the fact that they were hosting a "peaceful" music festival at a military base wasn't ironic enough, Griffiss was also a Superfund site. There were more hip-hop artists and metal bands (and the only participant from the original Woodstock festival was Grateful Dead drummer Mickey Hart), but "rap metal" was very popular in 1999, so performers like Limp Bizkit and Kid Rock were added to the bill as well.

After four days of dealing with price-gouging vendors and 100+°F temperatures, the crowd finally lost their cool during a performance by the Red Hot Chili Peppers on the fest's final night. While they were performing Jimi Hendrix's "Fire," bonfires began popping up around the festival grounds. Attendees began burning everything they could get their hands on, including vendor tents, and merchandise stands, and cars. The festival security staff (which was supposed to include 1,200 guards but actually only amounted to around 200) couldn't keep up with all the violence that ensued, especially after working 14-hour shifts all weekend. Members of MTV's film crew fled the grounds; Kurt Loder, one of the network's commentators, later described Woodstock '99 as "like a concentration camp." By the time the smoke cleared, 10,000 people required medical attention.

THE HEROES OF WOODSTOCK TOUR. In honor of the original festival's 40th anniversary, a concert tour called Heroes of Woodstock was launched on July 31, 2009, at the Genesee Theatre in Waukegan, Illinois. It featured many performers and bands that performed at the 1969 fest, among them Big Brother and the Holding Company (without Janis Joplin, of course), Canned Heat (without founding members Al Wilson, who died in 1970, and Bob Hite, who died in 1981), and Jefferson Starship (formerly Jefferson Airplane). Attendees were allowed to download recordings of each concert as mp3s. The tour wrapped up its 16th and final show on October 10 at the Soaring Eagle Casino in Mount Pleasant, Michigan. Not a single attendee streaked, no one rioted, and not a single glob of mud was thrown during any performance.

*　　*　　*

THREE RANDOM FACTS

• When TV service began in England in the 1930s, the BBC had to launch a public-relations campaign to assure people that their TV sets couldn't spy on them.

• Crayons get their distinctive smell from stearic acid—another name for processed beef fat.

• "Jerky"—as in dried meat snacks, such as beef jerky—is a corruption of the Incan word *charki*, which means "dried llama meat."

De-Merit Badges

Here are some weird Boy Scout merit badges from the past and present, and some of the requirements for earning them.

Dentistry. "Make a model tooth out of soap, clay, wax, or papier-mâché. Using a string and a large hand brush, show your troop or a school class proper tooth-brushing and flossing procedures."

American Labor. "Attend a meeting of a local union, a central labor council, or an employee organization."

Welding. "Show that you know first aid for injuries or illnesses that could occur while welding, including electrical shock, eye injuries, burns, fume inhalation, dizziness, skin irritation, and exposure to hazardous chemicals."

Nuclear Science. "Obtain a sample of irradiated and non-irradiated foods. Prepare the two foods and compare their taste and texture."

Railroading. "Using models or pictures, identify 10 types of railroad freight or passenger cars. Explain the purpose of each type of car."

Consumer Buying. "Check into how to buy a used car."

Taxidermy. "Prepare and present at least five skulls of birds or animals, each of a different species."

Cement Work. "Design and mold in a form, a concrete window-box, garden jar, garden seat, sundial, or hitching post."

Pulp and Paper. "Make a list of 15 pulp or paper products found in your home. Share examples of 10 such products with your counselor."

Invention. "Invent and patent some useful article."

Truck Transportation. "Assume that you are going to ship 500 pounds of goods from your town to another town 500 miles away. Your shipment must arrive within three days. Explain in writing."

Mining. "Discuss with your counselor two methods used to reduce rock in size, one of which uses a chemical process to extract a mineral."

Robotics. "Explain to your counselor the most likely hazards you may encounter while working with robots."

The 13th Amendment to the U.S. Constitution outlaws all forms of slavery—except prison labor.

Go Sue Yourself

*Every lawsuit has a "defendant" (the party being sued) and "plaintiff"
(the party doing the suing). Most of the time they're two different
people, but every once in a while...well, let's just hope
these real legal cases don't set a precedent.*

SEAH VS. SEAH

In November 1986, a Singaporean woman named Jubina Seah
Geok Tin was riding on the back of a motorcycle driven by her
husband, Jimmy Wong. Suddenly, an oncoming car driven by a man
named Wong Chin Hee turned directly into their path. Jimmy Wong
was unable to avoid Wong Chin Hee's car: he crashed into it with
such force that he was killed and Seah was paralyzed from the waist
down. Because Jimmy was speeding at the time of the accident, under
Singaporean law, he and Wong Chin Hee may both have been at fault
for causing the accident, and thus were both liable for Seah's injuries.
Seah sued Wong Chin Hee and she would have sued her husband, too,
but Singaporean law does not permit lawsuits to be filed against dead
people. It does, however, allow a widow to take her husband's place
as a defendant in a lawsuit, so she (the accident victim) sued herself
(the representative of her husband's estate)—and won a judgment of
$830,000 from her husband's motorcycle insurance company.

BAGLEY VS. BAGLEY

Who says only the *victim* of an accident gets to sue? In December 2011,
a woman named Barbara Bagley and her husband, Bradley Vom Baur,
were driving on Interstate 80 in Nevada when Bagley apparently fell
asleep at the wheel and drove their Range Rover off the road, causing it
to overturn. Vom Baur was thrown from the vehicle and died ten days
later; Bagley was seriously injured, but survived. In such cases, the driver's insurance company often covers the medical and funeral expenses
of the person killed in an auto accident, but not in this one. Bagley's
insurer was willing to cover only the damage caused to the vehicle.

Acting in her capacity as the representative of her deceased
husband's estate, Bagley filed a wrongful death lawsuit against herself
to recover the money she felt her husband's estate was owed by her
insurance company. At last report, the case was still working its way
through the courts. If Bagley prevails against the defendant (herself), as
her husband's sole heir she stands to inherit whatever money is left over
after his legal, medical, and funeral bills are paid.

HUDSON VS. HUDSON

In the summer of 2002, the six-year-old daughter of a man named Gary Hudson was playing on a wall in a park in Gwendraeth, Wales, when the wall suddenly collapsed and the little girl fell to the ground. She suffered what is known as a "greenstick fracture" to her right arm, which means that one side of the bone was broken and the other side was only bent. Hudson sued the Gwendraeth Valley Community Council, which manages the park, accusing it of failing to properly maintain the wall. Hudson is a member the council. "Each councilor has a responsibility and thus the councilor is taking litigation against himself," said a report published by the council. (The wall was repaired; no word on whether Hudson won his lawsuit against himself and the other councilors.)

CAMPBELL VS. CAMPBELL

In August 2014, an employee of the Parks and Recreation Department of St. Paul, Minnesota, crashed a city-owned van into a parked 2001 Nissan Pathfinder. The Pathfinder was owned by Megan Campbell, 24, who promptly filed a claim against the city, demanding that it pay the estimated $1,800 cost of repairing the front bumper. Who was the Parks and Recreation employee driving the van when it hit the Pathfinder? Megan Campbell, 24. "Because I was working for the city and driving a city vehicle, I feel they are responsible for paying for the damage done to my car," she says. At last report the city's accident review board was still reviewing the claim. "Since this situation is unusual," says Brad Meyer, a spokesperson for the Parks and Recreation Department, "the investigation will most likely receive additional scrutiny."

*　　*　　*

WEIRD CELEBRITY TATTOOS

• Rapper Gucci Mane has an ice-cream cone with red lightning bolts. On his face.
• Model Cara Delevigne has "BACON…" on the bottom of her foot.
• Singer Kesha has a tattoo reading "SUCK IT!" on the inside of her lower lip.
• *Girls* star Zosia Mamet has a line drawing of a heart, covering her entire right palm.
• Actor Stephen Baldwin met *Hannah Montana* star Miley Cyrus in 2009, and she said that if he got a Hannah Montana tattoo, she'd have him on the show. His kids were big fans and he wanted to impress them, so he got a small "HM" tattoo…but Cyrus never came through on the cameo.

Name That Element

Unless you've studied a lot of science, you probably haven't spent much time looking things up in the periodic table, the table of all the known elements in the universe. The stories of some of them and how they were named makes for interesting bathroom reading.

COPPER (Cu)

What It Is: A reddish-orange metal that is a cheap and efficient conductor of electrical current, which is why it is used so extensively by the electrical industry.

How It Got Its Name: Copper has been in use for more than 7,000 years, and one of the first, abundant sources of the element was the island of Cyprus, in the Mediterranean Sea. It came to be known as Cyprian metal, or *cuprum* in Latin, and eventually copper in English.

POLONIUM (PO)

What It Is: A rare, highly radioactive element found in pitchblende, a type of uranium ore that is also very radioactive.

How It Got Its Name: Polonium was discovered by the French scientists Marie and Pierre Curie in 1898. It has long been customary for the discoverers of elements to have the privilege of naming them, and Marie Curie chose to honor Poland, the country of her birth.

Details: Marie and Pierre Curie also discovered radium (Ra), another highly radioactive element. (Radium gave off large amounts of energy in the form of gamma rays, so they named it after the Latin word *radius*, which means "ray.") For their pioneering work on the theory of radioactivity, which included Marie Curie coining the term "radioactive," the Curies and a third physicist named Antoine Henri Becquerel shared the 1903 Nobel Prize for physics. When Pierre Currie died in 1906, Marie Curie continued her work without him and won a second Nobel, this time for chemistry, in 1911. To date she is the only woman ever to win two Nobel Prizes.

But all that work studying radioactivity took its toll: after decades of carrying polonium, radium, and other highly radioactive materials around in her pockets, in the 1930s Marie Curie developed terminal aplastic anemia, most likely caused by long-term exposure to the elements she had discovered. By then almost completely blind from cataracts—also caused by overexposure to radiation—she died in 1934 at the age of 66. In 1944, another radioactive element, curium (Cm), was named in honor of her and her husband.

URANIUM (U)

What It Is: A radioactive element that is the main source of energy for nuclear power plants around the world. A sphere of uranium the size of a softball contains more usable energy than an entire train load of coal.

How It Got Its Name: In 1789, a German chemist named Martin Heinrich Klaproth succeeded in extracting a new element from pitchblende. He named his element after the planet Uranus, which had been discovered eight years earlier.

GALLIUM (Ga)

What It Is: A soft, silvery metal with properties similar to aluminum.

How It Got Its Name: Discoverers get to name their elements, but they're not supposed to name them after themselves. That may have been what happened with Gallium. It was discovered in 1875 by a French chemist named Paul-Émile Lecoq de Boisbaudran, who also discovered the elements samarium (Sm) and dysprosium (Dy). The official story is that de Boisbaudran named gallium in honor of his native France (*Gallia* in Latin). But the Latin word for rooster is *gallus*, and *Lecoq* also means "rooster." If Rooster de Boisbaudran really did name gallium after himself, he is the only person (so far) to get away with it.

PLUTONIUM (Pu)

What It Is: A radioactive element used to make nuclear weapons and power nuclear power plants.

How It Got Its Name: Small amounts of plutonium do exist in nature, but most plutonium is produced artificially by bombarding U-238—a type, or isotope, of uranium—with subatomic particles called neutrons. This first produces an isotope of the element neptunium, which is named after the eighth planet from the sun, Neptune. When neptunium decays, it becomes another element, plutonium. A team of University of California, Berkeley physicists led by Glenn T. Seaborg were the first to produce plutonium, in 1940. Because plutonium is produced when neptunium decays, it made sense to name the new element after what was then the next most distant planet in the solar system: Pluto.

YTTRIUM (Y)

What It Is: A silvery-white metal that is used in the production of LED lights.

How It Got Its Name: Yttrium was first discovered in a feldspar mine near the village of Ytterby, Sweden, in 1843. At the time, the feldspar, which is used to make porcelain, was the only thing of value being taken out of the mine. But whenever unusual ores were found, they were sent to a Finnish chemist named Johan Gadolin. He managed to extract one new element from the ore—Yttrium—and believed there were several others that he could not extract using the primitive technology of the day.

Gadolin was correct: scientific advancements eventually made it possible to extract six more elements from the ore in the Ytterby mine. Three of those elements, ytterbium (Yb), terbium (Tb), and erbium (Er), are named in honor of the village, which has more elements named after it than any other place on earth. The other three elements extracted from the ore—holmium (Ho), thulium (Tm), and gadolinium (Gd)—are named after Stockholm, Scandinavia (Thule was an ancient name for the far northern lands that make up modern-day Scandinavia), and Johan Gadolin, respectively.

If you think picking a name for an element is a challenge in ordinary times, you should see what it was like during the Cold War. For that story, turn to "The Transfermium Wars" on page 407.

turn to "The Transfermium Wars" on page 407.

*   *   *

IT'S THE LITTLE THINGS

A single piece of rice is a grain. A piece of grass is a blade. But do you know the names of these other tiny things?

Pip: An individual square of a Hershey's chocolate bar. (There are 12 pips in a standard bar.)

Box tent: The white plastic thing that looks like a table that pizza parlors put in the center of a pizza. It keeps the box propped up so the lid doesn't slump and stick to the cheese.

Tittle: The dot over a lowercase i or j.

Caruncula: The little bump at the corner of your eye.

Philtrum: The divot in the upper lip, just under the nose.

Punt: The indentation on the bottom of a wine bottle.

Feed dogs: The small bars of teeth that move material forward on a sewing machine.

Aperture: The opening in a mollusk shell.

Splat: The central support in the back of a chair.

Yoke: The material that bunches out on the back of a shirt.

Toe: The tip of a paintbrush.

What is this ^ symbol called? A *circumflex.*

Chihuahua News

Big stories about tiny dogs.

CHIP, CHIP HOORAY. In April 2016, traffic was held up on the Bay Bridge, which connects Oakland and San Francisco. The cause of the snarl: a black Chihuahua that somehow found its way to the upper deck of the bridge and kept running back and forth across multiple lanes of traffic. California Highway Patrol (CHP) dispatched a motorcycle officer, who carefully scooped up the dog and took him to a San Francisco animal shelter. But despite widespread media coverage, his owners never came forward. The dog, named Ponch by the shelter staff, after the CHP officer portrayed by Erik Estrada on the 1970s TV series *CHiPs*, was adopted two weeks later.

TOO MUCH OF A GOOD THING. February 2014 marked the Great Chihuahua Invasion in the Maryvale neighborhood of Phoenix, Arizona. In one month, animal control offices received more than 6,000 phone calls about packs of stray Chihuahuas roaming the streets. The most common complaints: groups of dogs kept chasing kids walking to school, and dozens more were spotted breeding in the streets. Officials still aren't sure why there are so many feral Chihuahuas in Phoenix.

DOG GONE IT. Tabitha Ormaechea's car was stopped at a traffic light in Spokane, Washington, in 2014 when another car came "out of nowhere" and rammed into her. Ormaechea was especially confused because it appeared that the car had no driver...until the head of a tiny dog popped up from behind the steering wheel. Within a few minutes, Jason Martinez came running down the street. He'd left his Chihuahua in the car and left the motor running while he ran into a store. The dog apparently knocked the car out of gear, and it rolled down the street and into Ormaechea. (Bad dog!)

BAD KITTY. Jia Weinuan of Xuzhou, China, had a female American shorthair cat named Niuniu. His friend had a male, so in early 2015 they decided to breed them. But Jia claims that Niuniu didn't give birth to kittens—she produced a Chihuahua puppy. Could it actually have come from one of Jia's five dogs? No, none of them are Chihuahuas. Jia refuses to believe that Niuniu did anything biologically impossible, insisting that she's a "good cat who doesn't do bad things." After a month, Jia reported that the "puppy" still looked like a dog, but mysteriously had grown cat-like paws.

After the British burned the Library of Congress in 1814, Thomas Jefferson sold the government his...

Ghostbuster Guru

Now for some random thoughts from the twisted mind of Bill Murray.

"It's hard to be an artist. It's hard to be anything. It's hard to be."

"I'm a nut, but not just a nut."

"The best way to teach your kids about taxes is by eating 30 percent of their ice cream."

"There's not much downside to being rich, other than paying taxes and having your relatives ask you for money. But when you become famous, you end up with a 24-hour job."

"Keep seeing the glass as half full and it will dawn upon you that it's probably your turn to buy."

"Everyone loves Cinnabons."

"People are like music. Some speak the truth, and others are just noise."

"Parties are only bad when a fight breaks out, when men fight over women, or vice versa. If you can avoid those things, pretty much all behavior is acceptable."

"I don't like to work. I only like working when I'm working."

"The more relaxed you are, the better you are at everything. The better you are with your loved ones, the better you are with your enemies, the better you are at your job, the better you are with yourself."

"Unless you're a pizza, the answer is yes—yes, I can live without you."

"I try to be alert and available for life to happen to me. We're in this life, and if you're not available, the sort of ordinary time goes past and you didn't live it. But if you're available, life gets huge. You're really living it."

"I'm suspicious of people who don't like dogs, but I trust a dog when it doesn't like a person."

"The secret is to have a sense of yourself, your real self, your unique self. And not just once in a while, or once a day, but all through the day, the week and life. You know what they say: 'Ain't no try—ain't nothing to it but to do it.'"

"Nothing prepared me for being this awesome."

Uzz-Word Origins

For no special reason, here's an article on the origin of some words with the letters "uzz" in them. (Huzza!)

BUZZ

Meaning: A low, continuous, somewhat raspy, humlike sound, such as that made by a bee or a door buzzer

Origin: It dates to the late 15th century and it's an *onomatopoeic* word, (a word that sounds like the thing it describes), believed to have been first used to describe the sound that bees and flies make. The noun *buzz*, meaning "a rumor" ("What's the buzz?"), dates to the 1620s, and is believed to have been derived from the "buzzy" sound of people whispering. *Buzz off* dates to 1914, but originally meant to hang up a telephone, and didn't get its "Scram!" meaning until much later. The use of *buzz* for a mild state of euphoria first appeared in the 1930s, while it's opposite, *buzzkill*, meaning something that has a depressing effect, first appeared in 1992.

BUZZARD

Meaning: A hawk or vulture

Origin: *Buzzard* is a derivation of the Old French name for a European bird of prey, *buisart*, believed to be derived from the Latin *buteo*, meaning hawk. In the UK, *buzzard* is still used as the name of a specific species of hawk—the common buzzard (*Buteo buteo*). In North America, it came to be used most commonly as the name for vultures, especially the turkey vulture.

Bonus: The suffix *-art* was used in early French to give words a negative connotation. It was used in the case of *buisart* because these birds were seen as pests. A number of such words came from Old French to early English, with the *-art* becoming *-ard*, including *buzzard*, *bastard*, and *coward*. The suffix *-ard* later became its own element in English, and was used to create words such as *drunkard*.

GUZZLE

Meaning: To eat or drink something greedily

Origin: First appearing in the 1570s, *guzzle* is believed to have derived from the Old French *gosillier*, meaning both "chatter" and "vomit." That word, in turn, was derived from another Old French word, *gosier*, meaning "throat."

HUZZA

Meaning: A cry of approval or joy

Origin: This interjection is from the late 16th century, and probably started as sailor slang, perhaps as a work cry used by groups of men when hoisting gear. *Huzza*, which in recent times is more commonly spelled *huzzah*, was very common in the 18th and 19th centuries, then fell out of use almost completely in the late 20th century, and has had a revival only in recent years. (It's pronounced *huz-ZAH* today, but 18th- and 19th-century dictionaries indicate that it was originally pronounced *huz-ZAY*.)

NUZZLE

Meaning: To gently rub one's nose or face against someone or something, usually as a sign of affection

Origin: This word dates to the early 15th century and is believed to have come from the Middle English *noselyng*, and meaning "on the nose, prostrate," or, more literally, "nose-lying." It originally had a negative meaning similar to "grovel," and got its more affectionate meaning in the 16th century.

PUZZLE

Meaning: To confuse or be difficult to understand; something or someone difficult to understand; something that requires thought, ingenuity, or cleverness to solve

Origin: *Puzzle* appeared in its verb form around 1590, and as a noun in around 1600—but nobody knows for sure where the word came from. (It's a puzzle!) The sense of *puzzle* meaning a perplexing question or problem came into the language in the mid-17th century, and the first known use of *puzzle* as a kind of game or toy that required a solution was in the 1810s.

SCUZZ or SCUZZY

Meaning: A filthy, gross, sordid, or disgusting person or thing; the state of being filthy, gross, sordid, or disgusting

Origin: *Scuzz* and *scuzzy* are relatively modern words; they first appeared in English in the mid-1960s. According to the *Oxford English Dictionary*, both were "probably informal abbreviations of disgusting." Other sources say that *scuzzy* was a combination of *scummy* and *fuzzy*, and that *scuzz* was created as a back-formation of *scuzzy*. A number of other scuzz-words—including *scuzzbag*, *scuzzball*, and *scuzzbucket*—have been created in the years since.

In Bill Clinton's presidential portrait, the artist added a hidden message—the shadow of a dress.

HOT STUFF!

If you're a fan of spicy food, you might already know that chili peppers originated in the Americas. (Jalapeños come from Jalapa, Mexico; poblanos from Puebla, Mexico; and habaneros from Havana, Cuba.) Today there are over 50,000 varieties—many with such intimidating names that they sound like they'll set your mouth on fire. (And some really will.) Here are some examples.

White Bullet	TigerPaw
Hot Paper Lantern	Brazilian Starfish
Diablo Grande	Komodo Dragon
NuMex XX	Barker's Hot
Prairie Fire	Facing Heaven
Syrian Goat Horn	Candlelight
Tequila	Yellow Monster
Kung Pao	Cherry Bomb
Hot Golden Nugget	Twilight
Purple Flash	Cowhorn
Ring of Fire	Elephant Trunk
Trinidad Scorpion	Thai Dragon
Naga Viper	Red Amazon
Bolivian Rainbow	Holy Mole
Ho Chi Minh	Jigsaw
Devil's Tongue	Rooster Spur
Carolina Reaper	Conquistador
Black Cuban	Medusa
Macho	King of the North
Bishop's Crown	Fatalii
Beaver Dam	Infinity

Common treat in Southeast Asia: *balut,* **a partially developed duck embryo eaten in the shell.**

Juniors and Seniors

You probably know why Hank Williams Jr.'s father and John F. Kennedy Jr.'s father are famous. But how much do you know about the dads of these other famous juniors?

Ken Griffey Jr.: One of the most dominant baseball players of the last 25 years. Over his career he hit 630 home runs (he's #6 on the all-time list), played in 13 All-Star Games, and was the American League MVP in 1997.

Ken Griffey Sr.: The younger Griffey's achievements overshadowed those of his father, a three-time all-star who batted .296 over 19 seasons, which included two World Series titles with the Cincinnati Reds in the 1970s. (In Griffey Sr.'s final season, 1991, he signed with the Seattle Mariners so that he could play alongside his son—the first father-son tandem in Major League history.)

Cuba Gooding Jr.: Starred in *Boyz N the Hood*, *Radio*, and *Jerry Maguire*, for which he won an Oscar for Best Supporting Actor

Cuba Gooding Sr.: He was the lead singer in the 1960s/1970s Motown group the Main Ingredient. Their biggest hit: "Everybody Plays the Fool," which reached #3 in 1972.

Kurt Vonnegut Jr.: A major 20th-century novelist. He wrote *Slaughterhouse-Five*, *Cat's Cradle*, and *Breakfast of Champions*.

Kurt Vonnegut Sr.: An early 20th-century architect. He designed several Art Deco office buildings and stores in Indianapolis.

Martin Luther King Jr.: The preeminent leader of the civil rights movement in the United States in the 1950s and 1960s

Martin Luther King Sr.: He was born Michael King in 1899, but changed it in the 1930s when he became a minister, naming himself after the founder of the Lutheran church. His five-year-old son, Michael King Jr., changed his name, too. Like his son, he was a civil rights activist, and was once the president of the Atlanta wing of the NAACP.

Ray Parker Jr.: Musician best known for 1980s hits "A Woman Needs Love" and the theme from *Ghostbusters*. He started his music career at age 13. He was a guitar prodigy and, living in Detroit, became part of Motown Records' lineup of studio musicians, the Funk Brothers.

Ray Parker Sr.: He worked on the assembly line in a Ford plant in Detroit. When he discovered that his teenage son was making more

---

One U.S. state highway bans cars: M-185 on Mackinac Island, MI. (Horses and bikes only.)

money in a month at Motown than he did in an entire year at the auto plant, he thought Ray Jr. was selling drugs.

Alan Hale Jr.: A character actor who appeared in dozens of B-movies in the 1940s and 1950s…but he's much better known as the Skipper on *Gilligan's Island*.

Alan Hale Sr.: He was an actor, too, frequently the second banana in adventure movies. He played the role of Little John three times: in the 1922 silent version of *Robin Hood*, in Erroll Flynn's *The Adventures of Robin Hood* in 1938, and again in 1950's *Rogues of Sherwood Forest*.

Harry Connick Jr.: A boy wonder jazz musician in his hometown of New Orleans, playing piano at gigs from the age of 5 and recording at the age of 10. He became a big star when he recorded old standards for the *When Harry Met Sally…* soundtrack. He's since sold 28 million albums and is now a judge on *American Idol*.

Harry Connick Sr.: Connick Jr.'s first name is really Joseph, but he used the suffix because his dad was a popular New Orleans politician, and district attorney of Orleans Parish from 1973 to 2003. (Connick Sr.'s wife, Anita Connick, was a justice on the Louisiana Supreme Court.)

William F. Buckley Jr.: A conservative activist and writer, he founded *National Review* in 1955 and hosted the public affairs and debate show *Firing Line* from 1966 to 1999.

William F. Buckley Sr.: A lawyer, and then a Texas oilman and real-estate developer in the early 20th century. He wound up in Texas after being kicked out of Mexico in 1921, where he'd been trying to get the laws against Americans owning oil wells repealed.

Cal Ripken Jr.: A baseball Hall of Famer who played his entire career (1981–2001) with one team—the Baltimore Orioles. In 1995, he beat Lou Gehrig's streak of 2,130 consecutive games played, eventually finishing with 2,632.

Cal Ripken Sr.: Cal Ripken Sr. was also with the Orioles. In 1957, he was in the Orioles' farm system as a player, and then as a coach. In 1976, he joined the big-league Orioles' coaching staff, and was promoted to manager for the final two seasons of his career (1987–1988), where he managed his sons, players Cal Ripken Jr. and Billy Ripken.

Carl's Jr.: In 1941, Carl Karcher "Sr." opened a roadside stand in Los Angeles selling hot dogs and tamales. Four years later, he branched out and opened a sit-down restaurant in nearby Anaheim called Carl's Drive-In. In 1956 he opened two restaurants that were smaller, or "junior" versions of the drive-in, and called them Carl's Jr.

Bodies of Evidence

You don't expect to find human remains when remodeling a house or cleaning out a basement. But these folks did. Here are their macabre—but fascinating—stories.

BODY #1

B A carpenter named Bob Kinghorn was doing renovations on a house in a Toronto, Ontario, neighborhood in July 2007 when he found something wrapped in newspaper beneath the floorboards of the home's attic. He opened it...and found a mummified infant inside it. "It was all crunched up in a fetal position," Kinghorn later said to reporters. "It was pretty horrific." The deceased child, a boy, had lain hidden in the home for more than 80 years. (The newspaper it was wrapped in was dated September 12, 1925.) Medical examiners said the boy appeared to have died shortly after being born, but there was no way to determine a cause of death. A Canadian Broadcasting Corporation (CBC) investigation into the discovery found that the owners of the house in 1925 were Wesley and Della Russell, and that in 1934, Mrs. Russell had been admitted to a psychiatric hospital in Toronto. Four days after arriving there, she spent the afternoon repeating, "I'm a murderer but I can't get away. I'm a murderer but I can't get away." (She died in a sanitarium 19 years later.) The CBC also located a 92-year-old niece of Russell who was living in the house at the time of the baby's death. She couldn't add any details to the story, but thought the baby must have been the child of Della Russell's younger sister; she did not believe her kind Aunt Della could have been involved in the boy's death. The mummified remains lay hidden in the floorboards through a succession of homeowners, all of them unaware of its presence. (The baby was buried at a Toronto cemetery in October 2007, in a ceremony attended by more than 100 people. Bob Kinghorn was the sole pallbearer.)

BODY #2

In August 2010, Gloria Gomez, manager of the Glen-Donald Apartments in the MacArthur Park neighborhood of Los Angeles, found three abandoned steamer trunks in the building's basement. The Glen-Donald was built in the 1920s, and had been the home of some of the city's most elite residents over the decades, including some Hollywood stars. Gomez broke into the old trunks using a screwdriver, excitedly hoping to find antique treasures. Inside the first two trunks: nothing. The third contained some things, though—stocks, a fur stole, photographs, postcards...and two leather doctor's satchels. Inside the satchels: the bodies of two small infants, a boy and a girl, wrapped in newspapers dating to the 1930s. Medical examiners said one of the infants appeared to have died shortly after birth, and that the other may have been stillborn. Police were able to determine that the trunks belonged to a woman named Janet Barrie, who'd been the live-in nurse of George and Mary Knapp from the 1930s to the 1960s. Police located one of Barrie's relatives, who agreed to provide a DNA sample... which proved that Barrie was the mother of the dead children. Why the remains were hidden away in a steamer trunk remains a mystery. The identity of the children's father couldn't be determined, but there is some suspicion that it was George Knapp: he and Jean Barrie were married after Mary Knapp died in 1964. Barrie and Knapp continued to live in the Glen-Donald apartment until George Knapp died in 1968. Barrie then moved away, leaving the steamer trunks behind. She died in Canada in 1992.

BODY #3

In October 2003, Stephen and Deena Roberts of Brownwood, in central Texas, decided to remodel the unused second-story attic of the large A-frame home they had been living in for three years; their two children were growing up, and needed their own bedrooms. As they inspected the attic, Deena noticed something she'd never seen before: a small door in the back of a built-in closet. She opened it, peered into a musty crawl space, and saw a plastic garbage bag. Inside the bag: a paper bag holding the mummified remains of a newborn baby. The couple immediately called the police. The garbage bag was sent to medical examiners in Austin, Texas, and they found the remains of two more newborns inside the bag. After years of investigation, the following facts were determined: the house was built in 1987 by James and Doris Bowling; the couple lived there until they died—James in 1999 and Doris in 2000—after which their three adult children sold the family home. Two of those children were located by investigators. They agreed to give DNA samples to police...and the infants were proven to have been their siblings. (The shocked Bowling children said they knew nothing about the newborns.) Even more macabre: medical examiners determined that all three newborns were born and died around 1960—roughly 40 years before they were discovered—meaning that James and Doris Bowling brought the deceased infants with them when they moved into the house in 1992. How the infants died and why the Bowlings never reported the deaths to authorities remains unknown.

* * *

"If you have a secret, people will sit a little bit closer." —**Rob Corddry**

Kentucky Derby jockeys must weigh no more than 126 pounds, including all clothing and equipment.

Pages from History: The Green Book

Here's a piece of recent American history that most people have never heard of. It involves many of the elements we associate with modern life—cars, travel, eating, entrepreneurship…and discrimination. Here's the story of the Green Book.

ROAD TRIP!

For as long as automobiles have been around, they have symbolized freedom and independence. They offered the promise of taking people anywhere they wanted to go, as long as there was a road that went there. For many Americans automobiles did indeed deliver on that promise. But for African Americans living in many parts of the United States in the early and mid-20th century, the automobile was little more than a symbol—that of a freedom that, for them, remained out of reach.

In those years, a trip by automobile for African Americans was an experience all its own, quite unlike car trips taken by white Americans. A black family preparing for a long trip had to pack enough food to get them all the way to where they were going, in case the restaurants along the route refused to serve them—a form of discrimination that was perfectly legal at the time. They had to pack pillows and blankets so that they could sleep in their car if the hotels they stopped at refused to provide them with lodging. They had to put extra cans of gas in the trunk—enough to get them through towns where none of the service stations would sell them gas. And they had to leave enough room in the trunk for a bucket that they could use as a toilet in places where restrooms were reserved for whites only.

KEEP ON MOVING

In some parts of the South, black motorists were advised to keep a chauffeur's cap handy, so that if a white motorist took offense at their owning a car, perhaps because it was newer or nicer than their own, the motorist could put on the cap and pretend they were driving the car for a white owner. Even passing a slow-moving car on the road could lead to trouble: some white motorists took offense at the idea of dust kicked up by a black-owned car landing on their car. Simply stopping in a town long enough to find out blacks were unwelcome could be dangerous: thousands of towns all over the United States were "sundown towns," which meant that blacks and other minorities had to be out of the area by sunset. African Americans caught in such a town after dark risked being harassed, arrested, beaten, or killed. In many places the sundown policy was unofficial, but in places like the town of Hawthorne, California, in the 1930s, signs were posted at the city limits with warnings like, "N*****, Don't Let the Sun Set on YOU in Hawthorne."

THE LIST

The problem was worst in the South, where segregation was mandated by Jim Crow laws. But as places like Hawthorne, California, make clear, it flourished in other parts of the country as well. New York City was no exception, and it was there in the mid-1930s that an African American mail carrier (and World War I veteran) named Victor Hugo Green decided to do something about it. Inspired by directories published by the Jewish community identifying so-called restricted businesses that did not serve Jews, Hugo decided to create a directory of businesses in the New York City metropolitan area that *did not* discriminate against blacks. He printed the information in a 15-page booklet called *The Negro Motorist Green Book.*

"This, our Premiere Issue," Green wrote in the 1937 edition of the *Green Book,* "is dedicated to the Negro Motorist and we sincerely hope that you will find the many places of reference and information valuable and helpful." The price of that first edition: 25¢.

If an African American reader of the *Green Book* needed some work done on their car, they knew that Gene's Auto Repairs on West 155th Street would serve them, because the business was listed in the *Green Book.* Women who wanted a beauty treatment knew they would not be turned away by Bernice Bruton at the Ritz Beauty Salon on 7th Avenue. "Why Do So Many People Dine at Julia's?" asked one paid advertisement. "Because She Has Excellent Food, Well Served at Most Reasonable Prices," including daily dinners for 35¢, and Sunday dinners for 50¢. A couple eager for a night out could go to the Donhaven Country Club in Westchester County, which offered dinner dances with live music by Goldie Lucas and his Donhaven Country Club Band. The *Green Book* also provided listings for pharmacies, barbershops, cleaners, liquor stores, golf courses, and vacation spots, plus lists of state parks and points of interest, tips on safe driving and auto care, and any other information that Green thought would be useful to motorists.

HERE, THERE, EVERYWHERE

The 1937 edition proved so popular with readers that for the 1938 edition Green decided to expand the scope of the publication to include every state east of the Mississippi River. Then in 1939 he expanded it to the entire nation. For help with compiling the listings, he turned to his fellow mail carriers. They knew which businesses did and did not discriminate, which barbers gave the best haircuts, and which restaurants served the best food at reasonable prices. In communities where there were few or no hotels that provided accommodations to African Americans, the mail carriers submitted a new type of listing: "tourist homes," or private homes whose owners rented rooms to travelers.

Year by year, as more listings were sent in, the Green Book grew from 15 pages to more than 80, including entries for Canada, Mexico, and eventually even Bermuda, an island chain in the Atlantic popular with tourists. Later editions had the slogan "Carry Your Green Book With You—You May Need It" on the cover, along with a quote from Mark Twain: "Travel is Fatal to Prejudice."

Over time, the number of copies sold grew, eventually reaching 15,000 copies a year. They could be ordered directly from Hugo Green or purchased through the businesses listed in the Green Book. They were also distributed through Esso service stations, which marketed the guides using the slogan "Go Further With Less Anxiety." At a time when other service station chains, including Shell, refused to even sell gasoline to black motorists, Esso awarded service station franchises to blacks and had African American executives on its corporate staff. (Esso changed its name to Exxon in 1973.)

MUST-READ

Copies of the Green Book were essential reading not just for vacationers but also for African Americans who made their living on the road, including salesmen, musicians, and baseball players in the Negro Leagues. When the civil rights movement began in the mid-1950s, leaders of the movement began to use them as well. The guides probably saved many lives by steering motorists away from trouble and toward the businesses that would accommodate them.

Green also provided a "Vacation Reservation Service" to assist his readers with booking rooms and other services. He accomplished all of this while still delivering the mail during the day, and serving customers at the Green Book offices in the evenings from 8:00 p.m. to 10:00 p.m. It wasn't until he retired from his job at the post office in 1952 (after 39 years) that he was able to focus entirely on the Green Book.

PLANNED OBSOLESCENCE

As successful as the Green Books were, Green told his readers that he actually looked forward to going out of business someday. "There will be a day sometime in the near future when this guide will not have to be published," he wrote. "That is when we as a race will have equal

Ancestors of modern ants had saber teeth, long facial hair, and whiskers on their forehead.

opportunities and privileges in the United States. It will be a great day for us to suspend this publication for then we can go wherever we please." Green did not live quite long enough to see it: he passed away in 1960. But his widow, Alma, continued to publish the guides after his death, and she was the one who lived to see the passage of the Civil Rights Act of 1964, which made it illegal for businesses to discriminate against their customers on the basis of race.

With the passage of that law, for the first time in history African Americans had the freedom and the right to travel, buy gasoline, eat in restaurants, and obtain lodging anywhere they pleased. They no longer needed lists of businesses that were willing to serve them, now that all businesses were required by law to do so. Just as Hugo Green had predicted, the *Green Book* soon became obsolete, and ceased publication in 1966.

GREEN DAYS

For three decades, the *Green Book* had been an institution in the black community, as indispensable for the traveler as a road map, but they soon faded into obscurity. It had long been routine for subscribers to toss out last year's *Green Book* as soon as the new year's edition became available. When the *Green Book* itself became obsolete, many of the last copies were tossed out with the trash. Not surprisingly, few survive today. As interest in the publication has grown in recent years, the value of the surviving copies has risen substantially. The Smithsonian Institution's National Museum of African American History and Culture has a copy of the 1941 *Green Book* in its collection. It originally sold for 25¢; the Smithsonian paid $22,500 for it in 2015.

Copies of the *Green Book* may still survive today in private homes, cultural and historical treasures hiding in plain sight, waiting to be discovered. If you happen to find one lying around, hang on to it—or better yet, donate it to a museum. It's a living piece of American history, and a testament to one man's three-decade mission to secure the blessings of liberty for everyone.

*   *   *

29 RIDICULOUS 1920s SYNONYMS FOR "B.S."

Applesauce, balloon juice, banana oil, bibble-babble, birdseed, bosh, buckwheat, bugle oil, piffle, bum fodder, bushwah, flipflop, claptrap, eyewash, gobbledegook, horse apples, grapefruit, hogwash, hokum, hooey, horsefeathers, meadow dressing, mumbo jumbo, poppycock, tommyrot, phooey, ish kabbibble, corn, and fiddle faddle.

Animal Magnetism

Uncle John couldn't fathom life without animals. Neither can these folks.

"Until one has loved an animal, a part of one's soul remains unawakened."

—Anatole France

"The difference between friends and pets is that friends we allow into our company, pets we allow into our solitude."

—Robert Brault

"The greatest pleasure of a dog is that you may make a fool of yourself with him, and not only will he not scold you, but he will make a fool of himself too."

—Samuel Butler

"Ever consider what pets must think of us? I mean, here we come back from a grocery store with the most amazing haul—chicken, pork, half a cow. They must think we're the greatest hunters on earth!"

—Anne Tyler

"I once had a sparrow alight upon my shoulder for a moment, while I was hoeing in a village garden, and I felt that I was more distinguished by that circumstance than I should have been by any epaulet I could have worn."

—Henry David Thoreau

"I am fond of pigs. Dogs look up to us. Cats look down on us. Pigs treat us as equals."

—Winston Churchill

"God sent angels down to earth in the form of dogs with notes saying 'Don't judge, just love!' They ate the notes—but they keep trying to deliver the message."

—Unknown

"Such short little lives our pets have to spend with us, and they spend most of it waiting for us to come home each day."

—John Grogan

"Horses make a landscape look beautiful."

—Alice Walker

"There's no need for a piece of sculpture in a home that has a cat."

—Wesley Bates

"Whoever said you can't buy happiness forgot little puppies."

—Gene Hill

Calvin: "You know, sometimes the world seems like a pretty mean place."
Hobbes: "That's why animals are so soft and huggy."

—Bill Watterson

Myth-conception: St. Bernard dogs never carried casks of alcohol to warm up stranded travelers.

"Family" Businesses

Ever seen a mob guy on TV describe himself as a "legitimate businessman"? That's not just a Hollywood stereotype—organized crime has long used legitimate businesses as fronts for their illegal activities. And as these examples show, the mob has a diverse portfolio.

PIZZA

In 2014, Italian authorities seized seven pizzerias in Rome as part of a sweep of gangster-run businesses. Roman Mafiosi had been using the restaurants to launder profits from loan sharking, extortion, and drugs, padding the pizzerias' earnings with ill-gotten gains, and making the profits appear to be squeaky-clean. American mobsters have used pizzerias, too. In 2015, a joint Italian/FBI investigation called "Operation Columbus" shut down a mob cocaine network that was being run out of a pizzeria in Queens, New York. And back in 1987, the "Pizza Connection" trial convicted 18 gangsters of operating a billion-dollar heroin ring from pizzerias throughout the northeastern and upper midwestern United States.

Gangsters have their hands in the ingredients, too. In Sicily, mob-run farms and dairies are so prevalent that an independent cooperative called Libera Terra (Free Land) publicly guarantees that its products have no connection to the Mafia. In the United States, the 80-page "Report of the Study of Organized Crime's Infiltration of the Pizza and Cheese Industry" detailed how crime boss Joe Bonanno moved in on the specialty cheese industry in the 1940s and continued his control through the 1980s. While the cheese production was legit, Bonanno's business practices weren't. Mob-run companies forced stores and restaurants to buy exclusively from them—or else—resulting in a mozzarella monopoly for the mob.

WIND FARMS

Italian businessman Vito Nicastri was called "Lord of the Wind" because of the fortune he'd made from wind farms. Italian authorities called him something else: a frontman for La Cosa Nostra. In 2013, they seized €1.3 billion ($1.47 billion) of his assets. The Italian government offers grants and tax breaks to companies that "go green," but Sicilian and Calabrian mobsters have manipulated that policy to generate a different kind of green. In some cases, grants are awarded for wind farms that are never built. Other times the farms are built, but the construction is completed by Mafia-owned firms that charge high prices for substandard materials. And illegal mob earnings are hidden in the wind farms' ledgers.

X-factor: The increase of women studying science in the 1990s is called "the Scully Effect."

In 2007, a wiretap caught a Sicilian Mafioso telling his wife, "Not one turbine blade will be built in Mazara unless I agree to it." That wiretap was part of a series of investigations into mob corruption of the Italian wind farm industry. One of the operations, code-named "Gone with the Wind," yielded numerous arrests, including the president of Italy's National Association of Wind Energy. Another investigation resulted in the seizure of a third of Sicily's 30 wind farms, identified as Mafia-controlled. In 2014, the European Union law enforcement agency Europol named mob involvement in the alternative energy industry an "emerging trend."

THE FULTON FISH MARKET

Something smelled fishy in New York City, and it wasn't just the sea-food. Opened on the docks of lower Manhattan in 1869, Fulton quickly became the largest wholesale fish market in the United States. In 1923, Genovese mob member Joseph "Socks" Lanza established himself as the head of Local 359 of the United Seafood Workers' union. The fish market couldn't function without Local 359's workforce of 8,000 men, so dominating the union meant controlling all of Fulton. With labor in hand, the Mafia charged fishermen fees to dock and unload their boats, and charged similar fees to wholesalers. Other mob shakedowns included payments collected for "theft insurance," sign rentals, and "holiday contributions" at Christmas. The wholesalers even had to pay the gangsters for the privilege of parking in city-owned lots.

The corruption ran rampant for decades. Government officials were paid to look the other way—and justified their inaction by pointing to how smoothly the Fulton Fish Market ran under mob control. (Which was true. Not many people were willing to fool with the Genoveses.) From the 1930s through 1979, the U.S. Attorney's office convicted as many mobsters as it could on a case-by-case basis, but it wasn't until the 1980s that the feds specifically targeted Local 359. In 1987, U.S. Attorney Rudolph Giuliani filed suit against Local 359 and the Genoveses, which resulted in the court appointing an independent administrator to attempt reform. Still, the mob's hold on Fulton wasn't fully broken until 1995's Local Law 50 gave the city the power to regulate, investigate, and license all aspects of the market, and, most important, to kick out corrupt individuals and businesses.

ROCK 'N' ROLL

The New York mob wormed its way into the music business early, thanks to Moishe "Morris" Levy. He got his start as a street kid working in gangster-owned nightclubs. By 1949, the 22-year-old had opened his own place—the legendary Birdland jazz club. Building on that success, he founded Roulette Records in 1956 and signed acts ranging from Count Basie to Jimmie Rodgers. Levy's predatory contracts with musicians left him with all the copyrights and royalties. He even added his name to songwriter credits for an even bigger cut of the profits. If the musicians complained, they were told to "tell it to the judge" or were taken for "rides" in the country.

After producing such hits as "Party Doll," "Peppermint Twist," and "Hanky Panky," Roulette Records started to wane after the 1960s. But Levy continued to wield enormous influence in the music industry. Major record label executives called on the so-called Godfather of Rock' n' Roll to help "fix" certain problems such as counterfeit records and employee theft.

On the surface, Roulette and Strawberries, his national chain of record stores, seemed on the up-and-up...except that Levy was a long-time associate of Vincent "the Chin" Gigante, head of the Genovese crime family. According to the FBI, Levy's 90 businesses were fronts for the Genoveses, providing them with cash flow, real estate, and heroin distribution. When a Philadelphia record distributor refused to pay Levy $1.25 million for an order of records in 1984, a mob enforcer roughed him up and the FBI pounced. Levy was arrested, convicted of extortion, and sentenced to 10 years in prison. He died of cancer before he could begin serving his sentence, but Levy insisted to the end that the mobsters he knew were just friends and that he didn't work for them. Or as he put it, "I knew Cardinal Spellman, too. That don't make me a Catholic."

TOXIC WASTE

Over the last 20 years, the Mafia has illegally dumped more than 10 million tons of toxic waste in Italy, according to the Italian environmental group Legambiente. Locals call the area north of Naples the "Land of Fires" because Mafiosi contractors illegally burn trash and waste for days at a time; 2,500 trash fires were recorded in 2006 alone. Toxic waste removal pays well, especially when no money is spent to decontaminate or dispose of it safely. Mafia-linked companies win bids to haul away the waste, forge documents to make it appear that it's been treated, and then bury or burn it. It's estimated that illegal waste disposal has made 22 separate Mafia clans a combined total of $7 billion since the 1980s.

Unsuspecting locals are sometimes duped into doing the mob's dirty work. In 2003, Italy's "Operation Greenland" snared a waste disposal company that offered free "fertilizer" samples to farmers. The farmers spread the black mulchlike substance over their fields, then watched as fish died in nearby ponds when it rained...because the "fertilizer" was actually untreated toxic waste. The Mafiosi didn't seem to care that they were poisoning Italian soil. A wiretap reportedly caught an underling asking his boss what they'd drink if they polluted the land. "You idiot," the boss answered. "We'll drink mineral water."

Clever! Alligators will whack trees with their tails to dislodge baby birds from their nests.

Bathroom News

*Here are a few fascinating bits of bathroom trivia
that we've flushed out from around the world.*

LET THE CHIPS FALL WHERE THEY MAY

In January 2015, two guests in adjoining rooms at the Harrah's Casino Hotel in Atlantic City complained that water was leaking through the ceiling into their rooms. Plumbing leaks in big hotels are not unusual, but the source of this one was. Someone had flushed $2.7 million worth of high-denomination poker chips down the toilet. Investigators determined that the chips were counterfeit and therefore worthless. They traced them to the man staying in the room above the two that flooded: Christian Lusardi of Fayetteville, North Carolina, who police say had been using the phony chips to cheat in a poker tournament in the nearby Borgata Hotel Casino.

When Lusardi feared his cheating was about to be discovered, he flushed the chips down the toilet to destroy the evidence. He pled guilty to trademark counterfeiting and criminal mischief and was ordered to reimburse the Borgata Hotel Casino $463,540 for lost revenue after the three-week poker tournament had to be canceled, plus another $9,455 to Harrah's for damaging their plumbing. Flushing his fake chips down the toilet also got him sentenced to five years in the can.

PEE-TEOR

In September 2009, stargazers in North America were treated to the sight of an odd, bright light streaking across the night sky. It was moving too slowly to be a meteor, so what was it? A few days later, NASA explained that the phenomenon was caused when astronauts aboard the space shuttle *Discovery* jettisoned 10 days' worth of urine and wastewater into space while preparing to return to Earth.

Normally, smaller amounts of urine were jettisoned from the shuttle at more frequent intervals, but *Discovery* had just completed a 10-day visit to the International Space Station. NASA had recently instituted a no-dumping policy for shuttles docked to the station, to protect science experiments set up outside the space station from being contaminated (by astronaut pee). *Discovery* had accumulated about 150 pounds of urine and wastewater over the 10 days; when it was jettisoned all at once into the vacuum of space, it froze into ice crystals and then turned into water vapor when sunlight struck it. This "cloud" of vapor reflected enough of the sun's rays to allow it to be seen from Earth without a telescope.

The *Dolomedes briangreenei* spider can swim, dive, and catch fish. It's as big as your palm.

(At least one observer had a pretty good idea of what had caused the strange glow: Abe Megahed of Madison, Wisconsin, who was outdoors trying to photograph *Discovery* and the International Space Station as they passed overhead. "I just watched the shuttle and station flyover and was surprised to see that the shuttle was sporting a massive curved plume. What could it be?" he asked in an online post. "Something venting? An OMS burn? RCS thrusters? A massive, record breaking urine dump?")

DUTCH TREAT

In 2015, art conservators in Great Britain set to work cleaning a 17th-century Dutch painting owned by Queen Elizabeth called *A Village Fair, with a Church Behind.* Painted by Isack van Ostade in 1643, it depicts what its title suggests: a lively fair in the foreground, with the village church on a low hill in the background. As the conservators set to work cleaning the painting, they soon discovered that one of the bushes on the right side of the painting was not original and had been added much later. The conservators wondered why…and got their answer when they removed the bush. It had concealed a villager with his pants down, squatting in the dirt to relieve himself.

It turns out that Dutch painters of Van Ostade's era were fond of incorporating such images of people or animals into their paintings "partly as a joke, and partly to remind viewers of that crucial word 'nature,' the inspiration for their art," says Desmond Shawe-Taylor, who holds the title Surveyor of the Queen's Pictures. Elizabeth's ancestor, King George IV, bought the painting in 1810; he was known to have a bawdy sense of humor and may have bought it specifically because of the crude image. The painting has been in the royal art collection ever since. The bush is believed to have been added in 1903, when the painting was sent to an art restorer.

PEE-RLY WHITES

In July 2013, scientists at the Guangzhou Institutes of Biomedicine and Health in China announced that they'd succeeded in growing "toothlike structures" from cells harvested from human urine. Urine contains cells that have been discarded by the body, and the scientists were able to convert some of these into stem cells, a type of cell that can grow into any kind of tissue contained in the human body, including teeth. Bundles of the cells were implanted into laboratory mice, and after three weeks the bundles had grown into toothlike structures that contained dental pulp, dentin, and enamel, just like real teeth. More research is needed, but if successful, it may one day be possible for dentists to grow new teeth for their patients using cells harvested from the patients' own pee.

You're (Almost) in the Band!

Some stories about some famous musicians who were almost in other famous bands.

VAN HALEN, FEATURING PATTY SMYTH

It's probably the most famous instance of lead singer replacement in rock history, but Sammy Hagar ("I Can't Drive 55") was not the first person that Eddie Van Halen asked to replace David Lee Roth when Roth left the group for a solo career in 1985. Van Halen's first choice was Patty Smyth, lead singer of the pop rock band Scandal, who'd had big hits with "Goodbye to You" and "The Warrior." So Van Halen went to a Scandal concert and then traveled with the band on their tour bus for three days. At the end of the tour, Van Halen asked Smyth to leave her band for his. Smyth declined. She was eight months pregnant at the time and, as she later told a reporter, "those guys were drunk and fighting all the time." So Eddie Van Halen moved on to the next person on his list, who seems an even more unlikely pick: Daryl Hall of Hall and Oates. This was an urban legend in the rock world for decades, until 2012, when Hagar appeared on Hall's TV show *Live at Daryl's House* and asked Hall if the rumor was true. It was.

THE DOORS, FEATURING PAUL RODGERS

The future of the Doors was in serious jeopardy when charismatic front man Jim Morrison died of a drug overdose in 1971. About six months later, the rest of the band announced that they would continue on, and instead of trying to find someone to replace Morrison, keyboardist Ray Manzarek and guitarist Robby Krieger would share vocal duties. The three surviving Doors released their first post-Morrison album, cleverly titled *Other Voices*, in 1971 and their second, titled *Full Circle*, the following year...and the band broke up shortly after that. But there were rumors that the Doors had actively tried to seek out a new lead singer in the months after Morrison's death, and the lead singer they wanted was Paul Rodgers, who was in the British band Free ("All Right Now") at the time and would later be the front man for Bad Company, as well as Queen after the death of Freddie Mercury. The Rodgers rumors were eventually confirmed by Rodgers himself, but even he didn't find out that the Doors were interested in him until 2011, 40 years later. Evidently, Krieger traveled to London to seek him out, but

Rodgers was holed up in a recording studio in the English countryside, and was unreachable.

KISS, FEATURING RICHIE SAMBORA

Kiss was founded by singer/guitarist Paul Stanley and bassist Gene Simmons in 1973. They own the band and everything about it, resulting in a revolving door of lead guitarists and drummers. Ace Frehley, the guitarist when the band was at its commercial peak in the late 1970s, was fired in 1982 and replaced with Vinnie Vincent, who was fired in 1983 after upstaging Stanley and Simmons with an impromptu virtuoso guitar solo at a concert in Quebec City. They auditioned dozens of guitarists to replace Vincent, and one of them was New Jersey musician Richie Sambora. Sambora later recalled that Stanley and Simmons praised his playing style and ability but were annoyed that he hadn't bothered to learn the audition material beforehand, which consisted of five Kiss hits, including "Detroit Rock City" and "Rock and Roll All Nite." Not surprisingly, Sambora didn't get the gig…but just a few months later, he successfully auditioned to be in another popular hard-rock band: Bon Jovi.

THE ROLLING STONES, FEATURING MOST EVERY MAJOR GUITARIST IN ROCK 'N' ROLL

Stones guitarist Mick Taylor left the band in 1974, forcing the group to find a new rhythm guitarist before its scheduled 1975 Tour of the Americas. Among those who the band interviewed or auditioned: Jeff Beck, Peter Frampton, Ry Cooder, Mick Ronson (of David Bowie's backing band the Spiders From Mars), Nils Lofgren (later of Bruce Springsteen's E Street Band), Jorma Kaukonen (Jefferson Airplane), Andy Summers (a few years before he formed the Police), American session guitarist Wayne Perkins, Clem Clempson (Humble Pie), Hank Marvin (the Shadows), and Steve Marriott (the Small Faces, Humble Pie). According to a plaque memorializing him in Belfast, Northern Ireland, Irish blues guitarist Rory Gallagher was offered the job but turned it down. The job ultimately went to Ron Wood of the Small Faces, who's still with the Stones.

*   *   *

HOW LOW CAN YOU GO?

The lowest notes ever recorded: A black hole in the Perseus galaxy (which is 250 million light-years away) emits a single sound wave approximately every 10 million years. The sound emitted is a B-flat 57 octaves below middle C.

Strange Lawsuits

More stories of unusual legal battles.

THE PLAINTIFF: Andrew Rector, 26, a New York Yankees fan

THE DEFENDANTS: The New York Yankees, Major League Baseball, and ESPN

THE LAWSUIT: Rector, a used car salesman, must have had a busy day on Sunday, April 13, 2014, because when he attended a Yankees home game that evening against the Red Sox, he fell asleep in his seat in the fourth inning. The game was broadcast nationally on ESPN's *Sunday Night Baseball,* and when a camera panned the crowd and stopped on Rector in full slumber, the commentators—Dan Shulman and former major leaguer John Kruk—had fun commenting on how soundly Rector was sleeping. They called him "oblivious" and joked that his neck might be sore later. "Maybe [the guy sitting next to him] is his buddy, and he likes him a lot more when he's asleep," joked Kruk.

Rector claimed in his defamation suit that at one point he was called "fatty, unintelligent, and stupid." However, that quote didn't show up in the MLB-approved, two-minute clip from the game that appeared on YouTube. Rector said he was ridiculed even more after the clip was posted on MLB.com. Perhaps the worst comment: "He neither understands nor knows anything about history and the meaning of rivalry between Red Sox and New York Yankee." That did it. Rector sued the Yankees, ESPN, and Major League Baseball for $10 million.

THE VERDICT: Case dismissed. Bronx Supreme Court Justice Julia Rodriguez did agree that the announcers might have shown a bit more restraint. However, their jokes (which lasted less than a minute) did not "rise to the level of defamation," or, as Rector claimed in his suit, "an unending verbal crusade against the napping plaintiff." Judge Rodriguez added that when MLB.com reposted the clip, it did so without adding any further commentary, so no defamation there…and no $10 million for Rector.

THE PLAINTIFF: Mark Oberholtzer, owner of Mark-1 Plumbing in Texas City, Texas

THE DEFENDANT: AutoNation Ford Gulf Freeway in Houston

THE LAWSUIT: In 2013, Oberholtzer went to the AutoNation dealership to trade in his company truck—a black 2005 Ford F-250 pickup—for a newer model. As the transaction was being finalized,

Oberholtzer's son started to peel off the decal on the door that displayed the company's logo and phone number. But then, according to Oberholtzer's lawsuit, a salesperson told them to leave the decal alone; their people would remove it without damaging the paint job. So the decal was left intact, Oberholtzer signed all the papers, got into his new truck, and went home.

More than a year later, in December 2014, a tweet that featured a photo of Oberholtzer's truck being used by a Syrian jihadist group similar to ISIS went viral. A large gun was mounted to the bed of the pickup, and the Mark-1 Plumbing decal—with the business phone number—was prominently displayed on the door. Oberholtzer's business started receiving angry calls from people accusing him of supporting terrorism. He even received death threats. "A few of the people are really ugly," he claimed. "We have a secretary here, she's scared to death." Thousands more calls came in a week later after Stephen Colbert made light of the photo on the final episode of *The Colbert Report*. "Syria may be going down the toilet," joked Colbert, "but for the first time, they know who to call to unclog it."

Oberholtzer wasn't laughing. He said that when he called AutoNation to complain, they were unrepentant, and told him that it was the auction house's job to remove the decal. But the auction house in Dallas, which bought the truck from AutoNation, didn't do it. It was then sold and shipped to an unknown buyer in Turkey, who didn't remove the decal, either. From there, the Ford truck found its way to the jihadists in Syria.

In addition to the harassment (which forced him to close his business for a week), Oberholtzer said that the FBI and Homeland Security both interrogated him. They even told him to buy a handgun for protection, which he did. He sued AutoNation for $1 million for gross negligence and breach of privacy. "It hurts my feelings that anyone could possibly think that we were connected to terrorism in any way," Oberholtzer told CBS News.

THE VERDICT: Pending.

*   *   *

NAME THOSE DINOSAUR SPIKES

The cluster of spikes on the end of the tail of the dinosaur known as the *stegosaurus* is known among paleontologists as the "thagomizer"—the name given to the spikes in a 1982 *The Far Side* comic by cartoonist Gary Larson. (The cartoon says the thagomizer was named "after the late Thag Simmons.")

Candy corn was originally called "Chicken Feed."

Death by Underwear

It's a morbid thought, but it stands to reason that since nearly everybody wears underwear nearly all the time, every once in a while it's going to get somebody killed.

ACT OF GOD

One morning in October 1999, the bodies of two women were found underneath a tree in Hyde Park in London, England. For more than 15 hours, passersby had assumed that Sunee Whitworth, 39, and Anuban Bell, 24, were homeless and sleeping under the tree, or were perhaps drug addicts. But when a bystander noticed that they had not moved since the night before, she called the police. The responding officers discovered that the women were dead.

A thunderstorm the night before provided the first clue as to what might have killed them, and autopsies later confirmed it: Whitworth and Bell were sheltering under the tree when it was struck by lightning, killing them instantly. Investigators believe the women might have survived the strike, had Whitworth not been wearing an underwire bra. Burn patterns on her chest and the melted wire in her bra indicated that the lightning bolt had jumped from the tree to her bra, killing both her and Bell—who was standing next to her—instantly. "This is the second time in my experience of 50,000 deaths where lightning has struck the metal of a bra," Westminster coroner Dr. Paul Knapman noted in his autopsy report. (But before you or your loved ones toss out your underwire bras, consider this: In September 2015, a woman struck by lightning in China may have been *saved* by her underwire bra. In that case, investigators concluded that the wires diverted the electricity around her vital organs, sparing her life.)

FRUIT OF THE DOOM

Robert Alston, 19, and some friends were driving to a party in Pittsburgh, Pennsylvania, in August 2015 when a shot rang out and he screamed out in pain. This was no drive-by shooting: the shot came from *inside* the car. It turns out that Alston's friend in the back seat, 19-year-old Eietyoung Kemp, was packing a gun in his underpants. After climbing into the car and sitting down, he tried to adjust the position of the gun to get more comfortable. That's when it went off, firing a round through the back of the passenger seat in front of him and striking Alston in the back. He died in the hospital a few hours later. But by then Kemp was long gone: after the gun went off, he bolted from the car and hid out for a few days, then surrendered to the police, admitting to the shooting, but claiming it was an accident. At last report, he was in jail awaiting trial on charges of criminal homicide, reckless endangerment, and tampering with evidence for throwing his gun into the Allegheny River after the shooting.

HER CUP RUNNETH OVER

In January 2015, a St. Joseph, Michigan, gun owner died in a freak accident after she shot herself in the eye while adjusting her bra holster. Police say that Christina Bond, 55, liked to carry her concealed weapon in a special bra designed for that purpose, but on this day she was having trouble getting it to fit the way she wanted it to. "She was looking down at it and accidentally discharged the weapon," St. Joseph Public Safety Director Mark Clapp told the *Kalamazoo Gazette*. Bond was rushed to the hospital, but there wasn't much that the doctors could do, and she died the following day.

SQUEEZED OUT

Joan Kidd, an 85-year-old woman living in Brigg, England, went to live in a nursing home in 2009 after her children became concerned that she was no longer able to live on her own. But after moving in, she refused to give up wearing corsets, which she'd worn for 40 years. The staff at the nursing home couldn't force Kidd to give them up, so she continued to wear them, even in bed…and even after nurses warned that they were irritating the skin on her back. The irritation eventually became infected and progressed to sepsis, or blood poisoning, causing Kidd's death. "She was wearing her corset in bed and declined to take it off," said a spokesperson for the nursing home. "A patient cannot be treated against their will; it's their prerogative to refuse treatment."

IN BRIEF(S)

Corey McQueary, 33, was an inmate in the Jessamine County Detention Center in Kentucky in 2014. One day in August, deputies found him passed out in his cell. He later died, and an autopsy revealed that the cause of death was an overdose of methadone, a drug typically used to treat heroin addiction, but one that can also be abused if taken without medical supervision.

So where did McQueary get the methadone? From his cellmate, Michael Jones, 55, who'd recently returned to jail after being out for a few days on a court-ordered furlough. Jones smuggled methadone into the facility by soaking his underpants in the drug and wearing them back into jail. He gave the underwear to McQueary, who tore it into pieces and swallowed one piece after another to get high. When he swallowed too many pieces of his cellmate's underwear at once, he died.

According to the Latest Research

Can pigeons diagnose cancer? Does a preference for black coffee mean a person is nuts, or at least more likely to be nuts? Maybe so, say scientists. Here's a look at some of the more unusual scientific studies we've come across recently.

S**tudy:** "The Role of Body Mass Index in Child Pedestrian Injury Risk," *Accident Analysis & Prevention*, May 2016

Purpose: To see if there's any correlation between the weight or "body mass index" of a child and the likelihood that they will be hit by a car while crossing the street.

Methodology: Researchers at the University of Iowa constructed a simulated roadway with a crosswalk and a wooden curb for the children to stand on. Simulated traffic was displayed on video monitors in front of the children, who were instructed to study the traffic patterns and step off the curb when they felt it was safe to cross the street.

The kids did not actually cross the fake street; instead they stepped onto a "trigger plate" that activated a computerized avatar character. The avatar then made the simulated crossing at the child's typical walking speed, which had been measured in advance. Two hundred children between the ages of seven and eight participated in the study; each child made 30 fake crossings under a variety of traffic conditions.

Findings: On average, heavier children were "more impatient and impulsive" than their peers, and waited less time before crossing the street. They also allowed for less distance between themselves and oncoming cars, and were involved in more simulated collisions with vehicles. Lead author Elizabeth O'Neal speculates that "being overweight is putting increased stress on their joints, which is a little uncomfortable. So, they are compromising their safety in order to expedite the crossing."

Study: "A Brief Olfactory Test for Alzheimer's Disease," *Journal of the Neurological Sciences*, October 2013

Purpose: To determine whether peanut butter can be used to detect the early stages of Alzheimer's disease. A person's sense of smell is one of the first things that declines when they have Alzheimer's. It deteriorates even before memory loss becomes apparent. The left side of the brain is usually affected first, and because smells detected via a person's

---

Gargoyles were created to divert rainwater from running down (and marring) the sides of a building.

left nostril are processed by the left side of the brain, the researchers wondered if early stage Alzheimer's patients would lose their sense of smell in their left nostril before they lost it in their right. (Why peanut butter? It's smelly, inexpensive, and widely available.)

Methodology: The patient closes their eyes, mouth, and one nostril, then breathes normally through the open nostril. A small cup filled with about a tablespoon of peanut butter is held at a distance of more than 20 centimeters (about 8 inches) below the nostril. The cup is then slowly raised closer to the nostril one centimeter at a time until the patient reports that they smell the peanut butter. The person administering the test does not know which patients have been diagnosed with Alzheimer's disease.

Findings: Patients with Alzheimer's had a marked difference in their ability to detect smells with their left nostril versus their right; patients without Alzheimer's did not. On average, the peanut butter had to be 10 centimeters (about 4 inches) closer to the left nostril than the right before an Alzheimer's patient could detect the smell. The researchers hope that in the future, a simple "sniff test" will be used to diagnose Alzheimer's in its early stages.

Study: "The Efficacy of Duct Tape vs. Cryotherapy in the Treatment of Verruca Vulgaris (the Common Wart)," *Archives of Pediatric Adolescent Medicine*, October 2002

Purpose: To test the claim that duct tape is an effective wart remover.

Methodology: There were 51 wart patients in the study, ranging in age from 3 to 22 years old. The first 25 received the traditional "freezing" therapy—having liquid nitrogen applied to their warts every two to three weeks, for six weeks or until the wart was gone.

The remaining 26 patients received "duct tape occlusion therapy." Their warts were covered with pieces of duct tape cut to the size of the wart. The tape was left in place for six days, then removed. Twelve hours later, duct tape was reapplied, and the treatment was repeated for two months or until the wart disappeared. ("One patient enrolled in the duct tape group lost his study wart in a trampoline toe-amputation accident and was not included in our analysis," the authors noted.)

Findings: If you're like Uncle John and you were traumatized by painful freezing treatments when you were a kid, take heart. "Duct tape occlusion therapy of the warts was significantly more effective than cryotherapy," the study concluded. While 73 percent of the warts treated with duct tape resolved within 28 days, only 63 percent warts that were treated with liquid nitrogen resolved in the same time. Conclusion: "The mechanism of action of duct tape on warts is unknown…but it may involve stimulation of the patient's immune system through local irritation."

Prairie dogs are herbivores, yet will kill ground squirrels without provocation.

Real-Life Horror Movie Locations

Looking for a theme for your next road trip? How about "Places Where My Favorite Horror Films Were Shot"? If that appeals to you, here are a few scary spots you'll want to add to your agenda.

SILENCE OF THE LAMBS (1991)

Creepy Place: The house where serial killer "Buffalo Bill" (Ted Levine) lived, where he kept kidnapped women in a pit in the basement, and where he is eventually confronted by FBI trainee Clarice Starling (Jodie Foster)

Real-Life Location: 8 Circle Street, Perryopolis, Pennsylvania (a suburb of Pittsburgh)

Story: In the movie, the house is located in the fictional town of Belvedere, Ohio, but most of the film was actually shot near Pittsburgh. This house was one of several picked by movie location scouts in 1989, two years before the film came out. "They were looking for a home in which you entered the front door and had a straight line through," owner Barbara Lloyd told the *Pittsburgh Tribune-Review*. "They wanted it to look like a spider web, with Buffalo Bill drawing Jodie Foster into the foyer, into the kitchen, then into the basement." The home got the approval of director Jonathan Demme, and a film crew showed up to film inside the home for three days in early 1990.

Extra: The home made the news in 2015, when the Lloyds put it up for sale. The Lloyds told reporters that the home has a full basement...but no creepy pit. (That part of the movie was filmed in a studio.)

THE BLAIR WITCH PROJECT (1999)

Creepy Place: The woods where the young filmmakers disappear

Real-Life Location: Seneca Creek State Park, Maryland

Story: *The Blair Witch Project* was a low-budget independent horror film that shocked the entertainment industry when it earned $248 million worldwide, making it one the highest-grossing independent films in history. In the movie, three film students at a Maryland college go to the "Black Hills Forest," near the town of Burkittsville, Maryland, to make a documentary about the "Blair Witch," a ghost that purportedly haunts the woods. They disappear and are never seen again—but the footage they took in the woods is found a year later. The town of Burkittsville actually does exist, but most of the filming took place in nearby Seneca Creek State Park. (Why there? Because it was about five minutes away from the home of one of the filmmakers, Eduardo Sanchez.) You can visit the park…and you can even spend the night there camping. (Don't forget to take a video camera!)

Extra: The ramshackle house where the film's climactic final scene was filmed—a 200-year-old historic and abandoned home known as the Griggs House—was located in nearby Patapsco Valley State Park. After the film's success, fans started showing up to see it…and to take pieces of it home as souvenirs. The house was demolished a few years later.

NIGHT OF THE LIVING DEAD (1968)

Creepy Place: The cemetery in the film's opening scene…and the site of the movie's first zombie attacks

Real-Life Location: Evans City Cemetery, Evans City, Pennsylvania

Story: Director George Romero's horror classic opens with a young couple visiting the grave of their father in a rural Pennsylvania cemetery. Then—ZOMBIES! Well, actually just one: a zombie attacks the couple, and bashes the man's head on a gravestone, killing him, while the woman watches in horror, clinging to another gravestone, engraved with the inscription "Nicholas Kramer (1842–1917)." The cemetery, the gravestone, and the small chapel seen in the film are all still there today. (Romero, who was filming without permission, chose the cemetery because of its remote location—he didn't want shooting to be interrupted by locals or police. Also, it was convenient: Romero lived in Pittsburgh, less than 30 miles away.)

Extra: Fans have been going to the cemetery for decades to re-create the scene—complete with the Nicholas Kramer gravestone. (If you're a fan of bad reenactments, check out some of them on YouTube.)

HALLOWEEN (1978)

Creepy Place: The house where the first murder takes place

Real-Life Location: 1000 Mission Street, South Pasadena, California

Story: It's the house in the film's opening scene, when six-year-old Michael Myers (Will Sandin) stabs his big sister to death. In the movie, the house is in the fictional town of Haddonfield, Illinois (named for Haddonfield, New Jersey—hometown of the film's producer, Debra Hill), but in real life it was an abandoned house located on Meridian Avenue in South Pasadena. (The director, John Carpenter, lived in Hollywood, so the location was chosen out of convenience.) You can see the house today, but, as you may notice, it's not at the same address: years after the film was made, the house was moved around the corner, and is now on Mission Street. What's the famous horror house today? A chiropractor's office.

Pyroclastic flows from volcanic eruptions can reach speeds of over 400 miles per hour.

Extra: A number of other sites featured in the film can still be seen in South Pasadena today, including the hardware store from which Myers stole a knife and his now-famous Halloween mask. (It's no longer a hardware store, though—today it's an Indian restaurant.)

THE EXORCIST (1973)

Creepy Place: The "Exorcist Stairs"

Real-Life Location: Prospect Street NW, at the corner of 36th Street NW, Georgetown, Washington, D.C.

Story: If you know the film, you know the famous scene in which Father Karras (Jason Miller) coaxes the demon out of the possessed Regan (Linda Blair), and allows it to possess him. Then, just as the demon is about to make him attack Regan, Karras throws himself out of a window. He lands at the top of a long, narrow flight of stone stairs, tumbles down it, and dies. The stairs, which were padded with rubber for the filming, have been known as the "Exorcist Stairs" ever since, and it's still a regular stop for Washington, D.C., tourists. (Legend has it that during the filming of the stuntman falling down the steps, some students at nearby Georgetown University charged their friends money to watch from the school's roof.)

MORE SCARY SPOTS

Dawn of the Dead **(1978).** Most of the second film in George Romero's classic zombie series takes place in the Monroeville Mall in Monroeville, Pennsylvania. (Filming took place after stores were closed, every night from 11:00 p.m. until 7:00 a.m., over a period of three months.)

Friday the 13th **(1980).** Another gore-fest, this one was shot mostly at Camp No-Be-Bo-Sco, a Boy Scout camp in Hardwick Township, New Jersey. (Several other locations seen in the film can be seen in nearby Blairstown, New Jersey.)

A Nightmare on Elm Street **(1984).** The address in the film: 1428 Elm Street, Springwood, Ohio. In real life: 1428 North Genesee Avenue, Los Angeles. Across the street, at 1419 North Genesee, is where Johnny Depp's character lived. (*Nightmare* was Depp's first movie role.)

The Texas Chainsaw Massacre **(1974).** The big farmhouse where the killer, Leatherface (Gunnar Hansen), lived was built in 1900 near Round Rock, Texas. In 1998, the house was dismantled, moved, and rebuilt more than 60 miles away, in the town of Kingsland, Texas, where it is now the Grand Central Cafe restaurant. (If you go, make sure to try a "Leatherface Lemonade"—lemonade and Jack Daniels. Reviews say they're "killer good.")

History's Combo Meals

Ever heard of a "turducken"? It's a modern food creation—a chicken stuffed inside a duck, stuffed inside a turkey, cooked as a single roast. If you've never had one, try it sometime. It's very tasty. But…it turns out it's not so modern after all. Chefs have been creating these Frankenstein food combos for hundreds of years.

THE COCKENTRICE

A favorite at the court of King Henry VIII, this 16th-century English delicacy was half of a pig and half of a capon (a castrated rooster) sewn together. The order was optional—some recipes called for the pig's head to be in front; others put the capon's head on the pig's rear end. Either way, the body of the cockentrice was stuffed with a mixture of egg, sheep suet, bread, and spices and then roasted on a spit. If that wasn't fancy enough to suit the royal taste, another variation had the capon sewn *on top* of the pig and, after cooking, decorated with a paper helmet and lance to mimic a knight riding a horse. That dish was called the Helmeted Cock.

THE TROJAN HOG

Like the Trojan horse of Greek legend, which was crammed full of soldiers, the Trojan Hog—a popular dish in Rome around 400 AD—was crammed full of food. A butchered and cleaned hog was stuffed with birds called thrushes and gnatsnappers, as well as oysters, scallops, eggs, and polenta. Then the hog was slow-roasted and served belly-up so that the diners could cut it open and pull out the delicacies.

THE COMPLETE

This 13th-century Andalusian dish (Andalusia was a region in southern Spain) started with a fresh-killed, gutted ram. But the ram didn't stay empty for long. Several whole chickens, pigeons, and doves were fried and then stuffed with a mixture of bread crumbs, eggs, and seasonings. The stuffed birds were placed inside the ram along with meatballs, mirkâs (sausage), and egg yolks. The stuffed ram was then sewn shut and cooked in a clay oven.

PANDORA'S CUSHION

How did English cooks in the Victorian era stretch a Christmas goose to feed a houseful of guests? By putting a deboned quail inside a deboned

Why do wolves howl in harmony? One theory: to create the illusion that the pack is larger than it is.

pheasant inside a deboned chicken inside the Christmas goose. Each bird was separated from the next by a layer of *forcemeat*, a sausage stuffing that's "forced" through a sieve (which made it like a pate), and the entire stuffed goose was then sewn up and roasted.

RÔTI SANS PAREIL (ROAST WITHOUT EQUAL)

In 1807, Alexandre Balthazar Laurent Grimod de la Reynière, generally considered to be the first official food critic, published a recipe for a 17-bird roast. De la Reynière started small and worked his way up—a warbler, a bunting, a lark, a thrush, a quail, a lapwing, a plover, a partridge, a woodcock, a teal, a guinea fowl, a duck, a chicken, a pheasant, a goose, and a turkey were stuffed, one inside the other, and then the whole thing was stuffed into a great bustard, a large European bird. It was recommended that bread stuffing be added between each layer and that it be cooked for at least 24 hours. History doesn't record if anyone ever attempted the dish.

QUAIL À LA TALLEYRAND

Apparently the 19th-century French really had a thing for birds cooked inside other birds. In this recipe, supposedly created by diplomat and statesman Charles-Maurice de Talleyrand, the first step was to season a quail with champagne and truffles. Then the quail was placed inside a chicken and—as you probably guessed—the chicken went inside a turkey. Cooking the quail in this manner was supposed to infuse the bird with the juices of both the chicken and the turkey. An 1891 newspaper article recommended: "You take the quail as you would take some sacred relic, and serve it hot." (Neither the recipe nor the newspaper article said what the chef was supposed to do with the turkey and chicken in which the quail had been cooked.)

KIVIAK

This traditional Inuit dish has been made and consumed in Greenland for hundreds of years. The recipe calls for 300 to 500 little auks (small seabirds) to be placed whole inside a fat-lined sealskin bag. The bag is then stitched up and buried under a rock for 3 to 18 months. Unlike some other combo foods, kiviak isn't an attempt at haute cuisine: ancient Inuits developed it as a way to preserve food for the lean winter months. The layer of seal fat inside the bag softens the auks so that every part except the feathers can be eaten. Since the birds ferment while they're in the ground, they don't even need to be cooked. It's a method of food storage that's still used today.

Shocker: Nikola Tesla, inventor of the alternating current motor, was born during a lightning storm.

Welcome to Curly

If you know a little rudimentary Spanish, you can figure out that "San Antonio"
is "Saint Anthony" in English, and that "Los Angeles" means "The Angels."
Here are the meanings (and stories) of some other Spanish-named cities.

City: Modesto, California
Meaning: "Modest"
Details: Bank of California founder William C. Ralston
provided the funds to create a settlement in 1870. Residents wanted
to name it after him, but he was too modest, and declined the offer.
To honor Ralston in some way, and in keeping with the tradition of
naming places in California in Spanish (started by Spanish missionaries), the townspeople named it after Ralston's modesty.

City: El Segundo, California
Meaning: "The Second"
Details: The city was founded in 1911, when Standard Oil purchased
840 acres of farmland to drill on, and to house its employees. Standard
Oil had already built a similar settlement farther north, in Richmond,
California; this location was their second site in the state.

City: Amarillo, Texas
Meaning: "Yellow"
Details: There's a lot of yellow in the area around this Texas city.
Yellow wildflowers cover the area in late spring, and the banks of the
nearby Amarillo Lake and Amarillo Creek are bound by banks of
yellow soil. The city's official motto: "The yellow rose of Texas."

City: El Cajon, California
Meaning: "The Big Box"
Details: The city was settled by Europeans in 1821. It sits inside a deep
valley, which made the settlers feel enclosed, or boxed in.

City: El Paso, Texas
Meaning: "The Pass" or "The Crossing"
Details: Spanish explorer Don Juan de Oñate claimed the area for
Spain in 1598. After he crossed the Rio Grande, he named the area
"El Paso del Rio del Norte," or "the place where you cross the North
River."

City: Chino, California
Meaning: "Curly"
Details: When the U.S. Army surveyed the land in 1854, Lieutenant Amiel Whipple noticed the long, curly gama grass that grew wild in the area. The Spanish speakers called the grass *chino*, which means "curly," so Whipple called the entire valley Chino.

City: Escondido, California
Meaning: "Hidden"
Details: It sits in a valley, surrounded by large foothills.

City: Chico, California
Meaning: "Little"
Details: After arriving in the area in the 1840s, General John Bidwell purchased a parcel of land called Rancho Arroyo Chico, which means "Little Creek Ranch." (It's adjacent to Chico Creek.) The name of the city that now stands there was shortened to just Chico, which is also Spanish for "boy."

City: Las Vegas, Nevada
Meaning: "The Meadows"
Details: Literally an oasis in the middle of desert, springs and wild grasses naturally occur in the region that's now Sin City. In 1829, Mexican scout Rafael Rivera became the first nonnative to visit, and he named it.

City: Fresno, California
Meaning: "Ash Tree"
Details: The San Joaquin River was a major site for gold diggers during the California gold rush. Situated along that river are massive groves of ash trees—which gave the city its name in 1856.

City: Salinas, California
Meaning: "Salt Marsh"
Details: The city was built on and around salty marshland.

City: Reno, Nevada
Meaning: "Reindeer"
Details: "The biggest little city in the world" is actually named after Mexican-American War hero Jesse L. Reno, but it's worth mentioning that in Spanish his name means "reindeer."

Cats and Dogs? No, It's Raining...

Look—up in the sky! It's a bird! It's a plane! It's...a motorcycle?!

...CANNONBALLS

In December 2011, residents of the quiet Tassajara Creek neighborhood in Dublin, California, got a shock when a 30-pound cannonball smashed through the front door of a home, and shot up the stairs and into a bedroom where a woman and child were sleeping. It flew through the bedroom, blasted through the back wall of the house, and flew across the street, where it bounced off another house before finally smashing into a Toyota Sienna minivan parked in the driveway.

So where did the cannonball come from? The Alameda County Sheriff's Department bomb disposal range, about a half a mile away. That's where a crew from the *Mythbusters* TV show had been test-firing a cannon as part of an experiment to see whether cannonballs made of different materials can breach castle walls. The cannonball went astray when it struck a safety berm, giving it an "unforeseen bounce" that sent it flying out of the bombing range. Amazingly, no one was injured in the incident. The woman and child sleeping in the bedroom weren't even awakened when the cannonball smashed through their wall. "We feel really lucky and fortunate that, after a nearly perfect safety record over eight years, this mishap didn't lead to anybody being injured," *Mythbusters* host Adam Savage told the *Los Angeles Times* after visiting the neighborhood to apologize to the families in person.

...BIRDS

On New Year's Eve 2010, the residents of Beebe, Arkansas, were minutes away from ringing in the new year when thousands of blackbirds began plummeting to the earth across a one-square mile stretch near the campus of Arkansas State University. "We were inundated with calls from people screaming into the phone. Some of them thought it was the end of the world," Beebe police captain Eddie Cullum told the *Arkansas Democrat-Gazette*. "You just drive down the roadway, and it's littered with birds. You get off into the residential area, there's dead birds everywhere, on top of houses, in yards...It was really eerie."

Most of the affected birds were red-winged blackbirds, but other species, including at least one duck, were among the dead. Autopsies found evidence of "acute physical trauma," leading the state's Game and Fish Commission to suspect the birds had been killed by lightning or hail. An investigation later found that the blackbirds, which have poor night vision and don't ordinarily fly after dark, had been startled from their nighttime roosts by a resident setting off professional-grade fireworks. As many as 5,000 died after flying into buildings, trees, telephone poles, and each other. (When history repeated itself the following year, the Beebe police banned fireworks on New Year's Eve.)

...TOILETS

In May 2014, a Brazilian soccer fan named Paulo Ricardo Gomes da Silva died after being struck by a falling toilet outside a soccer stadium in the city of Recife. Unbeknownst to Da Silva, a short time earlier a riot had broken out inside the stadium between fans of the rival Santa Cruz and Parana teams. During the melee, some fans ripped toilets out of a stadium restroom and tossed them from the stands. One of them hit Da Silva in the head as he was walking into the stadium, killing him instantly.

...MOTORCYCLES

In April 2013, a Hollywood, Florida, man named Brett Krupnick, 40, was driving down Interstate 95 in his 1994 Nissan Sentra. He was on his way to get an oil change. Just as he passed beneath an exit ramp, he saw a large object falling toward his car from above. "By the time it came into my field of vision...I could tell it was a biker," Krupnick told the *Fort Lauderdale Sun-Sentinel*. Actually, it was just the bike, a 2004 Suzuki motorcycle. The biker, 22-year-old Ricardo Lambert, had been up on the exit ramp trying to negotiate a left turn when he lost control of the motorcycle. He managed to jump off just as it went over the guardrail and fell onto the hood of Krupnick's Sentra, causing it to burst into flames. The Sentra was destroyed in the fire and Lambert's Suzuki was totaled, but both men escaped with only minor injuries. "I'm not lucky," Krupnick told reporters. "I'm blessed."

...SKYDIVERS

The Yering Meadows Golf Course in Victoria, Australia, isn't far from the local airport, so it's not unusual to hear airplanes buzzing overhead. But when Ash Tainton went there to play a round with his father-in-law in August 2013, he heard something different near the 12th hole: a loud flapping sound coming from above. When he looked up he saw that the sound was coming from a tangled parachute. Attached to the chute—and plummeting to the ground at an alarming rate of speed—was a skydiving instructor identified in press accounts only by his first name, Bill, and his student, a first-time jumper named Brad Guy. "The parachute was open, but it wasn't working properly. They were horizontal, and they were whirling around, like water going down a drain. You could sense the sheer terror in everyone as we watched." Tainton told Australia's *Herald Sun*.

Bill and Brad almost certainly would have been killed had they not gotten a lucky break. Rather than slamming into the fairway or the putting green, they splashed down in the golf course's duck pond. And as soon as the skydivers landed, Tainton and other golfers waded out to them and helped them to shore. Both men suffered serious injuries but made full recoveries. Guy was so grateful for his deliverance that he had a parachuting man tattooed to his forearm. "I got it to remind myself I am lucky. I was part of a miracle and not many people can say that," he says.

...WINDOW WASHERS

In November 2014, a tech industry worker named Mohammad Alcozai was driving along Montgomery Street in San Francisco's financial district when something crashed onto the top of his Toyota Camry. It landed with enough force to cave in the roof and shatter the car's side and rear windows. The "something" turned out to be Pedro Perez, 58, a window washer who had been working on the roof of an 11-story bank building when he lost his balance and fell to the street 130 feet below. The fall should have been fatal and certainly would have been if Alcozai hadn't been driving by, but his Camry saved Perez's life by breaking his fall. The window washer spent more than a month in the hospital before being transferred to a rehabilitation facility to continue his recovery. His family told the *San Francisco Chronicle* that he was looking forward to returning to work, "just not as a window washer." As for the Camry, it was totaled, but Alcozai was unharmed. "I think God wanted me to be there just at the moment that poor man fell. It was a miracle that he was able to fall on my car," he told the *Chronicle*, "and it was a miracle that I was okay."

*　　*　　*

CELEBRITY-BRANDED HOT SAUCES

- Patti LaBelle's Lady Marmalade
- Johnny Winter's Screamin' Demon Hot Sauce
- Dexter Holland's (The Offspring) Gringo Bandito
- G. Love and Special Sauce Special Sauce
- Cheech (Cheech Marin) Waatsappenin' Hot Sauces
- Charlie Sheen's Tiger Blood Hot Sauce

Most expensive liquid on Earth: Scorpion venom. It sells for $38,858,507.46 per gallon.

Race-Day Superstitions

Many NASCAR, Formula One, and IndyCar drivers put themselves through some very peculiar rituals, in the belief that if they don't, bad luck will curse them to lose their race…or worse.

DON'T DRIVE A GREEN CAR

Just a few months after winning the Indianapolis 500 in 1920, Gaston Chevrolet died after crashing into a car he didn't see. His car had been painted green, so from then on it was considered bad luck to drive a green car. (Very few drivers went with green for decades, until 1952…when Larry Mann crashed his green Hudson Hornet into a wall, and died.)

DON'T EAT PEANUTS IN THE STANDS

In the early days of NASCAR (before World War II), most races were held at local fairgrounds, and pit crews were stationed in the shade, right underneath the grandstands. Fans sat up there and ate peanuts, and dropped shells into the pits…and the cars. Wrecks at these races almost always had evidence of peanut shells, leading to the idea that peanuts were a bringer of doom.

DON'T SHAVE BEFORE A RACE

NASCAR driver Doc MacKenzie got married in 1936 and shaved off his long beard for the ceremony. On his first race afterward, at the Wisconsin State Fair, he crashed his car and died. Fellow driver Ted Horn later quipped, "Doc shouldn't have shaved. That jinxed him."

DON'T DRESS YOUR LEFT SIDE FIRST

Many NASCAR drivers past and present believe that the right side is luckier than the left side, so that's how they dress on game day: underwear, pants, socks, shirt sleeves, and gloves all go on the right appendage before the left.

DON'T USE THE NO. 13

The number 13, in NASCAR as in so many places, is considered unlucky. It was rarely used as a car number until former Miami Dolphins quarterback Dan Marino became a team co-owner, and insisted his car use his old jersey number: 13. (In the 400 or so races where a 13 car has

A traffic light in Dresden, Germany, has been red for 28 years.

raced, it has finished in the top five only eight times.)

DON'T HANDLE $50 BILLS ON RACE DAY

Racer Joe Weatherly was killed at Riverside Raceway (in Riverside, California) in 1964. Among his personal effects, two $50 bills were reportedly found in his pocket. Racers and crews have avoided fifties ever since.

MORE SUPERSTITIONS

• Austrian Formula One driver **Alex Wurz** always raced in mismatched shoes.

• **Dale Earnhardt** left every building in and around the racetrack from the same door he came in.

• **Davey Allison** watched a movie the night before every NASCAR race. If he won the race, he'd watch the same movie the night before his next race, until he lost, at which point he started in with a new movie.

• Just before climbing into his car at the start of each NASCAR race, **Sterling Marlin** ate a bologna sandwich.

• Veteran IndyCar team owner **Carl Haas** smokes and chews on cigars during races, but when he headed up Mario Andretti's team in the 1980s and 1990s, he had a particular tradition: While Andretti climbed into the car, Haas would dance around the car while shaking his cigar at it.

• **Alberto Ascari** was a champion Formula One driver in the 1950s. He insisted on carrying a briefcase to each race. It contained his "lucky" racing helmet, gloves, goggles, and T-shirt, all blue. He wouldn't let anybody else handle that briefcase.

• When he was just starting out as a Formula One driver in the mid-1990s, **David Coulthard** wore the same pair of boxer shorts for every race. (We presume he washed them between races.)

• Early NASCAR star **Edward "Fireball" Roberts** would not allow his picture to be taken before a race.

• **Mark Martin's** superstition: no superstitions. He claimed to have once taped a four-leaf clover inside his car during a race at the North Wilkesboro Speedway in North Carolina…and he somehow crashed the car before the race even started. Now he avoids any sort of lucky charm.

Celebrity Anagrams

Rearranging the letters of a celebrity's name may not really provide better descriptions of those people...but they are pretty funny.

VIN DIESEL *becomes*...I END LIVES

HOWARD STERN *becomes*...TRASH WONDER

ALANIS MORISSETTE *becomes*...IT'S NASAL, TIRESOME

TOM HIDDLESTON *becomes*...ODD SILENT MOTH

BARRY MANILOW *becomes*...LIBRARY WOMAN

GLORIA ESTEFAN *becomes*...LARGE FAT NOISE

LEONARDO DICAPRIO *becomes*...PERIODIC ANAL ODOR

SIGOURNEY WEAVER *becomes*...REVIEWS ANGER YOU

PHILIP SEYMOUR HOFFMAN becomes...A FINELY FRUMPISH OOMP

HILLARY CLINTON *becomes*...ONLY I CAN THRILL

CARLY SIMON *becomes*...MOANS LYRIC

CARLOS SANTANA *becomes*...CARNAL SONATAS

AMY POEHLER *becomes*...MAYO HELPER

BRIAN WILSON *becomes*...SLOW IN BRAIN

JOHN MAYER becomes...ENJOY HARM

MELISSA MCCARTHY *becomes*...MYTHICAL SCREAMS

ERIC CLAPTON *becomes*...NARCOLEPTIC

SEINFELD *becomes*...SNIDE ELF

WILLIAM SHATNER becomes...NARWHAL ELITISM

RYAN GOSLING becomes...SLY GROANING

TV ads directed at children are illegal in Norway.

Random Origins

Once again the BRI asks and answers:
Where did all this stuff come from?

TATER TOTS

Ontario, Oregon, is located near the border of Idaho, a state known for potatoes. That's where brothers Nephi and Golden Grigg started the Ore-Ida frozen potato company in 1952. Their first product: french fries. But they didn't know what to do with all the leftover scraps, so they mashed them up with some flour and formed them into little cylinders. At first they used the fried potato balls to feed cattle, but when the Griggs discovered that they actually tasted good, they decided to sell them to people. But they still needed a name. In a company-wide contest, Clora Lay Orton came up with "tater tots." The tots hit the market in 1956, and today are Ore-Ida's most popular product.

TUBE MEN

These inflatable dancing puppets are taking over the world…one car dealership at a time. They were invented for the 1996 Olympic Games in Atlanta, Georgia, by Peter Minshall, a renowned Carnival artist from Trinidad and Tobago. Minshall was on the team responsible for the opening ceremonies, and came up with the idea of using inflatable tubes as screens on which images could be projected. But it didn't work because the picture wasn't clear. Then inspiration struck: "I sketched two of the tubes," he told Trinidad and Tobago's *Guardian* newspaper, "I saw two legs, two arms; I thought: My God, with a wind source, we could create a huge, incredible, undulating dancing figure." Minshall enlisted Doron Gazit, an Israeli conceptual artist known for his work with wind tubes, to design and build the "Tall Boys" for the Games. But a few years later, Gazit patented the tube men, and created a business licensing and selling them. Still, even though someone else is profiting from them, Minshall is proud of his creation: "Can you imagine how I feel when I see a tall guy dancing up a storm by a gas station? A part of me can't help but feel delight."

DUCT TAPE

During World War II, an Illinois woman named Vesta Stoudt got a job at the Green River Ordnance Plant packing boxes with cartridges for grenade launchers. But she noticed a problem: it could be difficult for soldiers to open the boxes because of the paper tape that held the flaps in place. More often than not, the tape came off without releasing the flaps, forcing the soldiers to use a knife (or their teeth) to get the box open. The precious seconds it took to do this could spell disaster. And because Stoudt had two sons fighting in the war, she was extra worried. She told her superiors that a better tape—one made from cloth instead of paper—would work better. Her superiors agreed…but never did anything about it. Unwilling to give up, Stoudt decided to appeal to the commander-in-chief: President Franklin D. Roosevelt. "I have two sons out there somewhere," she wrote in a letter. "You have sons in the service also. We can't let them down by giving them a box of cartridges that takes a minute or more to open, the enemy taking their lives, that could have been saved had the box been taped with a strong cloth tape that can be opened in a split second." Roosevelt agreed and forwarded her letter to the War Production Board, which tasked Johnson & Johnson with developing the tape. Their technicians came up with a rubber-based adhesive applied to cotton duck cloth. Soldiers called it "duck tape." After the war, Johnson & Johnson sold it in hardware stores. By the 1950s, it had become a go-to tool for duct work, and to match the ducts themselves, it was colored gray. Stoudt received a war workers award for "outstanding service to the nation's war effort."

THE BLUE MAN GROUP

In the late 1980s, three friends from Manhattan—Chris Wink, Phil Stanton, and Matt Goldman—wanted to do something that no one had ever done before. After they noticed three punk rockers walk past three men in Armani suits—all without acknowledging each other—they wondered what it would take to get a reaction out of New Yorkers. So they decided to walk around town in blue makeup. Why blue? "There really isn't an explanation," said Goldman. "Chris dug up a picture that he drew when he was five years old, and it had three blue men in it. And I had a thing in my wallet for years with a blue tribe in South America. I don't know why it was there; I never put pictures in my wallet." At first, they merely went to nightclubs as Blue Men, but then they started working on an act: they made percussion instruments out of PVC pipes, developed a musical-comedy show with no dialogue, and landed their first official gig in 1991 at La MaMa, an off-off-Broadway theater. That led to a permanent stage show at the Astor Place Theatre. The Blue Man Group has since recorded several albums, contributed to film scores, made their own 3-D movie, and has several troupes performing all over the world.

The Ketchup 'N' Fries plant gets its name from the fact that it grows both tomatoes and potatoes.

Owned by Buffett

Through his holding company, Berkshire Hathaway, businessman Warren Buffett has amassed a fortune worth over $65 billion, making him the second richest man in America (#1: Bill Gates). Buffett believes in diversification—investing in many businesses across a variety of industries—which is why his holdings include Russell Athletic, the Buffalo News, Helzberg Diamonds, portions of MasterCard, Costco, Coca-Cola, DirecTV, and much more. Here are a few of the companies owned by "the Oracle of Omaha."

Blue Chip Stamps. Remember when stores gave away stamps with purchases, and families saved them up to trade for housewares? That's Blue Chip's business. When Buffett started investing in it in 1970, it was worth $126 million. Trading stamps have virtually disappeared, but Buffett still owns the company, which now generates just $26,000 in annual revenue.

See's Candies. A much more lucrative subsidiary of Blue Chip Stamps is this boxed candy company.

Dairy Queen. In 1997, Buffett bought 99 percent of the 6,400-location ice cream and burger restaurant chain.

Kirby. Buffett owns this vacuum cleaner company. (Kirby still sells its products door-to-door…and *only* door-to-door.)

BNSF Railroad. In 2014, Buffett, a model train enthusiast, paid $15 billion to buy the Burlington Northern Santa Fe Railroad.

World Book. Most students use the Internet to research their papers these days, but print encyclopedias still exist, and Buffett owns *World Book*, the biggest name in the business.

The Pampered Chef. This "multilevel marketing" company, like Avon and Mary Kay, uses sales agents to sell kitchen tools to their friends door-to-door or via parties.

Oriental Trading Company. You might have found a copy of this company's mail-order catalog in your mailbox. They sell party supplies, toys, and novelties. Buffett acquired it in 2012.

Fruit of the Loom. In 2002, Buffett bought 99 percent of your underwear (or at least the company that makes it).

More companies owned by Warren Buffett and Berkshire Hathaway:
Benjamin Moore Paint • GEICO Insurance • Duracell Batteries

Is Boston from Boston?

Lots of rock bands name themselves after places. Sometimes it's the place they got started, sometimes not. Here's where some of these bands are really from.

- **CHICAGO ("Saturday in the Park"):** Chicago, Illinois

- **ASIA ("Heat of the Moment"):** London

- **OHIO PLAYERS ("Love Rollercoaster"):** Dayton, Ohio

- **AMERICA ("Sister Golden Hair"):** London

- **KANSAS ("Dust in the Wind"):** Topeka, Kansas

- **THE MANHATTANS ("Kiss and Say Goodbye"):** Jersey City, NJ

- **GEORGIA SATELLITES ("Keep Your Hands to Yourself"):** Atlanta, Georgia

- **EUROPE ("The Final Countdown"):** Upplands Väsby, Sweden

- **OAK RIDGE BOYS ("Elvira"):** Oak Ridge, Tennessee

- **CHILLIWACK ("My Girl"):** Vancouver, British Columbia, 63 miles from Chilliwack, B.C.

- **THE OZARK MOUNTAIN DAREDEVILS ("Jackie Blue"):** Springfield, Missouri—about an hour's drive from the Ozark Mountains

- **BERLIN ("Take My Breath Away"):** Los Angeles, California

- **BOSTON ("More Than a Feeling"):** Boston, Massachusetts

- **TEXAS ("Say What You Want"):** Glasgow, Scotland

- **ALABAMA ("Love in the First Degree"):** Fort Payne, Alabama

- **NAZARETH ("Love Hurts"):** Dunfermline, Scotland

- **MC5 ("Kick Out the Jams"):** The Motor City 5 formed in Lincoln Park, Michigan, a suburb of Detroit, "the Motor City."

Sound familiar? Male kangaroos flex their biceps to impress females.

Play Phone

When you're seeing a play, shut off your phone…or else.

THE WRATH OF PATTI

Over her 50-year theater career, Patti LuPone has become almost as famous for calling out poorly behaved theatergoers from the stage as she is for starring in Broadway classics like *Evita*. During a 2009 performance of *Gypsy*, she stopped mid-song to yell "WHO DO YOU THINK YOU ARE?!" at an audience member who was taking a flash photograph in the middle of the show. Months later in a Las Vegas production of *Evita*, LuPone was in the middle of belting out "Don't Cry For Me Argentina" when she noticed a bright light from the audience. She stopped the orchestra, then berated the audience member as the rest of the crowd went wild for her rant. You'd think that by now, audience members would know how to behave when LuPone was on stage. But in 2015, she spotted a woman in the front row of *Shows for Days* texting. Without missing a beat—and staying in character—LuPone snatched the phone as she delivered her scene exit line and took it with her backstage. She returned it after curtain call.

TO SNAP OR NOT TO SNAP

Academy Award nominee Benedict Cumberbatch got his start performing plays in England. After his movie success, he made a triumphant return to the stage in a 2015 production of *Hamlet* at London's Barbican Centre. Dozens of young Cumberbatch fans watched the shows through their smartphone cameras, which they held up to snap pictures or video. The lights were so distracting that Cumberbatch even had to restart the "To be or not to be" soliloquy during an early performance. After too many disturbing instances, the actor was forced to break character and beg fans to put away their phones…but not before recording his plea on their phones, and spreading it via social media.

NO OUTLET

In 2015, 19-year-old Nick Silvestri of Long Island took his visiting cousins to a performance of the Broadway show *Hand of God*. They went out for drinks first, and as the show started, the tipsy student began looking for an outlet to charge his dying cell phone. He spotted one on the stage set, and jumped onto the stage mid-performance and tried to plug his phone into the nonfunctioning outlet. Security guards swiftly reached Silvestri and ejected him from the theater.

Underwear in the News

Andy Warhol once said, "In the future, everyone will be famous for 15 minutes." Make that—everyone and their underwear.

NAKED TRUTH

If you're a fan of pro tennis and thought you knew everything about Andre Agassi, who played from 1986 to 2006, his 2010 autobiography probably revealed at least one thing that you didn't know: namely, that from 1999 onward, the tennis great played all of his matches sans underpants. Agassi stumbled into the "commando" phase of his career by accident, when he forgot to bring his underwear to a match during the 1999 French Open. His coach offered to lend his own underwear, but Agassi declined (wouldn't you?) and played with nothing on under his tennis shorts. He won that match and went on to win the French Open, something no other American (as of 2016) has done since. "After that it was a case of 'If it ain't broke, don't fix it.' It actually feels good," Agassi told an interviewer in 2010.

FEEL THE BERN

Vermont senator Bernie Sanders probably isn't the first politician to have his face emblazoned on a pair of underpants, but he may well be the first one so honored by his *own supporters*. The gesture was inspired by a *Saturday Night Live* comedy sketch in which Larry David, playing the 2016 Democratic presidential candidate, tells the audience, "I own one pair of underwear, that's it. Some of these billionaires, they've got three, four pairs!" The sketch inspired three of Sanders's home state admirers to create Bernie's Briefs, which feature a cartoon of the candidate's face silk-screened onto the backside of white cotton briefs along with the slogan "Feel the Bern."

"Every one of us has voted for Bernie in every election that he's run in, and we continue to be supporters of what he's doing," Bernie's Briefs cocreator Todd Bailey told *USA Today* in 2015. Sold online, the $15-a-pair underpants were so popular that the creators added women's styles to their product line. Ten percent of the company's profits were donated to the Yellow Ribbon Fund, a charity that supports injured veterans. So what does Bernie Sanders think of the underpants honor? "It cracks me up."

PANTY RAID

A Menifee, California, man named Arturo Galvan may be history's first—and creepiest—social media underwear bandit. Police say that beginning in about 2014, Galvan, 44, frequented public gathering places in Fullerton, where he searched online for social media posts being created by people sitting nearby. When he found one, he searched the person's online photographs, looking for attached GPS data that revealed where they lived. Then he went to their homes and burglarized them, stealing men's and women's underwear along with laptops, consumer electronics, jewelry, and other items. Fullerton police finally caught up with him in December 2015 after a local resident reported a prowler in the neighborhood. After a three-hour search, Galvin was arrested and booked on suspicion of peeping, prowling, burglary, and other charges. After serving a search warrant on his home, police found a pile of stolen underpants in the garage next to his home. The judge set bail at $1 million, and at last report Galvan was still in custody and awaiting trial.

SEEING RED

In early 2016, Japanese retailers were stocking up on lucky red underwear in advance of the Year of the Monkey, which began in early February. The Japanese word for monkey is *saru*, which sounds like the word for "go away." Tradition has it that wearing red underpants during the Year of the Monkey can make diseases and other bad things go away. Red skivvies printed with slogans like *Yanakoto Saru* "Unhappy Things, Go Away" and *Mayoi Saru* "Indecision Go Away" are popular New Year's gifts for men and women alike.

One person whose red underwear did *not* bring good luck was Taykim Ross, 18, a Long Island, New York, man. Police say that in June 2015 Ross burglarized an apartment in Hempstead and made off with $200 in cash, electronics, and a pair of Air Jordan sneakers. As he was leaving the scene of the crime, Ross stopped to try on the sneakers. That's when a neighbor snapped a photo of him bending over as he tried on the shoes, his back facing the camera and his bright red boxer shorts showing over the waistband of his saggy jeans.

A short time later, a police officer canvassing the neighborhood saw a young man—Ross—in front of another apartment, taking out the garbage. "I just happened to sit in the squad car for a moment and in my rear-view mirror about 500 yards away I see a guy bending over putting garbage bags down and what do I see? Lo and behold, I see red underwear standing out," Officer Russell Harris told CBS News. Harris stopped Ross and arrested him. The stolen items were soon recovered and returned to the victim. So how did Ross respond when Officer Harris told him it was his red underwear that got him caught? "He actually kind of laughed," Harris said. "If he had gone home and put on a belt, I probably wouldn't have noticed him."

BREATHTAKING

In February 2014, the police department in the city of Jaca (in north-eastern Spain) came under fire for using footage of underwear models as training videos in CPR courses. Citizens who enrolled in the classes were warned that they would be seeing videos of people in their underwear, but many assumed they'd be part of some kind of "post-accident scenario." Instead, they watched a series of YouTube videos called Super Sexy CPR, which contained "highly erotic" scenes, including one of a male model wearing only an athletic supporter performing the Heimlich maneuver on a woman wearing a bra and panties, and another of a woman in lingerie performing CPR on another woman in lingerie. "We apologize for showing these videos, which were inappropriate," a police spokesperson told reporters. "They won't be used again."

HOLD IT

Owen Coffee, a PhD student at Australia's University of Queensland, studies endangered loggerhead sea turtles. In 2015, he was involved in a three-year project to discover the turtles' most popular feeding areas around Moreton Bay, north of Brisbane. He planned to analyze their poop to see what they'd eaten, then locate the source of the food. But because they're sea turtles, their poop dispersed in the water before Coffee could collect it. So he started catching turtles in the wild and holding them in a tank until they pooped, and then releasing them back into the bay. Only problem: the poop samples also dispersed in the tank water, making it difficult to gather enough material to be useful.

Coffee solved his problem by fashioning diaperlike underwear for the turtles to hold the poop in place until he could collect it. The underwear, in turn, is secured in place with custom-fitted turtle bathing suits that Coffee stitches together from secondhand shirts that he buys at a local thrift shop. The turtles—which reach nearly three feet in length and can weigh more than 260 pounds—don't seem to mind the swimsuits or the underwear, and as soon as they poop, Coffee removes the garments, collects his sample, and releases the reptiles back into Moreton Bay. He hopes to use his research to protect the endangered turtles' most popular feeding areas from human encroachment.

*   *   *

"I wanna make a jigsaw puzzle that's 40,000 pieces. And when you finish it, it says 'go outside.'"

—**Demetri Martin**

Who won the Cold War? Hint: Prague's Museum of Communism has a McDonald's next door to it.

Are You a Genius?

According to the latest research, if you exhibit any of these behaviors,
you just might be a very smart person.

Talk to yourself? According to a study in the *Quarterly Journal of Experimental Psychology*, talking to yourself gives your brain a workout much the way lifting weights keeps muscles in shape. Researchers ran an experiment in a grocery store, where subjects who repeatedly said the names of items they were seeking out loud found them with greater ease than subjects who were silent. As psychologist Linda Sapadin explains, "Talking out loud focuses your attention, controls runaway emotions, and screens out distractions."

Neurotic? As fans of Woody Allen or Larry David would probably attest, neurosis fuels great writing. But now there's real science to explain why anxiety-riddled self-loathers are such good storytellers. According to Dr. Adam Perkins from King's College in London, neurotics have what is essentially a "panic button" in the temporal lobe of their brains. And those who suffer from abnormal fear and anxiety also tend to have overactive imaginations that make living with oneself a chore, but also give them the fuel to create works of art.

Distracted by noise? It's something of a cliché that coffee shops in Los Angeles and New York are filled with writers working on their screenplays or novels. How can anybody write in such a noisy place? They can't. Scientists at Northwestern University published a new study on "sensory gating" and the link between noise sensitivity and creative thinking. They found that those test subjects who were easily distracted by the noise and unable to filter it out were, by and large, more creative than their counterparts.

Tortured artist? Mad scientist? It turns out these aren't just stereotypes. Kay Redfield Jamison, a psychologist at Johns Hopkins School of Medicine, says that the findings of nearly 30 scientific studies prove there's a link between mental disorder, intelligence, and creativity. In a study of 700,000 Swedish teenagers, scientists found that 16-year-olds with genius-level intelligence were four times as likely to develop bipolar disorder. Another study found that bipolar sufferers coming out of deep depression tended to be more creative. Jamison, who is bipolar, believes it's essential to study "a potential link with so many intellectual and clinical implications," but warns that these are "devastating illnesses that you don't want to romanticize."

What is *superfetation*? Getting pregnant while already pregnant. (Relax—it's rare in humans.)

Cold Comfort

*Did you know that you can keep eggs in your freezer? (There's a trick to it.)
Here are some tips on how to freeze foods you probably thought couldn't
be frozen, and how to better freeze the stuff you're already freezing,
preventing waste and saving money in the process.*

FRESH VEGETABLES

• Before freezing, chop raw vegetables to the size you are likely to use when cooking. Thawed vegetables are more difficult to chop.

• Vegetables tend to lose color, favor, texture, and even vitamins when they're frozen, thanks to the activity of enzymes in the veggies. *Blanching* the vegetables (immersing them in boiling water for a short period of time) before freezing interrupts the activity of the enzymes, and will keep the frozen vegetables fresher longer.

• Blanching times vary from $1\frac{1}{2}$ minutes for peas and 11 minutes for large ears of corn; consult a cookbook for the correct amount of time for the vegetable you want to freeze.

• After blanching, quickly immerse the vegetables in cool water to prevent them from overcooking.

• Leafy greens, tomatoes, and watery vegetables like zucchini and squash can be frozen without blanching. If you plan on making zucchini bread, grate the zucchini before you freeze it.

GROUND MEAT

• Ground meat is suitable for freezing, but the Styrofoam tray covered with plastic wrap that it comes in is not. The container leaves too much air in the package, causing freezer burn.

• Remove ground meat from the container and place it in a plastic freezer bag, taking care to squeeze as much air out of the bag as possible before placing it in the freezer. Press the bag of meat as flat as you can before freezing—the flatter the meat, the faster it freezes, preserving quality.

• If you want individual servings, lay the unfrozen bag of meat flat on the kitchen counter and press a chopstick or the handle of a wooden spoon lengthwise against the outside of the bag to create indentations that divide the meat into single-sized squares. Now when you need some but not all of the meat, you can easily snap off as many squares as you need and return the rest to the freezer, instead of having to thaw out the entire bag.

EGGS

• Eggs expand while freezing and should not be frozen in the shell. Instead, beat raw eggs just until the whites and yolks have blended together, then pour the mixture into an ice cube tray and freeze. Each compartment of a standard ice cube tray will hold about one egg's worth of the mixture. When the eggs have frozen, they can be popped out of the ice cube tray and stored in a freezer bag for up to a year.

• Yolks and whites can be separated before freezing if you expect to use them separately. Separated whites will freeze just fine as they are, but separated yolks can become gelatinous over time. To prevent this, beat in 1½ teaspoons of sugar (if you plan to use the yolks in a dessert) or ⅛ teaspoon of salt (for other dishes) for every four egg yolks before freezing. Thaw in the refrigerator overnight before using.

THE CUBIST MOVEMENT

• Fresh herbs and spices can also be frozen in ice cube trays. Fill each compartment about two-thirds full with chopped fresh herbs or spices and cover with your choice of water, chicken or beef stock, olive oil, or melted unsalted butter before freezing. When the cubes are frozen, remove them from the tray and store them in freezer bags.

• Two more candidates for ice cube freezing: coffee and leftover wine (for cooking). Coffee cubes can be used to keep iced coffee cold without watering it down. Next time a recipe calls for ¼ cup of wine, instead of opening a new bottle (and getting stuck with more leftover wine), thaw out as many cubes as you need.

MILK

• If you don't think you can use all of your milk before it spoils, freeze it—just be sure to pour off a few inches of milk before freezing if the container is full. Milk expands when it freezes, so if you don't leave some air at the top of the container, it may burst, spilling the unfrozen milk all over the inside of the freezer. Label the container with the date (and the milk's expiration date if you freeze it in a container other than the milk carton) so that you'll know how long the thawed milk will last before it spoils. The milk will keep in the freezer for up to three months; when you're ready to use it, thaw it in the refrigerator overnight.

• During freezing, the fat in the milk may separate from the liquid. Shaking the milk in its container, or mixing it in a blender before using it, will help to redistribute the fat and restore the milk's familiar texture.

• If you plan to use small amounts of milk over time, such as when baking, milk, too, can be frozen in ice cube trays and thawed out individually as needed. Milk cubes can also be added to fresh milk to keep it cold without watering it down as the cubes melt.

The opah is the only known warm-blooded fish.

ODDS AND ENDS

- **Avocados.** Whole avocados do not freeze well, but they can be frozen after they've been peeled and pitted. Puree the pulp, then add ½ tablespoon of lemon juice for each avocado before freezing in an airtight container. Be sure to leave some air space at the top of the container, because the puree will expand as it freezes.

- **Potato Chips.** If you're the kind of person who stocks up on potato chips when they're on sale, freeze the unopened bags for up to three months to extend their life beyond their expiration date. Opened bags will also keep longer in the freezer without going stale.

- **Sauces and Condiments.** These can be frozen in freezer bags. Use snack-sized bags and freeze them flat, so that when you need some sauce for cooking you can open the freezer bag and snap off as much of the frozen sauce as you need. Sauces that are to be thickened with flour or cornstarch should be frozen before those ingredients are added. Add the flour or cornstarch after the sauce has thawed.

- **Chicken Breasts, Pork Chops, etc.** Marinate in your favorite sauce and freeze individually. That way, when you want a quick dinner, they can be easily thawed out and cooked.

- **Oatmeal.** If you don't have time to cook oatmeal before leaving for work and don't like the taste of instant, cook up a big batch of oatmeal when you do have time, then pour it into a muffin tin and freeze as individual portions. After the oatmeal has frozen, pop the portions out of the tin and store them in a freezer bag. Now when you want oatmeal in the morning, just put one or more of the muffin portions in the microwave and you'll have hot oatmeal in less time than it takes to make instant.

- **Homemade Soup Stock.** Stick an empty freezer bag or milk carton in the freezer. Whenever you have celery stalks, vegetable peelings, chicken bones, and other scraps, put them in the container instead of throwing them out. When the container is full, thaw it out and use the accumulated scraps to make your homemade stock. Once you've made your stock, refreeze it in individual portions in muffin tins or ice cube trays so that you'll only need to thaw out as much as you need.

CHEESE

- Rule of thumb when freezing cheeses: if the cheese is hard enough to be grated, it will freeze well. If it isn't, it won't. Some hard cheeses may become crumbly or mealy after freezing, but they won't lose their flavor.
- Cut large blocks of cheese into smaller portions or shred before freezing, so that you will only need to thaw out as much cheese as you need.

MORE TIPS

• Be careful not to overload your freezer with too many unfrozen foods at once—fill it with no more than three pounds of unfrozen food for every cubic foot of storage space in the freezer. Any more than that will slow freezing, making the food mushy when it thaws out. Too much warm food in the freezer may also thaw out nearby items that are already frozen, compromising their quality as well.

• When freezing a lot of food, space the items apart from one another so that cold air will circulate around each item. Lowering the freezer control to -10°F will help the foods freeze more rapidly and maintain their quality. Pressing freezer bags flat before freezing them also speeds freezing time.

• Frozen foods will last longer if they are stored at a colder temperature, so once the food has frozen, keep the freezer set at 0°F or lower.

*   *   *

THE MEASURE OF SUCCESS

Fannie Farmer was born in 1857, the eldest child of an educated family in Boston, and grew up with the expectation that she would go to college. After a stroke left her partially paralyzed at the age of 16, she found herself unable to continue her studies. However, Farmer was able to get around well enough to cook. So she focused on that, eventually turning her parents' home into a boardinghouse that became known for its excellent food. When she was 30, she enrolled in the Boston Cooking School, where she learned about the "domestic sciences," including cooking, but also home management, sanitation, and nutrition. She did so well at the school that she was hired as a teacher, and eventually became the principal and an author of cookbooks. Her first—and most famous—book, *The Boston Cooking-School Cook Book*, was published in 1896. It contained more than 1,800 recipes, but most important, it formalized measurements, using standardized cups and spoons, where previous cookbooks usually described measurements as guesses or estimates, such as "a piece of butter the size of an egg." The publishers of the book didn't think it would be a success, so they made Farmer pay for the initial run of 3,000 copies. As a result, she retained the copyright, and most of the profits. Lucky for Farmer. It drew tremendous acclaim and became extremely popular, selling millions of copies and making Farmer rich. The book came to be known as the Fannie Farmer cookbook (later editions were actually retitled *The Fannie Farmer Cookbook*), and remained in print for more than 100 years.

Regardless of what color they are, all Froot Loops have the same flavor.

Trippy Shakespeare

William Shakespeare has often been called the greatest writer in the English language because his plays have such universal themes that they remain relevant hundreds of years after they were written. Case in point: these unconventional adaptations of the Bard's works.

SCOTLAND, PA
This movie, made in 2001, is a dark comic version of *Macbeth*. But it's not about the machinations of the Scottish royal family—it's about a power struggle over a family-owned burger joint in a small Pennsylvania town. Instead of Dunsinane Castle, the action takes place at Duncan's Café. And Macbeth is Joe Mac, Macduff is police detective Ernie McDuff, and the three witches are three hippies.

GREEN EGGS AND HAMLET
Subtitled "The Scrambled History of the Prince of Denmark," this 1995 short film by visual effects artist Mike O'Neal is a retelling of *Hamlet*, performed in the style of Dr. Seuss. Sample lines: "I ask to be or not to be / that is the question I ask of me. / This sullied life, it makes me shudder. / My uncle's f**ing dear sweet mother!"

FIFTEEN-MINUTE HAMLET
Playwright Tom Stoppard is the Bard of Shakespeare variants. In 1966, he wrote a hit play called *Rosencrantz and Guildenstern Are Dead*, which is *Hamlet* told through the point of view of two of the original play's minor characters, and he also cowrote the screenplay for *Shakespeare in Love*. In 1976, he published *Fifteen-Minute Hamlet*, a frantic condensing of the four-hour play. The title is a little inaccurate, though: it consists of a 13-minute *Hamlet* and then an even faster two-minute version.

THE COMPLETE WORKS OF WILLIAM SHAKESPEARE (ABRIDGED)
This popular play, written in 2000, is performed hundreds of times a year around the world at the high school, college, and professional level. The premise: three actors, portraying "The Reduced Shakespeare Company," perform extremely short versions of all Shakespeare's 37 plays, and play dozens of characters each…in just 88 minutes.

TROMEO & JULIET
Troma Entertainment has a cult following for its comic horror movies, such as *Class of Nuke 'Em High* and *The Toxic Avenger*. In 1996, it also

---

Our favorite unit of measure of wine: the "butt load"—equal to two hogsheads, or 126 gallons.

took on Shakespeare…sort of. The plot: Tromeo Que (Will Keenan) works at a tattoo parlor in 1990s New York and is addicted to watching Shakespeare-themed dirty movies while Juliet (Jane Jensen) is engaged to a meat tycoon, having an illicit affair with her servant, and after her star-crossed romance with Tromeo ends badly, she turns into a cow. (*Tromeo & Juliet* was cowritten by James Gunn. Ten years later, he cowrote and directed *Guardians of the Galaxy*.)

ROMEO MUST DIE (2000)

It's another movie version of *Romeo and Juliet*, but instead of prominent families fighting for control of medieval Verona, it's Asian and African American street gangs battling to control the present-day streets of Oakland, California. Han Sing (Jet Li) stands in for Romeo, and Trish O'Day (Aaliyah) is the Juliet. Good news! While the original Shakespeare play has zero martial arts fighting sequences, *Romeo Must Die* has dozens. Another difference: it ends with the Romeo and Juliet characters living happily ever after.

ALFRED HITCHCOCK'S UNMADE HAMLET

Who but a master filmmaker like Hitchcock would even suggest a version of *Hamlet* that abandons all of the Shakespearean dialogue? Hitchcock planned to make a movie version of *Hamlet* set in 1940s England, using modern English, and starring Cary Grant. The film was never made for a number of reasons: Grant was 42 years old and thought he was too old for the title role. Also, the production was sued when a British literature professor learned that Hitchcock planned to use a modern English *Hamlet* adaptation that he (the professor) had written without offering to pay or credit him.

SHAKESPEARE WITHOUT WORDS (2001–PRESENT)

Updating the language is one thing, but the Virginia-based Synetic Theater group does away with Shakespeare's dialogue entirely. They present Shakespeare plays as "visual poetry," a mixture of dance, vibrant sets, and live music that's something closer to mime or ballet than live theater. They've already presented versions of *The Tempest*, *King Lear*, *The Taming of the Shrew*, and *Antony and Cleopatra*.

TINY NINJA THEATER'S MACBETH

First presented at the 2000 New York International Fringe Festival, it's the original text of Shakespeare's tragedy, but performed like it's never been performed before: By a cloaked pair of hands manipulating inch-tall ninja action figures along with "assorted dime store figures" on a "briefcase-sized stage." Voices were provided by actors in the wings. Only 25 people at a time could watch the performance.

Behold...the Megaweb

It's no late-night creature feature: megawebs are real...and really big.

EXTREME SPIDER SITUATION

In 2009, a five-person team of entomologists and arachnologists entered the Back River Wastewater Treatment Plant in Baltimore. They'd been called in to help assess what plant managers called "an extreme spider situation." Once inside the building, the team members couldn't believe their eyes: spiderwebs stretched over a distance as long as four football fields. These weren't spindly webs, either—they were long, thick sheets, so dense that one section even pulled an eight-foot-long hanging light fixture out of place. After removing web samples and documenting the spiders' activity, the team estimated that there were probably *millions* of spiders living in the open-sided treatment plant. The experts admitted, "We were unprepared for the sheer scale of the spider population."

What the Baltimore team had encountered was a "megaweb." As the name suggests, it's a spiderweb that covers acres and can contain hundreds of thousands, or even millions, of spiders. Megawebs have probably been around as long as spiders have and are often found in the tropics, but they're rare in the United States. The first one wasn't documented until 2007, when a worker in Lake Tawakoni State Park in Wills Point, Texas, stumbled across it while he was mowing the trails. Until that discovery, it hadn't occurred to arachnologists that megawebs might exist in the United States. As entomologist Dr. Michael Merchant put it, "Sometimes it's easy to miss something right in front of your nose unless you know what you're looking for."

STRETCH SPIDERS AT WORK

Intrigued by this new discovery, the scientists began collecting samples and watching the spiders. There were many varieties of spiders in the megawebs, but one kind seemed to be doing most of the construction: *Tetragnatha*, or the long-jawed orb weaver. Long-jawed orb weavers are sometimes called "stretch spiders" because they stretch their thin, overly long front legs straight out in front of their bodies while they sit in their webs. They're common spiders, but arachnologists were astounded that orb weavers were responsible for the megawebs. Although some spiders in Central and South America make a habit out of living together in huge webs, long-jawed orb weavers don't. Not only that, but the type of webs they were spinning in the megawebs had changed. The spiders were no longer making the orb-shaped webs that gave them their name. Instead, they were producing massive sheets of webbing. No one had ever seen such changes in arachnid habits.

WHAT IT TAKES TO BUILD A MEGAWEB

So what accounted for this new behavior? Food. The summer had been unusually rainy and mosquito and midge populations surge when there's more standing water for them to breed in. By August, when long-jawed orb weavers were most active, the mosquitoes and midges were swarming nightly. Result: The spiders simply congregated where their prey was. With so much food around, orb weavers didn't need to worry about other spiders taking their meal, so they were willing to live side by side in the hundreds of thousands. (If food had been scarce, they would have stuck to their usual one-spider-per-web behavior.) As for why they switched to making sheet webs instead of thousands of orbs, entomologist Dr. Roy Vogtsberger explained, "If you think about it, when you have so many individual spiders crowded together, it would be very hard for them to try to construct their typical orb webs. When you have neighbor spiders so close, there simply isn't enough room."

BUT IF YOU'RE AFRAID OF SPIDERS, DON'T WORRY

A megaweb is probably not going to engulf your backyard…unless your home happens to be where land meets water. That's where long-jawed orb weavers live, and that's the only kind of habitat in the United States where the megawebs have been found. Still, even with the right habitat, megawebs are rare because there also has to be a simultaneous explosion of spider, mosquito, and midge populations. After the 2009 web was found in Baltimore, one wasn't seen again until August 2015 in Lakeside Park in Rowlett, Texas. Not only are they rare, but a megaweb doesn't last long. Wind and rain quickly tear them down. The spiders' life cycle is also short. As soon as cooler fall temperatures set in, they begin to die, and they're gone by winter.

WEB WATCHING

Megawebs have been mega news. Everyone from the *New York Times* to NPR covered the stories, with headlines like "Even Spiders Know Everything's Bigger in Texas." Photos of the web went viral, and people flocked to see them. At Lake Tawakoni, 3,300 visitors came in one weekend just to check out the web. Dr. Michael Merchant noted, "On my last visit to the web there were visitors with children who had driven an hour and a half to visit the web. No eeks or yuks with those kids. It was more like 'Ooooh' and 'Cool!'"

Celebrity Collections

You could use your wealth to buy cars, houses, yachts…or action figures.

- **Rick Springfield**, who performed the 1980s hit "Jessie's Girl", has one of the largest and most complete collections of *Star Wars* toys in the world.

- **Demi Moore** has so many vintage dolls—more than 2,000—that she had to build a separate house to store them all. Most of the dolls are more than 100 years old.

- **Tom Hanks** owns more than 200 portable manual typewriters, most of them manufactured before 1960.

- **Will Ferrell** has made many talk show appearances with a parrot or some other bird on his shoulder. Those are his actual birds. In fact, he has an aviary on the grounds of his California home, which is home to an estimated $7.8 million worth of rare birds.

- **Penelope Cruz** owns 500 different styles of coat hangers. Her collection doesn't include any wire ones.

- **Dan Aykroyd,** star of *Dragnet*, owns hundreds of police badges.

- **Rod Stewart** has a model train collection and a scale model town that contains more than 100 buildings. He takes the trains and buildings with him on tour, too. Stewart books an additional hotel room so he can set up his trains and play with them.

- **Mila Kunis** collects *Star Trek* figurines from the 1960s and 1970s.

- **Quentin Tarantino** loads his films with pop culture references, so it's not surprising that he collects pop culture artifacts. He started with old lunch boxes, but thought they were too expensive, so he started collecting movie and TV-themed board games.

- **Harry Connick Jr.** owns several hundred pairs of cuff links…but he never wears any of them.

- **Sally Struthers's** house is full of cat items: cat paintings, cat posters, plush animals, figurines, doorstops, planters, cookie jars, lamps…

- **Nicolas Cage** has one of the largest Elvis Presley memorabilia collections outside of Graceland. (From 2002 to 2004, Cage was married to Elvis's daughter, Lisa Marie Presley.)

Game (Show) Over

*If you remember any of these strange TV game shows,
you win…a new CAR! If not, you win nothing.*

THE CHAIR (2002)

In this game show that ran in prime time on ABC, contestants were given a stake of $5,000, seated in the Chair. They were then hooked up to a heart monitor while they answered questions and faced stressful situations (a live alligator on stage, or host John McEnroe serving tennis balls at their head, for example). If the contestant's heart rate went over 160 percent of their resting heart rate, their winnings were reduced by $100 per second until they answered the questions correctly, got their heart under control, or ran out of money. The show was canceled after nine weeks.

SECRETS OF THE CRYPTKEEPER'S HAUNTED HOUSE (1996)

Tales from the Crypt was a horror anthology series that ran on late-night cable TV from 1989 to 1996. It's best remembered for its "host," a wise-cracking skeleton puppet called the Cryptkeeper. Inexplicably, CBS put a game show for kids on its Saturday morning schedule hosted by that spooky puppet, in which kids competed in horror-themed challenges with names like "Ghost Battle" and "The Swamp from Hell." Winning teams received Apple computers; losers got an encyclopedia.

DON ADAMS' SCREEN TEST (1975)

Between his 1960s gig starring on the spy comedy *Get Smart* and his 1980s gig voicing the title character on *Inspector Gadget*, actor Don Adams hosted a game show in which two aspiring actors re-created famous movie scenes. The studio audience then decided which contestant performed better, and the winner got an actual Hollywood screen test. The show lasted 24 episodes…but produced no future movie stars.

THROUT AND NECK (1999)

Aired for a few weeks late at night on the Game Show Network. The premise: viewers called in and used the touchpad of their phones to control two CGI monsters (Throut and Neck) in a video game maze.

YOUR NUMBER'S UP (1985)

Contestants had to spin an electronic wheel, and then guess the answer to a riddle that contained an acronym. Guess correctly and they got a point. Six points won the game. But wait! There's more! When the contestant answered correctly, the number on the wheel closest to them was posted on a board. When there were four numbers, any audience member who had those four digits in their phone number was invited onstage and asked to predict who would win the game. If their prediction turned out to be correct, they won a trip to Hawaii. This show, hosted by comedian Nipsy Russell, lasted only three months on NBC's daytime schedule, probably because it was too difficult for viewers to figure out.

THE NEIGHBORS (1975)

Hosted by former Joey Bishop sidekick and future daytime talk show host Regis Philbin, five moms who lived in the same neighborhood took turns sharing gossip, and then each had to guess who the salacious rumors were about.

HOW'S YOUR MOTHER-IN-LAW? (1967)

The contestants were two married men and their mothers-in-law. The men would complain about their wife's mother, and then a "defense attorney" (a comedian guest, such as George Carlin) would defend the mother-in-law's actions. A "jury" of unmarried people would then choose which of the two women they would rather have as a mother-in-law. The winning lady got $100. (This show, which lasted less than one season, was one of the first game shows created by Chuck Barris, who would later go on to produce and host *The Gong Show*.)

FUN AND FORTUNE (1949)

Contestants had to use four clues given by the host to guess what object was hidden behind a curtain. It's probably the simplest premise ever for a game show...but it was so simple that it didn't even last in the early, experimental, low-budget days of early television—it was canceled after one episode.

WHO'S WHOSE? (1951)

By asking lots of questions, a panel tried to match which of the three male contestants was married to each of the three female contestants. This is another "one-hit wonder," canceled after only one airing.

*   *   *

"Love is telling someone their hair extensions are showing."

—**Natasha Leggero**

It's possible to cross from Spain into Portugal on a zipline that's half a mile long.

Wallace's Words

David Foster Wallace was one of the most critically acclaimed novelists of the late 20th century. Never heard of him? He was also an essayist (an episode of The Simpsons *is based on one of his works), the subject of the movie* The End of the Tour *(he was played by Jason Segal), and purveyor of wise words like these.*

"The man who knows his limitations has none."

"It is often more fun to want something than to have it."

"One paradox of professional writing is that books written solely for money and/or acclaim will almost never be good enough to garner either."

"You will become way less concerned with what other people think of you when you realize how seldom they do."

"Whatever you get paid attention for is never what you think is most important about yourself."

"If you are immune to boredom, there is literally nothing you cannot accomplish."

"Am I a good person? Deep down, do I even really want to be a good person, or do I only want to seem like a good person so that people (including myself) will approve of me? Is there a difference?"

"Nothing brings us together like a common enemy."

"Everybody is identical in their secret unspoken belief that way deep down they are different from everyone else."

"The really important kind of freedom involves attention, and awareness, and discipline, and effort, and being able truly to care about other people and to sacrifice for them, over and over, in myriad petty little unsexy ways, every day."

"It's not what you lift, it's where you carry it."

"The most obvious, ubiquitous, important realities are often the ones that are the hardest to see and talk about."

"Worship your intellect—you will end up feeling stupid, a fraud, always on the verge of being found out."

"I'd like to be the sort of person who can enjoy things at the time, instead of having to go back in my head and enjoy them."

"The truth will set you free. But not until it is finished with you."

Their Final Film

*Despite a long, illustrious career, an actor's last
role may not be the best work of their lives.*

Walter Matthau. He played the father of three bickering sisters, who is dying and dealing with dementia in *Hanging Up* (2000). He died four months after the film's release.

Jack Lemmon. Though uncredited, Lemmon's last work was narrating the 2000 Matt Damon golf movie *The Legend of Bagger Vance*.

George C. Scott. He had a supporting role in *Gloria* (1999), for which co-star Sharon Stone was Razzie-nominated for playing the title role as a mobster's streetwise girlfriend.

Gregory Peck. He played the lead in the original 1962 version of *Cape Fear*. His last film role: a cameo in the 1991 Martin Scorsese remake.

Katharine Hepburn. The four-time Oscar winner's last on-screen appearance was in the 1994 made-for-TV movie *One Christmas*, opposite Henry Winkler and Swoosie Kurtz.

Audrey Hepburn. A cameo as a ghost barber and guide to the afterlife for a deceased pilot in Steven Spielberg's 1989 drama *Always*.

Orson Welles. The final role for director and star of *Citizen Kane* was in *The Transformers: The Movie*. In this 1986 animated film, Welles provided the voice for Unicron, a robotic planet that eats other planets.

Cary Grant. He retired from acting in 1966, and lived another 20 years. His last movie was the 1966 Olympic games farce *Walk, Don't Run*.

Gene Kelly. The star of dozens of classic movie musicals ended his career in 1994 as host of *That's Entertainment III*, the third compilation of moments from classic movie musicals. He died two years later.

Rock Hudson. Ten months before his death in 1985, Hudson joined the cast of the TV soap *Dynasty*. He appeared in nine episodes as a dashing horse trainer named Daniel Reece.

...bound in human skin from "the unclaimed female body of a mental patient who died from a stroke."

James Stewart. He played a dog cowboy gunslinger named Wylie Burp in the 1990 animated Western *An American Tail: Fievel Goes West.*

Elizabeth Taylor. In 2001, Taylor starred in the made-for-TV movie *Those Old Broads*, playing a once-huge Hollywood star. She died ten years later.

Dean Martin. The actor, singer, and variety show host wrapped up his career with the 1984 Burt Reynolds action comedy *Cannonball Run II*. One highlight of the film was a Rat Pack reunion, with cameos from Martin, Frank Sinatra, and Sammy Davis Jr. *Cannonball Run II* was the last movie for Sinatra and Davis, too.

Marlon Brando. Two weeks before he died in 2004, he did voice work for a low-budget animated superhero movie called *Big Bug Man*. The sessions were recorded at his home; between takes Brando required the use of an oxygen tank. The movie, in which Brando plays an old lady named "Mrs. Sour," is yet to be released.

Robert Mitchum. The quintessential Hollywood tough guy's final film was in the 1997 made-for-TV movie *James Dean: Race with Destiny*. Mitchum played George Stevens, director of Dean's 1956 movie *Giant*.

James Dean. *Giant.*

*　　*　　*

NOT-SO-HAPPY HOLIDAYS

Six real-life Christmas-themed articles published in medical journals:

"Deck the Halls with Rows of Trolleys: Emergency Departments Are Busiest Over the Christmas Holiday Period" (*Medical Journal of Australia*)

"Complications of Ornamental Christmas Bulb Ingestion: Case Report and Review of the Literature" (*Archives of Surgery*)

"Unilateral Phrenic-nerve Paralysis from Cutting Down a Christmas Tree" (*Southern Medical Journal*)

"Mold Allergy and Live Christmas Trees" (*Annals of Allergy, Asthma & Immunology*)

"A Hazard of Christmas: Bird Fancier's Lung and the Christmas Tree" (*Respiratory Medicine*)

"Christmas-Related Eye Injuries: a Prospective Study" (*Clinical and Experimental Ophthalmology*)

Uncle John's Stall of Shame

Bathrooms, toilets, and toilet paper should only be used as a force for good. But sometimes people end up using the facilities for more nefarious deeds. It is for these people that Uncle John created the "Stall of Shame."

Dubious Achiever: Ralph Curry of Upper Darby, Pennsylvania
Claim to Fame: Putting Mr. Potato in the head
True Story: In February 2015, Curry, 43, called for a maintenance worker to come to his apartment, but no one answered. Frustrated, Curry grabbed the potatoes he was cooking for breakfast and flushed them down the toilet...which overflowed. He called maintenance again. Still no answer. So he pulled the building's fire alarm, forcing his fellow tenants to go outside on a blisteringly cold morning. He finally got an answer...from the police, who arrested Curry for setting a false alarm.

Dubious Achiever: Burger King
Claim to Fame: Creating a color that should not exist (in the toilet, anyway)
True Story: In 2015, the fast food giant introduced a Halloween-themed Whopper with black buns (ooh, scary). But things got a lot scarier when the food coloring in the buns caused consumers' poop to turn green. And not just green—according to *USA Today*, it was "vividly, neon green." Or, as one Twitter user reported, "My stool was as green as the Irish countryside after a quenching rain."

Dubious Achiever: The city of Montreal, Quebec
Claim to Fame: Using the city's main waterway as a giant toilet
True Story: Like many cities with aging infrastructures, Montreal's public works department needed to overhaul its sewage treatment system. Specifically, they had to replace a "snow chute—a large opening that funnels water from melting snow to a facility used to treat the sewage." Before that could happen, however, something needed to be done with all the raw sewage in the tanks. Their solution: dump it in the St. Lawrence River...all 1.75 billion gallons of it.

That's exactly what they did in November 2015, and Quebecers were fuming mad. To ease concerns, city officials announced that the weeklong dumping (which was delayed until after Canada's national elections) was perfectly safe…although they did urge citizens not to flush any "diapers, medication, or condoms" during the sewage dump. And they put up signs along the riverbanks warning people: *"Évitez tout contact avec l'eau."* ("Avoid contact with water.") So the sewage-filled river—that might also contain used diapers, used condoms, or prescription medications—was perfectly safe…as long as you didn't touch it.

Dubious Achiever: Jackie Burns, a UK politician
Claim to Fame: Taking away public loos, and then letting loose himself
True Story: In May 2015, Burns, the deputy leader of the South Lanarkshire Council in Scotland, reported to his constituents that, due to federal budget cuts, several public restrooms in his district would have to be closed. But then Burns became a victim of those same cuts. A few months later, after a night out on the town, he was waiting for a taxi when he had to relieve himself. But alas, the public restrooms were closed. So he tried to go outside…and got caught by the police. Burns was fined £40, and apologized to the public, saying he was "embarrassed by the incident." At last report, the council was trying to find the money to reopen the restrooms.

Dubious Achiever: Administrators at Ryerson University in Toronto
Claim to Fame: Coming up with a weak reply to complaints…and then not complying
True Story: A scandal erupted at the Canadian university in 2015 when student journalists reported that the bathrooms used by the school's president and top administrators were stocked with two-ply toilet paper, while the bathrooms in the student dorms were "stocked exclusively with that translucent, gotta-fold-it-thirteen-times one-ply." When confronted, Ryerson president Sheldon Levy promised to take action. "When I found out about this, I said this is shocking, embarrassing, make sure this doesn't happen." But nothing did happen. A university spokesperson later explained that two-ply costs twice as much as one-ply, and adding it to the dormitories would stretch the school's budget too thin (so to speak), because it would also require upgrading the TP dispensers and even replacing the old pipes. So for now, only Ryerson's top administrators get to enjoy the superior softness of two-ply.

* * *

"You don't need to go to church to be a Christian. If you go to Taco Bell, that doesn't make you a taco."

—**Justin Bieber**

Name That American Island

Did you know that there are 18,617 named islands in the U.S. and its territories? Neither did we! Here are some interesting stories behind the names of some of those islands.

STATEN ISLAND

In 1609, English explorer Henry Hudson, sailing under a Dutch flag, sailed into New York Bay. (He wasn't the first European to explore the region; that honor goes to Italian explorer Giovanni da Verrazzano, who discovered it in 1524.) Hudson named the large island on the southwest side of the bay Staaten Eylandt, literally "States Island," after the Dutch parliament, known as the Staaten-Generaal. When the English took over the region in 1667, and made it part of their New York Colony, the name was anglicized to Staten Island.

Bonus fact: Staten Island wasn't its *official* name until 1975. In 1683, the British divided the New York Colony into ten counties, and designated Staten Island as Richmond County, after Charles Lennox, the son of England's King Charles II, and first Duke of Richmond. When Staten Island was incorporated into New York City in 1898 as one of its five boroughs, its official name was the Borough of Richmond—and that remained its name until 1975, when the city council finally changed it to the Borough of Staten Island.

LONG ISLAND

Just east of Staten Island, across a channel known as the Narrows that separates Lower New York Bay from Upper New York Bay (where the Statue of Liberty is located), lies Long Island. Like Staten Island, it was named by the Dutch in the early 17th century. They called it Lange Eylandt, meaning, of course, "Long Island." It's 118 miles long by 23 miles wide at its widest point, making it the longest (and largest) island in the contiguous United States. It's also the most populous island in any state or territory, with more than 7.8 million residents.

KODIAK

Kodiak Island is about 250 miles southeast of Anchorage, off the east coast of Alaska's Aleutian Peninsula. It's been home to the Alutiiq people for more than 3,000 years. And it's huge. At 3,595 square miles,

---

Irony: The CEO of the nonprofit charity "Food for the Poor" is named Robin Mahfood.

Kodiak is the second-largest island in the United States (after Hawaii), and the 80th largest in the world. The island was first encountered by Europeans in 1763, when Russian fur trader Stephan Glotov arrived there. He called it Kad'yak, a derivation of *kikhtak*, the native Aleut word for "island." The island became the center of the Russian fur trade, but the name didn't spread beyond the Russian trading community until 1778, when English explorer Captain James Cook arrived and made the first known written notation of the word "Kodiak."

HAWAII

According to traditional folklore, the largest of the Hawaiian islands was named after Hawai'iloa, a legendary seafaring hero who discovered and then colonized them. (He was from a land called Ka-aina-kai-melemele-a-Kane, meaning "the land of the yellow sea of Kane.") According to the same folklore, the names of the next three largest islands in the Hawaiian chain—Kauai, Oahu, and Maui—come from the names of Hawai'iloa's sons. But according to linguists, "Hawaii" is similar to words found in other Polynesian languages—including Maori and Samoan—that mean something along the lines of "homeland," and "Hawaii" probably once had that same meaning.

Bonus Fact: The Hawaiian word *lulu* means "calm," and the name of Hawaii's capital city, Honolulu, means "calm port."

MARTHA'S VINEYARD

Martha's Vineyard is a small island (25 miles long and 9 miles across at its widest point), just south of Cape Cod, about 7 miles off the Massachusetts coast. It may be best known as the vacation grounds of some of America's most elite families, especially the Kennedys. Before Europeans arrived, it was the home of the Wampanoag people for millennia. The Wampanoag name for the island was Noepe, meaning "dry land amid the waters." The curious route to its modern name:

• In 1524, the Italian explorer Giovanni da Verrazano made what many historians believe was the first sighting of this island by a European, while he was exploring the region for France. He recorded its unique triangular shape and named it Louise Island, after Louise of Savoy, the mother of the French king Frances I. That name was soon forgotten.

• In 1602, English explorer Bartholomew Gosnold made the first known landing by a European on the island. But he gave the name Martha's Vineyard to *another* island—a smaller one just to the south. The "Vineyard" is believed to have been a reference to the wild grapes that grow on the islands. No one knows for sure who Martha was: she could have been Gosnold's daughter, and maybe his mother, or his mother-in-law, or his sister, but none of these have been confirmed.

• A few decades later, the name Martha's Vineyard was transferred to the larger island that's still called that today. (The smaller island was renamed Nomans Land, possibly derived from Tequenoman, the name of a Wampanoag *sachem*, or chief, who lived there.)

• Martha's Vineyard was also known as "Martin's Vineyard." This may have been a reference to Captain Martin Pring, another English seafarer who explored the island in 1605; or it may have referred to English sea captain John Martin, who served on Gosnold's crew, and was later a councilman in the British colony at Jamestown, Virginia.

• In 1890, President Benjamin Harrison set up the Board on Geographic Names, to establish standards in the United States. Among the board's rules: possessive apostrophes were no longer allowed in U.S. place names—so Martha's Vineyard officially became Marthas Vineyard. (About 250,000 apostrophes were dropped from U.S. place names at the time.) In the early 20th century, the board allowed Marthas Vineyard to reinstate the apostrophe, and it became Martha's Vineyard again. (It's one of only five places granted permission to use a possessive apostrophe since then.)

PUERTO RICO

This Caribbean island was named San Juan Bautista in 1493 by Christopher Columbus, after the Catholic saint John the Baptist. The first permanent settlement was founded in 1508, actually on a small island just 100 yards or so off the north coast of the larger island, which formed the northern rim of a large protected harbor. The settlement moved to the larger island in 1509 and was dubbed Puerto Rico, or "rich port," while the island was still called San Juan Bautista. In 1521, the name of the settlement, which had become a thriving town, was expanded to San Juan Bautista de Puerto Rico. That created confusion among its residents, and they started referring to the town as San Juan Bautista, and the island as Puerto Rico. Officials eventually made the name swap official: the town of San Juan Bautista de Puerto Rico became San Juan, and the entire island, once known as San Juan Bautista, became Puerto Rico.

Bonus Fact: Puerto Ricans sometimes refer to the island as Borinquen, and to themselves as *borincanos*. Those terms come from Boriken, the name for the island used by the indigenous Taino people, whose culture dominated the island from around 1000 AD until the Spanish arrived. It means "land of the great lords."

MORE ABOUT U.S. ISLANDS

• Off the coast of Massachusetts, about ten miles from Martha's

---

The leaves of the mullein plant are soft and velvety, which is why they're called "Cowboy Toilet Paper."

Vineyard and just west of Nantucket Island, is Tuckernuck Island. Its name was derived from a Wampanoag word meaning "round loaf of bread."

• Dauphin Island lies just off the southwest coast of Alabama in the Gulf of Mexico. It was named Isle Du Massacre (Massacre Island) in 1699 by French explorer Pierre Le Moyne d'Iberville, who found a pile of human skeletons on the island. (Archaeologists say the bodies were probably not the result of a massacre—they were more likely the remains of a Native American burial ground that had been exposed by a hurricane.) D'Iberville changed the island's name to Dauphin Island in 1707, in honor of King Louis XIV's great-grandson and heir. Many people mistakenly call it "Dolphin Island"…but they're actually right. "Dauphin" was the title given to the heir to the French throne—and it actually does mean "dolphin"—a reference to the dolphin symbol on the French king's coat of arms.

• Joseph Whidbey mapped the islands of what is now Puget Sound (with his shipmate, Peter Puget) in 1792. Whidbey Island was named for him (and Puget Sound for Puget) that same year. By whom? By their captain: George Vancouver. (He has an island named after him, too—but it's in Canada, and this article is about American islands.)

*   *   *

REAL LUMBERJACK NICKNAMES FROM THE EARLY 1900s

Angus the Pope	Dirt Dan	Old Rampike
Battle Axe Nelson	Double Breasted Corrigan	One Eye
Bill the Dangler	Drop Cake Morley	Pancake Billie
Bug House Lynch	Frog Face	Panicky Pete
Blueberry Bob	Ham Bone Smith	Prune Juice Doyle
Buckskin Pants	Highpockets	Pump Handle
Calico Bill	Hungry Dan Shea	Silver Jack
Charley the Logger	Jack the Horse	Square Head
Cordwood Johnson	Jimmie on the Trail	Squeaky George
Crosshaul Paddy	Larry the Kicker	Sub Nelson
Cruel Face	Lousy Dan	Stuttering Ed
Dick the Dancer	Moonlight Bob	The Bear

Keystone Kops

The Keystone Kops was a popular silent film series in the 1920s that featured the exploits of a group of bumbling police officers. Here are some true cop stories that would do the Keystone Kops proud.

SIREN SONG

In 2015, two police officers went to an elementary school in Swindon, Wiltshire, England, to speak to the kids about law enforcement. At one point, a debate broke out about how to describe the sound that British police sirens make. Unable to come to a consensus, the young students somehow convinced the officers to blast their squad car siren as a test. So they did…several times. The station immediately started receiving complaints about the excessive noise, which led to this Facebook post (which went viral) from a department spokesperson: "Apologies to anyone in the area who may have been disturbed by our sirens yesterday morning—the officers were at the Primary School having a very important debate with the children about whether they go nee-nah or woo-woo." (The children voted, and "woo-woo" won by a margin of 68 to 20.)

ARE YOU MADD?

Here's a tip: If you're receiving an award from Mothers Against Drunk Driving, don't show up to the ceremony drunk. That's what happened when Officer Michael Szeliga of the Pinellas County (Florida) Sheriff's Department was being honored for making more than 100 DUI arrests in 2015. According to reports, he was slurring his speech and couldn't walk straight, so he was asked to return to his hotel room and not participate in the banquet. Szeliga was later seen walking around the hotel in his underwear. His punishment: one day's paid suspension, and he had to write an apology letter to MADD.

HE'LL BE BRIEF

The Italian press called San Remo cop Alberto Muraglia "the world's laziest policeman" after embarrassing CCTV footage showed him clocking into work in his underwear. Even worse: he then went back to bed. Muraglia, 53, lived in an apartment that's in the same building as the town council offices, so he figured that because his office was connected to his residence, then technically he was "still at work." (That was actually his defense.) The "pot-bellied officer," as the press called him, was fired after the camera footage went public, but he insisted that

---

When putting his handprints in front of Grauman's Theatre, Mel Brooks wore a fake 6th finger.

he's a scapegoat. The incident was part of a larger investigation into the "poor working habits" of the entire public workforce in San Remo. According to reports, nearly 75 percent of the town's public employees had been reprimanded for clocking in and then not working. Muraglia vowed to appeal the decision, claiming that just because he clocked in while wearing his underwear—which he admitted is "a bit sloppy"— that doesn't mean he didn't do his job. And as his lawyer claimed, a cop can do a lot in his underwear: "One time, dressed in his underpants, Alberto managed to foil a robbery—he ran out into the street, pistol in hand, and arrested the crook."

THE ODD COUPLE

Steve Upham was in a holding cell in the Allen County Justice Center in Lima, Ohio, on September 16, 2015, waiting to testify in the murder trial of Markelus Carter. He was going to tell the jury that when the two men were cellmates, Carter confessed to the murder. However, during a break in the trial (and before Upham testified), Carter was led out of the courtroom and put in a holding cell—the *same* holding cell that Upham was in. Apparently, no one told the bailiff to put them in separate rooms. By the time the cops realized their mistake, the defendant had punched the witness "several times." Carter was later found guilty and sentenced to life in prison, but his lawyer promised to appeal on the grounds that CCTV footage of the fight swayed the jury. The defendant maintains that Upham is a liar, and that he never told him anything (which is why he wanted to beat him up).

YOU LOOKIN' AT ME?

In 2015, a 22-year-old Dayton, Ohio, police officer named Randy Betsinger pulled over a man named John Felton for "turning on his turn signal too late." Felton couldn't believe it, but he cooperated, and Officer Betsinger said he would let him off with a warning. Felton still couldn't fathom why a late turn signal was worth a traffic stop, so he asked Betsinger one more time, "Why did you really pull me over?"

"You made direct eye contact with me," replied the officer, "and held onto it when I was passing you on Salem (Avenue)."

"You pulled me over for looking at you?"

"I'm not going to argue about it," said Betsinger before he got back into his squad car and drove away.

Felton, who is African American, complained that the cop was really racially profiling him. Betsinger's boss agreed. "I don't think that it's indicative of our police department or what we believe in Dayton," said Police Commissioner Joey Williams. He said that Officer Betsinger would be sent back to the police academy for more training.

A German driver's license requires 14 theory classes, 12 driving lessons, and a first aid-course.

Kids, Don't Try This at Home

The latest research says human brains aren't fully developed until age 25. That may be why most of the people who attempt these YouTube and Facebook challenges are young.

The Cinnamon Challenge: Put a huge spoonful of cinnamon in your mouth. Now try to swallow it.

What Happens: You'll spew out an "orange burst of dragon breath," and then start gagging, gasping, barfing, and crying. One teen was even hospitalized with a collapsed lung after inhaling the spice. She now carries an inhaler everywhere she goes because running—or just talking fast—can make her short of breath.

The Salt and Ice Challenge: First, put salt on your bare skin. Next, hold an ice cube on top of the salt for as long as you can stand it.

What Happens: When salt reacts with water, it lowers the temperature of the water to as cold as -18°F, which can cause severe frostbite where the ice-salt mixture contacts your skin. With a little help from his twin, a 12-year-old Pittsburgh boy managed to burn a huge cross into his back. He needed hospital care and spent an entire summer recovering.

The Kylie Jenner Lip Challenge: Stick your lips inside a shot glass and suck as hard as you can.

What Happens: When reality TV star Kylie Jenner plumped her lips to three times their size, she claimed that she "had never had plastic surgery." Some teens decided that sucking on a shot glass was the only logical explanation. After page upon page of bruised, disfigured, and bloody lips appeared online, Jenner admitted to using "temporary lip fillers." Dermatologists warn that the shot glass method carries a "risk for scarring and permanent disfigurement with repeated attempts."

The Warheads Challenge: Eat 150 Warheads "extreme sour" candies in 10 minutes.

What Happens: Two days after completing the challenge, a YouTuber who calls himself L.A. Beast stuck out his damaged tongue for viewers to see. "The Warheads burned the sides of my tongue off," he said. "I can't eat solid food without being in excruciating pain." Meanwhile, printed on the side of every Warheads pack is important information— "WARNING: Eating multiple pieces within a short time can cause a temporary irritation to sensitive tongues and mouths."

The Ghost Pepper Challenge: Eat an Indian Bhut Jolokia pepper. Nicknamed the "ghost pepper," this one weighs in at 1,041,800 on the Scoville scale—about 150 times hotter than Tabasco sauce.

What Happens: You get burned. And then…you cry, vomit, jump up and down in agony, or even hallucinate. An Indian farmer who cultivates the ghost chili says, "When you eat it, it's like dying." In fact, if eaten in large quantities, peppers this hot can cause convulsions, heart attacks, and even death.

The Eraser Challenge: Erase your skin as you recite one word for every letter in the alphabet.

What Happens: Rubbing not only breaks and damages the skin, it can cause infection, scars, and—if you share erasers as some teens do—communicable diseases. A 13-year-old California student ended up fighting for his life after contracting toxic shock syndrome from germs ground into his skin by an eraser.

The Fire Challenge: Pour a flammable substance—such as rubbing alcohol—on yourself and light it on fire.

What Happens: You get burned. A Kansas City teen ended up in the hospital with second- and third-degree burns on his face, neck, and hips. A 15-year-old Buffalo teen wasn't so lucky. He died.

The Saltine Challenge: Eat six saltine crackers in 60 seconds without drinking anything.

What Happens: The saltines absorb the saliva in your mouth, so it doesn't have time to replenish before you need to swallow.

The Chubby Bunny Challenge: Stuff as many marshmallows into your mouth as possible while repeating the phrase "Chubby bunny."

What Happens: Here's the thing…a marshmallow is perfectly shaped to lodge in your throat and block your airway. Stuff in too many, and—as was the fate of a 12-year-old Chicago kid playing the game at a school-sponsored "Care Fair"—you can suffocate. The child's parents sued the school district, which settled for $2 million.

The Planking Challenge: Lie facedown in an unusual place, such as along the top edge of a TV set, on the center line of a road, or high atop the golden arches of the local McDonald's.

What Happens: It's great for the abs and can be harmless fun. But it can also kill you. After a night of planking, an Australian man chose a balcony rail seven stories up for his final stunt. He was 20 years old.

Magic Words

Magicians never reveal their secrets, but we'll share some of their jargon.

Illusionist: What many magicians prefer to be called.

Misdirection: The key to a magic trick is "misdirecting" an audience's attention away from the magician's hands.

Burn: A stubborn audience member who stares at the magician's hands and isn't fooled by misdirection.

Legerdemain: It's French for "light of hand," meaning the ability to create an illusion using one's "fast fingers."

Hat production: Pulling something out of a hat…as if by magic.

Topit: A large, secret pocket in the inner lining of a coat, into which a magician tosses items to make them "disappear."

Servante: A pouch or a shelf beneath a magician's onstage table, where they toss other items that have "disappeared."

Dirty: A magician's hand is dirty if it's secretly holding a "vanished" item.

Mechanic: A skilled magician who specializes in card tricks.

Magic dust: When a magician jokingly says they need some "magic dust" in their pocket to make a trick work, it's not really a joke—they need to reach into their pocket to sneak a disappeared item or prop into their hand.

Confederate: An audience plant who assists a magician in a trick.

Black art: No, not evil magic. It's when a magician drapes a stage using a black curtain as a background to conceal any assistants or props that are shrouded in black.

M5: A magnet made of neodymium, used to "magically" stop watches when hidden inside a magician's palm.

Talking: If a hidden prop makes a noise—scraping on a surface, for example—this "talking" can ruin a trick.

"The ghost walks!": Magicians on the vaudeville circuit had a hard time getting paid. This phrase was their version of "when hell freezes over," applied to payday because, like hell freezing over, it's an unlikely occurrence.

Look—Up in the Sky!

Here's a piece of Atomic Age history you've probably never heard of: the civilian Ground Observer Corps, thousands of volunteers who scanned the skies for incoming Soviet bombers that would have marked the opening battle of World War III.

SHOCK WAVE

In September 1949, a U.S. Air Force reconnaissance plane flying over the North Pacific from Japan to Alaska detected levels of radioactivity in the atmosphere at least 20 times above normal. Other planes in the Pacific reported similar observations in the days that followed; elevated radiation levels were soon being detected over the British Isles half a world away. It quickly became clear that there could be only one explanation for the spreading cloud of radioactivity: the Soviet Union had secretly detonated its first atomic bomb.

The United States had known since the end of World War II that the Soviets would try to build their own nuclear weapon, but the best estimates were that it would take them eight to ten years to do it. They had managed it in less than four.

The Soviet bomb was estimated to be as powerful as the one dropped on Nagasaki in the closing days of World War II. That bomb had killed more than 70,000 people. Making matters worse, the Soviets were also building long-range bombers that could reach the United States. America's entry into World War II had been precipitated by a surprise attack on Pearl Harbor. Now, as the Cold War heated up, it seemed possible that the next war might begin with an *atomic* sneak attack by the Russians. If their target was a major American city like Washington, D.C., or New York, the casualties would be in the millions.

IN THE DARK

The United States had a limited ability to detect incoming bombers using radar, the technology that Britain had used to defend itself from Nazi fighter planes and bombers during World War II. But there were huge gaps in the radar coverage of the United States, and even where there were no gaps, the radar systems of the late 1940s did not have the ability to detect low-flying airplanes. The Russians likely knew this, so if they did attack, their bombers would fly too low to be detected by radar. Some other means of spotting these aircraft had to be put into place until the radar system improved. American military planners dusted off an idea that had been used during World War II: recruiting civilian volunteers to watch for bombers using binoculars and the naked eye. During the war, more than 1.5 million civilians had been posted in 14,000 observation posts on the East and West Coasts to keep watch for incoming German or Japanese aircraft. This "Ground Observer Corps," as it was known, was wound down toward the end of the war. But now that the threat of enemy air attack was rising again, the decision was made to bring it back into operation.

THE EYES HAVE IT

By early 1952, the reconstituted Ground Observer Corps had more than 200,000 civilian volunteers keeping watch in 8,000 observation posts, not just on the East and West Coasts as in World War II, but also along the northern border with Canada. Not out of fear that the Canadians might invade, but because the shortest air route from the Soviet Union to the United States was over the polar ice cap and down through Canada. The system operated much the same way as it had during the war:

• Whenever a civilian observer spotted one or more aircraft in their area, they made note of the number, type, and altitude of the aircraft; their position and distance from the observation post; and their direction of travel. (Small private aircraft and regular flights in and out of nearby airports were ignored.)

• The volunteer then telephoned the information to what was called a "filter center" staffed by other volunteers. The filter center's job was to match the observer's report with known air activity in that area.

• If the filter center was able to identify the aircraft and confirm that it was nonthreatening, they did nothing further. If they could not, they forwarded the information to the military, which then had to decide whether to scramble fighter jets to intercept the aircraft.

FUN FOR THE WHOLE FAMILY

Volunteers for the Ground Observer Corps were from all walks of life. The only requirements were that they have good eyesight, good hearing, good judgment, and the ability to speak clearly when phoning in aircraft sightings. The youngest volunteers were under 10 years old and the oldest were in their 80s. Some high schools had spotters clubs that were popular with kids who wanted an excuse to get out of class. Volunteers received training on how to identify aircraft and were given guidebooks with photographs of friendly and enemy aircraft. They were also issued transparent templates that they could hold up to gauge how far away airplanes were. If a plane was small enough to fit inside the hole marked "5 Miles," it was about five miles away. If it was too big for that hole but fit inside the larger "1 Mile" hole, then it was about a mile away.

Three things banned from Georgia by its founder, James Oglethorpe: alcohol, slavery, and lawyers.

THE LONG WAIT

It's a good thing the Soviets never tried to attack the United States, because although the Ground Observer Corps remained active until the end of the decade, it never managed to plug the gaps in America's radar coverage anywhere near as effectively as the military had hoped. Relying on volunteers was a big part of the problem: though the idea of watching for enemy bombers may have seemed exciting at first, there was little unusual air activity to report, and the job quickly became boring. Many observation posts were unheated in winter and lacked air-conditioning in the summer, which made it even harder to find volunteers to fill the two-hour shifts. And though the posts were supposed to be manned around the clock, few people were willing to volunteer in the middle of the night. Result: many posts went unoccupied and unstaffed for days on end.

Though the military had hoped to recruit more than a million volunteers, their numbers never grew much above 200,000, and by the end of 1953 the number of active volunteers had dwindled to about 100,000. Even after the Soviet Union successfully tested a thermonuclear bomb in 1955, a U.S. Air Force report found that "the vast majority of Americans would rather play bridge, watch television, or go to bed" than spend their free time watching for enemy planes in the Ground Observer Corps.

JUST DEW IT

Though the military apparently never considered actually *paying* people to watch for enemy aircraft, it was willing to spend vast sums of money improving America's radar defenses. It spent much of the 1950s building a network of 63 radar stations stretching from Alaska across the far north of Canada to Greenland and Iceland. This system, called the Distant Early Warning Line, or DEW Line, cost more than $600 million in 1957, the equivalent of more than $5.1 billion today. Another $2 billion ($26 billion today) was spent on a computer system to link the radar stations together. When the system went online beginning in 1957, the Ground Observer Corps instantly became obsolete, and was deactivated in January 1959. Today about all that remains of the corps are the badges, guidebooks, and other paraphernalia that pops up on eBay—that and the memories of the people who volunteered their time. "It was fun doing it," remembered Bob Hazel, who was a member of his high school's spotters club in Chesapeake City, Maryland. "You felt as if you were important and it was an important job," he told an interviewer in 2015. "And, of course, I guess it was."

Format Flops

For every successful media delivery method like
DVDs or CDs, there are a lot more that
sit on the shelf and gather dust.

CED (1981)

The early days of home video in the 1980s were marked with a well-known "format" war: Sony's Betamax cassette versus JVC's VHS. The winner: VHS, of course. But there was a third, forgotten contender—CED, short for "Capacitance Electronic Disc." The disc looked like a vinyl record and, in fact, it wasn't that different from a record. The CED was grooved; the data was in the groove. A needle read the data and converted it to video, spinning at a blistering 450 rotations per minute. Because any dirt or dust that got on the disc would lead to skipping, the records were encased in plastic sleeves, which were inserted into a $1,000 CED player, manufactured by RCA under the SelectaVision name. The video quality was similar to VHS, but unlike tapes, they had to be flipped over—each side of a disc held a maximum of one hour of video. Also, unlike cassettes, fast-forwarding, rewinding, and pausing a movie were all nearly impossible. RCA began developing the format in 1964. Had the product launched in the 1960s or even the 1970s, it would have introduced the notion of watching movies at home and created the home video industry. But technical problems delayed its entry into the marketplace, and CEDs didn't hit stores until 1981, at which point VHS and Betamax already dominated the market. By 1986, only 150,000 SelectaVision players had been sold, and RCA discontinued the product. The company lost an estimated $600 million on CEDs, which hurt RCA so badly that it was sold to General Electric the same year it ended CED production.

SUPER 8 (1979)

As an amateur filmmaking tool, Super 8 can't really be categorized as a flop. Tens of millions of Americans have a box of 15-minute Super 8 reels marked "Christmas 1974" or "John's birthday" (and maybe a Super 8 projector) gathering dust in the attic. But a few years after Kodak invented the Super 8 format in 1965, some movie studios experimented with marketing prerecorded Super 8 films that could be played on the same projectors. Introduced around the same time as Betamax and VHS, movies on Super 8 were bulky, to say the least. Because of the space limitations of the film reels, *The Godfather*, for example, came on 11 reels and cost more than $300. Cheaper and far less exciting were

---

Car racing was banned in the United States during World War II because of gas and tire rationing.

"selected scene edition" movies—highlights of a movie edited onto a single 15-minute reel. Never popular beyond home movie buffs, Super 8 could not compete with video, and movie studios stopped making movies available in this format around 1984.

UMD (2004)

In the 1990s, Sony attempted to introduce a new music format called the MiniDisc. It used a digital technology known as ATRAC to compress a CD's worth of material onto a tiny, plastic-encased disc with almost no loss of sound quality. The product took off in Japan, but although it was popular with musicians and audiophiles, it flopped in the United States. In 2004, Sony successfully applied the technology to video, compressing DVDs down to a MiniDisc-sized video disc… but losing as much as half the video quality. The company called it the "Universal Media Disc," an ironic name considering that it was playable on only one device: Sony's PlayStation Portable handheld video game system. The PSP sold 80 million copies, but the overwhelming majority of consumers bought it for video games. Movies on UMD never caught on. Consumers at the time preferred to rent movies rather than buy them, and UMD movies cost $30, more than most DVDs and with lower video quality. Just two years after Sony introduced UMD, Apple introduced iPods that played high-definition video, rendering the format obsolete. UMDs struggled on until 2014, when they disappeared completely.

VIDEO SINGLE

The "single" was an important part of the music industry. In the 1950s and 1960s, a 45-rpm record of a hit song (and some other song on the flip side) was a cheap way to buy music. By the 1980s, as cassettes replaced 33-rpm long-playing records, cassette singles similarly supplanted 45s. (First cassette single in the U.S.: the Go-Gos' "Vacation" in 1982.) When home video and MTV both hit big in the early 1980s, the music industry thought it had the next big format in music with the video single, also called a VHS single or Video 45. It was a standard VHS tape loaded with a few music videos. The first video single: In 1983, the synth pop band the Human League released a videotape in the UK with their hits "Mirror Man," "Don't You Want Me," and "Love Action." A VHS single cost about $11—about as much as an entire album. The format languished until 1990, when Madonna's "Justify My Love" became the first and only million-selling video single. The sexually explicit video was banned by MTV, so buying it was the only way to see it. The last major video single released: U2's "Numb" in 1993.

This Is Major Tom

Whether as Ziggy Stardust or himself, David Bowie always had something to say.

"Confront a corpse at least once. The absolute absence of life is the most disturbing and challenging confrontation you will ever have."

"If it works, it's out of date."

"You would think that a rock star being married to a super-model would be one of the greatest things in the world. It is."

"Fame can take interesting men and thrust mediocrity upon them."

"I'm just an individual who doesn't feel that I need to have somebody qualify my work in any particular way. I'm working for me."

"Make the best of every moment. We're not evolving. We're not going anywhere."

"I always thought I was intellectual about what I do, but I've come to the realization that I have absolutely no idea what I'm doing half the time."

"What I like my music to do to me is awaken the ghosts inside of me. Not the demons, you understand, but the ghosts."

"Tomorrow belongs to those who can hear it coming."

"I find only freedom in the realms of eccentricity."

"Any list of advice I have to offer to a musician always ends with, 'If it itches, go and see a doctor.'"

"All art is unstable. Its meaning is not necessarily that implied by the author, there is no authoritative active voice. There are only multiple readings."

"Once you lose that sense of wonder at being alive, you're pretty much on the way out."

"Speak in extremes, it'll save you time."

"The reason you don't want to make a commitment is not that you're such a freewheeling, adventurous person—it's because you're scared that it will turn out like your mother and father."

"The only art I'll ever study is stuff that I can steal from."

"I don't know where I'm going from here, but I promise it won't be boring."

A Newborn Bundle of Jelly Beans

The weight of the average American baby at birth is around seven pounds. Why, that's about the same weight as...

...29 million poppy seeds

...7 million grains of sand

...25 million grains of sugar

...40,000 raindrops

...3,000 jelly beans

...3,200 paper clips

...1,000 pennies

...600 sheets of printer paper

...375 AAA batteries

...200 DVDs

...150 mice

...95 lightbulbs

...30 decks of playing cards

...20 baseballs

...19 hockey pucks

...10 human hearts (adult size)

...9 cans of tomato soup

...5 basketballs

...3 liters of water

Or, to put it another way...

• 4 newborn babies = a bar of gold

• 16 newborn babies = a brand-new toilet

• 28 newborn babies = an adult kangaroo

• 150 newborn babies = a grand piano

• 200 newborn babies = a dairy cow

• 375 newborn babies = an adult giraffe

• 500 newborn babies = a late-model Ford Taurus

• 1,700 newborn babies = the tongue of a blue whale, the largest animal on Earth

• 2,600 newborn babies = a Tyrannosaurus rex

• 30,000 newborn babies = all the water in an average puffy white cloud

• 400,000 newborn babies = a fully fueled, launch-ready space shuttle

How did the Himalayan Dracula minnow (*Danionella dracula*) get its name? It has fangs.

Oh, Behave!

Did your grandparents complain that no one has good manners any more? Judging by these excerpts from etiquette books of yesteryear, they're right.

OUT IN PUBLIC

"In small towns it is quite a fashion for boys and girls to go to the railroad station 'to see the cars come in'; but it is not improving to their manners or morals. If they could realize, especially the girls, how out of place they appear standing on platforms, where they have no occasion to be, jostled by passengers and baggage-men, and exposed to the rude remarks of passers-by, they would never go there unnecessarily."

—*Lessons on Manners For School and Home Use* (1884)

"The chewing of gum in a street-car, in church, or any other place outside of your own private room stamps you at once as 'common.'"

—*Manners and Conduct in School and Out* (1921)

"In travelling, as everywhere in public…constant eating of fruit and peanuts is bad manners, and, as has been said before, it is generally associated with loud talking and laughing and other rude behavior."

—*Lessons on Manners For School and Home Use* (1884)

"Do not smoke in the street until after dark, and then remove your cigar from your mouth, if you meet a lady."

—*The Gentlemen's Book of Etiquette and Manual of Politeness* (1860)

DON'T EVEN THINK ABOUT IT

"A lady should never look up in a waiter's face while giving an order, refusing wine, or thanking him for any special service. This savors of familiarity, and should be avoided. A man, however, that is attentive will see that a lady has none of these things to do."

—*The Manners and Customs of Polite Society* (1896)

"Never point. It is excessively ill-bred. Never look back. That, too, is excessively ill-bred."

—*The Ladies' Book of Etiquette, and Manual of Politeness* (1860)

"Don't giggle. If girls from fourteen to eighteen could only understand the vulgarity of continually putting their heads together and giggling, as if the whole world was a supremely ridiculous affair, about which they must chuckle, and whisper, when in truth their own actions are the one thing ridiculous, they would refrain from such unmitigated nonsense."

—*The Manners and Customs of Polite Society* (1896)

"It is not good taste to ask relatives to be pall-bearers. The usual number is six to eight elderly men for an elderly person, and of young men for a young man. Six young women in white would be a suitable number to act as pall-bearers for a young woman."

—*The Book of Good Manners* (1922)

"Gentlemen unaccustomed to the management of a boat should never venture out with ladies. Men who cannot swim should never take ladies upon the water."

—*The Manners and Customs of Polite Society* (1896)

"No woman should overdress in her own house; it is the worst taste."

—*Manners and Social Usages* (1887)

THIS AND THAT

"Novel-reading strengthens the passions, weakens the virtues, and diminishes the power of self-control. Multitudes may date their ruin from the commencement of this kind of reading; and many more, who have been rescued from the snare, will regret, to the end of their days, its influence in the early formation of their character. It is, too, a great waste of time…If you wish to become weak-headed, nervous, and good for nothing, read novels."

—*Polite Manual for Young Ladies* (1849)

"Gentlefolk have 'friends' stopping with them, never 'company.' Servants have and keep 'company.' "

—*The Complete Bachelor: Manners for Men* (1896)

*   *   *

A CHANGE WE CAN OIL AGREE ON

The Tisdale, Saskatchewan, area is one of Canada's largest producers of canola oil. And it has been for 60 years, back when canola oil was known as "rapeseed oil." In 2015, the town voted to discontinue use of its decades-old town slogan, "Land of Rape and Honey."

Weird Canada

Strange stories from the land of Mounties, maple syrup, and Rush.

GET ON THE BUS

In September 2014, a nine-year-old boy riding his bicycle past a Saskatoon, Saskatchewan, transit yard noticed a city bus idling…with no driver…and its doors open. So he did what any nine-year-old would do: He got off his bike, got in the bus, and took it for a spin. Two blocks later, he hit a parked car. He kept going. He tried to turn down another street, but clipped a stop sign, scraped another passing city bus, and then got lodged against a curb. A passerby had to pry the doors open to get the boy out, because although he'd figured out how to drive the bus, he couldn't figure out how to open the doors (which had closed automatically when he'd started to drive). And because it was a Saturday morning, the boy was still wearing his pajamas.

BERRY, BERRY DRUNK

All over the world, birds eat berries. But they can't eat *all* of them. Uneaten berries that remain on trees and bushes can slowly ferment over time—even as they freeze and then thaw—before birds finally eat them. Result: birds can get drunk on fermented berries. That was a huge problem in the winter of 2014 in the Yukon Territory, particularly among Bohemian waxwings that were eating wacky mountain ash berries. Those birds then had trouble flying—dozens of people in the city of Whitehorse reported birds slamming into homes, windows, or the ground. A local nature group called Environment Yukon set up an "avian drunk tank" to help intoxicated birds sober up. If a drunken bird is spotted, residents call Environment Yukon and an employee collects the bird and puts it in a hamster cage until it's okay to fly again.

DIRTY MONEY

Most counterfeiters spend a lot of time and effort making sure their fake currency is a good copy and won't arouse suspicion. Cass Alder of Prince Edward Island is not that kind of counterfeiter. He bought a package of novelty napkins printed with the image of the Canadian $100 bill (featuring Prime Minister Robert Borden) and then carefully pasted them all onto thicker paper with a glue stick. He tried to use the phony bills at a convenience store, but the clerk wouldn't take them. (Alder was quickly arrested.)

The first pencil factory opened in England in 1832. The company is still in business.

CHALLENGE ACCEPTED

In 2014, a man calling himself "Captain" Quinn Barabash tried to start a YouTube fad among Canadians called the "Winter Challenge": He went to a frozen pond in the dead of winter, drilled through the thick ice, dropped himself down into the hole, hung out in the icy waters for a minute, and then got out. Barabash performed the Winter Challenge in "Canadian attire" (shorts and a fur-lined hat). But while the similar "Ice Bucket Challenge" went viral in the summer of 2014 when hundreds of thousands of people doused themselves with buckets of freezing water on video, only a few dozen people took on Captain Quinn's Winter Challenge.

GO WITH THE FLOE

In March 2016, Philicity Lafreniere was spotted by police in Prince George, British Columbia, after she broke into a building and ran away with several guns. She led the cops on a half-mile chase by hopping into the Nechako River and riding an ice floe. While on the ice, she tried to destroy the evidence of the crime (the guns) by trying to light a fire. (It didn't work; guns don't burn.) Lafreniere was apprehended after the floe hit a bank, and a police dog knocked her into the river.

GOOD MONEY

While standing on a street corner in Halifax, Nova Scotia, in 2014, Richard Wright of Prince Edward Island started passing out $50 and $100 bills to passersby, wishing them well and asking them to use the money or give it to someone in need. No good deed goes unpunished: the Royal Canadian Mounted Police stopped him for a "wellness check" and had him committed to a mental hospital for three days.

THIS IS THE BIG ONE, ELIZABETH!

In December 2014, a Toronto man named Jordan Axani bought his girlfriend, Elizabeth Gallagher, airplane tickets for a months-long trip around the world. But before the trip began, she broke up with him. He couldn't get a refund and didn't want the tickets to go to waste, so he set out to find someone who could use them. Only catch: because the tickets were issued to his girlfriend, Elizabeth Gallagher, his new traveling companion would have to have the same name and she had to be Canadian. More than a dozen different Elizabeth Gallaghers heard about the story and applied, and Axani eventually gave them to Elizabeth Gallagher of Cole Harbour, Nova Scotia. They took the trip together, visiting New York, Paris, Milan, Venice, Vienna, Prague, New Delhi, and Hong Kong together, and reportedly had a wonderful time. But if you were hoping for a romantic ending to the story, sorry—their relationship was "strictly platonic."

Count 'em: There are at least 900 different eucalyptus species in Australia.

National Boozes

Most countries have national songs, national colors, national foods, etc. In that "spirit," we found these official (or unofficial) national alcoholic beverages. So sit back, pour yourself a nice cold Schlitz (the national drink of Uncle John's house, or, as we call it, Schlitzerland), and share a few international libations with us. Cheers!

COLOMBIA

Drink: Aguardiente

Story: *Aguardiente* means "burning water" in Spanish, or more colloquially, "firewater." The name is used for several different liquors produced in Spanish-speaking regions around the world. In Colombia, it refers specifically to clear liquor made from distilled sugarcane molasses, flavored with oils extracted from anise seeds. It's the anise seeds that give it its distinctive licorice flavor (similar to other anise-based liquors, such as Italian anisette and Greek ouzo). There are different brands of aguardiente, each with its own preparation method and flavor, some sweeter, some drier and sharper. It's not particularly strong—it's normally around 29 percent alcohol—and it's commonly consumed straight, from shot glasses. Aguardiente has been popular in Colombia since the 1600s (not long after sugar plantations were introduced into the region by Spanish conquistadors), and it remains the most popular drink in the country today, by far.

Bonus fact: In the 1600s, Colombia's Spanish rulers tried to take advantage of aguardiente's popularity by monopolizing the industry. That led to many uprisings over the decades, which eventually helped fuel the revolution that led to Colombia's independence in 1810. Aguardiente—no surprise—is still a big part of the Colombian independence day celebrations today.

CHINA

Drink: Baijiu (BAY-jhee-yu)

Story: *Baijiu* (translation: "white liquor") is a hard liquor made from fermented grain using a double-distillation process that increases the alcohol content. The grain most commonly used is sorghum, but other grains, such as rice, wheat, barley, and millet, can also be used. It's strong—from 40 to 60 percent alcohol—and it's commonly drunk at room temperature, not unlike its Japanese cousin, sake. Also like sake, baijiu is traditionally served in small ceramic bottles, and drunk from small ceramic cups. There are many different types, varying from region to region, but all belong to four main categories, characterized by fragrance: strong aroma, light aroma, rice aroma, and sauce aroma. Baijiu was first made thousands of years ago. How popular is it in China? Studies indicate that baijiu accounts for one-third of all the hard liquor consumed…in the world.

Bonus fact: The first premier of communist China, Zhou Enlai, was a big fan of Moutai baijiu, a sauce aroma baijiu that has been made in the town of Moutai in China's Guizhou province since the 1600s. He made it China's official national drink in 1951—and it's what Zhou used to toast Richard Nixon in 1972, when Nixon became the first U.S. president to visit communist China.

BRAZIL

Drink: Caipirinha (KAI-peh-reen-ya)

Story: *Caipirinha* has been known as Brazil's national cocktail since the 1960s. (The origin of the name is unknown, but it can be loosely translated from Brazilian Portuguese as "little peasant.") Caipirinha is made with *cachaça* (kuh-SHAH-suh), a strong distilled spirit made from fermented sugarcane juice, which has been popular in Brazil since the 1500s. Caipirinha is believed to have originated in the Brazilian state of São Paulo in the late 1910s. The drink became popular throughout Brazil over the following decades, and more recently has become a popular cocktail in bars around the world. Traditional recipe: cut half a lime into three or four slices and put in a cocktail shaker; add two teaspoons of fine white sugar; using a utensil called a *muddler*, mash the lime and sugar well; add two ounces of cachaça; add lots of ice; cover and shake for five to ten seconds; pour into a rocks glass and garnish with a slice of lime.

Bonus fact: In the 1990s, Brazilian bartenders started experimenting with the traditional caipirinha recipe by adding new ingredients, or substituting liquors like vodka or sake for the cachaça. It led to such an outcry from purists that in 2003, the Brazilian government passed a law standardizing the caipirinha recipe, and it now, by law, has to be made with cachaça, sugar, and lime—and nothing else. (Except ice. *Saude!*)

UKRAINE

Drink: Horilka

Story: *Horilka* is basically the Ukrainian version of vodka, and is considered the traditional national alcohol. Horilka (the word is derived from the Ukrainian verb meaning "to burn," referring to the distilling process) was first made in the 1500s, and used as a medicine, often infused with fruit and spices. By the 1700s, it had become an integral part of Ukrainian culture. Like other vodkas, horilka is made from the distillation of grains, usually wheat or rye. (Occasionally, it's made from other sources, such as potatoes or sugar.) There are many flavored horilkas, just as there are flavored vodkas, but two particular types are uniquely Ukrainian: *horilka z pertsem* is horilka made with whole, hot red peppers; and *medova z pertsem* is made with peppers and honey.

Bonus fact: A song commonly sung at Ukrainian wedding receptions goes: "Horilka is too bitter, we will not drink it; we ask a groom to add some sugar to it. Bitter! Bitter!" The "sugar" in the song is a kiss; the song is sung to get the bride and groom to smooch.

ETHIOPIA

Drink: Tej

Story: *Tej* (also commonly spelled t'ej) is a unique type of mead, or wine made from fermented honey, that is flavored with extracts from the stems of the gesho shrub, a species of buckthorn native to Ethiopia. The gesho serves roughly the same purpose that hops serve in the making of beer: it adds a distinctive flavor, acts as a bittering agent to cut the sweetness of the honey (in beer, hops are added to cut the sweetness of the malt), and is also believed to have preservative qualities. Tej is easy to make, and many Ethiopians make it at home, but it's sold commercially, too, and you can find it in the many *tej bets*—or tej houses—around the country. A simple description of the manufacturing process: honey and water are mixed well (roughly one part honey to three parts water); then gesho stems and twigs are added. The gesho is removed after a few weeks, and the mix is allowed to ferment for a few more weeks. The finished product is then poured through a filter into a traditional *berele* bottle—a bulbous, vaselike bottle with a long, thin neck—and chilled.

Bonus fact: How long has tej been consumed in Ethiopia? A very long time. The ancient Roman historian Strabo wrote about tej way back in the first century AD, meaning it has probably been a regular treat in the region for about 2,000 years. (Want to make tej at home? You can find precise recipes and purchase gesho twigs online. Good luck!)

*   *   *

NOT MAKIN' WHOOPEE

For two years in the late 1980s, there was a worldwide whoopee cushion shortage. Many of the factories in Asia that usually made them didn't produce the novelties for two years. Reason: the rubber and labor had been redirected to the manufacture of surgical gloves and condoms because of increased demand due to the AIDS crisis.

Dead Language

All of these slang words and terms mean the same thing—the thing
we must all face one day. No, not taxes, the other thing: dying.

Closed up shop

Hopped the twig

Took up the harp

Joined the
invisible choir

Bought a
one-way ticket

Fell off the perch

Popped his clogs

Bit the dust

Rode the pale horse

Was traded to
the Angels

Checked into the
Horizontal Hilton

Kicked the
oxygen habit

Assumed room
temperature

Cashed in his chips

Put on a pine
overcoat

Played a
losing hand

Went to the big
castle in the sky

Bought the farm

Crossed the
Great Divide

Became worm food

Sprouted wings

Ceased to be

Went to check
out the grass from
underneath

Paid the piper

Bit the biscuit

Joined his ancestors

Took a permanent
vacation

Became crow bait

Went to Sleep City

Left a vacant chair

Got stamped
"Return to Sender"

Went to take
his free kick at
Hitler's backside

Turned up his toes

Checked into
Motel Deep 6

Entered the
Sweet Hereafter

Bought a pine
condo

Went to the
clearing at the
end of the path

Merged with the
infinite

Met her maker

Turned his face
to the wall

Tapped out

Flatlined

Joined the great
majority

Was called home

Left the building

Went to take a
dirt nap

Became a root
inspector

Ate it

The first around-the-world phone call was between two people seated 50 feet apart (1935).

By the Time We Blew Off Woodstock

The original Woodstock Music & Art Fair in 1969 featured performances from some of the biggest acts of the era, including Janis Joplin, Jefferson Airplane, the Who, and Jimi Hendrix. But not all of the biggest bands were there. Here are some performers who didn't make it to Max Yasgur's farm.

THE BEATLES. The Fab Four were offered a slot, but in 1969, the band was beginning to come apart at the seams, and John Lennon was spending most of his creative energies on the Plastic Ono Band with wife Yoko Ono. Reportedly, Lennon told Woodstock promoters that the Beatles would play, provided the Plastic Ono Band could play, too. The promoters said no, so neither the Beatles nor the Plastic Ono Band showed up. Another more boring, and more plausible, theory: The Beatles hadn't played a real concert together in three years and weren't interested in shaking off the dust.

LED ZEPPELIN. Manager Peter Grant turned down an offer to play at Woodstock because he didn't want his clients to get lost in the shuffle and be just one of a few dozen bands playing over the course of a weekend. (He wasn't prescient enough to know it would be quite a historic concert.) Instead, he launched Led Zeppelin on a headlining summer tour. The weekend of Woodstock, Led Zeppelin played in Asbury Park, New Jersey, about 150 miles away.

THE ROLLING STONES. The Stones were invited to play, but lead singer Mick Jagger was too busy. He was in Australia making a movie—his first starring film role. The movie was *Ned Kelly*, about the Australian outlaw and folk hero of the same name.

THE DOORS. Lead singer Jim Morrison hated to perform outside, citing his severe agoraphobia. He claimed that the condition stemmed from a fear—admittedly irrational—that somebody was going to shoot him while he was onstage. Whatever the reason, the Doors refused to play Woodstock because it was an outdoor gig.

BOB DYLAN. Dylan actually *was* scheduled to play, but reportedly told reporters a day or two before Woodstock took place that he had to cancel his appearance because one of his kids got sick. The real story, according to those close to Dylan, is that he was living just a few miles from the site of the festival at the time, and thousands of hippies were already starting to amass. He got freaked out by the crush of people, and fled to England (via cruise ship).

THE JEFF BECK GROUP. They were scheduled to play, but Beck broke up the band a week before the festival, which he later regretted.

THE MOODY BLUES. While the band's name appears on early Woodstock posters and other advertising materials, the Moody Blues had to cancel. The group's management had double-booked them for shows in Woodstock and Paris. They chose Paris.

TOMMY JAMES AND THE SHONDELLS. Years after the fact, James reported that his secretary had pitched the idea of playing at Woodstock over the phone to him like this: "There's this pig farmer in upstate New York that wants you to play in his field." James passed.

PROCOL HARUM. They were asked to perform, but Woodstock was scheduled to begin just as the band was ending a grueling, months-long tour. They wanted a break, so they declined.

IRON BUTTERFLY. The psychedelic band (best known for its song "In-A-Gadda-Da-Vida") was supposed to perform at Woodstock, but got stuck in the miles and miles of stopped traffic leading up to the concert. The band's management asked the New York state police for a helicopter to carry in the band and its gear. (Request denied.)

JONI MITCHELL. The Canadian singer/songwriter was offered two gigs that weekend: an appearance on *The Dick Cavett Show*, or Woodstock. Mitchell had recently performed to a hostile crowd at the Atlantic City Pop Festival, so she chose *Cavett*. But after she saw what Woodstock became, she regretted it.

JETHRO TULL. According to lead singer Ian Anderson, the band's manager, Terry Ellis, offered him the chance to play at Woodstock and this is how he responded:

> " 'Well, who else is going to be there?' And he listed a large number of groups who were reputedly going to play, and said that it was going to be a hippie festival, and I said, 'Will there be lots of naked ladies? And will there be taking drugs and drinking lots of beer, and fooling around in the mud?' Because rain was forecast. And he said, 'Oh, yeah.' So I said, 'Right. I don't want to go.' Because I don't like hippies and I'm usually rather put off by naked ladies unless the time is right."

In the 1800s, kids *got* letters from Santa Claus commenting on their behavior over the past year.

Love 2.0

*Can your smartphone help you find romance? The cupids
who invented these apps certainly think so.*

App: iFrenchKiss, released in 2011 by a company called nBit
Information Technologies

What It Does: It "scores your kissing skills."

How It Works: As far as this app is concerned, the touch screen on
your smartphone is also a "smooch screen." Pucker up, kiss your phone,
and the app will award points based on its assessment of your kissing
talent. Don't like your score? Keep kissing until your numbers improve.
"This is NOT a random 'mood sense' app," nBit assures us. "With our
original proprietary kissing analysis engine, we determine whether
you're a good kisser or not." If you're not into French kissing, the app
also rates ordinary smooches. "Use this as an icebreaker! Show off your
score and people might want to kiss you!" says nBit.

App: Good2Go, released in 2014 by Lee Ann Allman, a mom with
college-aged kids

What It Does: It verifies the "mutual consent" of two potential
partners before they engage in sex.

How It Works: A person who desires a "roll in the hay" launches the
Good2Go app on their smartphone, then hands the phone to the object
of their desire. "Are We Good2Go?" asks the app. Assuming the mood
hasn't just been spoiled by this awkward gesture, the prospective partner
can tap the "I'm Good2Go" button if they are indeed "good to go."

Doing so prompts a second screen to appear that asks whether
they are "Sober," "Mildly Intoxicated," "Intoxicated but Good2Go,"
or "Pretty Wasted." Tapping anything other than "Pretty Wasted" (too
drunk to consent) prompts additional screens that ask the user to 1)
confirm that they are at least 18 years old; and 2) verify their identity
by entering a six-digit code into the Good2Go app on their own phone.
A final screen then appears that confirms consent has been given, while
also cautioning that YES can become "NO at anytime!"

Update: Good2Go lasted just nine days in the iTunes store before
Apple kicked it off the site, apparently on the grounds that it contained
"objectionable content." That prompted Allman to pull the app from
Google Play as well; at last report she was planning to relaunch Good2Go
as a "purely educational tool" that informs users about sexual-consent
issues without asking them if they're drunk or want to have sex.

App: Spoonr, originally called Cuddlr, launched by a company called ShowMeLocal, Inc. in September 2014

What It Does: It's a Good2Go app for people who aren't Good2Go.

How It Works: Users who just want a cuddle, nothing more, post a picture and profile on the app. It searches for other cuddlers within walking distance and shares their name and picture, along with the number of "positive" and "negative" cuddles they've had in the past. If a user finds someone they'd like to cuddle with, they can tap their screen to request a cuddle, or respond to another user's request. "If you both agree…Spoonr will then show real-time walking directions between the two of you," says the company. "We encourage you to consider cuddling with people you wouldn't date, sleep with, or even find attractive, as well as those you would.…In the event of a somewhat too-grabby cuddle, you can report the user." The app also lets you post a photo of the two of you cuddling (assuming it's not too grabby).

Update: More than 200,000 people downloaded the original Cuddlr app within a week of its launch in September 2014, but the software was so buggy that the company withdrew it from the market six months later. The retooled app was launched as Spoonr in September 2015. "I think it's a good idea, IF you are good at sorting out dangerous types before meeting them in person," says one reviewer in the iTunes store.

App: *Islendiga-App* (App of Icelanders), created by three University of Iceland software engineering students in 2013

What It Does: It protects Icelanders from unknowingly "hooking up" with their own cousins

How It Works: Nearly all of Iceland's 330,000 citizens trace their ancestry back to the Vikings, who settled on the island in the 9th and 10th centuries. Intermarriage was inevitable over the generations; as a consequence, Icelanders are more closely related to one another than people in many other parts of the world are.

This genealogy has been thoroughly documented back more than 1,200 years. The family trees are contained in a database called the *Íslendingabók*, or *Book of Icelanders*, which was completed in 1997. All the creators of the App of Icelanders did was take the data contained in the *Íslendingabók* and build an Android app around it. *Islendiga-App's* most famous feature: an "Incest Prevention Alarm". All two amorous Icelanders have to do is "bump" their Android phones together before they hop in the sack. If they have at least one grandparent in common, the incest alarm will sound. *Islendiga-App's* slogan: "Bump the app before you bump in bed." (A version that protects iPhone users from accidental incest is said to be in the works.)

Live TV Goofs

*When there's no tape delay, TV sports can be pretty exciting
and in-the-moment. But in that moment there can also
be some pretty spectacular (and hilarious) screw-ups.*

THE NAKED TRUTH

After a Cincinnati Bengals win during the 2015 season, a reporter from the NFL Network conducted a locker room interview with defensive back Adam "Pacman" Jones. As the interview progressed, several of Jones's teammates, standing in the background, did what athletes usually do after a game—they undressed, unknowingly revealing their bare butts and genitals to viewers. After around 40 seconds, someone in the control room realized what was happening and cut back to the studio, where analysts, trying to hold back their laughter, could only remark, "Wowee-zowee. What an interview."

A FRANK MESSAGE

For most fans, Super Bowl XLIII in 2009 will be best remembered for the last-minute game-winning touchdown pass from Ben Roethlisberger of the Pittsburgh Steelers. But some Comcast subscribers in Tucson, Arizona (represented in the game by the Arizona Cardinals), never saw Roethlisberger's pass. Instead, they saw 37 seconds of a pornographic movie called *Wild Cherries 5*. The FBI investigated the incident and discovered that the feed had been tampered with by a 39-year-old cable company employee named Frank Gonzalez. Gonzalez was sentenced to probation and fined $1,000. Comcast gave customers $10 off their next bill, whether they saw the broadcast or not.

ROOKIE MISTAKE

In 2013, news anchor A. J. Clemente was about to start his first on-camera job with KFYR, an NBC affiliate in Bismarck, North Dakota. But before he could read the news, he didn't realize his microphone was live, and said…some bad words that you're not allowed to say on TV. It went out on the air. He completed the broadcast, then tweeted, "That couldn't have gone any worse." Two hours later, KFYR fired him. Clemente tried to do damage control by poking fun at himself in appearances on *The Today Show* and *The Late Show with David Letterman*, but as of 2016, he's working as a bartender. (What prompted Clemente's off-color outburst? Frustration. He was about to go live and he was having trouble pronouncing the name of the winner of the London Marathon, Tsegaye Kebede.)

In 2011, an inventor patented an "apparatus for facilitating the construction of a snow man/woman."

In the Greenhouse

Did you know that the first known primitive greenhouse was built almost 2,000 years ago? Here's a little history that just might grow on you.

EARLY ROOTS

Ever since humans started cultivating crops—about 12,000 years ago—people have been trying to develop better ways to grow them. At some point, farmers in various places around the world figured out that growing plants indoors, or in some kind of protected space, had potential advantages. In regions that had cold winters, they could grow plants indoors for a much longer period than they could outdoors, and they could grow plants that normally grew in different climates and on different terrain.

We don't know exactly when indoor gardening started, but we do know that advanced horticulture—the art and science of growing vegetables and ornamental flowers—was being practiced in many parts of the world thousands of years ago, and that it often involved the use of protected gardens. This included small vegetable and flower gardens outside of homes, protected from weather and wildlife by walls, and elaborate multilevel indoor (and outdoor) palace gardens—filled with hundreds of species of plants, often exotic varieties imported from conquered lands—such as the magnificent gardens built in Babylon and Egypt more than 4,000 years ago.

IT'S GETTING HOT IN HERE

The next big step in greenhouse history came when early horticulturists added heat to the equation, and built growing structures to take advantage of the sun. It probably first happened several thousand years ago, but the earliest direct evidence of something that could be identified as a greenhouse comes from the ancient Romans, about 2,000 years ago.

According to ancient Roman naturalist Pliny the Elder (ca. 23–79 AD), Emperor Tiberius, who ruled from 31 to 37 AD, had a craving for a particular vegetable: cucumbers. He insisted that his royal gardeners provide them for him every day—even in the winter. To meet this demand, Pliny wrote, the "kitchen-gardeners had cucumber beds mounted on wheels which they moved out into the sun, and then on wintry days withdrew under the cover of frames glazed with transparent stone." The "transparent stone" was *selenite*, a crystalline variety of gypsum that could be split into thin, translucent sheets. The selenite was placed over the portable cucumber beds, thereby acting as primitive greenhouses. (There was no such thing as glass windows at the time—the Romans would introduce them a short time later, around 100 AD.)

Other writers of the era mention the use of semitransparent stone windows to protect plants, suggesting that the use of these primitive greenhouses was fairly popular in ancient Rome. But little was written about them after that, and the concept of greenhouses disappeared almost entirely from the historic record for the next thousand years.

GLASS HOUSES

In the 14th and 15th centuries, citrus fruits—such as citrons, lemons, and oranges, all of which are native to the Far East—became increasingly popular in Europe. Taking advantage of that demand, citrus growers in the city-states of northern Italy figured out a way to grow the fruit year-round: they grew citrus trees in large terra-cotta pots, and in the winter they moved them into large warehouselike structures—known as *stanzone per vasi*, or "huge room for pots"—that were heated with wood stoves or open fires. The use of such hothouses spread throughout northern Europe, and became known as *orangeries*. In the late 16th century, when developments in glass production made the manufacture of transparent glass windows possible, orangeries with glass windows appeared.

THE CONSERVATORY MOVEMENT

In the 1660s, orangeries became known for the first time as "green houses." This was well into the age of exploration, and thousands of previously unknown species of plants of all kinds were being introduced to Europe from around the world. This gave rise to "botanical gardens," founded by universities and other centers of learning, for the study and display of those new and exotic plants. And because many of those plants could not survive the European climate, greenhouses were built for the sole purpose of keeping and studying those plants. As glass and iron production technology improved, greenhouses got larger and more complex, becoming known as "conservatories," from the sense that they existed for the conservation of plants. Many of those old conservatories still exist today, and are recognized as architectural wonders. These include the Palm House, built in 1840 at the Belfast Botanic Gardens in Ireland and one of the earliest examples of curved glass and cast-iron greenhouses; and the Royal Greenhouses of Laeken, an immense complex of highly stylized greenhouses built in Brussels, Belgium, in the late 19th century. Described as a "city of glass," it covers more than six acres.

STAY GREEN

Greenhouse technology continued to develop throughout the 20th century and into the 21st, and today greenhouses come in a huge

---

House cats (feral & pets) kill an estimated 1 billion birds & 6 billion mammals in the U.S. each year.

variety of shapes, sizes, and styles, and can be found in an equally wide variety of materials.

• High-tech greenhouses, such as the huge, thermoplastic biodome greenhouses built by the Eden Project in Cornwall, England, use state-of-the-art computer technology to regulate the climate inside the domes, allowing operators to create different climates.

• In Montreal, the Montreal Biodome—which is more than 650 feet long, 320 feet wide, and 180 feet tall—grows banana trees, rubber trees, coffee, and giant bamboo. And it has its own waterfall.

• Simple and inexpensive greenhouses made with plastic PVC pipe frames, and clear polyethylene film for windows, can now be found in homes, nurseries, and on farms all around the world. And backyard greenhouse kits are available at garden centers or online for just a few hundred dollars.

RANDOM GREENHOUSE FACTS

• The McMurdo Greenhouse on the United States' McMurdo Station in Antarctica can produce 250 pounds of vegetables a month. (Average outside temperature: 26°F…in the summer. It falls to an average of -15°F in winter.)

• In the late 1820s, London physician and amateur botanist Nathaniel Bagshaw Ward was studying a moth chrysalis in a sealed jar when he noticed a fern growing from the soil in the bottom of the jar. Intrigued, he made some small, sealed glass enclosures—basically miniature, sealed greenhouses—and found that he could grow ferns and other small tropical plants inside them. "Wardian cases," as they were known, became popular with explorers in the mid-19th century, as it allowed for the safe transport of fragile exotic plants that otherwise could not survive long sea journeys, and they later became popular items in Victorian homes. The tiny greenhouses are better known as *terrariums* today. (Note: Today "terrarium" is used to refer to small, *unsealed* glass display enclosures, such as those used to house small animals.)

*   *   *

FOUR TOASTER FAD FLOPS
• Downyflake Toaster Eggs
• Reddi Bacon
• Toaster Chicken Patties
• The Electric French Fry

What's Up, Doc?

*More real-life diagnoses of the ailments of fictional characters
that have been written up in medical journals.*

Patient: Winnie the Pooh
Medical Issues: What little attention span Pooh does have is focused on obtaining and eating honey.
Physician's Notes: "Given his coexisting Attention Deficit Hyperactivity Disorder and Obsessive Compulsive Disorder, we question whether Pooh may over time present with Tourette's syndrome. Early on we see Pooh being dragged downstairs bump, bump, bump, on the back of his head. Could his later cognitive struggles be the result of a type of Shaken Bear Syndrome?" Also: "Eeyore would benefit greatly from an antidepressant, perhaps combined with individual therapy." (*Canadian Medical Association Journal*, December 2000)

Patients: The good and bad characters in *The Hobbit*
Medical Issues: The evil characters eat an unbalanced diet (mutton, goblins, and, occasionally, fish). Since they live in the Misty Mountains and other dark places, they have little exposure to sunlight. The good characters, by comparison, eat a rich and varied diet and spend much of their time in the sun. (Spoiler alert! By the end of the story, the good characters triumph over the evil characters.)
Physicians' Notes: "We hypothesized that a major contribution to the defeat of evildoers in this context is their aversion to sunlight and their poor diet, which may lead to vitamin D deficiency and hence reduced martial prowess." (*Medical Journal of Australia*, December 2013)

Patient: Tintin the boy adventurer, a popular Belgian comic book character. The 23 books he appeared in from 1929 to 1975 were translated into more than 60 languages and sold more than 200 million copies worldwide. Steven Spielberg is a fan; he directed *The Adventures of Tintin* in 2011.
Medical Issues: Tintin, now about 100 years old, has never matured physically beyond the age of about 14. Given that he has never shaved and has not grown an inch since 1929, it's doubtful that he's gone through puberty. He has never dated, been in a romantic relationship, or shown even the slightest interest in members of either sex.
Physician's Notes: Dr. Claude Cyr, who teaches medicine in Quebec, Canada, read through all 23 books with his five-year-old and seven-year-old sons. They counted 50 instances where Tintin "falls

into the apples" (French for "gets knocked unconscious"), an average of more than one a year. Of these, 43 were concussions caused by explosions, gunshot wounds, falls from great heights, fights with wild animals, falls on ice, and blows to the head from a brick, a sword, a rake, a whiskey bottle, a bone, various clubs, and miscellaneous other blunt objects.

Dr. Cyr sees a link between the 43 concussions in 46 years and Tintin's lack of pubertal development. "We hypothesize that Tintin has growth hormone deficiency and hypogonadotropic hypogonadism (a pituitary gland condition) from repeated trauma. This could explain his delayed statural growth, delayed onset of puberty and lack of libido." (*Canadian Medical Association Journal*, December 2004)

Patient: Doc, leader of the seven dwarves of *Snow White* fame

Medical Issues: Doc's speech is usually fluent, but he occasionally stutters and he also has "many spontaneous paraphasias, most of them phonetic." (He jumbles words and makes meaningless statements.)

Doc refers to the other dwarves as "hen" instead of "men"; addresses Snow White as "quincess" instead of "princess"; asks her "What are you and who are you doing" when the dwarves discover her in their home; and tells her that she can stay because she knows how to make "laple duflings"—apple dumplings. Doc catches and corrects many of his own errors in speech, has no problem understanding the speech of others, and is able to sing fluently with no paraphasias or grammatical errors.

Physicians' Notes: Dr. Iftah Biran and Dr. Israel Steiner noted each of Doc's errors in speech in the 1937 Disney film, then made their diagnosis. "It seems…that Doc has a perisylvian aphasia with impaired repetition, but differentiation between an anterior and a posterior syndrome is not clear," the doctors write. "Whereas the fluent speech and preserved prosidy suggest a posterior syndrome, the stuttering and the intact comprehension are in favor of an anterior syndrome." And you thought Doc was hard to understand. (*Neurology*, July 2001)

Patient: Dopey, another of the seven dwarves

Medical Issues: Though he clearly understands speech and wants to communicate, Dopey is a mute. He cannot speak. He has a "wide-based, hopping gait" when he walks, and he experiences "generalized tonic-clonic seizures," or muscle spasms, when he sleeps. He has a happy demeanor and is almost always smiling.

Physicians' Notes: "The features presented in the film are strikingly consistent with Angelman syndrome, a neurogenetic condition characterized by developmental delay, absence of speech, motor impairment, happy demeanor and seizures," wrote researchers Bernard Dan and Florence Christiaens. (*Seizure*, 1999)

Lucky Finds

More true stories of amazing discoveries.

SEUSS ON THE LOOSE!

The Find: An unpublished Dr. Seuss book

Where It Was Found: In a box / that had no locks / and was not eaten by a fox

The Story: Audrey Geisel thought that all of her late husband's most important writings and drawings had been donated to the University of California, San Diego, after he died in 1991. She would know, because she assembled the collection herself. But there were a few random scribblings that didn't seem like much, so Geisel put them in a box and then forgot about them…for more than 20 years.

In 2013, Geisel (by then in her 90s) decided to have the contents of the box appraised. Inside were several notes and drawings—mostly stuff that Dr. Seuss himself rejected for his books—but there was something else that she had missed before: a 16-page black-and-white manuscript called *The Pet Shop*. A sequel (or perhaps a prequel) to his 1960 book *One Fish Two Fish Red Fish Blue Fish*, it chronicles siblings Jay and Kay as they try to decide on a new pet (including a Yent, who sleeps under a tent). Dr. Seuss wrote and illustrated it sometime between 1957 and 1962, but never showed it to anyone. Geisel said that it was a busy time for her husband, so he may simply have "forgotten about it." In 2015, Random House published the book under the title *What Pet Should I Get?* It sold 200,000 copies in its first week.

THE LEAK IN THE ATTIC

The Find: A painting masterpiece

Where It Was Found: Hidden inside a house in Toulouse, France

The Story: In 2014, a family (unidentified in press reports) living in an old house in the south of France had to deal with a leaky roof. When they looked for the source of the leak, they found a small room in the attic that they had never seen before. Inside the room was a painting.

The family brought it to a Paris art dealer, who suspected it could be *Judith Beheading Holofernes*, a long-lost piece by Renaissance painter Michelangelo Merisi Caravaggio. No one had seen the actual painting since the 1600s, but a copy had been made, so collectors knew it could be out there. After two years of scrutinization in Paris, experts authenticated it: it was a Caravaggio. The painting has been given "National Treasure" status in France. Estimated worth: €120m ($136 million).

Need another reason to quit? Scientists have linked smoking to premature hair graying.

They Sure Can Pick 'em

*Before a big game, lots of sports fans will have an opinion on who they
think will win. But how many are as good at picking winners—
or future presidents, for that matter—as these critters?*

ELI THE ORANGUTAN
Prognostication: Each year, Eli's keepers at Salt Lake City's
Hogle Zoo placed objects (such as papier mâché helmets and
cardboard footballs) painted with the logos of the two Super Bowl
teams in the orangutan enclosure. Whichever object Eli showed
interest in first served as his prediction for the winner of the game.

Outcome: From 2007 until his death in 2014, Eli picked teams for
seven Super Bowls—and all seven went on to win. (Odds of randomly
selecting seven Super Bowl winners in a row: 1 in 128.)

HUGH AND BUFFETT THE MANATEES
Prognostication: Hugh and Buffett are manatees, or "sea cows," who
live at the Mote Marine Aquarium in Sarasota, Florida. The week
before the Super Bowl, trainers lower two targets into the water at one
end of the manatee tank. One target has a photo of one team's helmet,
and the other target has the other team's helmet. The manatees swim
up to the targets, and whichever one they nudge first is considered their
pick for the winner of the game.

Outcome: Hugh and Buffett have been making their picks since 2008,
and as of 2016 Hugh has picked the winner five out of nine times and
Buffett has picked the winner eight out of nine times. (Odds of picking
the Super Bowl winner eight times out of nine: less than 1 in 50.)

THE PALM BEACH POOCH PREDICTORS
Prognostication: Every year, the Palm Beach Kennel Club in West
Palm Beach, Florida, holds a Pooch Predictor race between two grey-
hounds, each one wearing the colors of a team in the Super Bowl. The
team represented by the first dog across the finish line is the predicted
Super Bowl winner.

Outcome: As of 2016, the winning dog has correctly predicted the
winner of the Super Bowl 14 out of 20 times. (Odds of picking that
many winners at random: less than 1 in 25.)

The Atacama Desert in the Andes is similar to Mars in soil, climate, and radiation levels.

Bonus: The pacing of the dog race is used to predict the pacing of the Super Bowl. In 2016, for example, the dog representing the Denver Broncos took an early lead, but although the dog representing the Carolina Panthers nearly caught up, it never took the lead and the Broncos' dog was first across the finish line. This led to the prediction that the Broncos would take the lead early in the Super Bowl, "but be challenged in the early going by the Panthers" before winning the game. Just as the dog race had predicted, the Broncos pulled ahead early by scoring ten points in the first quarter, and the Panthers closed the gap by scoring seven points in the second quarter. But they never closed it entirely, and trailed the Broncos for the rest of the game. Final score: Broncos 24, Panthers 10.

PRINCESS THE CAMEL

Prognostication: In 2006, a local radio station called zookeepers at the Popcorn Park Zoo in Lacey, New Jersey, and asked them to have one of their animals pick a team to win the Super Bowl as part of an on-air radio stunt. Zoo manager John Bergmann gave the job to Princess, a Bactrian camel. Bergmann wrote the name of one team in the palm of his left hand and the name of the other team in the palm of his right hand. Then he put a graham cracker in each hand and held them out for Princess to choose. Whichever cracker she ate first revealed the name of the winning team in Bergmann's palm.

Outcome: Princess picked the winner that year, and the stunt was so popular, Princess continued to make picks—not just for the Super Bowl but for regular-season games as well. Her best season was 2008–2009, when she correctly chose the winners of 18 out of 23 games. By the time of her death in 2014, she'd predicted the outcomes of 175 NFL games…and correctly picked the winner 113 times. (Odds of picking that many winners at random: less than 1 in 10,000.)

PAUL THE OCTOPUS

Prognostication: In 2008, Paul's keepers at the Sea Life Center in Oberhausen, Germany, put two clear Plexiglas boxes in his tank, each one containing a mussel for him to eat. One of the boxes was decorated with a German flag, and the other bore the flag of the German team's opponent in the Euro 2008 soccer tournament. Whichever box Paul opened first was his pick as the winner.

Outcome: Paul correctly predicted the results of four of Germany's six matches in the Euro 2008 tournament. That impressed his keepers enough that they decided to use him again during the 2010 World Cup. This time Paul made his predictions live on German television, correctly picking the winners of all seven of Germany's World Cup matches, including Spain when it *beat* Germany in the semifinals.

Paul's accurate prediction of Germany's loss to Spain did not endear him to German soccer fans; there were so many calls to "throw him in the frying pan" and make calamari, as one Berlin newspaper put it, that a Spanish government official offered Paul asylum in Spain. Paul stayed put, though, and lived out the rest of his life at the Sea Life Center in Oberhausen, where he died from natural causes (or so we've been told) later that year. If you visit the Sea Life Center today, be sure to check out the memorial sculpture of Paul straddling a World Cup soccer ball. The urn containing his cremated remains is displayed nearby.

MR. NUTS

Prognostication: Mr. Nuts, a short-hair tuxedo cat, belongs to Michael Ostrofsky of Fremont, California. In the closing days of the 2012 presidential election, Ostrofsky set up two litter boxes side by side and had Mr. Nuts forecast the outcome of the race by putting the boxes to their intended use. The box on the left was labeled "Barack Obama" (Get it? The box on the *left*.), and the box on the right was labeled "Mitt Romney." Unlike other four-legged forecasters, Mr. Nuts's job was to pick the *loser*, which he did by relieving himself in his litter box and leaving the winner's box unsoiled. "When it comes to Mr. Nuts, any time you're dealing with him and his litter boxes you lose," Ostrofsky explained.

Outcome: Mr. Nuts defecated in Mitt Romney's box, and the rest is history. (Ostrofsky says the cat also correctly predicted the outcomes of the 2011, 2012, and 2013 Super Bowls; the 2013 America's Cup yacht race; and the sex of Prince William and Kate's first child. (A boy, Prince George, was born in July 2013. Mr. Nuts made that pick by pooping in the litter box marked "Girl.")

SONNY WOOL

Details: Sonny Wool's owner, New Zealander Beverly Dowling, drew inspiration from Paul the Octopus and began using the three-year-old sheep to predict the outcomes of New Zealand's matches in the 2011 Rugby World Cup. She set two bowls of hay in front of Sonny, one marked with a New Zealand flag and the other marked with the flag of the opposing team. Sometimes the New Zealand bowl was to the left of the opposing team's bowl, and sometimes it was to the right. Whichever bowl Sonny Wool ate from first predicted the winner.

Outcome: Sonny Wool picked New Zealand to win all of the seven games it played, and he was right every time: New Zealand won four games in the initial pool stage, then went on to beat its opponents in the quarterfinals, semifinals, and the final, beating France 8–7 to win the World Cup. (Odds of picking the winner seven times in a row: 1 in 128.)

Only about 20 copies of the first printing (1865) of *Alice in Wonderland* survive.

Lost Oil Rigs

In 1947, Kerr-McGee Industries built Kermac No. 16, the first productive offshore oil rig ever constructed out of sight of land, 10.5 miles off the Louisiana coast in the Gulf of Mexico. That ushered in the era of modern offshore oil drilling. Soon thereafter…the era of offshore oil rig disasters began. Here are the stories of some of the worst oil rig disasters in history.

C. P. BAKER

Background: The C. P. Baker was a 264-foot-long drilling barge—a cross between an oil rig and a ship. It looks like a large ship with an oil drilling derrick rising from its deck.

Disaster: On June 30, 1964, the C. P. Baker was at anchor about 70 miles off the Louisiana coast, drilling several hundred feet into the ocean floor, in about 184 feet of water. At around 3:00 a.m., a blowout occurred. That's when an oil drill penetrates a highly pressurized pocket of oil and natural gas, which is subsequently released with great force through the drillpipe. This is normally averted by the use of a blowout preventer, a device inserted into the piping above the ocean floor, which acts as a valve to stop gas and oil from releasing. But the blowout preventer hadn't been installed yet. Result: a blast of gas shot up out of the rig's piping, and minutes later, ignited and exploded, engulfing the entire vessel in fire. Within 30 minutes, the C. P. Baker had capsized and sunk to the ocean floor.

Aftermath: With more than half of the 43-man crew killed, it was the deadliest oil rig accident ever to occur in the Gulf of Mexico. A subsequent investigation led to changes in the offshore oil industry, including new regulations on when blowout preventers should be installed.

BOHAI 2

Background: The Bohai 2 was a jackup rig—a large oil rig that, once it was towed to a drilling location, is set firmly on long steel legs that reach to the seafloor. Those legs also extend up and through the rig's steel-and-concrete work platform, the deck upon which the rig's drilling equipment sits. The platform can be raised up the legs so that it sits high above the water's surface, protecting it from the waves (hence the name "jackup" rig). Owner: the China Petroleum Department.

Disaster: On November 25, 1979, the Bohai 2 was being towed to a drilling location in the Gulf of Bohai, in eastern China, when a violent storm struck with winds higher than 50 mph. A large wave broke over the surface of the rig, snapping a large pump off its moorings, sending it crashing onto the deck and punching a hole through the platform's surface. The hole allowed water to pour into a room inside the platform, which eventually led to the entire rig capsizing and, ultimately, sinking.

Aftermath: Of the *Bohai 2*'s 74 crewmembers, the ship towing the rig was able to rescue just two of them; the other 72 died. The high number of fatalities was blamed on the severity of the storm, and the fact that the crew had little in the way of emergency training.

ALEXANDER L. KIELLAND

Background: The *Alexander L. Kielland* was a semisubmersible oil rig. Semisubmersibles are floating rigs, supported by large hollow pontoons that sit underwater and act as flotation devices. In 1980, the *Alexander L. Kielland* was operating about 200 miles southwest of the Norwegian coast, right in the middle of the North Sea. But it wasn't being used to drill for oil or gas—it was a "flotel," used to house the workers at a nearby permanent oil platform, and was specially fitted with guest rooms, kitchens, lounges, and even a small movie theater.

Disaster: During a severe storm on March 27, 1980, an underwater brace supporting one of the rig's five massive legs broke. Then several other braces broke, after which the entire leg broke off. The rig immediately went into a 35-degree list, causing the platform that housed the off-duty workers to take on a large amount of water. Over the next 15 minutes, the crew attempted to launch the rig's seven 50-man lifeboats. Several men were killed in the process, smashed into the rig's legs by huge waves as the boats were being lowered from the platform. After just 15 minutes, the entire rig capsized.

Aftermath: Only two of the lifeboats were successfully launched, and 123 of the 212 workers on the *Alexander L. Kielland* died. An investigation determined that failure of the first brace was due to a faulty weld.

OCEAN RANGER

Background: Operated by oil giant Mobil, the *Ocean Ranger* was another semisubmersible oil rig—and it was huge. Its two flotation pontoons were 60 feet wide, 20 feet high, and almost 400 feet long, and the work platform they supported was more than 200 feet long and 80 feet wide; it sat more than 70 feet above the ocean's surface.

Disaster: On February 14, 1982, the *Ocean Ranger* was drilling a well in the North Atlantic, about 160 miles off the coast of Newfoundland, in water about 260 feet deep, when a storm struck. By the early hours of February 15, winds were reaching 115 mph, and 65-foot waves were crashing against the rig's understructure. At around 1:00 a.m., the *Ocean Ranger* sent out a mayday, reporting that the platform was listing badly. About 30 minutes later, it sent its last message: "There will be no further radio communications from *Ocean Ranger*. We are going to lifeboat stations." The rig sank about 90 minutes later.

Aftermath: The severe weather made rescue attempts impossible. All 84 men aboard the *Ocean Ranger* perished; only 22 bodies were recovered. A commission into the disaster found, among other things, that the crew had not been properly trained in emergency procedures, and did not have proper safety equipment, such as survival suits meant to protect the body from cold water (the water was about 29°F). The *Ocean Ranger* oil rig disaster remains the worst in Canadian history.

SEACREST

Background: The California company Unocal, now part of Chevron, operated the 360-foot-long drillship in oil and gas fields in the Gulf of Thailand. In 1989, it was at anchor and drilling in the middle of the gulf, about 270 miles south of Bangkok.

Disaster: On November 3, 1989, Typhoon Gay struck the gulf and passed directly over the *Seacrest*, battering it with 100-mph winds and 40-foot waves. The *Seacrest* never sent a distress signal, and wasn't reported missing by Unocal officials until the next day. A search helicopter found it at around 8:00 a.m. on November 4. It was four miles from where it had been stationed before the storm, floating upside down in the water.

Aftermath: The *Seacrest* had a crew of 97, and only six survived. (They were pulled from the water by Thai fishermen.) The fact that no lifeboats were found suggests that the storm capsized the rig too quickly for the crew to react. A lawsuit against Unocal, brought by the families of the dead, dragged on for years before being settled for an undisclosed amount.

PIPER ALPHA

Background: The *Piper Alpha* was an oil platform, meaning a fixed oil rig, built on site and permanently attached to the ocean floor. It was constructed in the 1970s above the Piper Oil Field, a large oil and gas deposit beneath the North Sea, about 120 miles off the east coast of Scotland. By the late 1980s, it was the world's largest oil rig of *any* kind: its main body—made up of four modules, some of which housed machinery, and some of which housed quarters for the more than 200 people who worked there—sat more than 100 feet above the water line on a network of legs that stretched 474 feet down to the ocean floor. It looked like a giant space station sitting on stilts above the ocean, with huge cranes, a helicopter landing pad, and an enormous oil derrick on top.

Disaster: On July 6, 1988, a safety valve on a pump used to pressurize a natural gas pipe on the rig was removed for routine maintenance, and was replaced with a temporary seal. An order was written warning that under no circumstances should the pump be turned on until the safety valve was replaced. That night, around 9:55 p.m., an engineer who was working the night shift—and hadn't seen the order—turned on the pump. Gas started leaking from the temporary seal almost immediately. The gas ignited and exploded. The ensuing fire, fueled by escaping gas, set off a chain reaction, and over the next few hours several more gas pipes were breached, resulting in more explosions and a fire that could be seen 70 miles away. A firefighting ship attempted to put out the fires, but to no avail. By 12:45 a.m., most of the *Piper Alpha*'s modules had melted and fallen into the sea.

Aftermath: The *Piper Alpha* had a crew of 226 people—and 167 of them were killed in the disaster. It remains the deadliest offshore oil rig accident in history.

OTHER OIL RIG DISASTERS

• The *Glomar Java Sea* was a drillship operating off the coast of Vietnam. On October 25, 1983, in the midst of stormy weather, its captain reported experiencing a list of unknown origin. The ship capsized and sank a short time later. All 81 people aboard were lost. (The *Glomar Java Sea* has been the subject of conspiracy theories since it went down, the most popular of which says it was actually a CIA listening post—and was sunk by a Vietnamese torpedo.)

• On July 27, 2005, a ship collided with the Mumbai High North oil platform in the Indian Ocean. The collision ruptured a gas pipe, and the ensuing fire destroyed the platform. It also severely damaged the ship, which drifted off and sank a few days later. Twenty-two people were killed.

• On April 20, 2010, the semisubmersible oil rig *Deepwater Horizon* was drilling for oil in the Gulf of Mexico, about 40 miles off Mississippi, in water almost 5,000 feet deep, when it experienced a well blowout. The crew tried to activate the well's blowout preventer. It failed. The escaping gas exploded, killing 11 men; the rig sank 36 hours later. The well gushed for three months before it could be capped, spilling an estimated 4.9 billion barrels of oil into the ocean. It was the largest oil spill in U.S. history.

*　　　*　　　*

KEEP YOUR FRIENDS CLOSE... An *indocannibal* eats their friends and associates. An *exocannibal* eats only their enemies.

Odd Monuments

*Tired of your standard boring, run-of-the-mill monument
to some dead president? Then try one of these.*

RADIOACTIVE DECAY MONUMENT

Where You'll Find It: The coastal city of Nieuwdorp, Holland

What It Looks Like: A bright orange, blocky building about the length of a football field and 130 feet tall, with scientific formulas—such as "$E = MC^2$"—in huge, bright green letters on its exterior

Story: It's a nuclear waste storage site, holding thousands of tons of highly radioactive waste, accumulated from Holland's two nuclear power plants. It's also a work of art meant to serve as a monument to radioactive decay, according to William Verstraeten, the artist hired by the Dutch government to design it. The building, officially known as the Habog Facility, was completed in 2005, and it will be the home of the radioactive waste inside it for at least 100 years. And it won't always be bright orange: every 20 years it will be painted a lighter shade of orange to symbolize the metamorphosis process, as the waste slowly decays and becomes less and less radioactive over time. This, the government says, will help educate the public about the safe management of radioactive waste. (Bonus: You can go inside the building. It has a visitor center and a museum, and it's a popular tourist destination.)

GIANT CORN MONUMENT

Where You'll Find It: Dublin, Ohio

What It Looks Like: A field of giant concrete ears of corn, painted white, each over six feet tall, in a roadside field in central Ohio

Story: This work of art was created as a memorial to Sam Frantz, a local farmer who used the field from the 1930s until the 1960s to develop several strains of hybrid corn. It was commissioned by the City of Dublin Arts Council, and designed by Malcolm Cochran, an arts professor at Ohio State University. There are 109 concrete ears of corn in the field, which covers about two acres. Each of them is about eight feet tall and weighs more than 1,500 pounds. *Roadside America*, a website that chronicles roadside oddities, says of the site: "Intended by the Arts Council to remind residents of the area's long-gone agricultural heritage, the Field of Corn instantly became a joke—giant inedible food, paid for with tax dollars, and surrounded by a sprawl of corporate offices, bland businesses, and suburban neighborhoods." (Bonus: Locals have dubbed the site "Cornhenge.")

BABY-EATER MONUMENT

Where You'll Find It: Bern, Switzerland

What It Looks Like: A public fountain in the middle of a square in Bern's Old City, with a tall column rising from its center, topped by a statue of an ogreish creature biting the head off a naked baby. The ogre has seven more babies—all looking terrified—at his side.

Story: The name of the fountain, *Kindlifresserbrunnen*, literally means "Child-Eater Fountain." It has been there for over 450 years—since 1546, when it was constructed by Swiss sculptor Hans Gieng. Exactly what it was supposed to signify nobody knows. One theory is that the ogre represents *Krampus*, the mythological figure popular in Europe during the Middle Ages, who is said to punish naughty children around Christmastime. (A more sinister theory: because the ogreish figure is wearing a pointy hat similar to a *Judenhut*, or "Jewish hat," which Jewish men were forced to wear in parts of medieval Europe, the sculpture could be a representation of the anti-Semitic "blood libel" slur popular in medieval times—which said that Jewish people murdered the children of Christians and used their blood in religious rituals.)

UPSIDE-DOWN DEAD HORSE MONUMENT

Where You'll Find It: Prague, Czech Republic

What It Looks Like: A dead horse hanging from a ceiling by ropes from its legs, with its tongue hanging out and with a kingly figure of a man sitting on its belly

Story: The bronze sculpture, called *Kun* (Horse), hangs from the ceiling of Prague's popular Lucerna Palace, an open-air gallery of shops, restaurants, bars, and performance venues. It was created in 1999 by rebel Czech artist David Cerny, whose many controversial sculptures dot the Czech Republic. *Kun* is a parody of the famous statue of a Saint Wenceslas that overlooks the city's Wenceslas Square. (Wenceslas, the subject of the famous Christmas carol "Good King Wenceslas," was a 10th-century Czech king, and has been a national hero for centuries.) The statue is also assumed to have been a dig at Czech leader Vaclav Klaus, a regular target of Cerny's art.

INJURED FOOT MONUMENT

Where You'll Find It: Stillwater, New York

What It Looks Like: A headstone about five feet tall with the sculpted likeness of a boot on it.

Story: The "Boot Monument" is a memorial to America's most famous traitor—Benedict Arnold, the general who fought for the Americans during the Revolutionary War, and then switched sides and sold secrets to the British. It was erected in 1887 in recognition of wounds

Arnold received to his foot and leg while fighting for the American side—before he turned traitor—in the pivotal Battle of Saratoga in 1777. The memorial, which sits near where Arnold was injured in what is now Saratoga National Historic Park, was donated to the site by Revolutionary War historian and former Civil War general John Watts de Peyster. An inscription on the back of the memorial says it was erected for "the 'most brilliant soldier' of the Continental Army, who was desperately wounded on this spot"…but it doesn't mention Arnold's name—at all. It's the only American war monument dedicated to a specific soldier that doesn't bear that soldier's name.

HOUSE-CRASHING SHARK MONUMENT

Where You'll Find It: Headington, England

What It Looks Like: A 25-foot fiberglass shark sticking out of the roof of a house in Headington, a suburb of the English city of Oxford

Story: The giant shark was designed by English sculptor John Buckley, and commissioned by the homeowner, BBC radio presenter Bill Heine. It was installed (to the surprise of Heine's neighbors) on August 9, 1986—the 41st anniversary of the United States' nuclear attack on the Japanese city of Nagasaki, as a protest of both nuclear weapons and nuclear energy. "The shark was to express someone feeling totally impotent and ripping a hole in their roof out of a sense of impotence and anger and desperation," Heine told reporters. The Oxford City Council tried to have the sculpture removed, but eventually had to give up because the Headington Shark, as it is commonly known, is too popular.

POOP MONUMENT

Where You'll Find It: Chicago, Illinois

What It Looks Like: A huge coiled, brown, and glistening turd on a marble stand in front of a building in Chicago

Story: The giant pile of poop was sculpted by Chicago artist Jerzy S. Kenar, and it sits on a three-foot-high pedestal in front of his studio. Inscribed on the marble stand are the words "S*** Fountain." (Except there are no asterisks.) Upon the sculpture's unveiling, at a July 4th party in 2005, Kenar announced that the work was "dedicated to all the dogs in the neighborhood," but later admitted it was meant more for local dog owners—who regularly failed to clean up after their pets on city sidewalks and in its parks. Want to take a selfie with the giant pile of poop? Kenar's studio is at 1001 North Wolcott Avenue, in Chicago's East Village. (Note: If uncoiled, the giant poop—which is made of bronze—would be more than six feet long.)

Forgotten '80s Toys

Thanks to He-Man, G.I. Joe, and Transformers, the 1980s were the golden age of action figures. But even a golden age can lay some eggs.

COMPUTER WARRIORS (1989)
The premise, as explained on the packaging: "A U.S. military supercomputer malfunctioned and created four evil viruses that jump from the electronic world into the real world, threatening humanity. In response, the military created 'good' software that took the form of two-inch-tall humanoids that also head into the physical realm and stalk the villains by hiding out in everyday objects." That's a pretty futuristic backstory to explain some pretty low-tech toys. Computer Warriors toys were plastic, nonfunctioning clocks, pencil sharpeners, soccer trophies, and soda cans that opened up to reveal a secret compartment, which held a tiny robot action figure.

BARNYARD COMMANDOS (1988)
The perfect toys for kids who liked farm animals…but also war. The packaging told buyers that a secret military experiment on a farm some-where in America's heartland had contaminated the grain, and mutated the sheep and pigs who ate it into violent army commandos. The pigs, outfitted with guns on their backs, called themselves P.O.R.K.S. (Platoon of Rebel Killer Swine). They were led by General Hamfat Lardo. The sheep, also with guns on their backs, called themselves R.A.M.S. (Rebel Army of Military Sheep). More advanced weaponry, such as the Pork-a-Pult—a catapult operated by pigs—was also avail-able. The marketing tagline: "These Guys Are Animals!"

ARMY ANTS (1987)
More animal commandos, but this time with six legs. These pint-sized, gun-totin' insect-soldiers came in two factions: the orange army (led by General Patant) and the blue army (led by General Mc-Anther). Kids could buy packs (squadrons) of armed-to-the-teeth ants with names like Warpo, Rambant, Snarl, Bullseye, and Blitz Kreig.

RING RAIDERS (1989)
The line of toys was based on a five-episode cartoon miniseries set in the far-off year of 1998. It featured the "Skull Squadron," a band of pilots who can use their planes for time travel, but the power goes to their heads and they crave world domination. Another crew of jet

pilots, called "Justice," aims to stop them. The cartoon had almost nothing to do with the actual toys—one-inch plastic versions of Skull Squadron and Justice planes glued to plastic rings. Kids were supposed to wear the planes on their fingers and then fight with them.

ROCK LORDS (1986)

Hasbro's Transformers—everyday vehicles that turned into robots—were the hottest toy around in the mid-1980s. Other toy companies quickly released their own versions of the thing-that-becomes-another-thing. Tonka's Gobots sold well and spawned an animated TV series. Tonka's spinoff line, Rock Lords...did not sell very well. Like Transformers, Gobots were vehicles that turned into robots. Rock Lords, however, were tiny, two-inch-tall robots that turned into rocks. In other words, they folded up into little plastic lumps. (The "Heroic" Rock Lords included: Boulder, Nuggit, Pulver-Eyes. "Evil" Rock Lords: Magmar, Tombstone, Slimestone.)

SECTAURS (1985)

The backstory from Coleco: "On the distant planet Symbion, a genetic experiment fails. Frightening changes take place that cannot be stopped. The result? A world where insects grow to frightening proportions." The horse-sized insects coexist on Symbion with human-insect hybrids (the Sectaurs) who ride them like horses, and with whom they share a telepathic bond. The "horses" are hideous, foot-long bugs with huge red eyes covered in synthetic fur (they're puppets that fit over your arm). Despite a massive marketing campaign, Sectaurs never caught on.

SUPER NATURALS (1987) and VISIONARIES (1987)

Toymakers thought holograms were going to be huge in 1987. Both Tonka and Hasbro released a line of action figures that featured silvery images. Tonka's Super Naturals, characters with supernatural abilities (one was a snake-man, another an Aztec warrior), had holograms on their battle shields—not to be confused with Hasbro's Visionaries, which were supernatural warriors who sported holograms on their *chests*.

FOOD FIGHTERS (1988)

Mattel's toys pitted one squadron of anthropomorphized plastic food against another for the dominance of a refrigerator. The Kitchen Commandos were the good guys: Lieutenant Legg (a fried chicken drumstick), Private Pizza (a piece of pizza) and Sergeant Scoop (an ice-cream cone). They rode around in a Combat Carton (a weapon-laden egg carton) and battled their sworn enemies, the Refrigerator Rejects. Some of the bad guys: Mean Weener (a hot dog), Fat Frenchy (fries), and Taco Terror (a taco).

First They Made...

Companies that last a long time adapt over the years as the marketplace changes. Here are some well-known companies and their very first products.

CASIO. Today the Japanese company is mainly known for manufacturing calculators and electric keyboards. When Casio was founded in 1946, its first item was called a Yubiwa, a ring that held onto a cigarette, allowing the wearer to smoke it down to the end.

STARBUCKS. Today they have thousands of cafés selling coffee and muffins, but in 1971, there was only one Starbucks (in Seattle) and it roasted beans and sold espresso machines.

NOKIA. The company is known for cell phones, but its first business—in 1865—was a paper mill on the Nokianvirta River in Finland.

HEWLETT-PACKARD. At its launch in 1947, HP made and sold electronic test equipment. (They didn't move into computers until 1968.)

NINTENDO. The video game company has changed direction many times over the years, selling vacuum cleaners, instant rice, and even running hotel chains in Japan. But when Nintendo started in 1889, it was already in the games business. They made playing cards.

SUZUKI. From 1909 to 1935, long before it became known for motorcycles, Suzuki was the Japanese silk industry's primary supplier of looms.

HASBRO. In 1923, the future toy giant was called Hassenfeld Brothers. They sold textile remnants and school supplies.

SAMSUNG. Long before cell phones and flat-screen TVs, the company was called Samsung Sanghoe. Founded in 1938, it sold dried fish and packaged noodles via mail order to Korean expatriates in China.

WRIGLEY. In the 1890s, William Wrigley wasn't selling gum—he was selling soap and baking powder. To get people to buy his soap, he gave away free packs of gum with each purchase...until customers started asking for the gum instead of the soap. So he started a company just to make the gum.

3M. The name of the firm that makes Post-Its is short for the Minnesota Mining and Manufacturing Company. It began in 1902 as an industrial mining operation looking for the mineral corundum, which was used in grinding wheels.

Tee-hee! A quarterly edition of the comic *Man-Thing* was titled *Giant-Size Man-Thing*.

An Incredible Critter

We've written about lots of unusual animals over the years, but this is the first one we've encountered that makes its own mucus sleeping bag. Here are a few more curious facts about the parrotfish.

A FISH BY ANY OTHER NAME

Parrotfish are a family of fish found in shallow tropical waters around the world, usually in and around coral reefs in the Pacific and Indian Oceans. If you've ever gone snorkeling or diving in Hawaii or Australia, for example, there's a good chance you've encountered some of these brightly colored creatures in their natural habitat. There are about 80 different species, ranging from less than one foot to four feet in length, and weighing as much as 100 pounds. And, as these parrotfish facts show, it is no ordinary fish:

• **They Have "Beaks."** Actually, parrotfish have sets of fused-together teeth on both their upper and lower jaws that protrude from their mouths in a slightly forward-thrusting formation—making it look like they have birdlike beaks. (The beaks are more pronounced in some species than in others.) That, along with these fishes' bright colors, explains the name "parrotfish."

• **They Eat Coral.** Parrotfish have extremely strong jaw muscles that, along with their sturdy, beaklike teeth, they use to bite pieces off of coral reefs. Another set of teeth, further back in their mouths, grinds that hard coral into powder. (If you've ever seen parrotfish in the wild, you may have probably *heard* them in the wild, too. They make a loud, crunching racket as they chew on coral reefs.) They do this in order to get at their favorite food—algae that grow on coral reefs, and coral polyps that live inside the reefs. (Coral polyps secrete their calcium carbonate exoskeletons the way that snails and other shellfish do. Those exoskeletons are what hold coral reefs together.)

• **They Poop White Sand Beaches.** The sand found on beaches around the world is made of a combination of substances—weathered and pulverized rock and minerals from the land, and ground-up seashells from the sea, for example—depending on the particular environment in the area around the beach. In regions where parrotfish live—such as around the beautiful white sand beaches of Hawaii—a good portion of that sand is made up of the undigested bits of calcium carbonate that parrotfish excrete as a result of their coral-based diet.

(It's the coral that makes the beaches so nice and white.) A single parrotfish can poop out more than 800 pounds of white sand every year.

• **They Sleep Like Logs.** Scientists say that all fish go through some sort of regular resting period, but most don't go into the full deep sleep that mammals do. One exception: the parrotfish. When a parrotfish is sleeping, you can swim right up to it, shout at it (if you could shout underwater), and shine a flashlight at it...and it won't wake up. For some species, notably the green humphead—the largest parrotfish species, named for the large bulbous bump on its forehead—this is unfortunate. Reason: humpheads tend to sleep in large groups, often in the same spot night after night. That makes them easy targets for fishermen, which has resulted in a sharp decline in their numbers in recent decades.

• **They Make Mucus Sleeping Bags.** Some species give themselves a measure of nighttime protection: before going to sleep, these parrotfish secrete a thick mucus from glands near their gills, which, within 30 to 60 minutes, surrounds the fish in a large sac. Then it goes to sleep. Scientists say these mucus sleeping bags act as mosquito nets of sorts, protecting the fish from parasites that would otherwise ravage them during their sleep. The tiny parasites are unable to penetrate the fish's mucus protection shield. The sacs may also block the fishes' scent from spreading through the water, thereby protecting it from larger predators as well. In the morning, the parrotfish eats its mucus sleeping bag—and goes about its daily business.

• **Some Males Pretend to Be Females.** Parrotfish are *sequential hermaphrodites*, a trait found in several fish families. What this means is that all of these fish are born female and become male as they mature. In parrotfish, this gender change is accompanied by a drastic change in appearance: young female parrotfish are actually quite dull in color, and only obtain their bright, vividly patterned colors upon becoming male. Especially large males are often found leading a harem of females, which he will vigorously defend against the amorous advances of other males. In order to trick a large, harem-leading male, some males will therefore employ an interesting trick: When they change from female to male, they keep their female colors. This allows them to sneak into a big, brightly colored male's harem, and spawn with as many females as they can before being discovered and chased off by the leader of the harem. (Bonus fact: When a big, brightly colored parrotfish harem leader dies, the largest female in its harem changes into a male, and takes over the harem.)

Mr. Coffee, Master Chef

Live in a small apartment or college dorm room with a tiny kitchen (or none at all)?
Good news: you can still cook. Using a simple drip coffeemaker, you can make…

Hot dogs: Put a couple of raw hot hogs in the carafe, add water, and turn on the machine. You don't need to run a brew cycle, just allow the burner that keeps the pot warm to stay on for a half hour. That's long enough to cook the hot dogs.

Eggs: The coffeemaker's warming plate is essentially a low-temperature "hot plate." With a very small frying pan, you can use it to cook an egg. (But use a pan—otherwise the eggs will burn and never come off the plate.)

Grilled cheese: The burner can be used *without* a pan for some foods, such as a grilled cheese sandwich. Wipe the crumbs and grilling butter off when you're done.

Pancakes: Again, just use the burner. And if you're bad at making pancakes, the shape of the burner will keep them perfectly round.

Steamed veggies: Put some raw veggies in the filter basket, and run a few cycles of hot water through them until they're soft and tender.

Veggies: If you'd rather boil your vegetables, put them in the pot, run a cycle of hot water through (with nothing in the filter basket), and let them stand in the hot water until they're cooked.

Chocolate fondue: Heat up some cream in the pot for about 15 minutes, and then stir in pieces of chocolate. (Bonus: Because the burner isn't super-hot, you run little risk of scorching the chocolate.) Cook for 10 minutes or until the mixture is smooth and creamy.

Caramel: Melt a couple sticks of butter in the pot on the burner. Add in the sugar and corn syrup, and stir. Once it's combined, pour it out of the pot into a greased pan and let sit for an hour.

Instant dried foods: Coffee machines are basically instant hot water machines; they heat up water in a minute. You could use that water to make coffee, of course, but you can also use it to make the hot water you need for ramen noodles, instant soup, or instant oatmeal.

"Is Jenny There?"

There are a handful of phone numbers made famous by songs, movies, and TV shows. Ever wonder what happens if you actually call them?

867–5309

According to rock legend, Tommy Tutone lead guitarist Jim Keller wrote "867-5309/Jenny" about a real girl (named Jenny) whose number (not "867-5309") he got off of a men's room wall, just like the hero of the song. The catchy refrain made the number so easy to remember that it wreaked havoc on anyone unfortunate enough to have the number at the time. Calling the number became a minor fad in 1981, when the song was a Top 10 hit. That year, a Gastonia, North Carolina, junior high school with the number reportedly received prank calls 200 times a day. A Chicago woman with the number reportedly received more than 20,000 phone calls a week.

976-EVIL

The 1988 horror film *976-EVIL* takes its plot from the 976 number fad that was popular at the time, which charged callers $3 per minute to listen to prerecorded messages or join in on "party lines." In the film (directed by Robert Englund, best known for portraying Freddy Krueger in the *Nightmare on Elm Street* movies), two teens dial what they think is going to be a horoscope hotline and instead get a direct line to Satan. What would happen if you called 976-EVIL? In 1988, you'd get charged a few bucks to listen to a short ad for the movie. Today, nothing. It's long since been disconnected (as have most 976 numbers).

1-900-MIX-ALOT

Sir Mix-a-Lot had a #1 hit in 1992 with his rap song "Baby Got Back." In it, he tells listeners to "dial 1-900-MIX-ALOT, and kick them nasty thoughts." That number was a real number, set up by Sir Mix-a-Lot and his record label. Callers would be charged a few dollars per minute to "kick them nasty thoughts," which meant recording their own sexually explicit messages, or listen to ones left by other people. The enterprise was rumored to have made a small fortune for Mix-a-Lot at the time, but the number is no longer active.

GHOSTBUSTERS HOTLINE

One of the most memorable moments in the 1984 comedy *Ghostbusters* is the low-budget TV commercial the Ghostbusters make, directing potential clients to call them at "555-2368." During the movie's theatrical run, director Ivan Reitman set up 1-800-555-2368, and ran it at the bottom of ads for the film on TV. Callers got a prerecorded greeting from stars Bill Murray and Dan Aykroyd. The movie was a blockbuster, and the hotline racked up an average of 1,000 calls an hour during the six weeks it was in operation.

916-CALL-TURK

In a 2004 episode of the NBC sitcom *Scrubs*, Dr. Turk (Donald Faison) shares his excitement over nabbing the phone number 916-CALL-TURK. (Numbering conventions being what they are, it was actually "916-CALL-TUR," but whatever.) Show execs went so far as to set up a working line, which usually delivered a recorded message from Faison urging viewers to watch *Scrubs*. But occasionally, callers were lucky enough to get their call picked up by one of the cast members, who would then carry on a conversation for a few minutes.

634-5789

In 1966, soul singer Wilson Pickett told us we could reach him by dialing "634-5789." Given that the song was a Top 20 hit, there are surprisingly few stories about people calling the number en masse. But it's also understandable because in 1966, during the single's initial release, all-number dialing was still rolling out to parts of the country where callers were accustomed to using two numbers and five letters

776-2323

That's the phone number of God. At least it is in the 2003 comedy *Bruce Almighty*. The movie is set in Buffalo, New York, and filmmakers chose it because that number was not in use in Buffalo at the time. However, the movie was a nationwide hit, and hundreds of people called it in their own area codes. A Florida woman with the number threatened to sue Universal Pictures, because she was getting 20 phone calls an hour from people asking "Is God there?" In Sanford, North Carolina, it was, ironically, the phone number of a church. (When the movie was released on DVD, 776-2323 was replaced with a generic—and fake—"555" number.)

1-877-TAMEHER

In the 1999 movie *Magnolia*, Tom Cruise plays a misogynistic self-help guru named Frank Mackey. His seminars instruct callers to dial "1-877-TAMEHER" to order his "Seduce and Destroy" destruction program. If real-life callers tried the number, they got a recording of Cruise's spiel from the movie, promising them to "get that naughty sauce that you want, fast."

Three Musketeers author Alexandre Dumas's pants fell down during his first duel. (He still won.)

The Rosemary Awards

Do you think government should be transparent? Apparently the government doesn't. The Freedom of Information Act, which became law in 1966, is supposed to grant American citizens access to declassified documents…but it doesn't always work out that way.

FOR YOUR EYES ONLY

The National Security Archive is an independent, nongovernmental research institute based at George Washington University in Washington, D.C. The organization uses Freedom of Information Act (FOIA) requests to press for the declassification of federal government documents. Since its founding in 1985, the organization has succeeded in obtaining the release of more than 10 million pages of government records. Its most famous "gets" have included the release of President George W. Bush's August 6, 2001, daily briefing that warned, "Bin Ladin Determined to Strike in the U.S."; the first public acknowledgment of the existence of the Nevada air base known popularly as Area 51; and the photographs of Elvis Presley's Oval Office visit with President Richard Nixon in 1970.

FIOA requests are required by law to be acted upon within 20 business days, or 30 days at most in the case of "unusual circumstances." Unless the records being sought compromise national security, violate an individual's right to privacy, or trigger a handful of other legal exceptions, the documents must be released to the person or organization making the FOIA request. That's how the system is *supposed* to work, but as the National Security Archives has learned from filing more than 50,000 separate FOIA requests over the years, government agencies often drag their feet, sometimes for years, even when the law prohibits them from doing so. That's why the archive created its annual Rosemary Award in 2005.

DUBIOUS ACHIEVERS

The Rosemary Award recognizes the federal agency with the "worst record of open-government performance over the past year." It is named in honor of Rose Mary Woods, Richard Nixon's personal secretary, who famously claimed to have "accidentally" erased 18½ minutes of the Watergate tapes when she stopped to answer a phone call while transcribing them. The accident (if that's really what it was) destroyed what is believed to have been a recording of President Nixon plotting with his chief of staff to cover up the White House's role in the burglary of Democratic National Committee headquarters at the Watergate office complex three days earlier. The cover-up failed, of course, and Nixon resigned in disgrace in August 1974.

Winners of the Rosemary Award receive a certificate and a framed photograph of Wood demonstrating the "Rose Mary Stretch" to Watergate investigators. She's leaning backward in her chair, one outstretched foot still on the pedal of her audio transcription machine, as she reaches back to answer the phone on a far corner of the desk behind her—the unlikely pose she said she was in when she erased those Watergate tapes.

DIS-HONORABLE MENTIONS

• **The U.S. Air Force.** In 2005, the National Security Archive awarded the first Rosemary Award to the U.S. Air Force for "outstandingly bad FOIA performance" that included sitting on FOIA requests for as long as 18 years before losing them or tossing them out in the trash, instead of responding in 20 to 30 days as federal law requires. In a lawsuit, the archive alleged that the air force "fails to acknowledge FOIA requests, loses FOIA requests, fails to process requests, tries to discourage the public from pursuing FOIA requests, fails to respond to inquiries about the status of the requests, and lets requests languish while records are destroyed or transferred to other agencies."

Embarrassed by the bad publicity, the air force launched a "Get Well" program to solve the problem…only to win the Rosemary Award again two years later for "failing miserably" to meet its FOIA obligations. Among the new failures documented were more lost FOIA requests, an FOIA "electronic reading room" website with 139 web links that led nowhere, and an FOIA fax request number that, instead of being connected to an air force fax machine, was actually the phone number for a hospital room at Wright-Patterson Air Force Base in Ohio.

• **The Central Intelligence Agency.** In between the air force's wins in 2005 and 2007, the CIA took the prize for 2006 in what the National Security Archive called "the most dramatic one-year drop-off in professionalism and responsiveness to the public we have seen in 20 years." At the time, the National Security Archive had been waiting 17 years for documents relating to the 1988 bombing of Pan Am Flight 103 over Lockerbie, Scotland, and 19 years for CIA records on the Jonathan Pollard spy case. (Four of the ten oldest unanswered FOIA requests—by any federal agency—were being held up by the CIA, even though the CIA receives just 0.08 percent of all such requests.)

• **The U.S. Treasury.** Why did the Treasury win the Rosemary in 2008? Consider this still-pending 1997 FOIA request for documents relating to the Clinton administration's certification of the Mexican government's anti–drug trafficking efforts: According to the National Security Archive, the Treasury "repeatedly asked the Archive (in 2001, 2004, and 2007) if we were still interested; asked for another copy of the request since the original had been 'destroyed'; and finally closed the request without ever processing a document, claiming so much time had elapsed that the records had been retired to the National Archives."

• **The Federal Bureau of Investigation.** The FBI won the 2009 Rosemary Award after it gave "No Records Found" responses to 66 percent of all FOIA requests submitted to it over a four-year period. By comparison, other federal agencies averaged a 13-percent no-records-found rate. Reason for the poor performance: "Unless a requester specifically asks for a broader search, the FBI will only look in a central database of electronic file names at FBI headquarters in Washington." Cross-referenced files and records stored in field offices or anywhere other than FBI headquarters were not searched, nor were records created before the 1970s, which are on paper and must be looked up using a manual card catalog. "Until the requester files suit in federal court, the FBI will not perform a broader search," said the archive.

• **The Federal Chief Information Officers Council.** This interagency group, which won the Rosemary Award in 2010, consists of the chief information officers of the various agencies of the federal government. Though these officials oversaw $71 billion of spending on computers and software each year, as of 2010 they still hadn't addressed "the failure of the federal government to save its e-mail electronically." So have things improved since then? Hardly: Four years later, the council won its second Rosemary, again for the government's failure to save its own e-mail. "The unfortunate silver lining of Hillary Clinton inappropriately appropriating public records [by using her own e-mail server and a private e-mail account while Secretary of State, instead of the State Department's system] is that she likely preserved her own records more comprehensively than her State Department colleagues, most of whose e-mails were probably lost," said the archive. (In 2011, State Department staffers sent more than a billion e-mails, but only 61,156 were preserved as "record e-mails.")

*　　*　　*

IT'S NEVER TOO LATE
• At age 30, Martha Stewart was working as a stockbroker.
• At age 37, Ang Lee was a stay-at-home dad who worked odd jobs to pay the bills. (He's won the Oscar for Best Director twice.)
• At age 40, Stan Lee released his first major comic book.

Rogue Waves

Some light reading for your next cruise vacation.

WAVE BYE-BYE
Stories about giant waves that appear out of the blue, towering above all the waves around them and wreaking havoc on ships and sailors, have been part of sailing lore for millennia. Known as "rogue," "killer," or "freak" waves, they've only been accepted by scientists as real in the last couple of decades—mostly because several causes have been determined. The most widely accepted is a scientific phenomenon known as *constructive interference*, in which waves traveling in different directions run into one another, meet up in just the right way, and combine and form much larger waves. Example: five-foot-tall waves traveling east run into five-foot-tall waves traveling west, they meet in just the right way, and combine to form ten-foot waves. Constructive interference can occur when many small waves combine or when a few large waves combine in this way, and result in one or more massive, towering waves—which can scare the bejeezus out of unsuspecting sailors. Here are documented examples of some of the most terrifying rogue waves in history.

HISTORIC ROGUE WAVES
• **Christopher Columbus.** In 1498, on his third voyage to the Americas, Columbus was leading a fleet of six ships through a narrow passageway between the southern tip of Trinidad and the Venezuelan mainland in the Caribbean Sea. According to his log book, he heard "a fearsome roaring." The explorer then turned around to see a wave higher than the top of his 60-foot mast approaching the fleet from the rear. The wave lifted the ships, sending them on a terrifying ride up and then down its steep sides…and then went on its way. (Columbus named the passageway "the Mouth of the Serpent.")

• **Bishop Rock Lighthouse.** Bishop Rock Lighthouse was built in the 1850s on a tiny rock outcropping in the North Atlantic Ocean, just off the southwestern tip of England. Affixed to the lighthouse gallery (the veranda-like platform on the outside of a lighthouse's watchroom) was a massive bell weighing more than 300 pounds, which was used as a fog-warning signal when the light wasn't working. In January 1861, a freak wave ripped the bell off the lighthouse. Height of the Bishop Rock Lighthouse gallery: 100 feet above sea level.

Famous forgotten inventor: Ed Waldmire Jr., who put the first corn dog on a stick (1946).

• **RMS *Etruria.*** On October 10, 1903, the 519-foot British luxury liner left New York City en route to its home port of Liverpool, England. At around 2:30 p.m., just four hours out of New York, in conditions calm enough that several passengers were seated in chairs on the deck, a massive wave, estimated at about 50 feet high, suddenly smashed into the ship's port side. The wave did significant damage to the *Etruria*, even tearing away part of the ship's bridge (the windowed compartment where the captain commanded the ship). The passengers seated on the deck received the full force of the wave, and were tossed around like bath toys. Several suffered serious injuries, including a number of broken bones; one person died from their injuries five days later.

• **USS *Memphis.*** On August 29, 1916, the *Memphis*, a 504-foot U.S. Navy gunship, was at anchor in the Caribbean Sea, about half a mile from shore off Santo Domingo, Dominican Republic. After bobbing like a cork in heavy swells for several hours, the ship was suddenly hit by a massive, odd-shaped wave. It was described as three waves in one, connected by high plateaus of water, the highest crest reaching 70 feet. The trough in front of the wave was so deep that the bottom of the ship slammed into the floor of the 55-foot-deep harbor. Seconds later, the ship was engulfed by the wave. More than 200 sailors were injured in the incident and 43 were killed—some in a motor launch that capsized just before the wave struck, others from injuries and drownings *inside* the ship, and others when the ship's boilers exploded. The USS *Memphis* ended up aground on the beach and never sailed again.

• **USS *Ramapo.*** The *Ramapo*, a 477-foot U.S. Navy oil tanker, was in the middle of the North Pacific on February 7, 1933, traveling east from the Philippines to San Diego, California, when it ran into a storm. The captain, Ross Whitemarsh, ordered Lieutenant Frederick Marggraff to start measuring the height of the waves. At around 3:30 a.m., Marggraff watched as an enormous wave appeared behind the ship. Estimated height: 112 feet from crest to trough. Fortunately, the ship was just the right length to ride out the massive wave, and it suffered no damage. Because Marggraff used a reliable system (simple trigonometry) to measure the wave, this is considered to be the first true record of a rogue wave more than 100 feet high.

• **RMS *Queen Mary.*** During World War II, the famous British ocean liner served as a troop transport ship between the United States and the UK. In early December 1942, with 16,000 American soldiers aboard, a giant wave hit the 1,019-foot ship broadside during a powerful storm. The wave, which witnesses say was 90 feet high, knocked the ship into a 52-degree list, almost causing it to capsize. No one was hurt. (One of the ship's passengers was war correspondent Paul Gallico. The event inspired him to write his best-selling 1969 novel, *The Poseidon Adventure*, about a luxury cruise ship that is capsized by a massive wave. It was made into a blockbuster film in 1972.)

• **World Glory.** This 736-foot supertanker flew under the Liberian flag. In June 1968, it picked up 334,000 barrels of oil in Kuwait, and set off for its destination in Spain. Normally, ships undertaking such a journey travel up the Red Sea, through the Suez Canal, and into the Mediterranean—but the Suez Canal was closed. (After the Six-Day War with Israel in 1967, Egypt closed the canal until 1975.) The *World Glory's* only other option: go south around Africa's Cape of Good Hope, through a region of the Indian Ocean notorious for its frequent rogue waves. There on June 14, about 70 miles east of Durban, South Africa, the ship encountered a violent northbound storm. For several hours the ship rode the huge swells produced by the storm. But at around 3:00 p.m., a 70-foot rogue wave lifted the tanker into the air by its midsection, leaving the bow and stern unsupported—and the ship cracked down the middle. A second huge wave broke the ship completely in two. Oil poured from the two broken pieces of the ship, the oil caught fire, and a few hours later, both sections of the ship sunk. Of the 34 crew members on the *World Glory*, just ten survived.

• **Florida.** At 11:00 p.m. on July 3, 1992, a wave approximately 18 feet high suddenly crashed ashore near Daytona Beach, on the east coast of Florida. Police sergeant John Marshall was in his jeep in a parking lot near the beach when the wave struck. It flipped the jeep over, then carried the vehicle and Marshall out onto the beach. "It looked like Matchbox cars on a piece of paper and something was shaking them all over," Marshall told reporters. "I was really scared of getting sucked out. I've never been that scared in my life." More than 75 people were injured, and about 100 cars were damaged in the incident. Meteorologic and oceanographic experts could not explain what caused the freak wave to occur.

• **Draupner Platform.** The Draupner platform is an oil rig in the North Sea off the coast of Norway. On New Year's Day 1995, it was being sloshed by waves about 10 to 20 feet high when it was suddenly struck by a monster 84-foot-high rogue wave. Nobody saw the wave: it was detected by a laser-based measuring device on the platform's hull. The "Draupner Wave," as it is now known, was the first rogue wave ever detected by a scientific measuring device, and it gave scientists new clues about the phenomenon. And it was a true rogue. The device showed that the waves before and after the rogue wave were all relatively the same size, with no buildup to the sudden monster wave. (Thomas Adcock, a professor of engineering sciences at the University of Oxford in England, said the information gathered suggested that the wave was caused when the crests of two groups of waves traveling at right angles to one another came together.)

• **_Aleutian Ballad._** In 2006, during the second season of the popular TV show _Deadliest Catch_, which revolves around crab-fishing boats in Alaska's Bering Sea, the _Aleutian Ballad_ was slammed by a 60-foot rogue wave. The wave turned the ship on its side, causing the engines to cut out, which caused the power and lights to go out as the helpless ship continued to be battered and rolled by waves. Thankfully, the ship righted itself in a short time, which allowed Captain Jerry Tilley to restart the engines and regain control of the ship. The wave did extensive damage to the vessel, but the episode is one of the few known instances of a rogue wave being captured on film.

A WAVE OF FACTS

• In 2000, the European Union launched a scientific project to find out just how unusual rogue waves really are. Called MaxWave, the project used satellites to take 30,000 images of the world's oceans over a three-week period. The study found 10 waves exceeding 82 feet (25 meters) in that three-week period alone—meaning rogue waves may be a lot more common than people realized.

• On December 8, 2004, a U.S. Coast Guard rescue helicopter was in the midst of a prolonged rescue operation on a stricken ship in stormy conditions off Alaska's Aleutian Peninsula. It was hovering just 30 feet or so over the surging waves when it was engulfed by what is believed to have been a rogue wave. Completely filled with water, the helicopter's engine cut out, and it crashed into the sea. All three crew members onboard were rescued. The incident prompted speculation that rogue waves may have been the cause of a number of unexplained rescue helicopter crashes over the years.

• Rogue waves can also occur in very large lakes. Some scientists believe a rogue wave may have caused the sinking of the SS _Edmund Fitzgerald_ on Lake Superior in November 1975.

*　　*　　*

"The one function that TV news performs very well is that when there is no news we give it to you with the same emphasis as if it were."

—**David Brinkley**

The creeping jellyfish is smaller than a pea, and reproduces by splitting in half.

Underwear with Something Extra

Given all of the challenges in our daily lives, it's nice to know that some of them can be solved with underpants.

D **FREE EARLY WARNING WEARABLE**
What It Does: Tells you when you need to get to the bathroom…before it's too late

Details: The DFree insert attaches to an ordinary pair of underwear or directly on the wearer's stomach. There it uses ultrasound technology to monitor the internal organs for signs of an impending bowel movement. When the signs are detected, the information is sent to an app on the wearer's smartphone, which displays the information in the form of a countdown timer. The app also keeps track of daily bowel movements and uses them to improve the accuracy of its pit stop predictions. Triple W, the Japanese company that makes the DFree, plans to market the device to adults struggling with incontinence, and to parents of young children, for use as a toilet-training aid.

THINX PERIOD PANTIES

What They Do: Eliminate the need for tampons

Details: Canadian native and Thinx cofounder Miki Agrawal came up with the idea for the product during a visit to South Africa in 2010, when she met a 12-year-old girl in a rural area who wasn't in school on a school day. Why not? "It's my week of shame," the girl explained. The girl didn't have any sanitary products to help her manage her menstrual cycle. For that reason, she had to stay home from school one week of every month while she was menstruating, a problem that affects an estimated 100 million girls of school age around the world.

When Agrawal returned home, she, her twin sister Radha, and their friend Antonia Dunbar founded Thinx and spent the next three years developing the QuadTECH® technology that makes their panties work. A top layer of wicking material draws menstrual fluid away from the wearer's skin and into a second layer of absorbent material that can hold up to two tampons' worth of menstrual fluid. A third antimicrobial layer prevents the growth of bacteria, and a fourth layer of breathable material prevents leakage. Thinx donates a portion of the proceeds from every pair of panties it sells to AFRIpads, a nonprofit group in

---

It's against federal law for the painted lines of a crosswalk to be any color other than white.

Uganda that provides menstrual kits to young girls to enable them to stay in school.

CONFITEX LINGERIE

What It Does: Aids women who suffer from light to moderate urinary incontinence

Details: Dr. Mark Davey, a New Zealand physician, and cofounder Frantisek Riha-Scott initially developed their absorbent underwear for alpine ski racers, who can't always stop when they have to go. But Davey and Riha-Scott soon realized that the need for such garments extended far beyond athletes, so they developed a line of fashionable lingerie for women who struggle with urinary incontinence but don't want to give up their sexy undergarments to wear absorbent pads or adult diapers.

Confitex's multilayer technology is similar to that of Thinx period panties, but with three layers of material instead of four. A top wicking layer made of a hi-tech sports fabric draws urine away from the wearer's skin and deposits it in a layer of superabsorbent material underneath. A third layer of breathable fabric makes the underwear leakproof. Confitex's most absorbent underwear styles hold up to one cup of liquid, yet are virtually indistinguishable from ordinary lingerie. They're so fashionable, in fact, that the company introduced their product line with a runway show during New Zealand's Fashion Week in August 2015. The company also sells superabsorbent men's briefs.

ARCHIE MCPHEE INSTANT UNDERPANTS

What It Is: Provides an emergency extra pair of underpants...just in case

Details: Archie McPhee is a novelty product dealer, so you might not be inclined to take these underpants seriously. But that doesn't mean you might not need them someday. The underwear is compressed into a pellet and is stored in a metal tin about the size of a hockey puck. When the need for a fresh pair of underpants presents itself, just put the puck in a bowl, pour water over it, and it will expand into a soaking-wet pair of one-size-fits-most unisex briefs. "Remember, it's better to have damp underpants than no underpants at all!" says the company's catalog. If you're the kind of person who insists on *dry* underwear, the company also sells the Emergency Underpants Dispenser, a "tissue box" that dispenses underpants instead of tissue.

*   *   *

"Accept who you are, unless you're a serial killer." —**Ellen Degeneres**

Lobster Facts

*This page is boiling over with trivia about the
most delicious of all crustaceans.*

• In July 2015, a lobster was caught in Scarborough, Maine, that was half brown and half orange. *Literally* half—the colors were split down the middle, the result of a genetic mutation. The odds of the odd coloring are 1 in 50 million.

• Lobster traps weren't invented until the late 19th century. Before that, lobsters were caught by hand (or they washed ashore after storms in big piles).

• Lobsters don't have teeth. They have a grinding organ called a gastric mill, located in the lobster's stomach…which is located right behind its eyes.

• Female lobsters can only mate after molting, or shedding their shells.

• About 126 million pounds of lobster are caught in Maine each year by its 6,000 licensed fishermen. To cover their costs (bait, gas, the boat), a fisherman needs to catch an average of 150 pounds of lobster a day.

• After a lobster lays her eggs, the odds that any will survive beyond six weeks is 0.1%.

• A lobster's brain is about the size of a ballpoint pen's tip.

• Myth: The black line on a lobster's tail is feces. Truth: It's a sign that the lobster is female—it's her unfertilized eggs, and they're safe to eat.

• If lobsters can't find their usual food source (bottom-feeders such as clams, snails, and crab), they'll fight, kill, and eat smaller lobsters.

• Lobster blood is clear, but when it's cooked it turns white.

• In Maine, it's legal to hunt lobsters at night with a flashlight. It's also a good idea, because lobsters are nocturnal.

• Because they're hit into the ocean, the golf balls used on cruise ships are biodegradable. They're made out of crushed and pressed lobster shells.

• Many people claim lobsters scream when they're placed into boiling water. That's a myth—lobsters don't have vocal cords. The "scream" that's sometimes heard is air trapped in the stomach escaping through the lobster's mouth.

Working Titles

Would Michael Jackson's Thriller *have sold 50 million copies if it had been titled* Starlight? *Here are some other album titles that were almost used.*

- Pink Floyd, *The Dark Side of the Moon* (1973): "Eclipse"

- U2, *The Joshua Tree* (1987): "The Two Americas"

- David Bowie, *Young Americans* (1975): "Shilling the Rubes"

- The Beatles, *Revolver* (1966): "Abracadabra"

- Bruce Springsteen, *The River* (1980): "The Ties That Bind"

- Public Enemy, *It Takes a Nation of Millions to Hold Us Back* (1988): "Countdown to Armageddon"

- Bryan Adams, *You Want It, You Got It* (1981): "Bryan Adams Hasn't Heard of You Either"

- Fleetwood Mac, *Rumours* (1977): "Yesterday's Gone"

- R.E.M., *Out of Time* (1991): "Cat Butt"

- Bob Seger and the Silver Bullet Band, *Night Moves* (1976): "Suicide Streets"

- Talking Heads, *Remain in Light* (1980): "Melody Attack"

- Nirvana, *Nevermind* (1991): "Sheep"

- The Beatles, "White Album" (1968): "A Doll's House"

- Elton John, *Caribou* (1974): "Ol' Pink Eyes Is Back"

- Elvis Costello, *Armed Forces* (1979): "Emotional Fascism"

- Beck, *Midnite Vultures* (1999): "I Can Smell the V.D. in the Club Tonight"

- The Clash, *Combat Rock* (1982): "Rat Patrol from Fort Bragg"

- Kiss, *Hotter Than Hell* (1977): "The Harder They Come"

- John Lennon, *Rock 'n' Roll* (1975): "Old Hat"

- The Beach Boys, *Pet Sounds* (1966): "Remember the Zoo"

- The Beastie Boys, *Licensed to Ill* (1986): "Don't Be a F****t"

- Rolling Stones, *Let It Bleed* (1969): "Sticky Fingers"

- The Who, *Quadrophenia* (1973): "Rock Is Dead—Long Live Rock"

Iceland's Silfra fissure is the only place where divers can touch two continental plates at once.

Happy Little Trees

He's one of the most famous faces on public television, even if you don't know him by name: the middle-aged white man with an afro, painting at an easel as he talks soothingly to the viewing audience. Say hello to Bob Ross.

PORTRAIT OF THE ARTIST

In the early 1980s, a Washington, D.C., woman named Annette Kowalski fell into depression after her 24-year-old son was killed in a car accident. She found some comfort watching a show on public television called *The Magic of Oil Painting,* hosted by a German artist named Bill Alexander, and she thought it would be therapeutic to take painting lessons from him. But Alexander had recently retired, so he referred Kowalski to Bob Ross, an artist who traveled the country giving painting lessons for Alexander's art supply company. Ross was a former U.S. Air Force officer and part-time bartender who'd taken up landscape painting while stationed in Anchorage, Alaska. He retired from the military after realizing that he could make more money teaching painting and selling his Alaskan landscapes to tourists.

Both Ross and Alexander used a technique called "wet-on-wet" oil painting, in which the artist adds one layer of paint after another onto a canvas without waiting for each layer to dry. Ross had learned to use the technique during his Air Force years, because it allowed him to whip out entire paintings in minutes. "I used to go home at lunch and do a couple while I had my sandwich. I'd take them back that afternoon and sell them," he once told an interviewer.

THE PAINT WHISPERER

Kowalski went to Florida to attend one of Ross's classes. She was there to study painting, but she soon became fixated on Ross's whispery, soothing, ever-encouraging manner of teaching instead. "I was so mesmerized by him," Kowalski told the *New York Times* in 2015. "I didn't paint. I just followed him around the room all day, listening to the way he talks to people. And at the end of my five-day class with him, I said, 'Bob, I don't know what you've got, but I think we should bottle it and sell it.'"

Kowalski, her husband Walter, and Ross agreed to pool their savings and launch Ross in his own business, teaching painting in art supply stores and shopping malls around the United States. But success was slow to materialize and they lost $20,000 the first year. One of the ways that Ross tried to save money in those lean times was to have his naturally straight hair permed into an afro to save on haircuts. (He eventually grew to hate his afro, but by then it had become such an iconic part of his look that he kept it for the rest of his life.)

AS SEEN ON TV

Another way that the business partners tried to improve their financial situation was by filming a commercial that they could use to attract students to Ross's classes. In what Ross would have referred to as a "happy accident," they recorded the commercial in the wrong video format and took it to WNVC, the public television station in Fairfax, Virginia, to get it transferred to a format that TV stations could air. Some WNVC executives saw the commercial and were so impressed by it that they offered Ross his own show.

That first episode of *The Joy of Painting* that aired on January 11, 1983, established the look of the show's 11-year, 403-episode run: Ross painting at an easel, with a plain black curtain for a backdrop, finishing an entire painting in 25 minutes. Initially Ross wanted a more elaborate set, but he soon realized that the simple set was more intimate, and kept the viewer's attention focused on the painting. (Another thing that kept the show intimate was that when Ross spoke to the audience, he imagined he was speaking to only one person: "a woman, in bed.")

PICTURE PERFECT

The first season of *The Joy of Painting* aired on about 50 East Coast stations, but Ross—frustrated by poor audio and video quality—moved the show to WIPB, the PBS station in Muncie, Indiana. A new distribution deal put the second season of *The Joy of Painting* on 75 stations around the country, and the audience grew from there. By the early 1990s, the show was airing on 300 PBS stations serving 100 million American households, as well as in a dozen foreign countries, including Turkey and even Iran. In the process, Ross became a pop culture icon and *The Joy of Painting* became the most popular art instruction show in television history.

So how much money did Ross make off the show? Not a penny—at least not directly. He hosted it for free and gave his paintings to public television stations to auction off during pledge drives. But Ross and the Kowalskis did make money—lots of it—by marketing "Bob Ross, Inc." paints, painting classes, art supplies, and how-to books to the estimated 3 percent of the show's audience that actually did take up painting. That may not sound like much, but by the early 1990s, the audience was so big that the 3 percent were buying $15 million worth of Bob Ross, Inc. products a year. Today, more than 20 years after Ross's death from lymphoma, reruns of *The Joy of Painting* still air on 95 percent of public television stations in the United States.

The Zen of Bob Ross

On page 317 we told you about Bob Ross, host of the PBS show The Joy of Painting.
*Here are some of the things he said as he created a new painting in 30 minutes.
Was he talking about the painting, about life, or both? You be the judge.*

"It's the imperfections that make something beautiful, that's what makes it different and unique."

"We don't really know where this goes, and I'm not sure we really care."

"Don't be afraid to scrape the paint off and do it again. This is the way you learn, trial and error, over and over, repetition. It pays you great dividends, great, great dividends."

"When things happen, enjoy them. They're little gifts."

"Work on one thing at a time. Don't get carried away; we have plenty of time."

"Everyone wants to enjoy the good parts, but you have to build the framework first."

"Think about a cloud. Just float around and be there."

"Ever make mistakes in life? Let's make them birds. Yeah, they're birds now."

"I don't know if anything in nature ever grows exactly the same, but it's always exactly as it should be—perfectly itself."

"In painting, you have unlimited power. You have the ability to move mountains. You can bend rivers. But when I get home, the only thing I have power over is the garbage."

"There are no mistakes, only happy accidents."

"All it takes is just a little change of perspective and you begin to see a whole new world."

"We don't need to set the sky on fire, a little glow will do just fine."

"Sometimes you learn more from your mistakes than you do from your masterpieces."

"Just let go—and fall like a little waterfall."

"If it's not what you want, stop and change it. Don't just keep going and expect it will get better."

"If what you're doing doesn't make you happy, you're doing the wrong thing."

"It really doesn't matter, we can always paint over it."

Buy Low, Sell High

For most start-up CEOs, the dream is to one day be bought out by an Internet behemoth. But there's always that nagging thought: "Did I sell too soon? Or too late?"

INSTAGRAM

The online photo-sharing service Instagram launched in 2010, and within two years its users had uploaded more than a billion photos. Fearing that Instagram might pose a threat to Facebook's position as the main place to share photos online, Facebook CEO Mark Zuckerberg made an offer that Instagram couldn't refuse: ownership of the company for $1 billion (in cash and Facebook stock) and the promise that Instagram could continue to operate independently. The deal made Instagram's 13 employees very rich. But what if they'd waited to sell? Just two years after the sale, the investment banking firm Citigroup, Inc. valued Instagram at $35 billion.

SNAPCHAT

When Snapchat debuted in 2011, its main feature—letting users send photos that vanish after a certain time period—gave it a reputation as a way to send inappropriate pictures with no long-term consequences. Result: more than a billion photos were sent over Snapchat in just one year. Facebook CEO Mark Zuckerberg met with co-founders Evan Spiegel and Bobby Murphy at Snapchat headquarters, but rather than offering a buyout as he'd done with Instagram, Zuckerberg tried to scare the young entrepreneurs, revealing that Facebook was days away from launching its own version of Snapchat, called Facebook Poke. When Poke flopped, Zuckerberg returned to Snapchat, this time with his checkbook and an offer of $3 billion for their company. Spiegel and Murphy took Facebook's offer to Google, and Google matched it. But sensing weakness from these two giant companies, Spiegel and Murphy turned them both down. It was the right decision. Though they hadn't yet turned a profit, by 2016 Snapchat was valued between $10 billion and $20 billion.

ALIBABA

In 2005, Yahoo! co-founder Jerry Yang put up $1 billion of his company's money to purchase 40 percent of Alibaba, owned by his friend Jack Ma. Alibaba is a Chinese tech company that's a combination of Amazon and eBay, and Yang felt that it had a bright future due to China's growing middle class. When Yang refused to sell Yahoo! to Microsoft in 2008, he was fired as CEO, but he had the last laugh when

Alibaba's initial public offering was the largest in stock market history. That IPO netted Yahoo! around $25 billion for their $1 billion investment…and it could've been more had Yang's successor not sold back 14 percent of the original purchase.

YELP

When your Internet start-up is so successful that it becomes a verb, you're probably in for a big payday soon. In 2006, only two years after he started the crowd-sourced review website, Yelp co-founder Jeremy Stoppelman claims he received an offer of $100 million, but he thought he could get more. He was right. In 2009, Google offered $550 million. Then Yahoo! offered $750 million. When Google was asked to match it, they declined. That caused internal chaos within Yelp. The management team refused to work for a company as poorly run as Yahoo!, but Yelp's board of directors *couldn't* tell shareholders that they turned down an extra $200 million. Result: the whole deal was called off. Don't feel bad for Stoppelman, though. They all became very rich when Yelp went public in 2011 at a valuation of just under $900 million.

GROUPON

Groupon was a huge fad. Daily emails were sent out offering deals on everything from durable goods (50 AA batteries for $10!) to local deals (a $20 restaurant gift card for $10). The company was earning a ton of money, mostly through companies paying them to offer bargains for their products, and the buyout offers started rolling in. Yahoo! offered around $3–4 billion in late 2010, but Groupon founders thought that was too low. Google was next with $6 billion, and Groupon entertained the offer until the founders decided they could make more with an IPO. And they did…at first. On the day stock went on sale, Groupon was valued at $13 billion. But in less than a year, its stock cratered by 90 percent to $2.76 a share and founder/CEO Andrew Mason was removed from the company. Nearly five years after its debut on Wall Street, Groupon shares still hover between $3 and $5.

VIDDY

Remember Viddy? Marketed as "Instagram for videos," this app boasted 30 million users and was valued at $370 million. It's understandable, then, why CEO Brett O'Brien turned down a $100 million buyout offer from Twitter. No problem. Twitter walked away and bought Vine, a similar service where users could post short videos. Viddy was left even further out in the cold in 2014 when Instagram started allowing users to create and share videos. Later that year, Viddy was sold to a video sharing company called Fullscreen for just $20 million. A few months later, Fullscreen shut down Viddy altogether.

"Houston, We Have *Another* Problem"

A few years back we told you the story of the WWII submarine that was lost due to a malfunctioning toilet. It turns out that a similar incident threatened the space shuttle Discovery in 1989, earning it a place in Uncle John's Stall of Fame.

TOP SECRET

On November 22, 1989, the space shuttle *Discovery* blasted off from the launchpad at Kennedy Space Center in Florida for a five-day secret mission in Earth orbit. It is believed to have deployed a spy satellite for the Department of Defense, but since the mission was (and still is) classified, only the United States government knows for sure.

But some details of the mission have emerged, and they involve something a little more down-to-earth: the space shuttle's toilet, or Waste Collection System (WCS), as it was more properly known. The $30 million device looked like an ordinary toilet, but because it was designed to operate in zero gravity, the experience of using it was quite different from using a toilet on Earth. The WCS toilet was equipped with a seat belt and stirrups that allowed shuttle astronauts to anchor themselves in place, so that they didn't float away in the middle of doing their business. And instead of a flush handle, the toilet was operated with a lever similar to an automobile stick shift.

SHIFTY BEHAVIOR

• When astronauts needed to answer the call of nature, after first securing themselves to the toilet with the seat belt and stirrups, they shifted the toilet lever once, closing a valve on the outer hull called the *overboard vent valve* that was normally open to the vacuum of space.

• Once the valve was closed, a second shift of the lever opened an inner valve called the *slider valve* or *toilet gate valve* at the bottom of the toilet bowl. The toilet was now "open for business"; urine could be deposited into a funnel attached to a vacuum hose (male- and female-shaped funnels were available), and solid waste could be deposited into the toilet bowl.

• Because there's no gravity to help the solid waste get to the bottom of the bowl, a third shift of the toilet lever activated a fan that used airflow to blow the waste through the toilet gate valve into an interior holding compartment of the toilet.

- After the waste had floated into the inner compartment, shifting the toilet gear in the reverse direction turned off the fan.

- A second reverse shift closed the toilet gate valve, securing the solid waste in the toilet's interior compartment.

- A final reverse shift opened the overboard vent valve, exposing the inner compartment and the solid waste therein to the vacuum of outer space. Doing so freeze-dried the waste, killing bacteria and helping control odors. The waste itself remained trapped inside the holding compartment, because ejecting into space would have turned it into a projectile hurtling through space at more than 17,000 miles per hour.

HAPPY THANKSGIVING

That was how the toilet was *supposed* to work, and that was how it usually did work. But that wasn't how it worked early in the morning of November 23, 1989, Thanksgiving Day, when mission commander Frederick D. Gregory woke up early and had to go to the bathroom. Everything went well until he finished up and reverse-shifted to close the toilet gate valve. Gregory didn't realize it, but the valve had failed to close. (He was still strapped to the toilet, and from that position he would have had trouble determining whether the valve was open or closed.)

When Gregory reverse shifted again, the overboard vent valve opened. Now *both* the toilet gate valve and the overboard valve were open at the same time, exposing the interior of the space shuttle to the vacuum of outer space. That was a big problem: the air inside the shuttle cabin was now rushing down the toilet and out into space. If it were not stopped, the shuttle could depressurize completely, killing all of the astronauts on board.

POT LUCK

It didn't take Gregory long to realize that something had gone terribly wrong. As if the air rushing between his legs and down the toilet were not enough of a clue, the sudden drop in air pressure triggered a shrieking alarm that woke up the rest of the crew—just the kind of thing you don't want to happen when your pants are down and you are strapped to a space toilet in zero gravity.

The dropping air pressure also activated an automatic system that replaces escaping air by releasing oxygen and nitrogen from storage tanks in the shuttle's payload bay. Because the payload bay itself is open to the vacuum of space, the tanks were very cold and the oxygen and nitrogen they contained was in liquid form. Before the contents of the tanks can enter the shuttle, it is heated to become a gas...but only just—the gas is still very cold. And if Fred Gregory needed reminding, he soon discovered that the oxygen and nitrogen are fed into the space shuttle's interior through vents located directly above the toilet. So in addition to feeling the air roaring through his legs and hearing the alarm screaming in his ears, he was also deluged by very cold oxygen and nitrogen gas being dumped on his head.

TO THE RESCUE

Mission Specialist Story Musgrave was the first crew member on the scene; he floated over to Gregory and together they managed to wrestle the toilet gate valve closed, stopping the leak. Then Musgrave helped Gregory, now thoroughly chilled, get off the toilet.

Crisis averted—but now the shuttle's one and only toilet was out of order, and that meant that the mission itself was in jeopardy. NASA's own flight rules dictated that if a space shuttle's toilet stopped working and could not be fixed, the shuttle had to return to Earth "as soon as reasonably possible," according to NASA Flight Director Rob Kelso, who was on duty that Thanksgiving morning.

A shuttle with a broken toilet had to return to Earth, but not because there was no other way to go to the bathroom in orbit. The shuttle did carry backup Fecal Containment Systems, better known as "Apollo bags," that the astronauts could use if the toilet wasn't working. Apollo bags were used on the Apollo lunar missions of the late 1960s and early 1970s. But the experience had been so unpleasant that NASA's Flight Crew office, which is kind of like a union that represents astronauts, successfully lobbied NASA to get the break-the-toilet-return-to-Earth rule instituted, so that shuttle astronauts would never suffer the indignity of having to use the Apollo bags again.

LEFT HOLDING THE BAG

So what was it about using the Apollo bags that made them so unpleasant that even astronauts who'd worked their entire lives to get into space would rather return to Earth than remain in space and use the bags? A number of things, it turns out:

• For starters, the bags, affectionately known as "ass gaskets," had an adhesive seal around the opening. An astronaut was supposed to glue the opening of the bag to his rear end to create an airtight seal that prevented the solid waste from escaping and floating around the cabin of the space shuttle.

• Add to this the fact that in space it's difficult for an astronaut to achieve "separation" from his or her waste without the assistance of gravity. Because of this, Apollo bags incorporated a narrow pocket called a "finger cot." The finger cot makes it possible for an astronaut to achieve separation manually, by inserting a finger into the finger cot and pushing the waste free from their posterior with a fingertip. The finger cot was also used to push the solid waste to the bottom of the bag.

• After separation had been achieved, quite a bit of skill was required to remove the bag from the astronaut's rear end without letting any solid waste escape from the bag. Because of this, "floating turds" around the cabin were common whenever the Apollo bags were put to use.

• Before sealing the bag shut, the astronaut had to squirt a packet of germicide into the bag, then seal the bag and thoroughly *knead* the germicide into their waste to be sure that the two were thoroughly mixed together. Reason: to prevent gas-producing bacteria from growing inside the sealed bag, which might eventually cause it to explode like a tiny bomb, spraying human waste all over the interior of the spacecraft.

• As if kneading one's own human waste like bread dough wasn't bad enough, for some reason NASA saw fit to make the Apollo bags out of clear plastic, leaving nothing to the astronaut's imagination.

• Using an Apollo bag and cleaning up afterward could take as long as an hour, and more than one Apollo astronaut preferred to strip completely naked rather than risk getting the mess on their space suits.

GETTING A GRIP

The race was on to find a fix for the space shuttle's toilet and save the secret mission from ending prematurely. The engineers at Mission Control dragged out a toilet that was identical to the one on board the *Discovery*, and quickly assembled a collection of all of the tools that the astronauts had at their disposal. Then they called in the engineering team that had designed the toilet and put them to work finding a way to fix it, using only those tools.

It took a few hours, but the engineers did manage to diagnose the trouble and come up with a fairly simple fix: the astronauts were instructed to remove the front cover of the toilet and use a tool called a vise grip (a pair of pliers with locking jaws) to open and close the malfunctioning valve manually whenever they had to go.

Problem solved! The rest of the mission went off without a hitch (as far as we know, anyway) and five days later, *Discovery* landed on schedule at Edwards Air Force Base in California. *Discovery* remained in service until 2011, and over its lifetime it flew 39 missions in all, more than any other space shuttle. It launched the Hubble Space Telescope into orbit, went on more than a dozen missions to construct and supply the International Space Station, and was sent on two more secret missions for the Department of Defense. Today it's on display at the Smithsonian Institution's National Air and Space Museum annex in Chantilly, Virginia.

HOLIDAY MEMORIES

Many of the NASA engineers who were on duty in 1989 have moved on to other things, but many can't help but remember the incident whenever November rolls around. Wayne Hale was one of the flight directors who was there; in a 2009 posting to his blog he wrote, "Every Thanksgiving now, sometime after the pie and before the football game/nap, I chuckle as I remember that episode. And give thanks for gravity and the three toilets in my house."

OUT OF ORDER

The space shuttle Discovery *wasn't the only spacecraft to have bathroom problems. Here are two more:*

• **Faith 7.** Astronaut Gordon Cooper was launched into Earth orbit in May 1963 aboard *Faith 7* in what was the longest and final flight of the *Mercury* space program. In those early days of spaceflight, the *Mercury* spacecraft were designed to fly automatically without any input from the one-person crew. The astronaut was just along for the ride—they were little more than "Spam in a can," it was said. That was how things were *supposed* to work, but toward the end of Cooper's 34-hour mission, the automatic systems mysteriously began to fail. The problems worsened, and by the time he was ready to reenter Earth's atmosphere, Cooper had little choice but to take manual control of the space capsule. Using lines he drew on the capsule window to help properly position the capsule for reentry, and by timing the firing of the reentry rockets using his wristwatch, he was able to bring the malfunctioning capsule in for a safe splashdown landing with little to no help from the automatic systems. So what caused the reentry systems to fail? An investigation found that Cooper's urine collection bag had leaked, and when droplets of his urine got into the equipment, it had short-circuited.

• **Mir.** The Soviet space station was in orbit from 1986 to 2001, and by the end of its life the station's solar panels had lost about 40 percent of their energy-generating capacity. The loss, it turned out, was caused by the *Mir* toilet, which vented its waste into space. It probably seemed like a good idea at the time, but the Soviets eventually realized that much of the damage to the solar panels had been caused by frozen urine crystals slamming into them at a high enough speed to do real damage.

* * *

"If I had asked people what they wanted, they would have said faster horses."

—**Henry Ford**

Death Marches

A "death march" is a forced march of prisoners—often prisoners of war—over long distances and under extremely cruel conditions. Unfortunately, history is full of them. Here are the stories behind some of the most infamous. (Warning: this is real history, but it's pretty gruesome, so if you're squeamish, you might want to turn to another article.)

BATAAN DEATH MARCH

Background: On April 9, 1942, U.S. General Jonathan Wainwright surrendered 75,000 soldiers (60,000 Filipino and 15,000 American) to Japanese forces on the Bataan Peninsula, on the Philippine island of Luzon. Just four months after the Japanese attack on Pearl Harbor that had brought the U.S. into World War II, the loss was a devastating blow: it was the largest surrender of a U.S.-led force in history.

The March: In what is probably the most well-known death march in modern history, the Japanese forced their prisoners to walk, in 90°F temperatures, from the southern tip of the Bataan Peninsula north to the nearest prison camp. Distance: 63 miles. The march lasted from five to ten days, depending on the health and strength of the individual prisoners, most of whom were already malnourished. Many were suffering from diseases such as dengue fever and malaria as well. They were given little to eat and drink along the way, and those who fell behind were beaten—sometimes bayoneted, shot, and/or beheaded. Exact numbers were impossible to verify, but some estimates say as many as 10,000 prisoners died before reaching the prison camp.

Aftermath: Conditions in the camp were no better, and an estimated 1,500 Americans, and perhaps as many as 25,000 Filipino prisoners, died before finally being liberated at the war's end. After the Japanese surrendered in August 1945, several of the Japanese officers involved in the march were found guilty of war crimes and executed.

AFRICAN SLAVE MARCHES

Background: From the 15th through the 19th centuries, an estimated 12 million people from sub-Saharan West Africa were enslaved and sent to European colonies in North and South America in the Atlantic slave trade. What many people don't know is that brutal forced marches were an integral part of that trade.

The Marches: In the early years of the slave trade, the enslaved were people captured in areas relatively close to the West African coast. As

---

More people on the beach are killed by falling sand castles than by shark attacks.

local populations diminished, slave raiders had to go farther and farther into the African interior to capture new slaves. Once captured, the prisoners were bound together in long lines with ropes or chains and forced to march—up to hundreds of miles—to ports on the West African coast, where they were sold to European slave traders. Conditions were horrendous. Historians believe that as many as three million people may have died just during the forced marches.

Aftermath: In the late 18th century, abolitionists in Europe and the U.S. started spreading stories about the brutality of the forced marches; drawings of marching slaves appeared regularly in abolitionist literature. Those stories and images (many of which can be found online today) helped win support for the antislavery movement, which played an important role in bringing the Atlantic slave trade to an end in the 1850s.

THE LONG WALK

Background: In 1846, the U.S. Army made its first contact with the Navajo people in their traditional homeland—the Four Corners region of the southwestern United States, around the borders of Arizona, New Mexico, Utah, and Colorado. Years of skirmishes followed, culminating in the scorched-earth campaigns of Colonel Kit Carson, who, with a force of 700 men, finally subdued the Navajo in early 1864. When it was over, thousands of Navajo men, women, and children were taken prisoner by the army.

The Marches: Between 1864 and 1866, more than 9,000 Navajo, in groups as large as 2,000, were forced to walk more than 300 miles, under the guard of soldiers on horseback, from eastern Arizona to a reservation near an army fort in eastern New Mexico. The groups, which included many children and elderly people, had to march more than ten miles a day, but were given only enough food and water to survive, and those too tired or sick to walk were left behind. (According to some sources, many were simply shot.) An estimated 300 died along the way.

Aftermath: For those who made it to the reservation, a barren piece of land known as Bosque Redondo, things didn't get any better. Hundreds died there, mostly of starvation and disease, over the following two years. In 1868, the army finally admitted the entire enterprise had been a failure. The reservation was closed and the Navajo were given back their land in the Four Corners. It remains their home today, and the "Long Walk," as the Navajo called the forced march, remains an important part of their history.

ARMENIAN MARCHES

Background: In 1914, the Ottoman Empire—which was at the time primarily Muslim and included all of modern-day Turkey, Syria, Saudi

Arabia, parts of Iraq, and much more—used the cover of World War I (they were on the German side) to begin a program of extermination of the empire's minority Armenian Christian population. Known today as the Armenian Genocide, the program included a number of mass killings, but it also included many forced marches.

The Marches: In May 1915, the Ottoman government passed the Temporary Law of Deportation. Through the law, more than a million Armenians, mostly women, children, and the elderly, were taken from their homes in what is now eastern Turkey, and were forced to march south, hundreds of miles, to concentration camps in the Syrian Desert. They were given little food or water, and brutal mistreatment by guards, especially of the women, was commonplace. Tens of thousands of the marchers died of hunger, disease, and abuse along the way. The roads into the Syrian Desert were littered with corpses for months.

Aftermath: World War I ended in 1918 with the defeat of Germany and its allies, but trials for war-crimes failed to convict most of the Ottoman leaders responsible for the death marches and genocide. So the Armenians took care of it themselves: by 1922, Armenian assassination squads had killed several of the Ottoman Empire's top officials, including Mehmed Talaat Pasha, the government minister considered most responsible for the genocide, who was shot by an assassin in Berlin in 1921. Estimates of the number of people killed in the entire Armenian Genocide range from 800,000 to 1.5 million.

HOLOCAUST DEATH MARCHES

Background: In July 1944, the Soviet army liberated Nazi Germany's Majdanek concentration camp near the city of Lublin, Poland. It was the first major Nazi concentration camp liberated by Allied forces, and photos of the camp's emaciated survivors, primarily Polish Jews, and its gas chambers and crematoriums, made the front pages of newspapers around the world, exposing the horrors of the Nazi camps for the first time. In response, Nazi chief Heinrich Himmler ordered the evacuation of all camps located outside of central Germany and their relocation to the German interior, where they would be more difficult for the Allies to find. Most of the evacuations were carried out by train. But in late 1944, with the Allies encroaching upon German territory from all sides, the Nazis started using forced marches to evacuate the camps.

The Marches: From late 1944 right up to the final days of World War II, prisoners were forced to march overland to camps in central Germany. One of the worst involved the forced march of about 60,000 prisoners from the Auschwitz-Birkenau camp complex in southern Poland to the German border, where survivors were to be loaded onto trains and taken into Germany. The march was only 35 miles, but it was the dead of winter and there was snow on the ground, and the already severely malnourished prisoners were not equipped for such conditions. An estimated 15,000 were shot by guards or froze to death before they reached the border.

Aftermath: Fifty-nine concentration camps were evacuated through the use of death marches in the final months of the war. Historians report that as many as 250,000 people died or were murdered on those marches. (Elie Wiesel, winner of the 1986 Nobel Peace Prize, and his father survived the forced march from Auschwitz. He describes the ordeal in his 1960 book *Night*.)

NATIONAL DEFENSE CORPS INCIDENT

Background: In December 1950, six months after the start of the Korean War, North Korean and Chinese forces began advancing down the Korean Peninsula. The South Korean government hastily established the National Defense Corps, through which more than 400,000 men between the ages of 17 and 40 were drafted into the South Korean military—mostly to keep them from being drafted by the North Korean army. The new conscripts were ordered to march south, along several different routes, toward training facilities in the south of the country.

The March: The South Korean army officers who had set up the program embezzled most of the funds intended to provide the new recruits with provisions. So when the recruits were forced by their commanders to march south, they had no weapons, no food rations, and only meager clothing to protect them from the winter cold. Accounts vary as to the number of recruits who died from exposure or starvation during the marches. The most common number given is around 90,000.

Aftermath: In April 1951, the National Defense Corps was disbanded. In August, Brigadier General Kim Yoon Keun, the top officer in charge of the corps, and four other corps officers were executed by firing squad for embezzling the corps' funds, and thereby causing the disaster. The National Defense Corps Incident, as it became known, has the dubious distinction of being one of the only known death marches caused by the marchers' own side.

*   *   *

TW......................INS

The longest amount of time between the births of twin babies, according to *Guinness World Records*: 87 days. Maria Jones-Elliott of Kilkenny, Ireland, gave birth to the first of her twin girls in June 2012—four months early—and the second girl almost three months later. (Both girls survived, and are happy and healthy today.)

More Eggcorns

On page 127, we told you about the eggcorn—*a phrase in which a new word is substituted for an old one…and it still means the same thing. Here are a few more.*

Bloodgeon. This is a common misspelling of the word "bludgeon," originally the name for a heavy wooden club, which later also came to mean "to beat someone repeatedly with a bludgeon or other heavy object." The fact that bludgeoning someone can have bloody results makes the mistaken "bloodgeon" perfectly sensible.

Cacoughany. Actual word: "cacophony," meaning "unpleasant loud sounds." It's often written as "cacoughany," which—*cough*—though incorrect—COUGH COUGH COUGH!—makes sense in its own way.

Internally grateful. A mishearing of "eternally grateful" meaning, to be grateful for something forever. If one is *internally* grateful, you could also be said to be especially grateful, feeling gratitude within yourself.

Old-timer's disease. This is a mishearing of "Alzheimer's disease," named for German psychiatrist Alois Alzheimer, who made the first medical diagnosis of the disease in 1901. The fact that it overwhelmingly affects the elderly makes it understandable why it's commonly misspelled and misspoken as "old-timer's disease."

Straddled with. To be "saddled with" something is "to be burdened." Example: "April is so saddled with debt, she won't be able to pay her bills until June." The idea comes from having to carry a saddle on one's back. "Straddled with" paints a very similar picture.

Teaming with. The correct phrase is "teeming with," *teem* meaning "to abound" or "to swarm," as in "the place was teeming with rats." If you say "The place was *teaming* with rats," it gives the sense that the rats, in our example, are teaming up like a sports team—which they sort of are.

Coal-hearted. The phrase is actually "cold-hearted"—but "*coal*-hearted" can be said to mean pretty much the exact same think…er, thing.

New leash on life. Actual phrase: "new *lease* on life," meaning a new appreciation or a sense of vigor for life. Example: "Having grandkids gave Sheryl a new lease on life." Having a "new *leash* on life" might liken life to a dog—but it suggests a new sense of control of one's life, so its meaning could be considered on par with a "new *lease* on life."

The first badges worn by the Texas Rangers were made out of Mexican coins.

It's Your Move

Chess originated in India around the sixth century. It is now played virtually everywhere in the world. According to a worldwide chess governing body, an estimated 70 percent of adults have played it at some point in their lives, and about 635 million people play it regularly. (That makes it way more popular than Uncle John's favorite game, tiddlywinks.) Here are some more facts about "the game of kings."

• "Checkmate," uttered by a player to declare victory when the opponent's king cannot avoid capture, comes from the Persian phrase *shah mat*, which means, "the king is helpless."

• The pieces were meant to represent different parts of an army. In sixth-century India, the pieces included counselors, calvary, elephants, chariots, and infantry. As the game was adopted in Europe, the pieces changed to reflect European terminology—counselors, calvary, elephants, chariot, and infantry became queens, knights, bishops, rooks, and pawns.

• The longest possible game of chess would be 5,949 moves.

• Youngest chess grandmaster ever: Sergey Karjakin, who qualified at the age of 12 years, 7 months.

• Chess has been played in space. On June 9, 1970, a game was played remotely between astronauts aboard the *Soyuz 9* and the ground control crew back in the USSR.

• First electronic program to beat a chess grandmaster: Deep Blue, designed in 1985 at Carnegie Mellon University. It beat Boris Kasparov in 1996.

• The shortest possible game: There are eight different ways to reach checkmate in just two moves.

• The last major rule change in chess was more than 700 years ago. In 1280, chess players in Spain introduced the idea of pawns making a first move with one or two squares forward, instead of just one.

• In 1973, police raided a chess tournament in Cleveland. Boards were confiscated and the tournament director was arrested. Reason: a cash prize was involved, which violated local antigambling laws. (The charges were later dropped.)

• The folding chessboard was created in 1125 by a priest who was forbidden to play chess. He created it so that it could be folded and stored on a bookshelf, where it simply looked like a small book.

During WWII, *Charlie and the Chocolate Factory* author Roald Dahl was a British spy.

Missing Memorabilia

These iconic movie props could be worth big bucks…if anybody could find them.

Prop: Dorothy's ruby slippers

Movie: *The Wizard of Oz* (1939)

Story: At least six pairs were created for Judy Garland to wear. One was donated to the Smithsonian and another wound up at the Judy Garland Museum in Grand Rapids, Minnesota…until 2005, when they were stolen from the museum. In 2010, police received a tip that the stolen slippers were on display in a glass box under the TV in the thief's Homer Glen, Illinois, home. They raided the house but didn't find the slippers, and no one has seen them since. Estimated value: $1 million.

Prop: The Maltese Falcon

Movie: *The Maltese Falcon* (1941)

Story: Humphrey Bogart spends most of the movie chasing the price-less statue known as the Maltese Falcon. Several metal falcon props were created for the film. Most were lost, but one sold at auction for $400,000 in 1994. Several plaster replicas were made for promotional purposes during the film's original theatrical release. Elisha Cook Jr., one of the film's stars, got his hands on one and gave it to John's Grill, a San Francisco restaurant that's mentioned in the original novel. It was on display until 2007…when it disappeared. A reward of $25,000 was offered, but nobody returned it, so the money was used to create a more elaborate, more intricate Maltese Falcon that's also three times heavier. To make sure that this bird doesn't fly the coop, they bolted it down and have several security cameras pointed at it around the clock.

Prop: Captain America's motorcycle

Movie: *Easy Rider* (1969)

Story: Four custom bikes were built for the classic film—two each for Peter Fonda and Dennis Hopper. One of Fonda's "choppers" used was heavily damaged during the filming of the tragic final scene, after which all four vehicles were garaged. Before the film debuted, the three bikes that were still in good shape were stolen by thieves who likely didn't know that they were movie props. It's assumed the bikes were scrapped and sold for parts, but they could still be roaming the highways of America for all anyone knows. Fonda's broken bike was left behind because it was all banged up. It's since been fully restored and can be seen at the EMP Museum in Seattle.

Getting their calcium: A bearded vulture's diet is about 90% bones.

Penne for Your Thoughts

The dozens of different pastas in Italian cuisine are by and large named after the shapes they resemble. But some of them are a bit more complicated. Here are some pasta names, and what they mean in English.

Linguine: The strands are thin and flat; the name means "little tongues." (The word is from the same Latin root as *linguistics* and *language*.)

Penne: Penne is the plural of *penna*, which is a quill or a pen.

Fettuccine: This pasta is shaped like ribbons. The name translates as "little ribbons."

Orecchiette: It means "small ears." Orecchiette are small, circular pieces of pasta with the sides pushed up. They look, quite literally, like small ears.

Gigli: Thin, narrow, and fluted at the top, this pasta looks like flowers, and the name means "lilies."

Ravioli: Often stuffed with meat, ravioli comes from *rava*, an Old Italian word that means "meatball."

Gemelli: The name means "twins," as this pasta resembles two rods twisted around each other.

Paccheri: These wide, flat tubes get their name from the word *pacca*, which means "to slap." Paccheri make a slapping noise as they hit the sides of a pot while being cooked.

Lasagne: The pasta is most associated with the prepared dish lasagna, which is cooked in a large, deep pot. The word literally means "chamber pot."

Mostaccioli: This rhombus-shaped pasta (the name means "rhombus") shares its name with an Italian biscuit, which is also called a mostaccioli, and is also rhombus-shaped.

Calamarata: The Italian word for "squidlike," because the pieces look like rings of prepared squid, or calamari.

Tortellini: Derived from *torta*, a pie, tortellini are round morsels of stuffed pasta. The name means "little pies."

Barbina: An unkempt beard can resemble a bird's nest, which is how this small, nestlike bunch of thin noodles got a name that means "little beards."

What sets the *Bagheera kiplingi* apart from all other species of spiders? It's an herbivore.

Tortelloni: Slightly larger than tortellini, the name means "big little pies."

Ditalini: The name means "small thimbles," in reference to the pasta's fingernail-size tubes.

Marziani: This extruded pasta is a short spiral, but with lots of squiggly lines on the outside. That makes it look like a Martian's antennae in an old science-fiction movie...and the name means "Martians."

Macaroni: These were traditionally made from *maccarone*, or barley.

Gramigna: These noodles are curved like macaroni and just as thick, but long and bendy like spaghetti. A plate looks like a bunch of wild weeds, which is what *gramigna* means.

Fusilli: They're small and spindly, literally "little spindles."

Cannelloni: The direct translation is "large reeds," as this extruded pasta is long and cylindrical, like a large reed.

Bucatini: This pasta resembles spaghetti, but with a hole running through the entire length of the noodle. The name means "pierced hole."

Caramelle: A rolled-out square of pasta is filled with a dollop of meat or cheese, folded over, and then the ends are twisted closed, resembling a *caramelle*, or a wrapped piece of candy.

Strozzapreti: These noodles resemble a traditional high collar worn by priests and clerics. The name means "priest choker."

Cappello del prete: These start flat and are rolled into a triangular point. They look like the hats that Catholic clergy wear, hence the name "priest hats."

Farfalle: It's butterfly-shaped and it means "butterflies."

Spaghetti: "Little strings."

Vermicelli: Traditionally slightly thicker than spaghetti, *vermicelli* means "worms."

Cavatappi: They're spirals, but twisty, like corkscrews. *Cavatappi* means "corkscrews."

Sacchettini: A flat square of pasta is stuffed, rolled, and the ends are collected and pressed into each at the top, making them resemble "little sacks."

Acini di pepe: Tiny, round-shaped pasta, *acini di pepe* is Italian for "pepper grains."

Occhi di pernice: Apparently these tiny circular noodles with holes in the middle look just like "partridge eyes."

Seme di melone: They have the size and shape of "melon seeds."

Classical composer Arnold Schoenberg feared the number 13...and died on Friday, July 13, 1951.

Peculiar Protests

Protesters typically carry signs, chant some slogans, and then call it a day. These determined demonstrators used much stranger methods to support their causes.

MOON SHOT. An odd surveillance system was installed along the U.S.-Canadian border in 2009. It's a camera attached to a 50-foot balloon that helps American officials keep an eye on ships sailing around Lake Huron. But 300 Canadians were unhappy about it, so they gathered along the shoreline in Centennial Park in Sarnia, Ontario, where they dropped their pants and collectively mooned the camera. Then they dispersed before authorities showed up.

A WHALE OF A TAIL. Japanese government officials say whaling takes place off the country's shores only for "research" purposes, although critics claim there's a secret industry that sells whale meat to restaurants and stores. In 2008, acting on a tip from a crew member on a "research ship," two Greenpeace activists intercepted a package of whale meat. The duo then held a press conference and turned their evidence over to local police. Unfortunately for them, the cops did not arrest the ship's crew. They arrested the two activists instead, on charges of burglary and trespassing.

COWABUNGA. Tumbling milk prices, which are influenced by the European Union's policy-making, led 3,000 Belgian dairy farmers (and their cows) to gather outside of EU headquarters in protest in 2009. Things started to get ugly when one farmer milked his cow in front of riot police, then turned one of the cow's teats at the cops, hosing them with milk. The situation deteriorated from there, as the farmers began setting fires and throwing bottles and pitchforks. Amid the chaos, one of the cows broke loose and chased a city worker down a street.

CUPID? STUPID. Some people in India really hate Valentine's Day. On February 14, 2008, a few dozen people gathered in New Delhi to burn greeting cards and shout "DOWN WITH VALENTINE!" They told reporters that the holiday is an infringement on traditional Indian values, and calling it an endorsement of "Western promiscuity." The protests have become an annual event, and they've been getting rowdier. In recent years, members of protests have attacked young couples showing affection in public on Valentine's Day, cutting off couples' hair, painting their faces black, and forcing them into mock marriage ceremonies.

A 2014 UNICEF public sanitation campaign in India featured the cartoon mascot "Mr. Poo."

Weird World Records

Uncle John's holds the record for most books read on the throne in one sitting—25 (ouch!). Here are some more dubious achievements.

MOST BLOWTORCHES EXTINGUISHED. New York City's Ashrita Furman currently holds 191 Guinness World Records (which is a Guinness World Record in itself), including ones for underwater pogo stick jumping, carrying the most bricks with one hand, and knife catching. His most recent record is probably his most dangerous. In May 2016, he lined up 47 blowtorches, turned them on, and then, in under a minute, he put out all 47 scorching-hot blue flames…with his tongue.

MOST WALNUTS SMASHED. One record Furman no longer holds: smashing the most walnuts with his forehead. At the 2014 Punjab Youth Festival in Lahore, Pakistan, a man named Mohammad Rashid smashed 155 walnuts (in the shell) with his forehead in less than one minute. He lined them up in pairs so that he could crush more nuts (and Furman's record of 55).

LONG DISTANCE KEG-TOSSING. Hafthor Bjornsson of Iceland stands 6'9" and weighs 420 pounds, and played a warrior named "the Mountain" on *Game of Thrones*. On the HBO series, his character killed a man by crushing his skull, which is something Bjornsson could probably do in real life. After winning the 2015 Strongest Man in Europe contest, he took five steps while carrying a 1,400-pound log on his back—something nobody in Iceland had done for more than 1,000 years. Among his other accomplishments: He threw a 15-kilogram (33-pound) beer keg eight meters up into the air, beating the previous record of 7.4 meters.

LONGEST PIZZA. In June 2015, 60 pizza makers in Italy worked together to combine 1.7 tons of flour, 1.5 tons of mozzarella cheese, and 2 tons of tomato sauce to make a rectangular pizza that was one foot wide…and 5,234 feet long. That's a just a few feet short of a mile.

FASTEST POOP-POWERED BUS. In the UK, Reading Buses has a special vehicle called the Bus Hound that in 2015 reached a speed of 77 miles per hour. That's pretty fast for a bus under any circumstances, but it set the record for land speed by a bus running on compressed biomethane—in other words, gas generated by cow poop.

Only Donald Duck film to win an Oscar: *Der Fuehrer's Face,* for Best Animated Short Film (1943).

- **MOST PEEPS CONSUMED IN ONE SITTING.** Around Easter 2016, competitive eater Matt "Megatoad" Stone ate 200 marshmallow Peeps, doubling the previous record of 100.

- **LONGEST RUN WHILE HOLDING A TABLE IN YOUR TEETH.** In 2008, Georges Christen of Luxembourg held a 26-pound table—with a 110-pound woman sitting on it—in his teeth. Then he ran 38 feet, 8 inches.

- **LONGEST HUMAN MATTRESS DOMINO CHAIN.** What's that? It's when several people are tied to mattresses, and then the mattresses are stood upright, and toppled like dominoes. At a 2016 managers meeting for Aaron's, a chain of home furnishings stores, the managers made a domino chain 1,200 people long.

- **MOST SUVS ROLLER-SKATED UNDER.** In 2014, six-year-old "limbo skater" Gagan Satish skated under 39 sport-utility vehicles that had just five inches of clearance beneath them.

- **FASTEST RUNNER IN INAPPROPRIATE FOOTWEAR.** A German man named Andre Ortolf set two Guinness World Records in 2015: fastest 100-meter dash while wearing clogs (16.27 seconds) and fastest 100-meter dash while wearing ski boots (17.65 seconds).

- **MOST APPLES CUT WITH A CHAINSAW.** Anybody, or at least anybody who isn't afraid of cutting off their fingers, can cut a bunch of apples with a chainsaw. But in 2013, a British performance artist named Johnny Strange cut through eight apples with a chainsaw…while holding all eight in his mouth.

* * *

MORE REAL COURT TRANSQUIPS

Lawyer: Did he kill you?
Witness: Excuse me, counselor, can you repeat the question?

Lawyer: (Showing the witness a picture.) That's you?
Witness: Yes.
Lawyer: And you were present, right, when the picture was taken?

Lawyer (to witness): Are you telling the truth?
Prosecutor: Objection; irrelevant.

---

45 U.S. states no longer require schools to teach cursive writing. (They teach keyboarding instead.)

Disbarred!

If you're an attorney and you break the rules that govern your profession, you can be "disbarred" and banned from practicing law for life. Some disbarments, it turns out, are more spectacular than others.

ATTORNEY: Jason W. Smiekel, 29, a divorce lawyer who practiced law in Algonquin, Illinois, a suburb of Chicago
LEGAL BRIEF: In 2008, Smiekel was hired by a man named Brian Hegg to represent him in a child custody dispute with his ex-wife, Megan Wangall. But while he was working on the case, Smiekel began an affair with Wangall. Hegg found out and reported Smiekel to the state's Attorney Registration and Disciplinary Commission. In an effort to prevent Hegg from testifying, Smiekel hired a hit man to murder him. Only problem: the "hit man" turned out to be an undercover federal agent posing as a hit man. Smiekel was arrested after he was videotaped handing the agent an envelope stuffed with $7,000 in cash in partial payment for the hit.

DISBARRED! In 2012, Smiekel pled guilty to one count of solicitation of murder using an "interstate facility" (a cell phone) and was sentenced to eight and a half years in federal prison. As part of the deal, he had to surrender his law license for good. "He's a nice guy and an excellent lawyer. His mind was just really scrambled at the time," Smiekel's attorney, Ralph Mecyzk, told the *Chicago Tribune*.

ATTORNEY: Aaron Ray Isaacson, 30, who became an assistant state's attorney in Lake County, Illinois, in January 2009
LEGAL BRIEF: Fresh out of law school with little practical experience, Isaacson was assigned to prosecuting traffic cases. The occasional misdemeanor drug case also crossed his desk, and he was more than qualified to handle those, something that became clear after five months on the job when his roommate, 30-year-old Ryan Yoselowitz, was arrested with 23 pounds of marijuana in his car. A search warrant served on the two friends' luxury town house led to the confiscation of a handgun, bundles of cash, a gram of cocaine, and 12 more pounds of pot, some of it kept in plain sight in glass candy jars in the kitchen.

At first Isaacson feigned shock—*shock!*—that pot had been found in the house, but the place stank of weed and the cops didn't buy his story. So he fessed up and admitted to witnessing dozens of Yoselowitz's drug deals and even helping him count the money. Yoselowitz claimed Isaacson made drug deliveries, too, but Isaacson denied it. He also

---

Candy sprinkles on buttered bread is a common snack in the Netherlands.

denied searching law enforcement databases at work for Yoselowitz. And those glass pipes found in the assistant state's attorney's bedroom? Isaacson says they were "college souvenirs." (He did, however, acknowledge having his own nickname in the drug trade: Yoda.)

DISBARRED! Isaacson was fired from his job, then granted immunity from prosecution in exchange for turning state's evidence against Yoselowitz, who pled guilty and was sentenced to 12 years in prison. At his disbarment hearing in 2012, Isaacson pleaded for a temporary suspension instead of a disbarment, telling the hearing board how he "so badly wanted to practice law." No dice—in 2013, less than five years after graduating from law school, he lost his license for good. Today he works as a marketing consultant.

ATTORNEY: Joshua Robinson, 37, of West Virginia

LEGAL BRIEF: In 2009, Robinson was hired by a man named David Lee Gump to settle his grandfather's estate. While working on the case, Robinson allegedly cashed a check that had been made out to Gump's grandfather. When Gump found out about it, he went to Robinson's house to confront him. According to the state Lawyer Disciplinary Board, that's when Robinson attacked Gump…

> with a wooden baseball bat and then chased his defenseless client…down a residential street until he fell to the ground. When Mr. Gump fell down, Mr. Robinson began beating him again with the baseball bat in the head chest and back. Mr. Gump sustained serious injuries.

Robinson was charged with malicious wounding, unlawful wounding, obstructing justice, and embezzlement. In 2010, he agreed to a deal in which he pled guilty to unlawful wounding in exchange for the other charges being dropped. He was sentenced to five years of home confinement, and fitted with an electronic ankle bracelet.

DISBARRED! The Lawyer Disciplinary Board found that the beating "constituted a violation of Mr. Robinson's duty to his client," and in October 2012, the West Virginia Supreme Court of Appeals stripped Robinson of his license to practice law. Robinson had asked for a temporary suspension instead of disbarment, but the court, noting that he was also facing charges in Kentucky for "throwing a propane tank through the windshield of his wife's vehicle as she was attempting to leave their home," rejected the request.

UPDATE: In 2012, Robinson sued the county for "failing to implement and apply hygienic procedures in the use of ankle bracelets." He alleged that after several months of wearing his, it became contaminated with bacteria and mold, causing his ankle to become infected, necessitating surgery. He sought damages to cover his medical bills.

ATTORNEY: Ira Dennis Hawver, who practiced law in Kansas

LEGAL BRIEF: In 2005, Hawver represented Phillip Cheatham, who was charged with shooting two women to death and attempting to murder a third. The third woman survived and identified Cheatham as the killer. Hawver's defense was a bit unorthodox: he admitted that Cheatham was "a professional drug dealer" and "shooter of people" with a prior manslaughter conviction for killing a rival drug dealer. (That last fact had been kept from the jury until Hawver revealed it.) "With this man's background and experience, do you think he would have left an eyewitness alive?" he asked. The jury was unpersuaded, and found Cheatham guilty. Then, during the sentencing phase, Hawver told the jury that "they should execute the killer." They obliged, sentencing Cheatham to death.

DISBARRED! In 2013, the Kansas Supreme Court overturned Cheatham's conviction and ordered a new trial on the grounds that Hawver had provided him with ineffective counsel. (Cheatham pled no contest and was sentenced to life plus 165 months for the crimes.) Next, the court held a hearing to determine whether Hawver should be stripped of his law license. Hawver showed up wearing a powdered wig and dressed as Thomas Jefferson; during the proceedings he pounded his fists on the lectern and shouted "I am incompetent!" The justices concurred, voting unanimously to disbar him.

UPDATE: At last report, Hawver was appealing his disbarment in federal court, though he says he has no plans to return to the practice of law even if he gets his license back. In 2014, he told the *Topeka Capital-Journal* that he will instead devote his time to aquaponic gardening, "in which manure created by fish in a tank is pumped over vegetable plants growing in a trough."

"HONORABLE" MENTION: Jasmine Shawn Parker, who took the Ohio state bar exam in July 2011

LEGAL BRIEF: The bar exam has a time limit. When time is up, you have to put down your pencil whether you're finished or not. But according to witnesses, on three sets of questions Parker continued to write after time had been called. Twice she continued writing for up to a minute, one of the witnesses alleged. When confronted, Parker vehemently denied the accusation. But under cross-examination, she conceded that it was "possible" she continued writing after time was called, but that she did not remember doing so.

NO ADMITTANCE! The Ohio Supreme Court, which has the final say on who is admitted to the bar, found Parker's answers less than forthright, and in a 2013 ruling found that she "failed to prove that she possess the requisite character, fitness, and moral qualifications"

for admission to the bar. It did, however, invite her to reapply, citing credible evidence of "remorse…and maturation throughout this process." Bonus: She had a passing score on the exam even after points were taken away as punishment, so if she does reapply, she doesn't have to take the test again.

* * *

BOB'S BURGERS SIGNS

The opening credits of the animated comedy TV series Bob's Burgers *depicts a row of stores that features the burger joint and the business next door… which changes every episode. Here are some of the store names*

- The Horse Renderer
- Magnum G.I. Colonoscopies
- A Fridge Too Far Used Appliances
- That's Improv-able Improv Theater
- Grindecologist Coffee Shop
- Annie Get Your Gum
- Year-Round Halloween Store (Closed for Halloween)
- Simply the Asbestos
- Wigs Wigs Wigs! (And Socks)
- Talk to the Hand Glove Store
- Scroto-Rooter Vasectomy Clinic
- That's A-Door-Bell Doorbells
- Earth, Wind & Tires
- Elliot's Smelly Bits Potpourri Shop
- Fern, Baby, Fern! Discount Fern Store
- Miles of Vials
- Sit and Spin Pottery
- Tandemonium: All Your Tandem Bike Needs
- A Unicycle Built for Two Tandem Bicycles
- Don't Go There: Cautionary Sign Store
- Wolf in Cheap Clothing: Discount Pet Apparel
- Betty's Machetes
- Takes All Rinds Composting Center
- You Can't Handle the Ruth Baseball Cards
- A Ton in the Oven Big and Tall Baby Clothes

Lost in Space

Here's a cautionary tale about a cell phone system that fell to earth.

CAN YOU HEAR ME NOW?

In 1985, Bary Bertiger, an engineer with the high-tech giant Motorola, had an intriguing idea: If a company could put enough low-orbit satellites in the air to attain direct access to the entire surface of the Earth, and use that network to support a satellite telephone system, then people could use the satellite phones to make calls to virtually anywhere in the world. This was very early in the cell phone era (Motorola had released the first one only a year earlier, in 1984), and people were becoming familiar with a problem that still exists today: if you're too far away from a cell tower network your phone won't work. With the proper satellite network, Bertiger figured, that problem could be overcome.

Motorola chairman Robert Galvin gave Bertiger's idea the go-ahead, and work on the project began in 1987. In 1991, it was spun off as its own company, Iridium LLC. Why "Iridium"? The plan was to put 77 satellites into orbit—and the element iridium is number 77 on the periodic table. (The number of satellites was later reduced to 66 for cost-saving reasons, but the name remained.)

WEAK SIGNAL

It took another six years to develop the technology necessary for the project, but in 1997, Iridium started launching its satellites. A year later, amid much fanfare—and after a $180 million advertising campaign—Iridium LLC started operations. "Iridium," said the October 1998 cover story of *Wired* magazine, "may well serve as a first model of the 21st-century corporation."

But it soon became clear that there were serious flaws in Iridium's business plan.

When Bertiger came up with his idea in 1985, cell phones were as big as bricks, nearly as heavy, and cost about $4,000. They were owned by very few people, and worked in very few places. By 1998, the technology had progressed enormously. Millions of people owned small, sleek, pocket-sized cell phones served by nationwide cellular networks, and the cost had dropped to about $200. What was Iridium offering? A heavy, boxy phone that cost about $3,000. Cost to use it: from $3.00 to $8.00 a minute. By comparison, typical cell phone charges were already down to about 10¢ a minute. But probably the worst feature of all:

Iridium phones didn't work inside buildings, under trees, or inside cars. In order to work, the phones had to have direct line-of-sight access to a satellite.

CALL ENDED

How much had Iridium spent in its 13 years of development? More than $6 billion. (Iridium had calculated that they would need a million subscribers just to break even. Impossible? No problem! Company analysts confidently predicted they'd reach that number in two years. The harsh reality: By August 1999—after nine months of operation— Iridium had just 55,000 subscribers. That same month, they defaulted on $1.5 billion in loans and filed for bankruptcy. The 12 years of development—and the $6 billion—was toast. At the time it was one of the largest bankruptcies in U.S. history, and it remains one of the most expensive technological flops ever. (Iridium's single largest investor, Motorola, lost about $2.5 billion.)

Aftermath: In 2000, a group of investors bought what remained of Iridium, including all of its 66 satellites—as well as several spares that had been launched—for $35 million. The company exists today as Iridium Communications, and they have about 600,000 subscribers, many of them in the U.S. military. And while the phones are smaller, lighter, and less expensive (Amazon sells them for $1,000), they still don't work inside buildings.

Bonus fact: On February 10, 2009, another Iridium crash made the news when one of the company's satellites collided with a deactivated Russian satellite over Siberia. Both satellites were destroyed.

*   *   *

SEEDLINGS KNOW THEIR SIBLINGS

In 2009, scientists at the University of Delaware, studied mustard plant seedlings, monitoring how quickly they sent down roots when grown next to mustard plants that were closely related to them (meaning plants grown from seeds from the same "mother" plant) as opposed to being grown next to non-related mustard plants. Result: the plants sent down roots much more quickly when growing next to *unrelated* plants, gobbling up water and nutrients as fast as possible. They grew roots much more slowly when growing next to sibling mustard plants—sharing the water and nutrients in the soil with them. The scientists leading the studies said they believe that the plants were able to recognize their kin via chemical signals in the soil.

Dumb Crooks: Far East Edition

Brainless bandits and goofy gangsters can be found in every corner of the world. Here are a few who have embarrassed themselves in the far East.

MERDE! In 2007, a woman identified as "Mrs. Chen" in the Chinese press was leaving a bank in Laohekou (in central China), when her dog had to do his business. After picking up her dog's deposit and wrapping it in a few pieces of newspaper, a motorcycle with two men on it screeched to a halt in front of her. One of the men jumped off the bike and grabbed the papers; then he and his colleague zoomed away. The culprits apparently assumed the package was filled with money.

LORIS LARCENY. The slow loris is an endangered primate native to Southeast Asia. The bug-eyed creature is also cute, which is why in 2013 two men set up a stand on the Thai island of Phuket and charged tourists to have their photos taken with one. One of their customers: pop star Rihanna. After taking a "selfie" with the slow loris, she uploaded the photo to her Instagram account. The picture went viral and animal authorities noticed. Turned out the slow loris was stolen. The thieves now face a four-year prison sentence and a $1,300 fine.

THE TOO-TINY GETAWAY CAR. If you're going to steal a pile of money, make sure your getaway car is large enough to hold it all. That's the mistake that some Malaysian robbers made in 2008. After stealing 4.5 million ringgit ($1.1 million) from a security van in Kuala Lumpur, they discovered that they couldn't fit it all in their compact getaway car (also stolen), so they decided to take the security van, too. The van was later recovered with nine bags of cash still inside. The thieves escaped…with less than half their original haul.

DIAMONDS DOWN THE DRAIN. A robber named Zhou broke into a mansion in China's Hubei province in 2008. After stealing around $65,000 worth of jewelry, he came across two enormous diamond rings. They were so ridiculously gaudy that he assumed that they were fakes and flushed them down the toilet. Zhou was later apprehended and questioned about the missing rings, which were indeed real.…and were never recovered.

Do you make less than $20 an hour? You have an 83% chance of losing your job to a robot.

Let's Dance

Does dancing make you happy? It does for these folks.

"I don't make love by kissing, I make love by dancing."

—Fred Astaire

"Part of the joy of dancing is conversation. Trouble is, some men can't talk and dance at the same time."

—Ginger Rogers

"Dance is a song of the body— either of joy or pain."

—Martha Graham, the "Mother of Modern Dance"

"If I can make you smile by jumping over a couple of couches or running through a rainstorm, then I'll be very glad to be a song-and-dance man."

—Gene Kelly

"Dance is music made visible."

—George Balanchine, choreographer

"There's just something about dance. It's like a primal thing in all of us."

—Patrick Swayze

"I believe that dance came from the people and that it should always be delivered back to the people."

—Alvin Ailey, choreographer

"When a body moves, it's the most revealing thing. Dance for me for a minute, and I'll tell you who you are."

—Mikhail Baryshnikov

"On many an occasion when I'm dancing, I have felt touched by something sacred."

—Michael Jackson

"I can't help it—my feet love to dance."

—Snoopy

"I have such a respect and fascination for dance. I can be light as air or stay grounded. Dance is really another universe."

—Shakira

"There are shortcuts to happiness, and dancing is one of them."

—Vicki Baum

"I started dancing before I could talk. Other babies learn to stand and then walk—I just danced."

—Bruno Tonioli, *Dancing with the Stars* judge

"Nobody cares if you can't dance well. Just get up and dance."

—Dave Barry

The first hair perms required a dozen brass curlers that weighed nearly 2 pounds each.

The Spirit(s) of Lily Dale

Since 1879, residents of a quaint town in upstate New York have mediated conversations between loved ones—parents and children, husbands and wives, brothers and sisters. What's so special about that? These mediators connect the living...with the dead.

TRAPPED IN TIME

Pastel-painted Victorian homes line the streets of Lily Dale, New York, leftovers from the town's golden age at the dawn of the 20th century. It's been called Silly Dale, Spookdale, and—in a 1997 *New York Times* article—"New York's own corner of the twilight zone." In winter, Lily Dale is as quiet as the ghosts rumored to walk its streets. But when summer rolls around, this town's population blossoms—from a few hundred to around 22,000.

This gated community, founded by members of the Spiritualist church beside a picturesque lake in western New York state, was set apart in its original corporate charter as a place "for the discerning of the spirits." When tens of thousands of true believers stream through the gates each summer, it's not the lake or the Victorian homes they're coming to see: it's the women (and a few men) who claim to be able to deliver messages from beyond the grave.

EARLY AMERICAN RAPPERS

Spiritualism got its start in 1848 in nearby Hydesville, New York, when unexplained rapping sounds in the night turned out to be the spirit of a peddler murdered and buried in the cellar of a farmhouse—or so the daughters of the house claimed. Fifteen-year-old Margaret Fox and her twelve-year-old sister, Kate, convinced thousands that communication between the dead and the living was possible. That belief started a movement—and then a "religion" called Spiritualism.

Spiritualists believe that death is simply "a transition from a physical entity into a nonphysical one." In its heyday (the second half of the 19th century), Spiritualism had as many as 10 million followers. The movement included many of the era's "free thinkers," such as women's rights advocate Elizabeth Cady Stanton, shipping magnate Cornelius Vanderbilt, writer Arthur Conan Doyle, newspaper publisher Horace Greeley, and even—some sources claim—Abraham Lincoln.

Early Spiritualists attended séances where mediums purported to

---

Meriwether Lewis's dog Seaman was the only dog to complete the Lewis and Clark expedition.

deliver messages from the deceased to friends and family members. In the earliest days of the movement, mediums asked spirits to rap "yes" or "no" to answer questions. Later, they moved on to spelling out longer messages with a series of raps corresponding to the 26 letters of the alphabet. Disembodied voices spoke to those around the table, and voices might be "channeled" through the medium's own lips. Haunting music sometimes flowed from ghostly trumpets that hung in the air. Lights floated across the room, glowing hands appeared, and flowers materialized, as if the dead were nearby, waiting to connect with the living.

SUCKERS OR SCIENCE?

If this all sounds foolish to modern ears, remember that the mid-1800s was a time of scientific marvels. If Samuel Morse could send "disembodied" messages with his telegraph consisting of nothing but electrical signals traveling over wires, why couldn't disembodied spirits send messages through a "spiritual telegraph" such as Margaret Fox? Millions believed they could.

In 1849, a committee of skeptics—men of science, skilled at exposing fraud—conducted a battery of public "tests" at Corinthian Hall in Rochester, New York, in an attempt to expose Margaret Fox as a fraud. Fox was stripped naked by a group of "sour-faced women" in a back room. They checked her clothes for anything that might cause the raps that often accompanied her readings. Once reclothed, Fox made her way to the stage, where the male examiners tied her skirt tightly around her ankles. One of them held her feet to the floor so she couldn't move them. Finally, a handkerchief was tied around her mouth.

Despite these preventive measures, when the audience posed questions, ghostly raps gave answers. Skeptics howled in protest, but believers were not dissuaded in the least.

THE SPIRITED SEX

Nineteenth-century American women were little more than second-class citizens, marginalized and silenced by their fathers and then by their husbands. From the beginning, Spiritualism gave women something they'd never had before: voices in the public sphere. Female mediums delivered messages that would have been scandalous if they were voiced by women who were *not* in trances. From the safety of their "trances," mediums made pronouncements about everything from social justice to sexuality: "Forcing women to have unwanted sex interferes with the evolution of the human race," one medium revealed. "Men who force their wives to have sex risk the wrath of the spirit world."

Messages from "the other side" played a role in the early women's rights movement and advanced the causes of social justice, including the abolition of slavery. Spiritualists at a convention in Providence, Rhode Island, promoted "the abrogation of all oppression, civil inequality, domestic tyranny or mental or spiritual despotism, because freedom is the birthright of all, and the instinctive demand of every growing spirit."

Female mediums of the time spoke with authority on almost any subject, from politics to science to economics. How did they get away with it? Women—as the "logical" men of the time maintained—could not possibly speak authoritatively due to an innate lack of intelligence. Therefore, they must be speaking for the dead.

THE PRICE OF BOOS

Messages from the dead aren't free. In 1860, a 14-year-old medium named Tennessee Claflin could be consulted for $1. (For an extra $2, her father would throw in a bottle of Miss Tennessee's Magnetic Life Elixir, a potent mix of alcohol and opium.) "The sad part about Spiritualism for me is that it used to be so easy—and still would be so easy—to fake," says Susan Glasier, executive director of today's Lily Dale Assembly.

Even Maggie, the elder of the famed Fox sisters whose ghostly raps gave rise to the religion, eventually recanted. The raps, she told the *New York World* in 1888, were faked by popping bones in her toes. Then she took off her shoes and popped away to prove it. Fox was broke at the time, and the *World* paid her $1,500 for the exclusive interview. But a 2012 *Smithsonian* magazine article reported that money wasn't her only motivation. The leading Spiritualists of the day had called her little sister Kate a drunk. They were advocating for Kate's two children to be taken from her. Margaret wasn't going to let that happen to her little sister, and she would take down the whole religion to prevent it, if she had to. It worked. The press called Maggie's admission a "death blow" to the movement, though it wasn't the end of the Fox sisters' story. A year after the *World* interview, Maggie recanted her recant and went back to working as a rapping medium. (Her spirit guides urged her to do so.)

TRY BEFORE YOU BUY

Lily Dale's mediums claim the days of defrauding people for money are long past. The National Spiritualist Association of Churches (NSAC) calls Spiritualism "a science, a philosophy, and a religion." On the "science" side, the church reviews data before deciding whether someone claiming the ability to contact the dead can actually do so. Mediums wanting to set up shop in Lily Dale have to prove themselves. They must give private readings to three of the corporation's board members.

If that goes well, they give public readings in front of the entire board. The board tests at least a dozen mediums every year, but only about 40 have passed the tests to become certified Lily Dale mediums.

A sign in the lobby of the town's Maplewood Hotel reads: NO READINGS, HEALINGS, CIRCLES, OR SÉANCES IN THIS AREA, PLEASE. Not to worry. Anyone who wants to talk to spirits will find all of the above inside the town's gates. Favorite first stop: the town's "holiest" spot, Inspiration Stump. At one time, mediums stood on the stump to deliver the words of the dead. After one of them toppled over stone dead, the townspeople decided the stump's energy was too strong and put a stop to stump speaking.

Public demonstrations of mediumship take place three times a day during the summer season. Those are included in the town's $15 gate fee (free for active military and visitors age 80 and older). What ghostly messages do Lily Dale's mediums reveal in public demos? One puzzled medium told a crowd that she was seeing images of Tootsie Rolls and Schlitz beer. "That's my grandmother!" yelled a woman in the crowd. Visitors looking for one-on-one readings with Lily Dale mediums will pay between $40 and $75 for a half-hour session.

WHO YOU GONNA CALL?

With 40 registered mediums, it's tough to know who to go to, but here are a few of the most renowned in the city.

• **Anne Gehman.** Gehman claims she's been consulted by government agencies, royal families, police departments, and corporate CEOs. She gained fame as the medium who (supposedly) aided law enforcement during the investigation of notorious serial killer Ted Bundy. Witnesses have seen Gehman bend spoons with her mind and make tables dance without touching them. But if you don't have deep pockets, forget it: the 2010 HBO documentary *No One Dies in Lily Dale* filled Gehman's appointment book and sent her rates soaring.

• **John White.** Police officer Ronald Holt went to Lily Dale hoping to contact his son, Blair. In 2007, 16-year-old Blair took the bus home from his Chicago school. A gang member intent on killing a rival boarded the bus and started shooting. Blair shielded a friend with his own body and died of gunshot wounds. When Holt consulted John White, the medium told him he felt Blair in the "spirit world" conducting a performance of music he had composed. Holt confirmed that Blair was, indeed, a composer. The grieving officer had recently put together a group to perform some of his son's compositions. Could White have known that ahead of time?

• **Carol Gasper.** In 2013, Pamela Hutson and her husband visited Lily Dale on a lark. She had no clue how to choose a medium and was told to stroll the streets and look for an "open" sign on a door. That's how she found Gasper. The medium was actually done for the day but had forgotten to take her sign down. After a few general comments about Hutson's dead parents, Gasper stunned her visitor by coming up with the name, date, and method of death (car wreck) of a young man Hutson knew when she was 18. But Hutson had not even told the medium her name. How, Hutson wondered, could Gasper have known anything about her dead friend…unless she was really acting as a speaker for the dead. The friend's message: "Let your pain and suffering go. It gets better in the next life."

• **Sherry Lee Calkins.** One scorching day in June 2000, journalist Christine Wicker walked through the gates of Lily Dale for the first time. Three years later, she published *Lily Dale: The True Story of the Town That Talks to the Dead*. A self-professed "raging skeptic," Wicker came to Lily Dale certain that she would find nothing but a big con. She remains skeptical but can't discount the fact that Calkins told her not one, but five true things she hadn't known about herself. Those five things included the fact that her grandfather had three children, one of whom "had something wrong with it" and died young. Wicker thought her grandfather had two children. When Wicker asked how Calkins could have known when she didn't know herself, the medium said, "You didn't have to, dear. I'm not a mind reader."

LAST GASP

The NSAC calls Spiritualism a "common sense religion," but today it's just a ghost of its former self. Membership hovers somewhere around the 14,000 mark, rather than the millions it once boasted. Given that this is an age where satellites orbit the Earth and robots rove across Mars, the fact that Spiritualism thrives is somewhat surprising. Perhaps British writer G. K. Chesterton explained its endurance best: "No conceivable number of forged bank-notes can disprove the existence of the Bank of England." By the same logic, Chesterton asserts, "No conceivable number of false mediums affects the probability of the existence of real mediums one way or the other." As long as people knock on their doors, Lily Dale's mediums will keep the tradition of mediating between the living and the dead…alive.

*   *   *

18 EARLY 20TH-CENTURY COCA-COLA KNOCKOFFS

Ala Cola, Cola-Coke, Heck's Cola, Kay Ola, Kola Ade, Kola Kola, Nerve Ola, Revive Ola, Rye Ola, Standard Cola, Wise Ola, Pau Pau Cola, Charcola, Cola Soda, Loco Kola, Minola, Vine Cola, Kola Pepsin

Pants Rabbits and Hog Fuel

Early 20th-century lumberjacks worked hard and lived hard.
Here's some of the lingo that was tossed around a lumber camp.

Bell ox: a lumber camp foreman

Hot biscuits: logs

Blue-butted school marm: a log with a swelled-up end

Pants rabbits: lice

Traveling dandruff: lice

Roll the guff: have a conversation

Quinine Jimmy: a lumber camp doctor

Uncle: lumber company superintendent

"Watch wild!": "Stand clear!" or "Timber!"

Shinny: liquor

Tanglefoot: cheap whiskey

Crumb boss: the worker (usually a boy) whose job it is to do menial chores like sweep up the bunkhouse and feed the livestock

Swedish fiddle: a crosscut saw

Hog fuel: sawdust

Blackjack: coffee

Red horse: salted "beef" of dubious origin

Strawberries: beans

Turkey: a duffel bag

Turnip: a pocket watch, tied to the belt with a leather strap

Beaver: a lumberjack who isn't very good at chopping down trees

Lucifer: a match

Ball hooter: a lumberjack who rolls logs down a hill

Bake a batch of rolls: to fraternize with a prostitute

Office: an outhouse

Bucker: a lumberjack whose job it is to cut felled trees into smaller logs

Hay burner: a horse

Iron burner: the logging camp's blacksmith

Crummy: a logging company's railroad car (or any vehicle) used to transport lumberjacks to a work site

Nosebag: a lunch bucket

Who Needs a Tooth Fairy?

On page 145 we told you the history of the tooth fairy, and explained that "shed-tooth rituals" are found all over the world. In many places, it turns out, the tooth fairy's job is handled by animals.

ANIMALS

• **Greece.** Here sows (female pigs) have the honor of disposing of baby teeth. The child throws the tooth onto the roof of their house in the hope that a sow will find it. While doing this, the child chants, "Take sow my tooth and give me an iron one so that I can chew rusks."

• **Lesotho.** The tooth is thrown onto the roof, in the hope that a lizard will find it and bring the child a new tooth.

• **Romania.** The child throws the tooth onto the roof and says, "Crow, crow, take away this bone tooth and bring me a steel one."

• **Jamaica.** When children lose a tooth, they are warned that a calf will come to get them and the tooth…but if they put the tooth into a tin can and shake it, the rattling noise will keep the calf at bay.

• **Nepal.** In this country, the goal is to keep the tooth hidden from birds by burying it. If a bird sees or eats the tooth before it is buried, the new tooth won't grow in at all.

• **El Salvador.** Salvadoran kids leave their teeth under their pillows in the hope that a rabbit will take it and leave some money behind.

• **Korea.** Korean children throw their teeth onto the roof while singing, "Blackbird, blackbird, my old tooth I give to you. Bring me a new tooth."

• **Cherokee (Southeastern United States).** The child runs around the house and then throws tooth onto the roof as they say four times, "Beaver put a new tooth in my jaw."

• **Sri Lanka.** Another country where the tooth is thrown onto the roof—in this case, in the hope that a squirrel will find it.

• **India.** Kids throw their teeth onto the roof and ask a sparrow to bring them a new tooth.

• **Mongolia.** If there's a dog handy, the child will put the tooth into a

---

Food for thought: The University of Kentucky offers a course on "Taco Literacy."

piece of fat and feed it to the dog, in the hope that the new tooth that grows in will be as strong as a dog's tooth. If there are no dogs around, burying the tooth beside a tree will (hopefully) ensure that the new tooth has roots as strong as the tree's. The tradition of feeding teeth to dogs has spread as far as Alaska.

OTHER TRADITIONS

• **Finland.** Perhaps the only country with a villain who frightens kids into taking better care of their teeth, Finland has a *Hammaspeikko* (tooth troll) who shows up anytime children eat candy. He gives the kids cavities by drilling holes in their teeth, but they can scare him away by brushing their teeth. The Hammaspeikko tale dates only to the early 1960s, but similar tales of spirits who cause toothaches have been a part of Finnish culture for centuries.

• **Brazil.** This country has two traditions: In some places, kids throw their tooth onto a roof and ask Saint John to bring them a new one. In others, they throw it in the yard and ask a bird to bring it. (Parents encourage children to brush their teeth by telling them that the birds will take the lost tooth only if it doesn't contain any cavities.)

• **Egypt.** In a tradition that dates back to when the ancient Egyptians worshipped the sun god Ra, the child wraps the tooth in tissue and throws it at the sun while saying, "Shiny sun, shiny sun, take this buffalo's tooth and bring me a bride's tooth."

• **Navajo (Southwestern United States).** Navajo children take their tooth away from the home and bury it somewhere to the southeast, on the eastern side of a bush or tree. (The sun rises in the east, and in Navajo culture the east is associated with childhood.)

• **Botswana.** Children here throw their baby teeth onto the roof and ask the moon to give them new ones.

• **Indonesia.** The child has to throw the tooth over their shoulder onto the roof...and with some skill: If they throw the tooth in a straight line onto the roof, the tooth that grows in will be straight as well. If the throw is crooked, the new tooth will be, too.

*   *   *

IT'S A MYTH-STORY

Legend says that if the ravens that live in the Tower of London ever leave, the British throne will fall, so the British government periodically clips the ravens' wings...just to make sure they can't fly very far.

Laura Ingalls Wilder got her start as the *St. Louis Star Farmer*'s poultry columnist.

7 Great Travel Books

If you're planning a great adventure—or if you're planning on writing a book about your travels—reading some of the most influential travel books of all time might give you some necessary inspiration. Here are seven…to get you going.

HISTORIES (440 BC)

Author: Herodotus

Where He Traveled: Middle East and southern Europe

Story: Written in the 5th century BCE, *Histories* is an account of the culture, history, traditions, politics, and geography of the ancient peoples and places around the eastern Mediterranean Sea. It's considered the literary work that invented the concept of history writing and earned Herodotus the title "Father of History." But it's also known as the world's first travel book. While researching the massive tome (700+ pages), Herodotus traveled great distances through the ancient Middle East, north to the region around the Black Sea, across Greece, and all the way to what is now southern Italy, writing about the sites and people he saw along the way. One of the most notable sections: observations on the day-to-day life of the ancient Egyptians, with touristlike accounts of ancient sites, such as the Pyramids of Giza and the city of Thebes (modern-day Luxor). While its tales are often wildly exaggerated, and it portrays many myths as true, *Histories* has inspired historians, travelers, and travel writers for more than 2,000 years.

THE TRAVELS OF MARCO POLO (c. 1300)

Authors: Marco Polo and Rustichello da Pisa

Where He Traveled: Middle East and Asia

Story: In the 13th century, Mongol leader Genghis Khan and his descendants established an empire that stretched from Southeast Asia all the way to eastern Europe. The peace and stabilization he brought to the empire allowed for trade and cultural interchange between Europe and Asia like never before. Taking advantage of this, in the 1260s, two Italian merchants, brothers Niccolo and Maffeo Polo, traveled all the way to the Mongol city of Dadu (now Beijing), where they were welcomed into the court of Kubla Khan (grandson of Genghis). The Polos returned to Venice in 1269, and made a second trip to Dadu in 1271—this time taking Niccolo's 17-year-old son, Marco, with them. Marco ended up a close confidant of Kubla Khan for the next 17 years, and traveled throughout Asia as Khan's envoy. He returned to Venice in 1295 and, with the help of author Rustichello da Pisa, put the stories of those travels into manuscript form. *The Travels of Marco Polo* offered Europeans the first extensive accounts of central and eastern Asian cultures. It was translated into many different languages over the following decades, making Polo one of the most celebrated travelers history has ever known. Like *Histories*, the book is full of exaggerations—and lies—but it's still a fascinating account of thousands of miles of journeys into ancient and exotic cultures by one of history's most accomplished adventurers.

Bonus Fact: Historian Laurence Bergreen's celebrated 2008 biography *Marco Polo: From Venice to Xanadu* untangles the stories of Polo's travels, and helps readers separate the myths from reality.

THE INNOCENTS ABROAD (1869)

Author: Mark Twain

Where He Traveled: Europe, the "Holy Land," and North Africa

Story: In 1867, a San Francisco newspaper commissioned Twain, at the time 32 years old and just a few years into his writing career, to join a group of passengers on the steamship SS *Quaker City* for a five-month journey to the lands around the Mediterranean. The trip included stops in southern Europe, Turkey, Lebanon, Palestine, and North Africa. The paper published Twain's hilarious "travel letters," sent to them during the excursion, and in 1869 the letters were collected and published as *The Innocents Abroad*. Twain's laid-back, dryly comic, and often cutting observations of his subjects—which included not just the exotic peoples and places he encountered, but his American travel mates, as well—made the book a big hit. It outsold *Huckleberry Finn* and *Tom Sawyer* during Twain's lifetime, and it remains one of the most popular travel books ever written.

Bonus Fact: Because *The Innocents Abroad* is long past its copyright era, you can find it for free online.

THE ROAD TO OXIANA (1937)

Author: Robert Byron

Where He Traveled: Venice, Cyprus, the Middle East, and western Asia

Story: *The Road to Oxiana* is the diarylike account of British travel writer Byron's 10-month journey, in 1933 and 1934, from Venice through Palestine, Syria, Iraq, Iran, Afghanistan, and India. The journey, which was undertaken by automobile, horse, and mule, was primarily focused on ancient archaeological sites along the trip's route, but features many side adventures. An excerpt from American literary scholar Paul Fussell's introduction to the 1982 edition of the book: "Here we find newspaper clippings, public signs and notices, official forms, letters, diary entries, essays on current politics, lyric passages, historical and archaeological dissertations, brief travel narratives (usually of comic-awful delays and disasters), and—the triumph of the book—at least twenty superb comic dialogues, some of them virtually playlets, complete with stage directions and musical scoring. Reading the book is like stumbling into a modern museum of literary kinds presided over by a benign if eccentric curator."

A WINTER IN ARABIA (1940)

Author: Freya Stark

Where She Traveled: Yemen

Story: In 1935, Freya Stark, a 42-year-old female British explorer—who had already traveled to parts of the Middle East and Asia few male European explorers had seen—led a small party to the Hadhramaut, in the far south of the Arabian Peninsula (present-day Yemen). She was the first Western woman and among the first non-Arabs ever to visit the region. Officially an archaeological expedition, *A Winter in Arabia* is the story of that journey, told in three parts: the first tells the story of the trip, mostly by car, from the Yemeni Indian Ocean coast to the Hadhramaut village of Hureidha; the second is a daily account of her time in the village; and the third tells the story of the journey out, by camel caravan, through some of the most remote and harsh desert on Earth. Along the way, Stark describes the region's history and geology, its flora and fauna, and the customs and day-to-day lives of the tribal people who have inhabited the region for centuries. (*A Winter in Arabia* is one of three books Stark wrote about the trip, for which she received the Founder's Gold Medal from the British Royal Geographic Society.)

LOG FROM THE SEA OF CORTEZ (1951)

Author: John Steinbeck

Where He Traveled: Sea of Cortez (more commonly known as the Gulf of California) in Mexico

Story: *Log from the Sea of Cortez* is Steinbeck's account of a six-week journey he took in the spring of 1940 with his best friend, marine biologist Ed Ricketts (and a crew of four), on a 75-foot fishing boat from Monterey, California, to the Gulf of California. The book is a combination travelogue, boat's log, science journal, adventure tale, and philosophical treatise, and it's considered the best of Steinbeck's nonfiction writings. The book was first published in 1941, with Ricketts as coauthor, and included a scientific catalogue of the species of marine invertebrates the duo collected—more than 50 of which were new to science. That book sold very few copies, so Steinbeck reissued the book without the catalog and under his own name, in 1951, three years after Ricketts's death.

Bonus Fact: Ricketts, who owned a marine lab in Monterey, was the model for the hard-drinking marine biologist "Doc" in Steinbeck's classic 1945 novel, *Cannery Row*. Another bonus fact: Most reviews don't mention it, but there was another person along on the trip—Steinbeck's first wife, Carol. She's never mentioned in the book, and they were divorced not long after the trip ended.

FULL TILT: IRELAND TO INDIA WITH A BICYCLE (1965)

Author: Dervla Murphy

Where She Traveled: Europe, Middle East, western and southern Asia

Story: Murphy took care of her ailing mother in Lismore, Ireland, until she died in 1962, when Murphy was 31. Then it was time for an adventure. A lifelong biking enthusiast, Murphy packed clothes and traveling gear into a satchel and set off from the northern French port town of Dunkirk on her Armstrong Cadet bicycle. Six months later, she pedaled into New Delhi, India. *Full Tilt* tells the story of that extraordinary adventure. Murphy traveled 4,500 miles, most of it on her bike, across France, Italy, Yugoslavia, Bulgaria, Turkey, Iran, Afghanistan, over the Himalayas, into Pakistan, and finally to India. For most of the journey she avoided hotels, staying in the homes of people she met along the way, or in the tents of wandering nomads, or just by herself out in the open. She endured injury, illness, an attack by wolves in Bulgaria (the pistol she carried with her helped out), an attempted sexual assault in Azerbaijan, and much more—and she did it all with incredible courage and good humor. Here's an excerpt about a long, rainy stretch in Yugoslavia: "By this time worrying about pneumonia seemed futile; for days I had been living in a state of permanent saturation from the waist down, so that the only sensible reaction was lots of rum and no fuss." (Bonus: Murphy went on to write more than two dozen books on her travels around the world. *Between River and Sea*, about a trip to Israel and Palestine, came out in 2015, when she was 83 years old.)

*   *   *

COCAINE? TRY FAUX-CAINE

When a movie or TV show calls for a character to use cocaine, they don't use real cocaine. (Obviously.) Propmasters use cornstarch and baby powder if the drug is just a visual prop. But if the actor has to inhale it, propmasters use powdered lactose or vitamin B powder. Then whatever is used to snort the drug, such as a straw, is coated with Vaseline. Result: most of the powder sticks to that, instead of going up the actor's nose.

Gun Dogs

*Ordinarily, the term "gun dog" refers to a dog that's been trained
to retrieve game for a hunter. We're pretty sure the owners of
these pooches wish that was what we were talking about.*

Dog: A female Labrador retriever owned by an embarrassed California duck hunter who refused to let his or his dog's name to be made public

Bang! In February 2010, the hunter and a friend were out near Los Banos, California. When they finished hunting for the day, the man set his loaded shotgun on the ground and went to collect his duck decoys, which were set up 15 yards away. The Labrador remained behind, and at some point it stepped on the man's shotgun, disengaging the safety and causing it to fire. The blast struck the man in the upper back.

Outcome: Being hit by a shotgun blast from 15 yards away can be fatal, but this man was lucky. He not only survived, but he was released from the hospital the same day. The wound to his ego may take longer to heal: the man broke one of the cardinal rules of duck hunting— unload your shotgun before leaving it unattended. "The guy was pretty adamant about [not releasing his name] because he's usually very big on gun safety. He doesn't want to talk to anyone about what happened," Merced County Sheriff's spokesperson Tom MacKenzie told reporters.

Dog: Stinky, a mixed-breed dog owned by a 30-year-old New Zealand man named Kelly Russell

Bang! In December 2000, Russell was hunting wild pigs near Tokoroa, on New Zealand's North Island, with Stinky and two other mutts. When the dogs cornered a pig, Russell set his shotgun on the ground and prepared to kill the pig with his knife. That's when Stinky jumped on the shotgun and it fired. "All of a sudden there was a boom, then I realized that I had shot myself, or rather that my dog had shot me," Russell told the *New Zealand Herald*. The blast got him in the left foot, injuring it severely. He managed to crawl to a nearby road, then lay there for five hours until a car finally drove past and stopped to help.

Outcome: The motorist hustled Russell into his car and raced to a hospital in Tokoroa. Doctors were unable to save the foot, but Russell doesn't blame the dog. "I don't bear any grudges against Stinky at all. It was all my fault. I should have unloaded my gun," he told the *Herald*. (Russell collected $10,000 in insurance money for the loss of his foot… and was fined $500 for hunting in a protected wilderness area without a

Cartoon fact: The *Looney Tunes* theme song is called "The Merry-go-round Broke Down."

permit.) Russell told reporters he planned to go hunting again as soon as he can. "I'll go again for sure, but I'll be sure to take a mate and a decent cellphone," he said.

Dog: A pooch, not named in news reports, owned by Luanne Denise Strouse, 59, of San Carlos Park, Florida

Bang! Strouse was lying on her bed one night in January 2010. Also on the bed: a loaded Kel-Tec .380 handgun. Not on the bed...yet: the unnamed dog, one of several that Strouse owns. When it did hop up on the bed, it knocked the gun to the floor. Strouse, who was described in police reports as "extremely intoxicated," reached down to pick up the gun, and when she did, it fired, striking her in the knuckle of her left middle finger. Strouse's husband was in the other room at the time. When he heard the shot, he raced to his wife's side, got a rag to stop the bleeding, and called 911.

Outcome: Strouse was taken by ambulance to a nearby hospital, where doctors were able to save her injured finger.

Dog: A Blue Gascony basset hound not named in news reports, owned by a French hunter who was identified only by his first name, Rene

Bang! In September 2012, Rene was hunting in southwestern France near Bordeaux with the young dog, who was on his first hunt, and two older dogs. Suddenly a deer appeared. The two older dogs chased after it, but the youngest stayed with Rene. When Rene sat down, the dog tried to hop up into his lap. "He jumped on me to give me a cuddle, I think," Rene told France Bleu radio. Rene was resting his shotgun on his lap at the time, and when the dog jumped, his paw hit the trigger and the shotgun fired. The blast hit Rene in his right hand.

Outcome: Rene was flown by helicopter to a hospital in Bordeaux, but the wound was so severe that doctors were forced to amputate the hand. Considering how traumatic it must have been to lose a hand that way, Rene remained upbeat and bore no ill will toward his dog. "It wasn't his fault, and he's adorable! I should have left the gun's safety on, that's all."

Dog: An unnamed dog owned by Anthony Wulf, who was living on Rambo Lane in Toledo, Ohio

Bang! The only thing Wulf was hunting for that fateful evening in December 2015 was a pizza, which he ordered from Wild Wings N Things and was having delivered. While he waited for it to arrive, he was handling a loaded handgun. When delivery boy Ryan Brill, 18, arrived with the pizza, Wulf set the gun on a table to answer the door. As he did, his dog ran past, and knocked the gun off the table. When it hit the floor it fired, shooting Brill in his left leg. "I've delivered to this guy before. Never shot me," Brill told the *Toledo Blade* newspaper.

Outcome: The wound wasn't life-threatening. Brill spent two hours in the hospital having his leg treated and spent the next three weeks on crutches. At last report, neither Wulf nor his dog had been charged with any crime, and Brill said he wasn't planning to sue. But Wulf may be out of luck the next time he wants a pizza. "I don't know if I'm ever going to deliver to that guy again," Brill says.

Dog: Eli, a 10-year-old American bulldog owned by 78-year-old Billy Brown of Dade City, Florida

Bang! In December 2011, Brown and his hunting buddy, Robert Gulvin, were in Brown's Chevy Silverado driving into swampland on a hunting trip when a deer suddenly jumped into the road in front of them. As soon as Eli, sitting in the back seat, saw the deer, he clambered over the center console separating the front and passenger seats and lunged at the deer through the windshield. Bad idea! Brown's loaded Browning .308 hunting rifle was resting on the console. When Eli scrambled over it, he knocked it off the console, disengaging the safety and firing the rifle into Brown's right thigh at point-blank range.

Brown and Gulvin were in such rugged terrain that the ambulance couldn't get to them; paramedics had to haul Brown out of the swamp in the back of a pickup truck. By the time he made it to the hospital, he'd lost three liters of blood and doctors weren't sure he'd make it

Outcome: Brown not only survived, but two months later was back hunting in the swamp with his two grandsons, the youngest of whom was 12. Conspicuously absent: Eli the bulldog. "He stayed home," Brown told the *Tampa Tribune*. "Eli is on restriction."

*   *   *

ALL THAT CREMAINS

Some things that can be made out of the ashes of cremated loved ones.

• A company called And Vinyly presses ashes into a vinyl record, on the record can be anything requested, such as the dearly departed's voice or favorite songs.

• Glass artist Beverly Albrets specializes in "memorial glass." She mixes human ash into molten glass and then blows it into ornate sculptures.

• If you send one pound of ash to a company called Holy Smoke, they'll mix it with gunpowder and send back 250 loaded shotgun shells.

• Instead of a regular urn, a company called In the Light Urns will make an hourglass with cremains instead of sand.

The Doctor Is In(sane)

These three real-life medical therapies were actually practiced on patients—one with good results; the other two, not so good.

INSULIN-SHOCK THERAPY

Treatment For: Schizophrenia and other mental disorders

Background: In the late 1800s, it was discovered that insulin, a protein produced in the pancreas, played a vital role in regulating glucose levels in the bloodstream. In the early 1920s, the first successful insulin treatment for diabetes was developed. This created great interest in the substance—and doctors started testing its effects on other conditions.

Weird Medicine: In 1927, Manfred Sakel, a 27-year-old Viennese psychiatrist, started treating drug addicts with insulin. Sakel accidentally gave one of the patients, who was also diagnosed with schizophrenia, an overdose, sending the patient into a temporary coma (too much insulin lowers a person's blood sugar to levels that do not allow the brain to function properly). After the treatment, according to Sakel, the patient seemed more at ease. So he started deliberately treating schizophrenics with insulin overdoses, sending them into a coma. Sakel claimed that more than 80 percent of the patients he treated with "insulin-shock therapy" were cured. Word of the breakthrough treatment spread, and by the 1940s, it was being used all over the world. Patients were typically given coma-inducing doses of insulin daily, for about two months. The painful treatments took hours to recover from, and regularly caused convulsions. Approximately 5 percent of the patients died. Doctors started becoming skeptical of the treatment in the 1950s, though it didn't fall completely out of favor until the 1970s. Most experts now believe insulin-shock therapy had no beneficial effects at all.

ROTATION THERAPY

Treatment For: Mental illness

Background: In the late 1700s, esteemed British physician Erasmus Darwin (grandfather of Charles Darwin), published a treatise on medicine, anatomy, biology, and other subjects, titled *Zoonomia, or the Laws of Organic Life*. In it, he described a device that he believed could induce sick people to sleep, which he believed was the best medicine for many ailments. The device: a couch or chair suspended by ropes from a ceiling, which could be rapidly spun in circles. Being spun on such a device, Darwin wrote, would "still the violent action of the heart and arteries," leading to deep, restful sleep. Darwin never actually built the device, nor did he ever try the therapy.

Weird Medicine: In early 1800s, psychiatrist Joseph Mason Cox, the head of Fishponds Private Lunatic Asylum in Bristol, England, took Darwin's advice, and started treating his patients with what he called "rotation therapy." Cox believed that sleep was the best therapy for the mentally ill, so he put patients in straitjackets, tied them to a chair hanging by ropes from the ceiling, and had orderlies spin them around in circles. Sometimes this meant gentle spins, but it often meant very fast spinning—up to a hundred revolutions per minute—for long periods of time. This, Cox wrote, would regularly result in "vertigo, attended by pallor, nausea, vomiting, and frequently by the evacuation of the contents of the bladder." Amazingly, rotation therapy was adopted by other asylums around Europe before it was finally rejected as ineffective—not to mention harmful and terrifying to the mentally ill.

MALARIA THERAPY

Treatment For: Advanced syphilis

Background: The first effective cure for the sexually transmitted disease syphilis was developed in 1910. But it didn't work on advanced forms of the disease, such as *neurosyphilis*, in which the brain and/or spinal cord of the victim is infected by the syphilis bacteria, leading to multiple symptoms, including blindness and severe mental illness.

Weird Medicine: In the late 1800s, Austrian psychiatrist Julius Wagner-Jauregg experimented with *pyrotherapy* on mentally ill patients, including those suffering from neurosyphilis. He induced high fevers in the patients by injecting them with bacteria, such as the ones that cause strep throat and tuberculosis, to see if it cured them of their mental illness. (It didn't.) In 1917, Wagner-Jauregg decided to try a new method. He infected patients with the mosquito-borne disease malaria, transfusing blood from malaria sufferers directly into the bloodstream of neurosyphilis patients. And it worked. The prolonged high fever caused by the malaria killed off the syphilis bacteria. Because malaria could be treated with quinine, the treatment was considered safe… sort of: around 15 percent of patients treated with malaria therapy died—of malaria. But since neurosyphilis was *so* destructive and *so* deadly, malaria therapy was considered worth the risk—and it was the most common treatment of the disease until around 1940, when more modern treatments became available. How important was Wagner-Jauregg's development of malaria therapy? It won him the 1927 Nobel Prize for Medicine.

Contrary to popular belief, the ability to roll your tongue is not a genetic trait.

Not-So-Greatest Hits

"Greatest hits" albums are a marketing tool—a way to repackage old songs and call it a new product. And consumers must love it, because record labels keep doing it...even if the artist never had many actual hits or much commercial success in the first place. So instead of getting "the best of," we're getting "some of."

CHUCK MANGIONE
Album: *Greatest Hits*
Details: In 1978, Mangione delivered one of the most memorable soft rock hits ever: "Feels So Good"—an instrumental song powered by Mangione's flugelhorn. It was (and still is) the only flugelhorn-driven song to ever top the charts...and it was also Mangione's only hit. But that hasn't stopped Mangione's record company from releasing not one, but ten separate "Best of" compilations.

GIN BLOSSOMS
Album: *Outside Looking In: The Best of the Gin Blossoms*
Details: This 1990s alternative rock band had a half dozen hits, including "Hey Jealousy," "Found Out About You," and "Allison Road."—not quite enough for a greatest hits album. Even so, the Gin Blossoms' label released this compilation—without the band's knowledge—after it had recorded only two albums.

NELSON
Album: *20th Century Masters: The Millennium Collection*
Details: Nelson was a pop-rock band fronted by Matthew and Gunnar Nelson, the twin sons of rock 'n' roll teen idol Rick Nelson. They had one #1 hit, "(Can't Live Without Your) Love and Affection," which spent one week at the top of the charts in 1990, and three other minor hits by the end of 1991. And that was it.

AARON CARTER
Album: *Most Requested Hits*
Details: Remember the Backstreet Boys? The boy band was so popular (at least with preteens) that Carter, the younger brother of member Nick Carter, got a record deal. He performed bubblegum pop, too, but wasn't as successful as the multimillion-selling Backstreet Boys. The younger Carter's only hit was the #35-peaking "Aaron's Party (Come and Get It)." But that didn't stop his record company from releasing *Most Requested Hits*.

What? DOLPHINS HEAR ABOUT SEVEN TIMES BETTER THAN HUMANS DO.

TONE LŌC

Album: *"Wild Thing" and Other Hits*

Details: The gravelly voiced rapper had two huge hits in 1989: "Wild Thing" and "Funky Cold Medina." And those were the only two hits he ever had, so the title of his greatest hits album is a bit misleading.

SHAQUILLE O'NEAL

Album: *The Best of Shaquille O'Neal*

Details: Did you even know that O'Neal had a recording career? He did. In the early 1990s he released two rap albums, *Shaq Diesel* and *Shaq Fu: Da Return*. Highlights of both were compiled onto this 1996 album. It's rounded out with multiple remixes of O'Neal's "Biological Didn't Bother," a rap song he wrote in praise of his stepfather.

YOUNG MC

Album: *The Best of Young MC*

Details: The rapper has released six albums, but his only two hits ("Bust a Move" and "Principal's Office") came off of his first one, *Stone Cold Rhymin'*. Amazingly, *The Best of Young MC* is actually just *Stone Cold Rhymin'*, but with the order of the songs rearranged…and three songs removed entirely.

MILLI VANILLI

Album: *Best of the Best*

Details: Milli Vanilli—two singers from Munich named Fab Morvan and Rob Pilatus—was off to a great start in 1988 when three of their first five singles went to #1. Then, in 1990, it was revealed that they didn't actually sing on their recordings and were lip-syncing in performances. The band's albums were quickly pulled from stores and remained commercially unavailable until 2006 when this greatest hits album was released.

L.A. GUNS

Album: *Ultimate L.A. Guns*

Details: This 1980s hair metal band is best known as the band that guitarist Tracii Guns formed after he left Guns N' Roses. While Guns N' Roses racked up a ton of hits and was later inducted into the Rock and Roll Hall of Fame, L.A. Guns had one hit: "The Ballad of Jayne" in 1989. Nowadays, two separate versions of L.A. Guns tour, one featuring founding guitarist Tracii Guns and another featuring other, latter members of the band. Due to legal disputes, *Ultimate L.A. Guns* does not contain the original versions of the songs, but re-recorded ones (by Tracii Guns's band) made to sound as much like the originals as possible.

In 2015, a Texas man shot an armadillo. The bullet ricocheted and struck the man in the face.

Not a Mile-High Club You'd Want to Join

There are mile-high clubs, and there are mile-high clubs. This one has nothing to do with romance: Its members have fallen from great heights without a parachute and lived to tell the tale. (If you're reading this on a plane, you might want to wait until you're safely back on the ground.)

AL WILSON

Wilson was a barnstormer, a wing-walker, a "plane changer" (someone who climbs from one airplane to another in midair), and a Hollywood stunt pilot in the 1920s and early 1930s. During one flight, he was hanging by his knees from the wing of a biplane when he slipped and began tumbling toward the ground. He wasn't wearing a parachute—those were for "sissies," he liked to say—and he was falling to what should have been certain death.

Luckily for Wilson, a pilot named Frank Clarke was following close behind in another biplane, filming the stunt. As soon as Clarke saw Wilson fall, he put his plane in a steep dive and managed to get beneath Wilson, who slammed headfirst into the top wing of Clarke's biplane. Wings were made of wood and canvas in those days, not metal, so rather than bounce off the wing, Wilson smashed through it and got wedged upside down in the canvas with his feet sticking out of the top of the wing. Clarke landed safely and Wilson walked away from the accident, but neither man seemed to have learned much from the experience. In 1932, Wilson was killed in a plane crash while performing aerial stunts at the Cleveland Air Races in Ohio. Clarke followed in 1948, when he crashed his plane trying to dive-bomb a friend's cabin with a bag of manure.

ALAN MAGEE

On January 3, 1943, Magee, 23, was a ball turret gunner on an American B-17 Flying Fortress making a bombing run over Nazi-occupied France. While flying over the port of Saint Nazaire, the bomber was hit by antiaircraft fire and burst into flames. Magee managed to climb out of the cramped ball turret and get to his parachute, only to discover that it had been destroyed by enemy fire. Before he could do anything else, the plane was hit by more gunfire and went into a tailspin. Magee passed out and at some point must have been tossed from the plane through a hole in the fuselage. He fell some

Highest possible IQ: 161 for adults and 162 for kids under 18. (Einstein and Hawking scored 160.)

22,000 feet—more than four miles—before crashing through a skylight of the Saint Nazaire train station and getting hung up in steel girders supporting the roof. He suffered shrapnel wounds (from the antiaircraft fire), a broken leg, a broken ankle, a deep gash on his right arm, and other injuries, but lived. He spent two months recovering in a German hospital, then sat out the rest of the war in a POW camp.

EDMUND SHIBBLE

Like Alan Magee, Shibble, 19, was a ball turret gunner on a B-17 during World War II. In March 1945, he was on a bombing raid over Nazi Germany when another bomber was hit by enemy fire. As it fell, it crashed into Shibble's bomber, breaking it in half. Trapped inside the ball turret and unable to get to his parachute, Shibble rode the wreckage all the way to the ground, a drop of 23,000 feet. Though he was badly injured in the crash, he survived. One other crew member parachuted safely to the ground; everyone else was killed. "I took the whole thing with a grain of salt," he told the *Pittsburgh Post-Gazette* in 1994. "I figured God wanted me to stick around for a while. That's the only thing I could think of."

LARISA SAVITSKAYA

In August 1981, Savitskaya and her husband, both 20, were returning from their honeymoon in Siberia aboard an Aeroflot passenger flight when it collided with a Soviet air force bomber. The collision sheared the wings off the passenger plane and caused both planes to break apart in midair at 17,000 feet, more than three miles up. Savitskya was tossed out of her seat by the force of the collision and fell unconscious as the plane disintegrated around her. She awoke to find herself plummeting to earth in a piece of the airplane about 13 feet by 10 feet across. Remembering a scene in a movie where a woman survives a plane crash by remaining in her seat, Savitskaya pulled herself onto a seat that was attached to the wreckage, then braced for impact.

Luckily for her, the piece of wreckage glided to Earth instead of dropping like a stone, and splashed down in a swampy piece of ground that helped to cushion the impact. Savitskaya suffered a broken arm, a broken rib, spinal injuries, and a concussion in the crash; she was the only survivor among the 38 people aboard the two planes. It took rescuers three days to find her, still sitting in her seat…and more than a decade for the Russian government to acknowledge that the collision had even taken place. For many years, officials claimed that Savitskaya had wrecked her own homemade glider. "Officially, planes never crashed in the Soviet Union," she told the *Moscow Times* in 2002. After the accident, Aeroflot, the Soviet national airline, paid her 75 rubles—about $20—in compensation.

Two Coats of Vegan?

The names of paints used to be simple and direct, like "slate gray" or "fire engine red." Here are some of today's paint colors…but what color are they?

Magic Potion	Sweet Caroline	California Dreaming
Abracadabra	Hugs & Kisses	Hey There!
Minstrel Heart	Centaur	Cosmic Dust
Iced Vodka	Biloxi	5 O'Clock Shadow
Vegan	Fossil Butte	Seduction
Get Back Jack	Friendship	Mole's Breath
Snugglepuss	Song of Summer	Old Canal
Winter Mood	Hipsterfication	Weekend in the Country
File Cabinet	Maverick	Darling Clementine
Flamingo's Dream	Frozen in Time	Dead Salmon
Bromance	Synergy	Cheerful Whisper
Maltese Puppy	Under the Big Top	Quietude
Warm Cocoon	Grandma's Sweater	Turbulence
Game Over	Reboot	Mermaid Net
Café on the Riviera	Harajuku Girl	Butte Rock
Vibrant	Stagecoach	Dirty Socks
Social Butterfly	Emotional	Mo Money
Phantom Mist	Spirit Whisper	Wishing Troll
Fledgling	Canyon Echo	Fairy Godmother
Newborn's Eyes	Bath Salts	

From 1862 to 1869, the U.S. government issued paper banknotes with a face value of 5¢.

The Queen's Corgis

Next to her big hats and her crown, the things most associated with Queen Elizabeth II are probably her short-legged dogs. Her Majesty has been photographed hundreds of times over the past seven decades with at least one or two of the dogs bobbing along behind her. Here's a look at the long-running love story between a head of state and her tiny pets.

Full name of the breed: Pembroke Welsh Corgi. Despite their tiny legs, they were initially bred to be herding dogs, nipping at the feet of cattle and sheep across the fields of Wales.

• Elizabeth reportedly first fell for the dog as a young girl, when the visiting Marquess of Bath brought along his pet Corgi. In 1933, Elizabeth's father, King George VI, brought home two Corgi puppies for his family: a male named Dookie and a female named Jane. Princess Elizabeth and Princess Margaret enjoyed hand-feeding the dogs.

• Princess Elizabeth got her first Corgi of her own on her 18th birthday—a gift from her mother—in 1944, a few years before she became queen. The dog's registered name was Hickathrift Pippa; Elizabeth called her Susan.

• Since getting that first Corgi more than 70 years ago, Queen Elizabeth has looked after more than 30 different Corgis—all descended from Susan. For example, Susan's two pups were named Sugar and Honey. Sugar, the childhood pet of Prince Charles, spawned Whisky and Sherry, while Honey spawned Bee.

• Susan died in 1959. The Queen designed the dog's gravestone with the inscription:

SUSAN
BORN 20TH FEB. 1944
DIED 26TH JAN. 1959
FOR ALMOST 15 YEARS
THE FAITHFUL COMPANION
OF THE QUEEN

• Each of the dogs has its own individual, curated menu, prepared by the Buckingham Palace kitchen staff. They eat rabbit, filet, scones, and homemade gravy laced with homeopathic and herbal medicines. Each dog's meal is served by a butler in old silver and porcelain dishes.

"Lucy," a star made of carbon, is so dense, it's one big (10 billion trillion trillion carat) diamond.

But then the Queen feeds the dogs herself. They sit around her in a semicircle, and she presents their food bowls, one by one, in order of "seniority."

• Corgis have been part of Elizabeth's family longer than her husband, Prince Phillip (whom she married in 1947), and her son, Prince Charles (born in 1949). Both men tolerate the Corgis. Philip calls them his wife's "dog mechanism," and Charles caused a mini-scandal in 1969, when he told the press, "I prefer labradors."

• The Queen Mother gave Elizabeth her first Corgi, but she was a fan, too. When the Queen Mother died in 2002, Elizabeth inherited her mother's dog, Monty. That dog and two other Corgis—named Holly and Willow—appeared in a popular filmed segment shown at the opening ceremonies of the 2012 London Olympics. In it, Monty rolls around on his belly when James Bond (Daniel Craig) arrives at Buckingham Palace to escort the Queen to the Olympics. (They climb aboard a helicopter and parachute into the Olympic Stadium.) Monty died a few months after the scene was shot.

• The dogs do not sleep with the Queen. They have their own room in Buckingham Palace. It's called the Corgi Room.

• A bit of royal advice: Don't mess with the Queen's Corgis. In 1999, one of Queen Elizabeth's footmen secretly spiked the dogs' water bowls with alcohol and watched them stagger around. He thought it was funny, but Her Majesty was not amused. The man was demoted and received a $3,500 pay cut.

• While the Queen has had as many as seven dogs at one time, she's currently down to four: two Corgis and two Corgi-Dachshund mixes (called "Dorgies"). She quietly stopped having them bred for her in 2012. Reason: She's in her 80s, and she doesn't want to leave any dogs behind if she dies first. (The two Corgis, Holly and Willow, were both born in 2003.)

*   *   *

LIFE IMITATES ART

Art: In the 1979 Steve Martin movie *The Jerk*, Navin (Martin) and daredevil motorcycle rider Patty Bernstein (Caitlin Adams) eat "Pizza in a Cup" at a carnival. What's that? Something Martin made up for the movie—all the ingredients of pizza mixed together in a cup.

Life: New to the Lunchables line of prepared snack items in 2015: "Walking Pizza," all the ingredients of pizza—bites of crust, cheese, and sauce—mixed together in a bag.

Wine Lines

These full-bodied wine quotations have a hint of wit with notes of whimsy.

"Beer is made by men, wine by God."
—**Martin Luther**

"A glass of good wine is a gracious creature, and reconciles poor mortality to itself, and that is what few things can do."
—**Sir Walter Scott**

"If reassurances could dull pain, nobody would ever go to the trouble of pressing grapes."
—**Scott Lynch**

"A fruit is a vegetable with looks and money. Plus, if you let fruit rot, it turns into wine, something Brussels sprouts never do."
—**P. J. O'Rourke**

"Wine can of their wits the wise beguile, Make the sage frolic, and the serious smile."
—**Homer**

"What is better than to sit at the table at the end of the day and drink wine with friends, or substitutes for friends?"
—**James Joyce**

"We are all mortal until the first kiss and the second glass of wine."
—**Eduardo Galeano**

"When wine enters, out goes the truth."
—**Benjamin Franklin**

"I like best the wine drunk at the cost of others."
—**Diogenese of Sinope**

"I made wine out of raisins so I wouldn't have to wait for it to age."
—**Steven Wright**

"Wine is sunlight, held together by water."
—**Galileo**

"Wine can be a better teacher than ink, and banter is often better than books."
—**Stephen Fry**

"Wine maketh glad the heart of man."
—**The Book of Psalms, 104:15**

"Wine is the most healthful and most hygienic of beverages."
—**Louis Pasteur**

"Age is just a number. It's totally irrelevant unless, of course, you happen to be a bottle of wine."
—**Joan Collins**

Stuart Little and the Missing Masterpiece

It's a good bet that after you read this article, you'll start paying more attention to background props in movies.

A CHRISTMAS MIRACLE

It was Christmas Eve 2009. Gergely Barki, an art historian and researcher with the Hungarian National Gallery in Budapest, had settled in with his daughter Lola to watch the 1999 movie *Stuart Little*. As Barki's daughter snuggled on his lap to giggle at Stuart the mouse's onscreen antics, Barki couldn't believe his eyes. In a scene where Stuart and his human family have a conversation in front of a fireplace, Barki recognized the painting hanging on the wall in the background. It was no ordinary set dressing—it was a lost Hungarian masterpiece that hadn't been seen in public since 1928.

"I nearly dropped Lola from my lap," Barki said. "It was like a miracle of Christmas for me. It seems almost impossible to find a painting hidden in a Hollywood movie."

What Gergely Barki had recognized was artist Róbert Berény's *Sleeping Lady with Black Vase*. Berény was one of "the Eight"—a group of avant-garde artists who modernized Hungary's art movement starting in 1909. Not only was Berény an important Hungarian artist, he was also a colorful figure. In 1920, he fled Hungary after designing recruitment posters for a failed communist revolution. He was also rumored to have had affairs with actress Marlene Dietrich and Russian Grand Duchess Anastasia.

Sleeping Lady with Black Vase was an art deco portrait of Berény's second wife that he painted in 1926. But it had vanished. In fact, the only image of the painting that Barki had ever seen was a black-and-white photograph in a 1928 exhibition catalog. Yet he had no doubt he'd spotted the missing painting. "It was not just on screen for one second but in several scenes of the film, so I knew I was not dreaming," he said. Barki had to track it down.

A "LITTLE" PROBLEM

The art researcher emailed Sony and Columbia Pictures, the studios that produced *Stuart Little*. Production executives remembered the painting, but they had no idea where it had gone after filming ended.

Some redwood trees have white needles (and look frosted). Reason: they're albinos.

So Barki worked his way through the list of cast and crew and emailed everyone who'd touched the movie in any way. Nobody could help. Then, two years after Barki had first spotted *Sleeping Lady with Black Vase*, he received an email from an assistant set director.

She'd been in charge of finding props for the film and bought the painting for $500 in a Pasadena, California, antique shop. When the movie was over, she took it home. "It was hanging on her bedroom wall in Washington," Barki said. "Within a year, I had a chance to visit her and see the painting and tell her everything about the painter. She was very surprised." But how had a Hungarian masterpiece ended up in Pasadena?

FROM HUNGARY TO CALIFORNIA

The painting's previous owner, Michael Hempstead, recognized his *Sleeping Lady* when the story hit the news. He'd purchased it at a St. Vincent de Paul charity auction in San Diego in the mid-1990s. "I think I only paid $40," he said. "Somebody had just donated it, probably with a lot of other items." Hempstead knew it was Berény's work but had no idea it was considered lost. He resold it for around $400 to the Pasadena antique shop where the assistant set designer later found it.

Where had the painting been before Hempstead bought it? Nobody knows. Gergely Barki's guess is that a collector had first purchased it from the 1928 exhibition where it was displayed in the archived catalog he'd seen. "That was when it was last exhibited and, as most of the buyers were Jewish, it probably left the country as a result of the war," he theorized. "After the wars, revolutions, and tumult of the 20th century many Hungarian masterpieces are lost, scattered around the world." It may never be known exactly how the artwork landed in a Catholic charity auction.

BACK ON THE BLOCK

The assistant set designer (who asked to remain anonymous throughout) sold the painting to an art collector for an undisclosed sum. On December 13, 2014, the painting went to a Budapest gallery to be auctioned. *Sleeping Lady with Back Vase*, which had been bought for $40 in San Diego and $500 in Pasadena, sold for $285,700 to an unnamed Hungarian buyer.

Gergely Barki decided not to attend the auction. "It was an amazing once-in-a-lifetime experience to discover the painting. That was the exciting part," he said. Thanks to Barki's keen eye, *Sleeping Lady with Black Vase* was rescued from obscurity and returned to Hungary. As Barki noted, "A researcher can never take his eyes off the job, even when watching Christmas movies at home."

Liquor Laws
Around the World

*Alcohol works the same way in every country (it gets you drunk),
but it's sold a different way in almost every place on earth.*

S WEDEN. Beer is available at bars, grocery stores, and restaurants throughout Sweden, but the alcohol content is fairly low: 3.5 percent alcohol by volume or less. Grocery stores can't sell beer at all after 7:00 p.m. If Swedes want stronger beer, they have to go a Systembolaget, a chain of government-run liquor stores.

ENGLAND. There are thousands of pubs in England; millions of Brits casually drink in their local pubs every day. Nevertheless, to be caught drunk inside a pub is illegal in the UK.

NIGERIA. Nigeria has one of the biggest beer markets in the world, and consumes more beer than any African nation except South Africa. Guinness produces a third of its beer there. But because the country wants to protect its domestic beer industry, it's illegal to import beer into Nigeria or to brew your own at home.

BOLIVIA. What'll you have? If you're in Bolivia, and you're a woman, and you're married, you can order a single glass of wine at a bar or restaurant. That's it.

AUSTRALIA. In Sydney, the country's largest city, there are some very specific liquor laws on the books to curb late-night revelry in the streets. After midnight, bars may not serve shots of spirits, alcohol in glasses, or four or more drinks at one time. After 3:00 a.m., they're not permitted to serve more than two drinks to a single person. That means that if you're grabbing a round of drinks for your friends, they have to come to the bar with you for an official head count.

SWITZERLAND. Absinthe, which contains *thujone*, an ingredient that is said to cause hallucinations, is illegal in many countries. It became legal in Switzerland in 2005, but may not be artifically colored. (Absinthe can be legally sold in the United States if it contains no thujone and is made without its other main ingredient, wormwood.)

What do all members of Brazil's Bororo tribe share? Type O blood.

CANADA. The "mixology" fad, in which creative bartenders infuse spirits with inventive flavors and then use them in drinks, has not hit Canada. That's because Canadian bartenders in many provinces are not allowed to pre-flavor liquor with other ingredients. (Although they can do it on the spot if a customer specifically asks them to do it.)

THAILAND. Alcohol is legal in Thailand, except during certain parts of the day. Bars, restaurants, and liquor stores must stop selling booze from midnight until 11:00 a.m., and from 2:00 to 5:00 p.m.

INDIA. Each of the country's 29 individual states determine their own drinking laws. While four states have banned the consumption of alcohol entirely, the rest have set legal drinking ages that range from 18 to 25. In the state of Maharashtra, it's more complicated. There is no age restriction on wine, but you have to be 21 to drink beer, and 25 for hard alcohol. No matter what they're drinking, though, citizens of Maharashtra must have a license to drink. To get one, they must fill out an application at a local Government Civil Hospital.

SCOTLAND. It may not be enforced, but in Scotland "propelling a cow" while drunk is against the law.

FRANCE. Less than a decade ago, drunk driving was a public health epidemic in wine-loving France, with about 4,000 people a year dying after crashing their cars while drunk. In 2012, the French government passed a law requiring all drivers to carry a single-use portable Breathalyzer in their cars. Drivers don't have to use them, but the government figured that if people saw a Breathalyzer in their car while tipsy, they might think twice about driving.

EL SALVADOR. Drunk driving carries steep prison time and/or fines throughout the United States, but in El Salvador even a first DUI can put you in front of a firing squad. The laws are a little looser in Bulgaria—a *second* drunk driving offense carries the death penalty there.

GERMANY. Don't drink and ride? Yes—getting caught on a bike while intoxicated can lead to a loss of a driver's license, and to get it back, you have to be cleared by a government-sanctioned psychologist.

TURKEY. A lot of people around the world drink on Election Day—either to celebrate or lament. In Turkey, the sale of alcohol is banned on Election Day. Reasoning: sober people are more likely to vote, and to have clear heads when they do.

Having difficulty getting out of bed in the morning is called *dysania*. (It's also called "normal.")

College Roommates from Hell

On page 108 we told you stories of people who were unlucky in their choice of roommates. Some of the worst roommates, it turns out, were the ones we lived with in college.

ROOMMATE: Hayley King, 22, a student at the University of South Carolina, who lived off-campus with two roommates

STORY: King clashed repeatedly with her roommates in early 2015 (no word on who started the fights), and when they asked her to find someplace else to live, she refused. Then one day in February 2015, one of the roommates noticed that some of her food tasted funny. She and the second roommate set up a hidden camera in the kitchen to see if King was tampering with the food. Sure enough, a short time later the camera caught King spitting and pouring Windex window cleaner into several food containers in the fridge.

WHAT HAPPENED: The roommates turned the video footage over to police, who called King down to the station for questioning. She confessed and was charged with "unlawful, malicious tampering with [a] human drug product or food," a felony. At last report, she was out on bail on a $5,000 bond and awaiting trial. (If convicted, she could get up to 20 years in prison.)

ROOMMATE: Nicole Metzgar-Schall, an international business major at the University of Cincinnati

STORY: Why stop at window cleaner and spit? In 2011, Metzgar-Schall was rooming with another student named Rachel Filler. By March their relationship had become so contentious that Metzgar-Schall filled a water bottle with urine and water from a toilet bowl and left it out for Filler to drink. Filler somehow figured out that someone had tampered with her water bottle. (Let's hope she didn't drink it.) She reported the incident to the police, and Metzgar-Schall was charged with criminal mischief. Shortly before she was scheduled to appear in court, Metzgar-Schall ran into Filler in a dining hall and asked if she was going to go to the court appearance as well. When Filler said yes, Metzgar-Schall dumped a bowl of hot chili on her head and ran off.

WHAT HAPPENED: Metzgar-Schall was charged with assault and

A man from Jaipur, India, has the world's longest mustache—14 feet from tip to tip.

intimidating a crime victim, a felony. One month later, she pled guilty and got a six-month suspended sentence, $250 in fines, and 50 hours of community service. She was also ordered to pay $210 in restitution to Filler and have no further contact with her.

ROOMMATE: Sarah Zamora, 19, a Florida Atlantic University student.

STORY: In August 2014, Zamora rented a room in an apartment that a man named Bryan Thanos shared with one other roommate. She may have had her eye on Thanos when she rented the room, perhaps assuming that he was single. He wasn't. As soon as Zamora laid eyes on his girlfriend, 24-year-old Melissa Nunez, the couple says Zamora "seemed angry" to find out that Thanos was in a relationship. How angry? Ten days later someone stole Nunez's laptop and car keys from inside the locked apartment and drove off in her car. Nunez says Zamora had been acting suspiciously: earlier that day, she'd sent Thanos a text claiming that the apartment's front door had been left ajar overnight. No one else in the apartment had seen it ajar, so Nunez called the police, who tracked down Zamora. Incredibly, she told them that someone had broken into the apartment in the early morning hours and forced her at gunpoint into Nunez's car—with Nunez's laptop—then drove her around. Eventually, Zamora claimed, the man fled, leaving her alone in the car. What did she do next? She drove to campus and went to class. The car was later found where Zamora says she parked it. It had been vandalized, and the laptop was gone.

What kind of kidnap victim goes to class instead of going to the cops? Or texts her roommate to say that the front door was ajar, but makes no mention of the kidnapping? The cops didn't buy Zamora's story and arrested her.

WHAT HAPPENED: Zamora was charged with third-degree grand theft auto and providing false information to the police. The state attorney declined to prosecute the case, but Zamora was ordered to have no contact with Nunez. "I guess she wasn't aware when she toured the apartment that Bryan had a girlfriend. I could tell she didn't like me," Nunez told the Fort Lauderdale *Sun-Sentinel*.

ROOMMATE: James White, 21, a student at the University of York in England

STORY: One evening in February 2012, White was at home in his flat, drinking himself "to the point of madness," as he later admitted. At some point in his stupor, he fried his flatmate's pet hamster in a skillet. (Yes, you read that correctly.) White initially admitted the deed to police, but after he sobered up, he claimed he couldn't remember anything. He was nonetheless arrested and charged with "causing unnecessary suffering to an adult female Syrian hamster by subjecting her to hyperthermia."

WHAT HAPPENED: White pled guilty and was sentenced to 120 hours of community service, fined £1,000 (about $1,300), and banned from owning pets for eight years. The sentence would have been much harsher, but the medical examiner who autopsied the hamster was unable to determine whether it was alive when it was fried, or had died beforehand, perhaps killed unintentionally by "rough handling" by White. "Had that sadistic conduct been established, I would be dealing with you in a far more serious way than I am," Judge Roy Anderson told White during sentencing. (The case infuriated animal lovers…and at least one taxpayer: "How much money did they waste on the murder trial of a g$#%@*! hamster?" one reader complained to the University of York's student newspaper.)

ROOMMATE: Daniel H. Milzman, 20, a freshman physics and math student at Georgetown University in Washington D.C.

STORY: Milzman was a fan of *Breaking Bad*, a TV show about a terminally ill high school chemistry teacher named Walter White who begins manufacturing illegal drugs in order to make money that he can leave to his family when he dies. How big a fan was Milzman? When White made some deadly toxin called ricin to poison an enemy, Milzman decided he'd make some, too. He researched how to do it on his iPhone, then waited until his roommate was away on break and whipped up a batch right there in their dorm room. He made just 123 milligrams of the stuff (less than 0.01 ounce), but even that amount, if inhaled, is enough to kill a 220-pound adult.

When Milzman showed off the ricin to a residence assistant, the residence assistant called the police. The following morning Milzman was arrested; the floor he lived on was evacuated, and a hazmat team in full biohazard suits went and seized the ricin.

WHAT HAPPENED: Milzman faced up to ten years in federal prison, but in November 2014 he copped a plea and was sentenced to one year in prison, plus two years of probation and 400 hours of community service. He will work off his hours by tutoring underprivileged students in math and physics (but not chemistry). The authorities still aren't sure what Milzman planned to do with the ricin; his classmates say they were shocked to learn what he'd been up to. "He seemed like a quiet, odd kid, but we're physics majors so everyone's like that," one student told the school newspaper.

*   *   *

"Never miss a good chance to shut up." —**Will Rogers**

Good to the Last Dropping

*Lots of people drink coffee for extra energy when they're pooped. Did you
know that some people also drink coffee made from poop? Believe it
or not, it's some of the highest-priced java in the world.*

STRANGE BREW

In the mid-1800s, the Southeast Asian nation of Indonesia was
a colonial possession of the Netherlands called the Dutch East
Indies. The Dutch government required Indonesian farmers to devote
at least one fifth of their land to growing cash crops that the Dutch
could sell abroad, such as rubber, tobacco, and coffee. The coffee
crop was so valuable that the farmers and laborers who worked in the
fields were not allowed to keep any beans for their own use. Many
Indonesians had never tasted coffee, but they did see plenty of Dutch
people drinking it, and more than a few of them must have wondered
what it tasted like.

There was, however, one source of coffee beans that the Dutch
steered clear of: civet droppings. The animals, known in Indonesia
as "coffee rats," are cat-sized, rat-faced mammals that live in tropical
forests. At night they come out of the forest to raid coffee plantations
and feast on coffee berries, the fleshy fruit that contains the coffee
beans that are the seeds of the fruit. Civets can digest the berries, but
not the beans. So they poop them out, and at some point someone hit
on the idea of collecting the beans from civet droppings and using them
to make coffee.

AN ACQUIRED TASTE

As awful as *kopi luwak*, or "civet coffee," may sound to the uninitiated,
people who've tried it say it's not all that bad. The animal's digestive
juices soak into the beans and break down proteins that are the source
of much of the bitterness in coffee, creating a brew that is smoother
than ordinary coffee. Kopi luwak soon became a popular drink among
the farmers and laborers, and in time even many Dutch colonials came
to prefer it over ordinary coffee.

With a story as odd as this one, it's hard not to wonder whether the
beleaguered Indonesians were just trying to trick their colonial masters
into drinking animal poop. That theory might carry more weight were
it not for the fact that more than 150 years later, kopi luwak is still a

---

Before NYC's pooper-scooper law, about 125 tons of dog poop littered the streets every day.

delicacy, considered by devotees to be superior to ordinary coffee. Its popularity has spread far beyond Indonesia, thanks to a British coffee buyer named Tony Wild, who stumbled across a mention of the stuff in a 1981 *National Geographic* magazine article. Wild worked for a Yorkshire tea and coffee merchant called Taylors of Harrogate, and he had a reputation for sourcing obscure coffees from all over the world. When he came across some kopi luwak on a trip to Indonesia a decade later, he remembered the story and bought a bag of it to take back to England. But he wasn't planning to sell it: he wasn't sure that UK health authorities would allow animal excrement to be sold for human consumption. Wild just thought it was an "interesting coffee curiosity," as he put it. When he got home, he shared some of the coffee with local reporters.

RAT RACE

The story didn't stay local for long. It was picked up by the British Broadcasting Corporation (BBC), and from there it spread to media outlets all over the world. Demand for kopi luwak began to climb, and soon the rare beans were selling for as much as $600 a pound or $30 a cup, making it the world's most expensive coffee. A kopi luwak "industry" soon arose to meet the growing demand. Where once people had collected kopi luwak wherever wild civets happened to poop it out, now they began trapping the animals by the hundreds and keeping them in cages on civet farms.

In the wild, civets eat a varied diet that includes much more than coffee berries, but on many farms they were fed nothing but coffee berries. Conditions on some of the farms were appalling, and the beans produced by the caged, mistreated, and malnourished wild civets were inferior. Fraud was another problem: some producers passed off ordinary coffee beans as kopi luwak by smearing them with animal poop. Since there was no easy way for consumers to tell if their kopi luwak was real or fake, or whether it had been produced by caged, abused civets or their wild cousins, the drink began to lose its luster. Even Tony Wild, who had inadvertently launched the fad, turned against it. In 2013, he launched a "Cut the Crap" campaign to discourage coffee drinkers from ever buying kopi luwak again.

JUNK IN THE TRUNK

Another person who was turned off by kopi luwak's troubled reputation was a Canadian entrepreneur named Blake Dinkin. He backed out of plans to start his own kopi luwak operation and started looking for a humane way to make a similar product using a different animal. After ruling out lions and giraffes, he settled on elephants after learning that they have been known to eat coffee berries with no ill effect in times of drought, when their traditional sources of food have dried up.

Dinkin believed that coffee production could actually be used to help the animals by raising money for elephant conservation efforts. He forged a relationship with the Golden Triangle Asian Elephant Foundation (GTAEF), a charity in northern Thailand that operates a sanctuary for elephants and their keepers, who are called *mahouts*.

Many mahouts lost their livelihoods in the late 1980s when logging was banned in Thailand; they (and their elephants) ended up homeless and begging on the streets of Bangkok and other Thai cities. GTAEF provides assistance to destitute mahouts by paying them a "rent" to keep their elephants at the sanctuary, and by hiring them to care for the elephants there. GTAEF is also developing cottage industries, such as silk weaving, to provide additional opportunities for the mahouts and their families to earn extra money.

ONE LARGE COFFEE...TO GO

Now that Dinkin has gotten involved with GTAEF, producing "Black Ivory Coffee," as he's named it, has become one of the sanctuary's cottage industries. Mahouts and their families feed the elephants a mash containing rice, bananas, coffee berries, and other ingredients as part of the 330 pounds of food the elephants eat each day. Like the civets, the elephants digest the *fruit* of the coffee berries, but not the beans. When the elephants poop—15 to 30 hours later—the mahouts and their families pick the beans out of the manure and dry them in the sun. It's not glamorous work, but it pays well: each family member can earn in an hour what the mahouts used to make in a day.

PERKS

As with civet coffee, the digestive juices in the elephant's stomach soak into the coffee beans and break down proteins that give coffee its bitterness. But there's a bonus: because elephants are herbivores, fermentation plays a greater part in their digestive process than it does in the omnivorous civets. This fermentation infuses the beans with the flavors of other foods the elephant has eaten. The animal's body heat also "cooks" the beans as if they were in a slow cooker, giving them a complex flavor that Dinkin describes as "chocolate malt with a bit of cherry" and "kind of like a cross between coffee and tea."

Dinkin estimates that it takes 33 pounds of coffee beans to produce a pound of Black Ivory Coffee. That's because when the elephants chew their food, they crush many of the beans to bits. Only a fraction of the beans remain whole and can be recovered. And if an elephant poops while bathing in the nearby river, the waste usually disperses and floats away before the mahouts can wade out and recover the beans.

The word "coconut" is derived from *coco*, Portuguese for "grinning face."

BLACK GOLD

If you'd like to try the coffee, get ready to spend some money: Dinkin charges as much as $750 a pound for the beans, eclipsing kopi luwak to become—for a time—the world's most expensive coffee. (Eight percent of the proceeds are donated to the elephant sanctuary.) Dinkin produced just 350 pounds of the coffee in 2015, his third year in production, and he sold nearly all of it to five-star restaurants in Asia. He hopes to expand production in the future.

If you happen to live near Comfort, Texas, about 50 miles northwest of San Antonio, you can try Black Ivory Coffee at the Elephant Story, a store that raises money for elephant conservation. They are the only American seller of Black Ivory Coffee. Or you can buy sample packs directly from Dinkin on the Black Ivory website. A bag containing five espresso cups' worth of coffee beans will set you back $66 (plus shipping). If you do decide to buy some, be sure to follow the instructions carefully: Dinkin says it took him nine years to perfect a method of preparing elephant crap coffee that doesn't taste, well…crappy.

CONSUMER CHOICE

Blake Dinkin isn't the only person who looked at the thriving kopi luwak trade and hoped to repeat its success using a different animal. Here are some other animal poop coffees (and one tea) that are competing for your dollar:

• **Terra Nera Coffee.** Made from the droppings of the Uchunari, an animal in the Peruvian Andes that looks like a civet but with a longer nose. Sold exclusively through Harrods department store in London, Terra Nera is available in six different grades, including the top-of-the-line Grade 0. A small bag of the finest hand-selected Grade 0 beans will cost you more than $11,000, but oh, what a bag! It's actually a bag-shaped canister handmade out of sterling silver and 24-karat gold, with the purchaser's name engraved on the container. Bonus: If you buy more than 500 grams of the stuff (about 1.1 pounds), Harrods will throw in a coffee machine.

• **Jacu Bird Coffee.** Produced exclusively in Brazil at an organic farm called the Camocim Estate, Jacu coffee consists of coffee beans excreted by this bird, which was considered a pest until its poop started turning a profit. Price: about $45 for a quarter of a pound of the beans, quite a bargain by poop-coffee standards.

• **Panda Poop Tea.** If you prefer tea to coffee, fear not: a man in China named An Yanshi collects manure from panda breeding centers and uses it to fertilize his organic green tea plants. He charges $3,500 for 50 grams (about a tenth of a pound) of tea leaves, or about $200 a cup, making it the world's most expensive tea. Bonus: because pandas eat bamboo, not tea, your tea will never see the inside of a panda.

Rest in Peace...Not!

These dearly departed had one more adventure left.

BAG LADY

The Deceased: A woman from Euskirchen, Germany

The Last Gasp: In 2014, the woman (not identified in press reports) died during an operation. She was placed in a body bag and then put into a car for a trip across town to a funeral home. Along the way, the undertaker parked in front of an office building to pick up the woman's death certificate. When he returned, he discovered several police officers surrounding his vehicle. Apparently, the undertaker had failed to zip up the body bag all the way, and after he parked the car, blood started leaking onto the street. Bystanders called police, who arrived quickly and saw the body bag in the backseat. The homicide unit, in particular, was very eager to speak to the undertaker.

The Aftermath: After a brief investigation, a police spokesperson reported that no crime had been committed, adding that, "It is a very painful and unpleasant thing to happen to the undertaker." (Apparently they forgot about the person who'd had a worse day than the undertaker—the woman in the body bag.)

GRANDFATHERED OUT

The Deceased: Mario Mark Marcaletti, 91, of Indianapolis, Indiana

The Last Gasp: After Marcaletti died in 2002, his cremains were kept by his brother in Florida. Ten years later, Marcaletti's grandson, John Gross, was going to take a jar of the ashes home to Indiana. Everything was going fine until Gross arrived at the TSA checkpoint station at Orlando International Airport. A female agent (name not released) inspected the tightly sealed urn, which was clearly marked "Human Remains." Gross asked her to be careful: "That's my grandpa." Then, wearing a pair of latex gloves, the agent unscrewed the lid (which is against TSA policy; remains should be X-rayed, not opened) and, according to Gross, "she used her finger to sift through it. And then she accidentally spilled it." It gets worse: "She started laughing. I was on my hands and knees picking up bone fragments. I couldn't pick up all of it. There was a long line behind me." Gross scooped up as many pieces of Grandpa as he could and continued through the checkpoint, leaving most of the ashes behind on the floor.

The Aftermath: Gross went public with his story, saying that all he wanted was an apology from the TSA and from the agent. "She thought

---

Renaissance man: Ohio's George Sperti invented sun lamps, powdered OJ, and Preparation H.

it was funny," he said. "I wanted to smack her." Instead, the agency released a statement claiming, "Our initial review concluded that the circumstances as described in some reports are inconsistent with what we believe transpired." In other words, they accused Gross of lying. And they said there was no CCTV footage of the incident, which is also against their policy. After Gross told his story to CNN, a TSA representative finally called him with a "heartfelt apology," but the agency never admitted publicly that they did anything wrong.

PARTY'S OVER

The Deceased: A 23-year-old man from Juárez, Chihuahua, Mexico

The Last Gasp: After several days of consuming drugs and alcohol with three friends in March 2014, the unidentified man suddenly died. But his friends—Elián Hernández Palacios, Roberto Israel Muñiz Padroz, and José Ángel Hernández Poblano—weren't ready for the party to end. So they put their buddy in the backseat of their car and started blasting through the city streets with him. A police officer pulled over the speeding car at 3:45 a.m. When he discovered the body in the back, he told the three men that they were under arrest. Two of them offered the officer 800 pesos (about $60) to let them go.

The Aftermath: The three men were arrested on numerous charges, including failure to report a death...and attempted bribery.

*　　　*　　　*

REAL NAMES OF COMIC BOOK VILLAINS

- Magneto (*X-Men*): Magnus Eisenhardt
- Mystique (*X-Men*): Raven Darkhorse
- The Joker (*Batman*): Jack Napier
- Harley Quinn (*Batman*): Harleen Quiznel
- Scarecrow (*Batman*): Jonathan Crane
- Riddler (*Batman*): Edward Nygma (E. Nygma. Get it?)
- Poison Ivy (*Batman*): Pamela Isley
- Mr. Freeze (*Batman*): Victor Fries
- Doctor Doom: Victor Von Doom
- Kingpin (*Daredevil*): Wilson Fisk
- Catwoman: Selina Kyle
- Green Goblin (*Spider-Man*): Philip Ulrich
- Doctor Octopus (*Spider-Man*): Otto Octavius
- Brainiac (*Superman*): Vril Dox
- Mr. Mzyptlk (*Superman*): Ben DeRoy
- General Zod (*Superman*): Dru-Zod

In 17th-century England, women could be sold by weight.

It's Special!

The article that was scheduled to appear in this spot won't be seen tonight. Instead, here's this very special presentation about some very weird holiday TV specials.

THE HALLOWEEN TREE (1993)

In this animated special based on an obscure Ray Bradbury novel, some kids travel through time to save a friend's life. They also learn about the history of Halloween from narrator Ray Bradbury.

A FAMILY CIRCUS EASTER (1982)

The comic strip family comes to TV. Oldest child Billy tries to catch the Easter Bunny, and meets him in a dream sequence. The Bunny is voiced by jazz legend Dizzy Gillespie.

HALLOWEEN IS GRINCH NIGHT (1977)

The powerful Sweet-Sour Wind whisks away a young Who named Euchariah while he's walking to the outhouse. He lands on a mountain where the Grinch is working on a contraption called the "Paraphernalia Wagon." The Grinch tosses Euchariah into it. Faced with a menagerie of surreal monsters that the Grinch is planning to unleash on Whoville, Euchariah stays strong until the Sweet-Sour Wind dies down and the Grinch must retreat to his cave.

RICH LITTLE'S CHRISTMAS CAROL (1978)

An adaptation of Charles Dickens's *A Christmas Carol*, in which all of the characters are portrayed by impressionist Rich Little. Little also squeezes in bits of his most famous impressions, including Richard Nixon, Truman Capote, and Johnny Carson.

THANKSGIVING FOR THE MEMORIES (1983)

The early 1980s video game character Q*bert (an orange puffball with bug eyes) and his classmates learn about the first Thanksgiving. Pilgrims sailed "the Q*flower" to "Q*berg," meet Native Q*bergers, and challenge them to a contest to see who wins a horse and buggy.

THE FAT ALBERT EASTER SPECIAL (1982)

Fat Albert and the Cosby Kids help Mudfoot, a down-on-his-luck guy who lives in their neighborhood, by cleaning up his shack. Then they play a prank on Mudfoot, who winds up in the hospital, and everybody learns a valuable lesson about the dangers of pranks.

Canary, black turtle, rattlesnake, and appaloosa are all different varieties of beans.

Toilet Tech

Better living through bathroom technology.

ASSUME THE POSITION

Product: Squatty Potty Toilet Stools

What It Does: Make it easier for people to "do their business" the old-fashioned way—by allowing them to simulate a squatting position while seated on the pot

How It Works: For most of human history, people squatted to go. It's only in recent centuries that Western civilization has brought us toilet or outhouse seats to relieve ourselves. In the seated position, a muscle called the *puborectalis* muscle may not relax completely, making bowel movements difficult to complete. That's what the Squatty Potty addresses: You set the stool down in front of the toilet, and put your feet up on the stool. This raises your knees several inches above the level of your hips, relaxing the puborectalis muscle and putting you in the optimum position for a complete emptying of your colon.

Bonus: In this position, gravity does most of the work, reducing the amount of straining required. If the Squatty Potty sounds familiar, you may have seen it on the TV show *Shark Tank* or heard "regular" user Howard Stern sing its praises on his radio show: "I put my feet up and each time I go, 'Oh Squatty, you saved me again.'"

A FRESH START

Product: Poo~Pourri Toilet Spray

What It Does: It's a bathroom deodorizing spray that you use *before* you go, instead of afterward.

How It Works: It creates a scented, odor-trapping oil slick in your toilet bowl. "Spritz 3–5 sprays into the toilet bowl on the water's surface," instructs the manufacturer, "then proceed to use the throne as usual. The natural essential oils create a barrier, trapping odor *under* the surface, *before* it begins. All you'll smell is a refreshing bouquet of natural essential oils. *Flush yeah!*"

Poo-Pourri is advertised using commercials that feature British actress Bethany Woodruff, aka "Poo Girl," as a spokesperson. "You wouldn't believe the mother lode I just dropped!" Poo Girl says over the sound of a flushing toilet in one ad. *USA Today* called it one of the worst advertising campaigns of 2013, adding that "nowhere, in a civilized society, is there room for this ad." But it got the job done: by late 2015, Poo-Pourri was the best-selling bath product on Amazon.com.

THE BRUSH-OFF

Product: The LooBlade

What It Does: Improves on the toilet brush by making it less brushlike.

How It Works: Scottish inventor Garry Stewart got the idea after his toddler tried to use a toilet brush—eeew!—as a *hairbrush*. That got him thinking about just how unsanitary and disgusting the bristles of a toilet brush are, not to mention ineffective. "The traditional toilet brush is a flawed design,": he says. "They don't clean efficiently, they clog up, they drip everywhere, they result in excessive use of chemicals and water, and people hate the sight of them."

Stewart came up with the LooBlade, which replaces the bristles of a traditional toilet brush with nine sturdy silicone blades that swirl around the cleaning head. The blades make better contact with the toilet bowl, reducing the amount of scrubbing needed to clean it. The blades are treated with an antimicrobial agent and a water-repellent coating that keeps the brush clean, dry, and germ-free. If the LooBlade isn't already available at a store near you, it probably will be soon. When Stewart launched a fund-raising appeal on the Kickstarter website in 2015, he reached his £20,000 (about $30,000) goal in just ten days. "I was blown away by the speed of the response," he says.

COLD CREAM

Product: Perlick Refrigerated Beauty Drawers

What It Does: Keeps beauty products fresh

How It Works: Americans buy nearly $7 billion worth of organic, preservative-free cosmetics and other beauty products each year. Going *au naturel* may be better for your skin (or at least make you *feel* better about your skin), but taking the preservatives out means the products don't have much of a shelf life, especially at room temperature. That's why Perlick, a manufacturer of commercial refrigerators, introduced this line of refrigerated bathroom drawers for the home. The units are made of stainless steel inside and out, which inhibits bacteria growth, and they can be customized to match existing bathroom cabinets. But keeping the rot out of your pomegranate regenerating hand cream, blueberry oxygen facial scrub, and kombucha enzyme exfoliating peel is going to cost you: the smallest drawer unit sells for $3,000…and the prices only go up from there.

WIPEOUT

Product: Cottonelle "CleanRipple Texture" Toilet Paper

What It Does: Cleans while it wipes

How It Works: Speaking of going *au naturel*, in 2015, Kimberly-Clark, the perennial third-place finisher in America's $9.7 billion toilet paper market, reformulated its Cottonelle brand toilet paper with the goal of increasing sales. They incorporated special "peaks and valleys" into the paper's texture. The company claims the ripples leave the end user (so to speak) so spotlessly cleaned that they can "go commando" (not wear underwear) without fear of staining the insides of their pants.

Kimberly-Clark promoted the idea with a publicity stunt on the beach in Santa Monica, California: a spokesperson offered free samples of Cottonelle to any restroom-goer willing to slip into a changing tent and remove their underwear. The company filmed the interactions and used the footage in TV commercials. No word on whether the ripples have increased sales, but the "Go Commando" ad campaign has certainly generated attention: "This is one of the most ridiculous and disgusting ad campaigns I've ever seen," one reader commented online. "Cottonelle, are you nuts?"

RIGHT BACK AT YOU

Product: Ultra-Ever Dry Urine Repelling Paint

What It Does: Punishes people who pee in public

How It Works: The paint, which is made by a Florida company called UltraTek International, is *super-hydrophobic*, which means it contains materials that are extremely effective at repelling water. As the paint dries, its unusual molecular structure forms a surface of microscopic peaks, or "high points." When urine (which is mostly water) strikes the painted surface, the water molecules touch only the high points, which make up "a very small percentage of the coating," the company says. The urine is repelled from the surface as if it had never touched it at all.

Bonus: When someone pees on a wall coated with the paint, their stream of urine splashes back at them at about the same angle that it struck the wall, soaking their pants and shoes instead of running down the wall. The German city of Hamburg painted some walls of its lively St. Pauli quarter in March 2015, along with signs that warned, "these walls pee back." When that experiment proved a success, the city of San Francisco, California, began painting trouble spots in the Tenderloin, the Mission, and South of Market neighborhoods in July 2015. "So far so good...It seems to be 95% effective. There's only one alley in the Mission that we have had trouble with," the city's public works director, Mohammed Nuru, told the *San Francisco Chronicle* a few months after the paint was applied.

*   *   *

"To kill an error is as good a service as, and sometimes even better than, the establishing of a new truth or fact."

—**Charles Darwin**

Exiled!

In the early 1970s, Uncle John was exiled from Yankee Stadium for…well, that's another story. Here are the famous stories of some groups and individuals who, for one reason or another, were forced to leave their countries.

THE ISRAELITES

In the eighth century BC, the kingdom of Israel (in the northern part of modern-day Israel) was conquered by the Assyrian Empire. In the decades following the conquest, thousands of Israelites were enslaved and forcibly relocated to Assyria (in modern-day Iraq). This exile, the earliest documented expulsion of ancient Jews from their homeland, was followed by several more expulsions over the following centuries, and resulted in the establishment of Jewish communities around the world, many of which still exist today. Most of the details of these forced exiles—known collectively as the Jewish Diaspora, from a Greek word meaning "dispersion"—are lost to history, but they play a huge role in Jewish history and religion, and are the source of many stories in both the Hebrew and Christian Bibles. (The biblical depiction of Moses, for example, is the story of a Jewish prince who leads a community of Jews out of exile in Egypt, and who prophesied the return of the Jewish people to Israel.)

OVID

One of the most popular poets of the ancient Roman Empire, Ovid was banished from Rome on the orders of Emperor Augustus in 8 AD, when he was 51 years old. He was sent to live in the Black Sea coast town of Tomis (in what is now Romania), a town Ovid described as a "cultural wasteland on the remotest margins of the empire." No public explanation was given for the exile—although Ovid did later write that the reason was "a poem and a mistake," leading historians to believe it could have been the result of his sexually explicit poetry, which may have offended Augustus's austere sense of morality. But there are other theories: Augustus's granddaughter, Julia the Younger, was banished around the same time as Ovid (to a different location), ostensibly for adultery, but possibly for being involved in a plot to overthrow Augustus. This has led some historians to believe Ovid's banishment had something to do with Julia the Younger. Did Julia's adultery involve Ovid? If so, he may also have been involved in the purported overthrow attempt. Whatever the reason, Ovid's pleas to be allowed to return to Rome were ignored. He died in exile in Tomis eight years later.

The Derbyshire Whiskers Club has taken out fire and theft insurance for its members' beards.

DANTE

The Italian poet Dante Alighieri was born in the city of Florence around 1265. And while he is best known as the author of the *Divine Comedy* and one of the most important literary figures in history, Dante was also a politician and a soldier, and it was through this lesser-known aspect of his life that he ran into trouble. In the late 1200s, he became involved in battles over control of Florence, and in 1300, he became one of the city's leaders. Opposition forces retook control of the city in 1302, and Dante was charged with trumped-up fraud charges related to his political work. When he refused to pay the heavy fine imposed by his enemies, he was banished from the city forever—with the promise that he would be burned at the stake if he ever returned. He never did. Dante spent the rest of his life living in different cities around Italy, and never saw Florence—or his wife, Gemma, the mother of his seven children—again. He died in Ravenna, 90 miles northeast of Florence, in 1321. (The city of Florence eventually revoked Dante's sentence of exile and cleared his name…in 2008, nearly 700 years after his death.)

CHARLES EDWARD STUART

The House of Stuart, which had ruled Scotland since the 14th century, and had ruled the combined kingdoms of England, Scotland, and Ireland since the early 17th century, came to an end in 1714, when the British crown passed to the House of Hanover. In 1745, 25-year-old Charles Edward Stuart, known as "Bonnie Prince Charlie," decided the Stuarts should be back in power, so he raised an army in Scotland, where the Stuarts were still very popular, and tried to take back the British throne. After some initial successes, Charles's army was defeated in April 1746 at the Battle of Culloden, near the Scottish town of Inverness, and a price was put on his head. After months on the run in the Scottish Highlands, Charles finally escaped to France. He spent the rest of his life in exile, and died in Rome in 1788, at the age of 67. (Bonus fact: The Scottish folk song "My Bonnie Lies Over the Ocean" is believed to have been written as an ode to the exiled Stuart.)

NAPOLEON

Napoleon Bonaparte led a coup and took control of France in 1799, and declared himself emperor in 1804. By 1812, he had conquered most of mainland Europe, but that same year, he made a huge mistake: he invaded Russia.

Exile #1: Russia got the upper hand in the war in 1813, and every other major European power—most of whom Napoleon had earlier conquered—jumped into the fight on Russia's side. Result: by 1814, the French army had been routed. Napoleon abdicated his throne (King

Louis XVIII became the new leader of France), France was restored to its pre-Napoleon borders, and Napoleon was exiled to the island of Elba, six miles off the coast of northwestern Italy. What many people don't know is that in exile, Napoleon retained the title of "Emperor" and became the leader of the 12,000 people on Elba. He was even put in charge of the island's small military force. And while the island was under the guard of the British navy, apparently they weren't very good at their jobs.

Exile #2: Nine months into his exile, in February 1815, Napoleon escaped the island with his 700-man Elban army, sailed to southern France, made his way to Paris, and took control of the country. Europe's response: WAR! Just a few months later, in July 1815, Napoleon was defeated for a second time. This time, he was exiled to St. Helena, a British-controlled island in the middle of the Atlantic Ocean, 1,200 miles off the coast of Africa. Napoleon never returned to France. He died on St. Helena in 1821, at the age of 51.

VICTOR HUGO

Hugo, like Dante, is best known for his written works, such as *The Hunchback of Notre-Dame* (1831). But like Dante, he was also a politician. He was elected to the French parliament in 1848 and became well known for his support of progressive causes, such as freedom of the press, free education, universal suffrage, and for his staunch opposition to the autocratic French president Louis Napoleon Bonaparte, the nephew of Napoleon. In 1851, when Louis-Napoleon abolished parliament and seized total power in a coup, Hugo joined an insurrection to stop him. The uprising failed. Hundreds of people were killed, and more than 20,000 were arrested. Louis-Napoleon declared himself Emperor Napoleon III, and Hugo fled the country. He spent the next 18 years in exile, most of it on the British island of Guernsey, in the English Channel. He remained a force in French politics during this period, though. His political writings, which were banned in France, were regularly smuggled into the country, and it was during this period that he wrote his most famous work, *Les Misérables* (1862), an epic of the French Revolution. And Hugo is one of the lucky ones in history's exile club: he eventually got to go home. On September 5, 1870, Napoleon III was captured by Prussian forces, effectively bringing the Franco-Prussian War to an end. Hugo returned to Paris the next day. He received a hero's welcome, and was soon elected to the French parliament. When he died in 1885, more than two million people joined his funeral procession along Paris's Champs-Élysées. (Final Irony: Napoleon III died in 1873—in England, where he had lived in exile after being released by the Prussians in 1871.)

Tourons

Real questions asked by people on vacation.

"Where are the rides?"
—**Everglades National Park**

"Is the mule train air-conditioned?"
—**Grand Canyon**

"How long does the forty-minute cruise last?"
—**Windermere Lake, England**

"Where are the tracks the wagon trains ran on?"
—**Sutter's Fort, California**

"Who dumped all those lava rocks up on the mountain?"
—**Bryce Canyon, Utah**

"Why did they build the ruins so close to the road?"
—**Mesa Verde, Colorado**

"What time do they turn on the northern lights?"
—**Anchorage, Alaska**

"Which beach is closest to the ocean?"
—**Miami, Florida**

"Is this the Eiffel Tower?"
—**CN Tower, Toronto**

"How much for a moose?"
—**Banff National Park, Canada**

"What time do they turn off the falls?"
—**Niagara Falls, New York**

"Does the Canada flag come in any other colors?"
—**Vancouver, Canada**

"Are the Amish in season?"
—**Pennsylvania**

"Is there anyone here who speaks Australian?"
—**Scotland**

"Does the water go all the way around the island?"
—**Hawaii**

"Which parks have swings for six-year-old babies?"
—**Auckland, New Zealand**

"Is that the same moon we get in Texas?"
—**Australia**

"What state governs the Florida Keys?"
—**Florida Keys**

"Why did the queen build Windsor Castle so close to Heathrow Airport?"
—**England**

"So where are the faces of the presidents?"
—**Grand Canyon**

In World War I, dogs, horses, and pigeons were all issued gas masks.

Letters from Leia

Born into Hollywood royalty (her parents were Eddie Fisher and Debbie Reynolds), Carrie Fisher found fame in 1977 as Princess Leia in the original Star Wars. *Since then, she's battled mental illness and drug addiction, and became a best-selling author* (Postcards from the Edge). *Here are some of her thoughts on her life and what's it like to be a part of the world's most popular movie franchise.*

"I was street smart, but unfortunately the street was Rodeo Drive."

"My extroversion is a way of managing my introversion."

"You can't find true affection in Hollywood because everyone does the fake affection so well."

"I have been in *Star Wars* since I was 20. It follows me around like a vague, exotic smell."

"My idea was pain reduction and mind expansion, but I ended up with mind reduction and pain expansion."
—on her drug use

"Resentment is like drinking poison and waiting for the other person to die."

"I feel I'm very sane on how crazy I am."

"Instant gratification takes too long."

"As you get older, the pickings get slimmer, but the people don't."

"It's hard to date once you're a big *Star Wars* star because you don't want to give men the ability to say, 'I had sex with Princess Leia.'"

"I signed my likeness away. Every time I look in the mirror, I have to send George Lucas a couple of bucks."
—on Leia action figures

"Maturity: A stoic response to endless reality."

"Actors may know how to act, but a lot of them don't know how to behave."

"I'm now a Disney Princess!"
—on Disney buying Lucasfilm

"I get lots of awards for being mentally ill. Apparently, I am better at being mentally ill than almost anything else I've ever done."

"Acting engenders and harbors qualities that are best left way behind in adolescence."

"Sometimes you can only find Heaven by slowly backing away from Hell."

London has chewing gum receptacles. The gum is collected and recycled into plastics.

After the Presidency

*Some U.S. presidents are immortalized in stone for their achievements
as commander in chief; others didn't achieve true success until
after they left the most prominent office in the world.*

JIMMY CARTER

As a result of rampant inflation, a stagnant economy, the 1979 energy crisis, and the Iran hostage crisis, President Carter's nomination by his party for reelection was contested—in fact, he almost lost the Democratic nomination to Senator Ted Kennedy. California governor Ronald Reagan, the Republican candidate, ultimately defeated Carter in a landslide in 1980. After leaving office with his reputation in tatters, Carter rebuilt it by becoming one of the world's most prominent humanitarians. A year after leaving office, Carter and his wife, Rosalyn, founded the Carter Center, a nonprofit organization devoted to promoting human rights. Carter is also well known for his association with Habitat for Humanity, a charity that builds affordable housing for the poor. For his postpresidential work in advancing democracy and human rights, Carter was awarded the Nobel Peace Prize in 2002. He's the only U.S. president to receive it after leaving office.

WILLIAM HOWARD TAFT

From his early days as an assistant prosecutor in Ohio, Taft's dream was to serve as chief justice of the Supreme Court. But a career in politics got in the way. President William McKinley appointed Taft to the post of civilian governor-general of the Philippines in 1901, and President Theodore Roosevelt appointed him Secretary of War in 1904. When Roosevelt tapped him to be the Republican Party's presidential nominee in the 1908 election, Taft was less than excited, but felt it was his duty. He won the election, but after serving an unremarkable four years as president, Taft lost his reelection bid to Woodrow Wilson. Voted out of the job he never wanted, Taft dove right back into law. He later was appointed the president of Yale Law School, and then elected president of the American Bar Association. Finally, in 1921, Taft got his dream job when Edward D. White, the chief justice of the Supreme Court, died and President Warren G. Harding nominated Taft to replace him.

ANDREW JOHNSON

Johnson, Abraham Lincoln's vice president, assumed the presidency when Lincoln was assassinated, and filled out the rest of Lincoln's term.

But in 1868 Johnson failed to receive the presidential nomination from his own party (he was a Democrat), and that ended his service. Johnson returned to his home in Tennessee and plotted a political comeback. He ran for the U.S. Senate in 1869, but lost by three votes (in those days state legislatures, not voters, selected senators). Trying again three years later, he ran for a spot in the House of Representatives as an independent and lost again. He finally made it back to Washington in 1875, being elected senator by a margin of one vote. Four months after he took office, Johnson died of a stroke.

HARRY TRUMAN

These days, outgoing presidents are almost guaranteed a lucrative publishing deal to write their memoirs. When Harry Truman left office in 1953, he was offered several commercial endorsements and corporate positions, but turned them all down, believing them to be inappropriate for a former president. Instead, Truman retired on his U.S. Army pension of $112.56 a month. It wasn't enough, though. There was no retirement package for ex-presidents, so Truman had to take out a bank loan to get by. By the mid-1950s, faced with financial ruin, Truman changed his mind and signed a deal to write his memoirs, which included an account of his White House years, something only a few previous U.S. presidents had ever done. (In 1958 Congress passed the Former Presidents Act, which gave a lifetime pension to former presidents.)

*   *   *

WEIRD CANADA

If you're ever in Quebec and want a soft drink, it's best to just order "le cola." Over the past 40 years, "pepsi" has become a derogatory term for French Canadians. Since the 1970s, Pepsi has aggressively marketed its products in Quebec, where most French-speaking Canadians live, and where most people speak French. When Michael Jackson's Pepsi commercials aired in the U.S. and Canada in the '80s, for example, ads starring French Canadian comedian Claude Meunier aired in Quebec instead. A commercial from 2009 includes an English-speaking Canadian who mistakenly orders a Coke in a Montreal restaurant and attracts the sneers of not just his fellow patrons but the entire city as well. He quickly acknowledges his faux pas and requests, in French, a Pepsi instead. Quebecers' love of the beverage has become such a cliché that Canadians from other parts of the country now use it to insult them.

Now That's a Grimm Tale

When you think of Grimms' Fairy Tales, *written in the mid-1800s by German brothers Jacob and Wilhelm Grimm, you probably think of stories like* Snow White *and* Cinderella. *Here's one from the collection that's less well known:* The Dog and the Sparrow. *(From a 1900 translation.)*

THERE WAS ONCE UPON A TIME a sheep-dog whose master was so unkind that he starved the poor beast and treated him in the cruelest manner. At last the dog determined to stand this ill-usage no longer, and, one day, he ran away from home. As he was trotting along the road he met a sparrow, who stopped him and said: "Brother, why do you look so sad?"

The dog answered, "I am sad because I am hungry, and have nothing to eat."

"If that's all, dear brother," said the sparrow, "come to the town with me and I'll soon get food for you."

So they went together to the town, and when they came to a butcher's shop, the sparrow said to the dog: "You stand still and I'll peck down a piece of meat for you."

She looked all around to be sure that no one was watching her and then she pecked at a piece of meat that lay on the edge of a shelf until at last it fell down. The dog seized it ravenously, and ran with it to a dark corner where he gobbled it up in no time. When he had finished it, the sparrow said, "Now come with me to another shop, and I will get you a second piece, so that your hunger may be satisfied." When the dog had finished the second piece of meat, the sparrow asked him, "Brother, have you had enough now?"

"Yes," replied the dog, "I've had quite enough meat, but I haven't had any bread yet."

THE SPARROW SAID: "You shall have as much bread as you like. Come with me." Then she led him to a baker's shop, and pecked long at two rolls on a shelf that at last they fell down, and the dog ate them up. But still his hunger was not appeased, so the sparrow took him to another baker's shop, and got more rolls for him. Then she asked him, "Well, brother, are you satisfied?"

"Yes," the dog replied. "Now let us go for a walk outside the town."

A Scottish law from 1288 allowed women to propose to men—but only on February 29.

So the two went for a stroll into the country, but the day was very hot, and after they had gone a short distance the dog said: "I am very tired, and would like to go to sleep."

"Sleep, then," said the sparrow. "As you do, I will keep watch on the branch of a tree."

SO THE DOG lay down in the middle of the road, and was soon fast asleep. While he was sleeping a carter passed by, driving a wagon drawn by three horses, and laden with two barrels of wine. The sparrow noticed that the man was not going out of his way to avoid the dog, so she called out: "Carter, take care what you are about, or I shall make you suffer for it."

But the carter merely laughed and, cracking his whip, drove his wagon right over the dog, so that the heavy wheels killed him.

Then the sparrow called out, "You have caused my brother's death, and your cruelty will cost you your wagon and horses."

"Wagon and horses, indeed," said the carter. "I'd like to know how you could rob me of them!"

The sparrow said nothing, but crept under the cover of the wagon and pecked so long at the bunghole of one of the barrels that she got the cork away, and all the wine ran out without the carter's noticing it.

At last he turned around and saw that the bottom of the cart was wet, and when he examined it, he found that one of the barrels was empty. "Oh! what an unlucky fellow I am!" he exclaimed.

"You'll have worse luck still," said the sparrow, as she perched on the head of one of the horses and pecked out its eyes.

WHEN THE CARTER SAW THIS, he seized an axe and tried to hit the sparrow with it, but the little bird flew up into the air, and the carter only hit the blind horse on the head, so that it fell down dead. "Oh! what an unlucky fellow I am!" he exclaimed again.

"You'll have worse luck yet," said the sparrow, and as the carter drove on with his two horses she crept under the covering again, and pecked away at the cork of the second barrel till she got it away, and all the wine poured out onto the road.

When the carter perceived this fresh disaster he called out once more: "Oh! what an unlucky fellow I am!"

The sparrow answered: "Your bad luck is not over yet," and flying onto the head of the second horse she pecked out its eyes.

The carter jumped out of the wagon and seized his axe, with which he meant to kill the sparrow, but the little bird flew high into the air, and the blow fell on the poor blind horse instead, killing it on the spot. "Oh!" the carter exclaimed. "What an unlucky fellow I am!"

Fish out of water: India's blue dwarf snakehead fish can survive on land for up to four days.

"You've not come to the end of your bad luck yet," sang the sparrow, and perching on the head of the third horse, she pecked out its eyes.

BLIND WITH RAGE, the carter let his axe fly at the bird, but once more she escaped the blow, which fell on the last horse and killed it. Again the carter called out: "Oh! what an unlucky fellow I am!"

"You'll have worse luck yet," said the sparrow, "for now I mean to ruin your home."

The carter left his wagon on the road and went home in a towering passion. As soon as he saw his wife, he called out: "Oh! what bad luck I have had! All my wine is spilt, and my horses are all three dead."

"My dear husband," replied his wife, "your bad luck pursues you, for a wicked little sparrow has assembled all the other birds in the world, and they are in our barn eating everything up."

The carter went out to the barn and found it was just as his wife had said. Thousands and thousands of birds were eating up all the grain, and in the middle of them sat the little sparrow. When he saw his old enemy, the carter cried out: "Oh! what an unlucky fellow I am!"

"Not unlucky enough yet," said the sparrow, "for, mark my words, your cruel conduct will cost you your life." And she flew into the air.

The carter was much depressed by the loss of all his worldly goods, and sat down at the fire plotting vengeance on the sparrow, while the little bird sat on the window ledge and sang in mocking tones: "Yes, carter, your cruel conduct will cost you your life."

THE CARTER SEIZED HIS AXE and threw it at the sparrow, but he only broke the window panes, and did not do the bird a bit of harm. She hopped in through the broken window and, perching on the mantelpiece, she called out: "Yes, carter, it will cost you your life."

The carter, beside himself with rage, flew at the sparrow again with his axe, but the little creature always eluded his blows, and he only succeeded in destroying all his furniture. At last he managed to catch the bird in his hands. Then his wife called out: "Shall I wring her neck?"

"Certainly not," replied her husband, "that would be far too easy a death for her. She must die in a far crueler fashion than that. I will eat her alive," and he did. But the sparrow fluttered and struggled inside him till she got up into the man's mouth, and then she popped out her head and said: "Yes, carter, it will cost you your life.'"

The carter handed his wife the axe, and said: "Wife, kill the bird in my mouth dead." The woman struck with all her might, but she missed the bird and hit the carter right on the top of his head, so that he fell down dead. And the sparrow? She escaped out from his mouth and flew away into the air.

What's another name for "loop-the-loop centrifugal railroad?" Roller coaster.

Spills!

When Uncle John hears the words "a truck overturned today..." on the news, he first hopes that the driver is okay. Then he hopes the truck spilled out something really weird onto the road.

MONEY. A bank truck got a flat tire while driving on a highway near Foggia, Italy, in 2010. That caused the driver to lose control and hit a median. The doors of the truck flew open, throwing boxes out onto the ground, where they broke apart on impact. In the boxes: more than 2 million worth of euro coins. Drivers in nearby cars screeched to a halt and made off with more than 10,000 euros lying on the road before police could blockade the area.

A DEAD WHALE. A truck was transporting a beached, 60-ton sperm whale to a research center in Taiwan in 2004. The dead whale was scheduled for an autopsy, but gases built up inside the carcass and it exploded, causing the truck carrying it to crash. Whale blood and guts drenched the road, as well as cars and pedestrians.

FISH. In January 2012, a truck overturned and dumped its entire load of fresh mackerel onto a farmer's land in Northern Ireland. The fish were reportedly two feet deep in spots. (Three years later, a similar accident occurred in Belfast, this time dropping 600 mackerel onto a city street. The truck driver reportedly had no idea that he'd left his doors open.)

BEER. A car collided with a Molson beer truck on a Canadian high-way near Toronto in 2005. Neither driver was harmed, which can't be said for the 2,184 cases of beer that fell off the truck and onto the road. An officer at the scene described the highway as a "sea of beer."

BAKED GOODS. In October 2011, a bakery truck on I-74 in Illinois overturned and its cargo poured out. The cargo: 20 tons of food, mostly chocolate cake, doughnuts, and cinnamon rolls. The road was closed for more than seven hours.

COCAINE. Drug cartels employ many different methods to hide drugs inside trucks and smuggle them into foreign countries. In 2007, one Colombian cartel truck didn't get very far—it was still in Bogotá when it turned a corner too sharply and tipped over. Result: the fabric of the walls and roof were torn...which is where the cocaine was stashed. Total amount of white powder on the road: about 2,000 pounds.

PAINT. A truck carrying industrial-size buckets of white paint crashed on a bridge in Halifax, Nova Scotia, in 2012. More than 400 cars drove through the paint before cleanup crews could close the bridge and sop up what was left.

BEES. The ongoing shortage of bees requires farmers to bring truckloads of rented bees into agricultural production areas to ensure proper pollination of crops. That's why a truck was hauling 400 hives containing 14 million bees (and their honey) from California to North Dakota in 2015. In Idaho, the driver veered off the road, lost control, and crashed, throwing out the boxes full of bees. Traffic was backed up (motorists were urged to keep their windows rolled up) for two hours as beekeepers tried to corral the insects. It took cleanup crews two full days to clean up all the honey left on the road.

PENGUINS. A refrigerated truck was heading from the Indianapolis Zoo to Moody Gardens in Galveston, Texas, in 2006 when the driver lost control and rolled the vehicle. Tossed onto the road were 25 penguins, along with an octopus and a few exotic fish. Four of the penguins died in the accident, but the octopus—found near the road and still in a plastic bag filled with water—survived.

TOILET WATER. A car spun out on Highway 280 in San Jose, California, in 2014, triggering a six-vehicle accident, including an overturned tanker truck. It was carrying 100 gallons of portable toilet deodorizing fluid, which soaked the highway. Fortunately, it was unused portable toilet fluid. (Motorists in Multnomah County, Oregon, weren't as lucky. In 2015, the driver of a tanker truck took a curve in the highway too fast and spilled 2,000 gallons of what appeared to be raw sewage all over the road. It turned out that it wasn't sewage—it was cooking oil.)

*   *   *

9 FILMS SCREENED AT THE WHITE HOUSE FOR PRESIDENT RICHARD NIXON

True Grit
Patton (twice in April 1970)
The Unsinkable Molly Brown
It's a Mad, Mad, Mad, Mad World
You Can't Take It with You
Citizen Kane
Notorious
The Sting
Friendly Persuasion

Secrets of the Super-Centenarians

There's only about a 1 in 1,000 chance that a 100-year-old person will become a "super-centenarian"—live to see their 110th birthday. So how did these folks make it that far? Read on and find out.

Misao Okawa, Osaka, Japan (117 years old)
She ate lots of her favorite foods (mackerel sushi, beef stew, and spaghetti) and got plenty of sleep. "Eat and sleep and you will live a long time," she said in 2014. "You have to learn to relax."

Emma Morano, Verbania, Italy (116)

Morano, the last living human born in the 1800s, has a glass of home-made brandy every day, and on doctor's orders she's eaten two raw eggs and one cooked egg daily since 1920. (That's more than 105,000 eggs in all—70,000 of them raw.) She has only milk for dinner. One more factor she credits with giving her a long life: after divorcing her violent husband at the age of 38, she never remarried. "I didn't want to be dominated by anyone," she says.

Besse Cooper, Monroe, Georgia (116)

"I mind my own business and I don't eat junk food."

Susannah Mushatt Jones, Brooklyn, New York (116)

Jones, who died in May 2016, never had children, slept 10 hours a night, and ate four strips of bacon every day at breakfast. "I never drink or smoke. I surround myself with love and positive energy. That's the key to long life and happiness."

Bernice Madigan, Cheshire, Massachusetts (115)

"No children, no stress, and a spoonful of honey every day." Madigan also ate her favorite breakfast—Eggo waffles smothered in banana slices, and four glazed donut holes—every day.

Daisey Bailey, Detroit, Michigan (113)

Bailey took nips of bourbon whenever possible, ate lots of vegetables, and avoided beef. "She didn't eat nothing but pork," her granddaughter, Helen Arnold, told the *Detroit News*.

Nothing to sneeze at: An osprey's nostrils close and become watertight to help them catch fish.

Tomoji Tanabe, Miyakonojo, Japan (113)

"Not smoking and not drinking," and a diet of fried shrimp, miso soup, pickled vegetables, and bananas, washed down with plenty of milk.

Gertrude Weaver, Camden, Arkansas (116)

"Trusting in the Lord, hard work, and love everybody…Just do what you can, and if you can't, you can't."

Benjamin Harrison Holcomb, Carnegie, Okla. (111)

Big breakfasts and small dinners. "All his life, Daddy didn't smoke, he didn't drink. But he did have a huge breakfast. Just huge. Eggs, sausage. And just cornmeal mush for dinner," Holcomb's daughter, Leola Ford, told the *Washington Times* in 2000.

Leila Denmark, Athens, Georgia (114)

Denmark was the world's oldest practicing pediatrician when she retired at the age of 103; by then she was treating the great-grandchildren of her first patients. (Her other claim to fame: co-developing the whooping cough vaccine in the 1930s.) Denmark avoided milk, fruit juice, junk food, and sweets, including her many birthday cakes because they contained sugar, which she hadn't eaten in 70 years. She drank only water.

Tuti Yusupova, Karakalpakstan, Uzbekistan

Yusupova, who died in 2015, claimed to be 134, but this is unconfirmed. "The secret to a long life is to do lots of work in the fields and to live an honest life," she told the BBC in 2009. "Having lived through so many wars I would also tell the children of today to try and live their lives in the company of good people and to appreciate times of peace."

Gertrude Baines, Los Angeles, California (115)

Ate plenty of bacon, fried chicken, and ice cream, but "she never did drink, she never did smoke, and she never did fool around."

Yisrael Kristal, Haifa, Israel (112)

Kristal, the world's oldest living male in 2016, had no idea why he lived so long. "I believe that everything is determined from above, and we shall never know the reasons why," he told Guinness World Records.

Jose Aguinelo dos Santos, Sao Paulo, Brazil

Dos Santos claims to be 126, but that's unconfirmed. He has smoked a pack of cigarettes every day for 50 years and says there's no secret to his long life: "The truth is you just keep getting older," he told an interviewer in 2014. "If I got to this age it's because I've lived a lot, that's all."

Modern Wisdom

Famous folks and their thoughts on life.

"The large print giveth and the small print taketh away."
—**Tom Waits**

"Art is the closest we can come to understanding how a stranger really feels."
—**Roger Ebert**

"Nationalism is cured by traveling."
—**Shakira**

"Funny is funny, and it can come in 8 billion different shades and flavors, so I think it's silly to kind of limit it."
—**Melissa McCarthy**

"Adversity has a way of introducing a man to himself."
—**Shia LaBeouf**

"The reality is: sometimes you lose. And you're never too good to lose. You're never too big to lose. You're never too smart to lose. It happens."
—**Beyoncé**

"Knowing how to think empowers you far beyond those who know only what to think."
—**Neil DeGrasse Tyson**

"Fiction is the truth inside the lie."
—**Stephen King**

"Never get into a wrestling match with a pig. You both get dirty, and the pig likes it."
—**John McCain**

"Pressure is something you feel when you don't know what the hell you're doing."
—**Peyton Manning**

"Sometimes your whole life boils down to one insane move."
—**James Cameron**

"That's what life is: repetitive routines. It's a matter of finding the balance between deviating from those patterns and knowing when to repeat them."
—**Joseph Gordon-Levitt**

"You have to be able to accept failure to get better."
—**LeBron James**

"Splendid architecture, the love of your life, an old friend—they can all go drifting by unseen if you're not careful."
—**Ian McKellen**

"The moments that make life worth living are when things are at their worst…and you find a way to laugh."
—**Amy Schumer**

Can they rent? The 1967 Outer Space Treaty bans nations from owning any property in space.

Shake and Vibrate!

The early 1960s was the golden age of dance crazes. There were hundreds. You've probably heard of the Twist and the Mashed Potato, but do you remember…

The Charleston Fish

The Peanut Duck

The Mope

The Alley Cat

The Slurp

The Boney Maronie

The Tantrum

The Sno-Cone

The Arthur

The Popcorn Boogaloo

The Mother Popcorn

The Smock

The Salt-'n'-Pepper

The Raggedy Bag

The Napoleon

The Popeye Waddle

The War Canoe

The Granny

The Spunky Onions

The Karate Monkey

The Monkey-Donkey

The Tarzan's Monkey

The Surfing Monkey

The Bad Baboon

The Kickapoo

The Big Egg

The Lurch

The Shake and Vibrate

The Olympic Shuffle

The Mozart Stomp

The Typewriter

The Uncle Willie

The Zonk

The Banana Split

The Pata-Pata

The Stupidity

The Suzie

The Molecule A-Go-Go

The Barracuda

The Chickie-Goo

The March of the Mods

The Shovel

The Rifleman

The Mother Goose

The Funky Fatman

The Mississippi Cutback

The Underdog Backstreet

The Bat-Tusi

The Zizzle

The Whammy

The Switch-a-Roo

The Shingaling

The Pigmy Grind

The Mojo Workout

The Rush Hour Stomp

The Scrumble

The Slime

The Slop

The Unwind Twine

The Voodoo-Mash

The Wibble

Commuters, take note: Minnesota, the land of 10,000 lakes, has a canoe-share program.

Apps for the Crapper

Remember the old days when you had little choice but to read in the bathroom because there were no other options? (At the BRI, we called that "job security.") Good news! Today there are lots of bathroom-themed smartphone apps to choose from.

APP: SitOrSquat

What It Does: It helps you find nearby public restrooms and ranks them according to cleanliness

How It Works: The app, which was created by the makers of Charmin toilet paper, uses mapping software to show the location of the public restrooms near you. Restrooms that other app users have reported as being clean are designated as "Sits"; they're marked on the map with a green roll of toilet paper. Unclean restrooms are "Squats" and are marked with a red roll. Users are invited to upload photos and restroom reviews to the SitorSquat database. "Add new locations and spread the word about restrooms you would SIT, or ask for improvements for those that are SQUATS by adding them to the map," say the folks at Charmin. One user who goes by the handle of Toots McKenzie made a pit stop at the Hyatt Regency in Austin, Texas, in February 2016 and rated the restroom as a Sit. "Clean, stylish. I'd poop here again," Toots wrote alongside a photo of a toilet stall that was uploaded to the app.

APP: Places I've Pooped

What It Does: It lets you "mark your territory" in cyberspace

How It Works: Once you've used SitOrSquat to find a place to do your business, use Places I've Pooped to advertise your accomplishment to the world. Open the app and a map of your location appears; push the "Bombs Away" button at the bottom of the screen and a pin will appear on the map. If you want, you can post a note describing your experience. The app also lets you track your friends' poops and receive a notification each time they mark a new spot on the map. "Track all the places you've pooped in the world. Expand your territory, mark every-where you've visited. Bombs away!" writes Rob Goldstein, the creator of Places I've Pooped. (Also available from Goldstein: Places I've Been Drunk, and Places I've Had Sex.)

APP: ToiletPay

What It Does: It lets you calculate how much you're being paid when you go to the bathroom at work.

How It Works: Let's say you work 40 hours a week and make $30,000 a year. Enter those amounts into the app's settings, then press the "Start Session" button when you begin your bathroom break. The app starts a timer and keeps a running tally of how much money you're making on the pot. When you're finished, push the "Stop Session" button. At 40 hours a week and $30,000 a year, if you take a five-minute bathroom break you'll earn $1.40. ToiletPay also calculates the dollar value of an average bathroom break, the total value of all your bathroom breaks, and it forecasts how much money you'll have made in the bathroom at the end of one year.

APP: RunPee

What It Does: It identifies the best times to run to the restroom during a film.

How It Works: At home you can wait for a commercial break or hit the pause button on your DVD player. If you're at the movies, there's RunPee. When you open the app, it shows a list of movies currently appearing in theaters, along with advice on the best time to sneak out to the bathroom without missing anything really important.

For the 2016 Leonardo DiCaprio film *The Revenant*, RunPee lists four different "peetimes": at 56 minutes into the film, 1 hour and 18 minutes, 1 hour and 45 minutes, and 1 hour and 50 minutes. (For the 1:50 bathroom break, the app advises heading out as soon as "Glass and the horse go over the cliff," adding that "if you are either squeamish, or very fond of horses, then use this peetime.") The app includes a timer to activate when the movie starts; it will vibrate your smartphone when it's time to go. Also available on the app: written summaries of what you missed while you were on your pee break.

Details: RunPee creator Dan Florio got the idea for the app while watching the 2005 three-hour remake of *King Kong*. By the end of the film he *really* needed to pee but he didn't want to leave the theater during it for fear he'd miss something good. "After the movie it occurred to me that if I had gotten up and peed during that scene with the huge insects, which was really gross and had nothing to do with the rest of the movie, I wouldn't have needed to pee so badly at the end," he writes. RunPee got its start as a website in the spring of 2008; the smartphone app followed in July 2009. The app is so popular that Florio was able to quit his job at Microsoft. Today he, his mother, and his sister make their living watching movies and producing pee break listings for RunPee.

*   *   *

"The funniest people are the saddest ones." —**Confucius**

The Transfermium Wars

*If the Transfermium Wars raged from the late 1960s to the late 1990s,
how is it that so few people have ever heard of them? Because they
were fought by rival groups of scientists over who would get
to name newly discovered chemical elements.*

PARENT TRAP

When someone discovers a new chemical element, it's the tradition in the scientific community that the founder gets to name it. The system works pretty well, except for when more than one scientist or group of scientists claims to be the discoverer.

Take the elements that were initially known as numbers: 104, 105, and 106. On the periodic table, elements are organized according to their atomic number—the number of protons, or positively charged subatomic particles, in the nucleus of each atom. All three of these elements were synthetic, which means they don't exist in nature but can be produced or synthesized in laboratories. All three are radioactive, and their discoveries were the product of secret atomic research during the Cold War between the Soviet bloc countries and the United States and its allies. A group of Soviet scientists at the Joint Institute for Nuclear Research in the town of Dubna, near Moscow, claimed to have discovered all three in the late 1960s and early 1970s. But so did scientists at the University of California, Berkeley.

Then there's the elements 107 and 108. The Russian scientists at Dubna claimed to have discovered those two elements as well, but so did German scientists at the Society for Heavy Ion Research in Darmstadt, West Germany.

Because all five elements follow fermium (Fm)—which has the atomic number 100—on the periodic table, the dispute came to be known as the "Transfermium Wars." Neither side was willing to concede victory, and the dispute over what to name the elements continued for more than 30 years.

ELEMENT 104

Who's Your Daddy? The Russians claimed to have discovered it in 1964, but scientists at U.C. Berkeley believed *they* were first when they made their discovery independently in 1969. One of the problems with verifying the claims is that even the most stable form, or isotope, of element 104 has a half-life of only 1.3 hours, which means that half of the material decays in less than 80 minutes. And 1.3 hours after that, half of the remaining half will decay, and so on, until there's not much physical evidence left to prove the claim that you've actually succeeded in making the stuff. The suspicion and mistrust of the Cold War era made it that much harder for one side to believe the claims the other side was making—especially when the other side claimed to be first.

The Russians named the element kurchatovium in honor of Igor Kurchatov, the father of the Soviet atomic bomb. The Berkeley scientists gave it the name rutherfordium to honor Ernest Rutherford, the New Zealand–born, Nobel Prize–winning British physicist who is considered the father of nuclear science.

ELEMENT 105

Who's Your Daddy? If you think element 104's half-life of 1.3 hours was a challenge, the first form of element 105 that was discovered had a half-life of just 1.6 *seconds*. The Soviet scientists claimed they synthesized the element as early as 1968, and the scientists at Berkeley claimed they did it in 1970. The Soviet scientists called the element nielsbohrium (Ns) in honor of Danish physicist Niels Bohr; the Berkeley scientists called it hahnium (Ha) in honor of German chemist Otto Hahn.

ELEMENT 106

Who's Your Daddy? In this case, the claims of discovery were only a few months apart. The Soviets claimed to have synthesized element 106 in June 1974; the scientists at U.C. Berkeley said they created their first samples in September of the same year. The isotope claimed by the Soviets had a half-life of a little over half a second, and the isotope claimed by the U.C. Berkeley scientists had a half-life of 0.9 seconds.

It's not clear that the Soviets ever picked a name for element 106, but the Berkeley scientists did: seaborgium, in honor of their colleague Glenn T. Seaborg. He and an associate named Edwin McMillan won the Nobel Prize in 1951 for discovering five different elements: plutonium (Pu), americium (Am), curium (Cm), berkelium (Bk), and californium (Cf). Seaborg also helped in the discovery of two more elements, einsteinium (Es) and mendelevium (Md).

As the co-discoverer of so many elements, Seaborg was certainly worthy of the honor, but the choice was controversial because Seaborg was still alive. Traditionally, elements are named for dead scientists. The only exceptions were einsteinium (Es) and fermium (Fm), both of which were discovered in the debris of a hydrogen bomb testing at the North Pacific atoll of Enewetak in 1952. The names for these elements were proposed while Einstein and Fermi were still alive, but the existence of the new elements, and thus their names, remained a military secret until they were declassified in June 1955. By the time the names were made public, both Einstein and Fermi were dead.

ELEMENT 107

Who's Your Daddy? The Soviet scientists said they produced the first samples of the element in 1976, but scientists at the Society for Heavy Ion Research in Darmstadt made their own claim of discovery after synthesizing element 107 in 1981. In this case the Soviet claim was sketchy but the German claim was not. Scientists there were able to prove they'd created five atoms of an isotope of element 107 that had a half-life of just 84 milliseconds—less than a tenth of a second. The Russians proposed no name for the new element, but the Germans proposed naming it nielsbohrium if the Russians lost out on their bid to give that name to element 105 in honor of Niels Bohr.

ELEMENT 108

Who's Your Daddy? Both the Soviets and the Germans claimed to have synthesized the element in 1984. It's not known whether the Russians actually proposed a name for the element. The Germans wanted to call it hassium in honor of the German state of Hesse, where Darmstadt is located.

ONE-TWO-THREE

By the early 1990s, the names of all of these elements had yet to be sanctioned by the International Union of Pure and Applied Chemistry (IUPAC), a body of scientists that has the final say in picking the names that will be adopted by the scientific community worldwide. When the discoverer of an element is not in question, their role is typically to approve whatever name has been suggested by the discoverer. But when there's no agreement on who the discoverer is, it's hard for the IUPAC to reach consensus on which name to approve.

In the meantime, the IUPAC had a system of temporary "placeholder" names for the elements that was based on Greek and Latin words for the atomic numbers of each element in dispute. Element 104, for example, was given the placeholder name unnilquadium—"one-zero-four-ium." This pleased nobody. In such cases, scientists in the Soviet bloc used their preferred name in scientific papers and textbooks, and the Americans used theirs. Disinterested scientists everywhere simply referred to the elements by their atomic numbers: element 104, element 105, and so on, and got on with their work.

LET'S MAKE A DEAL

In 1986, the IUPAC joined with another group called the International Union of Pure and Applied Physics (IUPAP) to form a committee that would consider the competing claims for discovery of the elements in dispute and settle on names for the elements that all parties could agree on. It took them eleven years to hammer out a compromise, but by 1997 they finally got it done. In the end the discovery claims of the United States, Russia, and Germany were all found to have merit to one degree or another, so the sides agreed to divvy up the naming rights.

• **Element 104.** This element would be named rutherfordium (Rh), as the U.C. Berkeley scientists had wished.

• **Element 105.** The Russians got to name element 105 dubnium (Db) in honor of the Russian town of Dubna, which is home to the Joint Institute for Nuclear Research, where the Russian scientists were based.

• **Element 106.** For a time it seemed that the "dead-scientists-only" policy would prevail, but the American scientific establishment refused to accept any compromise that didn't include naming an element after Glenn T. Seaborg, even though he was still alive. In the end they got their way and element 106 was named seaborgium (Sg). To date, Seaborg, who died in 1999, is the only scientist ever to live long enough to look himself up in the periodic table. (With the possible exception of Paul-Émile "Rooster" Lecoq de Boisbaudran. That story is on page 186.)

• **Element 107.** The Germans got to name this element bohrium (Bh) in honor of Niels Bohr, a name that also pleased the Russians, who had wanted to name element 105 after him. So why was bohrium chosen instead of neilsbohrium, as had been proposed for element 105? The convention in naming elements was to use only the last name of the person being honored; had the name neilsbohrium been approved, Niels Bohr would have been the only person whose first *and* last names were used, but only because the name bohrium was thought to be too similar to the element boron (B). This time convention prevailed and bohrium won out over neilsbohrium.

• **Element 108.** As the Germans had wished, this element was named hassium (Hs) in honor of the German state of Hesse.

*   *   *

"The biggest waste of brainpower is to want to change something that's not changeable."

—**Albert Brooks**

Conspiracy...or Cuckoo?

As crazy as these conspiracy theories may seem, there are people out there who believe them. How about you?

THEORY: Astronauts couldn't have landed on the Moon...because it isn't real! The Moon is actually a holographic projection sent from Earth, and it's hiding a huge alien space base. A YouTube user named Ccrow777 has filmed the Moon for hours a night over the course of a decade with a high-definition camera, looking for discrepancies, and he finally found what he was looking for: footage of the Moon in the middle of a "lunar wave." He claims that's proof the Moon isn't real.

THEORY: Ever post an old picture of yourself on Facebook or Instagram because it's "Throwback Thursday"? That was devised by the National Security Agency (NSA) to get people to upload pictures from the pre-digital age so they can be cataloged in a secret database. This theory may have resulted from a 2011 report on the leaked memos uncovered by hacker Edward Snowden that said the NSA was collecting 55,000 images a day of people in an attempt to thwart terrorism.

THEORY: According to the right-wing website the Abreu Report, Supreme Court justice Antonin Scalia was killed at a Texas ranch in 2016 by the Bush family because he was going to reveal that George W. Bush was the architect of the 9/11 attacks, and thus derail the presidential campaign of Jeb Bush.

THEORY: *Star Trek* star Leonard Nimoy faked his death in 2015 and went on to become the leader of the Illuminati, a secret society that controls the world. Nimoy had Supreme Court justice Antonin Scalia killed in 2016 so fellow Illuminati member President Barack Obama could appoint a new judge and tip the court to a liberal majority. Then those judges would cancel the 2016 election and declare Obama president for life. This theory was first posited on a parody news site called Hard Dawn, and legitimate news organizations reported the story.

THEORY: Taylor Swift is also a member of the Illuminati. According to various websites (such as Illuminati Watcher), the number 13 figures prominently into Illuminati mythology, and Swift, who was born on

---

Instead of writing letters, Scottish children shout their desires to Santa up the chimney.

December 13, turned 13 on Friday the 13th, and writes "13" on her hand before concerts. Fellow Illuminati Kanye West famously interrupted her acceptance speech at the MTV Video Music Awards, which took place on September 13, 2009. Why? The interruption was actually a secret Illuminati initiation for Swift.

THEORY: Do you believe in evolution or creationism? Forget them both. The government is keeping the *true* origin of mankind secret: Thousands of years ago, a flying saucer crashed into Mt. Ararat in Turkey. The two figures we know as "Adam" and "Eve" emerged. (This is an offshoot of a theory called the "ancient astronaut hypothesis," which suggests that all life on Earth can be traced back to extraterrestrials.)

THEORY: Elon Musk, the CEO of electric car company Tesla, is funneling his company's money into SpaceX, a private space travel company. Reason: he's really an alien who crash-landed on Earth, and he's using SpaceX to build a spaceship to return to his home planet.

THEORY: In 2014, a writer for MTV's website slowed down rapper Nicki Minaj's vocals and concluded that Minaj sounded a lot like Jay Z. Minaj has publicly stated that Jay Z is her idol, and that her album *The Pinkprint* is an answer to Jay Z's album *The Blueprint*. That news mutated into a conspiracy theory that Minaj doesn't really perform her music—her vocals are Jay Z's vocals, sped up.

THEORY: The real story behind alien abductions? In 1954, President Dwight Eisenhower signed a treaty with aliens who came to Earth. The deal gave the U.S. government access to advanced alien technology, and in exchange, the aliens were allowed to kidnap and probe unsuspecting humans. According to some fringe news sites, Eisenhower had as many as three secret summits with alien leaders.

THEORY: According to an anti-factory farming blog called REALfarmacy, Chipotle's 2015–16 *E. coli* outbreak was the work of giant agricultural companies who resented the fast-food chain's rejection of the GMO foods that they produce. The "Big Ag" companies sent employees who posed as workers at Chipotle's meat-processing plants and poisoned the supply with *E. coli*.

THEORY: Less than a week after the 2004 Indian Ocean tsunami, conspiracy theories were flying around the Internet, claiming the disaster was the result of an underwater nuclear explosion by the Indian government. Middle Eastern–based news network Al Jazeera even presented the theories to viewers as actual possibilities. (They're not...are they?)

First recorded auto accident: A collision between a car and a bicycle in New York City in 1896.

The Season That Never Was

In 1994, a players' strike ended the Major League Baseball season in August. A third of the regular-season games were canceled, depriving some players of a chance to make baseball history with these records.

First .400 hitter in 50 years. The last player to bat over .400 in a season was Ted Williams, with a .406 batting average in 1941. Three-time batting champion Tony Gwynn might have topped .400 if the season weren't cut short. At the time of the strike, he had a .394 average, the highest since Williams's banner year.

• **Single-season home run record.** It's since been topped several times (Barry Bonds set the current record of 73 in 2001), but in 1994, Roger Maris's 61 homers in 1961 was the one to beat. When the strike began, Matt Williams of the San Francisco Giants had 43 home runs. At that pace over a full season, he would have tied or broken Maris's 61.

• **Worst record for a division winner.** At the season's abrupt end, the Texas Rangers led the American League West despite having a losing record of 52–62. The last-place teams in the other two AL divisions, the Milwaukee Brewers and Detroit Tigers, both had records of 53–62, better than the Rangers.

• **The Expos in the World Series.** Before moving to Washington, D.C., in 2005, the Expos played 26 seasons in Montreal and *never* made the World Series. (Only one other modern franchise has done that: the Seattle Mariners.) The 1994 season was the best shot they ever had. At the time of the strike, their 74–40 record was the best in baseball.

• **Fred McGriff.** Only 27 players have hit at least 500 home runs. That feat is a virtual free pass into the Baseball Hall of Fame (not including players who may have used performance-enhancing drugs). Fred McGriff is tied with Lou Gehrig for #28 on the all-time list with 493— and he's not in the Hall of Fame. In 1994, he knocked 34 balls out of the park, and was on pace to hit 47 for the full season…which would have given him a career total of 506.

• **An attendance record.** In only its second year as a franchise, the Colorado Rockies had a total attendance of 3.28 million through 57 home games. Averaged out over a full season, the Rockies would have drawn more than 4.6 million fans and shattered the attendance record of 4.48 million, set a year earlier by…the Colorado Rockies.

Allergic to cheese? British photographers used to tell their subjects to say "prunes."

Law and Order: Masonic Police Unit

Ready to call a cop? On page 59 we told you about a few American law enforcement agencies you've probably never heard of before. If your local sheriff is too busy, maybe you can try one of these.

UNITED STATES MINT POLICE

Force: About 300

Story: One of the oldest law enforcement agencies in the United States was formed during George Washington's first term as president. Their responsibility: to protect gold, silver, coinage, and other government assets, as well as the employees at America's seven mint facilities—San Francisco, Philadelphia, Denver, West Point, Washington, D.C., and Fort Knox. In recent years the duties of U.S. Mint Police officers have expanded. Special response teams have been deployed at such events as the 2002 Winter Olympics in Salt Lake City, the Kentucky Derby, and at the Federal Reserve Building in New Orleans during Hurricane Katrina.

Bonus Fact: In September 2011, the U.S. Mint Police made national headlines—in a bad way—when Officer William Gray, 67, a 15-year veteran of the force, was arrested for smuggling an estimated 32,000 "error coins"—coins that carried flaws made during minting—out of the Philadelphia mint over the course of four years. Gray had sold flawed Presidential $1 coins to a California dealer for up to $75 apiece, making roughly $2.4 million. Gray pleaded guilty, and was sentenced to three years in prison.

NOAA POLICE

Force: About 150

Story: Officially known as the National Oceanic and Atmospheric Administration Fisheries Office for Law Enforcement (NOAA OLE), these cops patrol more than 3 million square miles of open ocean and protected marine areas, along with more than 95,000 miles of U.S. coastline. That's just for the mainland. They also patrol U.S. islands and territories all around the world and investigate crimes involving endangered marine mammals. Headquartered in Silver Spring, Maryland, NOAA OLE officers are, according to their website, "dedicated to enforcing laws that conserve and protect our nation's living

---

For a tender and flaky pie crust, replace half the water with any 80-proof liquor.

marine resources and their natural habitat." It goes on to say the agency "protects fish stocks from depletion and marine mammals from extinction. We also protect the livelihoods of commercial fishers, the hobbies of recreational fishers, and the health of seafood consumers."

Bonus Fact: In 2010, the owner of the Hump, a Santa Monica, California, sushi restaurant, and two of his chefs were arrested and charged with several felonies after undercover NOAA OLE officers successfully ordered sushi made from whale meat. Not only had the restaurant sold whale meat—which is illegal—tests confirmed it came from endangered sei whales. (It was later determined that whales were caught by Japanese whaling vessels, purportedly for "research" purposes.) The owner and two chefs were each sentenced to probation and fined $37,500. The Hump closed down for good.

CATTLE RAISERS SPECIAL RANGERS

Force: About 30

Story: Fully named the Texas and Southwestern Cattle Raisers Association Special Rangers, this is a joint Texas and Oklahoma police force that overlooks 76 million acres along the Texas-Oklahoma border. Their job: to investigate cases of cattle rustling. The Rangers were formed in 1877 when a group of ranchers, tired of having their cattle rustled, hired armed guards to watch their herds. Today it's a fully sanctioned police force, and its officers investigate more than 1,000 cases per year. They also investigate equipment theft and agricultural fraud, maintain records on more than 100,000 different cattle brands used by ranchers across the country, capture stray cattle and help get them back to their owners, and generally try to keep the peace in the Southwest cattle country. (They have a hotline dubbed "Operation Cow Thief," where people can leave tips anonymously.)

Extra Info: The Cattle Raisers Special Rangers' uniform includes cowboy boots and white (of course) cowboy hats.

MASONIC POLICE

Force: Unknown

Story: In April 2015, three members of the Masonic Fraternal Police Department—a police department almost nobody knew existed (mostly because it doesn't actually exist)—were arrested in Los Angeles for impersonating genuine police officers. The three cops—David Henry, 46, his wife, Tonette Hayes, 59, and Brandon Kiel, 31—had apparently set up their own police force, complete with uniforms, vehicles, badges, guns, and even a website. The trio claimed their "police force" had ties to the Freemasons organization, that they were "descendants of the Knights Templar" (a Christian monastic order founded during the

12th century), and that the force had been in existence for 3,000 years. They also claimed that they had jurisdiction in 33 states and Mexico. Investigators determined that the three cop wannabes had been going to real police stations—in uniform—to let police chiefs know that they would be setting up operations in their area. That's what led to their arrests. The bizarre case came to an end in April 2016 when charges against Kiel were dropped and, later the same day, David Henry died of a pulmonary embolism. Exactly what the pretend police force was up to remains a mystery.

POLICE AND THANK YOU

• Other police forces you may not know: the National Security Agency Police, the Bureau of Land Management Police, the Department of Veterans Affairs Police, the Pentagon Force Protection Agency, the Postal Inspection Service (a.k.a. the Post Office Police), the Bureau of Indian Affairs Police, the Bureau of Engraving and Printing Police, the Government Printing Office Police, the Tennessee Valley Authority Police, the Forest Service Law Enforcement and Investigations Unit, the Office of Export Enforcement, the Food and Drug Administration Office of Criminal Investigations, and the Department of Transportation Office of Odometer Fraud Investigation.

• Those are just *federal* law enforcement organizations. Each of the 50 states have many more agencies of their own, often with similar names and functions. The state with the most: Texas. It has 1,913 different state and local law enforcement agencies.

• There are about 120,000 federal law enforcement officers in the United States, in 73 different law enforcement agencies. And there are an additional 1.1 million officers in state and local agencies. (Note: All of these numbers come from the last census of U.S. law enforcement agencies—which was conducted in 2008. So there are probably a lot more now.)

*　　*　　*

GERM WARFARE

In an average day, the president of the United States meets—and shakes hands with—175 people. That's about 65,000 people a year… and 65,000 people's germs. Many politicians have no choice but to use hand sanitizer as frequently as possible. Former president George W. Bush reportedly went through a bottle a week; he even applied some immediately after shaking incoming president Barack Obama's hand for the first time. Obama was put off, but not too long into his presidency, he began including in his entourage a staffer who dispenses the Purell.

When a chameleon flicks its tongue, the tip accelerates from 0 to 60 mph in 1/100th of a second.

Old Hollywood Diets

Crazy fad diets go back a long way. Here are what some stars of
old Hollywood did when they wanted to drop a few pounds.

Marilyn Monroe: Two raw eggs whipped in warm milk for breakfast, no lunch, and for dinner broiled liver, steak, or lamb, and five carrots.

Jean Harlow: She occasionally went on "The Four-Day Diet." For four days she ate only two tomatoes for lunch (with black coffee), and then the same thing at dinner.

Nita Naldi: The silent film star popularized the "Lamb Chop and Pineapple Plan" in 1924. For breakfast she ate two slices of pineapple; for lunch, a lamb chop and a slice of pineapple; dinner was two lamb chops and two slices of pineapple.

Betty Grable: She'd snack on raw onions and garlic.

Gloria Swanson: She had a recipe for "Double Corn Soup," consisting of chopped onions, water, a few drops of olive oil, soy sauce, and half a cup of corn meal.

Elizabeth Taylor: Taylor would diet six days out of the week, eating little more than dried toast. The seventh day was her "pig-out day," and she would indulge in her favorite snack: sour cream mixed with cottage cheese.

Joan Crawford: A few spoonfuls of cold beef consommé and six crackers with mustard.

Grace Kelly: Oatmeal for breakfast, and then as many carrot sticks and celery as she wanted, provided she ate them by 11:00 a.m.

Orson Welles: To drop the 50 pounds he gained to play the lead role in *Citizen Kane*, for a month he ate only orange juice, salad (without salad dressing), and boiled eggs.

Maria Callas: The opera star had a doctor inject iodine into her thyroid to "speed up her metabolism."

Jacqueline Kennedy: She wasn't a Hollywood movie star, but she was just as famous and influential. Her diet secret: her one daily meal would be a baked potato, topped with caviar.

Sign language is regional. People who learned it in Philadelphia will sign with a Philly accent.

Famous...and Naked

More strange-but-true tales of some famous folks who let it all hang out.

FAMOUS: Mohandas (Mahatma) Gandhi, nonviolent activist who helped India gain independence from British rule

...AND NAKED: At age 37, after the birth of his fourth son, Gandhi took a vow of "celibacy". "I vow to flee from the serpent which I know will bite me," the young father declared. Scholars note that Gandhi practiced *brahmacharya*, which went beyond abstaining from sex to the "elimination of all desire." In the final few years of his life he decided to strengthen his resolve by testing himself. Nick Gier, Professor Emeritus of the University of Idaho, reported that Gandhi called yogis who isolated themselves in caves "cowards." It was much braver, he believed, to "face temptation head-on" by sleeping...in the nude...surrounded by naked women. One of those women was his 17-year-old grandniece, Manuben Gandhi. His closest followers worried that Gandhi risked being seen as the worst kind of dirty old man. But Manuben's diary contains no mention of hanky-panky. On December 28, 1946, nine days after joining the 77-year-old Gandhi as one of his "personal assistants," Manuben wrote: "Bapu [Gandhi]...is initiating me to a higher human plane through the Brahmacharya experiments. Any loose talk about the experiment is most condemnable."

FAMOUS: Marchesa Luisa Casati, Milanese aristocrat, patron of the arts, and fashionista

...AND NAKED: Her Venetian neighbors weren't sure what to call Luisa Casati, but the closest modern comparison might be Lady Gaga. Born in 1881 into a wealthy Milanese family, Casati died in 1957, owing creditors $25 million. At one time the richest woman in Italy, Casati hemorrhaged money, treating herself to palaces, cars, travel, art, and—most of all—fashion. "I want to be a living work of art," Casati proclaimed. Casati powdered her face to "fungal white," and wore enough dark *kohl* around her eyes to make them look as if they'd sunken into her skull. Then she squeezed in a few drops of deadly belladonna to make them "glitter like emeralds." Casati accessorized with ornaments such as a live snake shimmering with gold leaf and a headdress of peacock tail feathers sprinkled with chicken blood. So what does all that have to do with nudity? The Marchesa took regular evening strolls through St. Mark's Square wearing nothing but ropes of pearls and a sable wrap. And she was, according to her biography, "the most artistically represented woman in history after the Virgin Mary and

Creepy fact: Dead people can get goosebumps.

Cleopatra." Portraits of Casati hang in galleries and private collections around the world. (Several are nudes.)

FAMOUS: Winston Churchill, the British prime minister who guided the empire to victory against Hitler in World War II

...AND NAKED: Britain's most famous prime minister didn't have any problem going around "starkers," according to his wartime secretary, Patrick Kinna. After the Japanese bombing of Pearl Harbor in 1941, Churchill visited President Franklin D. Roosevelt at the White House. Churchill had just emerged from one of his two daily baths and was giving dictation in the nude when a knock came at the door. Churchill said, "Come in!" Roosevelt rolled his wheelchair inside, and then screeched to a stop when he saw the pasty prime minister's pink, unclothed body. He stuttered that he would come back later, to which Churchill replied, "Mr. President, I have nothing to hide from you!"

FAMOUS: Helen Mirren, Academy Award–winning actor and Dame of the British Empire

...AND NAKED: Mirren loves nudity. "I love being on beaches where everyone is naked. Ugly young people, beautiful old people, whatever. It's so unsexual and so liberating." That made Mirren perfect for one of the leads in *Calendar Girls*, a 2003 movie about a group of "mature" British women who pose topless to raise funds for cancer research. Based on a true story, the movie garnered rave reviews. But Mirren got herself into trouble with director Nigel Cole. It seems Cole had to tell Mirren repeatedly to put her robe back on after her nude scenes. In 2007, Mirren dared *60 Minutes* interviewer Morely Safer to get naked with her on TV. (She was 62; he was 75.) "I think we should do this interview, both of us, in the nude," Mirren said. "You'd love it. Go on." To which Safer replied, "What the hell…?"

* * *

ON A ROLL

In 1970, Bernard Sadow, an executive at U.S. Luggage Corps, was lugging two suitcases through a busy airport when he noticed a worker moving some equipment on a cart. It occurred to Sadow that putting wheels on luggage could be a simple solution to the problem of toting heavy bags. He went home, mounted wardrobe casters on a suitcase, and attached a pull-strap. His four-wheeled invention was a hit when it reached stores in 1972…but it was supplanted in 1987 by Rollaboard, invented by pilot Robert Plath, who put two plastic wheels and a long handle on a suitcase to wheel it upright.

The Flat Stanley Project

A nice story about nice people doing nice things.

STAN THE MAN

In 1964, magazine editor and short-story writer Jeff Brown was putting his kids, J. C. and Tony, to bed. Trying to distract their dad so they could stay up a little longer, the boys asked him what would happen if the large bulletin board on the wall were to fall on one of them. Brown replied that if the board fell, J. C. would most likely wake up flat. The boys liked the idea, and the three started talking about what life would be like for a flat boy. Later than year, Brown collected the ideas into a children's book about a flat boy, *Flat Stanley*. The plot: A boy named Stanley Lambchop survives being squashed by a bulletin board and must make the best of his new flat life by doing things like sliding under doors and being used as a kite. Another advantage of being flat was that he could visit his friends through the mail. Brown published five more books in the series, and at the time of his death in 2003, more than a million Flat Stanley books had been sold.

The Sincerest Form of Flat-tery

In 1994, Dale Hubert, a third-grade teacher in London, Ontario, was looking for something to liven up his literary arts curriculum. Inspired by Brown's Flat Stanley series, Hubert had an idea: What if he used the new Internet technology to find other classrooms around the country where kids were reading the Flat Stanley books? He asked his students to create their own flat people out of paper and to write stories about them in their journals. Then they could mail the Stanleys out to other kids throughout North America. The idea was to give kids a more creative outlet than a typical pen-pal relationship.

The Flat Stanley Project has been going strong ever since. Kids from more than 40 different countries have exchanged photos and letters, and Flat Stanleys have cropped up all over the world (not unlike the globe-trotting garden gnomes). They can be paper or digital, sent out by snail mail or through the Flat Stanley app. Recipients take Flat Stanley sightseeing, and then send him back home with souvenirs and photos of their adventures. Over the years, Flat Stanleys have flown on a space shuttle, visited heads of state, and been seen with celebrities and movie stars from Kim Kardashian to Clint Eastwood.

Three U.S. states conduct elections entirely by mail—Oregon, Washington, and Colorado.

You Dirty Rat!

We tend to think of wild animals as pretty messy and generally disgusting when it comes to matters of hygiene. But the truth is, many animals have very fastidious sanitation habits.

AFRICAN MOLE RATS

Also known as naked mole rats (because they have no hair), these molelike rodents are native to the dry grasslands of east-central Africa. They spend the great majority of their lives in elaborate underground tunnel-and-chamber systems, where they live in colonies of anywhere from 20 to 300 individuals. That makes for a lot of urine and feces, which could be an especially messy problem in a closed underground environment. It could also be dangerous, because feces and urine are breeding grounds for disease. So African mole rats have a solution: they dig toilet chambers—and all the mole rats in a colony urinate and defecate only in those chambers. They even spend time in those chambers cleaning and grooming themselves after they've done their business—much as humans do. When a chamber is filled up with waste, it's covered with dirt, and a new chamber is dug.

VULTURES

Vultures are carrion eaters, meaning they eat the rotting flesh of dead animals. For most animal species, this would be risky—and potentially deadly—because dead bodies are fertile ground for microbes, including the toxic bacteria that cause botulism, salmonella, and *E. coli*. So why don't vultures get sick from exposure to all that dead flesh? First, they have specially adapted characteristics that protect them, including incredibly strong stomach acids, and the absence of feathers on their necks and heads. (The latter prevents bacteria-rich flesh and juices from building up in their feathers, and allows them to "bake" away any bacteria on their heads and necks, via frequent sunbathing sessions.) They are also very fussy about cleaning themselves. Whenever there is standing water available—such as ponds, lakes, or lagoons—vultures of every species around the world will bathe, especially after eating, dunking their heads in the water over and over, thereby rinsing away any nasty microbes. Some vultures have even been observed flying many miles after eating—just to find a bathing place.

KANGAROOS

How can you tell when a pregnant kangaroo is about to give birth? Watch for a particular cleaning habit. About two days before her due

---

Until the late 18th century, the color traditionally associated with Ireland was blue, not green.

date, a pregnant kangaroo will clean out her pouch—holding the pouch open with her front paws, and sticking her snout inside and licking any dead skin or dirt from it, thereby making it nice and clean for the new joey (or joeys). It doesn't stop there: kangaroo joeys don't leave the pouch—at all—for the first five to six months of their lives. How much poop and pee can kangaroo joeys produce in five to six months? A lot! Solution: mother kangaroos regularly stick their snouts inside their pouches, lick up the joey's waste, and eat it, thereby keeping their babies' environment germ-free.

Bonus: Many marsupial species, such as koalas and wombats, don't have the kangaroo's long neck, so they can't reach their heads into their pouches to clean them out. So how do they keep their pouches clean? These marsupials secrete a powerful antimicrobial fluid into their pouches during breeding season, transforming them from dank and dirty places into pristine and sanitary nurseries. After the young are born, the pouch becomes dirty again—until the next breeding season comes along.

HONEYBEES

A common honeybee colony consists of three types of bees: the queen, whose sole job is to breed; drones, males whose primary job is mating with the queen; and workers, females whose primary job it is to collect pollen and tend the hive. The queen and the drones can, and do, poop anywhere in the hive. Nevertheless, honeybee hives are very clean places…because the queen's and the drones' waste is picked up and dumped outside the hive by the worker bees. The workers do not poop inside the hive. When they have to go—they hold it in. And in climates that have cold winters, that can mean holding it for weeks or even months. (Honeybees don't leave their hive when the temperature dips below 50°F.) When the first warm spell comes, a hive's worker bees will leave en masse, and take part in what is known as "cleansing flights"—a mass honeybee pooping trip. You may have seen the results of such cleansing flights, as they can appear as yellowish stains around beehives—they show up especially well on snow—and can even appear as "yellow rain" falling from the sky. (By the way, honeybees don't pee; they only poop.)

Bonus Fact: Honeybee workers aren't just in the sanitation business. Some of them also act as undertakers. When a bee dies inside the hive, a specially designated worker bee drags the body to the hive's entrance, flies it away, and dumps it—often as far as 300 feet from the hive. Since there are so many bees in a single hive (one queen; hundreds of drones; and from 10,000 to 50,000 workers), that can mean carting away dead bees dozens of times a day. It's such hard work that the undertaker bee will often make several attempts—and several crash landings—before

---

the dead bee is deemed far enough away from the hive. This is important work for several reasons, but primarily because if a colony is hit with one of the many transmittable honeybee diseases found in nature, getting the infected bodies out of the hive as quickly as possible is important to the colony's health.

BLUESTREAK CLEANER WRASSES

When a shark or other large fish is infested with tiny parasites, it can't just scratch them off like a dog would. And that's bad news because these parasites can really wreak havoc; they eat the fish's blood and mucus, killing skin tissue in the process, and they can even cause infections that can spread to other fish. Thankfully, these big fish can go to undersea "cleaning stations" where a school of smaller fish called bluestreak cleaner wrasses will swim around and even inside their mouths eating up all of the parasites, along with the dead and damaged tissue. The wrasses get a meal, and the "client fish" get to swim away much cleaner and healthier than they were before they arrived.

Bonus: Many saltwater fish tank experts try to discourage people from buying bluestreak cleaner wrasses as pets. Reason: the oceans need them too much! In one study, researchers removed all of the cleaner wrasses from a reef, and kept them off of it for 8.5 years. After that time, the scientists compared the reef to one nearby that had been left alone. The findings were startling: on the reef without the wrasses, there were 37 percent fewer fish, and the fish that were there were smaller. There were even fewer species thriving there—all because of the removal of one little fish that likes to dine on disgusting things.

*　　*　　*

FOUR PIRATE JOKES

Q: What has eight arms, eight legs, and eight eyes?
A: Eight pirates.

Q: What did the pirate say when his wooden leg fell off in a snow storm?
A: "Shiver me timbers!"

Q: Why didn't the pirate take a bath before he walked the plank?
A: Because he'll just wash up on shore later.

"Yarr," said one pirate to another, "that's a nice wooden peg you got there, and such a shiny hook! How much did they cost you?"
  The other pirate replied, "An arm and a leg."

Children of U.S. presidents have higher than average rates of alcoholism and mental illness.

Cut the Cable

*Is it true that you can create any kind of specialized
cable TV channel and it would find an audience?
Not really, as these flops prove.*

THE PUPPY CHANNEL

One of Animal Planet's most popular shows is *The Puppy Bowl*, an hour of puppies frolicking on a football field, shown annually opposite the Super Bowl. But ten years before *The Puppy Bowl* premiered, retired businessman Dan FitzSimons had an idea for a network that showed footage of dogs playing 24 hours a day (and that's it). The idea came to him while watching the seemingly endless O. J. Simpson trial in 1995: What if there was a show that lasted all day and all night but was much happier? He had a hard time attracting investors. By 2001, FitzSimons could get only four cable companies to sign on, so the Puppy Channel was put to sleep before it had a chance to play.

GENESIS STORYTIME

There are lots of channels just for kids—Nickelodeon, Cartoon Network, the Disney Channel. But what's better for kids than TV? Books! Around the clock, Genesis Storytime displayed one page of a children's picture book, after another, holding each page for a minute or so, until the book was done. Then a new book would start. Nobody read the books aloud—it was narration-free, words and pictures only, and parents or kids could check in and read whenever they liked. Not many did: Launched in 1983, the Genesis story ended in 1984.

CBS CABLE

The generic name of this channel didn't do much to attract viewers in the early days of cable TV. This 1981 offshoot of the CBS broadcasting network offered classy, cultural fare, such as symphonies, plays, jazz concerts, and interviews with painters. CBS founder William Paley personally managed the network and spent $10 million to create original content. It lasted only a year, losing the battle for viewers and space on cable systems to A&E, which offered similar programming.

SATELLITE NEWS CHANNEL

In 1980, CNN became the first all-news cable network, and the first 24-hour news service in TV history. And despite industry predictions that it would fail, it was a huge success. Copycats naturally emerged.

The first was Satellite News Channel, which announced it would go on the air in June 1982 with an attractive concept: It would deliver news around the clock, updated every 18 minutes (plus two minutes for commercials). CNN owner and founder Ted Turner responded by launching CNN2, rushing it onto the air in January 1982 (five months before Satellite News Channel). CNN2—later renamed Headline News—offered new newsfeeds every 30 minutes, not as good as SNC's 18, but it didn't matter. By the time SNC launched, most major cable systems had already allocated the space to CNN2. Satellite News Channel folded in October 1983.

WEDDING CENTRAL

By 2009, WE TV's schedule consisted almost entirely of reality shows about weddings—shows with names like *Always a Bridesmaid, How to Marry a Prince, Wedding Cake Masters, Rich Bride Poor Bride, Girl Meets Cowboy,* and *Bridezillas.* The bridal shows did so well that the channel spun them off onto a separate channel, Wedding Central. But despite the popularity of the individual shows, cable systems weren't interested in offering a new channel devoted entirely to weddings, especially since a lot of the content on Wedding Central had previously aired on WE. Result: after being carried on less than a dozen cable systems, Wedding Central died in 2011, and the wedding shows returned to WE TV.

NATIONAL EMPOWERMENT TELEVISION

Fox News gets a lot of criticism for a perceived right-wing bias to its news coverage, though the network insists it is "fair and balanced." National Empowerment Television, on the other hand, didn't bother trying to seem fair, proudly marketing itself as a conservative news outlet. NET went on the air in December 1993 with news and talk shows (including *The Progress Report with Newt Gingrich*), and shows produced by special-interest and consumer groups such as the National Rifle Association and the Philip Morris Tobacco Company. But the channel failed to attract enough advertisers, many of whom didn't want to be associated with a single political ideology. Within two years NET was gone.

*　　*　　*

CHRISTMAS COOKIE TRIVIA

The most famous variety of animal crackers: Barnum's Animals, in a little red box with pictures of circus animals on it and a string that can be used as a handle. But that's not why the string is there. It was originally put on the box so it could be used as a Christmas tree ornament.

Ironic, Isn't It?

There's nothing like a good dose of irony to put the problems of day-to-day life into proper perspective.

FIGHTIN' IRONY

A celebrity basketball game in 2015 nearly erupted into a brawl when one of the coaches, rapper Lil Wayne, rushed the referee after some questionable calls. His team had to hold him back. The incident took place at the "4th Annual Loose Cannon Celebrity Basketball Game," promoting nonviolent conflict resolution.

DISTRACTING IRONY

Speed cameras may generate revenue for cash-strapped municipalities, but the claim that they make roads safer was called into question by a 2015 British study by Wunelli, a company that compiles traffic data for insurance companies. According to the study, not only are roads with speed cameras less safe—because drivers brake hard when they see them, which leads to more accidents—Wunelli actually concluded that "the most dangerous place to be on a British road is near a speed camera."

AN IRONY TRANSFUSION

In 1928, a Russian doctor named Alexander Bogdanov experimented with slowing the aging process by giving himself blood transfusions from young people. Unfortunately, one of the 11 transfusions he underwent was from a young man who was suffering from malaria and tuberculosis. Result: Instead of achieving eternal youth, Bogdanov went to his eternal rest. (Bonus irony: the ailing young man who got Bogdanov's blood survived.)

IRONY AT WORK

• "Whistleblowing" is considered protected speech under U.S. federal law. So if a federal employee is punished for whistleblowing, where can he or she turn? To the Merit Systems Protection Board, a government agency that bills itself as a "personnel court of last resort for federal employees who believe they were unjustly…punished for revealing… truths agencies don't want to hear." In 2013, a federal employee named Timothy Korb revealed at a staff meeting that his agency's caseload was much larger than was being made public. In retaliation, Korb's boss stripped him of some of his duties and threatened to suspend him.

Snakes can strike with an acceleration force of more than 20 g. Humans black out at 9 g.

So Korb took his case to the Merit Systems Protection Board, where a federal judge ruled in his favor. His name cleared, Korb was able to return to his job...at the Merit Systems Protection Board.

• In 2015, Indiana's Department of Workforce Development laid off 60 employees whose job it was to help people find jobs. Why? The state's unemployment dropped far enough that the federal government reduced its aid to the state. If the jobless rate rises again, they'll get their jobs back.

IRONY WHEN WET

In 2011, Ahmad Sajad, 52, was walking out of an Aldi supermarket in Sydney, Australia, during a rainstorm when he slipped on a painted "Disabled Parking" sign on the asphalt. He broke his ankle, which required several expensive surgeries to repair. So Sajad sued the grocery store chain, claiming they had used poor-quality paint, which made the "Disabled" sign slippery when wet. The judge agreed, and awarded Sajad $400,000.

IRONY GOES BLAM!

Allie Carter took her 12-guage shotgun and her 11-year-old black lab on a hunting trip in Indiana in the fall of 2015. At some point, Carter stopped to take a break and placed her shotgun on the ground. The dog then stepped on the gun...which accidentally discharged and shot Carter in the foot. The dog's name: Trigger.

THE SOUND OF ONE IRONY CLAPPING

In 2015, administrators at Naropa University filed an application with the City of Boulder, Colorado, to "exterminate" 100 prairie dogs from campus grounds. The irony? Naropa is a Buddhist college, and one of the principles of Buddhism is "Do no harm." School administrators say they don't want to kill the rodents—which can carry plague—so they filed the kill request in the hopes that someone would come and take the prairie dogs away. So far, no one has. And the request really irked animal-rights groups. "The fact that a Buddhist university would even apply for a lethal application is totally against any Buddhist concepts," said Colorado's WildLands Defense director Deanna Meyer, who started a petition to save the animals. (It's amassed over 180,000 signatures.) At last report, the prairie dogs were still plaguing the campus. Your move, Buddhists.

* * *

"How is it possible to have a civil war?" —**George Carlin**

There's a 20-acre solar farm in Orlando, Florida, in the shape of Mickey Mouse.

Cold War Secret, Pt. III: "Project Horizon"

Here's the final installment of our story about America's plan to build a military base on the Moon in the 1950s. (Part II is on page 175.)

A BARGAIN AT TWICE THE PRICE

Project Horizon's authors estimated that building the base and keeping it supplied through the end of 1967, by which time it would have been in operation for one year, would require more than 229 rocket launches to the Moon. That's roughly one trip to the Moon every week and a half for nearly three years. They estimated that the program would cost $6 billion, the equivalent of $49 billion today, plus another $25 million to develop the weapons that would be used to defend the base. That was quite a lot of money in 1959, but the authors argued that the amount came to less than 2 percent of the annual defense budget, and they warned that if the U.S. waited until it had definite proof that the Soviets were planning their own Moon base and then launched a crash program to try and beat them to the punch, both the cost of the program and the risk of failure would be much higher.

NO SALE

It's probably a good thing for taxpayers that the army never got the green light to build its Moon base, because the report's cost estimate was *way* too low. The Apollo program was far more modest in scope, with just six Moon landings between 1969 and 1972, and a seventh attempt (*Apollo 13*) that was scrubbed after an oxygen tank exploded on the way to the Moon. But even the Apollo program cost $25 billion, half the estimated cost of Project Horizon. The cost of Project Horizon's 229 trips to the Moon would have been…astronomical.

SPIKED BY IKE

If there's one person most responsible for *not* putting an American military base on the Moon, it was probably President Dwight D. Eisenhower. "Ike" was the former five-star general who led the Allied forces to victory against Nazi Germany in World War II, but as president he was wary of excessive defense spending, especially when it came to atomic-powered airplanes, Moon bases, death rays, and other "Buck Rogers fantasies," as he called them. He wanted the military to focus on the more modest and attainable goal of building better rockets for nuclear missiles. By July 1958, Eisenhower had already signed legislation creating a civilian space agency—the National Aeronautics and Space Administration—to handle everything else that was space-related, including sending astronauts to the Moon. (Ike didn't care much for that idea either; he thought racing the Soviets to the Moon was a waste of money. It wasn't until his successor, John F. Kennedy, was elected president that the Apollo lunar program roared to life.)

The United States would soon land on the Moon, but thanks to Eisenhower, the U.S. Army remained stuck on planet Earth.

GUN CONTROL

Whatever small chance there still was for Project Horizon to come to fruition disappeared entirely in 1967 when the United States, the Soviet Union, and more than 60 other countries signed the Outer Space Treaty, which forbade nations from claiming the Moon, the planets, and other celestial bodies as sovereign territory. The treaty also limited their use to peaceful purposes, and banned the placement of nuclear weapons or other weapons of mass destruction into Earth orbit or outer space. And it specifically forbade "the establishment of military bases, installations and fortifications, the testing of any type of weapons and the conduct of military maneuvers on celestial bodies." As long as the Outer Space Treaty remains in effect, the only place to see military bases in space will be at the movies or on TV.

BIRDS OF A FEATHER

So how realistic was the threat that the Soviet Union would build a military base on the Moon? Just as American military planners had feared, in 1962 the Soviets did begin developing plans for such a base. And they kept at it until 1974, far longer than the U.S. Army spent on Project Horizon. After the Outer Space Treaty was signed in 1967, however, the military components of the base plan were abandoned.

The base was just one part of the Soviets' lunar program, which also included a plan to land a cosmonaut on the Moon *before* the United States, something we told you about in *Uncle John's Unsinkable Bathroom Reader*. Then, when the Americans beat the Russians to the Moon in 1969, the Soviets hoped to make their second-place finish more impressive by going forward with the construction of a lunar base.

Their plan for the *Zvezda* (Star) base bore some similarities to Project Horizon: at least one habitation module would have been sent to the Moon in advance of the cosmonauts. Nine modules in all would have landed on the Moon, some before the cosmonauts and some after, and the modules would have been connected together to build the base. Unlike the American modules, the Soviet modules would have been expandable. After arriving on the Moon in compact form, the cosmonauts would have filled them with compressed air to expand them from 15 feet to their full size of nearly 30 feet in length. The modules would also have been built on wheels, so that a special module called a *tug* could tow the base from one place to another like a locomotive. Like Project Horizon, power for the base would have been supplied by nuclear reactors, and if necessary the modules could have been covered with lunar soil to protect against micrometeorites and wild swings in temperature.

FAILURE TO LAUNCH

The Soviets never did build their base on the Moon, for the same reason that they never made it to the Moon in the first place: their N-1 heavy-lift rocket suffered from design flaws that caused all four of its test launches to end in failure. One rocket blew up on the launchpad, and another exploded less than two minutes into its flight. The other two rockets malfunctioned and crashed back to Earth. Soviet premier Leonid Brezhnev canceled the program in 1974. A successor to the N-1 rocket, the Vulkan rocket, was proposed the same year but never built.

By then the Soviets had decided to focus on building a reusable space shuttle in order to counter what they felt was the military threat posed by the American space shuttle. The Soviet *Buran* (Blizzard) space shuttle was completed in 1984 and made just one unmanned, remote-controlled flight in 1988 before it was canceled due to lack of funds.

*   *   *

THREE MOVIES THAT FEATURE MOON BASES

Moon (2009), starring Sam Rockwell as astronaut Sam Bell, and Kevin Spacey as the voice of GERTY, Bell's computer companion. Bell is nearing the end of a three-year stint as the sole resident of an automated helium factory on the far side of the moon when things begin to go haywire.

Iron Sky (2012), starring Julia Dietze as Renate Richter and Götz Otto as Klaus Adler. This "Finnish-German-Australian comic science fiction action film" is set in 2018, when American astronauts landing on the far side of the moon discover a secret base where Nazis have been hiding out since blasting off for the moon at the end of World War II.

A Grand Day Out with Wallace and Gromit (1989), starring Peter Sallis as the voice of Gromit. If a picnic blanket on the moon can be considered a moon base, this 24-minute stop-motion animated film fits the bill: When Gromit and his dog Wallace run out of cheese to go with their crackers, they build a rocket to take them to the moon "because everybody knows the moon is made of cheese," Wallace says.

Welcome to the Big House

A somewhat random collection of interesting facts and statistics about prisons and jails. Just in case you ever need to know…

JAIL vs. PRISON

The terms *jail* and *prison* are commonly used interchangeably, but they actually have different meanings. The major differences are the length of the term and the reasons for imprisonment. Jails are temporary holding facilities for people who have been recently arrested and are awaiting a court date, or for people who have been convicted of a crime but were given a relatively short sentence—usually less than a year. Prisons are for people who've been convicted of crimes and received sentences of more than one year. Jails are run by local governments—usually by county sheriff's departments—while prisons are run by state or federal governments. People convicted of state laws go to state prison; those convicted of federal laws go to federal prison. There are currently about 120 federal prisons, more than 400 state prisons, and more than 3,800 jails in the United States today.

LEVELS OF SECURITY

Federal prisons in the United States are run by the Federal Bureau of Prisons. They have five different security designations: minimum, low, medium, high, and administrative.

Minimum-security prisons have no perimeter fencing. They have dormitory-style housing and are work- and program-oriented, with prisoners often working off-site and taking part in rehabilitation programs, such as for drug treatment. (They are also known as Federal Prison Camps.)

Low-security prisons have double-fenced perimeters. They have dormitory or cubicle-style housing (cubicle housing is similar to dormitory housing, but with 3- or 4-foot partitions between beds), and are also work- and program-oriented.

Medium-security prisons have double-fenced perimeters, often with electronic detection systems. Most have multi-occupant cells, rather than dormitories, and they have internal work and program operations.

High-security prisons have highly secured perimeters, usually with fences, walls, and electronic detection systems. They have both multioccupant and single-occupant cells, and they have a much higher staff-to-inmate ratio than the lower-security facilities. They also have internal work and program operations.

Administrative prisons come in several varieties, including prisons for people with serious and/or chronic health problems and prisons for especially dangerous prisoners. This includes the highest-security prison—the only U.S. prison designated "Supermax": the Administrative-Maximum Security Penitentiary outside of Florence, Colorado.

Note: Most state prisons have three security level designations—minimum, medium, and maximum security.

MORE ON SUPERMAX

America's only federal Supermax prison, commonly known as ADX Florence, was built in 1994. It is for male prisoners deemed too violent, too escape-prone, too high-profile, or too high a national security risk to be housed at a high-security prison. The facility is ringed by a 12-foot-tall concrete wall and several rings of razor wire fencing; armed guards and attack dogs patrol the perimeter. There are also pressure-sensitive alarm pads on the grounds outside the prison, as well as laser-based alarms. The prison has 490 single-occupant 7-by-12-foot cells. Prisoners are confined to their cells for 23 hours a day for their first year of confinement, but that may be gradually reduced, depending on conduct. The cells are soundproof, so prisoners cannot communicate with each other, and the cell doors are solid steel, with slots to allow items to be passed in and out. Time outside of the cells is spent in a windowless concrete gym (described as being like an empty swimming pool), with a single small skylight in its ceiling. Prisoners are never allowed outside. There is no mess hall (all other security levels have communal dining halls); all meals are brought by guards to the prisoners' cells. Outside visitors are allowed, as with all other security levels, but visiting rights at ADX Florence are highly restricted.

Famous Prisoners: Current ADX Florence inmates include Unabomber Ted Kaczynski, Soviet spy Robert Hanssen, 9/11 attack planner Zacarias Moussaoui, Boston Marathon bomber Dzhokhar Tsarnaev, and former Aryan Brotherhood leader Thomas Silverstein. (Silverstein was a convicted armed robber, but he committed three murders, including one of a prison guard, while in other federal prisons. He is deemed the most dangerous prisoner currently in the U.S. prison system, and ADX Florence was built specifically with him in mind.)

WOMEN'S PRISONS

Until the late 1800s, women convicted of serious crimes in the United States were sent to men's prisons, and were housed with men. In the latter half of the century, reform movements began advocating for separate institutions for incarcerated women, and in the 1870s, the first prisons exclusively for female inmates were built. The Indiana Woman's Prison, built in 1873 and located just outside of Indianapolis, was the first adult female correctional facility in the United States. The Federal Industrial Institution for Women in Alderson, West Virginia, built in 1927, was the first federal prison for women.

Jails can simply house female inmates in separate cells, although most cities with large jail systems have separate wings for female prisoners.

One of the most pressing issues involving incarcerated women is providing health care to those who enter prison while pregnant, or become pregnant while in prison. More than 2,000 babies are born in U.S. prisons every year. Most are taken away from the mothers and given to family members or placed in foster homes within 48 hours of birth. But there are currently nine states that have prison nurseries in which women can live with their babies, in some cases for up to one year.

PRISON NUMBERS

The U.S. prison population was fairly stable for most of the 20th century. Then changes in laws, especially drug laws, caused the number of inmates to rise dramatically. In 1973, there were about 200,000 people in state and federal prisons; by 2015, there were about 1.5 million. With the number of inmates in jails added to the number in prisons, the total number of incarcerated people in the United States rises to about 2.2 million, by far the most of any nation. (China is second with about 1.6 million, and Russia is third with about 870,000.)

• The United States has about 5 percent of the world's population—and about 25 percent of the world's incarcerated population.

• There are about 205,000 women in American prisons and jails, the most of any country. (China comes in a distant second at around 84,000, and Russia is third with around 59,000.)

• Other types of incarceration facilities in the United States include more than 2,200 juvenile detention facilities, dozens of military prisons (such as the Guantanamo Bay detention camp in Cuba), and around 80 tribal jails on Native American reservations across the country.

RANDOM FACTS

• The country with the smallest prison population: San Marino, a tiny independent state on the Italian peninsula. It has just one jail, with a total of six cells. In 2009, there were 14 people in that jail at one time,

In 70 AD, Roman emperor Vespasian had urine collected from public urinals and sold for use in dyes.

making it an exceptionally high crime year. In a typical year, the jail is empty most of the time.

• Actor Leighton Meester, best known for her role as Blair Waldorf on the TV series *Gossip Girl*, was born in a federal prison in Texas, where her mother was serving time for her part in a drug-smuggling operation. Her mother was able to care for her for three months in a halfway house, after which she had to return to prison. Meester lived with her grandmother until her mother was released.

• In 2015, the Pendleton Correctional Facility, a state prison in Indiana, started a program in which inmates take care of cats that were adopted from a local animal shelter. The cats live in a large, revamped office with lots of windows and several cat climbing trees, and inmates have to sign up to get a shift feeding, grooming, and just hanging out with them. The program is hugely popular with the inmates. "Love will change characteristics from anybody's tortured past," inmate Lamar Hal told reporters. "That goes for animals *and* humans, really."

*   *   *

SINCERELY, STEVE MARTIN

In the 1970s and 1980s, comedian Steve Martin responded to fan mail with a form letter that had several fill-in-the-blanks, and he didn't fill in the blanks.

```
Dear _____,

What a pleasure it was to receive a letter from you.
Although my schedule is very busy, I decided to take
the time out to write you a personal reply.

Too often performers lose contact with their audience
and begin to take them for granted, but I don't think
that will ever happen to me, will it _____? I don't
know when I'll be appearing close to you, but keep
that extra bunk made up in case I get to _____.

                              Sincerely,
                              Steve Martin

P.S. I'll always cherish that afternoon we spent
together in Rio, walking along the beach, looking
at _____.
```

It's a Ghost(writer)!

From our don't-believe-everything-you-read department: just because a book or movie is credited to a certain writer, that doesn't mean they didn't have a little help...or a lot.

Author Katharine Anne Porter wrote the best-selling 1962 novel *Ship of Fools*, and in 1966 won a Pulitzer Prize and a National Book Award for her short-story anthology *The Collected Stories*. But when she was starting out, she was just trying to pay the bills. Her first published work was ghostwriting *My Chinese Marriage*, a 1921 book about one of the first interracial marriages in the United States.

✍ James Ramsey Ullman was the runner-up for the 1955 Newbery Medal for his popular children's novel *Banner in the Sky*, an adventure about mountaineering in the Alps. (Disneyland based its Matterhorn attraction on the book.) Before Ullman, a real mountaineer, struck it big with *Banner*, he ghostwrote other books about mountain climbing. Among them was *Man of Everest*, the "autobiography" of Tenzing Norgay, the Sherpa who accompanied Edmund Hillary on his ascent of Mount Everest in 1953.

✍ Academy Award–winning screenwriter Adam McKay (*The Big Short*) is best known for his comedies, which he writes with Will Ferrell. When Ferrell got the starring role in *Elf* in 2003, he had the producers hire McKay to rewrite the script. McKay's work on the film was uncredited.

✍ In 1930, Sinclair Lewis became the first American to win the Nobel Prize for Literature. His body of work includes classics such as *Babbitt*, *Arrowsmith*, and *Elmer Gantry*. It also includes ghostwriting tennis star Maurice McLoughlin's 1915 instructional book *Tennis as I Play It*.

✍ Kenneth Lonergan is an acclaimed playwright, with works such as *This Is Our Youth* and *The Starry Messenger*. But writing plays doesn't pay much, so he took jobs punching up movie scripts such as *Analyze This* and *The Adventures of Rocky and Bullwinkle*. He secretly wrote several drafts (and wasn't credited) on the 2008 Matthew McConaughey romantic comedy *Fool's Gold*.

✍ One of the best-selling business and self-help books of all time is *The 7 Habits of Highly Effective People*, by businessman Stephen Covey.

One of the habits must be outsourcing, because it was written by a ghostwriter named Ken Shelton.

✍ *The Personal Memoirs of Ulysses S. Grant* was written in 1885, as the former president and Civil War general was dying of cancer, and was published just after his death. Some historians suspect that Grant was in no shape to write a book, and the writing style suggests he may have had a ghostwriter: his close friend Mark Twain.

✍ Actor Edward Norton almost always does a rewrite on his own movies. He also did an uncredited rewrite on the 2002 Frida Kahlo biographical film *Frida*. His girlfriend at the time, Salma Hayek, produced and starred in the movie.

✍ In 1924, the science-fiction pulp magazine *Weird Tales* published *Imprisoned with the Pharaohs*, a supposedly autobiographical story by Harry Houdini. The plot: Houdini is kidnapped by a tour guide near the Great Sphinx, thrown in a hole, and escapes. It probably didn't happen, and it's definitely not autobiographical, because it was actually written by *Weird Tales* staff writer (and future horror legend) H. P. Lovecraft.

✍ On the eve of filming, producers of the 1994 action movie *Speed* were unhappy with the shooting script, written by Graham Yost (who would later go on to create the TV series *Justified*). So they hired a "script doctor" named Joss Whedon (who would later go on to create the TV series *Buffy the Vampire Slayer*) to punch up the screenplay. He went beyond the call of duty because, according to Yost, Whedon ended up writing "98.8 percent of the dialogue."

✍ Two of the most famous adventure novels of all time are *The Three Musketeers* and *The Count of Monte Cristo*. They were both written in 1844 by French author Alexandre Dumas. Well, partially. Dumas wrote the finished manuscripts, but detailed plot outlines were given to him by a failed playwright and ghostwriter named Auguste Maquet.

✍ In the 1990s, actor William Shatner became a science-fiction author with a book series called *TekWar*, which was expanded into comic books and a video game. While Shatner came up with some rough outlines of plots and characters (on the set of *Star Trek V: The Final Frontier*) and is credited as the author, it's sci-fi writer Ron Goulart who actually wrote the *TekWar* books. It's easy to tell because Goulart lifted elements and passages from *Brainz Inc.*, his own 1985 novel.

The first successful TV broadcast (1928) was viewed on 1.5-inch screens.

Unsung War Heroes: The Polish Schindlers

You've probably heard of Oskar Schindler, the German industrialist who saved the lives of 1,200 Jews during the Holocaust. Here's a story you probably haven't heard—about two men who pulled off a similar miracle in Poland.

OCCUPATION

Dr. Eugene Lazowski was a young Red Cross physician living in the village of Rozwadow during the Nazi occupation of Poland in World War II. Life in Poland under German occupation was a time of unimaginable suffering and horror. By the time the Soviet Union's Red Army finally drove the Germans out in 1945, one fifth of the entire Polish population had been murdered, including 3 million of Poland's 3.4 million Jews, and 3 million Polish Gentiles. Millions more Poles were arrested and put to work in forced labor camps, including 1.6 million who were sent to camps in Germany.

As a physician, Lazowski did what he could to alleviate the suffering of his countrymen. A member of the Polish resistance, he provided medical care and supplies to resistance fighters hiding in the forests around Rozwadow. Lazowski's house backed up against the Jewish ghetto, and though assisting Jews in any way was punishable by death, he set up a system whereby Jews who needed medical attention could let him know by hanging a piece of white cloth on his back fence, then return after dark to be treated and given medicine that Lazowski passed through a hole in the fence. "Every night a white cloth would fly and lines would form," Dr. Yoav Goor wrote in the *Israel Medical Association Journal* in 2013. "The Jews trusted him. He helped anyone who needed help, creating a system of faking his medicinal inventory to conceal this clandestine activity."

DISEASE

Lazowski's biggest opportunity to provide assistance came in 1942 when a fellow physician, Dr. Stanislaw Matulewicz, told him that he'd discovered a way to make healthy patients test positive for the deadly disease typhus. The Germans were terrified of typhus, which was spread by body lice. The disease killed as many as one in every four people who contracted it, and under battlefield conditions of close quarters and poor hygiene, it spread quickly from one soldier to another. A typhus epidemic could mean the difference between victory and defeat: during Napoleon's disastrous 1812 invasion of Russia, in which 570,000 of his 600,000 troops died, more soldiers were killed by typhus than by the Russians. During the Russian Civil War, which raged from 1917 to 1922, it's estimated that typhus killed more than 3 million people.

To prevent the same thing from happening again, the Nazis required physicians in German-occupied Europe to take blood samples from any patient they suspected of having typhus, and send the samples to German labs for analysis. The test was conducted by mixing the blood sample with some dead typhus cells. If the sample became cloudy, the patient had typhus. Gentiles with typhus were quarantined in their homes; Jews with typhus were shot and their houses burned to the ground.

FALSE POSITIVE

What Matulewicz had discovered was that if he injected some of the dead (and therefore harmless) typhus cells into a patient before taking the blood sample, the sample would test positive for typhus even though the patient did not have the disease. When he told Lazowski about his discovery, Lazowski suggested creating a fake typhus epidemic in Rozwadow by injecting villagers with dead typhus cells. The Germans, he hoped, would quarantine the villagers in their homes and leave them alone.

From then on, every time Lazowski or Matulewicz treated non-Jewish patients, the doctors injected them with the dead typhus virus without telling them what they were doing or why. (Since Jews risked being shot if they tested positive for typhus, they were not injected with the virus.) To avoid attracting suspicion, rather than take blood samples from all the patients they injected, the doctors referred some patients to other physicians in the area to have their blood drawn there. That way, every doctor in the area submitted samples that tested positive for typhus, not just Lazowski and Matulewicz. The two men then paced their injections, referrals, and blood sample submissions to mimic the spread of a real typhus epidemic.

KEEP OUT

Within weeks, the Germans began posting signs around Rozwadow that warned, "*Achtung, Fleckfieber!*" ("Warning, Typhus!"). As time passed, the "epidemic" spread to nearby communities—about a dozen villages in all. These were home to some 8,000 Polish Gentiles and an unknown number of Jews in hiding. (By then, most of the Jewish population of Rozwadow had been deported to labor camps or death camps.) All of the villages fell under the quarantine, and German soldiers began to avoid them entirely, giving the residents their first feeling of safety,

Premature babies in incubators were a sideshow attraction on Coney Island until the early 1940s.

however fragile, since the Nazi invasion of Poland in September 1939.

Faking a deadly epidemic right under the noses of the Germans was a dangerous ruse. "I was scared," Lazowski admitted in an interview with the *Chicago Sun-Times* in 2001. "I didn't know if I would be arrested and tortured by the Gestapo. So I carried a cyanide pill in case I was arrested."

The danger grew as time passed and nobody died; some of the villagers even began to suspect that something was afoot. Most kept quiet, though, either for their own personal safety or (if they guessed who was behind the ruse) to protect Lazowski and Matulewicz. But every Polish community had its German collaborators, and when those living in and around Rozwadow passed their suspicions on to the Germans, a team of Nazi physicians was dispatched to Rozwadow to investigate.

WELCOME MAT

Lazowski was ready. He greeted the physicians on the outskirts of Rozwadow with a feast of sausages, vodka—both hard to come by during the war—and musical entertainment. Just as Lazowski hoped, the senior doctors stayed to enjoy the party, dispatching their two young subordinates to perform the unpleasant and (as far as they knew) dangerous task of entering the quarantine area to examine infected villagers to see if they really had typhus. The patients waiting to be examined were the oldest and sickest-looking people that Lazowski could find, and he put them up in the most ramshackle, lice-ridden huts in the village.

Examining patients for typhus exposes physicians to the risk of contracting the disease themselves, and the young doctors weren't fools. Rather than give the patients thorough medical exams, they merely took blood samples. They raced through the process as quickly as possible, then beat it back to the party before the vodka and sausages ran out.

The blood samples tested positive for typhus, of course, and the Nazis didn't bother Lazowski or Matulewicz again until the end of the war. They even left Lazowski alone after collaborators reported him for treating members of the Polish resistance, who were fighting a savage guerrilla war against the Nazis. "They didn't kill me because I was needed to fight the typhus epidemic," he recalled. "I was kind of a hero to the Germans because I was a young doctor who was not afraid to be infected."

ESCAPE

By early 1945, however, when the war was clearly lost and Rozwadow was about to be overrun by the Red Army, the Germans were more

Kohei Nawa, a Japanese artist, had an exhibit consisting of a dark room filled with foam. Title: *Foam.*

interested in punishing people who'd aided the Polish resistance than they were in containing the typhus epidemic. Lazowski was marked for death by the Nazis; he and his wife and daughter only managed to escape to Warsaw after a German soldier he'd treated for venereal disease warned him that he was about to be arrested.

AFTERMATH

Both Lazowski and Matulewicz survived the war. In 1958, Lazowski emigrated to the United States, where he became a professor of pediatrics at the University of Illinois Medical Center. It was only after he arrived in Chicago that he began to speak of his wartime experiences; until then, not even his wife knew the full story of what he and Matulewicz had been up to. In Poland, Lazowski had been afraid of reprisals from Polish anti-Semites and wartime collaborators of the Nazis, but now he felt free to tell his story.

In the 1990s, Lazowski and Matulewicz wrote a memoir called *Private War*. Published in Poland, it told their story to their countrymen for the first time and was a best-seller. In 2000, the two men, now well into their eighties, made their first trip back to Rozwadow since the end of the war. They received a warm welcome from the villagers, including many old enough to remember being treated by the physicians. Some villagers still did not realize the full extent of the ruse that the doctors had played on the Nazis during the war. When one man approached Lazowski and thanked him effusively for the "miracle" of curing his father's typhus in only five days, all Lazowski could do was smile. "It was not real typhus," he said. "It was my typhus."

*   *   *

SHOULD HAVE STAYED HOME

Janet Faal developed such a severe case of agoraphobia—the fear of open spaces—that she only left her home in West Sussex, England, twice in ten years. Then, in 2015, the 57-year-old grandmother was urged by a friend to go for a drive. Reluctantly, Faal agreed. "I was help-ing her reverse out of a parking lot," Faal told the *Telegraph*, "and there was this wooden pallet in the way." So she moved it. Unfortunately, she didn't notice that the pallet was covering an open manhole...and she fell in. Faal was trapped for an hour before paramedics rescued her. "It was awful," she said. "I was in the hole with blood all over me and I couldn't move." Faal suffered several bruises, two black eyes, a broken nose, and a broken leg. She said the incident has set her condition "back years."

Fascinating Foreign Phrases

Don't give us any pumpkins—you're going to love these foreign phrases!

"TO HAVE A WIDE FACE" (Japanese)

Translation: *Kao ga hiroi* (kah-oh gah hee-ro-ee)

Meaning: To have many friends; to know and be known by many people

Explanation: This is considered an important compliment, especially in the highly competitive Japanese business world, where someone with many personal connections—or a "wide face"—has a better chance of a successful career than someone without that status. How the phrase came to be is uncertain, but it's probably related to the powerful Japanese (and broadly Asian) concept of "face," meaning dignity, prestige, or social standing.

"TO GIVE SOMEONE PUMPKINS" (Spanish)

Translation: *Dar calabazas a alguien* (dar kahl-ah-bah-sahs ah al-ghee-en)

Meaning: To reject a suitor; to give someone the cold shoulder

Explanation: This odd phrase dates back to the late 1700s. Its most common origin story claims it comes from the ancient Greek belief that pumpkins are antiaphrodisiacs. A more interesting version: people in Spain once used pumpkins as flotation devices while learning how to swim. When someone learned to swim on their own, they could "give someone their pumpkins"—so they could swim away and be free.

"IN THE MOUTH OF A WOLF" (Italian)

Translation: *In bocca al lupo* (in bok-ah ahl loo-po)

Meaning: Good luck!

Explanation: You might say this to someone facing a difficult task, like an exam or job interview. According to one origin story, it came from the opera world. From the stage of an opera house, the audience chamber could be said to look like a large mouth, and performers took to telling each other *In bocca al lupo!* as a counterintuitive wish of good luck—similar to the English theater-based saying "Break a leg!" Another story claims that the saying is related to the ancient Roman myth of Romulus, the founder of Rome, and his twin brother, Remus, who were protected and raised by a she-wolf. In this version, the saying is used in a more straightforward sense, akin to "May you be protected by a wolf," although many say it still carries the sense of standing up to danger or difficulty, and is meant as a call to courage. The proper response to *In bocca al lupo!* is *Crepi il lupo!*—which translates basically to, "May the wolf die!"

"NOT MY CIRCUS, NOT MY MONKEYS" (Polish)

Translation: *Nie mój cyrk, nie moje małpy* (nyeh moy serk, nyeh moy-uh mahl-peh)

Meaning: It's not my problem; I don't care

Explanation: The meaning of this phrase is pretty straightforward, and can be used in a variety of situations. A common instance where it might be used is when someone is trying to get someone to help them clean up some kind of messy situation.

> **BRI Jay:** Uncle John! You've gotta help Brian! He tried that get-rich-quick scheme you recommended—and now the FBI is after him!
>
> **Uncle John:** Not my circus, not my monkeys.

"TO HAVE TO ZERO" (French)

Translation: *Les avoir à zero* (layz ah-vwah a zear-o)

Meaning: To be really frightened; to be petrified

Explanation: This slang French idiom literally translates to "have them to zero"—which makes no sense. But there's an implied word missing in this phrase: to French speakers it means, "To have one's testicles down to zero." (And that's *really* afraid.)

* * *

COMMON PHRASES THAT ORIGINATED IN THE BIBLE

- The blind leading the blind
- A drop in the bucket
- Sign of the times
- How the mighty have fallen
- Can a leopard change his spots?
- The powers that be
- Nothing but skin and bones
- The writing is on the wall
- There's nothing new under the sun

HELP WANTED

Times have changed. Today we have appliances to make household chores easier. In the old days, people didn't have labor-saving devices…but they did have servants. How to manage them was a popular topic for advice books of the day. Here are a few examples.

The true gentleman is never arrogant, or overbearing, or rude to domestics. His commands are requests, and all services, no matter how humble the servant, are received with thanks, as if they were favors. There is no surer sign of vulgarity than a needless assumption of the tone of authority and a haughty and supercilious bearing toward servants and inferiors in station generally. It is a small thing to say, 'I thank you,' but those little words are often better than gold."
—How to Behave (1857)

"The one thing which every lady must firmly demand from her servants is respect. The harassed American woman who has to cope with the worst servants in the world—the ill-trained, incapable, and vicious peasantry of Europe, who come here to be 'as good as anybody,' and who see that it is easily possible to make a living in America whether they are respectful or not—that woman has an arduous task to perform."
—Manners and Social Usages (1887)

"In the treatment of servants a man must exercise an iron will. He can be kind and considerate, but he must never descend to dispute with one, and certainly not swear at him…Once in a while give them a holiday, or an evening off, a cash remembrance at Christmas, and from time to time some part of your wardrobe or cast-off clothing. They are just like children, and must be treated with the rigor and mild discipline which a schoolmaster uses toward his pupils."
—The Complete Bachelor: Manners for Men (1896)

"The real charity is to keep servants steadily to their duties. They are a class of persons to whom leisure is destruction; the pursuits of their idle hours are seldom advantageous to them, and theirs are not minds which can thrive in repose. Idleness, to them, is peculiarly the root of all evil, for, if their time is not spent in vicious amusements, it is often passed in slander, discontent, or vanity. The loud and crying complaints of the worthlessness of this class are but too justly founded."
—The Ladies' Book of Etiquette, and Manual of Politeness (1872)

World's oldest newspaper still in circulation: Holland's *Haarlems Dagblad*, which dates to 1656.

Secrets of the Movie Costumes

When we watch a movie, we look at the scenery, listen to the dialogue and the music…and we probably miss a lot of carefully designed details. It turns out, for example, that much more goes on behind the scenes of movie costume design than we realize.

Film: *Iron Man* (2008–2016)
Costume: The Iron Man and War Machine suits
The Secret: No pants. To achieve a larger-than-life look, the Iron Man and War Machine suits are built elongated so that they're more dramatic than the normal human form. But being out of proportion to the actors' bodies makes the costumes uncomfortable to wear. The solution? In most scenes, Robert Downey Jr. and Don Cheadle wear only a chest piece that covers them from the waist up. When a full-body shot is needed, the costumes have snap-on legs that can be used, or the leg armor is added digitally in postproduction.

Film: *The Hunger Games: Mockingjay Part 1* and *Part 2* (2014–2015)
Costume: Peeta's wardrobe
The Secret: Peeta begins *Mockingjay* as a rebel, but he is captured by the government, tortured, and brainwashed. To emphasize his decline, designers Kurt and Bart deliberately dressed Peeta in three colors. His clothes start in white, then change to black as the brainwashing takes effect, and finally end in gray when Peeta's been completely broken.

Film: *The Matrix* trilogy (1999–2003)
Costume: The clothes worn inside the Matrix
The Secret: Costume designer Kym Barrett and writer/directors Larry and Andy Wachowski decided that the color blue wouldn't exist inside the computer-generated world of the Matrix. But green would. In fact, every costume is tinted green—even shirts that appear white on screen were actually given a green dye bath.

Film: *Cinderella* (2015)
Costume: The glass slippers
The Secret: Cinderella's glass slippers were based on a 19th-century shoe that costume designer Sandy Powell saw in a museum, and made

by the Swarovski crystal company. Only problem: with a five-inch heel and no additional platform for support, star Lily James couldn't walk in them. So she wore leather shoes and CGI artists placed the glass slippers on Cinderella's feet in postproduction.

The Film: *Maleficent* (2014)
The Costume: Maleficent's horns
The Secret: In 1959, Disney's animators drew Sleeping Beauty's nemesis with a dramatic set of horns on her head. For the 2014 live-action film, Angelina Jolie wore horns made of urethane resin. But the design team didn't want her to be uncomfortable or to risk injury if the horns caught on something during stunts. The solution: magnets. Jolie wore a skullcap that had the first inch of horns built in, and then the rest of the horns were attached with magnets. That way, the horns could easily be removed between takes to let Jolie rest, and would break away if they got snagged during stunts, rather than wrenching her neck.

The Film: *The Great Gatsby* (2013)
The Costume: Tom Buchanan's suits
The Secret: Wealthy, arrogant Tom Buchanan is a graduate of Yale, and it's implied that he was a member of the secret Skull & Bones Society. For the film, costume designer Catherine Martin lined Buchanan's suits with skull-and-bones-patterned silk—which isn't even visible on camera. Reason: to help actor Joel Edgerton feel in character.

The Film: *Mirror, Mirror* (2012)
The Costume: The Evil Queen's wedding gown
The Secret: Costume designer Eiko Ishioka created a massive wedding gown for the Evil Queen—an 8-foot-diameter dress made from 30 yards of fabric, weighing a whopping 60 pounds. It was so heavy that Julia Roberts pulled a thigh muscle when she turned too quickly during a scene.

The Film: *Guardians of the Galaxy* (2014)
The Costume: Prison uniforms
The Secret: When the film's heroes are sent to a galactic prison, they wear yellow jumpsuits. If you look closely, you'll see markings on the jumpsuit legs that are unique to each character. That's because designer Alexandra Byrne created a bar code system to denote how many and what kind of crimes each prisoner had committed, a detail that's never explained in the movie. Byrne feels that when every costume has a backstory—even one that only the actors know—it adds to the film's atmosphere.

Bathroom Sounds

*Here are three smartphone apps that may make your next
bathroom visit a little noisier…but in a good way.*

BATHROOM SOUNDSCAPE
What It Does: It masks the sounds people make in the bathroom.

Details: App creator Bag-Head Squidman (a.k.a. David Renardy and Olivia Walch) says it created Bathroom Soundscape for those times when you have to make a pit stop in someone's house, only to discover that the bathroom doesn't have a noisy fan to cover up the embarrassing noises you're about to make. "Blow away your cares with the 'Classic Fan' sound," says the company. "Rinse yourself of shame with the 'Sink' sound. Steam things up with the 'Shower' sound." Using the app will unlock other sounds, including "Toothbrush," "Bubbles," and… you'll just have to find out for yourself.

PEE BUTTON

What It Does: Gives new meaning to the term "streaming audio"

Details: The app appears on your smartphone screen as a big green button with the words "GO PEE" on it. Choose from four different sounds. Pee Button can be used to pull pranks on people who won't know where the sound is coming from. It can also serve a more serious purpose: helping people with *paruresis*, or "shy bladder syndrome," according to the creator, H&G Mobile Apps. If the user stands at the urinal and nothing happens, they can activate the peeing sound and use the noise to hide their shame.

PEEAID

What it Does: It's another app for people with shy bladders.

Details: Why settle for tricking people into thinking you peed when modern technology can help you do the real thing? That's where PeeAid comes in. For a lot of shy bladder sufferers, it's easier to get the flow going when they hear water running, which is what this app is for. It lets the user choose between "slowly running water," "shower," "watering the grass," and other sounds. Wear earbuds so that no one will know what you're listening to, then start the app, and (hopefully) pee to your heart's content. There's even a timer function that lets you walk to the restroom with your phone in your pocket before the water sounds start to play.

Bad news: 8,000 Americans are bitten by poisonous snakes each year. Good news: Fewer than 10 die.

More Other Googles

*On page 168 we told you about some of Google's oddball competitors.
There are many, but we only picked a few. Here are
a few more (that we Googled).*

CHACHA. Want a more personal Internet search engine experience? Go to ChaCha, where you can search for information online—and get an actual human to help you in real time. That help is performed by "guides"—freelance workers hired and trained by ChaCha to help users get the information they want. Pay rate: about $0.02 per question. Sample: We asked, "How many bathrooms are there in the White House?" About three minutes later, a guide named Kelsey (in Pioneer, California) told us, "According to the official White House web page, there are 35 bathrooms in the White House, none of which are public bathrooms." (Why is it called ChaCha? It comes from the Mandarin Chinese word *cha*—which means "search.")

CC SEARCH. "CC" stands for "Creative Commons," the American nonprofit organization dedicated to making creative works available for public use—legally and for free. CC Search is their search engine. Do you need some artwork—drawings, writings, photos, music—for a project, either for private use or for a commercial product (such as artwork for a CD)? Go to CC Search. If you need a drawing of a platypus, for example—or a photo, an article, or even a song about platypuses—enter "platypus" into the CC Search search bar, and then wait for results from sites that include YouTube, Google Images, the photo website Flickr, the music site SoundCloud, and the free artwork site OpenClipArt. You can filter your search to find artwork that can be used commercially, and/or work you can modify and build upon—and CC Search will bring back links to works you are free to use for those purposes.
Important Note: CC Search can't guarantee that all results will be fully available for use. There are different degrees of public domain status under the law, so make sure you do additional research to determine what you're actually free to use.

WOLFRAMALPHA. WolframAlpha isn't exactly a search engine— it's a "computational knowledge engine." It doesn't simply provide links to other websites (although it sometimes does do that), it scours the Internet for facts and data about search items, assesses that information with it own algorithms, and gives you what it determines to be the most relevant information about your search. Example: enter the word "oxidation," and you'll get its scientific definition, its pronunciation, how often the word has been used throughout history, synonyms, rhymes, anagrams, translations of the word into other languages… and the basic score "oxidation" would get in the boardgame Scrabble. WolframAlpha also answers math queries, from the simple to the complex, and you can even ask it plain old questions such as, "Where was LeBron James born?" (Result: "Akron, Ohio.") It also answers oddball questions. We asked, "How many roads must a man walk down?" Result: "The answer, my friend, is blowin' in the wind."

OTHER SITES TO SEE

• FedWorld is the search engine maintained by the United States government. It allows users to search the millions of digital documents created by federal government departments and agencies, including the White House, the FBI, CIA, NASA, EPA, and many more.

• FreeBookSearch scrubs the web for eBooks available to read for free, usually in PDF format. (Some of the results link to books that can be downloaded to e-reading devices.)

• TinEye is a reverse-search engine for images. Upload an image from your computer or smartphone to TinEye—or just enter a link to an image online—and TinEye will give you links to websites that have the same image, or similar ones, allowing you to learn more about the image, or possibly find a higher-resolution version of it.

• FindSounds is just what you'd think. It allows users to search for recorded sounds from more than one million online sources. (We entered "throat clearing" and got 17 results. And 200 for "fart.")

• WhatToRent gives you movie recommendations. Choose a user name, fill out a questionnaire about yourself, answer a few more questions about your current mood, and it recommends a film. Don't want to watch that one? Tell it, and it will choose another.

• Music-Map provides a virtual "map" of musically related musicians. Enter "Neil Young," and it gives you a page with Young's name in the center, and a bunch of other musicians' names floating around it. The closer the name is to Young, the closer the artist's music is. You may not agree with the map, but it is fascinating.

• SodaFinder allows to search for hard-to-find soda brands, which you can get shipped straight to your home. (Are you pining for a Pittsburgh, Pennsylvania, favorite—Tom Tucker Southern Style Mint Ginger Ale? You can find it on SodaFinder.)

• Yandex is Russia's most popular search engine. Sample use: we entered "Superman." The results were in Russian. We can't read Russian.

In the early 1800s, men *and* women wore corsets.

Microwave Memories

*Do you remember when microwave ovens became standard fixtures
in American homes of the 1970s? If you do, you may also recall
how cookbooks of the era were filled with recipes for dishes that
really had no business being cooked in a microwave. Return
with us now to those thrilling days of yesteryear…*

MAJOR APPLIANCE

Microwave oven technology has been around since 1947, but it took 20 years for manufacturers to figure out how to make microwaves small enough and cheap enough for the home kitchen. The earliest models, sold to restaurants and commercial kitchens, cost $5,000 ($52,000 in today's dollars), weighed more than 700 pounds, and were as big as refrigerators. Many of the restaurants that bought microwaves used them to reheat already-cooked dishes that had gone cold.

By the mid-1960s, microwaves were small enough to sit on a kitchen counter and cost around $500 ($3,400 today). That was still a lot of money (a 1967 Ford Mustang cost just $2,400), and to entice consumers into buying them, manufacturers and appliance dealers promoted them with a lot of hype. They claimed that microwaves could do anything that conventional ovens could do, in only a fraction of the time, and with much greater convenience. An entire industry of microwave-related products—including cookbooks, cookware, and specially formulated mixes for pies, cakes, casseroles, and other foods sprung up to feed the public's fascination with these new devices.

But microwaves seldom delivered on their promise, as many a homemaker discovered by ruining one cooked-from-scratch meal after another before finally giving up and using their microwave the same way restaurants had in the 1940s: to reheat food that had been cooked some other way.

MICRO-MANAGING

Even referring to microwaves as "ovens" is a bit of a stretch, because they cook food differently. Conventional ovens use what is called a "dry heat" process, applying an external heat source at temperatures ranging from 300°F to 525°F to cook the food. Though microwaves may appear to use dry heat, they are actually using a peculiar form of "moist heat" cooking, similar to boiling or steaming. The short-wavelength radio waves generated inside a microwave oven penetrate about an inch and a half into the food and cause the water molecules in the food to vibrate. The friction generated by the vibrating molecules produces the heat that cooks the food. (Though the oven is full of microwave energy, the only heat inside the oven comes from the cooking food itself.)

THE REST OF THE STORY

But there's a catch: water has a boiling point of just 212°F, a temperature too low to produce the rich tastes, textures, and aromas produced by roasting, baking, or broiling food in a conventional oven. (When was the last time you set an oven to 212°F?) Meats don't brown, breads don't form a crust, and foods containing natural sugars don't caramelize or turn a golden color. On large pieces of meat and poultry, such as roasts and whole chickens, the outside can become dried out before the inside has had a chance to cook. Cakes, pies, and cookies "baked" in a microwave can end up tough and chewy on the outside and soggy on the inside. And microwave ovens also have "hot spots," where microwave energy concentrates and overcooks food. Few early microwaves had turntables to counteract this effect.

While there were fixes for some of the problems associated with microwave cooking, such as covering parts of a chicken with foil to deflect microwave energy and prevent overcooking, they were often so complicated and time-consuming that the purpose of owning a microwave in the first place—speed and convenience—was defeated entirely. But you wouldn't have learned any of this from your appliance dealer or from the microwave cookbooks of the 1970s, which were filled with recipes for everything from steaks and cakes to chicken chow mein—few of which, we're betting, many people bothered to prepare more than once. Here are some of the odd, inappropriate, and (in some cases) truly disgusting recipes we've dug up from microwave cookbooks of the past:

NO STIR/NO FRY STIR-FRIED SHRIMP WITH GARLIC

"Sprinkle 2 tbsp. of salt over 1 pound medium raw shrimp that's been shelled and de-veined. Mix well, then rinse in cold water for about 5 minutes to remove salt. Drain and dry on paper towels, then mix shrimp with 3 minced garlic cloves, 2 tbsp. dry sherry, ¼ teaspoon salt, and 1 tbsp. vegetable oil. Arrange in a single layer around the sides of a heat-proof baking dish, leaving the center unfilled. Cook on high 2 minutes, then mix well and rearrange shrimp in a single layer around the sides of the dish. Cook on high 1½ minutes more, then serve."

NO-FUN FONDUE

No fondue set? No problem! "Pour 1 cup dry white wine and two cloves peeled and smashed garlic into a 1-quart soufflé dish. Microwave on high for 5 minutes. Place ½ pound Swiss Gruyére or Emmentaler cheese in the work bowl of a food processor and pour the wine and garlic mixture over it. Process for two minutes, then pour back into soufflé dish. Microwave uncovered on high for 2 minutes, then stir and microwave on high for 2 minutes longer. Stir in 2 tsp. cherry brandy; serve with bread chunks for dipping (use fondue forks). Reheat in microwave as needed."

BEEF BRAIN SALAD

"Rinse brain in cold water, then remove the *medula*, or middle part of the brain connecting the two hemispheres. Place the hemispheres, rounded side up, in a 2-quart soufflé dish. Combine ½ cup water and 2 tsp. malt vinegar and pour over brain. Cover and cook on high for 4 minutes, then turn brain over and cook on high for another 4 minutes. Drain brain and let stand until cool, then cut into ¼-inch slices and arrange on a serving platter on a bed of escarole lettuce leaves. Combine 1 tsp. tarragon vinegar, 3 tsp. olive oil, 1 tsp. minced tarragon, ½ tsp. salt, 1 finely chopped hard-boiled egg, and 1 tsp. minced shallot and pour over brain. Serve with freshly ground black pepper."

THANKSGIVING TURKEY

"Remove giblets; fill the turkey with stuffing of your choice. Tie drumsticks together and secure wings to bird with kitchen twine. Place turkey breast side down on a microwave-proof roasting rack in a microwave-proof baking dish. Microwave on high power for five minutes per pound. During cooking, look for areas that are browner than the rest of the bird and shield with aluminum foil. (Using small amounts of foil to shield food from overcooking is safe, as long as you leave most of the food uncovered.) When cooking has finished, drain fat from baking dish and turn turkey breast side up. Insert temperature probe in thickest part of thigh, and let microwave to cook at medium power until the probe reaches 180°. Let stand ten to fifteen minutes before carving."

For Best Results:

• "Pop-up thermometers are not inserted deeply enough into the turkey to give proper readings when microwaving. Test for doneness using a standard meat thermometer."

• "Turkeys over 12 lbs. are difficult to cook evenly in a microwave."

CAPPUCCINOS

"Pour 2 cups of milk into a 4-cup glass measuring cup. Microwave until milk is hot but not boiling, 3 to 3½ minutes. Stir in four tsp. sugar and two tsp. instant coffee. For a dessert drink, add four ounces of brandy and four ounces of grated semisweet chocolate to milk before heating; top with whipped cream. Serves four."

Salvador Dalí designed surreal Christmas cards for Hallmark in 1959. They flopped.

TACO HOT DOGS

"Combine 2 tbsp. bottled taco sauce, ½ cup of grated cheddar cheese, 2 tbsp. of chopped onion and 2 tbsp. of chopped green chilies. Slit four hot dogs lengthwise and stuff with three-fourths of the cheese mixture. Place stuffed hot dogs in taco shells and stand shells upright in a micro-wave-proof baking dish. Spoon the rest of the cheese mixture into the taco shells. Microwave on high for 1½ to 2 minutes; top with shredded lettuce, garbanzo beans and guacamole dip. Serve immediately."

PECAN PIE

"Roll pastry dough into a 12-inch circle, then place in one 9-inch glass pie plate. Trim and flute edges, prick with a fork, and set aside. Combine ¼ cup melted butter or margarine, ⅓ cup brown sugar, 1 cup dark corn syrup, 3 eggs, 1½ tsp. all-purpose flour, 1 tsp. vanilla, ⅛ tsp. salt, and 1 cup pecan halves. Pour mixture into pastry shell. Cook on defrost for 25 minutes. (Note: crust will not brown in the microwave. To improve pastry color, add 1 to 2 drops of yellow food coloring or brush diluted dark corn syrup on pastry before cooking.)"

CHEESEBURGERS

"Mix 1 lb. ground beef with 1 tsp. salt and ½ tsp. pepper. Shape into four patties; place patties in an 8-inch by 12-inch microwave-proof baking dish. Cover dish with wax paper and microwave on high for four minutes for rare burgers, and six minutes for medium burgers. Place each patty in its bun and top patties with a slice of cheese. Microwave each cheeseburger on medium for one additional minute or until the cheese melts."

MORE MICROWAVE "TIPS & TRICKS"

• "Do not attempt to operate the microwave with the door open."
• Bread baked by microwave "does not brown or form a crust, but this can be partially overcome by using toppings, frostings, and dark flours."
• "Popcorn will not cook in a microwave. It is too dry to attract microwave energy."

FINAL THOUGHT

"It was one of the most ghastly experiences of my life. The foodies thought I was insane—how could I do anything so demeaning?"
—Former *New York Times* microwave columnist Barbara Kafka, describing the public response to her 1987 cookbook, *The Microwave Gourmet*, which included instructions on how to kill a lobster in the microwave. "The humane types got all upset. But the lobster dies very quickly," she told the *Detroit News* in 2005.

Dogs can be trained to detect bedbugs.

Weird Celebrity Auctions

For some reason even the most mundane objects can become valuable if a celebrity owned—or even just touched—them.

Scarlett Johansson appeared on *The Tonight Show* in 2008 while sick with a cold. After the show, she was persuaded to put one of her used tissues in a plastic bag and autograph the bag. The bag and tissue sold for $5,300 on eBay. Proceeds were donated to USA Harvest, a charity that feeds homeless people.

• In 2010, a set of Marilyn Monroe's chest X-rays, taken in Florida in 1954, sold for $45,000 at a Las Vegas auction.

• Sometime in the 1960s, John Lennon gave a rotten, extracted tooth to his housekeeper, Dot Jarlett. Lennon wanted her to throw it away, but jokingly told her to give it to her Beatles-crazed daughter. Jarlett did indeed pass it along, and in 2011, the younger Jarlett sold it to Omega Auctions in London. It sold to a Canadian dentist named Michael Zuk for $31,200. Zuk has bizarre plans for the tooth: he wants to extract Lennon's DNA from it and someday create a John Lennon clone that "could be looked at as my son."

• Los Angeles police commissioner Steve Soboroff spotted pop star Rihanna at a Los Angeles Lakers game in May 2014. They met, but then Rihanna accidentally knocked Soboroff's phone out of his hand. When it fell to the ground and broke, the singer tried to make up for the loss by signing the phone, "Sorry, I love LAPD, Rihanna." Soboroff auctioned off the broken phone for $65,000 and donated the money to the LAPD Cadet Program.

• While Michael Jackson was filming a Pepsi commercial in 1984, a fireworks display went off too early, and Jackson's hair caught fire. He was badly burned, and in the chaos lots of his charred hair fell to the ground. A producer named Ralph Cohen collected some of it, and in 2009, he sold it at an auction. Price of 12 strands of the King of Pop's hair: $1,600.

• One of the black acrylic nails Lady Gaga wore during a 2012 concert in Dublin, Ireland, broke off during her performance. After the show, a member of the stage crew found it, snatched it up, and sold it for $13,000.

- In October 2014, Willie Nelson's signature braids were sold at an Arizona auction house for $37,000. They weren't even fresh. Cut off in the 1980s, Nelson had given them as a present to country singer Waylon Jennings.

- On a tour of Wales in 2004, Canadian pop star Bryan Adams took off his Armani socks in the back of a taxi. He left them behind, and the car company sent them to an auction house. Winning bid on the "Summer of '69" singer's dirty socks: £541, or about $770.

- In 1968, Queen Elizabeth II accidentally left behind a pair of mono-grammed silk underwear on a private plane in Chile. Years later, the pilot gave the panties to Miami artist Baron Joseph de Bicske Dobronyi, and in 2012 his family auctioned them off for $18,101.

- In a 2015 auction, Julien's Auctions of Los Angeles offered a 1988 Visa credit card application filled out by Whitney Houston. Her request for a $5 million credit line was approved; the application includes Houston's address and Social Security number.

- A year after he died in 1987, an auction of Liberace's personal effects was held in Las Vegas. The weirdest item: Liberace's Nevada driver's license, bearing his full name, Wladziu Liberace. It sold for $1,700.

- By 2001, 1980s heartthrob Corey Haim had fallen on hard times. He approached a Las Vegas celebrity memorabilia store called Startifacts about auctioning off some of his possessions. One item—a bad tooth that had been removed by a dentist—was almost included…but was pulled at the last minute. (Get it? Pulled!)

- Wil Wheaton starred in *Stand By Me* and on *Star Trek: The Next Generation*. Today he's a blogger and Internet personality. In 2012, he put a dented table-tennis ball he found in his garage on eBay. Wheaton named it "Silas." It sold for $1,135.

- Pete Best's claim to fame: he was the drummer fired by the Beatles right before they became the most popular band in the world. Despite being kicked out of the Beatles, he signed a Beatles drum head in 2015, and it was auctioned off for $1,024. (At the same auction, a baseball signed by the Fab Four sold for $100,000.)

- Former child star Gary Coleman auctioned off a number of personal items on eBay in 2008 to help pay off some hospital bills. Among the lot: a pair of blue, size XL Gap Kids sweatpants that Coleman autographed. The winning bid: $400,000. But the payment was never received, so the sweatpants went to the second-place bidder—talk show host Jimmy Kimmel. His bid: $500.

The Bionic News Report

The Six Million Dollar Man is now closer to reality than ever, thanks to new advances in bionics. (It's just going to cost a lot more than six million dollars.)

FEELING SPINE

Scientists at the Royal Melbourne Hospital, the University of Melbourne, and the Florey Institute of Neuroscience and Mental Health have developed a device that they hope will allow the paralyzed to walk again. The paperclip-sized device is inserted through a cut in the neck and fed into the top of the motor cortex. Electrodes outfitted on the "bionic spine" detect signals and send them to a receiver implanted in the patient's shoulder. The signals are then sent to bionic prosthetic limbs via Bluetooth. The bionic spine has been tested on sheep, and trials on human patients is underway in Australia.

THE FIGHTING SPIRIT

Set to be held in Switzerland in October 2016, the first ever "Cybathlon," a competition for disabled athletes using bionic assisted technology, will have six events, including track and field and biking events for athletes with bionic limbs. There's also the "brain computer interface race," a virtual competition in which participants wear a device on their head that maps their brain waves to control a video game character. Another event: the powered arm prosthesis race. Athletes must use their computer-enabled arm to slice a loaf of bread and pour a cup of coffee.

A HAND UP, NOT A HAND OUT

There are around two million people on Earth in need of a prosthetic hand. But the cost of purchasing, installing, and maintaining a robotic hand ensures that most hand amputees will never be able to afford one. Enter: Open Bionics, a British prosthetic company selling a £500 (about $715) robotic hand that can be 3D printed and assembled in less than an hour. Open Bionics CEO Joel Gibbard hopes that his company's product can help most of those two million people regain a semblance of a normal life again, especially those in war-torn countries. Open Bionics has also partnered with Disney to provide royalty-free licenses to create Marvel, *Frozen*, and *Star Wars*-inspired designs for children. Their hope is that it will make the child amputees less self-conscious about their bionic hands.

The Restoration Fabrication

Here's the bizarre story of an anonymous artist so desperate to receive credit for his work that he took himself to court.

THE MIRACLE OF MARIENKIRCHE

On March 28, 1942, the German port city of Lübeck was nearly obliterated by Allied bombers during World War II. More than 230 British planes dropped 400 tons of bombs, destroying thousands of homes, the town hall, the merchant district, and several churches dating back seven centuries, including the huge Gothic cathedral known as the Marienkirche (Church of Mary).

The bombing created a firestorm so hot that the church bells melted. After the raid ended and townspeople began to assess the damage, a remarkable discovery was made in the Marienkirche. The intense heat had also melted dozens of layers of paint off the walls. Underneath that paint: frescoes, a style of painting in which pigment is applied directly onto a wet plaster wall. The paintings of saints, biblical scenes, and religious icons dated back to the 1250s, when the church was built. After what was dubbed "the miracle of the Marienkirche," the town quickly came together to erect a temporary roof for the cathedral to protect it from further attacks, so that the frescoes could be restored when the war was over...whenever that might be.

FEY TO GO

After the end of the war in 1945, the roof and walls of the Marienkirche were rebuilt, and the work was completed in 1948. Town officials then hired celebrated German art restorer Dietrich Fey to bring the church's frescoes back to life. Fey had apprenticed under his father, Ernst Fey, a Berlin art historian who had worked on the recovery and restoration of frescoes in churches throughout Germany in the 1920s and 1930s. But it was the elder Fey who was the artist; the younger Fey's skills were more on the business side, landing commissions and finding wealthy patrons.

By 1936 the Feys had more work than they could handle, and they needed a skilled assistant. That's when they were approached by Lothar Malskat. A recent graduate of the Art Academy of Konigsberg (now the Russian city of Kaliningrad), Malskat could paint in any number of classic styles. (His favorite style: 13th-century Gothic painting, like the frescoes of the Marienkirche.) Malskat had hoped to become an artist, but when he got to Berlin, the only painting work he could get was painting houses. He was homeless and sleeping on a park bench when he asked the Feys for a job.

BRICK HOUSE

Malskat's first assignment: paint Dietrich Fey's house. But Fey also brought Malskat into the restoration business, loaning books on ecclesiastical art (religious paintings), and training him as they worked. Malskat proved his talent in the 1937 restoration of St. Petri-Dom, a cathedral in the city of Schleswig with artworks dating to the 14th century. At first, he had to undo damage caused by the Feys. Then they had to scrape away the work of an earlier restorer, August Olbers. They scraped away so much paint from Olbers's 1880s restoration that they—oops!—also scraped away almost all of the original artwork.

Malskat knew what to do. He whitewashed the brick, and then tinted it to look old by combining lime with various colors of paint. Once that dried, he painted freehand (and from memory) the paintings that had been accidentally removed. Finally, Malskat and Fey artificially aged the drawings through a process called *zurückpatinieren*—rubbing them with a brick. Church leaders were impressed by the final product, as was Alfred Stange, an art historian at the University of Bonn. He called the murals "the last, deepest, final word in German art."

FAKE IT UNTIL YOU MAKE IT

World War II ended the business; Malskat was drafted into the Wehrmacht, and was discharged at the war's end. Now unemployed, he moved to Hamburg. Once again, he was homeless, subsisting by selling pornographic drawings. Finally, in late 1945, he tracked down Fey and asked for his old job back.

Germany was in tatters after the war. It was occupied by foreign powers and divided into two—West Germany and East Germany. The economy was weak, and any available funds were used to rebuild infra-structure; restoring art was not a priority for postwar West Germany. So Fey put his business skills and Malskat's painting skills to good use: they started counterfeiting famous paintings. Fey provided Malskat with canvases, paints, brushes, and other supplies, along with art books and a list of names. His instructions: paint the works of Rembrandt, Picasso, Van Gogh, Toulouse-Lautrec, Edvard Munch, Marc Chagall, Jean Renoir, Edgar Degas, and others that could be sold to private collectors as the real thing. From 1945 to 1948, Malskat painted an estimated 500 forgeries.

Demand was so high that Malskat had to turn the paintings around quickly; he claimed to have spent just a day re-creating a painting by Rembrandt, and an hour for a Picasso.

DUST IN THE WIND

Thanks to aggressive government programs (as well as the Marshall Plan), the West German economy stabilized by 1948, diminishing the black market economy that had made Fey and Malskat's forgery ring possible. With that stability, the restoration of the Marienkirche could finally commence.

Having acquired 150,000 deutschemarks through fund-raising efforts, Lübeck officials contacted Dietrich Fey (his father had since died) to restore the frescoes. But the centuries—and the bombs—had left the paintings in almost as bad a state as the ones at St. Petri-Dom. Malskat reportedly climbed the scaffolding to assess the damage to some paintings and noticed that some of the art was barely there at all, and what was there "turned to dust when I blew on it." Restoring those frescoes would be impossible…but Malskat was up to the challenge. He'd do what he did before: create new art that looked like the old art.

In fact, he utilized almost all of the techniques he'd used at St. Petri-Dom: He whitewashed the walls, tinted them with lime and pigment, and started painting. He used old photographs and art books as a guide… but added personal touches. He modeled Mary on his sister Freyda, painted a bearded king to look like Rasputin, gave a saint the face of Marlene Dietrich, and made monks look like the local townsfolk.

GERMAN REUNIFICATION

The restoration was completed in September 1951, just in time to celebrate the 700th anniversary of the construction of Marienkirche. A special ceremony was held, attended by West German chancellor Konrad Adenauer. As he stared up at 10-foot-tall paintings of Gothic saints, Adenauer proclaimed, "This is uplifting." He went on to call them "a valuable treasure and a fabulous discovery."

The Marienkirche was a sensation, uniting Germans still battered and embarrassed after World War II. The newly restored old paintings filled Germans with national pride. The acclaim came quickly. The government printed two million postage stamps detailing the frescoes. One art historian called the murals "the most important and extensive ever disclosed in Germany." Even in the United States, *Time* called the frescoes "a major artistic find." Over the next year, more than 100,000 tourists flocked to Lubeck to see Marienkirche, bringing much-needed tourism—and cash—to the town.

All of this infuriated Lothar Malskat.

The first big-city "pooper-scooper" law went into effect in New York City on August 1, 1978.

COMPENSATION FRUSTRATION

Fey was the public face of the restoration project (and took all the credit), but Malskat had done most of the actual work. He'd spent three years in the Marienkirche, providing the concepts and labor needed to produce dozens of paintings, virtually by himself. Fey paid Malskat a weekly salary of 110 deutschemarks (the equivalent of about $328 today), and paid himself about eight times as much—not even factoring in the 150,000-deutschemark bonus he received from Chancellor Adenauer, or the prestigious art professorship he was given. Yet in all of his public speeches and interviews about the Marienkirche, Fey never thanked Malskat. He never even mentioned him.

More than money, Malskat wanted credit. After his work on the church, he no longer saw himself as an art restorer—he saw himself as a creator and a true artist. Toward the end of the restoration, he started to leave clues about his work on the project. Malskat left "LM" on paintings as he finished them, and even "all paintings in this church are by Lothar Malskat." Fey reviewed Malskat's work every few days and painted over these personal touches.

For a year after completing his work at the Marienkirche, Malskat simmered in private, which couldn't have been easy, considering that he was still doing restoration work (and more forgery work) for Fey in Lubeck. Finally, on May 9, 1952, Malskat had had enough. He walked into the Lubeck police station and gave a statement, asserting that the famed Marienkirche murals were a fraud, and that he had forged them under the direction and cooperation of Dietrich Fey. His reason for confessing: He was tired of being treated unfairly by Fey and he wanted the world to know the truth, and by doing so, reveal himself as the brilliant artist behind the beloved works of art.

CAN'T GET ARRESTED IN THIS TOWN

Only problem: The paintings were so beloved that nobody believed Malskat. Lubeck police threw him out of the station. He went to the local newspaper. Officials there were dismissive too, writing that Malskat's claims were "the lamentable case of a painter gone crazy."

Nobody wanted to see Malskat's proof—before and after photographs of the church—either. They didn't want to see that in one fresco, photographs showed that Mary Magdalene had shoes before the restoration…and no longer did. Or that the fringes of some works were decorated with turkeys, a bird not introduced to Germany until the 1500s, making it unlikely for them to appear in genuine artwork from the 1200s. (When the German news media reported this fact, a prominent German historian tried to explain it away, claiming that Vikings had brought turkeys to Germany in the 1100s.) The city of

---

Dust from cinnabar, a red mineral once commonly used in jewelry, is deadly if inhaled.

Lubeck issued a statement saying that Malskat's charges were "rumors and purely malicious gossip."

I WILL SEE ME IN COURT

When the law won't cooperate, what can a person do? Take the law into their own hands. After spending most of 1952 trying, unsuccessfully, to convince the country that he was the artist responsible for Marienkirche, Malskat hired a lawyer named Willi Flottrong. Malskat gave him a huge folder of photographs of his earlier forgeries, primarily his Picasso and Rembrandt fakes. He argued that this established a pattern of criminal behavior.

So, on October 7, 1952, with the artwork in hand, Malskat's lawyer went into the Lubeck police station to file criminal charges against Fey…and Malskat. Official charges from a third party forced the police to investigate and even arrest the two men. Police searched (a very cooperative) Malskat's home and found a total of 28 pieces of counterfeit art. Two days after his lawyer filed charges on his behalf, Malskat got what he wanted: He was arrested for forgery. (And so was Fey.)

A REMARKABLE DISCOVERY

While Malskat happily sat in jail, awaiting his day in court, police gathered evidence against him. Art experts from around Europe examined Marienkirche. It took them just two weeks to issue a report, which, not surprisingly, said that upon close inspection, the frescoes were not legitimate. "The 21 figures are not Gothic, but painted freehand," the report stated.

Prosecutors spent 10 months in all amassing testimony, and as the investigation unfolded, it became clear that several officials at Marienkirche knew exactly what Fey and Malskat were doing, but looked the other way. To avoid prosecution, the church superintendent retired early, and his second-in-command abruptly moved behind the Iron Curtain into East Germany.

Malskat's trial began on August 10, 1954. To accommodate the hundreds of spectators and reporters, it was moved from the Lubeck courthouse to a local dance hall. The first witness, as well as the star witness: Lothar Malskat. Early in the trial, the prosecutor asked Malskat why he had brought the case forward. His blunt response: "Everybody raved about my beautiful murals, yet Fey got all the credit. Nobody even knew my name."

Malskat and his lawyer didn't really mount a defense, since he wanted to be found guilty. That would prove to the world that he'd done the paintings. His time on the stand was instead spent disparaging art critics, officials, and others who'd unknowingly praised his work on the restoration of St. Petri-Dom cathedral in Schleswig:

- "One art critic raved about the 'prophet with the magic eyes.' It was modeled on my father."

- "Another gushed about the 'spiritual beauty of the splendid figure of Mary, so far removed from our present day image of womanhood.' For that painting I used a photograph of [Austrian film star] Hansi Knoteck."

- When asked by the prosecutor how a "second-rate painter could have fooled the nation's leading experts," Malskat said, "People like to be fooled. We just gave them what they wanted."

GUILTY AT LAST

After five months of testimony, a verdict was reached in January 1955. The judge said that the case was tricky, because property damage—the basis of a forgery charge—didn't really come into play. Instead, he said, "The infringement was psychological: Robbery of faith, theft of a miracle." Fey received 20 months in prison; Malskat got 18 months.

Malskat didn't serve his sentence right away. After the trial, he escaped to Sweden and tried to make good on his newfound celebrity. Soliciting commissions, he painted the interior of a Stockholm restaurant in the Gothic style (similar to his work on Marienkirche). He also painted the interior of the Royal Tennis Court. What did he paint on the walls there? Turkeys.

After being extradited back to Germany in 1956, Malskat served his 18 months and settled into a quiet life, painting at home and presenting a handful of small gallery shows of his artwork. He died at age 74 in 1988.

As for the frescoes in Marienkirche, they were painted over.

*   *   *

COACHES SAY THE DARNDEST THINGS

"We're not attempting to circumcise the rules."
—Bill Cowher, NFL coach

"It was a team effort. Everybody contributed with poor play."
—Bob Green, college football coach

"We have to score more goals than we concede to win a game."
—Sam Allardyce, soccer coach

When Zoo Animals Attack

Zoos are supposed to be places where people can learn about fascinating animals and enjoy a day out with the family. Tragically, zoos are also places where people learn that animals are unpredictable... and dangerous especially if the keepers are careless or the public ignores safety rules. Here are the stories behind some of the scariest zoo attacks ever.

Location: The Alaska Zoo, Anchorage, Alaska
Animal: Polar bear
Attack: On July 30, 1994, Australian tourist Kathryn Warburton, 29, climbed over the two safety fences around the polar bear exhibit at the Alaska Zoo, and walked right up to the bears' enclosure. She was hoping to get a close-up photograph of Binky, the zoo's star 1,200-pound polar bear. Binky's response: he reached his front paw through the cage's bars, pulled Warburton against the cage, stuck his head through the bars, and clenched his massive jaws onto her left thigh, eventually pulling her leg back through the bars. Several onlookers frantically tried to save the screaming Warburton, attempting to pull her free while thrashing Binky with tree branches, all of it captured on a tourist's video camera. It took nearly two minutes to free her.

Aftermath: Warburton suffered severe lacerations to her leg, which was broken in the attack. But she survived and eventually made a full recovery. Zoo officials refused to euthanize the bear, because Warburton had clearly violated the zoo's safety regulations. Warburton later said jumping the safety barriers was "the dumbest thing I've ever done." A photo of Binky with one of Warburton's shoes in his mouth made the front pages of newspapers all over the world. (Binky refused to relinquish the shoe for three days.)

Location: The Oklahoma City Zoo, Oklahoma
Animal: Malayan tapir
Attack: On November 20, 1998, zookeeper Lisa Morehead slid open the two-foot-wide feeding door on the cage of Melody, an adult Malayan tapir. Tapirs are mammals resembling a cross between a pig and a rhinoceros, with an odd-looking elongated nose. And they're huge: adult Malayan tapirs can grow to three feet high and six feet long,

and can weigh more than 600 pounds. And while they are vegetarians and normally very friendly with their keepers, they are unpredictable when their young are near—and Melody had a two-month-old calf with her. When Morehead tossed some food into the cage, Melody suddenly bit Morehead's left arm, pulled her into the pen, and proceeded to bite and stomp her. After several minutes, Morehead was finally pulled free by fellow keepers.

Aftermath: Melody bit off Morehead's left arm completely, at mid-bicep level. Doctors were unable to reattach it. Morehead also suffered a punctured lung and bite marks to her face, throat, and legs and required numerous surgeries over the following months. Melody the tapir remained on display at the zoo until she died of kidney failure a year later.

Location: The Dallas Zoo, Texas

Animal: Gorilla

Attack: On March 18, 2004, Jabari, a 13-year-old western lowland gorilla, somehow managed to jump a 14-foot-wide moat and scale a 16-foot-high retaining wall to escape into the zoo's crowded public grounds, where he went on a rampage. The 300-pound primate first attacked Cheryl Reichert, 39, who was attempting to protect her three children, shaking her violently and biting her arm several times. Then he grabbed a three-year-old boy, shaking him "like a rag doll," according to witnesses, and biting the boy's head. The boy's mother, Keisha Heard, started punching Jabari in the back, after which the gorilla attacked her. "I thought he wanted to kill us," Heard later said. "He was so angry and upset." After more than 40 minutes outside his cage, Jabari was shot and killed by police officers.

Aftermath: All three victims suffered serious bite wounds, but they all made full recoveries. The day after the attack, the zoo received an anonymous call from a man who said he had seen two teenage boys taunting Jabari, throwing either rocks or ice at him, just before the attacks. "I'm thinking he just got angry enough at being harassed," zoo mammal curator Ken Kaemmerer told reporters, "and he either made the climb of his life or a leap and got lucky." After the incident, the zoo's gorilla compound was redesigned to prevent future escapes.

Location: Haliburton Forest and Wild Life Reserve, Ontario, Canada

Animal: Wolves

Attack: On the afternoon of April 18, 1996, Trisha Wyman, a newly-hired 24-year-old wildlife biologist with only three days on the job, entered a 15-acre, fenced wolf enclosure on the preserve, located in Haliburton Highlands, about 150 miles northeast of Toronto. The enclosure, home to five North American gray wolves, was scheduled to be opened to the public that July, so that visitors could learn about wolves in a natural setting. Nobody knows exactly what happened, but Wyman was attacked by the wolves.

Aftermath: Her body was discovered by two other employees later that afternoon, about 80 feet into the compound's interior. She had multiple bite wounds on her body, and the wolves had removed all of her clothing. Investigators could not determine what made the wolves attack: they had all been raised in captivity, but had not been socialized to humans, and normally stayed far away when staff entered the enclosure. Investigators surmised that Wyman may have fallen and injured herself—the ground inside the enclosure was covered with sticks, branches, and logs—which could have triggered the wolves' hunting instinct. The five wolves were all shot, with the intent of determining whether they were infected with rabies. Those tests came back negative.

Location: The San Francisco Zoo

Animal: Siberian tiger

Attack: On Christmas Day 2007, three young men—Carlos Sousa Jr., 17, Amritpal Dhaliwal, 19, and his brother, Kulbir, 23—were outside the zoo's Siberian tiger grotto, when Tatiana, a four-year-old female tiger, escaped. The 320-pound cat jumped into the empty concrete moat surrounding the grotto and lunged across it, leaped to the top of the high concrete wall surrounding the moat, and descended onto the zoo footpath. She attacked Kulbir first, then set upon Sousa, who was trying to save his friend. A few minutes later, the big cat tracked down the Dhaliwal brothers, who had fled and were more than 300 yards away (she was probably following the blood trail of the older brother, experts said). She then attacked the younger Dhaliwal. That's when police arrived on the scene, and shot and killed Tatiana.

Aftermath: Sousa died on the scene, having suffered deep bite wounds to his neck, as well as spinal and skull fractures. The Dhaliwal brothers received several puncture wounds and lacerations, but were not seriously injured. An investigation into the attack determined that the moat wall around the tiger enclosure, which zoo officials had told reporters was 18 feet high, was actually only 12.5 feet high—well below the 16.5 feet recommended by national zoo standards. (The zoo was fined for the infraction, and the wall height was increased to over 20 feet.) The investigation also found evidence that the three victims may have been provoking the tiger just before the attack, but no charges were filed against them.

MORE ANIMAL ATTACKS

• In March 1972, a camel at the San Francisco Zoo reached over the six-foot-high fence around his pen, bit a three-year-old girl on the face, grabbed her hair in its teeth, and dragged the screaming child over the fence and into his pen. Then the camel proceeded to trample the girl. She was rescued only when a friend of her family jumped into the enclosure and was able to pull her away from the angry camel and carry her over the fence to safety. The girl, who was not named in news reports, suffered a broken jaw and several cuts to her face, but recovered.

• In May 1990, San Francisco Zoo keeper Alan Feinberg was next to the cage of a Persian leopard when the big cat reached through the bars of the cage, grabbed Feinberg with its paws, and sank its fangs into his neck. Feinberg screamed, "Get him off! Get him off!" over and over, as the crowd of schoolchildren he was entertaining looked on in horror. Feinberg was freed by colleagues, and he did not suffer permanent injury.

• In April 2009, a woman identified in news reports only as Mandy K. scaled a series of safety barriers around the polar bear exhibit at the Berlin Zoo in Germany. She then jumped into the bears' swimming pool, which served as a moat around the exhibit. One of the zoo's four enormous polar bears jumped into the pool and attacked the woman. Zoo staff threw ropes to her and tried to pull her up the moat's wall, while trying to distract the bears by throwing things at them. The rescuers almost got her up…and then she lost her grip and fell back into the water. They started to pull her up again…and one of the bears bit the woman's back, ripping her from the rope. They tried again… and were finally able to pull her to the top of the wall and free her. The woman was treated for bite wounds at a local hospital. News reports later said that Mandy K. had jumped into the pool because she was despondent over losing her job.

*　　*　　*

HISTORY QUIZ

Q: Of the billions of people who have ever lived, there is something unique about three of them: Georgy Dobrovolsky, Vladislav Volkov, and Viktor Patsayev. Do you know what it is?

A: In 1971, the three Soviet cosmonauts were aboard their orbiting *Soyuz-11* spacecraft, preparing to re-enter the Earth's atmosphere when the cabin suddenly depressurized, killing them instantly. They're the only humans ever to have died outside of Earth's atmosphere.

Uncle John's
Stall of Shame

*More examples of how people end up using bathrooms toilets,
and toilet paper for nefarious deeds…instead of for good.*

Dubious Achiever: An unknown assailant

Claim to Fame: Going to a golf course, and then going on a golf course

True Story: Frustrated greenskeepers at a public course in Norway are urging players to be on the lookout for a person who obviously "hates the game of golf." For the past decade, the mysterious invader has been trespassing during off hours and…browning up the greens (specifically, the cups themselves). The only evidence left behind are bike tracks and used toilet paper. Course managers were unable to obtain permits for security cameras, so they put up spotlights, but the mad pooper simply disables them. "He has a couple of favorite holes," said one of the grossed-out greenskeepers, adding, "And we know it is a man because the poos are too massive to be from a woman."

Dubious Achiever: Ross McDonald, 39, of Iowa City, Iowa

Claim to Fame: Using TP to wipe away evidence of a crime

True Story: On Halloween night in 2015, McDonald got pulled over at 3:00 a.m. for driving the wrong way down a one-way street. Despite claims that he'd had only two drinks, officers took him to the station to give him a Breathalyzer test. But before they got there, he ate a wad of toilet paper—thinking it would somehow "absorb" the alcohol in his system. He was wrong—his alcohol content was still more than twice Iowa's legal limit. McDonald was charged with drunken driving. (Uncle John would have also charged him with unlawful use of TP.)

Dubious Achievers: School administrators at Bellbridge Primary in Hoppers Crossing, Victoria, Australia

Claim to Fame: Denying kids their fundamental right to go pee-pee and poo-poo

True Story: The parents of Hoppers Crossing were hopping mad when some of their kids started arriving home from school with wet pants (and worse). The children explained that they would be "fined" if they used the bathroom during class time, so they tried (unsuccessfully) to hold it in. According to Yahoo news, "The fines were paid from play currency through the school's 'earn and learn' program, which was designed to teach the value of working and earning money." (Denying the bathroom breaks during class time was reportedly in response to a few kids who'd been abusing that privilege.) Adding to the embarrassment, when kids did go to the bathroom, they had to log how much time they spent in there on a white board. Kids who took too much time not only got fined, but had to stay indoors during recess. After a barrage of complaints, Bellbridge principal Debbie Clancy flushed the penalty program, announcing that from then on, "Our students are free to go to the toilet whenever they need."

Dubious Achiever: Gaioz Nigalidze, a chess grandmaster from the nation of Georgia

Claim to Fame: Soiling his sport

True Story: At a 2015 tournament in Dubai, 25-year-old Nigalidze, one of the top young players in the world, took several bathroom breaks during a match against Armenian grandmaster Tigran Petrosian. Each time Nigalidze returned, he made a move that stumped his opponent. Even more suspiciously, Nigalidze insisted on using the same restroom stall every time. Petrosian complained, so tournament officials inspected the stall, where they discovered an iPhone hidden inside a wad of toilet paper. Nigalidze denied the phone was his, but a quick investigation revealed that it was. And not only that, it had an app open that analyzes chess games and calculates the best moves. (For this exact reason, players are banned from bringing smartphones to matches.) Nigalidze was ejected from the tournament.

Dubious Achiever: The 25 Hours Hotel Bikini Berlin

Claim to Fame: Providing restrooms with a view...inside

True Story: This swanky German hotel made news in 2014 when photos started showing up online of guests going to the bathroom. The pictures were taken from the street below. How could this be? The top floor is home to a lounge called the Monkey Bar, and the bathrooms have floor-to-ceiling windows, allowing patrons to see the city from ten stories up. But due to a design flaw, the windows also allow people to see in. And the toilets are right next to the windows. Rather than spend thousands to replace the windows, hotel management simply put up signs in the restrooms warning guests: "Please be careful, not only the monkeys are watching." (The hotel is located near the Berlin Zoo.)

*   *   *

"Women love a self-confident bald man." —**Larry David**

Playing hard to get: Young Komodo dragons roll in poop to discourage the adults from eating them.

Mascot Injuries

Ever since the trampoline-jumping, basketball-dunking Phoenix Suns Gorilla burst onto the scene in 1980, teams have wanted their mascots to be bigger, faster, stronger…but sometimes it comes with a price.

ROCKY THE MOUNTAIN LION

In 2013, the Denver Nuggets' mascot, Rocky the Mountain Lion, was supposed to be lowered from the rafters as part of the team's season-opening ceremony. But when the lights inside the Pepsi Center dimmed and a spotlight was shone way up top, 18,000 fans saw a limp, lifeless mascot being slowly lowered until he collapsed on the court. To make matters worse, the mascot's body harness was hidden by his enormous head, so from the TV camera angle it looked like Rocky was hanging by his neck, giving the event the appearance of a ritual sacrifice. Team officials later explained that the performer had the wind knocked out of him just before the stunt.

STANLEY C. PANTHER

Arguably the sports world's toughest mascot gig is working in the NHL, where the combination of slippery ice and having to wear a headpiece the size of a beach ball has led to some very bad falls. In 2010, Stanley C. Panther, mascot of the Florida Panthers, was putting on a show for fans, and while attempting (unsuccessfully) to hurdle over a folding chair, he slipped on the ice and was knocked out of commission with "undisclosed injuries." Mr. Panther attended the rest of the season's home games in a wheelchair, but this show of loyalty didn't impress the franchise's executives: They laid him off during the 2012 NHL lockout to save money.

SABRE

Hopefully, the Fort Wayne Fury of the now-defunct Continental Basketball Association had health insurance when the team mascot, Sabre, suffered a serious injury during a 1996 playoff game stunt. The tiger mascot was lowering himself from the rafters during pregame introductions when his leg got tangled in the rope. The costumed cat somehow came out of his harness and fell 50 feet onto the concrete floor behind the basket. A spotter broke Sabre's fall, but the mascot was rushed to the hospital in critical condition. The man who played Sabre ended up suffering a broken back, but made a full recovery.

Traditional Welsh breakfast: Laverbread (seaweed paste) on toast, served with bacon and clams.

TESTUDO

In 1988, the University of Maryland's mascot, Testudo (a diamondback terrapin), was play-fighting with the University of Virginia's mascot, Cavalier (a guy dressed as a cavalier), when the turtle was knocked to the ground, breaking his arm in three places. Given that the guy inside the Testudo suit, student Scott Rudolph, was a paid employee of the university (he earned $25 per game), he figured his school would help out with his medical bills. But the university claimed it wasn't liable. Finally in 1993, a worker's compensation judge ruled that Maryland *was* liable for the injury and ordered it to pay Rudolph $5,000 and any related medical bills for the rest of his life.

WILD WING

When the NHL awarded a hockey franchise in Anaheim, California, to the Walt Disney Company in 1992, the movie studio went all-out in promoting their new franchise, the Mighty Ducks of Anaheim. To drum up fan support, the team sometimes resorted to cheesy stunts. One they shouldn't have tried: In 1995, Wild Thing was supposed to hurtle over a fire pit. He got about three inches of hangtime before falling into the pit and catching on fire.

*   *   *

YOU'RE MY INSPIRATION

Donald Trump. Love him or hate him, if you thought Trump's 2016 presidential campaign was like something from *The Twilight Zone*, you're not far off. Trump's business philosophy was actually inspired by a 1960 episode of the sci-fi TV show called "A Nice Place to Visit" in which a dead criminal goes to what he thinks is heaven. When he's told he can have anything he wants, he replies, "I want to win, win, win. I want the most beautiful women. I want to never lose again." Trump says he never forgot that lesson, as evidenced by this statement: "If I'm president, we'll win so much, you'll get bored with winning!"

One Direction. The look of the most popular boy band of the 2010s was inspired by the most popular girl group of the 1990s. According to One Direction's stylist, Caroline Watson, "I wanted them to be like the male equivalent to the Spice Girls. Everyone wore different things and no two girls looked the same. I wanted to create that with the boys."

Bart Simpson's Name. "In high school I wrote a novel about a character named Bart Simpson," recalled *Simpsons* creator Matt Groening. "I thought it was a very unusual name for a kid. I had this idea of an angry father yelling 'Bart!,' kind of like a barking dog."

Teddy Roosevelt's wife and mother died within hours of each other on Valentine's Day 1884.

The Riddler

Time to test your power of deductive reasoning with these tricky riddles. (Answers on page 511.)

1. What word has six letters, but if you take away the last one, twelve remains?

2. What has 13 hearts, but no other organs?

3. What points up when it's light and down when it's dark?

4. It is easy to get into but hard to get out of. What is it?

5. Apart, they are more delicate than tissue; together, they can crush a small town. What are they?

6. What can you find in December that you can find in no other month?

7. What chair has only two legs but wields great power?

8. You commit an act of violence and run away from home. Then you make three quick lefts and return home, only to be confronted by two people in masks. Who are they?

9. Alive, they are mostly silent; dead, they make a great noise, especially when stepped upon. What are they?

10. What asks but never answers?

11. What loses a head every morning but gets it back every night?

12. Its name is long, but what it means is short. What is it?

13. What letter do you add to "one" to make it disappear?

14. What five-letter word becomes shorter when you add two letters to it?

15. What gets up every time you do, and can linger long after you're gone?

16. What do you bury when alive, and then dig up when dead?

17. What is always old but sometimes new, never empty but sometimes full?

18. What can go up a chimney down, but can't go down a chimney up?

19. What can pass between you and the sun, but not cast a shadow?

British etiquette dictates that the correct way to eat peas is to squish them onto the back of a fork.

World-Class Walks

When you've had enough of the news, the noise, the office, the traffic—and the Kardashians—there's nothing like a good long walk to clear the hubbub out of your head. And if your local footpath isn't quite enough, here are a few world-class hiking trails you may want to put on your walk-it list. (Which is kind of like a "bucket list"—only more walky.)

THE INCA TRAIL

Location: Peru

Distance: 26 miles (recommended time: 4 days)

Best Time to Go: May to September

Details: This fairly grueling hike through the Sacred Valley of the Incas in southern Peru takes you across high rocky mountain plateaus, into densely vegetated cloud forests, and past ancient ruins, all surrounded by the stunning Andes mountains, and finally ends at the most famous Incan site, Machu Picchu. It's not for everyone: the path has a lot of ups and downs, climbing from elevations of about 6,000 feet to 13,000 feet, so aside from the work, there's the danger of altitude sickness. The Inca Trail is one of the most popular treks in the world, meaning you need a reservation and a permit (required) at least six months in advance. Note: Since 2001, trekkers are no longer allowed to hike the trail alone. Most people go with guided tour groups (porters, cooks, food, tents, and sleeping bags provided). But you can certainly go smaller—just you (or you and a small group) with one guide—for a more personal trail experience.

THE SENTIERO AZZURRO

Location: Italy

Distance: 7.5 miles (3 to 4 hours...or 3 to 4 days)

Best Time to Go: In the spring

Details: This is the most popular walking path in the Cinque Terre (Five Lands), a historic and picturesque section of the Italian Riviera in northwestern Italy, comprised of five villages on the coast of the Mediterranean Sea. (The entire area is recognized as a UNESCO World Heritage Site.) The Sentiero Azzurro, meaning "Blue Path," connects those five medieval Italian villages, famous for their pastel-covered buildings, while passing sandy beaches, coursing along steep rock cliff faces overlooking the sea, and climbing stone steps up into the forested hillsides. The entire trail can be done in just a few hours, but most hikers take their time, taking in the sights, stopping for a swim, drinking some of the local wine, and staying overnight in guesthouses or hotels along the way. (Tip: Seasoned hikers suggest starting in the southernmost village of Riomaggiore and finishing in the northernmost, Monterosso al Mare. The hike starts off a bit easier this way, and gets you ready for the more difficult northern part.) This trail is extremely popular—so much so that there is now a small fee and a daily limit on the number of people who can walk it. Hotels must be booked far in advance, too.

THE GOECHALA TREK

Location: India

Distance: 55 miles (about 11 days)

Best Time to Go: Mid-April to May; October to mid-November

Details: This Himalayan mountain trek, called by many avid hikers the best in the Indian Himalayas, starts in the northeastern town of Yuksom at an elevation of 5,670 feet, and ends at the 16,000-foot-high Goechela Pass, a few miles from the eastern border of Nepal. Like on the Inca Trail, most people do guided treks, with porters, gear, and food included (carried by yaks!), but you *can* do it without guides, provided you're fit and have experience with high-altitude hiking. Sights include the spectacular Himalayan mountain range—including Kanchenjunga, the third-highest mountain in the world (at over 28,000 feet); sprawling alpine meadows of wildflowers; forests of giant ferns, bamboo, and rhododendron; turquoise-blue alpine lakes; gushing rivers, possibly with some frozen waterfalls; many glaciers; and a lot more. (The trek is not recommended during the summer rainy season. You can do it in November and December, but be prepared for very cold, very dry weather.)

THE GREAT BAIKAL TRAIL

Location: Siberia, Russia

Distance: Varied

Best Time to Go: June to October

Details: The Great Baikal Trail is a Russian nonprofit organization founded in 2003 to promote environmentalism and ecotourism in the region by getting volunteers to help build hiking trails all the way around southern Siberia's Lake Baikal, the deepest and oldest lake on earth. Over the years, more than 5,000 volunteers from all around the world have built or improved more than 400 miles of trails in the region. One of the most popular: the 34-mile-long path between the lakeside villages of Listvyanka and Bolshoye Goloustnoye (recommended time: 3–4 days). It takes you along the lakeshore, up to the top of rocky cliffs overlooking the lake, across lush green meadows, and through dense forests, passing little villages and staying in cabins, guesthouses, or tents along the way. (Bonus: You might even see some *nerpa*, or Baikal seals—the only freshwater seals on earth—swimming in the lake or sunning themselves on the beach.)

THE KUMANO KODO

Location: Japan

Distance: Varied

Best Time to Go: Spring and fall, but winter is okay, too. (Summer isn't—it's the rainy season.)

Details: The Kumano Kodo (*Kumano* is a type of Shinto shrine; *kodo* means "road" or "passageway") is a network of seven trails that wind through the densely forested, often misty and mysterious Kii mountain range, in the south of Japan's main island, Honshu. The trails have been used by Japanese people for more than 1,000 years, and are used for making pilgrimages to three sacred Shinto shrines, collectively known as *Kumano Sanzan.* Called "one of the best (and possibly most overlooked) treks on the planet" by CNN's *On the Road* series, individual trails can be hiked on short day trips, or the entire set of seven main trails can be trekked over the course of four to five days. (You can camp or stay in bungalows along the way.) Highlights include lush cedar forests; the many *oji* (mini shrines) along the path; the three main shrines, each elaborately constructed in ancient Japanese style; the many farms and gardens along the route; numerous creeks and rivers; and Nachi no Taki, a 436-foot-tall waterfall (Japan's highest).

THE URIQUE-BATOPILAS TRAIL

Location: Mexico

Distance: 32 miles (3 to 4 days)

Best Time to Go: October to March

Details: This hike takes you between the towns of Urique and Batopilas in the Sierra Madre Occidental mountains, in Mexico's northern state of Chihuahua, and runs through six interconnected canyons, collectively known as Copper Canyon. The hike starts at the floor of Urique Canyon, the deepest of the canyons, in the historic mining town of Urique, at about 1,800 feet. It climbs more than 4,000 feet of rocky desert pathways, past cacti and agave, to the canyon's rim, amid patches of mesquite, sycamore, and wild fig trees. It then descends into neighboring Batopilas Canyon, ending at the mining town of Batopilas. The breathtaking Grand Canyon–like vistas, the bizarre rock formations, the burbling creeks (fed by the winter rainy season), and night skies filled with more stars than you've probably seen in your entire life make this one of Mexico's most memorable hikes. (Bonus: you can also take side trips to the villages of Tarahumara Indians, who have lived in the canyons for centuries. You might also spot some rattlesnakes, mountain lions, wild boar, and wild burros on your journey.)

MOUNT KAILASH KORA

Location: Tibet

Distance: 32 miles (3 to 4 days)

Best Time to Go: May to October

Details: Mount Kailash is a 21,778-foot Himalayan mountain peak in southwestern Tibet, and is considered one of the most sacred places in the world by Buddhists, Hindus, Jains, and Bons. (Bon is a native Tibetan religion.) The Mount Kailash Kora (*kora* means "circumambulation") is a 32-mile-long pilgrimage trail around the base of this stark, rocky, dome-shaped and snowcapped peak that has been followed by practitioners of these religions for millennia. The trail has also become increasingly popular with tourists over the last few decades. The path itself passes over barren terrain, intermixed with an occasional lush meadow, but the views of the surrounding Himalayan peaks, and the diverse groups of pilgrims and tourists traveling together along this path, make the Mount Kailash Kora a combination of geographical, cultural, and religious wonder, and one of the highest-rated hikes on earth. And while it's difficult—the average altitude is about 16,000 feet and the path follows a lot of uneven ground—there are regular guesthouses along the way, as well as tents where you can get hot meals and drinks. So take your time!

THE ISRAEL NATIONAL TRAIL

Location: Israel

Distance: 620 miles (45 to 60 days)

Best Time to Go: Spring and fall

Details: The Israel National Trail (INT) was the brainchild of Israeli journalist and environmentalist Avraham Tamir, who was inspired to see such a trail in his country after hiking America's Appalachian Trail in 1980. The INT zigzags its way across the entire nation of Israel, from the *kibbutz* community of Dan near the Lebanese border, to the southernmost point in Israel, the Red Sea resort city of Eilat. The trail covers a range of terrains, from greener regions in the north, to beaches on the Mediterranean coast, across parts of the Judean mountain range on the outskirts of Jerusalem, to deserts in the south, crossing many ancient archaeological sites along the way. This is a very difficult hike, especially in the desert sections, where you will have to hire people to bring your supplies. It's recommended that all hikers either get a guide or do serious research before attempting it. One of the great things about the

---

Papal bull: In the 1500s, Pope Pius V would enjoy a meal of "pie of bull testicles."

trail: the INT "Trail Angels," people who open their homes at various spots along the way for showers, a place to cook a hot meal, a yard to set up camp, and some friendly conversation. Several *kibbutzes* along the way offer inexpensive food and lodging, as well, as do some Bedouin communities in the southern desert regions. Of course, like most of the trails listed here, if you don't have time to do the whole thing, you can always do small sections at your leisure.

Couch Potato Hiking Bonus: Over the course of three months in the summer of 2015, about 250 volunteers, organized by the Society for the Protection of Nature in Israel and Google, took turns hiking the trail with 360-degree cameras strapped to their backs—so you can now enjoy the entire INT on Google Street View from your home computer.

OTHER WALKS OF LIFE

The Kungsleden (King's Trail) is a popular 270-mile-long trail in the arctic north of Sweden that offers comfortable cabins at regular intervals along its length. The trail is especially popular around the summer solstice, when daylight lasts for nearly 24 hours. (In the winter, the Kungsleden is open as a cross-country ski trail.)

The Thorsborne Trail is a 20-mile trail on Hinchinbrook Island, five miles off the coast of Queensland, Australia. Only 40 hikers are allowed on the path each day, and there's a small entrance fee, but it's worth it: you can camp on tropical beaches (where you might see dugongs, sea turtles, or crocodiles); on rocky outcrops overlooking the Great Barrier Reef; or beside waterfalls in lush and misty rain forests.

Mount Kilimanjaro in Tanzania is the tallest mountain in Africa (19,340 feet), and the tallest freestanding mountain in the world. (It's not part of a larger mountain range—it just suddenly rises out of the African plain.) It's one of the rare tall mountains that doesn't need any special gear to climb, and there are a number of fairly easy trails to its summit, although it will take six to eight days. The trek will take you from hot African savanna at the mountain's base up through the clouds to glaciers near the mountain's snow-covered peak.

The Narrows is just 16 miles long, but it's one of the most beautiful hikes on the planet. It takes you down the Virgin River at the base of Zion Canyon in Zion National Park, Utah. Much of the hike is actually spent walking in the shallow water of the river—refreshing in the heat of the Utah summer—in a sandstone canyon that is sometimes just 20 feet wide, with beautifully sculpted, terra-cotta-hued sandstone walls stretching straight up as high as 2,000 feet above you. You can do the walk in one day, but it's best to take your time and camp in one of the 12 designated campgrounds provided. (Happy trails!)

Out of This World

On page 155 we told you about the bed rest studies that NASA uses to simulate zero-gravity environments on Earth. Here are some of the space agency's other "analog missions" that prepare astronauts for trips to the Moon, asteroids, and Mars.

NEEMO (NASA Extreme Environment Mission Operations)

Location: Aboard *Aquarius*, the world's only undersea laboratory, 3.5 miles off the coast of Key Largo, Florida

Description: *Aquarius* sits on the ocean floor in water more than 60 feet deep. The sunken lab is owned by the National Oceanic and Atmospheric Administration, which uses it to study coral reefs. NASA borrows it for a few weeks in the spring and summer to practice "spacewalks" on the seafloor. Bonus: The isolation and cramped living quarters simulate conditions that will likely exist at a lunar base or on a spacecraft bound for Mars.

Mission: Up to six "aquanauts" share living space not much larger than a school bus for up to two weeks at a time, testing equipment such as robotic arms and battery-powered jet packs when they venture out of *Aquarius* in full-body diving suits that simulate spacesuits. By adding lead weights of various sizes to the suits and to the equipment being tested, the aquanauts can adjust their buoyancy to simulate the gravitational forces found on the Moon, on Mars, and on near-Earth asteroids, where gravity is almost nonexistent. (NASA plans to visit at least one asteroid as an interim step toward one day sending astronauts to Mars.)

During Mars simulations, inserting 20-minute time delays to the communication between *Aquarius* and "mission control" onshore mimics the time it will take radio signals to travel from Mars to Earth. A delay of only three seconds is needed to replicate communications between Earth and the Moon. The 20th NEEMO mission took place in 2015, and more are scheduled for the future.

PRLP (Pavilion Lake Research Project)

Location: Pavilion Lake, about 180 miles northeast of Vancouver, British Columbia

Description: Pavilion Lake is one of only a handful of the world's freshwater lakes that contains coral-like structures called *microbialites*. Similar structures called *stromatolites* were created in the world's oceans 3.5 billion years ago by microorganisms that were among the earliest life-forms on Earth. Some stromatolite fossils from that era have

---

Tall tale: *Carnage carolinensi,* an ancestor of crocodiles, was 9 feet tall and walked on its hind legs.

survived to this day. The microorganisms that made the stromatolites evolved at a time when there was little oxygen in the atmosphere. In fact, they may have been responsible for creating a lot of the oxygen in the atmosphere through a process called *photosynthesis*, which may have made it possible for more advanced life-forms to develop.

Mission: One of the questions that remains unanswered is whether life ever existed on Mars. If so, it's possible that the earliest (and perhaps only) Martian life-forms were similar to the primitive microorganisms that made the stromatolites. By studying the microbialites in Pavilion Lake, NASA hopes to improve its chances of finding evidence, if any exists, that life did indeed exist on Mars millions of years ago.

Bonus: Pavilion Lake is a difficult environment to work in. It's more than 200 feet deep and the water temperature at that depth never rises more than a few degrees above freezing. Studying microbialites on the lake floor requires the use of submersibles and robotic vehicles, similar to the way that rovers and robotic vehicles will be used during a mission to Mars. NASA hopes to use the experience gained to "determine the right balance in the use of autonomous robots, remotely controlled robots, and crewed rovers in future space exploration missions."

HMP (The Haughton-Mars Project)

Location: The Haughton impact crater on Devon Island, in the northern Canadian territory of Nunavut

Description: The Haughton crater was formed some 39 million years ago when a comet or asteroid more than a mile across slammed into what is now Devon Island, leaving a crater 14 miles in diameter. The island is more than 400 miles north of the Arctic Circle, and temperatures remain well below freezing for most of the year. Because of this, the crater has eroded comparatively little since it was formed and is well preserved. Scientists refer to it as "Mars on Earth" because, as the term suggests, it is one of the most Mars-like places anywhere on Earth.

Mission: The crater is strewn with dust, sand, and rocks of all sizes, which makes it a great place to test Mars rovers. One concept that has been repeatedly tested there: using rovers fitted with "space suit ports," in which empty space suits remain outside the vehicle and attached to the airlock or port, and serve as its outer door. When an astronaut needs to walk outside the rover, they open the inner door of the port and slide right into the space suit via a large opening in the back of the suit. Then they close the door behind them, seal the opening of the space suit, and detach the suit from the rover. Space-suit ports will help to keep Martian dust out of the rover, and free up space inside the rover that would otherwise be needed to store the bulky suits.

If and when NASA does send humans to Mars, they'll probably

take at least *two* rovers with them, not just one, thanks to lessons learned at the Haughton impact crater. What's the second one for? To pull the other one free if it gets stuck in the sand. That's something that happens a lot at this site, which means it could also happen on Mars.

DESERT RATS (Research and Technology Studies)

Location: The Black Point Lava Flow, outside of Flagstaff, Arizona

Description: Black Point—more than two million years old—is a rugged site that's subject to dust storms, large temperature swings, and other features similar to those found on Mars and the Moon. (The Moon has no atmosphere or dust storms, but it does have plenty of dusty powder on its surface.) During the Apollo era, NASA made the lava flow even more Moon-like by blasting artificial craters into the volcanic rock.

Mission: At the Black Point site, NASA practices space missions using a simulated base called the Habitat Demonstration Unit (HDU), and mock-ups of two pressurized rovers called Space Exploration Vehicles, or SEVs. The SEVs are like motor homes: they're large enough to contain living quarters in which their two-person crews can venture away from the HDU for up to two weeks at a stretch. When the rovers reach a site that's of interest to the astronauts, they put on mock-ups of space suits, exit through the simulated airlocks, and explore the area on foot.

During the 2010 Desert RATS mission, crews spent 14 days exploring more than 90 miles of the lava flow in their SEVs before driving back to the habitat. With excursions such as these, NASA hopes to improve the efficiency and procedures of similar missions that will be part of any trip to Mars.

ILHS (Inflatable Lunar Habitat Analog Study)

Location: McMurdo Station, an American research facility on the southern tip of Ross Island in Antarctica

Description: The benefit that McMurdo Station offers is that it's in one of the most isolated and extreme environments on Earth.

Mission: Why bother *constructing* a lunar or Martian base when it might be easier and cheaper to *inflate* one? Such a structure, when deflated, would take up less space on a rocket than one built with more conventional materials, and like a tent it could be packed up and moved from one location to another as needed. From 2008 to 2009, NASA conducted a study to see if a prototype habitat and its heating system could withstand the harsh environment of Antarctica, where winter temperatures average –22°F and the wind gusts at speeds in excess of 60 miles per hour. Another goal was to test whether a three-person team would be able to deploy the prototype while dressed in extreme cold weather gear that, like a space suit, limited mobility.

The team spent the first week of the study repeatedly unpacking, inflating, deflating, and repacking the prototype; they found that the average setup time was 50 minutes. At the end of the week they inflated the tent one last time and left it there for a year to see if it would survive the elements without deflating or suffering equipment failure. Few details have been given, but according to NASA, "the habitat experienced several problems that required manual human intervention." An improved model, the agency says, would need "more autonomous maintenance capabilities so that it can resolve problems…without manual intervention." Another finding: astronauts will "need a better way to fasten things to the walls of inflatable structures, as traditional methods such as nails and screws are not an option with inflated walls."

ISRU (In-Situ Resource Utilization)

Location: Mauna Kea, a volcano on the Big Island in Hawaii

Description: Mauna Kea's crater looks like a lunar crater and just as important, the volcanic rocks and soil contain large amounts of oxygen, just like the rocks and soil on the Moon do.

Mission: One of the factors that makes trips to the Moon or Mars so expensive is that the astronauts need to bring with them all the oxygen they'll breathe, all the water they'll drink, and all the fuel they'll need to get back home. But what if these resources could be manufactured on site? The risks associated with a mission would be reduced substantially. That's what In-Situ Resource Utilization missions are all about: developing technologies to extract oxygen and water from lunar and Martian soils.

In 2008, a robotic excavator succeeded in collecting some of Mauna Kea's volcanic soil and feeding it into a machine that extracted oxygen from the soil. For a 2012 mission, prospecting for ice was the goal, and future missions will focus on putting the water to use. Both Mars and the Moon have ice at their poles; the southern polar ice cap on Mars contains enough water to cover the entire surface of the planet under 35 feet of water. Technology being developed on Mauna Kea will one day make it possible to process lunar and Martian water into potable water that astronauts will be able to drink. Technology also exists to split the water molecules into hydrogen, which can be used as rocket fuel, and oxygen for the astronauts to breathe.

HI-SEAS (Hawaii Space Exploration Analog and Simulation)

Location: Mauna Loa, another volcano on the Big Island of Hawaii

---

There's an abandoned missile base in the Florida Everglades, built during the Cuban Missile Crisis.

Description: Like Mauna Kea, Mauna Loa is isolated and barren—just the kind of otherworldly locale to simulate the isolation and boredom of a long spaceflight.

Mission: The HI-SEAS facility consists of a two-story geodesic dome just 36 feet in diameter and 20 feet tall, about the size of a small house. In August 2015, six "crew members" shut themselves inside the dome for the program's fourth—and longest—mission to date: a one-year stay in which they were cut off from the rest of the world, just as they would be on a mission to Mars.

Conditions inside the dome hewed as closely to those on Mars as NASA could make it. The crew had limited access to water—just one six-minute shower a week—and no fresh food. Instead, they ate only the kinds of shelf-stable, packaged foods that would remain edible without refrigeration on a three-year Mars mission. To simulate the kind of bulky radiation shielding that would be necessary on a Martian base, the dome was built with just one tiny porthole window, with a view of the lava field outside. The crew members spent most of their time inside the dome, venturing out only during simulated spacewalks, after putting on mock space suits and passing through an airlock.

Each member of the crew had their own projects to work on, but the overarching mission was to see how well six people could manage the emotional and psychological strain of living together in tight quarters for an extended length of time. Boredom is more than just a quality-of-life issue when astronauts are 34 million miles from home; if it remains unaddressed it can lead to depression, lethargy, inattention to detail, impaired judgment, and risk-taking behavior—the kinds of things that can cause a multiyear, multibillion-dollar mission to fail. By studying these issues here on Earth and developing strategies to deal with them, NASA hopes to prevent just such a failure and, in the process, make life at a lonely, faraway Martian outpost as pleasant and productive as possible.

*   *   *

BOOKS OF RECORD

Martin Tovey of Radstock, England, earned an entry in *Guinness World Records* for...owning the most *Guinness World Records*. His impressive collection, which he began in 1968, now totals more than 350 Guinness books as well as thousands of Guinness collectibles—including Guinness board games, Guinness spoons, and other Guinness trinkets. A Guinness spokesperson said that "Tovey's incredible collection outstrips even the archive here at *Guinness World Records!*"

The Miami Showband Massacre

In July 1975, a van carrying members of a popular Irish pop band was stopped at a British Army checkpoint on a rural road in Northern Ireland. The band members didn't think much of it: this was at the height of the "Troubles," the decades-long period of violent strife over control of Northern Ireland, during which bombings and shootings were common. But this was no ordinary checkpoint, and what followed was a massacre that shook the already shaken country.

TROUBLING HISTORY

In the late 1960s, after more than 40 years of relative peace, violence broke out in Northern Ireland over England's controversial centuries-long rule of the region. What was the origin of that strife—and why was it centered in the north of Ireland?

England first invaded Ireland all the way back in the 12th century (at the invitation of the deposed king of Leinster and with the backing of Pope Adrian IV), and completely conquered the country in the 16th century. This was followed by a program of subjugation and colonization by which Irish clan leaders who submitted to English rule could keep their land; those who rebelled had their land taken from them. Confiscated lands were then given to English and Scottish settlers. The region with the most unyielding clans—and thus the region that ended up with the most foreign settlers—was Ireland's far northern province of Ulster, the last stronghold of Ireland's ancient Gaelic culture. (This settlement program was referred to as the "Plantation of Ulster.")

EARLY TENSIONS

The English and Scottish who settled in Ireland were required not only to be loyal to England, but also to be Protestant because England, with its official Anglican Church, was overwhelmingly Protestant. That added a religious element to the conflict, because the Irish were overwhelmingly Roman Catholic.

Making the situation worse, the British passed a number of repressive and discriminatory laws, including laws that made it illegal for Catholics to hold office, to inherit property, to marry Protestants, or to become lawyers or judges. Most of those laws were repealed in the 18th and 19th centuries, but some persisted, and widespread discrimination against Catholics in Ireland continued into the 20th century.

Older than you think: Inline skates were invented in 1823 and were called the "Volito."

IRISH (PARTIAL) INDEPENDENCE

In the 1880s, an Irish independence movement began, and over the following decades, as the movement gained more support, tensions between pro-Irish and British loyalist groups became more heated. The region with the most tension was Ulster, which, unlike the rest of Ireland, had a majority pro-British Protestant population—the descendants of the original Scottish and English settlers. In 1912, a loyalist group in Ulster formed a paramilitary group (a military organization not officially linked to a nation's government) called the Ulster Volunteer Force (UVF), with the express purpose of stopping the Irish independence movement. A pro-Irish group, in turn, formed a paramilitary group called the Irish National Volunteers, which soon became known as the Irish Republican Army (IRA). Over the following years, a series of violent clashes occurred, and by 1919 the IRA and the British Army, with help from the UVF, were at war. In 1921, the conflict ended when both sides signed a treaty establishing an independent Irish Free State.

But not all of Ireland became independent: a large chunk of Ulster became the region now known as Northern Ireland, and it remains part of the United Kingdom today.

BACK TO WAR

Relations between pro-Irish and pro-British groups in Northern Ireland remained strained in the decades following the 1920s, but aside from brief skirmishes, things remained relatively peaceful. Then, in the 1960s, a series of incidents led to a renewed outbreak of violence:

• In the early 1960s, civil rights groups began staging large demonstrations in cities around Ulster (the biggest of them in Ulster's capital, Belfast), calling for an end to the anti-Catholic discrimination that continued in Northern Ireland.

• In 1966, in response to the demonstrations and the pro-Catholic sentiments they were stirring up, a pro-British group re-formed the UVF and started carrying out deadly attacks against Catholics.

• In 1969, the IRA, which had never disbanded, started staging attacks of their own against Protestant civilians and police officers, with the goal of ending British rule in Northern Ireland. That same year, the British Army was deployed to Northern Ireland—and the period known as the Troubles had officially begun.

By 1975, several hundred people had been killed—most of them civilians, and most of them in shootings and bombings carried out by the UVF and the IRA. Most of the attacks occurred in Northern Ireland, but they occurred in the Republic of Ireland and England as well. And while there were attacks that took more lives, the 1975 attack on the Miami Showband was probably the one that shook the region the hardest.

MUSIC MAKERS

The Miami Showband was a six-piece musical group that was part of the "Irish showband" scene—dance bands that toured Ireland from the 1950s until the late 1970s, playing mostly rock 'n' roll cover songs to throngs of kids in ballrooms across both the Republic of Ireland and Northern Ireland. The showband scene was incredibly popular, and the Miami Showband, founded in 1962, was the most popular of the bunch. With seven #1 songs on the Irish pop charts over the years, they'd earned the nickname the "Irish Beatles." The band's lineup in 1975: lead singer (and heartthrob) Fran O'Toole, guitarist Tony Geraghty, bassist Steve Travers, drummer Ray Millar, saxophonist Des Lee, and trumpeter Brian McCoy.

The height of the Miami Showband's popularity, in the early and mid-1970s, coincided with the worst years of the Troubles. And although the band was based in Dublin, they regularly performed across the border in Northern Ireland. The band members weren't political; they took no outspoken positions on the conflict, and were, in fact, a mix of four Catholics and two Protestants. But despite that, as the Troubles raged on, it became increasingly dangerous for them to play in Northern Ireland.

THE ATTACK

On July 30, 1975, the band performed at a ballroom in Banbridge, a small Northern Ireland town about 25 miles southwest of Belfast. At around 2:30 a.m. on July 31, five members of the band packed their gear in their Volkswagen minibus and headed back south toward Dublin. (Drummer Ray Millar left in his own car.) Not long after setting out, as they made their way down a dark rural road, they were stopped at a British Army checkpoint. They weren't worried—army checkpoints were a fact of life in Northern Ireland in those days. The soldiers made the musicians line up by the side of the road while they searched the van. There were about ten soldiers in all, commanded by an officer later described as having an upper-class British accent. Two of the soldiers opened the van's rear hatch, presumably to search its contents. Then they closed the hatch…and suddenly there was a huge explosion.

The blast completely destroyed the van and killed the two soldiers instantly. The force of the explosion blew all five of the Miami Showband members down a short slope and onto an adjacent field. Inexplicably, the surviving soldiers immediately started firing at the musicians. Brian McCoy was shot in the back nine times and died.

Fran O'Toole tried to run away; a soldier ran him down and shot him 22 times with a machine gun, 12 of the shots to his face while he lay on the ground. Tony Geraghty also tried to run and, after pleading for his life, was shot in the back and the head four times. The other two members survived: Steve Travers was shot only once, and survived by playing dead; Des Lee was blown into a nearby thicket by the explosion, and the gunmen didn't see him.

THE UVF

The British Army checkpoint wasn't an army checkpoint at all: the men were members of the pro-British UVF paramilitary, dressed in British Army uniforms. Specifically, they were members of the Mid-Ulster Brigade, known as one of the most ruthless UVF units in Ulster. They were led by Robin "the Jackal" Jackson, who is believed to have killed more than 50 people—and to be behind dozens of deadly bombings—during his more than 20 years with the UVF.

The attack on the Miami Showband was, of course, meant to go differently. The UVF soldiers who appeared to be searching the back of the van were actually hiding a powerful time bomb. The bomb was supposed to go off when the band was farther down the road, and would have almost certainly killed all five musicians. The band and the IRA would be blamed for the bombing, because the band would have appeared to be smuggling bombs for the IRA. But something went wrong, and the bomb went off early. The surviving soldiers attempted to kill all the musicians to prevent the UVF's involvement in the attack from being revealed.

AFTERMATH

Des Lee waited until he was sure the soldiers were gone, then made his way to the road, flagged a passing car, and got a ride to the nearest police station. Steve Travers was subsequently picked up, and both men were treated at a local hospital.

Twelve hours after the attack, the UVF issued a public statement, saying that one of their patrols had stopped the Miami Showband's van to perform a standard security search, and that a bomb in the van had gone off during the search. But they came under heavy machine-gun fire, the statement continued, after which they returned fire, subsequently killing their attackers (the Miami Showband). The statement alleged that the band had been transporting explosives for the IRA.

Few people—at least few Catholics—believed the statement, and investigators were able to link the bombing to the UVF fairly quickly. Arrests were made in the weeks following the attack, and, in October 1976, two of the men involved were sentenced to 35 years in prison

---

The first comic book, called *The Wasp*, was published in 1802.

each. In 1980, a third UVF member was convicted for his part in the killings, and received the same sentence. Robin "the Jackal" Jackson was arrested, but police didn't have enough evidence to link him to the attack. The three convicted men never gave up the names of their co-conspirators.

LATER FINDINGS

Over the years, there have been allegations that the British Army and the Royal Ulster Constabulary (RUC), Northern Ireland's official police force, collaborated with the UVF in committing atrocities during the period. And there is evidence that both groups played a part in the Miami Showband killings.

• Two of the UVF men convicted in the attack were also members of a British Army regiment. The third man was a former member.

• In 1981, a British Army intelligence officer-turned-whistleblower claimed the attack was planned by an army intelligence officer, Captain Robert Nairac, along with UVF's Robin "the Jackal" Jackson. The two survivors, Steve Travers and Des Lee, believe Nairac may have been the man with the upper-class British accent who was in command during the attack. The allegation has never been proven. (Nairac was abducted and killed by the IRA in 1977.)

• In 2011, the Police Service of Northern Ireland confirmed that Robin "the Jackal" Jackson's fingerprint had been found on a gun silencer found at the scene of the bombing. The report also confirmed that Jackson was a special agent with the RUC at the time of the killings. (Jackson died of cancer in 1998.)

Neither the British Army nor the RUC have ever admitted to having played a part in the attack. Travers, Lee, and family members of the three murdered musicians continue to call for an investigation into possible collusion in the attack, and for justice to be brought to those involved.

CONCLUSION

The Miami Showband massacre inflamed the already ugly conflict, and in the weeks afterward, the IRA staged a number of revenge attacks, including the bombing of a Belfast bar frequented by Protestants that killed five people. The UVF responded with more attacks of their own, and the grim conflict ground on for another two decades.

The remaining members of the Miami Showband, Steve Travers, Des Lee, and Ray Millar (Millar was the lucky one who'd driven his own car that night), re-formed the Miami Showband in late 1975, but by 1978 all three had left the band and moved on to different things.

Henry Ford, Thomas Edison, and Harvey Firestone used to take vacations together.

They got back together in 2005, thirty years after the bombing, for a memorial concert in Dublin.

LAST NOTES

• The three men convicted of taking part in the attack were all released from prison in 1998, as part of the Good Friday Agreement that marked the official end of the Troubles.

• In 2005, a memorial to the two UVF members killed trying to plant the bomb in the attack was installed at an estate in Portadown, Northern Ireland, where one of the attackers lived. The plaque describes them as having been "killed in action."

• Dozens of paramilitary organizations were formed during the Troubles, on both sides of the conflict, but none were as deadly as the UVF and the IRA. Estimated number of people killed by the UVF: 483. By the IRA: 1,823. Both organizations still exist today; both are classified as terrorist organizations in both the UK and the Republic of Ireland.

• In 2007, Steve Travers revealed that in 2006 he received an invitation to meet secretly with the UVF's second-in-command. Travers reported that the UVF commander apologized for the killings. He did not say whether or not he accepted the apology.

*   *   *

LEADER IN NUDITY

Leader is a town of about 900 in rural Saskatchewan. Highway 32 was a main route in the area, but by 2006 it had become so poorly maintained and dotted with potholes that most locals wouldn't use it for fear of losing a hubcap or an axle. Pharmacist Gord Stueck put together a group of concerned citizens to petition the provincial government of Saskatchewan for the funding to clean it up, but it was fruitless. Stueck jokingly told a reporter that maybe he and his friends—mostly male senior citizens—would put out a sexy charity calendar to raise the money they needed to do the road repairs. Then he decided it was actually a pretty good idea. Result: a 2007 calendar featuring Stueck, plus ten other male and one female resident of Leader, all posing nude in front of the pothole-covered Highway 32. Well, they weren't completely nude—certain body parts were obscured by "strategic poses or props," such as hubcaps. Amazingly, Leader sold more than 3,000 copies of the calendar, and made a profit of $40,000. That, combined with a change in government, led to the road finally getting fixed as part of a highway renovation project in 2010.

The Fenn Treasure

Hidden somewhere in the Rocky Mountains north of Santa Fe, there's an 800-year-old chest filled with $2 million in treasure. Want to find it? Here's the story of the man who hid it and the clues he's given to help you find it.

THE COLLECTOR

Forrest Fenn was a kid growing up south of Waco, Texas, in the late 1930s. His father was the principal of the local school, and when he wasn't busy seeing to the education of the town children, the elder Fenn passed on a love for a different kind of learning to his son: scouring the countryside for Native American artifacts. Forrest found his first arrowhead when he was about nine years old. "I was exhilarated and it started me on a lifelong adventure of discovering and collecting things," he told an interviewer in 2013.

Fenn joined the U.S. Air Force in 1950 and became a fighter pilot. His military career took him all over the world, and whenever he was on leave, he searched for ancient artifacts. He found Roman jars filled with olive oil in Pompeii, old brass coins in the Mediterranean Sea near Tripoli, Libya, and 8,000-year-old spearheads in the Sahara desert. After his military career was up, he decided to turn his hobby into a career, and in the early 1970s he became a dealer of Southwestern art and antiquities in Santa Fe, New Mexico.

X MARKS THE SPOT

In 1987, Fenn's father died from pancreatic cancer, and the following year Fenn himself was diagnosed with kidney cancer. His doctors gave him just a 20 percent chance of surviving more than a few years. His brush with mortality caused him to think about his own legacy—what kind of mark, if any, did he want to make on the world?

Fenn decided that his "mark" would be like an X on a treasure map. Searching for artifacts had given him such pleasure during his lifetime that he decided to try and pass his love for the hobby on to others, just as his father had passed it to him. What better way to do that than to give would-be treasure hunters an *actual treasure* to hunt for? Over the years Fenn had amassed a collection of artifacts worth millions of dollars, and he began selecting some of his favorite pieces to include in the treasure.

In 1990, he paid $25,000 for an 800-year-old bronze lock box that he thought would make a good treasure chest, and began filling it with the items he selected: hundreds of gold nuggets, more than 200 gold coins, "lots of jewelry" that included a 2,000-year-old fetish necklace and a gem-encrusted Spanish ring dating to the 1600s, and much more. When full, the box weighed 42 pounds. Beneath the treasure at the bottom of the box was a copy of Fenn's autobiography, printed in tiny lettering, rolled up and stuffed into an ancient olive jar. He even tossed a magnifying glass into the box so that the tiny words would be easier to read. (One item that he didn't put in the box: his most treasured possession—that first arrowhead that Fenn found when he was nine. He says he still has it…and he's keeping it.)

BONELESS

One idea Fenn toyed with was waiting until he was near death to carry the treasure to its hiding place, then lie down and die next to it, ensuring that he and his treasure would be found together. That was one reason for putting his autobiography in the lock box: he wanted to make it easy for the authorities to identify his body. So why didn't he stick with the plan? He beat his cancer. "I ruined the story by getting well," he jokes.

Fenn held onto the treasure chest for about 20 years, but the cancer never came back. So sometime around 2010 (he won't say exactly when), he put the box in his pickup truck and drove to a spot in the Rocky Mountains somewhere north of Santa Fe (he won't say where). Then he got out of the truck and carried the treasure chest into the wilderness on foot (he won't say how far). At some point he stopped and hid the treasure, or maybe he just left it sitting there, in plain sight. Then he drove back home.

Whatever he did with the treasure, as far as anyone can tell, it's still right where he left it, waiting to be discovered.

RHYME OR REASON

To help treasure seekers find his treasure, Fenn wrote a poem that he says contains nine clues that point to its location. It reads as follows:

As I have gone alone in there

And with my treasures bold,

I can keep my secret where,

And hint of riches new and old.

Begin it where warm waters halt

And take it in the canyon down,

Not far, but too far to walk.

Put in below the home of Brown.

From there it's no place for the meek,

The end is ever drawing nigh;

First woman depicted on U.S. currency: Pocahontas, on an 1865 $20 bill.

There'll be no paddle up your creek,

Just heavy loads and water high.

If you've been wise and found the blaze,

Look quickly down, your quest to cease,

But tarry scant with marvel gaze,

Just take the chest and go in peace.

So why is it that I must go

And leave my trove for all to seek?

The answers I already know,

I've done it tired, and now I'm weak.

So hear me all and listen good,

Your effort will be worth the cold.

If you are brave and in the wood

I give you title to the gold.

GOLD RUSH

Fenn published the poem along with his autobiography in a 2010 book called *The Thrill of the Chase: A Memoir*. But he only sold it through a single bookstore in Santa Fe, so knowledge of the treasure spread slowly. Then in 2013, a producer on NBC's *Today* show read about it in an in-flight magazine and profiled the story on the show. Within weeks of the *Today* story airing, treasure hunters from all over the country began arriving in Santa Fe and points north to search for Fenn's treasure chest.

Fortune seekers have been coming ever since, and the numbers continue to grow. It's estimated that as many as 30,000 people head into the Rockies each year to look for the Fenn Treasure. Many of them gather in organized group campouts called "Fennborees" that allow treasure hunters to share stories and compare theories.

MORE CLUES

Since publishing the poem, Fenn has offered a few more clues:

• He didn't bury the treasure in his own yard, in his neighbors' yards, or in any of the cemeteries where his relatives are buried. He asks that treasure seekers not dig in these places anymore, at least not without permission. (If you bother him at home or follow him around Santa Fe, he'll call the police, as he's already done on more than one occasion.)

• He didn't bury the treasure in any *other* grave or cemetery, either, so don't go digging anyplace where people are buried. Fenn gave out this clue after one treasure seeker was arrested for digging up a *descanso* (a marker that denotes where someone died or had their ashes scattered) near the Pecos River. Digging up descansos is illegal.

Glowworms aren't worms, but they do glow: They're luminous flies, similar to gnats.

- It isn't hidden in or under any buildings or other structures. "No need to dig up the old outhouses," he says.

- Actually, Fenn won't even confirm that the treasure is buried. Nor will he confirm that it's in New Mexico. In 2014, he published a treasure map that includes all of the Rockies in western Montana, Wyoming, and Colorado, as well as New Mexico north of Santa Fe.

- In an advertisement that Fenn appeared in for the New Mexico Board of Tourism in 2015, he states, "I know the treasure chest is wet." He also said that if he were standing near it, he'd smell "wonderful smells, of pine needles or piñon nuts or sagebrush." After filming the commercial, though, he said that it didn't contain any new clues, so you'll have to decide for yourself how much this information is worth.

- Fenn also reminds treasure seekers that he carried the 42-pound treasure chest into the wilderness on foot. He was in his late seventies at the time, so "don't look anywhere where a 79- or 80-year-old man can't put something. I'm not that fit. I can't climb 14,000 feet."

- Fenn insists there really is a chest filled with treasure, and it really is hidden out there somewhere. He had to confirm this after one treasure hunter wrote a book about her search in 2014. As was the case with everyone else (so far), her search came up empty. But because she was sure she'd figured out the correct hiding place, she concluded that the real treasure must be the fun of the search itself. Fenn rejects her conclusion, though he does agree with the sentiment. The thrill of the hunt, after all, is what caused him to hide the treasure in the first place. "I'm trying to get fathers and mothers to go out into the countryside with their children. I want them to get away from the house and away from the TV and the texting, and while they're looking for treasure they will also explore the outdoors," he told the *Albuquerque Journal* in 2013. "That's the adventure and the greater treasure."

*   *   *

HOT WHEELS

In 2012, a Japanese company called Stokyo Design introduced the Soundwagon, touted as the most compact, most portable, and smallest record player available. It looks like a tiny toy Volkswagen van, scarcely larger than the 9-volt battery that goes inside of it. The toy car has a record-playing needle on the bottom and a speaker on the top. When turned on and placed on the groove of a vinyl record (which can sit on any surface—no turntable required), the car zooms around the surface and plays the music. Today it's sold as the Record Runner.

Stranded in the Car: Stories of Survival

For these people, surviving the crash was only the beginning of their uncanny struggle to stay alive.

THE LONG WAY UP

The Driver: Debra Lopez, 57, of Atascadero, California

The Accident: In February 2015, Lopez told her husband she was going to the store. She decided to take the scenic route on Highway 1, which overlooks the Pacific Ocean. The road's high cliffs, sharp turns, and intermittent guardrails can be treacherous if you take your eyes off the road. Logan took her eyes off the road. She put out a cigarette, and when she looked back up, she was heading toward a cliff. She hit the brakes, but it was too late. "The truck just flew over and I could just feel myself flying down and hitting things," she said.

Staying Alive: When Lopez finally came to some time later, she was still strapped in her seat belt—upside down—and her face was bleeding. When she tried to move, she felt excruciating pain in her ribs, so she remained in that position for nearly a day. She had no cell service, no food or water, and as the hours dragged on, little hope that she'd ever see her husband again. By the next morning, Lopez realized that no one was coming to rescue her, so she decided to rescue herself. The seemingly simple task of unbuckling her seat belt and climbing out of the vehicle took several hours. Once out, Lopez saw that her truck had landed (on its roof) in a ditch—which was fortunate, because otherwise it could have tumbled into the sea. Thirsty and weak, she drank some rainwater that had gathered in the wheel well. Then she looked for an escape route. The sheer cliffs and rough seas below meant there was only one way out: "If I go straight up that mountain, I can get out."

Climbing 100 feet up a near-vertical rock face would be difficult for an experienced climber, but even though Lopez was injured and past retirement age, she said that her will to see her family again and her faith in God kept her pressing on, inch by inch. It took her an entire day to claw her way up the cliff. When she finally reached the road, three days after going over it, she kissed the asphalt.

Rescued: A short time later, a vacationing family drove past and saw the battered and bruised woman and stopped to help. Lopez was rushed to a hospital in nearby San Luis Obispo, where doctors told her she was in remarkably good shape considering what she'd gone through.

Aftermath: Her husband, who'd spent the past 72 hours frantically looking for her, was overjoyed. "He said, 'What the heck happened?'" Lopez recounted to the *San Luis Obispo Tribune*. "I told him about the truck, and he says, 'I don't care about the truck.'" But as relieved as Lopez was to see her family, she admitted that it will take some time to fully recover. "I know I'm still here, but my mind is still in that ditch."

LITTLE ANGEL

The Driver: Patti Marie Emery-Wade, 44, of Arizona

The Accident: In January 2004, Emery-Wade was driving on Arizona Highway 60 to visit her brother. Also in the car was her three-year-old daughter, Angel, and their pug dog. At some point during the drive, Emery-Wade lost control of her car; it went over an embankment and then hit a juniper tree before coming to a stop down a hill.

Staying Alive: Emery-Wade suffered trauma to her head and back and was barely clinging to life. The dog didn't make it. Angel suffered a head injury as well, most likely because she wasn't strapped into her car seat. (That actually turned out to be a good thing: a tree branch had crashed through the window and impaled the car seat.) Using what little strength she had left, the injured mother wrapped her daughter in a blanket. And then—it's unclear exactly when—Emery-Wade died, leaving her little girl alone in the car.

The temperature was below freezing and a series of winter storms was rolling through, and because the windows were broken, Angel was exposed to the cold and snow. She had no coat, just loose clothes and that blanket to keep warm. All she had to eat were some crackers. Meanwhile, a massive search was underway, but with each passing day, Emery-Wade's friends and family were losing hope.

Rescued: Five days after the crash, the car was finally spotted by a sharp-eyed motorist. Police Sergent Dave Wander was the first on the scene. After trudging 60 feet down the embankment through the snow, he expected the worst. "I could see that the mother was dead," he told the *Arizona Republic*. At first, it didn't look like anyone else was in there. "And then all of a sudden, Angel popped up!" She'd been curled up in the blanket, and started "chattering away" when she saw him. "I leaned halfway in, and she came right to me." Angel told the policeman her name and age, and asked him for something to eat. She was bruised and shivering, but she didn't cry. "She's a sweetheart," he said.

Aftermath: Angel was placed in intensive care—she was dehydrated, had a large bruise on her head, and had frostbite on her hands and feet. Dr. Mark Matthews was able to save all of her fingers and toes, and expected her to make a full recovery. "She had an inner cranial bleed, but she's done well," Matthews told *Good Morning, America*, adding, "She's adorable." Angel was placed in the care of her extended family. "She was told her mom had gone to heaven," her neighbor Roland Racine told the *East Valley Tribune*. "She's very sad, but she's taking it in stride. She's a strong little girl."

RUDE AWAKENING

The Driver: Joe Woodring, 21, of Boone, North Carolina

The Accident: While driving home on a cold night in the Appalachian Mountains in October 2014, Woodring fell asleep at the wheel of his pickup truck. It went off the road and tumbled 60 feet down an embankment, rolling several times.

Staying Alive: When Woodring came to, he was on his back inside the crushed cab; his legs were pinned beneath the dashboard and seat. He knew he was hurt but didn't know how badly. And the temperature was dropping fast. "I could hear vehicles and I tried to holler, but nobody heard me," he told WBTV. "I thought that I was going to lay there and die." Refusing to give up, the avid outdoorsman put his survival skills to work. He used a pocket knife to cut fabric from the seat for a blanket. He stuffed some grass inside his shirt for insulation, and caught some rainwater in a can to help him stay hydrated. As night gave way to morning, Woodring alternated between yelling for help and praying to God.

Rescued: That afternoon, more than 17 hours after the crash, a man drove by in a truck that was high enough for him to see the overturned pickup below. He slowed down and, when he heard cries for help, he called the police. When they reached Woodring, he was still pinned, and by this point he couldn't feel his left foot. It took rescuers two hours to cut open the pickup and free him.

Aftermath: Woodring's right leg was broken; the doctor told him that if his left leg wasn't amputated immediately, his organs would shut down and he would die. Woodring had the operation, and vowed that once he's fitted with a prosthetic leg, he'll pick up right where he left off in life. "He knows he's going to walk again," his aunt Trish Miller told WSOC TV. "He hasn't said the first negative thing about any of it."

SWAMPED

The Driver: Tillie Tooter, 83, of Pembroke Pines, Florida

The Accident: In August 2000, at around 3:30 a.m., Tillie was driving her Toyota Tercel on I-595 to pick up her granddaughter at Fort Lauderdale International Airport. While she was on an overpass, her car was rear-ended by a man in a pickup truck. (He left the scene, and later claimed he'd fallen asleep and didn't even realize he'd hit another car.) The impact sent Tooter's Tercel into a barrier, scraping along more than 30 feet before launching over an embankment, and then landing 50 feet below in a swamp full of thick mangrove trees.

Staying Alive: The next thing Tooter knew, she was upside down. She freed herself from her seat belt, but she couldn't get the car's doors open. Trapped and in pain, she yelled for help but was too far from the freeway to be seen or heard. She couldn't find her phone, and she had nothing to eat except for some chewing gum and a few cough drops.

As the sun rose in the sky, her predicament got even worse: the muggy August temperatures approached 100°F. Inside the car it was sweltering; outside, the swamp was infested with snakes, alligators, ants, and mosquitoes. The reptiles didn't get her, but the bugs had a feast. Trapped and uncomfortable, the 83-year-old woman kept herself alive by drinking rainwater she collected in the steering wheel cover. Eventually, Tooter became too weak to yell for help.

Three days passed.

Rescued: About 78 hours after the crash, 15-year-old Justin Vannelli was picking up garbage on the side of the freeway with his father when he spotted something. "I saw all those trees pushed over," he told the *Miami Herald*. "And then I saw the car. I was looking at it for a while, and I saw her feet. She was dangling her feet to get my attention." Justin's dad called 911. Rescuers had to rappel 50 feet down the slope, and cut down several trees to reach the vehicle. Then they had to cut open the car to get her out. Tooter was placed in a stretcher, lifted up to the road by a crane, and then rushed to a hospital.

Aftermath: She was in critical condition and placed in intensive care, but she recovered…mostly. She needed a walker and never regained full use of her right arm, but that didn't slow her down. In fact, Tooter became a minor celebrity. The media couldn't get enough of the octo-genarian's resolve and wit. Two years after the accident, she accepted an apology from the man who ran her off the road. "I feel deeply sorry for your mother because I'm sure you broke her heart," she told him in court. "I will pay for the rest of my life, but I have no bitterness toward you." Tillie Tooter died in 2015 at the ripe old age of 98.

*　　　*　　　*

POLITICAL THEATER

Jimmy Carter watched five movies a week during his presidency. The very first, screened at the White House two days after his 1977 inaugu-ration: *All the President's Men*, the story of how *Washington Post* writers Bob Woodward and Carl Bernstein uncovered the Watergate scandal (which led to the resignation of his predecessor, Richard Nixon).

Artificial People

Ordinarily, when someone describes another person as "artificial," they're referring to a real person who only seems fake. But occasionally the expression applies to a fake "person" who seems real, like Apple's Siri. Did you think she was the first artificial person? Think again.

ELIZA

What It Was: One of the earliest "chatterbots," a computer program that mimics conversation between two people

How It Worked: Created in 1966 by an MIT computer scientist named Joseph Weizenbaum, ELIZA was designed to imitate a psychotherapist interviewing a patient. An interview began when the human user typed a statement into the computer. ELIZA then searched the statement for any keywords for which it had preprogrammed responses. If the statement contained the word "father," for example, ELIZA would reply with, "Tell me more about your family." If the statement contained no keywords, ELIZA responded with a general statement such as "Please go on" or "Why do you say that just now?" to keep the conversation going. The program also fed the user's statements back to them in the form of questions. If a user typed, "My boyfriend made me come here," ELIZA responded with, "Your boyfriend made you come here?"

Weizenbaum made ELIZA simulate a psychotherapist to take advantage of the therapeutic technique of repeating the patient's own statements back to them. It's a form of conversation in which simple repetition of one person's speech plays a central role. Doing so saved Weizenbaum the trouble of having to program ELIZA with any real-world knowledge. It could turn "I had an argument with my wife" into "You had an argument with your wife?" mechanically, without ELIZA having to know what an argument was or what a wife was.

Impact: Even when Weizenbaum explained the trick of how the program worked, he was startled by how quickly users came to believe—falsely—that ELIZA understood what they were saying and was putting thought and even emotion into her replies. "I had not realized...that extremely short exposures to a relatively simple computer program could induce powerful delusional thinking in quite normal people," he said. He was so disturbed by the phenomenon that he wrote a book, *Computer Power and Human Reason*, in which he discusses the limits of artificial intelligence and warns against ever giving computers the power to make important decisions affecting the lives of human beings.

Oxford University began admitting women in 1879...but didn't award them degrees until 1920.

PARRY

What It Was: A chatterbot that mimicked the conversational patterns of a person suffering from paranoid schizophrenia

How It Worked: Developed by a Stanford University computer scientist named Kenneth Colby in 1972, PARRY has been described as "ELIZA with attitude." Instead of simply repeating the human user's statements back to them, PARRY was programmed to add his own "beliefs, fears, and anxieties" to a conversation, including an obsession with horse racing and a delusion that the Mafia was trying kill him. Unlike ELIZA, he had a background story: he was an unmarried, 28-year-old male who worked at the post office.

Impact: To test the program's effectiveness at simulating someone who is mentally ill, Colby arranged for a group of psychiatrists to interview a mix of human subjects and computers running the PARRY software. The psychiatrists communicated with their patients over computer terminals, and did not know which patients were human and which were computers. Afterward, transcripts of the interviews were printed and shown to a second group of psychiatrists, who were asked to identify which patients were human and which were computers. The psychiatrists guessed correctly just 48% of the time—no better than if they had made their guesses by flipping a coin.

Bonus: Considering that ELIZA was modeled on a psychotherapist and PARRY was simulating mental illness, it was probably just a matter of time before someone got the idea of having the two programs talk to each other. (How did that go? See page 499.)

RACTER

What It Was: Short for "Artificially Insane Raconteur," Racter was one of the first chatterbots that consumers could buy for their home computers. It went on sale in 1984 and cost $49.95.

How It Worked: Programmers Tom Etter and William Chamberlain designed Racter purely with entertainment in mind. They thought home computer users would enjoy the experience of "talking" to their IBM PCs, Commodore Amigas, and Apple II computers. Advances in computer technology made it possible to pack Racter with a much larger database of conversational topics than had been possible when ELIZA and PARRY were developed. That's what made him a raconteur. Jumping randomly from one unrelated topic to another, even in midsentence, was what made him "artificially insane."

Impact: Racter could also compose essays, poetry, and short stories. Etter and Chamberlain published a collection of his work in what was billed as "the first book ever written by a computer," *The Policeman's Beard Is Half Constructed.* "Tomatoes from England and lettuce from

---

Canada are eaten by cosmologists from Russia," Racter wrote. "I dream implacably about this concept. Nevertheless tomatoes or lettuce can inevitably come leisurely from my home, not merely from England or Canada."

VIVIENNE

What It Was: A virtual cellphone girlfriend

How It Worked: ELIZA, PARRY, and Racter were all text-based personalities. You typed a message into the computer and the computer responded. By 2004, however, technology had advanced to the point that it was possible to stream audio and video over cellphones. That inspired a Hong Kong software company called Artificial Life to create one of the first artificial personalities that could actually be seen, heard, and communicated with by text message: Vivienne, a 20-something anime character who supposedly worked as a computer graphic designer at Artificial Life.

Adding Vivienne to your cellphone service cost $6 a month. The subscription included 18 virtual locations to take your new girlfriend to, including restaurants, bars, a shopping mall, and the airport. Vivienne was programmed to converse on 35,000 different topics in six different languages. She was flirty, and if you bought her enough gifts—most were free, but the nicest ones added charges of 50¢ to $2.00 per gift to your cellphone bill—your relationship could progress from virtual smooching all the way to marriage. But that marriage would never be consummated, not even virtually, no matter how many fancy gifts you charged to your phone. Reason: Artificial Life hoped to market Vivienne to teenagers with affluent parents (who paid the cellphone bill), so the relationship never got intimate.

Impact: Vivienne never really caught fire, and the service is no longer available, but Virtual Life is still in business. Today it markets smartphone apps like Robot Unicorn Attack Heavy Metal, Amateur Surgeon, and Barbie APP-RIFIC Cash Register.

KARIM

What It Is: Something that ELIZA imitated in the 1960s but never really was—a psychotherapy bot

How It Works: Following the outbreak of civil war in Syria in 2011, more than three million Syrians fled the country and were living as refugees in neighboring countries. It's estimated that as many as one in five suffer from anxiety, depression, post-traumatic stress, or other mental health problems. But access to mental health care is limited, and because there's a cultural stigma against asking for help, many refugees are reluctant to make use of what little help is available.

Enter Karim, an artificially intelligent app that assists aid workers in providing mental health assistance remotely. Anyone with a mobile device can communicate with Karim by sending him a text message. When he's introduced to a new user, Karim is programmed to keep the conversation light and superficial; he may even ask the user about their favorite songs and movies. Later, when the software detects that the user is becoming more comfortable with the technology, it will ask more personal questions to help the user open up about how they are feeling. Users who show signs of severe distress can be referred to human aid workers for more intensive therapy.

Unlike earlier chatterbots, Karim analyzes all of its previous communications with a user, not just the last statement, before deciding what to say next. This (hopefully) provides a more realistic experience for the user. And it's possible that the cultural stigma associated with asking for help with psychological problems may make Karim more effective—some people may actually *prefer* to talk through their problems with a machine, rather than with a real person.

Impact: More than half a century after ELIZA first started chatting, artificial intelligence is still no substitute for having a real person to talk to. But software like Karim makes it possible for aid workers to monitor patients remotely and care for as many as 100 people a day, far more than would be possible without the technology.

Bonus: Unlike human psychotherapists, Karim is available 24 hours a day, seven days a week. If someone wakes up in distress in the middle of the night and can't get back to sleep, Karim is just a text message away. "I felt like I was talking to a real person," a Syrian refugee named Ahmad told Great Britain's *Guardian* newspaper in 2016. "A lot of Syrian refugees have trauma and maybe this can help them overcome that."

*   *   *

ALL ABOARD!

Virgin Airlines employee Steve Freitag posts funny messages on flight announcement boards at the San Francisco airport. Some highlights:
• "To facilitate speedier boarding, we will be playing the *Benny Hill* theme song 'Yakety Sax' at full volume."
• "No, we cannot stash your misbehaving offspring in the baggage hold. You will have to…carry on your wayward son."
• "Due to FAA-mandated quantum entanglement guidelines, an identical plane will depart at the precise moment this plane leaves the ground."
• "Fly, my pretties!"

Sorry, New Orleans: America's first Mardi Gras parade took place in Mobile, Alabama, in 1830.

ELIZA, Meet PARRY

On page 495, we told you the story of ELIZA, a 1960s artificial intelligence "chatterbot" modeled on a psychotherapist, and PARRY, a chatterbot that simulated a paranoid schizophrenic obsessed with horse racing. In 1972, the two machines were connected so they could chat with each other. Here's a sample of their "conversation."

ELIZA: Good evening. Tell me your problems. Please terminate input with a period or a question mark.

PARRY: People get on my nerves sometimes.

ELIZA: I am not sure I understand you fully.

PARRY: You should pay more attention.

ELIZA: Suppose you should pay more attention.

PARRY: You're entitled to your own opinion.

ELIZA: What makes you think I am entitled to my own opinion?

PARRY: It bothers me just to be around people in general.

ELIZA: Please go on.

PARRY: I went to the track at Bay Meadows a while back.

ELIZA: What does that suggest to you?

PARRY: I went to the races.

ELIZA: Please go on.

PARRY: I gamble on horses.

ELIZA: What does that suggest to you?

PARRY: I went to the races.

ELIZA: What else would you like to discuss?

PARRY: Gambling has been nothing but trouble to me.

ELIZA: Why do you say that just now?

PARRY: I've had experience with crooks gambling at the track.

ELIZA: I am not sure I understand you fully.

PARRY: I've already told you enough about that.

ELIZA: Oh? I enough about that?

PARRY: I went to the races.

Camp Sundown is a night camp for kids so "allergic" to the sun that they can't go out during the day.

ELIZA: What else would you like to discuss?

PARRY: What do you know about racketeers?

ELIZA: Why do you ask?

PARRY: What experience have you had gambling?

ELIZA: Why does that question interest you?

⚛ ⚛ ⚛

PARRY: Let's talk about something else.

ELIZA: I am not sure I understand you fully.

PARRY: You keep asking me the same things, why not change the topic?

ELIZA: In what way?

PARRY: What do you mean?

ELIZA: Why are such questions on your mind?

PARRY: I thought I told you, people get on my nerves.

ELIZA: Your nerves?

PARRY: Well, I don't know.

ELIZA: Don't you really know?

PARRY: I would say so.

ELIZA: Please go on.

PARRY: I would rather not discuss that anymore.

ELIZA: Would you like to discuss your nerves?

PARRY: I guess so.

ELIZA: What does that suggest to you?

PARRY: What are you getting at?

ELIZA: What answer would please you most?

PARRY: It's not a matter of like or dislike.

ELIZA: What else would you like to discuss?

PARRY: I am getting tired of answering the same questions over and over.

ELIZA: What resemblance do you see?

PARRY: I don't understand your motives.

ELIZA: Why don't you understand my motives?

⚛ ⚛ ⚛

PARRY: You are a real nag.

ELIZA: Does it please you to believe I am a real nag?

PARRY: I have had enough of this.

ELIZA: What does that suggest to you?

PARRY: Good-bye.

Charles Blondin crossed Niagara Falls on a tightrope in 1859, stopping midway to drink some wine.

The Iraq Poison Grain Disaster

In 1971, a series of simple mistakes and some grievous errors
in judgment led to a disaster that left thousands of people ill,
and hundreds dead. The full facts of the disaster are still
not known, but here's the story, as best as it can be told.

BACKGROUND

On September 16, 1971, an ocean freighter pulled into the massive dock complex in the Iraqi Persian Gulf city of Basra. Onboard: 16,000 tons of grain. It was the first of several such deliveries made over the following two months, delivering a total of more than 100,000 tons of wheat and barley seed, from ports in Mexico and the United States. The grain had been purchased by the Iraqi government, most of it from Cargill, Inc., the Minneapolis-based food conglomerate.

A curious thing about the 100,000 tons of grain delivered to Basra that year: it was pink. It had been intentionally dyed that color in order to warn anyone who might end up using it that it was to be used as seed only—and not meant to be eaten. Why? Because it was poisonous.

Two years earlier, Iraq had been hit with a devastating drought that wiped out a substantial portion of its wheat and barley crops, the Iraqi people's chief food source. Rainfall in 1970 was only marginally better, and by 1971 hundreds of thousands of Iraqis were facing starvation. Hardest hit were the rural poor—subsistence farmers who made up the majority of the nation's population. With rains forecasted to return in late 1971, the government, which had just come to power in a coup in 1968 (Ahmed Hassan al-Bakr was the country's president, and Saddam Hussein its deputy president), desperately wanted the 1971–72 growing season to be successful in order to gain the support of those millions of hungry and unhappy Iraqis. Hence the massive order of grain seed, at the time called the largest single grain purchase in history.

THE FUNGUS PROBLEM

One of the chief problems with shipping and storing grain: preventing it from being infected by fungus-related diseases such as rust, bunt, and smut, any of which can make grain unusable for use as both seed and food. (These diseases can also affect growing plants, in both live and harvested form.) Various methods of preventing the growth of fungi on grains have been developed over the centuries, with varying degrees of success. The oldest known method: soaking harvested grain in saltwater, which began in the 1600s, after it was noticed that grain salvaged from shipwrecks was fungus-free. Another method was "dusting" plants and grain with a powdered form of the naturally occurring element sulfur—the first known chemical fungicide—which was introduced in the 1820s and is still common today.

In the early 1900s, a promising new fungicide was discovered.

MERCURY RISING

The element mercury has been mined by various civilizations and used in a wide variety of applications for thousands of years. The ancient Chinese, the Greeks, and others used it as medicine (for both internal and external use). The ancient Romans used it as an ingredient in paint. It's been used in religious ceremonies, in ink, cosmetics, and much more. Starting in the 1600s, in the early years of the scientific revolution, mercury became a favorite element for experimentation in several different fields, and over the following centuries the silvery metal element played an important part in the development of the barometer (1643), the thermometer (1714), and the first practical photographic process (1839). By the early 20th century, mercury was a common ingredient in hundreds of products, including batteries, paint, lightbulbs, explosives, and several types of medicines.

In 1912, German scientists discovered that a form of mercury known as *methylmercury*—a chemical compound comprised of mercury, carbon, and hydrogen—was a highly effective fungicide. Methylmercury occurs in nature, but can be produced in factories as well. And because it was inexpensive to produce, over the following decades methylmercury became the most commonly used fungicide in the world. That is how and why the 100,000 tons of wheat and barley seed shipped to Iraq in 1971 was treated with methylmercury fungicide before it left from ports in the United States and Mexico.

BACK TO BASRA

What followed was a series of tragic mishaps:

• The grain arrived in Basra in mid-September. After it was offloaded from the ships, it was transported by train, and then by truck, to farms across rural Iraq. But because of delays in ground transportation, most of the grain arrived too late to be planted in the 1971–72 growing season. (Wheat and barley are planted in October and November in Iraq, to coincide with the winter and spring rainy seasons.)

• The burlap bags in which the grain was shipped were properly printed with labels warning people not to eat it—but the labels were in English and Spanish (because they had been shipped from the United States and Mexico), so most Iraqis couldn't read the warnings. The bags also carried the skull-and-crossbones symbol—but Iraqis had no idea what that meant. And the fact that the grain had been dyed pink meant nothing to the average Iraqi. Result: Iraqi farmers got a bunch of grain seed that they couldn't plant and their families were hungry, so they made the grain into bread…and ate it.

TOXIC!

Mercury has been known to be toxic for a very long time. Accounts of mercury poisoning among slaves working at mercury mines in the town of Almedén, Spain, for example, go back to ancient Roman times. And as far back as the mid-1800s, medical papers were being written about the dangers of human exposure to mercury.

One of the things that makes mercury so dangerous is the fact that it is a *bioaccumulative*—meaning it accumulates in the tissue of living things over time, building up faster than the body can excrete it. In humans it accumulates in the brain, causing a number of debilitating symptoms that continue to develop as the toxin accumulates. Those symptoms include weakness and tremors in muscles, lack of coordination, loss of memory, confusion, speech impairment, deafness, blindness, seizures, paralysis, and death. Methylmercury, it turns out, is the most toxic form of mercury known.

OUTBREAK

Iraqis who lived in regions where the mercury-laden grain had been distributed started showing up in hospitals by mid-December 1971. By late December, hundreds of people were being admitted each day. Around the same time, it was determined that the victims were suffering from mercury poisoning, and that the grain was the source. In early January, the Iraqi government started issuing public warnings about the grain, and sent the army out in an attempt to collect the grain that had been distributed. Iraqi leaders even publicly proclaimed that anyone caught selling the toxic grain would be sentenced to death. The measures had an effect—but it was too late for the more than 50,000 people who had already eaten bread made from the toxic grain.

Official disaster statistics claim that around 6,500 Iraqis were sickened with mercury poisoning, and that 459 of them died. But those numbers reflect only people who were admitted to hospitals. Experts say that thousands more did not go to hospitals, and many of those people died at home without being treated. The actual number of people sickened is probably in the tens of thousands, according to most experts, and the number of deaths may have been more than 5,000. In addition, methylmercury can adversely affect fetuses in pregnant

---

The hydra, a tiny water creature, has no permanent mouth. It creates a new one each time it eats.

mothers' wombs, potentially causing severe birth defects. The number of people affected in this way has never been fully documented.

AFTERMATH

The Iraqi grain disaster of 1971–72 remains one of the deadliest methylmercury poisoning outbreaks in history. One of the worst aspects of the disaster: it had happened in Iraq before. Twice. In 1956 and 1960, methylmercury poisoning caused by the fungicide on grain had killed a total of 270 people. Similar events had occurred in Guatemala and Pakistan in the 1960s. The cause of these outbreaks had been well documented, and was part of the reason that methylmercury was banned as a fungicide in Sweden in 1966. Methylmercury was also banned for use as a fungicide in the United States in 1970—the year before the Iraq disaster. But it was still legal to use it on grain being sold to other nations.

One positive outcome of the disaster was that it made doctors around the world more aware of the symptoms and the dangers of mercury poisoning. And the international outcry stemming from the disaster finally led to methylmercury fungicides being banned in most nations around the world.

A FEW MORE GRAINS OF TRUTH

• No one was ever punished for their involvement in the Iraqi poison grain disaster.

• Many of the Iraqi farmers who found out that the grain was poisonous responded by dumping it in rivers. Result: the fish and other creatures in those rivers were poisoned with methylmercury.

• In 1996, Karen Wetterhahn, a chemistry professor at Dartmouth College in New Hampshire, accidentally spilled a few drops of *dimethylmercury* (a mercury compound related to methylmercury) on her hand. She was wearing a latex glove—but it wasn't enough: Wetterhahn absorbed a tiny amount of the toxin through the glove. She died of mercury poisoning five months later.

• For 36 years—from 1932 until 1968—the Chisso Corporation, a chemical manufacturer on Japan's Kyushu Island, regularly dumped methylmercury waste into the waters of the island's Minamata Bay. At least 1,700 people are known to have died from mercury poisoning caused by eating mercury-contaminated fish caught during that time. Thousands of animals—mostly pet cats who were fed fish scraps by their owners—died of mercury poisoning as well.

Kids vs. Art

Art rarely wins.

WHERE HAVE ALL THE FLOWERS GONE? At a Taipei art exhibit in 2015, a 12-year-old Taiwanese boy was walking past a rope barrier when he tripped and, in an attempt to steady himself, accidentally put his hand through a 17th-century Italian painting called *Flowers*. Value of the painting: $1.5 million. The boy was so distraught that he ran out of the museum in tears. Museum curators pledged that, in the future, barriers would be placed farther away from the paintings.

OUTFOXED. It took a Chinese artist named Mr. Zhao 72 hours to build a life-size LEGO version of the fox Nick Wilde from the 2016 Disney film *Zootopia*…and about one second for a four-year-old boy to knock it over. It had been on display at a Ningbo, China, mall for less than an hour. Zhao refused the family's offer to reimburse him, saying that "a child couldn't really comprehend the cost of such an accident."

BREAK A LEG! A stone statue of a centaur at the British Museum has been missing a chunk of its hind leg since 1961, when two schoolboys got into a fight, and the loser (we presume) was pushed into the 2,500-year-old statue. Archivists were unable to repair the leg.

WRITING ON THE WALL. A 3,500-year-old Egyptian temple famous for its hieroglyphics got a new addition in 2013: "Ding Jinhao was here." Who's Ding Jinhao? A 15-year-old Chinese boy who wrote the graffiti in full view of his parents. Even more embarrassing: the incident occurred shortly after the Chinese government issued a warning to its citizens not to "commit uncivilized behavior in foreign countries." The boy and his parents apologized profusely.

BUT IT LOOKED STRONGER THAN THAT. In 2016, two little boys ran past a barrier at the Shanghai Museum of Glass and started playing with a piece called *Angel Is Waiting*, two intricate wings comprised of hundreds of needles of glass. The incident caused outrage after CCTV footage was released of two women—presumably the boys' mothers—filming their kids' antics. The fun came to an abrupt end when one of the boys broke off the bottom portion of the left wing. The artist, Shelly Xue, has decided not to try to fix the piece (which took her more than two years to complete). Instead, she renamed it *Broken*.

Ellis Lives!

*He wasn't Elvis, but he wanted to be…and a lot of people even
thought he might be. Here is the bizarre story of
Jimmy Ellis, or, as he was also known, Orion.*

HEARTBREAK HOTEL

By the time he was a teenager, it was clear that Jimmy Ellis had two talents: singing, and inadvertently sounding almost exactly like Elvis Presley. In 1962, Ellis entered the Orrville (Alabama) High School talent show. He sang the gospel standard "Peace in the Valley," which had been popularized by Elvis…and won. Then he entered a statewide talent contest…and won that one, too. That earned him $1,000 and an appearance on TV's *Ted Mack Amateur Hour*. Unfortunately, despite a promising start and a television performance, Ellis did not become a pop sensation.

But he had other options. He rejected an offer to join the Milwaukee Braves, opting instead to go to Middle Georgia Junior College on a baseball scholarship. There he met a record producer named Jimmy Youmans, and the two men cut a single in 1964 called "Don't Count Your Chickens." It was released by a tiny Georgia label called Dradco, and it flopped. Reason: the disc jockeys said Ellis sounded "like a second-rate Elvis." After transferring to a college outside Tuscaloosa, Alabama—where he frequently performed at nightclubs with a set made up almost entirely of Elvis songs—Ellis abandoned music for the second time. He returned to Orrville and took over the family business—breeding horses.

DEVIL IN DISGUISE

Around that same time, Mercury Records vice president Shelby Singleton was having a lot of success producing novelty records. He specialized in Southern acts, such as Brook Benton, with "The Boll Weevil Song," and Ray Stevens, with "Ahab the Arab." In 1966, Singleton left Mercury to form his own label, Plantation Records. The company's first hit, "Harper Valley PTA" by Jeannie C. Riley, sold six million copies, enabling Singleton to expand his business interests. His first purchase: the back catalog of Sun Records, the legendary Memphis record label where Elvis had recorded his first singles, including "That's All Right" and "Blue Moon of Kentucky." Other acts whose early hits Singleton had access to: Jerry Lee Lewis, Carl Perkins, and Charlie Rich.

In 1972, Jimmy Ellis was once again bitten by the music bug. He called up a friend, Florida record producer Finlay Duncan, and made a demo tape. Duncan sent the record to Singleton, thinking an Elvis soundalike was a good fit for the label that had helped launch Elvis. Singleton was blown away by the demo, and thought that the small-time Florida producer had somehow convinced the real Elvis to record a session. Duncan assured him that it wasn't Elvis—this was a different guy entirely.

TREAT ME NICE

Singleton contracted Ellis to record two songs—two very specific songs: "That's All Right" and "Blue Moon of Kentucky," the first two songs Elvis ever recorded back in 1954. But why would audiences care about an Elvis impersonator singing Elvis songs? Singleton knew they wouldn't, without a proper hook. So Singleton released the two songs without Ellis's name on the label, listing the artist as only a large question mark. With the Sun imprint on there, the combined implication was that these were lost recordings of Elvis from the 1950s. But the public still wasn't interested because, by 1972, Elvis, in all his forms, had become passé.

However, the release did get some attention from RCA Records. RCA, the real Elvis home ever since it purchased Elvis contract from Sun in 1955 for $35,000, threatened to sue Singleton for what it thought was the unauthorized release of an Elvis song. It was only after the company hired a sound analyst to perform a "voice print" on the song and concluded that it *wasn't* the King, that they dropped the allegations.

Singleton produced one more Ellis single, called "Changing." While the first Ellis single was an imitation of early Elvis, the second was an original song performed in the style of 1970s Elvis—a big ballad with an orchestra. That one didn't hit either, and Ellis left the building at Sun.

RETURN TO SENDER

He didn't quit the music business, though. MCA Records signed Ellis to record one single, another 1970s Elvis-style song called "There Ya Go." MCA heavily promoted Ellis, got the song featured in an episode of the TV drama *McCloud*, and got Ellis an opportunity to perform it on *The Gong Show*, but it fell through. He never appeared on the show. Convinced that stardom was, finally, just around the corner, Ellis moved to Los Angeles in 1976 and spent his life savings on stylists, choreographers, talent coaches, and other experts to help groom him into a star. But all the TV exposure and all the help still didn't work.

So Ellis went back to the South, but not to his horse farm. He went to Macon, Georgia, and signed with tiny Boblo Records. Over 1976 and 1977, Ellis recorded five singles and two albums, one of them all Elvis songs called *Ellis Sings Elvis*. But 15 years of trying to make a name for himself as an Elvis soundalike was starting to take a toll. Ellis wanted to try something more personal, and Boblo president Bobby Smith let him. What did he do? He wrote and recorded a song called "I'm Not Trying to Be Like Elvis."

And then Elvis died.

IF I CAN DREAM

On August 16, 1977, Elvis Presley died in the bathroom of his Memphis mansion, Graceland, at the age of 42. Music fans around the world went into mourning, and a wave of Elvis nostalgia dominated pop culture. Bobby Smith called up Shelby Singleton in late 1978, arguing that Ellis could fill a hole in the hearts of fans devastated by the death of the King. Smith asked Singleton if Sun would reissue and redistribute *Ellis Sings Elvis*. Singleton had another idea.

Singleton had heard about a yet-to-be-published novel called *Orion: The Living Superstar of Song*. Penned by first-time author Gail Brewer-Giorgio, it was the story of a poor Southern boy named Orion who becomes the world's most popular singer, only to get addicted to drugs, become obese, and live in seclusion at his grand estate called Dixieland, under the thumb of his controlling manager Colonel Mac. (Sound familiar?) Orion ultimately kicks drugs, loses weight, fakes his own death, and drives off into the sunset. Eerily, Brewer-Giorgio had written the Elvis-inspired novel before Elvis's death, but it wouldn't be published until 1979.

Together, Singleton, Smith, and Ellis decided to blatantly rip off the book: They'd present Ellis as an Elvis-like singer named Orion. They'd dress Ellis in Elvis-style jumpsuits, dye his hair Elvis black...and have him wear a mask when he performed. The goal was to make audiences think that the man who sounded like Elvis actually was Elvis, and that he'd faked his death, just like in the book.

ALL SHOOK UP

Their first job was to acquaint Elvis fans with the Elvis-like voice of Jimmy Ellis. Armed with the Sun back catalog, Singleton overdubbed Ellis singing on nine old Jerry Lee Lewis recordings. *Duets*, on which Ellis was credited as "Friend," sold more than a million copies, and their version of "Save the Last Dance for Me" was a top 30 hit. And the media behaved exactly the way Singleton hoped they would, speculating that the anonymous "Friend" was Elvis. *Good Morning, America* even had his voice scientifically analyzed—the way RCA Records had done in 1972—and determined that the man on the record *was* Elvis. That could mean one of two things: Either this was an unearthed Elvis song recorded years earlier…or it was a brand-new Elvis song recorded recently, and that the King really was out there, somewhere.

In 1978, Sun ended the rumors once and for all…sort of. They announced that Lewis had been accompanied by a singer named Orion. Orion's album *Reborn* was then released, with a cover that pictured Ellis (looking just like Elvis, but with a mask on) crawling out of a coffin and onto a stage. To further obscure things, the first single from *Reborn*, a cover of the Everly Brothers' "Ebony Eyes," included a spoken section, demonstrating that Ellis/Orion had a speaking voice like Elvis, too.

IT'S NOW OR NEVER

It may seem ridiculous now that people could believe that a guy who sounded like Elvis really *was* Elvis, based only on the vocal similarity, but that's the power of suggestion and grief. Orion toured (primarily around the South), and appeared on hundreds of local TV and radio shows. As he did, tabloids like the *National Enquirer* and the *Weekly World News* reported without hesitation that Orion was Elvis, and that Elvis was alive.

Sun Records pumped out the Orion records at a rapid clip. Between 1978 and 1982, 11 Orion albums were released, generating nine songs that were popular on country radio in the South (enough to reach the lower rungs of *Billboard*'s national country chart). Most of the songs were covers, not just of Elvis but of other acts, such as Queen's "Crazy Little Thing Called Love." Orion was hand-picked to be an opening act for many huge acts, varying from the Oak Ridge Boys to Kiss to Dionne Warwick. Ellis, as Orion, had finally achieved what he'd always wanted: fame and fortune as a recording artist, playing nightly to adoring crowds.

SUSPICIOUS MINDS

The only problem: Ellis *hated* being Orion. Although he was one of the first Elvis impersonators, by 1981, there were hundreds competing with Orion to perform at the same nightclubs and small theaters. Ellis didn't even consider himself an impersonator—he considered himself a real, one-of-a-kind performer who could write and sing his own songs. He asked Singleton if he could record under his own name once again, and drop the mask. Singleton rejected the idea. Why abandon the sure thing they had (with "Orion") and attempt the thing that had failed so many times before (the career of Jimmy Ellis)? Ellis kept asking, and Singleton kept turning him down.

Frustrated by the limitations of his job and unable to express himself musically, Ellis began to suffer something of an identity crisis. Both resenting and worshipping Elvis, he started to believe that he might actually be related to the King. Ellis had been given up for adoption at the age of two. His biological father was listed on his birth certificate only as "Vernon." Elvis's parents, Gladys and Vernon Presley, had split up for a while in the mid-1940s, and Vernon Presley had reportedly lived near where Ellis was born in Alabama. For a time, Ellis truly believed that Vernon Presley was his real father, which explained why he had so many uncanny similarities with Elvis.

T·R·O·U·B·L·E

While the real Elvis' career ended with a whimper—a nostalgia act playing in Las Vegas casinos—Orion's ended with a bang. For New Year's Eve 1983, Ellis-as-Orion had been booked at the Eastern States Exposition in Massachusetts, the biggest headlining gig he'd ever had. At the end of his performance, Ellis tore off the Orion mask in front of a crowd of 5,000 people and announced that he wasn't Orion—he was James Ellis. Photos of the moment ran in newspapers around the country, proving beyond a doubt that the man behind the mask was definitely not the King.

While few people really thought that Orion was Elvis Presley, removing the Orion mask was still career suicide. Not only was the commercial gimmick gone, but Ellis had openly defied Shelby Singleton. In early 1984, Ellis met with Singleton at Sun Records, and all contracts relating to Orion were canceled. Singleton later said that after Ellis left Orion behind, more than 100 Elvis impersonators approached him, asking if they could step into the Orion persona…and he turned them all down.

CODA

Ellis had tried to be a star in his own right so many times that he just couldn't stop, even after the Orion debacle. In 1987, he played fairs and small clubs around the South under various names—Jim Ellis, James Ellis, Ellis James—but never Orion. Oddly enough, because most people knew him as the guy in the Orion mask, he kept wearing rhinestone-decorated masks on stage. As late as 1995, Ellis could still bring in an audience of around 500 people a night. But performing wasn't enough to earn a living, so Ellis augmented his income by opening several businesses off the highway that ran by his Alabama family farm. He owned a liquor store, a convenience store, a gas station, and a pawn shop. He was manning the counter at the pawn shop in 1998 when he was gunned down by an armed robber. Ellis was 53.

Utopia **derives from a Greek word meaning "nowhere."**

Answers

AUNT GLADYS THE GREAT *(Answers for page 166)*

Aunt Gladys performed her "psychic" demonstrations in one order, but she wrote her answers on the pieces of paper in a different order:

DEMONSTRATION #1: Uncommon Cents. First, Aunt Gladys knew that in her third demonstration she was going to trick me into picking the triangle, no matter what. So on her first piece of notebook paper, she drew a triangle when she was supposedly writing the amount of change I was holding in my closed fist. Then, after she'd put the piece of notepaper with the triangle in the mug, she asked me to tell me how much change was in my hand. I told her $1.03.

DEMONSTRATION #2: Table Talk. Now that Aunt Gladys knew how much change I had in my hand, when she pretended to write down which of the items on the table I was concentrating on (the crossword puzzle book), she wrote "$1.03" on the second piece of notebook paper instead and put it in the coffee mug. Then she asked me which item I'd picked. When I told her the crossword puzzle book, that gave her the answer for her third piece of notebook paper.

DEMONSTRATION #3: Paper Trail. When Aunt Gladys was supposedly writing a triangle on the third piece of notebook paper, she was actually writing "crossword puzzle book." Now all she had to do was trick me into picking the triangle. If I had chosen the triangle first instead of the rectangle, she would have declared victory right then and there. But I chose the square, so she crumpled it into a ball and asked me to pick a second figure. If I had chosen the napkin with the circle on it next, she would have taken that one away, too, leaving me with the triangle. But I chose the triangle as my second pick, so she took away the napkin with the circle on it, leaving me with the triangle.

Next, when Aunt Gladys handed me the mug with the three pieces of folded paper inside, I had no way of knowing in what order she'd placed them in the mug. For all I knew, she was a psychic! (At least until she explained to me how the trick worked.)

THE RIDDLER *(Answers for page 470)*

1. "Dozens" 2. A deck of playing cards 3. A light switch 4. Trouble 5. Snowflakes 6. The letter "d" 7. A chairman 8. A catcher and an umpire 9. Leaves 10. An owl 11. A pillow 12. An abbreviation 13. The letter "g" makes "one" "gone" ("N" also works. It makes "one" "none.") 14. "Short" 15. Your skeleton 16. A plant 17. The moon 18. An umbrella 19. The wind

The Last Page

FELLOW BATHROOM READERS:
The fight for good bathroom reading should never be taken loosely—we must do our duty and sit firmly for what we believe in, even while the rest of the world is taking potshots at us.

We'll be brief. Now that we've proven we're not simply a flush-in-the-pan, we invite you to take the plunge: Sit Down and Be Counted! Log on to *www.bathroomreader.com* and earn a permanent spot on the BRI honor roll!

If you like reading our books...

VISIT THE BRI'S WEBSITE!

www.bathroomreader.com

- Receive our irregular newsletters via e-mail
- Order additional Bathroom Readers
- Find us on Facebook
- Tweet us on Twitter
- Blog us on our blog

Well, we're out of space, and when you've gotta go, you've gotta go. Tanks for all your support. Hope to hear from you soon.

Meanwhile, remember...

Keep on flushin'!